ENCYCLOPEDIA OF
INVASIONS
AND
CONQUESTS
FROM ANCIENT TIMES
TO THE PRESENT

ENCYCLOPEDIA OF
INVASIONS
AND
CONQUESTS
FROM ANCIENT TIMES
TO THE PRESENT

Paul K. Davis

Grey House
Publishing

Millerton, NY

PUBLISHER: Leslie Mackenzie
EDITORIAL DIRECTOR: Laura Mars-Proietti
PRODUCTION EDITOR: Toby Raymond
MARKETING DIRECTOR: Jessica Moody

Grey House Publishing, Inc.
185 Millerton Road
Millerton, NY 12546
518.789.8700
FAX 518.789.0545
www.greyhouse.com
e-mail: books @greyhouse.com

Publisher's Cataloging-In-Publication Data
(Prepared by The Donohue Group, Inc.)

Davis, Paul K., 1952-
   Encyclopedia of invasions and conquests from ancient times to the present / Paul K. Davis. -- 2nd ed.

   p. : ill., maps ; cm.

   ISBN: 1-59237-114-0
   Originally published: Santa Barbara, Calif. : ABC-CLIO, 1996.
   Includes bibliographical references and index.

1. Military history--Encyclopedias. I. Title. II. Title: Invasions and conquests from ancient times to the present

D25.A2 D38 2006
355/.003

ENCYCLOPEDIA OF INVASIONS AND CONQUESTS
FROM ANCIENT TIMES TO THE PRESENT
SECOND EDITION

SECTION ONE: ENTRIES

PART 3 THE DARK AND MIDDLE AGES 57

SECTION THREE: READINGS

PREFACE

The greatest difficulty in undertaking a work such as this is defining the terms *invasion* and *conquest*. Both have overtly military connotations, though not all conquests are accomplished totally through military means. Still, *conquest* can best be described as the occupation and long-term domination of one country by another. Using this criterion, colonization can be defined as conquest, especially because most examples of colonization have a military aspect. Hence, the Spanish occupation of the New World, the British occupation of America, Canada, India, etc., all constitute conquests. If the colonization takes place with little military activity, the term *occupation* is used.

The definition of invasion is much more difficult to nail down. Any battle involves invasion of territory, even if it is only enemyheld ground on the other side of the battlefield. To narrow our field, we will deal only with the violation of national borders - one country invading another. This immediately removes from consideration all civil wars, since a nation fights such a war against itself. While many would argue that Union forces attacking the Confederacy constituted an invasion, this cannot fit our criteria because the Confederate States of America was never officially an independent nation. This further removes from consideration most revolutions, unless they are against a foreign power and the revolutionaries achieve national status. The American Revolution would be covered, because the United States became a nation in the midst of revolution with formal recognition by other countries. The Texas Revolution, on the other hand, would not because Texas did not gain international recognition until after hostilities ended.

Additionally, the placement of national boundaries creates another question. For most of its history, modern Italy has been a collection of nation-states trying to establish domination over one another. Do conflicts among these neighbors constitute invasions? Would the fighting between Serbs, Croats, and Muslims in post-Communist Yugoslavia be considered a series of territorial invasions, or simply a struggle for local control? Is an attack against a neighbor, conducted with no intent of conquest (for example, Prussia versus Austria in 1866), considered an invasion?

These are some of the considerations to be faced in defining the scope of this work, and in some cases, inclusion ultimately comes down to an editorial judgment call. What some might view as an invasion, we might decide was a dynastic squabble among rival factions, and modern national identities may at times be overlaid on a set of historical states that no longer exist. In general, we will explore actions by one nation against another with the intent or result of establishing the attacker's domination over the defender. By this definition, invasions almost always will be military, but ultimate conquests may be political or economic, as in the U.S. intervention in Latin American nations. Because the establishment and fall of empires normally involve the conquests of numerous enemies, these events are covered by the names of the empires, rather than by the listing of each conquest involved in the process of empire building.

Every effort has been made to cover as much history of the world's invasions as possible - from the time Sargon the Great first expanded the borders of Akkadia to the American-led coalition effort to overthrow Saddam Hussein and establish democracy in Iraq.

I would like to thank all the contributors who aided in the production of this work: John Adams, Gary Botello, Ed Davis, Thomas E. Davis, Allen Hamilton, James L. Iseman, Edward Maier III, Rhett Michael Schall, Deborah Palacios, Travis Denzer, Michael Barden, and Kyle Matheu.

I very much want to recognize the efforts of my wife, Jerri, for her patience with me during the research and writing of this work.

List of Contributors

John Adams
Michael Barden
Gary Botello
Thomas E. Davis
Thomas E. Davis, Jr.
Travis Denzer
Allan Lee Hamilton
James L. Iseman
Edward L. Maier III
Kyle Matheu
Deborah Palacios
Rhett Michael Schall

List of Maps

PART 7 – THE TWENTIETH CENTURY

The Twentieth Century – Maps 1-5
Numbered locations on these maps correspond with all entries contained in Part 7.

SECTION ONE: ENTRIES

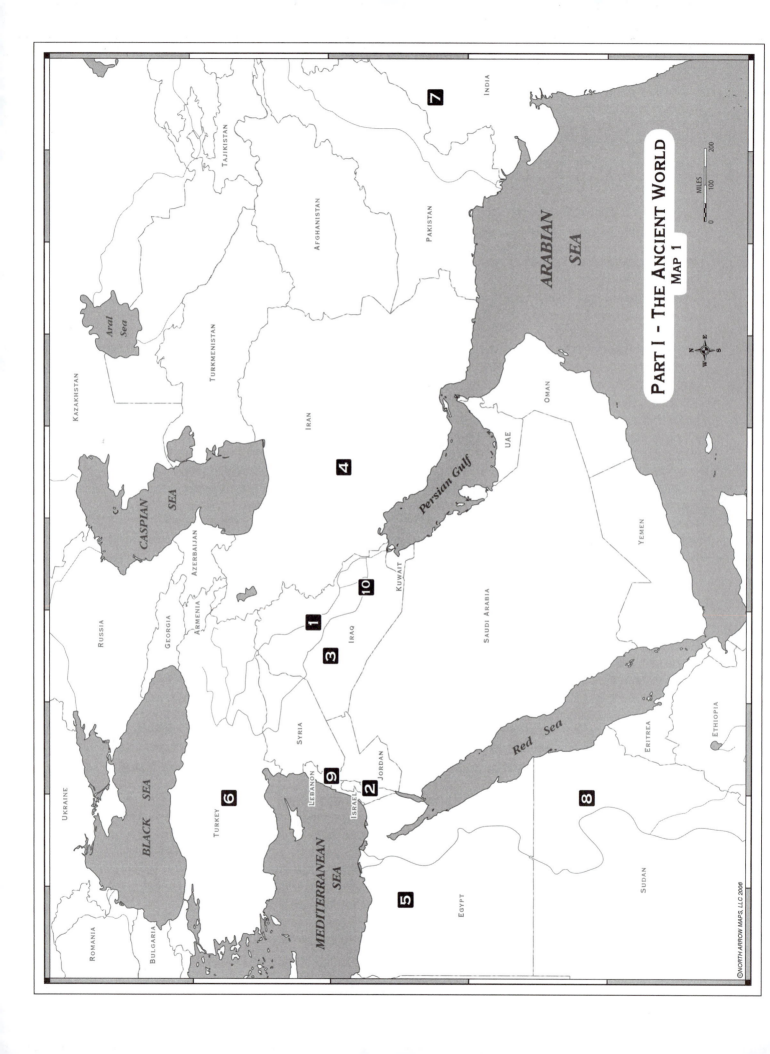

PART I – THE ANCIENT WORLD
MAP 1

PART 1
THE ANCIENT WORLD

1

1   ASSYRIAN EMPIRE

The first strong Assyrian state was formed in the late Bronze Age in the wake of the decline of the Mitanni, a confederation of tribes living along the upper reaches of the Tigris River. In the fourteenth century B.C.E., Ashururballit led his people in an expansion westward, during which they came to control the upper arch of the Fertile Crescent for approximately a century. The Assyrians ran up against the power of Aram (situated in modern-day Syria), which blocked their access to western trade routes. Still, the early success coupled with the continued fighting against Aram made the Assyrian army strong and experienced, able to defend itself and mount major raids far to the south and west. With this powerful military, Assyria dominated the Near East by the 900s B.C.E.

Initially, the Assyrians' main objective was to expand to the Mediterranean coast in order to control the major trade routes of ancient times. Assyrian armies finally overcame the resistance of nations led by Aram, and they captured the major city of Damascus in 732 B.C.E. Old Testament accounts tell of Assyrian attacks into Samaria and Judah, and fighting against the Egyptians. Assyria established empire status under the leadership of Sargon II (722–705 B.C.E.), who named himself after the Sumerian leader Sargon the Great, the first well-known conqueror. Sargon II's son Sennacherib maintained the lands his father had conquered, and raided Asia Minor after 700 B.C.E. Sennacherib established control over Phoenician towns on the Mediterranean coast all the way to the Egyptian frontier. The last of the great emperors was Esarhaddon (681–668 B.C.E.), who came to the throne by murdering his father, Sennacherib. To secure his frontiers, Esarhaddon coupled diplomacy with warfare. He entered into agreements with the Medes to the east and the Cimmerians to the north, but also invaded Egypt, a nation seemingly always in rebellion against the Assyrian demands for tribute. By the end of Esarhaddon's reign, Assyrian territory stretched from the Persian Gulf across the Fertile Crescent and halfway down the Nile in Egypt.

Assurbanipal was the last of the Assyrian kings. More of a scholar than a warrior, he let his generals punish the rebellious while he established a large library at Nineveh.

The Assyrian Empire came to an abrupt end in 612 B.C.E. Three hundred years of warfare, both conquests and the suppression of almost constant rebellions, had put a serious strain on Assyrian manpower. The birthrate had not kept up with the casualty rate, and the Assyrians had been obliged to use conscript troops, who proved of doubtful loyalty. Agreements with neighbors lapsed, and enemies pressed from all directions. Ultimately the Medes led a coalition that laid siege to the Assyrian capital city of Nineveh, which fell after three months, spelling the end of the empire, an end more celebrated than lamented. The biblical prophet Nahum wrote, "All who hear the news of you clap their hands over you. For upon whom has not come your unceasing evil?" Nahum summed it up perfectly; Assyria had built and maintained its empire by military force and terror, showing no mercy to any defeated foe, whether in conquest or rebellion.

The Assyrians were the first people to institutionalize cruelty to control the lands they acquired. Towns destroyed in battle were left in ruins as an example to other possible foes. Ashurnasipal bragged, "I caused great slaughter. I destroyed, I demolished, I burned. I took their warriors prisoner and impaled them on stakes before their cities. . . . I flayed the nobles, as many as had rebelled, and spread their skins out on the piles [of dead bodies]. . . . Many of the captives I burned in a fire. Many I took alive; from some I cut off their hands to the wrist, from others I cut off their noses, ears and fingers; I put out the eyes of many soldiers. I burnt their young men and women to death." This boast was not just Ashurnasipal's; every leader acted in the same fashion. It is not surprising that they had to deal with constant rebellion; they certainly inspired no loyalty from their subjects.

Despite this negative characteristic, the Assyrians contributed to society and culture. Some of the world's oldest roads were built in the time of Sargon II. This road system allowed for freer trade and the development of a postal system. The Assyrian Empire was the first to

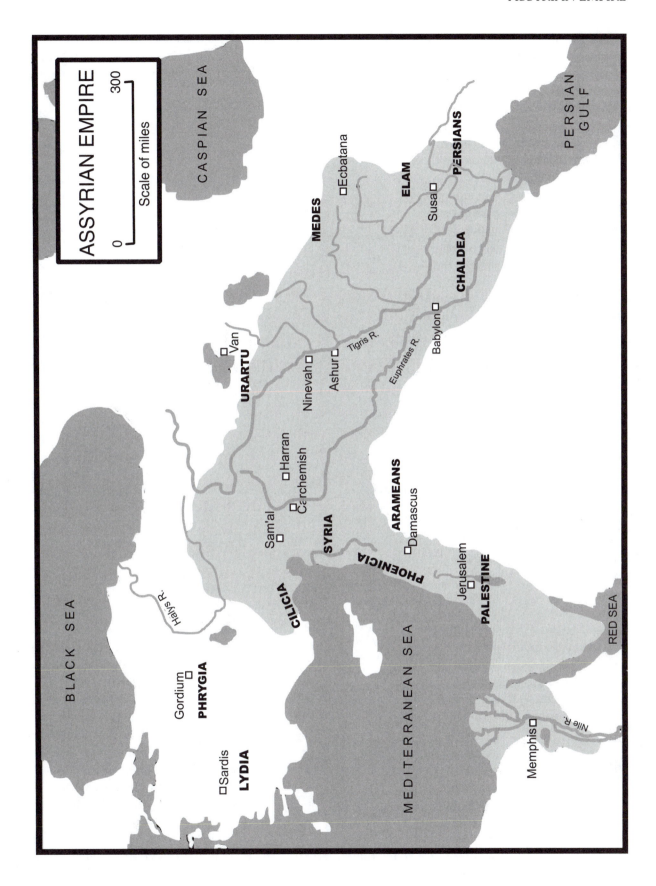

ASSYRIAN EMPIRE

Scale of miles

0   300

CASPIAN SEA

PERSIAN GULF

PERSIANS

MEDES

ELAM

□Ecbatana

□Susa

CHALDEA

□Babylon

Tigris R.

Euphrates R.

URARTU

□Van

Ninevah□   □Ashur

□Harran

□Carchemish

Sam'al□

ARAMEANS

□Damascus

SYRIA

PHOENICIA

Jerusalem□

PALESTINE

CILICIA

BLACK SEA

Halys R.

PHRYGIA

Gordium□

□Sardis

LYDIA

MEDITERRANEAN SEA

RED SEA

Nile R.

Memphis□

construct aqueducts. Adopting cuneiform script from the Babylonians, the Assyrians became the world's first serious historians. They established a number of libraries, where they recorded scientific knowledge acquired on their own and from Babylon. They also inaugurated the first widespread use of iron. Though iron was used by the Hittites, the Assyrians were the first to use the metal for weapons. As more iron-producing territory came under their control, it became the most common metal in tool production, far outperforming anything made from bronze. Their artists are regarded as masters of relief work, with realistic and emotional portrayals of kings at war and sport.

The Assyrians are best remembered, however, for their accomplishments in warfare. Using chariots (already invented), they were the first to add cavalry to their army, which often proved the decisive factor in their victories. Assyria was the first state, but certainly not the last, to build its society around the armed forces. They established what may be called the first true empire, because whereas most previous warriors cam paigned mainly for loot and tribute, the Assyrians established political control by appointing governors in conquered lands. Had they had the statesmanship skills to match their military prowess, they could not only have lasted longer as an empire, but they would also have had an even greater impact on the progress of ancient society and culture.

See also Hittites; Sargon the Great.

References: Bury, J. B., S. A. Cook, and F. E. Adcock, eds., *The Cambridge Ancient History: The Assyrian Empire* (Cambridge: Cambridge University Press, 1923–1939); Laessoe, Jorgen, *People of Ancient Assyria, Their Inscriptions and Correspondence* (London: Routledge & Kegan Paul, 1963); Saggs, H. W. F., *The Might That Was Assyria* (London: Sidgwick & Jackson, 1984).

CANAAN, ISRAELITE INVASION OF

Throughout history, nations have gone to war against their enemies in the name of God, whether for punishment, revenge, or greed. Seldom has there been a war in which one or all of the participants did not try to invoke God's blessing or intercession on their behalf, no matter who their god may have been. Worse yet, a holy war is usually fought with more ferocity and less mercy.

The Israelite invasion of the area that has come to be known as the Holy Land was probably as genocidal as any in history, but it seems to have been conducted with less malice. As a racial and religious group, the Hebrews considered themselves to have been chosen by the one and only God, who had promised their forebear, Abraham, that they would have a country of their own. Thus, it became a tradition covering several centuries that the Hebrews had a mandate from God to possess this land. The people who inhabited the land were virtually unknown to the Israelites, and the only indication that the invasion was conducted with moral overtones is the biblical statement that God was punishing the local inhabitants for their idolatry.

Forty years before the invasion began, the Israelites were a captive people serving Egyptian masters in the Nile Delta region. In response to intolerable treatment, they came together under the leadership of a man named Moses, who had been raised and educated in the household of the pharaoh. Though not always popular with the rank-and-file Israelites, Moses was able to secure their release from bondage during a time of turmoil and plague, which had been attributed to God's intercession.

According to the Bible, the Israelites left Egypt some six million strong, but were unable to muster the resolve necessary to invade their objective immediately. They spent 40 years wandering about the Sinai desert, and by the time the actual invasion began, their numbers had considerably decreased. The Bible states that they were fielding an army of about 40,000 men as they approached Canaan, the Promised Land. The Israelites had apparently come out of Egypt unprepared for the hardships of the Sinai or the rigors of battle, but during the 40 years of wandering through the territories of various kingdoms, they had been toughened and their fighting skills sharpened by encounters with nomadic tribes.

At a date scholars place variously from the sixteenth to the thirteenth century B.C.E., the Israelites arrived in the area south of the Dead

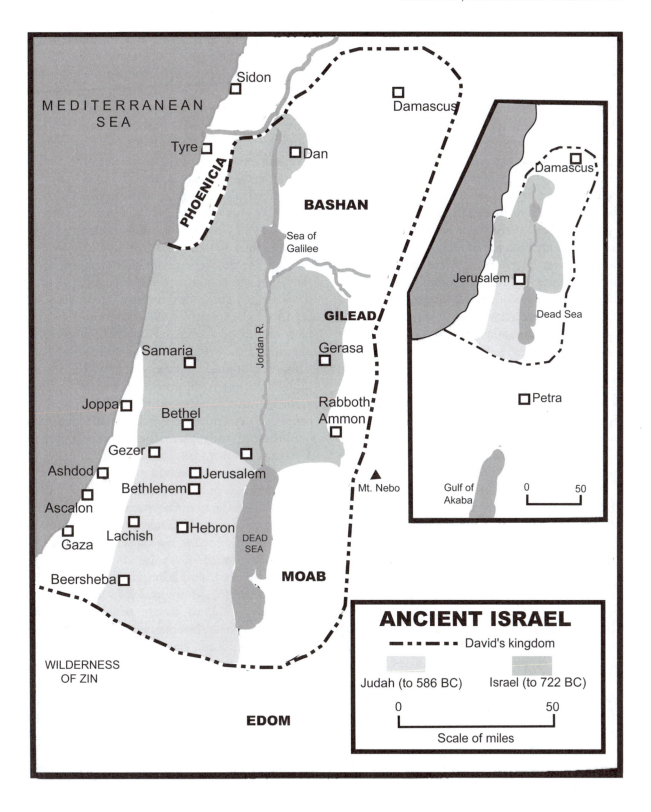

MEDITERRANEAN SEA

Sidon

Damascus

Tyre

PHOENICIA

Dan

BASHAN

Sea of Galilee

GILEAD

Samaria

Jordan R.

Gerasa

Joppa

Bethel

Rabboth Ammon

Gezer

Ashdod

Jerusalem

Bethlehem

Mt. Nebo

Ascalon

Hebron

Gaza

Lachish

DEAD SEA

Beersheba

MOAB

WILDERNESS OF ZIN

EDOM

ANCIENT ISRAEL

—··—··— David's kingdom

Judah (to 586 BC) Israel (to 722 BC)

0   50

Scale of miles

Damascus

Jerusalem

Dead Sea

Petra

Gulf of Akaba

0   50

Sea, Canaan's southern limit. They encountered two Amorite kingdoms, Sihon and Og, and defeated both. According to God's instruction, through Moses, those occupying the land of the ancient mandate were to be killed to protect the Hebrews from contamination by idol worshippers. All the people were put to the sword, thus clearing the land, which reached from the Dead Sea to well north of the Sea of Galilee and from the Jordan River eastward almost to the Euphrates.

Though the territories of Sihon and Og were vast and a part of the Promised Land, the symbolic point at which the Israelites began the invasion was on the Jordan River just south of the ancient walled city of Jericho. Moses passed the mantle of leadership to Joshua, the general of his army, and died without ever having crossed the Jordan. Joshua gathered all his people together and instructed them to follow the priests who were carrying the Ark of the Covenant, the sacred chest containing holy relics, the most important of which were the tablets containing God's laws, the Ten Commandments. As the priests stepped into the water, the Bible says that the river ceased to flow, and all the people passed through the riverbed dry-shod.

Once across the river, Joshua ordered an altar to be built and the proper sacrifices made. He reinstituted the ancient rite of circumcision, which had been abandoned during the years of wandering. He also reconsecrated himself and his family to God and the task before them, and preparations soon began for the assault. Jericho was a strong, walled city founded on the site of an abundant spring and surrounded by palms. Seeing the Israelites' approach and terrified by the disasters that had befallen Sihon and Og, the local inhabitants fled into the walled city. They had heard that the Israelites crossed the Jordan on dry ground, and had seen with their own eyes how the Jordan had ceased to flow.

Joshua instructed his people to march around the city silently for six days; on the seventh day they would give a great shout, and the walls would fall down. This happened as Joshua predicted, and the people in the city perished—save for one family, who had harbored Israelite spies.

After the sacking of Jericho, Joshua planned to climb from the river valley to high ground and swing south, clearing the land of its inhabitants as he went. Standing in his way was the city of Ai, another walled city partway up the mountain slope. He sent only part of his army (about 3,000 men) and was repulsed. Joshua returned with the bulk of his army, and by a ruse enticed the defenders out of the city. Cut off from the protection of the city fortifications, they were ambushed; once again, all the inhabitants were killed. Archaeologists dispute the existence of Ai, but reputedly it was very near the city of Bethel; possibly the conquests of both cities were accomplished at the same time. Whatever the explanation, the Israelites unquestionably stormed the heights, and Joshua continued his conquest.

The only exception to the policy of genocide apparently occurred at this time. The inhabitants of Gibeon took advantage of the Israelites' unfamiliarity with the country. Sending out emissaries dressed in rags and professing to be travelers from a distant land, they exacted a pledge from Joshua that he would spare their people. When Joshua learned that they lived just over the next ridge, he honored his pledge, but sentenced them to be slaves, forever "carriers of water and hewers of wood."

The land of God's mandate, now called Israel, extended roughly from the Dead Sea in the south past the Sea of Galilee in the north; it was bounded by the Mediterranean on the west and by some portion of the Euphrates on the east. After passing Gibeon, Joshua continued south along the mountains and then dropped into the lowlands, taking all the land to the south and west. Retracing his steps, he conquered most of the land in the north. In all, the Bible lists 31 kingdoms that were conquered, including Jericho. No peace treaties were made, except for that with the Gibeonites, and no one was allowed to surrender. Though the Bible states that the conquest was complete after six years and that the Israelites then rested, it is clear that some resistance still remained even when Joshua died, 25 years after the invasion began.

The chief problem lay with the Philistines, a non-Semitic people of mysterious origin occupying the area along the southern seacoast. So stubborn was their resistance, so superior their iron weapons over the bronze implements of the Israelites, and so devious their tactics that the term Philistine has come to mean a person of crass and base instincts. The Philistines fought against the Israelites in the time of the judges (the two centuries or so after invasion), and brought about Samson's downfall. A giant Philistine from Gath was killed by young David, setting the boy on the path to power. Not until David was king did the entire Promised Land come under complete Hebrew control. The genocidal policy was never fully implemented, and the Bible blames many of the later problems of the nation on interracial marriages, economic ties, and the worship of false gods.

For more than 3,000 years the descendants of the Israelites have possessed (in their own minds and that of many others) the Promised Land, if they have not always controlled it. This land was the geopolitical center of the then-civilized world: exposed to all cultures and religions, crossed by most of the trading caravans, and host to ships from the far places of the sea. Christianity began here and, though dominated by the Romans for centuries, this product of the land conquered and eventually possessed even that great power.

The Israelite conquest that came sweeping out of the desert one and a half millennia before the time of Christ has had more far-reaching consequences on the entire world than any other conquest in history. Though the land today is of relative insignificance in an economic sense, it continues to be a force in world affairs—a magnet for Jews, Muslims, and Christians, many with the old antipathies and genocidal tendencies intact.

References: Gaubert, Henri, *Moses and Joshua, Founders of the Nation* (New York: Hastings House, 1969); Grant, Michael, *The History of Ancient Israel* (New York: Scribner, 1984); Miller, James, *A History of Ancient Israel and Judah* (Philadelphia: Westminster Press, 1968).

CHALDEAN (NEO-BABYLONIAN) EMPIRE, EXPANSION OF

3

Many memorable civilizations arose in the area known as Mesopotamia, the land lying between the Tigris and Euphrates rivers above the Persian Gulf. The Bible frequently mentions Mesopotamian civilizations, especially the spectacular city of Babylon. The city lay some 150 miles south of Sumer, site of the world's first civilization. The ruins of the ancient city visible today were left by the Chaldeans, or Neo-Babylonians, another Semitic group that came to prominence after the first Babylon settled by the Amorites.

The Assyrians, a warrior race based some 200 miles north of Babylon, were in total control of Mesopotamia around 750 B.C.E. Being a people dedicated to conquest and plunder, the Assyrians maintained a mighty army but made no loyal allies among their conquests. Hatred of the Assyrians by their conquered subjects ultimately weakened the civilization. Being forced to deal with almost continual rebellions laid them open to conquest from the outside, an invasion that came from the Chaldeans and Medes. The Chaldeans had lived in the Persian Gulf area for centuries and the Medes lived in the foothills of Persia. Together, led by the Chaldean king Nabopolasser, they destroyed the Assyrian capital at Nineveh in 612 B.C.E.

With the Assyrians removed from power, the Chaldeans and Medes split the territory; the Chaldeans occupied the area around Babylon, and the Medes settled in the northwest. King Nabopolasser established his capital at Babylon, ascending the throne in that city in 604 B.C.E. Defeat of the Assyrians did not bring peace to the Chaldeans, however. Assyria's fall encouraged the expansion of Egypt, under Pharaoh Necho, into Syria. Nabopolasser wanted to resist, but failing health caused him to send his son Nebuchadnezzar to fight the Egyptians. The Chaldeans won a major battle at Carchemish, but the Egyptians remained covetous of Syria. Allying themselves with Phoenicia and the kingdom of Judah, the Egyptians returned to the area. Again they met defeat at Chaldean hands. Nebuchadnezzar captured the capital of Judah, Jerusalem, and took a large part of the nation's population into captivity in Babylon in 597 B.C.E. When the Egyptians tried a third time to take Syria—and were a third time defeated—Nebuchadnezzar again took Jerusalem by siege and removed the remainder of the population.

While Nebuchadnezzar was in the Mediterranean coastal area, he made war against Phoenicia, capturing the port city of Sidon. He was unable to capture the fortress city of Tyre, though he disrupted their trade. During this expedition, Egypt caused little trouble. Nebuchadnezzar's successor, Neriglassar, took military action to defend his national borders from an invasion in the west. Neriglassar's successor, and the final Chaldean king, was Nabonidus, who spent much of his reign putting down Syrian rebellions and capturing the town of Shindini in Edom.

Though the Chaldean Empire was not as large as that of the Assyrians, the former were known as the great conquerors of the Middle East because of better documentation, especially in the Bible. Nebuchadnezzar destroyed Jerusalem, burned the temple of Solomon, and hauled the people into captivity, but he was also famous for beautifying Babylon and transforming it into the cultural and economic center of its time. The city was about 81 square miles in area and surrounded by a defensive wall of brick. Eight gates into the city were dedicated to eight Chaldean gods. Babylon not only had a royal residence along the Euphrates, but sophisticated, multistory housing and paved streets. Such architectural marvels as the Hanging Gardens and huge temples (possibly even the Tower of Babel) were located in Babylon.

The city became the trade center of the Middle East, bringing in goods from India and Arabia. The people excelled in science, especially astronomy and astrology. Babylon became the center of learning in Mesopotamia, and the beginnings of literature can be traced there. The king, though not considered divine, was believed to be a mediator between the gods and the people, and he had to perform rituals worshipping Ishtar, Marduk, and Shamush.

Despite this cultural advancement, or perhaps because of it, the Chaldeans became the targets of yet other invaders. In 539 B.C.E., the Persian king Cyrus attacked from the east and overwhelmed the Chaldean military, which had been neglected in favor of science and the arts.

See also Assyrian Empire; Palestine, Egyptian Invasions of.

References: Falls, Cyril, *The First 3000 Years* (New York: Viking Press, 1960); Mac-Queen, James, *Babylon* (New York: Praeger, 1965); Seignobos, Charles, *The World of Babylon* (New York: Leon Amiel, 1975).

4 · CYRUS THE GREAT

Texts sing with endless praise of the accomplishments of Cyrus, king of Persia. One would think, therefore, that there would be few unrecorded aspects of his life. However, it appears that relatively little is known of his early life and many of his achievements. The contemporary coverage focused on three battles that led to the creation of the Persian Empire and on a few decisions made at the beginning of his reign. His birth and death are shrouded in myth.

Some have speculated that Cyrus was the son of a sheepherder who migrated from the mountains north of modern-day Iraq to the plains of the Tigris River valley. We do know that his father, Cambyses, ruled over a small Persian tribe in the southern Tigris-Euphrates area. When Cambyses died, Cyrus took over and united all of the Persian tribes under his rule in 559 B.C.E.

The first of the three battles in which he is known to have fought received limited coverage, Supposedly, Cyrus moved against Astyages, king of the Medes, capturing the capital city of Ecbatana in 550. This aggressive act caused the Lydian King Croesus to turn his attention toward the rising Persian threat. The Lydians were allied with the Medeans and, through Croesus's conquests, the Lydian boundaries had been extended to the Halys River, west of the newly acquired kingdom of the Persians. Croesus wasted no time in hiring Spartan mercenaries to mount an offensive against Cyrus. When he learned of this, Cyrus led his forces into Lydian territory, demanding that Croesus surrender and become his royal vassal. After a series of battles, Croesus was crushed and the Lydian capital at Sardis was captured in 546. Cyrus's generals extended his empire to the Hellespont while he attempted conquests in the east. Again, the details of his exploits have escaped modern historians. Evidently, he succeeded in extending the boundaries of the empire to the Indus River in the east and the Oxus River in the northeast.

Cyrus now sought to bring the Babylonian Empire under his control. In 539, conflict began when Belshazzar, the emperor's son and the reigning governor of Babylon, confronted Cyrus at Opis. Belshazzar was soundly defeated and the city of Babylon was captured without a fight. Cyrus entered the city several days later, proclaiming himself liberator. Several factors contributed to the fall of Babylon. Nebonidus, its emperor, raised heavy taxes to pay for personal religious expeditions. He also introduced the gods of Ur, Uruk, and Eryden, which angered Babylonian priests. These actions encouraged dissidents to aid the Persians in the overthrow.

The first of Cyrus's great qualities was his ability to lead in battle. Through the strategies employed in the three battles, one can see his genius. Against the Lydians he marched his troops several thousand miles through winter snows, after a standoff at Pteria, in order to surprise Croesus at Sardis. Croesus had sent most of his troops home, thinking the Persians would be delayed by the weather and terrain. Cyrus's military vision also can be appreciated in the fall of Babylon. To capture the city, he diverted the waters of the Euphrates, which flowed through the city, so his troops could enter under the wall. Cyrus organized and trained his troops better than any other ruler of his day. Organization proved to be a problem because the Persian army was composed of several different tribal and ethnic groups. Cyrus divided these groups by tribes, allowing some of their own tribesmen to lead them. The familiarity of a local leader aided the troops in their ability to trust Cyrus's decisions.

The last qualities relate to one another. They were policies that grew from an attitude of openness and toleration. The ritual of conquering nations dictated that a vassal state surrender all customs and national identity to the conquerors. The Assyrian and Babylonian empires practiced displacement of peoples and the destruction of their cultures by carrying off their gods to their respective capitals. Conversely, Cyrus allowed the conquered peoples of Babylon to return to their homeland with their gods. The Hebrew people particularly benefited from these policies, as they had been prisoners in Babylon for 70 years. When Cyrus came to power, he permitted them to return to Palestine with the sacred elements of their temple. Cyrus also funded the rebuilding of the Temple in Jerusalem, issuing a decree that gave Jewish leaders the power to secure the materials needed for construction.

Cyrus the Great, founder of the
Persian Empire.

These policies of tolerance led to this proclamation after the fall of Babylon: "Come forth, collect your herds, draw water for the animals, and give your families to eat. The disturbance is ended, the peace of Archaemedia prevails." The kingdom of Cyrus would be the precursor of many tolerant empires to come. Cyrus would have been forgotten as an insignificant character, and not assigned the status "the Great" afforded him today, were it not for his tolerant policies. The familiarity of his name in the Western Hemisphere grows largely out of the praise given to him in the Old Testament. The Book of Ezra elevates him to an exalted status: ". . . the Lord God of Heaven . . . appointed me [Cyrus] to build a Temple for Him at Jerusalem." The Jewish and Christian faiths recognize Cyrus as not only the king of Persia, but also "the Great" because of his benevolent and tolerant policies, which led to the propagation of both faiths.

See also Assyrian Empire; Chaldean (Neo-Babylonian) Empire, Expansion of.

References: Huart, Clement, *Ancient Persian and Iranian Civilization* (New York: Barnes & Noble, 1972); Lamb, Harold, *Cyrus the Great* (New York: Doubleday, 1960); Sykes, Sir Percy, *Persia* (Oxford: Clarendon Press, 1922).

5 EGYPT, HYKSOS INVASION OF

Power slipped from the pharaohs of Egypt in the late Middle Kingdom, during the Twelfth Dynasty, in a relatively easy victory for the Hikau-Khoswet,

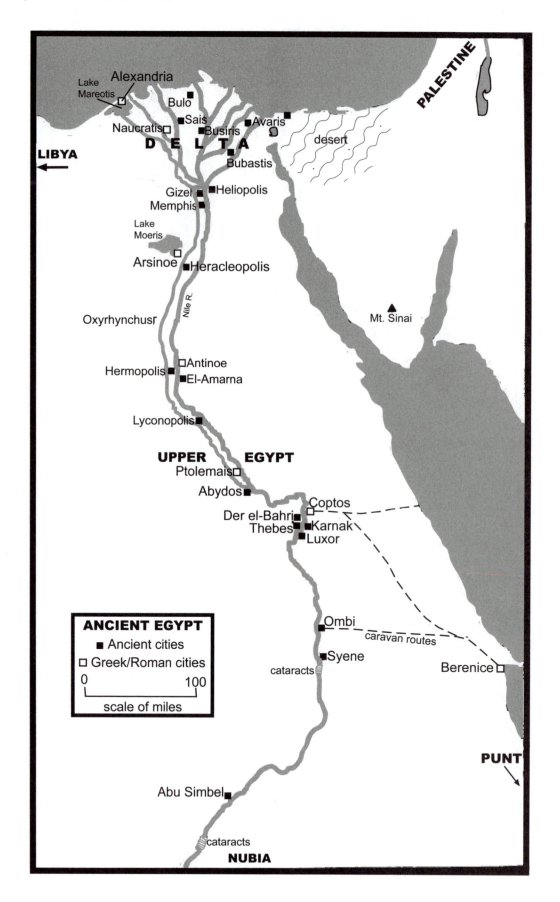

ANCIENT EGYPT

■ Ancient cities

□ Greek/Roman cities

0   100

scale of miles

a name originating from the Egyptian phrase meaning "rulers of foreign lands." An Asiatic group composed primarily of Semites, the Hikau-Khoswet, or Hyksos, reigned over Egypt for well over 100 years, beginning from about 1750 B.C.E. and ending with the establishment of the New Kingdom in 1567 B.C.E. The main catalysts that enabled the Hyksos to invade the Nile Delta so easily were the internal dissent among the Egyptians themselves, a counterrevolt of the nobility, and the weakening power of the pharaohs. Additionally, the Hyksos were said to be well trained and well armed, using tactics that included the introduction of the horse and chariot to Egypt.

During the course of their invasion, towns and cities were burned, temples damaged, and the native populations subjected to severe hardships and cruelties. Once the Hyksos gained control, they imposed heavy taxes as well as a strong military dominance. Surprisingly, the majority of Egyptians accepted this style of leadership without much resistance.

The Hyksos were not entirely preoccupied with military goals. According to William Hayes, "The Hyksos kings of the Fifteenth Dynasty brought about the construction of temples, production of statues, reliefs, scarabs, and other works of art and craftsmanship," some of which are regarded as the best examples of Egyptian literary and technical works of that time. Practical and useful inventions such as the well sweep, the vertical loom, and the composite bow, as well as the introduction of new religious and philosophical concepts, were Hyksos legacies. Until this time, Egypt was comparatively slow in its technological advancements in relation to the Middle Eastern civilizations. Egyptians were now able to learn of bronze working, the potter's wheel, and the use of arsenic copper. The Hyksos also introduced humpbacked cattle and fruit crops, and taught the Egyptians new planting and harvesting skills. Evidence suggests that the Hyksos encouraged exercise through dance and expression with new musical instruments.

On the whole, the Hyksos seem to have been a powerful and influential people, but only a few rulers can take credit for these advances. One of the six Hyksos rulers was Prince Salatis, a name that has been interpreted to mean "Sultan."

During his rise to power, he banned the contemporary Egyptian rulers from the capital city of Memphis and extended his rule over most of Middle Egypt, eventually taking over Upper Egypt and Nubia as well. In the meantime, Hyksos rulers had moved the capital to Avaris, the location of which remains a mystery. Though these Semitic invaders were eventually overthrown by the Egyptians in the late 1560s, they left behind the tools and knowledge that helped build Egypt's future empire. Little information exists on the Hyksos invasion itself, but their overall accomplishments were dynamic and paved the way for future Egyptian glory.

References: Baines, J., and J. Malek, *Atlas of Ancient Egypt* (New York: Facts on File, 1980); Hayes, W, *The Scepter of Egypt* (Cambridge, MA: Harvard University Press, 1959); Van Seeters, J., *The Hyksos* (New Haven, CT Yale University Press, 1966).

6   HITTITES, EXPANSION OF

The Hittites probably originated northeast of the Caucasus. They migrated into Asia Minor circa 1900 B.C.E. and established a kingdom. They occupied the Anatolian plateau, ultimately extending their influence toward Syria. Their migration may have pushed other populations southward, creating the Hyksos invasion of Egypt. The Hittites probably took their name from the Plain of Hatti, which they occupied and upon which they imposed their culture and Indo-European language. Their first conquest was the town of Nesa (near modern Kayseri, Turkey), followed by the capture of Hattusha (near modern Bogazkoy).

Little is known of them until the seventeenth century B.C.E., when Labarna (ruled circa 1680–1650) established the Old Hittite Kingdom and set up his capital at Hattusha. Labarna was the first major conqueror for the Hittites, spreading their control throughout Anatolia to the coast. His successors pushed their borders southward to Syria. Mursili (or Mushilish) raided deep into the Old Babylonian Empire, captured Aleppo, and set the kingdom's southern boundary in Syria. This proved to be the extent of their conquest, for they spent the next two centuries quelling internal disturbances and fighting the Mitanni of upper Mesopotamia.

Around 1500 B.C.E., the kingdom returned to some stability under the leadership of Telipinu, who laid down strict succession guidelines and possibly established a law code. Some 50 years later, the New Hittite Kingdom was established. The Hittites had just suffered a defeat at the hands of Egyptian pharaoh Thutmosis III and had begun paying them tribute. One of the key figures in the New Kingdom was Suppiluliuma (Shubbiluliu), who seized power about 1380 B.C.E., reestablished Hittite authority in Anatolia, and defeated the Mitanni. He was unable to defeat the Egyptians, however, and the two powers remained rivals for the next century. During a time of Egyptian weakness under Akhenaton, the Hittites made gains in Lebanon at Egyptian expense; they also spread their power to the Aegean, Armenia, and Upper Mesopotamia.

The key battle in the ongoing conflict with Egypt took place in 1294 B.C.E. at Kadesh, on the Orontes River. Pharaoh Rameses II led his army of Numidian mercenaries north to force his will on the Hittites once and for all. He captured two Hittite deserters, who informed him that their army was still many days' march away, so Rameses rode ahead of his army to set up camp near Kadesh. The two prisoners had been planted by the Hittite king Muwatallis, and the pharaoh, without most of his troops, was attacked by the Hittite army. Rameses fought bravely until his men arrived, and their appearance forced a Hittite retreat into the city of Kadesh. Without siege equipment, Rameses could not force their surrender, so he withdrew. Shortly thereafter, the two nations signed a peace agreement: The Egyptians recognized Hittite sovereignty in Syria in return for Hittite recognition of Egyptian dominance in Palestine. The alliance was sealed by a dynastic marriage, and the two nations remained at peace until the fall of the Hittite Empire, which came at the hands of the "Peoples of the Sea," about 1200 B.C.E.

The Hittite legacy showed itself in a mixed culture in the region of northern Syria. Some of their written and spoken language remained in the region, as did their last remaining city-states, which were ultimately overrun by the Arameans

(forerunners of modern Syrians) and then by the Assyrians in the eighth century B.C.E. The Hittites used both cuneiform writing adopted from Mesopotamia and hieroglyphics influenced by Egypt, and their formal political writings were in Akkadian. They had a highly developed literature and historical writing. Their main strength lay in their administration; their law codes were based on those of Babylon, but depended less on retribution than on compensation. Their artwork, though recognizable as their own, was heavily influenced by Babylon, as was much of their pantheon. The Hittites are believed to have been the first to smelt iron, which would account for some of their military superiority at a time when their enemies, especially Egypt, were still using bronze. Apparently, it did not prove a sufficient advantage to save their civilization from invasion.

See also Assyrian Empire; Egypt, Hyksos Invasion of.

References: Ceram, C. W, *The Secret of the Hittites*, trans. Richard Winston and Clara Winston (New York: Alfred A. Knopf, 1956); Lehman, Johannes, *The Hittites: People of a Thousand Gods*, trans. J. M. Brownjohn (New York: Viking Press, 1977); MacQueen, J. G., *The Hittites and Their Contemporaries in Asia Minor* (London: Thames & Hudson, 1968).

7   INDIA, ARYAN INVASION OF

The earliest known civilization in India was that of the Harappans, who established well-organized cities in the valley of the Indus River in the third millennium BCE. By about 2000 BCE, the civilization was beginning to fade, probably because of climatic changes, which brought about shifts in the rivers and widespread flooding. By sheer coincidence, as the Harappans were weakening, a group of invaders appeared from the steppes of the Caucasus. The Aryans were mostly nomadic-herding sheep, horses, and cattle-and, like most nomadic peoples, more warlike than the agricultural inhabitants of northern India. Both by migration and by force of arms, they dominated the area of the upper Indus valley and over time spread eastward down the Ganges.

The Aryans take their name from the word in their Sanskrit language meaning "noble." The Aryans themselves are identified as a language group, not a racial one. The fact that their area of origin made them lighter-skinned than the people they conquered has nothing to do with the language they spoke, so equating "Aryan" with "white" is incorrect; this nineteenth-century concept was reinforced by some twentieth-century racists. However, the original Aryans instituted a practice that called for separation of their peoples from the conquered. Their society was based on four basic classes that are the basis of the caste system that dominates India to this day: priests, warriors, merchants/artisans, and laborers. This class division did not include the conquered peoples of India, who became "outcast[e]s," or the "untouchables" of modern India.

The Aryans ultimately settled down to an agricultural way of life, but their early years in India resulted in the perpetuation of their herding ways. The plains of northern India provided good grazing land, and their herds of horses and cattle grew. Cattle became the most valuable of commodities, possibly foreshadowing the sacredness of cattle in the Hindu faith. The Aryans' famous horsemanship was a major reason for their military successes, as the Harappans had neither cavalry nor chariots. A military society built around the upper-class warriors was reflected in the rowdiness of the Aryans, who celebrated life with drinking, horse racing, and gambling; the last was a national obsession.

The greatest legacy of the Aryans is the religious works passed down originally through the priesthood. The Vedas are a collection of religious rituals handed down through oral tradition and finally committed to writing when that skill was introduced about 700 BCE. The ceremonies practiced and the gods worshipped through the Vedas laid the groundwork for the introduction of the Hindu faith, the dominant religion of India for some 2,000 years.

Though they were conquerors of northern India early in the second millennium BCE and of the northeastern plains and Ganges River valley between 1000 and 500 BCE, the Aryans became the dominant inhabitants of India as they settled into agricultural pursuits. This less mobile pastime bred, as it almost always does, a less martial society, but the Indians managed to remain fairly isolated from later conquerors. Alexander the Great spent two years fighting and negotiating in northwestern India, installing a Greek administration in some areas. After his death, however, Chandragupta Maurya overthrew the bureaucracy and established an Indian empire. Not until the Islamic invasion of India in the 800s CE did outside forces have much luck in penetrating the subcontinent.

All that being said, there has been strong debate starting in the 1990s about the entire story. Some modern scholars argue that there was no serious migration into India between 4500-800 BCE, and the whole thing is a nineteenth-century construct based on misreading the Vedas. The latest interpretation is as follows: "Rig Veda verses belie the old chronology (VI.51.14-15 mentions the winter solstice occurs when the sun rises in Revati nakshatra, only possible at 6000 BCE, long before the alleged invasion). Carbon dating confirms horses in Gujarat at 2400 BCE, contradicting [the old] model [claiming that] Aryans must have brought them. NASA satellite photos prove [that the] Sarasvati River basin is real, not a myth. Fire altars excavated at Kali Bangan in Rajasthan support existence of Rig Veda culture at 2700 BCE. Kunal, a new site in Haryana, shows use of writing and silver craft in pre-Harappan India, 6-7000 BCE." (Hinduism Today)

The latest evidence does, indeed, seem strong, although critics counter that the claims are Hindu revisionism attempting to discredit European influence in India since the 1500s.

See also Mauryan Empire [27]; India, Muslim Invasion of [53].

References: Gokhale, Balkrishna, *Ancient India: History and Culture* (Bombay and New York: Asia Publishing House, 1959); Wheeler, Radha, *Early India and Pakistan* (New York: Praeger, 1959); Wolpert, Stanley, *India* (Englewood Cliffs, NJ: Prentice Hall, 1965); "Hindu Timeline Reconstruction", *Hinduism Today*, December, 1994, www.hinduismtoday.com/ archives/1994/12/, 14 March 2006.

8   KUSH, EXPANSION OF

About 1500 B.C.E., Egypt conquered the area above the cataracts known as Kush. The purposes of this expedition were to establish frontier forts to protect against the aggressive Nubians and to gain access to the gold of Kush. Egypt dominated the area for about 400 years, until the collapse of the New Kingdom. In the meantime, they introduced Egyptian civilization into Kush, and the Kushites found it attractive. By the 700s B.C.E., Kush had grown in power and invaded Egypt in turn. Starting about 725 B.C.E., Kushites conquered Thebes and Memphis, establishing themselves as rulers of Egypt and beginning the Twenty-fifth Dynasty. Their occupation was relatively short-lived, thanks to the Assyrians who invaded in 664 B.C.E. and forced the Kushites to return home, behind the protective barriers of the Nile cataracts.

Though no longer a major factor in Egyptian history, the Kushites established a strong civilization along Egyptian lines. They copied Egyptian religion and government, and built temples and tombs heavily influenced by Egyptian architecture. Their capital at Napata, just south of the fourth cataract, was a major religious center for the worship of Amonre. When a later Egyptian ruler raided into Kush with the aid of Greek mercenaries, the capital was moved from Napata to Meroe, which became not only the political but the mercantile center of the Kushite Empire. In the few centuries prior to the Christian era, a succession of kings established their control over outlying areas and peoples, and recorded these exploits on inscribed memorials.

Kush reached the height of its civilization at the beginning of the Christian era, when a series of military encounters with Roman forces in Egypt brought about a treaty establishing exact borders between the two powers. By this time, Meroe was the major supply center for gold as well as precious and semiprecious stones from the interior of Africa to the Mediterranean world. The profits from this trade translated into elaborate buildings and artwork. Kush made a name for itself throughout the known world, and references and artistic depictions of them spread widely. Indeed, it is from the Greeks that the name for the peoples of this area comes: Ethiopians, or "men with burnt faces." Kush was the first essentially Negroid nation to reach a powerful status. They were the first Africans to mine and smelt iron; that, in addition to their ability to buy horses, gave them a better armed, more mobile army than any of their neighbors.

Kush eventually fell owing to circumstances beyond its control. The area the Kushites controlled was fertile enough to support extensive agriculture and flocks at the time, but today it is almost totally desert. Historians hypothesize that overgrazing and a shift in weather patterns began to rob the land of its fertility, making it impossible to support the population. Also, the trade routes Meroe controlled along the Nile began to fall from favor after easier, seagoing trade established itself along the Red Sea coast. This lack of income, coupled with decreasing arable land, spelled the Kushites' doom, and they fell easy prey to Axum about 350 C.E.

For 2,000 years, Kush had been virtually the only point of contact between Africa's interior and the civilizations of the Middle East. Almost nothing is known of their posterity, though legends relate that the ruling families traveled west into the Sudan and were instrumental in establishing nations in central Africa.

See also Assyrian Empire; Axum, Expansion of.

References: Hallett, Robin, *Africa to 1875* (Ann Arbor: University of Michigan Press, 1970); Mokhtar, G., *Ancient Civilizations of Africa* (Paris: UNESCO, 1990).

9 PALESTINE, EGYPTIAN INVASIONS OF

Considering the number of times Egyptian armies entered Palestine, it is somewhat ironic that the spur for their activity was an invasion that probably came from Palestine. For about 100 years the Egyptians had been ruled by the Hyksos, who introduced new weaponry (especially the chariot) to Egypt. As is often the case, the rulers became lazy and corrupt, and in the middle 1500s B.C.E., Egyptian rebels overthrew them. The Egyptian army that chased them back to their homeland was the first in a long line of forces to cross the Suez into Palestine.

The Theban prince Ahmose chased the Hyksos out of Egypt and established a foothold on the eastern Mediterranean coast. Tuthmosis I led his army as far as the Euphrates River, and set up a monument to himself. His immediate successors had little to do with the area, but in the reign of Tuthmosis III (1490–1436 B.C.E.), 17 expeditions entered Palestine or Syria, and the Egyptians fought several times against the Mitanni, a confederation of Hurrian tribes living north of the Euphrates who raided or forced tribute from a large area in the Middle East. Tuthmosis's eighth campaign resulted in a major defeat of the king of Kadesh at the plain of Megiddo, or Armageddon. Tuthmosis personally led a flanking maneuver that crushed his opponents in what became the first recorded battle in history. He pushed Egyptian influence to the edge of Hittite authority in Asia Minor and into northwestern Mesopotamia. This proved to be the greatest distance the Egyptian army ever traveled, because Tuthmosis III's successors merely maintained Egyptian influence in Palestine, and signed a treaty with the Mitanni in the late fifteenth century B.C.E.

Egypt ruled the area with a number of garrisons under the direction of provincial governors, who worked with the local princes to con trol the larger population centers, holding their princes' children hostage in Egypt to ensure cooperation. The governors' main duty was to provide annual tribute from the conquered territories. What, if anything, the conquerors brought to Palestine is unknown, for there are no written records from this area in that period. The Egyptians probably gave little to the people besides a military presence, but they took with them knowledge, which Egypt, long isolated from the rest of the world, used along with the tribute money to build a civilization rich in architecture and culture. The Egyptians grew so accustomed to the tribute that, over time, less attention was paid to the army in Palestine, and Egyptian control began to wane.

After a series of introspective pharaohs, Egypt returned to Palestine in force during the reign of Seti I (1305–1290 B.C.E.), who launched a number of expeditions to reestablish Egyptian authority. The Egyptians ran into difficulties with the Hittites north of Syria and were ultimately forced to come to a settlement with them. It would not last. Rameses II returned to Palestine with a large army in 1286 B.C.E. and marched to the city of Kadesh on the Orontes River. He walked into a trap, but managed to survive with the timely arrival of reinforcements.

Rameses's future forays were less ambitious, and he finally signed a treaty with the Hittites in 1269 B.C.E. The treaty gave Egypt a nominal role in the area, but the Hittites gave little away.

Egypt's influence soon faded. Pressures from desert tribesmen to the west occupied much of their attention, and the Egyptians spent much time trying to maintain the gold supply from the southern territory of Nubia. Many historians believe the Jewish exodus, leading to the establishment of the state of Israel, took place during the reign of Rameses II. Rameses III was the last New Kingdom pharaoh to enter Palestine in order to retain it as part of the empire; he beat back several threats to his frontiers and reconquered Palestine. By the eleventh century B.C.E., however, Egypt had withdrawn into its shell, coming out only occasionally to unsuccessfully challenge the Assyrians or the Persians. Pharaoh Necho regained temporary sway over Palestine by defeating King Josiah in 609 B.C.E., but his defeat at the hands of Nebuchadnezzar of Babylon in 605 ended Egypt's role in Palestine's history.

See also Assyrian Empire; Canaan, Israelite Invasion of; Cyrus the Great; Egypt, Hyksos Invasion of; Hittites; Kush, Expansion of.

References: Hawkes, Jacquetta, *Pharaohs of Egypt* (New York: American Heritage, 1965); Matthew, Eva, *The Mediterranean World in Ancient Times* (New York: Ronald Press, 1951); North, Martin, *The Old Testament World* (Philadelphia: Fortress Press, 1962).

10 · SARGON THE GREAT

As is the case with many ancient figures, Sargon's early years are somewhat of a mystery. He was born around 2350 B.C.E. of undetermined parentage. Some historians theorize that he had either a pastoral upbringing or that he was the child of a temple prostitute, for he did not know his father. According to legend, the boy began life as Moses did: cast adrift on the Euphrates by his mother. He was rescued and raised by others—in this case a farm family, not a royal one. However, he managed to become cupbearer to Ur-Zababa, the king of Kish. He came to power either by overthrowing the king himself or by assuming the king's throne when Ur-Zababa was

Bronze Head of the Akkadian ruler Sargon the Great
(Scala/Art Resource, NY)

killed by the invading king of Sumer. He took the name Sargon, meaning "King of Universal Dominion," and made war against Sumer.

Sargon united his Semitic people into history's first empire: the Akkadians. Sargon set about conquering, quite successfully. He captured cities up the Euphrates River, then crossed to the Tigris River and worked his way up to Ashur. From there he conquered eastward to the Persian hills, then south to defeat Sumer, possibly gaining revenge for the death of Ur-Zababa. He symbolically washed his weapons in the Persian Gulf, marking the limit of his conquests in that direction. After consolidating his hold on Sumer, he marched west to conquer Mesopotamia and possibly as far as Syria and Lebanon, with rumors of conquests in lands as far-flung as Egypt, Asia Minor, and India.

In order to control this vast amount of territory, Sargon appointed representatives of the conquered peoples to governing positions, and they answered only to him. He stationed troops in posts around the empire, garrisoning them with forces of all nations, though some soldiers were forced to join his armies. Sargon was successful in battle because he initiated new tactics. He abandoned the standard tight, phalanx-style formation in favor of a looser one, and he adopted the use of javelins and arrows shot from com pound bows. He also maintained the first standing army, a force of 5,400 men.

By placing so much land under one ruler, previously uncooperative peoples became more open to relations with neighboring tribes, and the freer exchange of goods and ideas resulted. New gods and religions were adopted from conquered peoples, as were cuneiform writing and art. The Akkadians were the first to use writing for more than keeping temple records. Because of this, we have the first recorded actions of royalty; hence, Sargon is regarded as the first clearly identified individual in history. He set an example for later royal chroniclers, as seen here: "He spread his terror-inspiring glamour over all the countries. He crossed the Sea in the East and he, himself, conquered the country of the West…He marched against the country of Kazalla and turned Kazalla into ruin-hills and heaps of rubble. He even destroyed there every possible perching place for a bird."

Having acquired vast amounts of land, Sargon's empire was exceedingly wealthy, controlling the known world's gold, silver, copper, and stone. With the abundant agriculture of Mesopotamia and plenty of forage to the north, Sargon seemingly had it all. He maintained control by appointing loyal governors and visiting parts of his empire on occasion to let the people know he was interested in them. He ruled for 56 years, but his reign ended with parts of the empire in revolt. The Akkadian empire lasted some 200 years, only to be overthrown by those who had originally been defeated—a resurgent Sumerian society.

References: Edwards, I. E. S., ed., *The Cambridge Ancient History* (Cambridge: Cambridge University Press, 1980); Gabriel, Richard, *The Culture of War* (New York: Greenwood Press, 1990); Gabriel, Richard, *From Sumer to Rome* (New York: Greenwood Press, 1991).

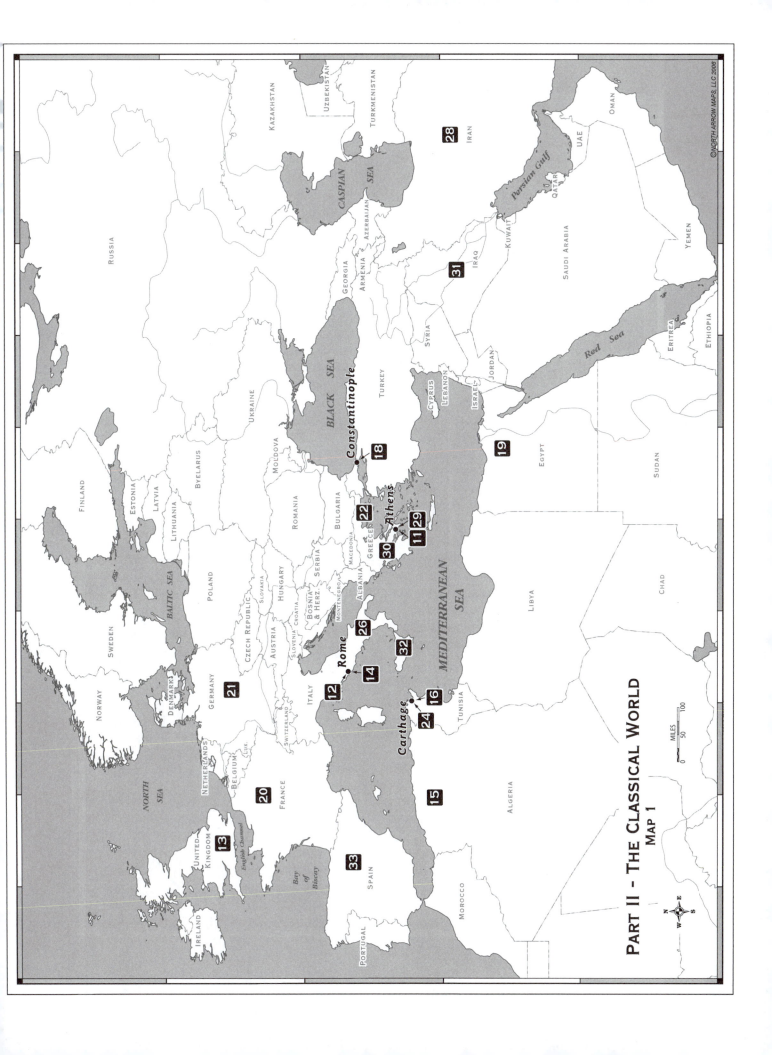

PART II - THE CLASSICAL WORLD
MAP 1

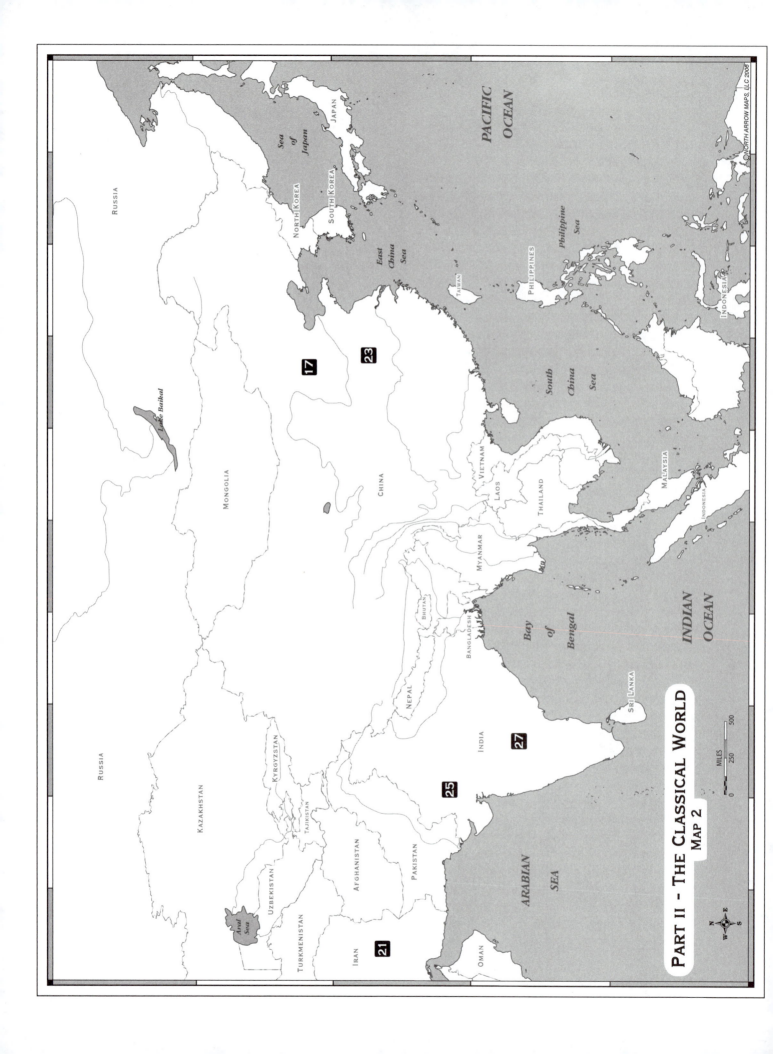

PART II - THE CLASSICAL WORLD
MAP 2

PART 2
THE CLASSICAL WORLD

11 ALEXANDER THE GREAT

Alexander was born to rule and to conquer. He was the son of the great military and political leader Philip of Macedon and his first wife, Olympia. Philip was organizing the remote province of Macedon into a military powerhouse and using his well-trained and well-disciplined army to beat back the more barbaric tribes of Macedon and attack the more civilized polises of Greece to his south. He defeated the disorganized Greek city-states and obliged them to recognize him—not as their king, but as the defender of the Greek way of life against outside threats, notably from Persia. He convinced most of his defeated enemies to accept this and treated them with magnanimity, but he never converted the Athenian leader Demosthenes, who spent his life opposing Philip and Alexander. It was in the battle of Cheronaea, in which the Macedonians defeated the Athenians, that Alexander first distinguished himself in battle.

He was only 18 years old when he commanded a wing of the Macedonian army at Cheronaea in 338 B.C.E., but he gained the respect of all who fought with him. His father trained him well in both military and political strategies, but the two fought. Alexander's mother, Olympia, told him that his true father was not Philip but the supreme god Zeus (Ammon to the Egyptians). She also plotted against Philip and may have been responsible for his murder in 336 B.C.E., an act that brought Alexander to the throne. He quickly put down revolts that sprang up throughout Greece upon the news of Philip's death, then marched north to defeat the tribes on Macedon's frontiers. While there, the false report of his death was circulated in Athens and Demosthenes stirred up rebellion, which Alexander suppressed as soon as he returned from the north. Like his father, he spared Demosthenes's life and left a constant irritant in Greece.

Once the rebellions were put down, Alexander marched to the Hellespont, where his father had been preparing to lead the united polises of the Corinthian League against Persia. Alexander marched into Asia Minor in 334 B.C.E. with 35,000 men, liberating the coastal Ionian provinces from Persian rule. His first serious encounter with Darius III, the Persian emperor, occurred at Issus in northeastern Syria. Contemporary accounts of the Persian force claim it was 500,000 strong, but few historians believe it. Still, although it was probably larger than Alexander's force, the battle proved a fairly easy Macedonian victory. Alexander positioned himself to be in the thick of the fighting, encouraging his comrades and striking fear in his enemies. Darius abandoned the field and ran, leaving behind not only his army but his family, whom Alexander took to his camp and treated like royalty.

Rather than pursue Darius deeper into the countryside, Alexander turned south to capture the coastal cities and deny the harbors to the Persian fleet. Capturing the eastern Mediterranean coast, he entered Egypt and wintered there in 332–331. He established the city of Alexandria (the first of many) and led a small column into the desert to visit the temple of Ammon. What transpired inside the temple is unknown, but many think Alexander communed with the great god and received confirmation that he was indeed of divine parentage as his mother had told him. True or not, he did nothing to stop those who deified him. This may have been megalomania or a clever ruse to awe his enemies; no one knows for sure.

Leaving Egypt, he marched into Persia and met a new army under Darius at Gaugamela along the Euphrates River. Again, the contemporary estimates are too fantastic to believe, but Darius proved no match for Alexander. The latter marched on to the Persian capital at Babylon and occupied it, then captured the Persian treasury at Persepolis. With the Persian empire well under his control, he finally cornered Darius near the Caspian Sea, but lost him to the swords of Darius's minions, who murdered him rather than be caught with him. From here, Alexander meandered eastward until he made his way through Afghanistan into India. Here he won victories, but they proved too costly; his army convinced him to abandon the expedition and return to Persia. He did so, taking the desert route, which proved much more difficult than he had anticipated.

Back in Persia, Alexander began to show his brilliance as a statesman. He had a vision for a

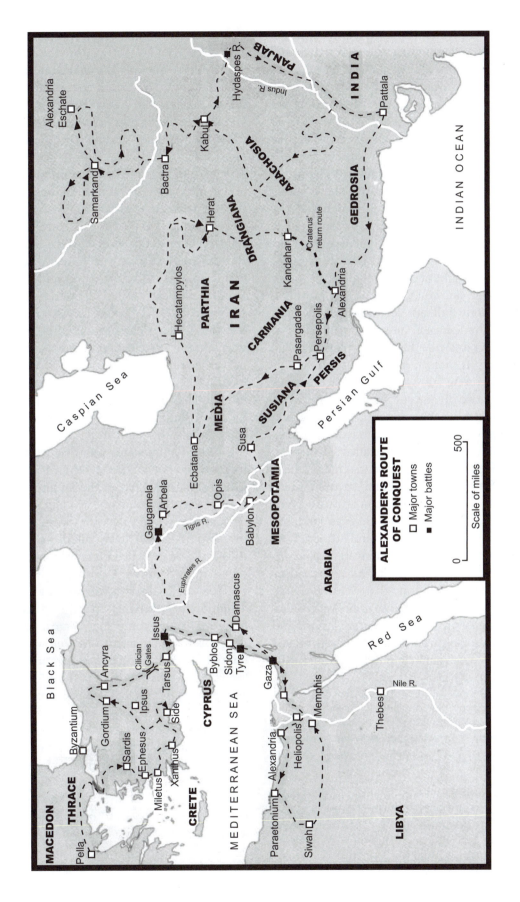

ALEXANDER'S ROUTE OF CONQUEST

☐ Major towns
■ Major battles

Scale of miles

0 · · · · 500

world empire in which the wealth and culture of the East would meld with the rationality and drive of the Greeks. He encouraged his veterans to marry Persian women in order to facilitate the integration of the two societies. He began to act more like an Eastern potentate than a Greek general, and his men grew weary of that. He shamed them into remaining loyal, but his time was limited. Not long after his return from India, the wounds he received in battle there, along with the difficulty of the desert march and the fever he had developed in Babylon, conspired to ruin his health. The stress of combat and leadership was not aided by his prodigious thirst; alcoholism, too, brought about his demise.

Alexander can be regarded as one of only a handful of truly brilliant leaders. Like Genghis Khan and Charlemagne, he was equally adept at both conquest and rule. He was ruthless in battle but forgiving in victory, gaining converts to his cause from among his opponents. His dream of blending the two diverse cultures of East and West was successful for some centuries, for his successors (the Ptolemaic Dynasty and Seleucid Empire) created a Greek-like society called Hellenism, which blended the perspective and scientific bent of the Greeks with the beauty and grace of Eastern philosophies. The intellectual and artistic accomplishments of the Hellenistic societies surpassed anything that had come before and attracted the future power of the Mediterranean, Rome, to desire and fight for the mystic East. Alexander's generalship created an army that was unbeatable and soldiers who were second to none, but his successors learned only from his military lessons and not from his political acumen. They fought among themselves, and by doing so, laid themselves open to defeat by Rome.

See also Egypt, Alexander's Conquest of; India, Alexander's Invasion of; Persia, Alexander's Conquest of; Philip of Macedon; Ptolemaic Dynasty; Seleucid Empire; Carolingian Dynasty; Genghis Khan.

References: Arrian, The Campaigns of Alexander, trans. Aubrey de Selincourt (New York: Penguin, 1958); Keegan, John, The Mask of Command (New York: Viking, 1987); Tarn, W W, Alexander the Great (Cambridge: Cambridge University Press, 1948).

12   AUGUSTUS, CAESAR

Gaius Julius Caesar Octavianus, or more simply Octavian, was the grandnephew of Julius Caesar and was named in his will as heir. After Julius Caesar's assassination in March 44 B.C.E., his killers left Rome, Cassius going to Syria and Brutus to Macedonia. Mark Antony, consul under Julius and one of his most trusted advisers and generals, saw himself as the rightful political successor, and he was not happy to see Octavian present himself to the Senate as such. After some fighting between them, Octavian finally invited Antony to join forces with him and another general, Lepidus, to form the Second Triumvirate. With Senate approval, they marched to do battle with Cassius and Brutus. In October 43 B.C.E., the forces met near Philippi, in Greece. They were evenly matched in numbers, but Antony proved the more able general. Two battles were fought; the first was a draw in which Cassius killed himself, and the second was a clear victory for the Triumvirate, resulting in Brutus's suicide soon after.

The Triumvirate soon quarreled among themselves, but at the signing of the Treaty of Brundisium in 40 B.C.E., the empire was divided among the three members: Lepidus controlled Africa, Octavian ruled the western provinces from Rome, and Antony ruled the provinces of the east. Antony aided Octavian in suppressing a revolt from Sardinia, Corsica, and Sicily led by the son of Pompey, a member of the original Triumvirate with Julius. In return, Octavian supported Antony's campaigns against Parthia.

Antony's popularity with his troops and his relative success in the east gave him the impetus for more power. He allied himself (personally and politically) with Cleopatra of Egypt, who urged him to seize power. Octavian convinced the Senate that Antony planned to establish rule of the empire from Alexandria in Egypt and name his sons by Cleopatra as his heirs, which motivated the Senate to support Octavian's call for war. Between 33 and 30 B.C.E., the two sides maneuvered for position until 2 September 31, when Octavian's forces won the naval battle of Actium, defeating Egypt's navy. Octavian proceeded to invade Egypt against a disheartened

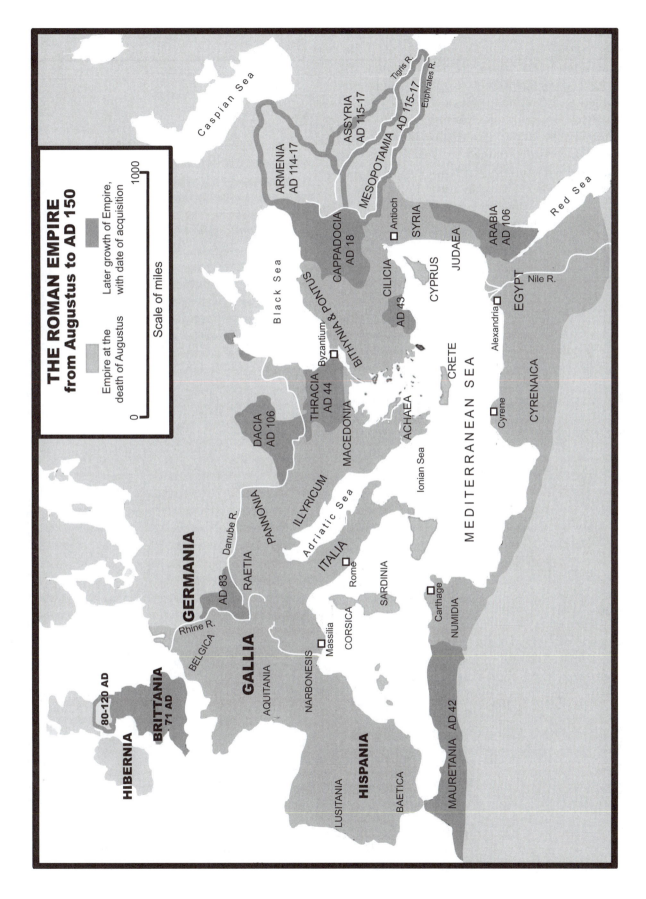

THE ROMAN EMPIRE
from Augustus to AD 150

Empire at the death of Augustus

Later growth of Empire, with date of acquisition

Scale of miles

0   1000

Caspian Sea

ARMENIA AD 114-17

ASSYRIA AD 115-17

Tigris R.

MESOPOTAMIA AD 115-17

Euphrates R.

CAPPADOCIA AD 18

Antioch

SYRIA

ARABIA AD 106

Red Sea

Black Sea

BITHYNIA & PONTUS

Byzantium

CILICIA AD 43

CYPRUS

JUDAEA

EGYPT

Nile R.

Alexandria

THRACIA AD 44

MACEDONIA

ACHAEA

CRETE

MEDITERRANEAN SEA

Cyrene

CYRENAICA

DACIA AD 106

ILLYRICUM

Adriatic Sea

Ionian Sea

PANNONIA

Danube R.

RAETIA

GERMANIA AD 83

Rhine R.

BELGICA

ITALIA

Rome

SARDINIA

CORSICA

Massilia

Carthage

NUMIDIA

GALLIA

AQUITANIA

NARBONESIS

80-120 AD

BRITTANIA 71 AD

HIBERNIA

MAURETANIA AD 42

HISPANIA

LUSITANIA

BAETICA

Antony and a desperate Cleopatra. After suffering reverses at Roman hands, the two killed themselves and left Octavian supreme. He looted the Egyptian treasury, which was immense, and returned to Rome.

After years of turmoil under the Triumvirates, Rome was finally at peace, and Octavian was determined to keep it that way. Though he had not shown himself to be an outstanding soldier, Octavian used the services of able leaders, proving his eye for talent. Thus, his importance lay not in his military ability but in his political acumen, which was extensive. Octavian inherited a republic with far-flung responsibilities, and he turned it into an empire. In 27 B.C.E. he was named Augustus by the Senate, a title of divinity that he graciously accepted, though he preferred the title First Citizen, princeps of the Senate. Octavian thus avoided Julius's mistake of giving the appearance of grasping for power, and his power ultimately far exceeded that of his granduncle. Through lavish spending of his Egyptian wealth, he stimulated a lagging economy, and by forgiving debts he stimulated investment; Rome's financial state was soon healthy. He dismissed 60 percent of his half-million-man army, giving them rewards and lands for pensions. He paid the remaining 200,000 men well, and distributed them around the frontiers to maintain what became known as the Roman Peace, the Pax Romana. He maintained a Praetorian Guard of 10,000 with which to tacitly keep control of Rome and Italy. After a 20-year enlistment, retiring veterans received land; citizenship was granted to foreigners who served in his army.

Caesar Augustus's most lasting accomplishments were the Roman Empire and the formulation of Augustan law. By synthesizing legal codes from around the known world, he created a system in which all men were treated equally before the law in a manner that did not seem alien to any of the subordinate cultures. The resulting peace created an atmosphere in which trade boomed, as did cultural advancements. Until his death in 14 C.E., Caesar Augustus oversaw the largest and most placid empire up to that time. He wisely maintained the forms of republican government to which Roman citizens were accustomed, while working through those institutions to impose his will. Rarely has one man exercised so much positive influence on the world. Not until the reign of Constantine or Justinian would the Mediterranean world come close to being ruled by such a man of vision.

See also Caesar, Julius; Constantine, Emperor; Justinian.

References: Campbell, J. B., *The Roman Army, 31 B.C.E.–AD 337* (London: Routledge, 1994); Earl, Donald C., *The Age of Augustus* (New York: Crown, 1968); Jones, A. H. M., *Augustus* (New York: Norton, 1970).

BRITAIN, ROMAN CONQUEST OF

13

Between 58 and 50 B.C.E., prior to the time of his rise to power in Rome, Julius Caesar undertook the conquest of Gaul, an extensive territory roughly corresponding to modern-day France. He did this in order to enhance his financial and political status within Rome's governing elite. The conquest of Gaul brought Britain to Caesar's notice because of the assistance the British gave the Celts of Gaul. Rome had had a strong desire to grow from a republic to an empire, which necessitated the invasion and conquest of other territories to amass land and riches. As Virgil wrote, "Forget not, Roman, that it is your special genius to rule the peoples; to impose the ways of peace, to spare the defeated, and to crush those proud men who will not submit." Along with the land and wealth that came to Caesar and his successors came power and glory, all of which fueled the desire to "rule the peoples."

Beginning with Julius Caesar and ending with Honorius, the conquest of Britain and its transformation to Roman rule was a process that took centuries. Caesar's invasion was almost an afterthought. During his successful conquest of the Gauls, he recognized that Britain was rich with deposits of tin and iron ore, and that, from a financial standpoint, their resources and prosperity would make Roman conquest worth the effort. Also, from a geographic perspective, England's southeastern shore was only 21 miles across the Channel from Gaul, easily visible on a clear day. During the Gallic campaign, British tribes fought among themselves, and appeals for Roman support from defeated British chieftains indicated that a conquest should not be too difficult. Finally, in light of the Celts' support of their brothers-in-arms across the Channel in Gaul, Caesar no doubt wished to teach some respect for the might of Rome.

Caesar made two forays into Britain, the first in 55 B.C.E. and the second a year later. Both expeditions were of minor consequence, because Rome's interest in the Britons was just beginning. On both of these attacks, Caesar crossed the Channel and entered Britain by way of Deal, after first being turned away at the cliffs of Dover. Once on land, British forces were overwhelmed and victories came easily. As was the case with all Roman conquests, demands for hostages and regular tribute followed. The significance of Caesar's invasions would not be realized immediately, but the die was cast. Britain had been brought to Rome's attention and, with the organization of Celtic Gaul into Roman provinces, the British began to feel the impact of Roman civilization.

A century went by before the emperor Claudius turned his attention to Britain, in 43 C.E. He sent four Roman legions under the command of Aulus Plautius across the Channel into Kent with the intention of bringing Britain under Roman authority. The Claudian invasion, which lasted 15 years, marked the real beginning of Roman Britain. From this point on, the primitive culture of the British Celts was transformed by the conquering legions of a huge cosmopolitan power, and by the administrators and entrepreneurs who followed them. The invasion forces represented the best Rome had to offer: Many of the legionaries were specialists such as engineers, architects, masons, clerks, and medical staff. This mixture of soldiers was in keeping with the Roman policy of ensuring that its soldiers were highly trained, long-term professionals whose skills were as important to Rome in peace as in war. Even while garrisoned, the troops sometimes practiced digging defensive works or assisted civil authorities with building projects. This practice and experience in building and construction work made it possible for Roman armies to construct siege-works, build bridges, and lay roads very quickly during invasions.

In contrast to the highly skilled and organized Roman legions, the British had no standing armies. Lengthy campaigns were impractical for British troops because the majority of them were farmers, and they would leave the fields of battle for their fields of crops. During the Roman march through the British lowlands, in which there was little resistance, the British tried to fight with chariots. One of their favorite stratagems was to feign retreat to draw off small groups of Romans, and then attack them with chariotborne troops, dismounting to fight hand-to-hand.

Following the years of war after the Claudian invasion, there were intermittent rebellions against Roman rule. These conflicts were peacefully resolved for the most part, but there was one significant uprising known as Boudicca's Rebellion, which took place in 60 C.E. in the British province of Iceni. This rebellion represented a critical turning point for the Romans in their quest to establish rule. Ironically, the rebellion was organized and led by Boudicca, widow of Prasutagus, king of the province of Iceni, a tribe friendly and loyal to Rome from the beginning of the Claudian invasion. Shortly before Prasutagus died, Nero ascended the Roman throne and appointed C. Suetonius Paulinus, a man of excellent military credentials, as governor of Britain. During this unstable transitional period of Roman rule in Britain, the Roman military and civil officers ransacked the Iceni kingdom of all its wealth, confiscated Queen Boudicca's property, raped her two daughters, and flogged the queen herself. Simultaneously, her neighbors, the Trinovantes of Essex, were becoming impatient with Roman rule. Many Roman soldiers had retired and settled in the colony at Colchester and, in so doing, drove the native Trinovantes from their homes and land, and treated the natives as captives and slaves. These abuses of power and the instability of Roman rule fostered the perception by the natives that perhaps now the time was ripe to rid Britain of the invaders and regain control of their homeland.

In the year 60, the uprising commenced. On the Roman side, considerable confusion reigned at first. The British force, led by Boudicca, was a coalition of a half-dozen tribes consisting of 230,000 men, women, and children—farmers, peasants, and soldiers. They advanced on Londinium (London), a city without colonial or municipal status at the time, but already a large and attractive prize for plundering armies. Suetonius realized he did not have a force large enough to repel the British, so he retired and left the city to its fate. Londinium fell to the rebels, and many of the same atrocities and bestialities the Iceni had suffered at Roman hands now befell the residents.

The only way to defeat the overwhelming British force was with superior Roman discipline and tactics. Suetonius could now choose the location of the decisive battle, and he drew up his 10,000 troops in a defensive position to face a force of over 200,000. He placed his men on a hill with woods behind to protect his flanks and rear, then lured the British into attacking uphill. Suetonius drove through Boudicca's force in a tight wedge, the infantry doing serious damage with the glddius, a short sword. The Roman cavalry next attacked the flanks of the disorganized British force. Unable to retreat, the British were butchered. Boudicca escaped, but she committed suicide shortly thereafter. Romanization recommenced in full force under peaceful conditions.

Another turning point took place during the reign of the emperor Hadrian in 117. His reign concentrated on consolidation of the empire rather than expansion—securing the borders of Roman Britain rather than conquering new lands—and he made use of the military to restore order in those parts of the empire with violent disaffection. The main effect of this emphasis on defense was three-quarters of a century of peace throughout the empire. Hadrian accomplished this goal in Britain by commissioning the construction of a wall 70 miles long, spanning the narrow neck of land between Solway Firth and the mouth of the Tyne. The consequences were immense. Protection from the hostile tribes of Scotland brought general prosperity, which in turn caused the provincials to more readily identify with the empire, and it created a unified governing class. The universal extension of Roman citizenship to free inhabitants of the empire would be a direct result of Hadrian's reforms. An air of security allowed economic development by the southern tribes because it allowed them to concentrate on trade, farming, and manufacturing rather than be preoccupied with village defense. A long period of peace and prosperity followed, the likes of which had not been seen for almost 160 years.

For the next two and a half centuries, Roman Britain prospered. The Romans contributed greatly to the development of the British economy, and not only in agriculture. Britain had been mining long before the Claudian invasion, but the Romans introduced more efficient mining technology. They also contributed to the cultural development of Britain by introducing language, theater, art, and trade skills to its labor force. Rome's greatest contribution, though, was peace. Ironically, this reduction of military force led to the successful Visigothic invasion of Britain.

During the reign of Emperor Honorius (395–423) came the beginning of the end of Roman rule in Britain. Many of the highly skilled and trained professional Roman legionaries were replaced by local tribesmen and Saxon mercenaries, who were unable to fend off attacks by the Visigoths. Honorius rejected pleas from Britain in 410 to help defend its borders, and the barbarians ultimately prevailed. Urbanization, one of Rome's greatest contributions, halted completely, and cities and towns withered and died.

See also Gaul, Roman Conquest of.

References: Fry, Plantagenet Somerset, *Roman Britain, History and Sites* (Totowa, NJ: Barnes & Noble, 1984); Holder, P A., *The Roman Army in Britain* (New York: St. Martin's Press, 1982); Salway, Peter, *Roman Britain* (New York: Oxford University Press, 1981).

14   CAESAR, JULIUS

Gaius Julius Caesar was born 13 July 100 B.C.E. At age 16 he took over as head of the family upon his father's death and tended to his mother and two sisters. At age 19 he married Cornelia, the daughter of a Roman consul. After her death, Julius made a politically significant match by marrying the granddaughter of the great consul Sulla. (He divorced her after five years.)

Through these contacts, and his military abilities, he rose from the relative unimportance of an impoverished noble family to contacts with the most powerful men in Rome.

Early in his military career, Julius saw service in Asia and Cilicia and was involved in battles against the Persian leader Mithradates. His accomplishments on the battlefield and his political contacts put him in position to be elected tribune in 73 B.C.E. As this was an elected position, it showed his growing popularity with the public. He later held other elective and appointive offices, including aedile (city administrator), pontifexmaximus (head of the priests), and proconsul in Spain. He reached for the top when he allied himself with the two consuls Pompey and Crassus, forming the Triumvirate in 60 B.C.E. With their support in the Senate, he received the proconsulship of Gaul. There, he could enforce Roman rule and make a name for himself as a general, which was fast becoming the path to political power.

Between the years 58 and 51, he subdued Gaul, challenged marauding Germanic tribes, and mounted an expedition to Britain. He also tried to mediate between the increasingly hostile Crassus and Pompey.

Their failing relationship was the catalyst that ultimately led Julius to power. When Julia, Julius's daughter and Pompey's wife, died in 54 B.C.E., and Crassus was killed on a campaign in 53, the ties binding Julius and Pompey were broken. Pompey appealed to the Senate to remove Julius from his position in Gaul, a move designed to destroy any chance Julius might have to reach the highest government position: consul. Rather than accept his recall, Julius crossed the Rubicon River and led his forces into Italy, a treasonable act that led to direct military confrontation between himself and Pompey.

Julius's reputation had preceded him, and many cities welcomed his arrival as Pompey's forces fled. Their forces finally fought at Pharsalus, where Julius was victorious. Pompey fled to Egypt, but was murdered upon his arrival. Julius followed, and fell under the spell of the Egyptian Queen Cleopatra; when her brother dethroned her, Julius helped her regain the throne. Cleopatra considered a close relationship with Caesar the best

Bust of Julius Caeser, dictator for life of the Roman Republic before his assassination in 44 B.C.

security for her country, which was a declining power. After a quick campaign against the Persian Mithradates VI, Caesar returned to Rome.

Caesar did much to improve the lot of the Roman citizen. He established two colonies to drain off surplus population, and revived an old law requiring one-third of all agricultural laborers to become free men, cutting into the widespread use of slave labor long practiced by estate owners. He worked on codifying Roman law, opened the first public library in Rome, drained marshes around the city, and surveyed and mapped the empire. His longest lasting contribution was the Julian calendar, which remained the standard for date-keeping until the Middle Ages.

As a military man, Caesar is best known for his Gallic War, mainly because he wrote about it first-hand in his Commentaries. While in service in Gaul, he promoted the engineering aspect of Roman armies by modifying camp structure and weaponry. He improved the gathering of intelligence, the methods of training, and the art of military speechmaking. He promoted loyalty by increasing pay and benefits, and by his increased respect for the rights of soldiers. His campaign in Gaul secured the region for the Roman Empire for centuries and set up the later Roman conquest of Britain.

Rather than claim the position of king, which had been banned by the Roman Republic at its birth centuries earlier, Caesar took the title Dictator. He had himself elected to this position for single-year terms, then for a 10-year term; shortly afterward, he accepted the position for life. The difference in terminology between king and dictator was too indistinct for the Roman Senate, which Caesar had reduced to an almost powerless body. On the Ides (fifteenth) of March 44 B.C.E., Caesar was assassinated on his way to address the Senate. The conspirators, led by Marcus Junius Brutus and Gaius Cassius Longinus, removed the man who threatened to return the Republic to the status of a kingdom, but they had no contingency plans of their own. They were defeated shortly after by Caesar's grandnephew and appointed heir, Octavian, who instituted the position of Emperor and, as Caesar Augustus, took Rome to its greatest power. Julius Caesar did not make the Roman Empire himself, but his actions laid the groundwork for the successes of Augustus.

See also Augustus, Caesar; Britain, Roman Conquest of.

References: Bradford, Ernie Julius Caesar: *The Pursuit of Power* (New York: Morrow, 1984); *Caesar, Julius, Commentaries,* trans. John Warrington (New York: Heritage Press, 1955); Wiseman, Anne, and Peter Wiseman, *Julius Caesar: The Battle for Gaul* (Boston: David R. Godine, 1980).

15 CARTHAGE, EXPANSION OF

The city of Carthage was established by the Phoenicians late in the ninth century B.C.E. as a stopping place for eastern Mediterranean traders plying their business with the inhabitants of Spain and the western Mediterranean. Tyre was the parent city to Carthage, which is the Latinized version of the Phoenician Kart-Hadasht, or New City. The trading empire of Phoenicia, dealing in various metals, was well established in Spain; it also had settlement/trading posts in Sicily, Corsica, and Sardinia.

Carthage represented the first major attempt to settle along the North African coast outside the Egyptian sphere of influence.

The inhabitants of Carthage lived peacefully for more than two centuries because the local Libyan population was not organized enough to resist them and whatever military action was necessary was directed from Tyre. When Phoenicia came under Babylonian control, however, Carthage lost its connection with the homeland and came into its own. While Babylon was conquering the Levant, the Greeks stirred up trouble in Sicily, where their colonies attacked Phoenician settlements around 580 B.C.E. Carthage provided the defensive forces for Sicily and for threatened towns in southern Sardinia. In 553 B.C.E. Carthage allied with the Etruscans of Italy; together, they inflicted a major defeat of a Greek fleet off Corsica. That battle made Carthage master of the western Mediterranean and gave it dominance over the Spanish trade.

Like Phoenicia, Carthage's major expansion was in the form of settlement and trade. The society was so involved in trade that its military forces were almost always mercenaries. After a defeat of its army and navy at Himera in Sicily in 480 B.C.E., Carthage focused its attention on expansion in North Africa, spreading its influence from Libya to the Atlantic coast of modern Morocco. The Carthaginians made little attempt to enter the interior, so their dominance was almost exclusively along the coastal strip. Though Carthage maintained settlements in western Sicily after the defeat at Himera, it took as small a part as possible in the island's politics, rising only to defend its settlements from attack by Syracuse in the east.

Carthage's relationship with Rome proved its ultimate undoing. Though the two cooperated against Greece, they had little other contact because their spheres of influence did not overlap. That came to an end in 264, when both Carthage and Rome sent forces to save a band of Roman mercenaries, employed by Carthage, fighting around Syracuse. The result was the First Punic War, which lasted 23 years and was followed by two more Roman-Carthaginian wars, the latter of which resulted in Carthage's utter destruction.

Carthage was unique in ancient history for having its wealth built almost completely on trade. Carthaginians became the middlemen for almost all Mediterranean trade west of Sicily, reaching as far as Cape Verde on the Atlantic coast of Africa and possibly as far as the Atlantic coast of France. Carthage displayed little in the way of culture that was particularly their own, but they served as disseminators of eastern cultures to the western reaches of the known world. The language and sciences of the East were made available to the West, and the Carthaginians established urbanization in northern Africa, where before only tribal villages had existed. The transformation to "modern" civilization in northern Africa, Spain, Corsica, and Sardinia was due to Carthaginian merchants.

See also Carthage, Roman Invasion of (Third Punic War); Italy, Carthaginian Invasion of (Second Punic War); Sicily, Roman Conquest of (First Punic War).

References: Charles-Picard, Gilbert, and Collette Picard, *The Life and Death of Carthage*, trans. Dominique Collon (London: Sidgwick & Jackson, 1968); Warmington, B. H., *Carthage: A History* (London: Robert Hale, 1960).

CARTHAGE, ROMAN INVASION OF (THIRD PUNIC WAR)

16

After Rome was victorious in the Second Punic War, Carthage recovered well and quickly under the leadership of Hannibal. He was as able a political leader as a military one, but as he learned in his campaign in Italy, the people of Carthage would not give him sufficient support. The Carthaginians' return to economic health made them believe that they could return to military health as well, though the terms of the treaty ending the Second Punic War denied them the ability to make war at all outside Africa, and only with Rome's permission on the continent. This control over Carthage's foreign policy laid the groundwork for the city's doom.

The Numidian king Masinissa, a one-time ally of Carthage against Rome, changed sides during the later stages of the last war and was now trying to expand his kingdom at Carthaginian expense. He periodically demanded lands, which

Carthage ceded because of Roman support of Masinissa's claims. The demands were not extravagant, but over time they chipped away at Carthage's homeland. As Carthage grew surly at this loss of territory, Rome became jealous of the revived Carthaginian economy. In Rome a merchant class arose, gaining influence in the government, and the merchants had a powerful mouthpiece in M. Porcius Cato. Cato wanted Carthage destroyed, and Masinissa's claims proved the vehicle for that destruction.

In 156 B.C.E. the Carthaginian government demanded that a Roman envoy come to Africa to rule on Masinissa's latest demand. Cato got the job, and observed first-hand the revival of Carthage's power. He ruled for Masinissa, provoking war. In 151 B.C.E. Carthage invaded Numidia, but it was a disastrous campaign and their army was virtually destroyed. As they had gone to war without Roman permission, Rome declared war on them. To Roman surprise, Carthage put up no resistance, depending on a complete surrender to guarantee lenient terms. The Romans restored lost territory to the Carthaginians, but demanded that the city itself be abandoned. The citizens would not concede their city, so Rome laid siege from 149 to 146 B.C.E.

The city finally fell to P. Cornelius Scipio Aemillius, son of a hero of Rome's war against Macedon and grandson of the Scipio Africanus, who defeated Hannibal. Just as Rome had demanded, no one lived in Carthage afterward because the Roman government ordered Aemillius to raze the city and sell into slavery the 10 percent of citizens who survived the siege. The destruction of the Carthaginian empire brought its territory under direct Roman control, and the city of Utica became its new capital. The province proved a valuable source of grain for Rome's expanding empire, and a century after the city's fall it was rebuilt under orders of Julius Caesar, who settled some of his veterans there. The North African coast was so Romanized that any remains of Carthaginian influence virtually disappeared. Whatever chance Carthage had had of dominating the western Mediterranean and bringing the culture and religion of the East into Europe halted. Roman power and civilization were reconfirmed and remained dominant until the 400s C.E., when the Vandals conquered the area.

See also Hannibal; Italy, Carthaginian Invasion of (Second Punic War); Vandals.

References: Bagnall, Nigel, *The Punic Wars* (London: Hutchinson, 1990); Caven, Brian, *The Punic Wars* (London: Wei-denfeld & Nicolson, 1980); Dorey, T. A., and D. R. Dudley, *Rome against Carthage* (London: Seeker & Warburg, 1971).

17   CH'IN DYNASTY

The Chinese had been under the leadership of the Shang and Chou dynasties, but neither dynasty had been able to maintain a strong hold over a large amount of territory or protect the citizens from nomadic raiders. The Chou dynasty established a capital at Hao, near modern Sian, in the eleventh century B.C.E., but was forced to move eastward in 770 B.C.E. by the pressure of barbarian invaders, coupled with some rebellious provinces. The eastern capital at Loyang oversaw a smaller Chinese state until 476 B.C.E., when the Chou emperor was reduced to the status of prince. For another 250 years, the provinces warred among themselves until one fought its way to the top in 221 B.C.E.: the Ch'in.

The Ch'in learned from the nomads the successful military use of cavalry. They also developed a militaristic society under the leadership of Shang Yang, who removed the traditional power of the aristocracy and replaced it with a ruling class based on success in battle. All the adult males were liable for military service and could rise in status by showing bravery in combat. Any member of a ruling family who engaged in private quarrels or did not fight well in battle would be punished. With an increasingly powerful military, the Ch'in also worked diplomatically to keep the other states at odds with one another so they could not combine in opposition. In 278 B.C.E. the Ch'in attacked and seized the capital of their neighbors, the Chou. The Chou leader fell to Ch'in aggression in 256 B.C.E., and the last of the five opposing states fell in 222. The next year, China was declared united under one lord, who took the title Ch'in Shih Huang-ti, or Ch'in First Emperor.

Shih Huang-ti implemented a centralized bureaucracy, removing the aristocracies from the conquered states. He brought their leaders to his capital and built them luxurious homes—not from kindness, but to keep them under his watchful eye. He appointed governors to the provinces he created in his now-unified state. These governors had the duty of enforcing the law and mobilizing the local population for military duty. Shih Huang-ti ordered a census with such depth that it rivaled the Domesday Book of William the Conqueror in England. He also began the construction of a large series of internal improvements, and mandated standards for construction, language, and coinage. His administration was based on the Chinese philosophy of legalism, which punished lawbreakers but also rewarded those who aided in law-keeping. Easily, the most famous of the Ch'in projects was the construction of the Great Wall to protect the Chinese from northern nomadic raiders. Shih Huangti's military power took his armies as far south as the Red River valley in modern Vietnam and on to the Korean peninsula. Campaigning and the construction of large palaces reflected his power but cost a substantial amount of money, which came from increasingly high taxation. His burial in 210 B.C.E. also became famous; he was interred with thousands of terra-cotta soldiers and horses.

Shih Huang-ti's sons proved weak and oppressive, and soon provoked a peasant uprising. Knowing that defeat against the rebels would be rewarded with beheading, many Ch'in generals decided to change sides, and the opposition strengthened. Finally, in 206 B.C.E., a peasant rebel leader named Liu Pang captured the Ch'in capital at Hsienyang, and the Ch'in dynasty ended, leaving an empire that Liu Pang, who established the Han dynasty, would enlarge upon.

See also Han Dynasty; Britain, Norman Invasion of.

References: Cotterell, Arthur, *The First Emperor of China* (London: Macmillan, 1981); Hookham, Hilda, *A Short History of China* (New York: St. Martin's Press, 1970); Twitchett, Denis, and Michael Loewe, *The Cambridge History of China, Vol. 1: The Ch'in and Han Empires* (New York: Cambridge University Press, 1978).

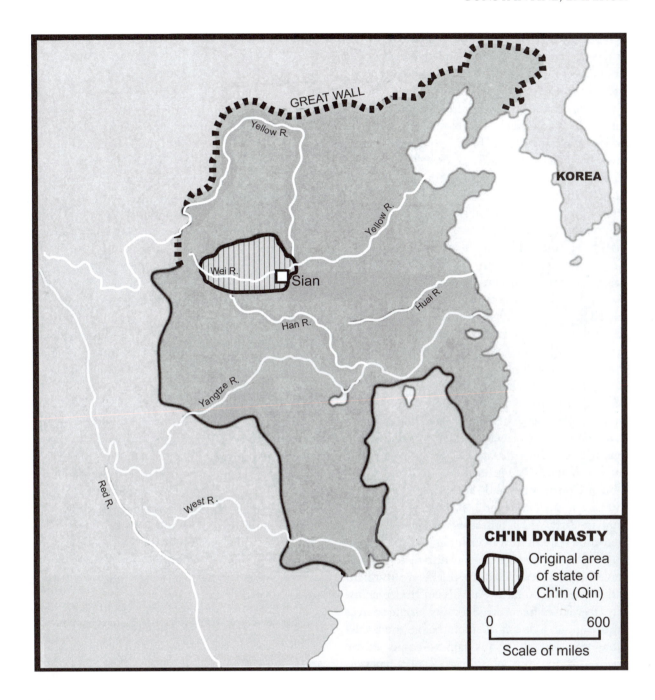

18   CONSTANTINE, EMPEROR

Constantine was born Flavius Valerius Constantinus about 272 C.E. in Moesia, the area of modern Serbia or Macedonia. His mother Helena bore him illegitimately, but he was adopted by Constantius I when Helena became Constantius's chief concubine. Constantius was named caesar in 305 under the newly reorganized power structure of the Roman Empire. Emperor Diocletian had divided power in the empire between two people, himself and Maximian, who were called augusti. They each appointed a subordinate, a caesar, who would rise to the position of augustus upon his superior's death or retirement. Under this system, Constantius was named caesar by Maximian, while Diocletian chose Galerius. When Diocletian retired (and forced Maximian to do likewise), Galerius and Constantius rose to become augusti. The sons of Constantius and Galerius hoped to be named caesars, but were disappointed when two others got the jobs. What Diocletian had hoped would become a peaceful progression of power became instead a struggle for inheritance.

Constantine had little formal education and turned to soldiering early. He fought with his father in a campaign in Britain, where his father died. Popular with the legions, they named Constantine augustus in his father's place. Instead, he took the title caesar rather than directly challenge the ultimate authorities in Rome. His assumption of the title, though reluctantly recognized by Rome, added fuel to the succession fire. Constantine stayed with his troops and campaigned against incursions by the Franks in Gaul.

In 306 the Praetorian Guard in Rome supported a new candidate for augustus, and the scramble for power that ensued virtually defies rational description. Not until Renaissance Italy would the world see another such convoluted struggle for leadership. At one time six men all claimed the title augustus. Constantine's army won victories at Aries and Marseilles over his rival and father-in-law Maximian in 310; the following year Galerius died, and four possible augusti remained: Maxentius and Daia, allied against Constantine and Licinius.

Learning of Maxentius's movements against him, in early 312 Constantine marched 40,000 men into Italy and won victories at Susa, Turin, Milan, Brescia, and Verona. He also recruited supporters along the way and entered his greatest fight with some 50,000 men. At Milvian Bridge across the Tiber River he received a vision; some sources say it came in a dream the night before the battle. More traditionally, it was said to come in the bright sun in front of thousands of witnesses. However it appeared, Constantine was convinced by this vision that if he placed the symbol of Christ on his soldier's shield, he would be victorious. He did so, and won. As in Julius Caesar's campaign across the Rubicon into Italy, Constantine now became the master of Rome. He named Licinius augustus of the east.

After Licinius defeated Daia, it seemed inevitable that he and Constantine would oppose each other rather than return to Diocletian's original framework. They fought a series of indecisive battles until, in 323 at Adrianople, Constantine

personally fought with his forces in a victory that forced Licinius into Byzantium. Constantine besieged the city and fought a final engagement at Scutari, where Licinius surrendered and was executed. Constantine was now the sole emperor.

Constantine's importance was in his role not only as the final leader of a unified Roman Empire, but also as the founder of Constantinople as the new seat of empire, a second Rome. From there he directed the affairs of empire, the most important of which was his support of Christianity. In 313 he and Licinius had issued the Edict of Milan, which guaranteed religious freedom; however, Constantine became an open supporter of Christianity, and by the time of his death it was the state religion. He remained sole leader of the empire for 13 years, during which time he continued military reforms begun when he first occupied Rome. He defended the frontiers from barbarian attacks by constructing a series of forts to create a defense in depth, with mobile reserves stationed to come to the aid of any that were attacked. This strategy worked well in his time, but ultimately the increasing use of frontier recruits and the difference in pay between frontline and reserve forces created problems. To a great extent the establishment of a second capital promoted the idea of a divided empire, and after Constantine's death, the empire gradually split, with Rome ruling the west and Constantinople ruling the east. The eastern Byzantine Empire would survive until the fifteenth century, whereas the west would fall to barbarian invasions within a century.

See also Caesar, Julius; Byzantine Empire; Franks.

References: Barnes, Timothy, *The New Empire of Diocletian and Constantine* (Cambridge, MA: Harvard University Press, 1982); Dorries, Herman, *Constantine the Great* (New York: Harper & Row, 1972); MacMullen, Ramsay, Constantine (New York: Dial Press, 1969).

EGYPT, ALEXANDER'S CONQUEST OF

19

The Persian Empire had ruled Egypt since Cyrus the Great's son Cambyses conquered the country in 525 B.C.E. Cyrus's occupation was brutal, but later Persian emperors were occasionally more tolerant. Under Darius the Great, the Persians allowed unrestricted worship of the Egyptian gods. Darius studied native writing and theology, encouraged commerce, and completed a canal between the Nile and the Red Sea. The administration of his successor, Xerxes, was marked by its cruelty; he enslaved the people and robbed their temples. By the time of Darius III, Alexander the Great's Persian foe, the Egyptians had had more than enough of their rule.

The occupation of Egypt was the culmination of the first phase of Alexander's campaign against the Persian Empire, 334–331 B.C.E. The Persian navy far outclassed anything the Greeks could muster, so Alexander decided to control the Mediterranean coastline and occupy the port cities, thereby denying the Persian navy any base of operations. Rather than chase the defeated Darius II after the Greek victory at Issus, Alexander turned south to complete his coastal strategy. After capturing Tyre and Gaza, Alexander's forces marched into the Egyptian city of Pelusium. The city surrendered to him without a fight; indeed, the Egyptians viewed Alexander more as a liberator than a conqueror.

From Pelusium, Alexander proceeded to Memphis, on the Nile River. The inhabitants welcomed him and, so grateful were they for their deliverance from Persia, the Egyptians made Alexander pharaoh. Alexander endeared himself to the Egyptians by honoring their gods, and it was by way of religion that he not only solidified his dominance over Egypt, but also laid the groundwork for his own future adulation. Alexander's mother, Olympia, claimed that Alexander had been fathered not by her husband Philip but by the god Zeus, and therefore Alexander was semidivine. This claim fit neatly into the Egyptian view of pharaoh as a mixture of god and man. Prior to leaving Greece, Alexander visited the Oracle at Delphi and was told to pay close attention to the Egyptian deity Ammon-Zeus.

When Alexander decided to spend the winter of 332–331 B.C.E. in Egypt, he traveled to the remote desert site of the temple of Ammon-Zeus at the oasis of Siwah. The journey had all the marks of a divinely led pilgrimage. The Greek force was saved from dehydration by a freak rainstorm in the desert. A sandstorm obscured landmarks and made navigation in the desert virtually impossible, but the Greeks followed birds, which flew to the oasis. At the temple, Alexander left everyone outside and entered to commune with the priests of Ammon-Zeus. What passed between them was never revealed, but from then on Alexander did nothing to discourage the growing belief of many in the east that he was a god.

After the journey to Siwah, Alexander laid plans for the construction of a new city named—as so many of his cities were—Alexandria. The city was designed in a grid pattern to create well-organized thoroughfares. He made sure that temples to both Egyptian and Greek gods were con structed. He oversaw the start of construction prior to his return to Memphis, where he established a government to administer the country. He appointed several locals to important positions while leaving several garrisons of Greek soldiers. In the spring of 342, he left Egypt in pursuit of Darius, never to return.

After his death, Alexander's conquests were divided among three of his generals. Egypt and much of the Mediterranean coast went to Ptolemy, whose descendants ruled Egypt as pharaohs until the days of Caesar Augustus. Alexander's virtually bloodless occupation of Egypt changed both the conqueror and the subdued. Coins minted from this time depict Alexander with rams' horns (the symbol of Ammon-Zeus), and Alexander notified Greece that they could now worship him as a god. Egypt benefited greatly from the Greek occupation. Alexandria became not only one of the great cities of the ancient world, but it was also the site of the greatest library of antiquity, housing some 700,000 scrolls. The city became the center of learning for centuries, with public buildings, parks, and the first museum. Alexander's legacy was one of knowledge and culture, but that of the Ptolemies was also one of exploitation of the Egyptian population and economy.

See also Cyrus the Great; Alexander the Great; Augustus, Caesar; Philip of Macedon; Ptolemaic Dynasty.

References: Bosworth, A. B., *Conquest and Empire* (New York: Cambridge University Press, 1988); Green, Peter, *Alexander of Macedon* (Los Angeles: University of California Press, 1991); Lane Fox, Robin, *The Search for Alexander* (Boston: Little, Brown, 1980).

GAUL, ROMAN CONQUEST OF

20

In Roman times, Gaul made up the area now encompassed by France, Belgium, Luxembourg, and Germany west of the Rhine River. It was divided into four general areas: Provincia, Aquitania, Celtica, and Belgica. The first to come under Roman domination was Provincia, whose capital, Massalia (or Massilia), was the site of modern Marseilles. Massilia had long served as a trading center for Phoenician and Greek merchants before Rome took over; it remained a financial but not a military center. The remainder of Gaul, having less contact with Mediterranean cultures, became known as Gallica Comata, or Long-Haired Gaul. The "barbarian" tribes of that area included the Suebi, Sequani, Arverni, Aedui, and Helvetii.

Population pressures forced the Gallic tribes into expansion, with the Helvetii allying with the Sequani and Aedui to escape the pressures exerted by the Suebi and other Germanic tribes pushing westward.

This combination of conquest and migration soon put pressure on Provincia, and that attracted the Roman military.

Rome had been undergoing political upheavals with a rivalry between the elected senate, which served in a strongly advisory capacity, and the growing power of individuals who hoped to exercise expanded if not supreme power. By 60 B.C.E., the three major figures in this rivalry were Pompey, Crassus, and Julius Caesar. Their cooperation (the Triumvirate) was unconstitutional but effective in the face of a weakening senate. Their personalities, however, guaranteed that the trio could not rule together indefinitely. The junior partner of the Triumvirate was Caesar, who lacked Pompey's military experience and Crassus's wealth. In order to gain both, he lobbied for and received the position of governor and commander of the Roman forces in Gaul. His accession to the political position in Gaul coincided with the arrival of the Helvetii, so his chance for glory beckoned.

There was no better infantry force in the world than the Roman legions, but at first they had difficulty in dealing with the aggressive cavalry of the Helvetii and their allies. Still, Caesar was successful in forcing their withdrawal in 58 B.C.E., while capturing the Suebi leader Ariovistus after a campaign in Alsace. The following year, Caesar marched north and defeated the Belgae and Nervii, establishing Roman control over the lands of modern Belgium and northern France. He spread Roman power to the Atlantic coast in 56 B.C.E., thereby isolating the central Gallic tribes. An invasion by the Usipites and Tencteri forced his return to Belgium, but Caesar defeated them as well and kept his hold on the province. Campaigns in Germany and Britain accomplished little of immediate importance, but they gave Caesar more experience and publicity.

With most of Gaul under his control, Caesar spent the years 54–51 suppressing revolts. The most serious was a coalition of Gallic tribes led by Vercingetorix. Caesar cut off their supplies with scorched-earth tactics and starved them into submission, defeating them at Alesia in 53 B.C.E.

The immediate effects of Caesar's campaigns were to expand Rome's northwestern borders all the way to the Atlantic and beyond, laying the groundwork for a later, more successful invasion of Britain. His success and personal appeal made him immensely popular with his troops; that and the wealth he accumulated through his victories translated into personal power, for money and military support were soon to be the main factors necessary to advance in Roman politics. The death of Crassus in 53 B.C.E. and Caesar's military success created a rift between him and Pompey that exploded into civil war in 49. Rather than leave his army outside Rome's borders (as the law demanded) and appear before the senate alone, Caesar crossed onto the Italian peninsula at the Rubicon River and challenged Pompey and the government. Caesar proved the superior general, quickly establishing his power in Italy and Spain, chasing Pompey to Greece, and then to Egypt. Defeating Pompey, his allies, and later his sons gave Caesar ultimate power in Rome, and he became the first emperor.

In Gaul, Romanization proceeded fairly quickly in the south, mainly through the retirement and settlement of many of Caesar's veterans. In Gallica Comata, however, anti-Roman sentiment died hard. Caesar sponsored settlements only along the frontier between Provincia and the interior. The tribes so lately defeated kept nominal power in their lands, and Rome allowed them to exercise local autonomy in return for trade. These tribes also acted as a buffer against possible Germanic invasions of Roman settlements. The main part of Gaul, however, remained fairly independent. Under the reign of Claudius I, some 100 years after Caesar's conquest, the provinces of Belgica, Lugdenensis, and Aquitania emerged, and they were eventually allowed to send nobles to the senate. The Roman pantheon and emperor worship were encouraged, to the detriment (and occasional persecution) of other religious practices. The later Roman Empire introduced Christianity and Latin, both of which further eroded Gallic culture. Though Gaul prospered through trade with Rome, it ultimately suffered by being first in line during the Germanic and later barbarian invasions. The territory finally was settled and divided among the new tribes, mainly the Vandals and Visigoths in the south of France and Spain, and with the Franks, Alamani, and Burgundians in the upper portion of Gaul.

See also Britain, Roman Conquest of; Caesar, Julius.

References: Caesar, Julius, *The Gallic War*, trans. H. J. Edwards (Cambridge, MA: Harvard University Press, 1966); Drinkwater, J. E., *Roman Gaul* (London: Groom Helm, 1983); King, Anthony, *Roman Gaul and Germany* (Berkeley: University of California Press, 1990).

GERMANY, ROMAN INVASION OF

21

Though Julius Caesar had conquered Gaul in the middle of the first century B.C.E., the Roman attitude toward Germany remained undefined. Under the direction of Caesar Augustus, Rome began campaigns against German tribes in 12 B.C.E., ostensibly to protect Gaul from attacks by aggressive German tribes, but actually to establish a new frontier along the Elbe River. Augustus chose two generals—Tiberius and Drasus—to carry out the campaign.

The Germanic people were composed of a number of independent tribes, most of them mutually antagonistic, which kept them from making any real progress in acquiring Gallic lands or cooperating in the face of Roman attacks. Individually the Germans were courageous, but they were impaired by a lack of unity and discipline.

The Roman armies began their offensive with Tiberius pushing eastward through Switzerland to defeat the Pannonians (residing in modern-day Austria), thereby securing the southern frontier by placing Roman troops on the Danube. Drasus, meanwhile, marched north through the Brenner Pass, then down the Rhine. In a series of rapid thrusts he mastered western Germany and raided as far as the Elbe. Roman advances stopped here because Drasus's death in 9 B.C.E. terminated the invasion. Not until two years later did they take the offensive again, this time with Tiberius in overall command.

Tiberius consolidated the Roman hold along the Rhine by transplanting uncooperative German tribes to Gaul, where superior Roman forces could keep an eye on them. Two years later Tiberius advanced from the upper Danube into the valley of the Saale River. He also sent columns toward the Elbe River, defeating German tribes and forcing most of them to recognize Roman overlordship by 4 B.C.E. Rome held this position for nearly a decade, assuming that Germany had been pacified. Roman merchants began to operate in the area, and forts and trading posts were constructed. The German tribes did nothing to give the impression that they resented Roman rule, and Rome took many of the German leaders and their families to Rome to teach them "civilized" behavior and language. Some of the Germans learned the Roman way of war and fought in the Roman army, sometimes with Roman troops and sometimes in command of native auxiliaries. One of the more successful students of Roman warfare was Arminius of the Cherusci. He commanded German cavalry forces in support of Roman operations; the Romans were strong on infantry and tended to use foreign troops as mounted soldiers.

Plans finalized in 5 C.E. called for Roman forces to occupy all of Germany. Again Tiberius was placed in command, but he was unable to

Bust of Roman Emperor Tiberius, who consolidated the Roman hold over Germany.

undertake this mission because of a revolt in Illyrica (modern Yugoslavia). The operation was reinstated the following year under the command of Quintilius Varsus, who was ordered to conquer all German territory, no matter the cost. By this time, the Germans seem to have learned some lessons from the Romans, for they had formed alliances to face this threat. Led by the Cherusci tribe, the Germans launched a surprise attack on Varsus in the Teutoburger Forest. The Cherusci prince Arminius, leading the cavalry contingent of the Roman force, had lured his commander into a trap. Unable to use their standard tactics in the rugged, wooded terrain, the Romans were overwhelmed, losing three legions.

This was a major blow to Rome's prestige. The Romans feared that the Germans would follow up this victory with an invasion of the Rhine area or Gaul, but it did not happen. The Germans seemed satisfied with defending their own lands. Tiberius was soon reassigned to the

area, but he decided not to push Roman luck. He solidified Rome's hold along the Rhine, but refrained from entering the Germanic wilderness. In 14, Germanicus was ordered to the region to avenge Varsus's defeat, but after campaigning among the tribes with mixed success, he withdrew to the better defended Rhineland. Tiberius, successor to Augustus as emperor, realized that if Rome did not offer a visible threat, the feuding German tribes could not maintain a solid front or pose a serious threat to Rome's frontiers.

Rome's goal became the maintenance of German recognition of their power without Rome's having to hold the ground to prove it. The frontier remained relatively peaceful until the Roman Empire began to decline in the third century. By the 220s the Goths, descended from Scandinavian immigrants, broke through the frontier and drove the Romans out of Germany, the Balkans, and central Europe.

As Roman power declined over the succeeding centuries, former enemies of Rome became allies. Rome hired German mercenaries to man its legions, and in the process the Germans became acquainted with Roman civilization and advances. Later, Roman generals assigned to frontier garrisons became caesars, thanks to the skill of their German soldiers. The people who occupied what is modern-day Germany came under a variety of influences as various peoples migrated through their territory, so Roman input into Germanic culture was but one factor among many. Germans were sufficiently impressed with Roman wealth to lust after it, and the Germans were among many who invaded and looted the Italian peninsula. They took treasures, but not much culture, and not until the Christian church came to be a dominant force in Europe did the tribes of Germany rise to the level of outside cultures.

See also Caesar, Julius; Gaul, Roman Conquest of; Ostrogoths.

References: Balsdon, J. B V D., *Rome: The Story of an Empire* (New York: McGraw-Hill, 1970); Dudley, David, *The Romans: 850 B.C.E.–AD 337* (New York: Knopf, 1970); Salmon, Edward, *A History of the Roman World from 30 B.C.E. to AD 138* (London: Methuen, 1972).

GREECE, PERSIAN INVASION OF

22

Thanks to the efforts of Cyrus the Great and Darius the Great, the Persian Empire stretched from the borders of India to Egypt and from the Caspian Sea to the Hellespont by 500 B.C.E. However, spelling ultimate doom for the Persians was the crossing of the Hellespont into Europe. Once across that narrow strait, they faced the determined people of Hellas, ancient Greece. Though the Greeks were divided into independent city-states that were often antagonistic toward each other, in the face of an outside threat, they banded together. The Greeks had attracted Darius's attention when Athens gave support to former Greek colonies in Ionia, along the western Asia Minor coast. Because they were under Persian rule, Athenian and Eretrian support of the Ionian rebellions of the 490s B.C.E. demanded punishment. Darius was determined to invade Greece and bring the country to heel. He sent his general, Mardonius, to subdue the northern provinces of Thrace and Macedon in 492 B.C.E., and massed an invasion force for an amphibious assault on Greece.

Darius gathered 50,000 men for the attack, which was commanded by Datis. With the Persians was Hippias, a former Athenian tyrant who had been deposed some years earlier and now returned with his patrons to engage in some behind-the-scenes agitation and reestablish his power. Only after the Persians attacked Eretria on the island of Euboea did the Greek mainland learn of the invasion. The Athenians prepared for battle and dispatched a messenger to the southern city-state of Sparta for assistance. The militant Spartans responded that they would arrive as soon as they had completed some necessary religious festivals. Thus, Athens marched out alone to battle. They made their way westward to the high ground overlooking Marathon, the only available port near Athens, where the Persians had debarked their forces. Once the Athenians arrived (and were joined by a small force from Plataea), the Persians implemented their strategy. The city of Athens now stood undefended, so they embarked about half their force to sail for the city while the remainder held the Athenian army in place. The Athenian leader Callimachus ceded command of the force to Miltiades, who argued for a bold attack on the Persian force, now reduced to 20,000; that number was still half again the size of the Greek force. The Athenians advanced in a long, line-abreast formation with stronger flanks. The Persians struck the weaker center, but found their own weak flanks surrounded by the Athenians. The result, intended or accidental, was a perfect double envelopment, which broke Persian morale. They raced for the safety of the ships on the beach and escaped only by a strong holding action. The main, relatively contemporary source for the battle is the Greek historian Herodotus, who numbered the casualties as 192 Greek dead versus a loss of 6,400 Persians. The Persians sailed away, and the victorious Athenians met the Spartans arriving just after the battle's end. The Persian fleet sailed for Athens but arrived too late; the army had returned and taken defensive positions, so the Persians sailed for home.

Darius was not about to let this defeat go unavenged, but he was diverted from immediate counterattack by a revolt in Egypt. In the process of subduing the rebellion, Darius died, so the duty of punishing Greece fell to his successor, Xerxes. Xerxes planned an even larger invasion force, of probably 200,000, who marched around the Aegean, supplied by the Persian fleet sailing along the coast. At the Hellespont, he ordered a bridge of boats constructed, and the Persian army marched into Europe in 480 B.C.E. The Greeks had spent the last 10 years fighting among themselves, and now had to bury their differences to meet the foreign threat. The Persians marched through northern Greece, gaining the voluntary or grudging assistance of virtually every city-state. This time the Spartan army marched to the fore, while the Greek fleet sailed to impede the Persian navy. The Greek strategy was to separate the Persian army from its food supply onboard the ships, so the Greek fleet blocked the straits between the mainland and the island of Euboea. The Persian army continued along the coast to the pass of Thermopylae, where a Greek force commanded by the Spartan leader Leonidas awaited them. Leonidas stood on the narrow

ANCIENT GREECE

Athenian empire, 450 bc

■ BATTLE SITES

0   50

Scale of miles

defile between mountains and sea, and for three days his 6,000 men repulsed the might of the Persian army. With the aid of a local Greek shepherd, the Persians learned of a track around the Greek roadblock and marched to surround their opposition. Learning of this move, Leonidas sent most of his force to meet it. They failed to stop the encirclement by the superior Persian force; Leonidas and his few hundred men held the pass until all were killed. The news of the Persian victory at Thermopylae convinced the Greek fleet to withdraw, so the Persian advance continued.

The Athenians had earlier consulted the Oracle at Delphi on the best strategy for meeting the invaders, and in true Delphic style they were told to seek refuge behind wooden walls. The debate over this response led the Athenians to determine that the oracle meant the wooden walls of ships rather than the walls surrounding the city of Athens, so the city was abandoned to the advancing Persians. The Athenians led a combined Greek naval force in the waters off Athens, but it was only about half the size of the Persian navy. Their only hope was to use the superior maneuverability of the smaller Greek triremes in the narrow waters off the island of Salamis, near Athens. Xerxes sat atop his throne on the hillside to watch his fleet's victory, but he was disappointed. Lured on by a false promise of turncoats within the Greek fleet, the Persians found themselves unable to maneuver their unwieldy ships in the straits. Herodotus claims that the outcome was 40 Greek ships sunk for a loss of 200 Persian ships, and the remainder sailed away home. Xerxes withdrew much of his army, but left a force in the northern provinces; it was defeated in 479 B.C.E. The battle of Plataea broke the back of the remaining Persian force, and the Greek victory at Mycale a month later brought about the final destruction of Persian forces in Greece.

The Persian Wars rate among the most important in history. They proved the worth of the western military mind and infantry soldier against a previously undefeated foe. The chance to continue the experiment of democracy continued unburdened by Oriental despotism, and the philosophy and culture developed by the Greeks influence Western civilization to this day. As the historian J. F. C. Fuller wrote in his *Military History of the Western World*, "With these battles we stand on the threshold of the western world to be, in which Greek intellect was to conquer and to lay the foundations of centuries to come. No two battles in history are, therefore, more portentous than Salamis and Plataea; they stand like the pillars of the temple of the ages supporting the architecture of western history."

See also Cyrus the Great.

References: Burn, A. R., *Persia and the Greeks: The Defence of the West* (London: Arnold, 1962); Fuller, J. F. C., *Military History of the Western World* (New York: Minerva, 1954-1956); Grant, Michael, *The Rise of the Greeks* (New York: Scribner's Sons, 1987); Hignett, Charles, *Xerxes' Invasion of Greece* (Oxford: Clarendon, 1963).

23 HAN DYNASTY

After the successful reign of Shih Huang-ti, founder of the Ch'in dynasty, his two successors failed to live up to his standards and became the objects of rebellion. Liu Pang, one of the rebel leaders, seized power in 206 B.C.E. and began the Han dynasty, taking the regnal name of Kao-tsu. Kao-tsu was able to take advantage of the territorial consolidation of the Ch'in dynasty; he took over almost all of the Ch'in lands, except Yueh in the south, which he ceded to another general, Chao To, for his support in the rebellion. Kao-tsu spent the early years of his reign consolidating his power and protecting his frontiers.

Kao-tsu's main rivals on the frontier were the Hsiung-nu, known to Europe as the Huns. Dominating the steppes north of the Great Wall and often raiding south of it, their cavalry numbered as many as a quarter million. Kao-tsu's first campaign against the Huns was very nearly a disaster, for they drew him into a trap and took him prisoner. He made peace with them and sealed a treaty with the marriage of one of his harem to the Hsiung-nu leader, which secured the north for some years. Following Kao-tsu's death in 195 B.C.E., the Hsiung-nu honored the agreement, but after 176 B.C.E., new leaders began raids into China almost as far as the Han capital at Loyang. Rather than attack the northerners directly, the Han leaders often paid other tribes to harass them.

With the accession to the throne of Wu Ti in 140 B.C.E., the Han challenged the might of the Hsiung-nu. Wu Ti, also known as the Martial Emperor, took the Han dynasty to its heights of power. He launched attack after attack against the nomads, but was beaten back by their superior numbers or the hostility of the terrain. Wu Ti sought allies against his enemy, sending the envoy Chang Chien to the west to broker a pact with the Yueh Chih, or Kushan Empire, of Bactria. Chang Chien was captured by the Hsiung-nu, but escaped and made his way to Kushan. The Kushans' disastrous encounters with the Hsiung-nu convinced them not to ally themselves with China. Finally, Wu Ti led an invasion and succeeded in defeating the nomads between the Great Wall and the northern bend of the Yellow River in 127 B.C.E. Six years later, Wu Ti sent the 20-year-old general Ho Ch'u Ping with 100,000 men to attack the Hsiung-nu capital. He was so successful that the nomads were driven north of the Gobi Desert; this victory

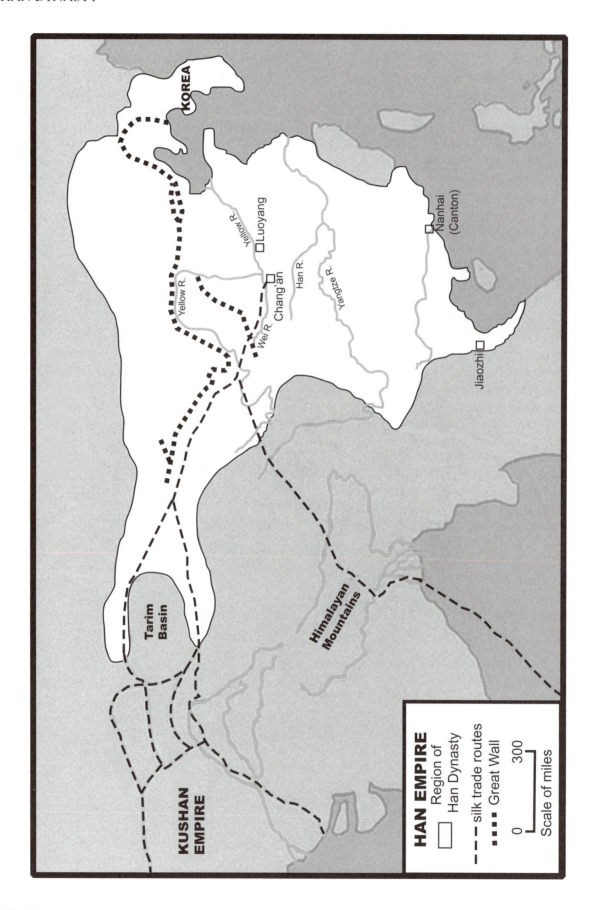

KOREA

Yellow R.

☐Luoyang

Han R.

Wei R. ☐Chang'an

Yangtze R.

Nanhai
(Canton)

☐Jiaozhi

Tarim
Basin

Himalayan
Mountains

KUSHAN
EMPIRE

HAN EMPIRE
☐ Region of
Han Dynasty
--- silk trade routes
▪▪▪ Great Wall

0   300

Scale of miles

opened the land route westward for both invasion and trade.

Wu Ti learned the value of cavalry from the Hsiung-nu, and he spent much time breeding horses and training horsemen. This proved successful in beating the Hsiung-nu at their own tactics, and gave Wu Ti the ability to defeat other, less prepared enemies. He campaigned in the south against the former Ch'in province of Yueh, capturing it, and drove southward as far as Annam and Tonkin by 109 B.C.E.; the chieftains of that region acknowledged Chinese suzerainty and paid tribute. The next year, Wu Ti focused his attention on the north, conquering Manchuria and northern Korea.

Not content with merely dominating China and its immediate environs, Wu Ti sent Li Kuang Li on an expedition to the west. Li Kuang Li drove into central Asia and defeated a number of tribes in the Jaxartes River region before being forced to withdraw into Sinkiang. After regrouping there, he reinvaded the region of Ferghana and forced the inhabitants to acknowledge Chinese dominance. The expedition was expensive, as only 10,000 of the original 60,000 soldiers returned to China, but they brought back excellent breeding stock for Wu Ti's increasingly important cavalry.

Wu Ti spent the last years of his reign consolidating his empire, which had tripled in size under his rule. The constant warfare had cost huge fortunes, and he dedicated himself to restoring financial stability, but the overworked bureaucracy and overtaxed peasantry staged a series of rebellions. Nevertheless, China generally enjoyed relative peace with its neighbors and an expansion of trade, most notably along the Silk Road to India and the Middle East.

Internal troubles brought about more rebellions in the first century C.E. and led to the establishment of the Second Han dynasty in 24 C.E. under the leadership of Kuang Wu Ti. During his reign, Chinese forces under General Ma Yuan campaigned in the south and reestablished dominance in Annam and Hainan. The return of the Hsiung-nu at mid-century provoked Chinese punitive expeditions that drove the nomads farther west. Later in the first century, Chinese armies drove even deeper west, conquering Turkestan and scouting as far as the Caspian Sea. Around the year 90, Chinese armies inflicted the final defeat on the Hsiung-nu, expelling them from central Asia and starting them on a migration that ultimately reached Europe and produced the great leader Attila. This abandonment of the high plains opened the area to habitation by the Mongols, who began their long rise to prominence.

After the first century, the Han dynasty began to decline, mainly because of internal strife. It had been the most successful Chinese dynasty thus far, and had opened China to influences outside its culture via the Silk Road and naval expeditions into the South China Sea and beyond. Representatives of the Roman emperor Marcus Aurelius are reported to have visited Han territory. However, the internal unrest caused by the recurring problem of overtaxation weakened the dynasty, as it did so many others. Military dictators ruled at the end of the second century, but after 220 the empire broke into warring states, not to be reunited, by the Sui and T'ang dynasties, until the late sixth century.

See also Ch'in Dynasty; Huns; T'ang Dynasty; Vietnam, Chinese Conquest of.

References: Hookham, Hilda, *A Short History of China* (New York: St. Martin's Press, 1970); Twitchett, Denis, and Michael Loewe, *The Cambridge History of China, Vol. 1: The Ch'in and Han Empires* (New York: Cambridge University Press, 1978).

24   HANNIBAL

Often compared to Alexander the Great, Julius Caesar, or Napoleon, Hannibal dominated the military scene of his day. With the possible exception of his father, Hamilcar, Carthage never had a better political leader. Even more remarkably, this reputation was established strictly by the accounts of his enemies, because Carthaginian sources on his life do not exist.

Hannibal was born to fight Rome: At age nine his father made him swear eternal enmity to that trans-Mediterranean power. At the age of 26, Hannibal became leader of the Carthaginian Empire. He combined the policy of his brother-in-law, Hasdrubal, of building Carthaginian power by diplomacy with that of his father, who sought military conquest. Hannibal took control of Carthage's major possession, Spain, by marry-

Hannibal, famous for introducing a new weapon to ancient warfare–the elephant. (Detail from a fresco ca 1510, Palazzo del Campidoglio [Capitoline Museum], Rome)

ing a Spanish princess and demanding hostages of the major tribes.

With this as a base, he challenged Roman authority along the Pyrenees and provoked the Second Punic War, where he established his reputation as a commander.

Hannibal seemed to have had neither personal nor strategic fear. He invaded Italy virtually without supply lines, as his crossing of the Pyrenees and Alps made resupply extremely difficult. He made the best use of his enemy's weaknesses, striking where they had the fewest forces, and he encouraged Rome's vassals to rebel and join him. He instituted a new weapon to ancient warfare—the elephant.

Hannibal knew when to take risks, and he knew his enemy. Recognizing that he might lose half of his 100,000-man army crossing the mountains to Italy, he proceeded anyway, aware that the Gauls on the other side would gladly make up his losses for the opportunity to fight their Roman overlords. Even though he lost massive numbers of men in the march, he did everything possible to take care of his troops. "In all his operations, we see supreme excellence, skill, resource, daring, an heroic spirit, the faculty of command in the very highest degree, caution, sound judgement, extraordinary craft, and last but not least, watchful and incessant care in providing for the requirements of his troops."

Hannibal's greatest legacy to military history came from his tactics at Cannae, his greatest victory and Rome's worst defeat. By withdrawing the center of his forces from Roman attack, he drew the Romans into the center of the field, where the cavalry on either end of his line could attack both Roman flanks and rear, a double envelopment that came to be known as the "Cannae maneuver." Rome entered the battle with 60,000 men and left with only 10,000. Hannibal did not follow up this victory with an assault on Rome itself, for he knew the city's defenses were too strong. He contented himself with rampaging around the countryside, living off the land, denying the Romans badly needed food supplies, and provoking rebellions against Roman rule for 15 years (218–203 B.C.E.). Hannibal's successes were insufficient to persuade his government in Carthage to provide him with reinforcements. All his successes went for naught when he had to return to Carthage to save the city from a Roman attack. At Zama he lost his only battle, at the hands of the Roman general Scipio.

Defeated in battle and owing the Romans tribute, Hannibal strove for seven years to rebuild his nation's fortunes. He concentrated on the traditional Carthaginian pastime—trade—to stabilize his society. He challenged the authority of the corrupt oligarchy, which had placed an intolerable tax burden on the people to pay the tribute to Rome, and forced an almost democratic system on them. His economic leadership and evenhanded treatment of the public were so successful that Carthage made enough money to pay the Roman tribute years early. But once again, Hannibal was betrayed by his own government. Unable to exist in his just society, the country's leaders plotted against him by telling Rome that he was planning another war. Hannibal had to flee for his life; rather than fall into Roman hands, he ultimately committed suicide.

See also Alexander the Great; Caesar, Julius; Italy, Carthaginian Invasion of (Second Punic War); Napoleon Buonaparte.

References: Baker, G. P, *Hannibal* (New York: Barnes & Noble, 1967); Lamb, Harold, *Hannibal* (New York: Doubleday, 1958); Morris, William, *Hannibal: Soldier, Statesman, Patriot* (New York: Knickerbocker Press, 1978).

INDIA, ALEXANDER'S INVASION OF

25

With the entire Middle East under his control, Alexander the Great looked for more land to bring under his domination. Determined to conquer the entire Persian Empire, he needed to occupy all the territory to the Indus River. He marched his men toward India at the urging of one of his new allies, Taxiles, who had a dispute with an Indian king, Porus. In November 326 B.C.E., the Greeks and their auxiliaries took two routes through modern Afghanistan: Hephaestion through the Khyber Pass to establish a bridgehead across the Indus, and Alexander paralleling him a bit to the north to defeat the tribes in the hills and secure the left flank. When the two columns reunited, Alexander's force numbered 5,600 cavalry and 10,000 infantry. Taxiles had provided a number of elephants, but Alexander used them only for transport.

Just past the Indus, the Greeks found Porus encamped on the southern side of the Hydapses (modern Jhelum) River. It was late spring and the river was rising, so Alexander had to act quickly. He spread rumors that he was going to wait until the river fell to cross, yet at the same time he built boats in plain sight of Porus's army. Unsure of Alexander's intentions, Porus reacted to Alexander's ploy of marching up and down the river, feinting at a number of places yet never attacking, in order to tire the Indians so they would soon give up following his marches and countermarches. When they stopped reacting to his moves, Alexander took advantage of a well-timed storm to move his cavalry and 6,000 infantry upriver, where they crossed in the night. Spotted early the next morning, Alexander soon faced a 2,000-man cavalry force sent by Porus's son to investigate. After easily defeating them, Alexander marched downriver. The covering force he had left behind made threatening moves to cross the river opposite Porus's camp, so the Indians had to decide which threat to meet—a tactic taught in infantry schools to this day.

Porus turned to face Alexander. He stretched his men across an open plain with his anchors on the river to his left and a chain of hills to his right. He placed 300 elephants along the front of his line, supported by infantry; his 3,000–4,000 cavalry were in two equal units on the flanks. Unknown to Porus, however, Alexander had detached a cavalry force to ride behind the hills and strike the Indians from the rear after Alexander struck along the river to draw the entire Indian cavalry to that side. The assault from the rear collapsed the Indian line from the right, and the elephants ultimately lost control when the Greeks killed their handlers. The wounded Porus surrendered, but as was his wont, Alexander restored the gallant enemy to his kingdom in return for an alliance, and he settled the differences between Porus and Taxiles.

Alexander established two towns in the neighborhood of his victory and divided his force: Under Hephaestion, one-half moved down the Hydapses to its juncture with the Indus, and Alexander took the other half southeastward to the Hyphasis (Beas) River. After he defeated a force of Cathaeans there, he wanted to proceed in his search for the Indian Ocean, but for the first time, his men would not follow him. This river was perhaps the extent of the Persian Empire, and they were homesick. Alexander sulked in his tent for three days, but his men would not relent, so he finally left to rejoin Hephaestion. With his force divided, as well as hurt by unrevealed casualties he suffered at the Hydapses, certainly Alexander could not have fought his way to the ocean, though he was convinced it was not far away. Once again reunited with the entire army, Alexander ordered ships built. The fleet was to carry many of his troops to the mouth of the Indus at Karachi and up the coast toward the Persian Gulf. While the ships were being built, he launched his last great campaign, this time against the Malli tribe, probably subjects of the old Persian Empire. He crossed to the Hydraotes (Ravi) River and attacked their main city, which fell easily. The Indians retreated to their citadel, and here the fighting was the fiercest. Alexander led the assault, but found himself inside the citadel walls with only three other soldiers. He fought with his usual tenacity even though wounded by an arrow. Finally, his army broke through the walls and killed all the defenders. This campaign was marked by more than the usual slaughter, perhaps an indication that the Greeks wanted to go home and not leave trouble behind.

Alexander nursed his wounds until the fleet was prepared in the autumn of 325 B.C.E. He intended to march along the coast and establish supply depots for the ships, but the terrain forced him to swing north. He and his troops suffered terribly from the heat and lack of supplies, but finally reached the shore and met the fleet at the Gulf of Hormuz. From there they returned to the Persian capital at Susa.

The Greek expedition to India was in some ways a reunion, because the Aryan conquerors who had established themselves in northern India a thousand years earlier may have had the same roots in the steppes of western Asia as did the forebears of the Greeks; certainly there were similarities of language that suggest the possibility. As Alexander was intent on spreading Greek culture wherever he went, the establishment of cities and garrisons left some Greek imprint in the north Indian states. Though Alexander's death a few years later brought an end to Greek dominance, the Mauryan Empire that succeeded it left art and sculpture heavily influenced by Greek styles. Alexander's love of knowledge led him to debate Indian philosophy at every chance, but the long-lasting interchange of ideas is hard to pin down. Though the Greek invasion did not have abiding effects, it created a power vacuum in northern India that allowed the Mauryans to come to power, and their domination of India had positive results.

See also India, Aryan Invasion of; Alexander the Great; Mauryan Empire; Persia, Alexander's Conquest of.

References: Bosworth, A. B., *Conquest and Empire* (Cambridge: Cambridge University Press, 1988); Keegan, John, *The Mask of Command* (New York: Viking, 1987); Tarn, W. W., *Alexander the Great* (Boston: Beacon Press, 1948).

ITALY, CARTHAGINIAN INVASION OF (SECOND PUNIC WAR)

26

After the First Punic War, Carthage had domestic problems to overcome, mainly concerning the mercenary forces with whom it fought its wars. In the later part of the war, these men had gone unpaid, and therefore they rebelled against Carthage. When many of the towns under Carthaginian control rebelled as well, in sympathy with the mercenaries, the appointment of Hamilcar Barca to head Carthage's defense proved a wise move. Hamilcar put down the revolt and cemented his leadership of Carthage at the same time.

Though neutral throughout the revolt, Rome soon made advances in Sardinia to support discontented Carthaginian subjects there. Rome claimed that this was part of its spoils from the first war, and Carthage could do little about it. Rome's additional demand for control of Corsica and a higher indemnity served to reignite hostility. Because Carthage was in no position to challenge Rome immediately, Hamilcar focused Carthaginian attention on expanding its power base in Spain throughout the 230s B.C.E. After Hamilcar's death in 229, his son-in-law, Hasdrubal, continued his work by establishing the port city of Nova Carthago (modern-day Cartagena). Rome watched with interest, as the Romans were beginning to look outward from Italy for the first time and were anxious to establish their own contacts in Spain. They entered the Iberian peninsula from Gaul as the Carthaginians were consolidating the south.

In 226 B.C.E., the two powers agreed to establish the Ebro River as the border between their domains, and for a few years this worked well. Hasdrubal's assassination in 221 B.C.E. brought Hamilcar's son Hannibal to power, and he soon had to deal with Roman expansionism. Rome persuaded the town of Saguntum, south of the Ebro, to elect a pro-Roman government. Hannibal viewed this as a violation of the spirit of the 226 B.C.E. treaty, and responded by laying siege to the city in 219 and capturing it eight months later. As the siege continued, the militant faction came to power in Rome and declared war against Carthage.

Carthage had ceased to control the waters of the northwestern Mediterranean, so Hannibal had to move his forces overland to invade Italy, preempting a Roman invasion of Spain. He surprised everyone by clearing away resistance and moving his army, complete with elephants, through the Alps into northern Italy by November 218 B.C.E. Fighting local tribes in the

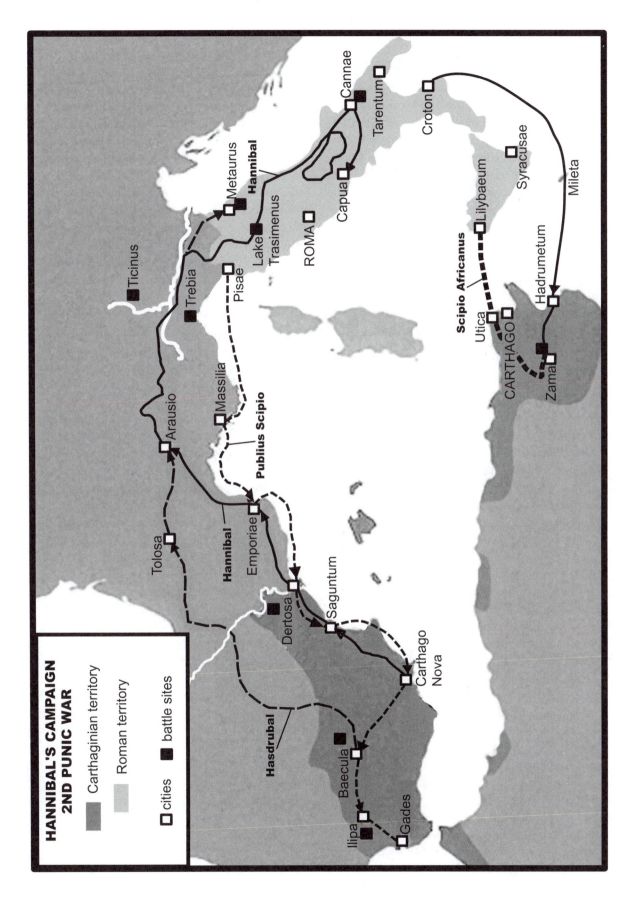

HANNIBAL'S CAMPAIGN
2ND PUNIC WAR

- Carthaginian territory
- Roman territory
- □ cities   ■ battle sites

Ticinus

Metaurus

Hannibal

Trebia

Lake
Trasimenus

Pisae

ROMA

Cannae

Tarentum

Croton

Capua

Mileta

Massilia

Arausio

Publius Scipio

Scipio Africanus

Lilybaeum

Syracusae

Hadrumetum

Utica

CARTHAGO

Zama

Tolosa

Hannibal

Emporiae

Saguntum

Dertosa

Hasdrubal

Carthago
Nova

Baecula

Ilipa

Gades

mountains, coupled with the onset of winter weather, killed many of his men, but he entered Italy with 20,000 infantry, 6,000 cavalry, and a number of elephants. He quickly won two battles and went into winter quarters in the Po Valley. Hannibal's strategy was to provoke the subject tribes of Italy into revolt against Rome, which would simultaneously weaken its power and enlarge his. His apparent goal was not to destroy Rome as a major power, but to limit it to the peninsula and regain territory lost since the first war.

The Romans were unable to defeat Hannibal as he rampaged through Italy, defeating every Roman army sent against him. In 216 at Cannae, he won one of ancient history's most brilliant victories by executing a double envelopment of the Roman forces in which he inflicted 60,000 casualties for a loss of only 6,000 of his own men. The Romans appointed Fabius as occasional consul/occasional dictator during Hannibal's campaign. Fabius decided that the best way to fight Hannibal was to avoid pitched battles, and instead to settle into defensive positions in cities and wait for the Carthaginians to wear themselves out. His method became known to history as Fabian strategy, and it proved successful. Hannibal neither gained as many local allies as he had hoped for, nor accumulated a sufficient siege train to assault the well-defended cities. He had to content himself with living off the countryside and attacking the occasional city, usually with mixed results.

Meanwhile, Rome committed its reconstituted military to Spain, attempting to deny Hannibal his base of operations. Hannibal's brother, also named Hasdrubal, fought a long and inconclusive war against Roman forces under the Scipio brothers. Both Spain and Italy saw much fighting, but no force became dominant until 209 B.C.E., when the son of one of the now-dead Scipio brothers came to command in Spain. Publius Scipio proved to be a match for the Carthaginian generals. He captured Nova Carthago, the capital of Carthaginian Spain, and forced Hasdrubal and his brother Mago to go on the defensive in southwest Iberia. In 207, Hasdrubal attempted to march through the Alps to reinforce his

brother, but at the Metaurus River, he was defeated and beheaded. Hannibal learned of his brother's fate when a Roman horseman threw Hasdrubal's head into his camp.

The fighting continued, without much success on either side, until 206 B.C.E., when Scipio finally consolidated Roman power in Spain. In 204 he sailed for Africa, where he gained Numidia as an ally. Scipio failed to impose his will on Carthage, but he frightened the inhabitants considerably. Carthage ordered Hannibal home to defend the city, but he could not comply; Rome still controlled the sea lanes. Scipio's capture of Tunes, very near Carthage, forced the Carthaginians to agree to terms. Hannibal returned to Carthage under the terms of the ceasefire to negotiate with Scipio. When they could not agree, the two powers fought the battle of Zama. Scipio, with the assistance of Numidian cavalry, became the first Roman to defeat Hannibal in open battle.

Though Hannibal had campaigned through Italy for 17 years, causing immense destruction and hundreds of thousands of deaths, the peace terms were fairly easy. Carthage lost its possessions in Spain, but maintained its merchant navy (however, the war fleet was reduced to 10 ships) and trading connections. Carthage also was to pay Rome reparations amounting to 10,000 talents (more than 500,000 pounds of silver) over a 50-year period. Rome could have annexed Carthage into its new empire or denied the Carthaginians the ability to trade, the latter of which would have proven deadly. Rome did neither, and under Hannibal's political leadership Carthage was able to recover economically. The Carthaginians also recovered militarily and challenged Rome once more—a decision that would be fatal. The main result of the Second Punic War was the establishment, somewhat by default, of the Roman Empire. Though overseas possessions had not been sought intentionally, Rome now controlled the islands of the Mediterranean as well as Spain. For the next 600 years, Rome would be the dominant power in the world.

See also Carthage, Expansion of; Carthage, Roman Invasion of (Third Punic War); Hannibal; Spain, Roman Conquest of.

References: Charles-Picard, Gilbert, and Collette Picard, *The Life and Death of Carthage*, trans. Dominique Collon (London: Sidgwick & Jackson, 1968); Dorey, T A., and D. R. Dudley, *Rome against Carthage* (Garden City, NY: Doubleday, 1972); Lamb, Harold, *Hannibal* (New York: Doubleday, 1958).

27 MAURYAN EMPIRE

After the decline of the Harappan civilization in India, little or no organized political system existed until the arrival of Alexander the Great. Though northwestern India was considered a part of Alexander's empire, after his death the struggling inheritors of his lands could not pay attention to the distant reaches of India. The consolidation that had taken place gave an opportunity to a regional Indian prince, Chandragupta, to fill the power vacuum left by Alexander's death. He came to power in 323 B.C.E. and cleared the northwest regions of India of Greek troops. One of Alexander's successors, Seleucus, reinvaded India

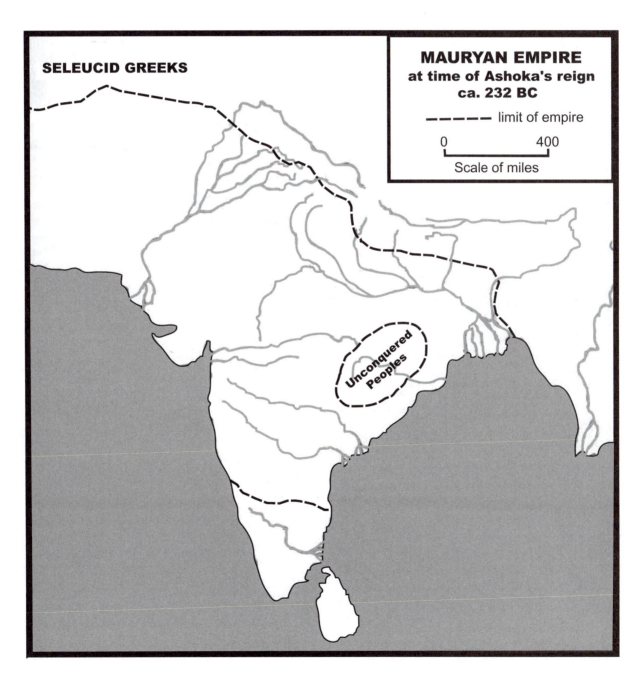

in 305 B.C.E., but could not defeat Chandragupta's forces. Seleucus agreed to cede the Indian lands Alexander had conquered in return for 500 war elephants. This action confirmed Chandragupta's power and extended the reach of his control.

Once solidly in control, Chandragupta organized an efficient government machinery to oversee economic and military affairs. He kept a standing army of about one-quarter the size of his wartime conscripted army, described by a Seleucid ambassador as 600,000 infantry, 30,000 cavalry, and 9,000 elephants. He also maintained a river fleet for both the Ganges and Indus, which may have protected the coastlines as well. His reserves were in the form of "guild levies," groups of craftsmen who trained together and were called up in time of emergency. One of history's first political manuals was written for Chandragupta by his closest adviser, Kautilya: the *Arthasastra*, or *Manual of Politics*. Like Machiavelli's *The Prince*, it spelled out the necessities for a ruler to maintain power, and included extended sections on military organization, structure, and function.

Chandragupta began the Mauryan Empire, but its greatest expansions came through his successors. His son Bindasura attacked southward and brought almost all of India under his rule, excepting only the subcontinent's southernmost tip and the island of Ceylon. Bindasura's son Asoka (or Ashoka) accomplished the last conquests, securing the eastern coast. Under Asoka, the Mauryan Empire was not only at its political extreme, it reached cultural heights previously unknown in India. Asoka became disgusted with the destruction caused by warfare and turned to Buddhism. He mandated the establishment of a Buddhist bureaucracy to maintain honesty in government affairs. Asoka spent his wealth on the construction of monasteries and temples and the erection of inscribed stone pillars extolling his accomplishments. He sent Buddhist missionaries to Ceylon, Burma, and Java, and stretched India's trading empire to those distant areas.

It is difficult to know for certain how strong the Mauryan hold in India was, or if the emperors were lords to vassal nobles who exercised local power. Whatever the case, the empire did not last long after Asoka's death in 232 B.C.E. The succeeding emperors lacked the will or

vision of the first three, and local revolts coupled with a return of the Seleucids in 206 B.C.E. brought the empire down.

See also Alexander the Great; India, Alexander's Invasion of; Seleucid Empire.

References: Allan, John, *The Cambridge Shorter History of India* (Delhi: S. Chand, 1964); Mookerji, Radha, *Chandragupta Maurya and His Times* (Delhi: Motilal Banarsidass, 1966); Wheeler, Robert, *Early India and Pakistan to Ashoka* (New York: Praeger, 1959).

28   PERSIA, ALEXANDER'S CONQUEST OF

Upon the death of Philip of Macedon, his 20-year-old son Alexander inherited his throne and his army. Though still young, Alexander had gained combat leadership experience from the battle of Cheronaea two years prior to his accession. His first task, however, was to restore Macedonian control over those provinces that had rebelled upon hearing of Philip's death. That accomplished, he set out to attain his father's dying goal: the conquest of Persia. Historians argue whether Alexander was originally intent on world conquest, Persian Empire conquest, or merely defeating Persian forces and gaining control of Asia Minor. Successive victories took him deeper and deeper into Persian lands, so it is difficult to gauge his original design by the outcome of his campaign.

Whatever his original motivation, he crossed the Hellespont in 334 B.C.E. The Persian emperor, Darius III, left his satraps (governors) to deal with Alexander's invasion. They met him quickly; within three days of his entrance into Asia Minor, Alexander faced a mixed force of Persian cavalry and Greek mercenary infantry at the river Granicus. Twenty thousand Persian cavalry aligned themselves along the eastern bank of the Granicus, with the infantry arrayed in phalanx formation well behind them. Alexander ignored advice to wait for dawn to make a surprise attack, and advanced immediately. He had the phenomenal ability to pick out his enemy's weak point and strike it; in this case it was the center of the Persian line, usually a strong point. Because the Persians were at the water's edge, however, they were unable to use their cavalry to build momentum for a charge. Coupled with the lack of close infantry support, this made them vulnerable to a determined assault by a mixed cavalry/infantry force. Once the center was broken, the Persians fled, and the Greeks were surrounded and slaughtered.

Alexander quickly proceeded along the coast, liberating the Greek cities of Ionia. Those that surrendered, he treated kindly; those that resisted, he pillaged or destroyed. His goal was not merely to free Greeks from Persian rule but to control the coastline so completely that the Persian navy would become superfluous. After capturing Helicarnassus, he drove inland to seize Gordium, in the heart of Asia Minor, in April 333 B.C.E. There he cut the Gordian knot, a feat legend said would indicate the king of Asia. He worked his way southward and then eastward to Tarsus by the autumn of 333 B.C.E. At this point, where the coast of Asia Minor turns southward to become the Levant, Darius arrived to fight him.

Darius reached the coast at Issus a few days after Alexander had passed, thus cutting him off from his line of communication back to Ionia and Macedon. Alexander turned about to fight at the River Pinarus, which feeds into the Gulf of Issus. Again, Alexander chose to charge the Persian center in mid-afternoon, and again he was successful. Darius soon dropped his weapons and fled, abandoning his army and his family. A determined counterattack by Greek mercenaries forced Alexander to stand and fight rather than pursue, and Darius escaped. The sudden collapse of the Persian center and Darius's quick flight demoralized the Persians, and the battle was over by nightfall. Estimates of the size of the Persian force vary wildly, but it is generally agreed that it far outnumbered Alexander's, and therefore his quick victory was correspondingly amazing. The victory at Issus took Darius out of the Levant for a year and gave Alexander time to continue his conquest of the coast.

Sidon and Byblus surrendered without a fight, but Tyre resisted. The Persian garrison manned a walled fortification on an island just off the beach. The only way Alexander and his army could approach it was to build a causeway, which he began constructing in January 332 B.C.E. Its

Alexander (left) stabs a Persian soldier as he rushes to battle Darius, the Persian king, in a mosaic depicting the Macedonian victory at Issus. (Erich Lessing/Art Resourc, NY)

construction, and the defection of Phoenician ships from the Persian navy to his cause, gave Alexander the tools necessary to assault the fort. Tyre resisted for seven months before succumbing to Alexander's men; for their resistance, they suffered 8,000 dead and 30,000 sold into slavery. Jerusalem fell without a fight, but Gaza resisted. Its capture and destruction in November 332 B.C.E. gave Alexander mastery of the eastern Mediterranean coast and open access to Egypt.

After almost a year in Egypt, Alexander marched his forces back up the coast, supplying them by sea. From Syria he struck inland for the Euphrates with 47,000 men. He marched along the edge of the Armenian hills rather than attack down the river into the waiting arms of Darius's newly raised army on the plains around Babylon. Darius grew impatient, and marched away from friendly and favorable ground to move on Alexander near the Tigris. In late September, Alexander crossed the river first and encamped near Gaugemela, just upriver from Darius's army. Darius chose the battleground, however, and placed his men in two long lines. Arrian, traveling with Alexander, numbered the Persian army at one million, but modern historians discount this figure and estimate between 100,000 and 250,000, a number still significantly larger than Alexander's.

Early in the battle, Darius ordered the commitment of his secret weapon—scythed chariots—but Macedonian skirmishers and light infantry disabled the horses or drivers, and they proved useless. Though Persian attacks on the Macedonian left almost broke Alexander's line, the Persian desire for loot overcame their discipline and they drove for the rear rather than turn to envelop their enemy. Alexander saw a growing gap in their line and attacked there, once again breaking the Persian lines and panicking Darius into flight. The need to protect his forces kept Alexander from pursuing, but the battle was won. After Gaugemela, Darius could do nothing but keep running. Alexander caught up to him a year later, but could only claim the body of Darius; he had been killed by his few remaining courtiers.

Meanwhile, Alexander marched on and occupied Babylon and the Persian capital at Susa, then captured the city of Persepolis, site of the Persian treasury. In January 330 B.C.E., he destroyed the royal palace at Persepolis and declared Persia to be his. Some Persian vassals resisted their new lord, and Alexander had to fight a guerrilla campaign in the northeast until 327. After that, he was poised for India.

After his return from India, Alexander ensconced himself in Babylon and proceeded to remake the known world. He dreamed of a new worldview blended from Eastern culture and Greek rationality, and Hellenism was the result. For 300 years after his death, until the Middle East came under Roman sway, Hellenism was the dominant culture of the world. The infusion of Greek settlers brought literacy and new sciences, and the massive treasury of Persepolis provided an enormous economic boost to the region that brought the expansion of trade and patronage of the arts. Though Alexander's political bequest was one of dissension, the cultural heritage brought about new philosophies, scientific discoveries, and an atmosphere of learning that was not matched again until the Renaissance.

See also Alexander the Great; Egypt, Alexander's Conquest of; India, Alexander's Invasion of; Philip of Macedon.

References: Hammond, N. G. L., *Alexander the Great: King, Commander, and Statesman* (Park Ridge, NJ: Noyes Press 1980); Keegan, John, *The Mask of Command* (New York: Viking, 1987); Tarn, W. W., *Alexander the Great* (Cambridge: Cambridge University Press, 1948).

29   PHILIP OF MACEDON

Philip was born in 382 B.C.E. in Macedon. In 359, he became regent for his young nephew. The arrangement proved unworkable for the stability of the kingdom, and Philip was named the new king. At this time the Macedonian state was not unified, and the area was under incessant attack from barbarian tribes. Macedon had never been known for its military abilities and could rarely field a large force. This changed under Philip, when he quickly proved his leadership abilities. He used bribery and diplomacy to keep most of his enemies at a distance while he concentrated on the nation's greatest threat, the Illyrians. Within 18 months of his accession to power, Philip defeated the Illyrians in one battle in 358, and celebrated the victory by marrying the first of seven wives, Olympia.

Philip proposed to unify Greece, not so much for the sake of conquest as for making sure his rear was secure for a future invasion of Asia. He gained control of Amphipolis, which provided him with the necessary wealth to continue his campaign. By capturing Pydna and Methone, he obliged the Athenian forces to withdraw southward. He next captured Chalcidice, then Thessaly. Philip made himself leader of the Thessalian League and married a Thessalian princess. This leadership position gave him access to fine herds of horses, which he used for his cavalry. After defeating a northern threat at Olynthus, he turned toward Athens. Philip laid siege to cities vital to Athens's survival and ultimately attacked Athens itself; after its capture, he surprised the inhabitants with his lenient surrender terms.

With Greece under his domination, Philip made himself leader of the Corinthian League. He hoped to use the combined power of the Greek city-states to wage war against Persia, which they voted to do in 337 B.C.E. Philip returned home to Macedon to prepare for the invasion, but was assassinated before the operation could start. Though Philip's death is the subject of some debate, historians generally believe that his first wife, Olympia, was behind the murder, as she feared for the future of her son, Alexander, because Philip was producing sons by other wives.

In his 46 years, Philip accomplished a great deal. He turned a floundering kingdom into a military power and made Greece a unified state for the first time. His military organization changed the nature of classical warfare. He adopted the standard phalanx formation of the time, but lengthened the spears the formation infantry carried to between 16 and 23 feet. The extra length made it much more difficult to attack the phalanx, and extended the killing range of the Macedonian unit. Philip also made his infantry wear lighter armor so that they could maneuver more quickly than his enemies. He used cavalry wisely in support of his infantry and employed engineers for the construction of siege engines, including the first torsion catapult. He placed members of the same community in regiments to promote unit cohesion. Troops under Philip's command were well known for their discipline, training, and loyalty.

Able as he was in military affairs, Philip preferred diplomacy and bribery to warfare. He was an intelligent leader who knew when to back away from a battle as well as when to join one. He maintained a large network of spies, and often knew his enemies' abilities better than they themselves did. He also used marriage to cement alliances and bind newly conquered states to his cause. His civil works were also notable: He founded new towns and encouraged cultural advances. Most of all, he trained his firstborn son, Alexander, to succeed him, and provided the best-trained army in the world for Alexander's own dreams of conquest. Though Philip never saw the destruction of Persia, his son accomplished that goal beyond Philip's wildest dreams.

See also Alexander the Great.

References: Borza, Eugene, *In the Shadow of Olympus: The Emergence of Macedon* (Princeton, NJ: Princeton University Press, 1990); Cawkwell, George, *Philip of Macedon* (Boston: Faber & Faber, 1978); Perlman, Samuel, *Philip and Athens* (New York: Barnes & Noble, 1973).

30   PTOLEMAIC DYNASTY

Late in Egypt's New Kingdom period, the ancient civilization came under the domination of foreign invaders. In the seventh century B.C.E. the Assyrians ruled Egypt, so weakening the local culture that the Egyptians could not withstand the onslaught of the Libyans or the Empire of Kush. When the Persians took over in the sixth century B.C.E., Egypt chafed under their rule, though Persia was more lenient than were other empires that had conquered the Nile Valley. When Alexander the Great entered the country in 331 B.C.E., the locals viewed him as a liberator and welcomed him without resistance. Alexander's rule proved short, but Greek rule did not; Ptolemy, one of Alexander's generals, succeeded to the Egyptian throne on his leader's death in 323 B.C.E. Ptolemy and his heirs ruled Egypt for three centuries, until they succumbed to the power of Rome.

Having served as governor for Egypt under Alexander's administration, Ptolemy declared himself the independent ruler of Egypt in 305 B.C.E., taking the regnal name of Ptolemy I Soter (meaning "preserver"). He ruled as pharaoh, the divine leader recognized by Egyptian culture for two millennia. This may not have endeared him to the Egyptians, but at least it made his rule acceptable.

Ptolemy I Soter fought with his fellow successor generals, the Diodachi (Seleucus and Antigonus), who had each inherited a third of Alexander's empire. He maintained almost constant conflict with the Seleucids, in particular, over control of Syria and the eastern Mediterranean coast, and he managed to establish control over Rhodes and Palestine. Most famous for establishing the Library of Alexandria, Ptolemy I Soter resigned in favor of his son in 285. Ptolemy II Philadelphus (meaning "brotherly") continued his father's wars with the Seleucids. He established Egypt as the major maritime power of the Mediterranean at the expense of the Seleucid king Antiochus I. He also followed in his father's academic footsteps by enlarging the Alexandrian Library and sponsoring literary and scholarly endeavors. He was also responsible for the Pharos, or great lighthouse, one of the seven wonders of the ancient world. His reign of nearly 40 years made Egypt the cultural center of its time. He was outdone only by his own son, Ptolemy III Euergertes (meaning "benefactor"), who reunited Cyrenaica (modern Libya) with Egypt and invaded Syria. Egyptian naval power grew to dominate the Aegean Sea. Ptolemy Euergertes spent even more time and money improving the library and patronizing the arts, making his 25-year reign the height of Ptolemaic power and prestige.

Successive rulers of the dynasty made alternate peace and war with the successors of the other Diodachi, as each attempted to match the empire founded by Alexander. Though they brought wealth and fame to their own spheres of influence, they could not match Alexander's military accomplishments. Frontiers moved back and forth, but the Ptolemies usually maintained control of African territory even when they occasionally ceded authority across the Suez. The Ptolemies maintained their Greek heritage by following the Egyptian practice of family intermarriage. It was a brother-sister/husband-wife combination who controlled Egypt in the middle of the first century B.C.E. when Julius Caesar focused Roman attention on the Egypt of Cleopatra and Ptolemy XII.

Though the Ptolemies could not be considered cruel masters, their three centuries of rule certainly did not benefit the common inhabitant in Egypt. Almost constant warfare cost significant tax money and necessitated conscription for public service, which the commoners were obliged to provide. The cultural advancements typified by the Library of Alexandria benefited only the upper classes. However, the Ptolemies maintained strict observance of Egyptian religious rites, and provided a steady flow of money to the temples for maintenance and improvement, which kept the people relatively quiet, if not happy. Rebellion was always close at hand, but the Egyptian people never had the power to defeat their Greek masters. The takeover of the country proved almost as easy for Rome as it had for Alexander, but the locals viewed them as new masters rather than liberators.

See also Assyrian Empire; Kush, Expansion of; Alexander the Great; Augustus, Caesar; Caesar, Julius; Egypt, Alexander's Conquest of; Seleucid Empire.

References: Seven, Edwyn, A History of Egypt under the Ptolemaic Dynasty (London: Methuen & Co., 1927); Foster, Edward, Alexandria, a History and a Guide (Gloucester: Doubleday, 1968).

31 · SELEUCID EMPIRE

The death of Alexander the Great brought a struggle among his subordinates for succession to his throne. As many as 11 of his commanders vied for position, but it finally became a struggle among three: Antigonus controlled Macedon, Seleucus took over most of what had been the Persian Empire, and Ptolemy became ruler of Egypt. Not satisfied with their holdings, the three fought among themselves for more land; often, two of them allied against the third in an ever-changing set of partnerships. Seleucus controlled the largest of the three domains, but his successors had the most difficult time in maintaining it. Seleucus established his capital at Babylon in 312 B.C.E., but spent most of the rest of his life suppressing revolts by provincial governors. Syria was a continual source of trouble. His victory at the battle of Ipsus in 301 B.C.E. gave him control of the important trade center, but keeping it was another matter.

Upon Seleucus's death, his son Antiochus I inherited the throne and had to fight on all frontiers. He was the first to war with Egypt over Syria, losing it to Ptolemy II in the First Syrian War of 280–279 B.C.E. Antiochus allied himself with Antigonus after the Macedonian had to suppress several Greek rebellions subsidized by Ptolemy. Antiochus invaded Syria in 260 B.C.E., and Antigonus engaged and defeated the Egyptian fleet off the island of Cos in 258. Ptolemy sued for peace in 255. Ptolemy III regained Syria in a Third Syrian War, 246–241 B.C.E., while Seleucus II was busy fighting a civil war against his brother. Seleucus was aided in this by the city-state of Pergamum on the Turkish Adriatic coast, which had a brief career as arbiter of Asia Minor politics.

The Seleucid Empire reached the height of its power under Antiochus III, called "the Great." He regained territory in Asia Minor from Pergamum; he fought yet another Syrian war to little effect; he suppressed a rebellion in Asia Minor (216–213); he defeated Armenia and forced them to recognize his suzerainty; and he invaded Parthia, the power that had succeeded the Persians in the east. At the battle of the Arius

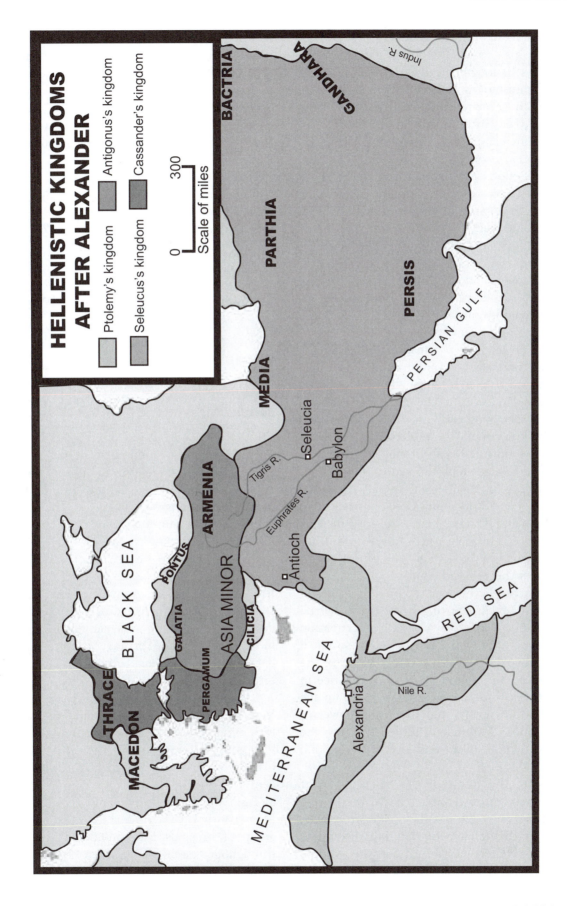

HELLENISTIC KINGDOMS
AFTER ALEXANDER

Ptolemy's kingdom
Antigonus's kingdom
Seleucus's kingdom
Cassander's kingdom

0   300
Scale of miles

BACTRIA

GANDHARA

Indus R.

PARTHIA

PERSIS

PERSIAN GULF

MEDIA

Seleucia

Babylon

Tigris R.

Euphrates R.

ARMENIA

ASIA MINOR

PONTUS

GALATIA

PERGAMUM

CILICIA

Antioch

BLACK SEA

THRACE

MACEDON

RED SEA

MEDITERRANEAN SEA

Alexandria

Nile R.

in 209, he forced the Parthian king Araces III to become his vassal. Moving farther east, Antiochus III fought the Bactrians (in modern-day Afghanistan) and forced their submission, after which he marched down the banks of the Kabul River into northwestern India. In 205–204, he campaigned down the Persian Gulf to conquer Gerrha (modern Bahrain). His final successful effort was another war in Syria, in which he took advantage of the infant king Ptolemy V. Again allying his nation with Macedon, now under Philip V, Antiochus easily defeated Egyptian forces in the key battle at Panium in 198, which gave him control over Palestine, Syria, and Asia Minor. Macedon was of little assistance because it lost battles to Pergamum and Rome.

The rising power of Rome spelled the end of Seleucid power. After defeating Philip V, the Romans continued onward toward Syria. The Romans and Seleucids fought their major battle at Magnesia in December 190 B.C.E. After achieving the upper hand early on, Antiochus's forces were broken when their elephants suddenly became uncontrollable and trampled their own army. The Romans took the victory, but did not take territory for themselves. Instead, they gave Asia Minor and Antiochus's Greek possessions to Pergamum and Rhodes at the Peace of Apemeax in 188 B.C.E. This defeat and Antiochus's death the following year brought about a general revolt throughout the Seleucid domain.

Antiochus IV managed to hold on to power for a while, even defeating Egypt twice, but he was forced by Rome to evacuate. His occupation of Palestine after that evacuation was so harsh that it provoked a Jewish revolt: the war of the Maccabees. He restored Seleucid dominance in the east, but a succession struggle broke up the empire. More revolts and the rising power of Parthia under Mithradates served to bring the Seleucid dynasty to an end late in the second century B.C.E.

Despite the fact that the Seleucids spent almost their entire tenure in wars, there were some positive results of their time in power, mostly in the implementation of Alexander's legacy of Hellenism throughout the Middle East. Greek settlers and retired veterans estab-lished Greek communities throughout the area, making Greek the language of science and the arts. Greek schools kept alive the sciences and philosophies of Greece and served to introduce Stoicism to the region, an outlook that had effects on the establishment of Christian doctrine. Without strict religious oversight or strong polit-ical order, the citizens of the empire were able to explore the ideas of both Eastern and European cultures and blend them into views unique to the area. Especially in religion, these views would arise as rivals to the gods of Rome and heresies to Orthodox and Roman Christianity.

See also Alexander the Great; Ptolemaic Dynasty.

References: Bar-Kochva, Bezalel, *The Seleucid Army* (London: Cambridge University Press, 1976); Sherwin-White, Susan, *From Samarkand to Sardis* (London: Duckworth, 1993).

32 · SICILY, ROMAN CONQUEST OF (FIRST PUNIC WAR)

Prior to 264 B.C.E., the Mediterranean Basin and Asia Minor were dominated in large part by either Hellenic or Hellenistic military force and culture. However, the status quo had been inexorably changing, owing to the growing strength of agricultural Rome and commercial Carthage. According to the historian Polybius, these two powers negotiated three separate treaties prior to the outbreak of this war. The first two were basically nonaggression pacts, and the third was a mutual-defense agreement designed to neutralize or defeat a perceived com-mon enemy, King Pyrrhus of Epirus. Rome's defeat of Pyrrhus removed the common threat, setting the stage for the Punic Wars.

Many historians believe that the First Punic War began by mistake, and some writers label the initial conflict an "accidental war." This viewpoint stems from the Roman and Carthaginian encounters in Sicily, which were centered on the Mamertine city of Messana along the Sicilio-Roman border. The Mamertines ("Men of Mars") were an unruly group of brigands who plundered and looted throughout coastal Sicily, provoking the ire of Syracuse, the dominant force on the island. The

Mamertines induced Carthage to protect them from Syracuse; then, during the Carthaginian occupation, they persuaded the Romans that the citizens of Messana were Roman allies or even of Roman blood. Rome intervened on their behalf, starting the 23-year-long war. Other historians speculate that the move to save their supposed brothers in Sicily was merely an excuse for an aggressive Roman Centurial Assembly, made up of wealthy plebeians, to force the senate into a war to expand Roman power.

From Consul Appius Caudex's defeat of a combined Syracusan-Carthaginian force at Messana in 264 B.C.E. to the decisive naval battle at Lilybaeum, won by Consul Catalus in 242 B.C.E., no previous war had cost so much in lives and materiel. During the conflict at sea, the Romans lost an estimated 250,000 men and the Carthaginians 210,000; no estimate has been made regarding personnel losses suffered on land. The Romans were thought to be stronger on land and their adversary stronger at sea, but the conflict became a seesaw affair, with Rome winning many naval battles and Carthage defeating a number of Roman armies in the field. Consul Regulus, for example, soundly defeated Hamilcar's fleet off Sicily in 256 B.C.E.; in turn, his army was beaten and captured by Xanthippus at the Plain of Tunis.

The Romans had no navy before 260 B.C.E., so it is quite remarkable that they became a maritime power virtually overnight. Two key reasons for Roman success in naval warfare were their development of a boarding platform, called a "raven," and the courage, discipline, and training of the average Roman soldier or marine. The only serious naval defeats the Romans suffered came from either poor leadership or disdain for the power of nature: The majority of Roman naval losses were incurred during storms.

The Carthaginian government greatly aided the Roman cause by crucifying their own most capable admirals and generals after the loss of a single engagement, thus depriving themselves of their best leadership. They also refused to support their most successful general, Hamilcar Barca. After a series of successful raids against Roman outposts along the Italian coast, he landed his force to occupy a Roman force at Palermo. His government refused to send aid or reinforcements.

Two battles in 249 B.C.E. brought a major naval loss for each side, after which ensued a ceasefire of almost nine years, time the Carthaginians wasted, while the Romans rebuilt their forces. In 241 B.C.E., with a new 200-ship armada, the Romans sailed secretly to Sicily, caught a Carthaginian fleet unaware, and overwhelmed it. The Carthaginian admiral Hanno was crucified upon his return to Carthage following this loss to Consul Catalus. This defeat swung the balance firmly in Rome's favor, forcing the Carthaginians into peace negotiations.

The immediate effects of the victory were to give Rome complete hegemony over Sicily and to provide its coffers with 2,200 talents (125,400 pounds) of silver in Carthaginian reparation payments over 10 years. In the long term, Rome would henceforth view Sicily as vital to its national security. The Sicilian client-states, established after the war, would become models for Rome's governance of conquered territories during the life of the Roman Empire.

In North Africa, the Carthaginian government continued to be its own worst enemy. When the mercenaries, who made up most of the army, demanded their back pay, the government prevaricated and provoked a rebellion. Hamilcar again proved himself their most able commander. He raised a force to restore order, then convinced the government to send him to Spain to reestablish Carthaginian dominance. That move helped to provoke the Second Punic War.

Although, as stated, the First Punic War may have been accidental, it is far more likely that such a conflict was inevitable. The residents of Messana merely provided the spark to put the two powers at loggerheads. Carthaginian claims on Sicily were tenuous at best, because the powerful Syracusans lived in closer proximity to Rome than to Carthage. Polybius's writings notwithstanding, it is likely that the powerful, aggressive Romans had already decided to expand their borders beyond the Italian coast. The voices of senators who called for peace in 265 B.C.E. were drowned out by those clamoring for war. With consuls eager to gain fame and riches through warfare, it seems logical that they would look toward Carthage for fulfillment. At any rate, the First Punic War set the stage for Carthage's ultimate destruction and established the framework for Roman dominance in the Mediterranean.

See also Carthage, Expansion of; Italy, Carthaginian Invasion of (Second Punic War).

References: Charles-Picard, Gilbert, and Collette Picard, *The Life and Death of Carthage*, trans. Dominique Collon (London: Sidgwick & Jackson, 1968); Errington, R., *The Dawn of Empire: Rome's Rise to World Power* (New York: Cornell University Press, 1972); Gruen, E. S., ed., *Imperialism in the Roman Republic* (New York: Holt, Rinehart & Winston, Inc., 1970).

33 SPAIN, ROMAN CONQUEST OF

During the First Punic War, Rome and Carthage battled each other from 264 to 261 B.C.E. The cause of that conflict was Rome's discontent with Carthaginian expansion into Sicily, and ultimately, Rome forced Carthage back into its African domain. In 218 B.C.E., Rome interpreted a Carthaginian attempt to rebuild a power base in Spain as a threat to Roman interests, forcing another declaration of war on Carthage. Early in the contest, Roman success was minimal. In fact, the famed Carthaginian general Hannibal wreaked havoc across the Italian countryside. Looking for new leadership, the Roman senate arranged for Publius Cornelius Scipio's son, Scipio Africanus, to be elected proconsul to Spain. Unlike most Romans, he realized that Spain was the key to the struggle against Hannibal: Spain would serve as his main base of operations and provide most of his replacements.

Scipio's first target in Spain was New Carthage (modern-day Cartagena). New Carthage was the capital, and the only Spanish port able to handle a large fleet. Furthermore, it possessed other strategic aspects: It provided a direct sea link to Carthage, the Carthaginians kept the bulk of their gold bullion and war materiel there, and it would give Scipio an essential base from which he could conduct his campaign into the south of the peninsula.

Scipio's success at Carthage was the result of his talent for deception. Cartagena was surrounded by water on three sides—a lagoon on the north, a canal on the west, and a bay and the open sea on the south. The winter prior to his assault, Scipio made careful topographical inquiries about the area. He learned from local fishermen that the lagoon was easily fordable at low tide. In the spring of 209 B.C.E., he launched a frontal attack on the gates of the city, which faced east, to divert their forces. He then sent a party of 500 men with ladders across the lagoon. Quickly clearing the wall, his men took the Carthaginians by surprise and opened the way for the main body of Roman troops to overwhelm the city.

This victory, coupled with Hannibal's eventual withdrawal back to Africa, left Rome in control of Spain. Rome had not intended to conquer all of Spain, but the law of expansion forced the Romans either to commit themselves totally or surrender what they had captured. The more civilized eastern and western portions of Spain submitted easily to Roman rule, but it took more than 60 years to gain firm control of the country because the warlike tribes of the interior would not give in. Engaging in tribal warfare against militant Spanish bands throughout the countryside was a challenge to Rome. Coping with the type of warfare the Spanish practiced was difficult for the legionaries because the Spanish fought in small groups, taking advantage of their knowledge of the terrain to cut off and surprise Roman detachments. These tactics, employed often in the future, were given the name guerrilla, Spanish for "little war." Until 132 B.C.E., Roman armies were often defeated in the Spanish hinterland and were obliged to concede peace terms on many occasions. Nevertheless, each time, the treaties were disavowed by the government in Rome or by Roman generals on the scene.

The process of Romanization was slow, not only because of the native opposition, but also because Roman ideas themselves continued to evolve until the second century C.E. Their initial contributions dealt with law and administration. Rome's administrative abilities were passed on to the Spanish through their organization of cities, towns, and governmental institutions. Even the Christian Church, introduced to Spain by the

Romans, was organized on the basis of Roman administrative districts, employing Roman methods and Roman law.

Thanks to agricultural and commercial successes during Roman rule, Spain amassed considerable wealth. The public works projects undertaken during Roman rule were among the most significant contributions to Spanish society. New roads and bridges—some existing in whole or in part to this day—permitted the peoples of Spain to communicate freely with one another as never before. The construction of aqueducts served as both a necessity and a convenience for expanding cities. Roman architecture in Spain had the characteristics of massiveness and strength, borrowing structural principles from the Etruscans and decorative forms from the Greeks. These qualities were most evident in theaters, amphitheaters, temples, triumphal arches, and tombs.

Spain was invaded by the Visigoths in 409 C.E., but by that time, most Roman characteristics were permanently engraved in Spanish society. Despite further invasions by barbarians from the north and the Muslims from the south, Roman influence endured. Whether or not Rome had a concrete reason for invading and occupying Spain in the beginning, the Romans were so successful in planting their culture and institutions during six centuries of occupation that much remains to this day.

See also Hannibal; Italy, Carthaginian Invasion of (Second Punic War); Sicily, Roman Conquest of (First Punic War); Visigoths.

References: Chapman, Charles E., *A History of Spain* (New York: Free Press, 1966); McDonald, A. H., *Republican Rome* (New York: Praeger, 1966); Scullard, Howard H., *A History of the Roman World: From 753 to 146 B.C.E.* (London: Methuen & Co., 1969).

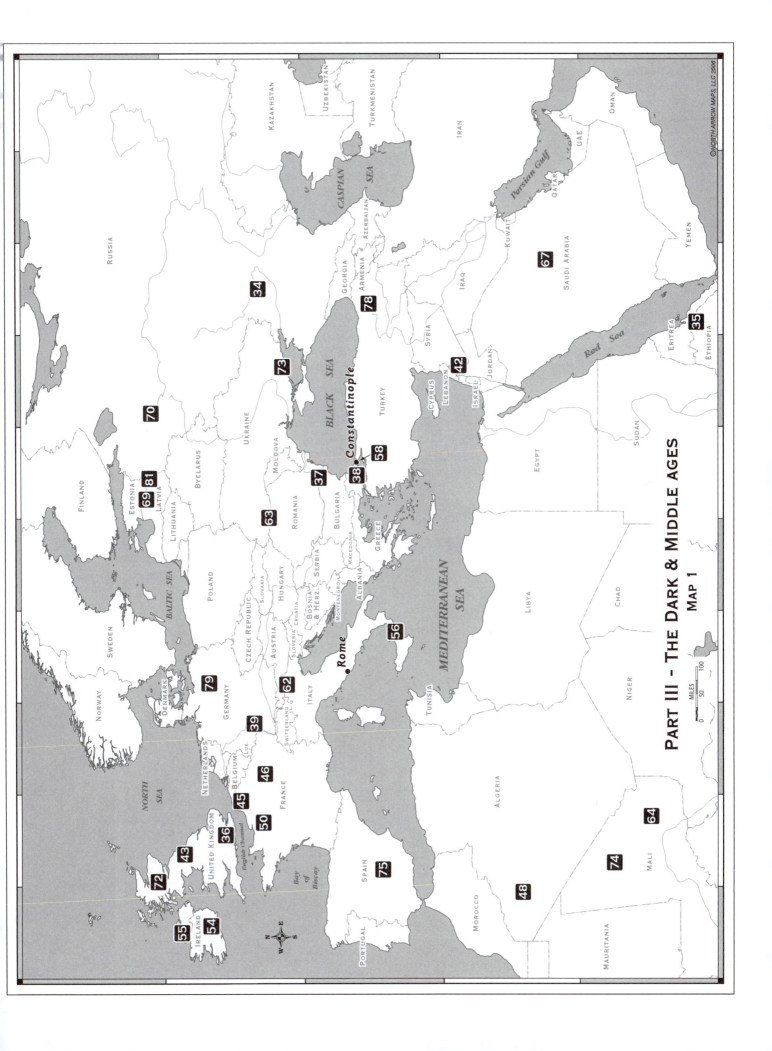

PART III – THE DARK & MIDDLE AGES

MAP 1

©NORTH ARROW MAPS, LLC 2006

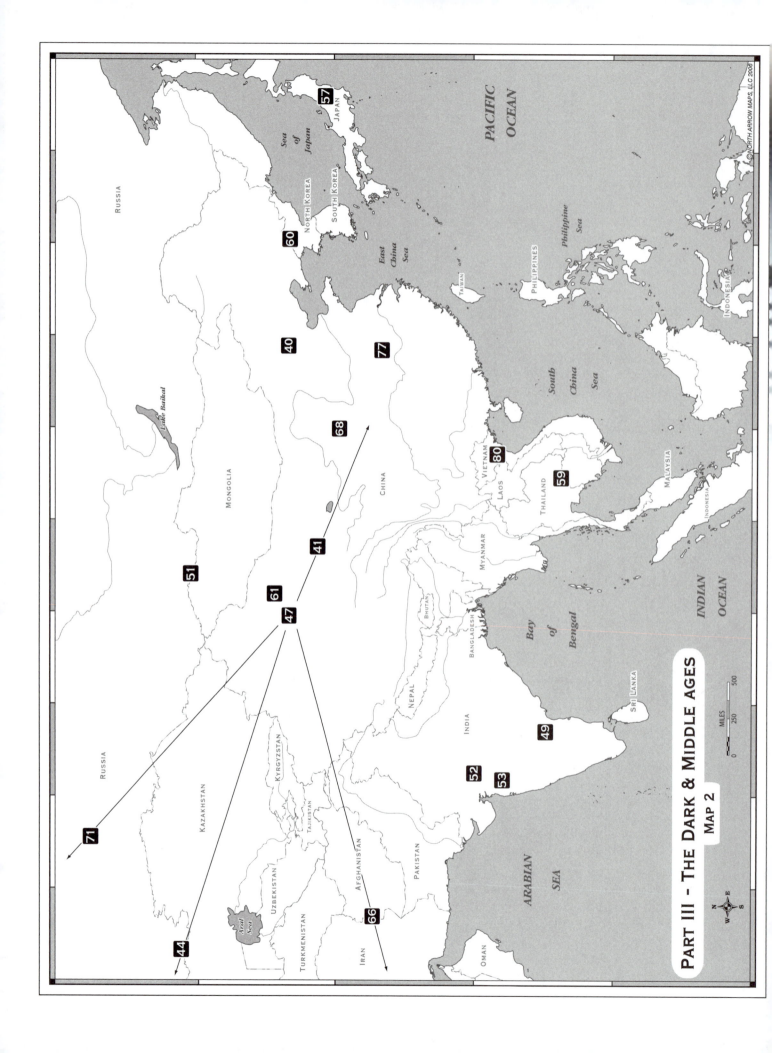

PART III - THE DARK & MIDDLE AGES

MAP 2

PART 3
THE DARK AND MIDDLE AGES

AVARS

34

A people ethnologically related to the Huns, the Avars are first mentioned in the fifth century C.E. as living east of the Volga River in Russia. Their first contact with Western society came in the mid-sixth century when they appeared in the Caucasus. The Avars invaded the territory west of the Dnieper River, defeating the Utigurs (the last of the Huns) and the Antes. They pillaged this territory so thoroughly that those two tribes disappeared, and the Avars then made demands on the Byzantine Empire. For a while, the Avars served the Byzantine Empire as mercenaries, but over time they grew too strong. In 561 Khagan Baian, the major Avar leader, received tribute from Emperor Justinian to stay away from Constantinople, so the Avars moved north and west. Though they met defeat at the hands of the Franks in Thuringia in 562, they allied with the Langobards in 565 to make war on the Gepids, inhabitants of the Danube valley. Together they crushed the Gepids in a huge battle in 567 and split Gepid lands between them. Rather than face a potential new enemy, the Langobards ceded their newly acquired Gepid lands to the Avars and migrated to Italy, where they became better known as Lombards.

With this cession from the Langobards in addition to their initial conquests, the Avars now controlled land stretching from western Rumania through Hungary to Bohemia and on to the Elbe River in central Germany. After attacking the Byzantine fortress at Sirmium, the Avars extorted an increased tribute from Emperor Justin II. Only on their southern frontier was there a challenge to their power: the Sclavini, the forerunner of the Slavs. This tribe had pillaged throughout the Balkans and Danube valley for years, growing wealthy in the process. Khagan Baian offered to accept the Sclavini as vassals if they would pay him tribute; they rejected his offer by killing his envoy. That was all the excuse the Avars needed. They quickly went to war against the Sclavini by moving tens of thousands of men overland and down the Danube River into their territory. The Avars made short work of the Sclavini, pillaging their land and forcing them to run for the hills of northern Greece. Justin had hoped to play the Sclavini against the Avars, forgoing the need to commit his own forces, but the Avar victory ended that hope.

Perhaps earning the respect of the Sclavini, the Avars soon joined with them and came to be known as Avaro-Slavs. Together they invaded the Balkan peninsula, wreaking havoc everywhere. They rampaged from Constantinople to Thrace to Greece for four years, then returned across the Danube. Emperor Maurice paid the Avars tribute in return for being allowed to claim the land to the Danube as his own. In 601 Maurice's generals defeated the Avars, neutralizing the Avar threat, but a mutiny the following year gave the Avars the opening to recover their strength and counterattack. In the first decade of the 600s, the Avaro-Slavs defeated Byzantine forces in several cities along the Adriatic coast, leaving only ruins in their wake. The Sclavini returned to ravage Greece between 610 and 626. With Avar aid, they laid siege to Thessalonika for 33 days, ending the siege with a treaty in 626 that gave the surrounding territory of Illyria to the Avars while allowing Thessalonika to remain free. That proved to be the high point of Avar power. In 626 they were defeated while attacking Constantinople. From that time forward they had to face rebellious tribes, including the Sclavini, who sapped their power. Migrations of Bulgars and Magyars ultimately took over Avar holdings. The final war the Avars fought was against Charlemagne in 805; after that, they ceased to exist.

The main result of the Avar conquests was the establishment of a Slavic population in eastern Europe. The remains of Avar cemeteries show a high quality of metalwork in the form of bridle bits, saber-daggers, spear points, and three-barbed arrowheads. This artistry reflected the style of eastern Asian nomads rather than any influences adapted from the peoples they conquered. Dedicated mainly to conquest and plunder, the Avars left virtually no architectural legacy.

See also Byzantine Empire; Carolingian Dynasty; Franks; Huns; Justinian; Lombards.

References: Gimbutas, Marija, *The Slavs* (New York: Praeger, 1971); Hosch, Edgar, *The Balkans*, trans. Tania Alexander (New York: Crane, Russak & Co., 1972); Obolensky, Dimitri, *Byzantium and the Slavs* (London: Variorum Reprints, 1971).

35   AXUM, EXPANSION OF

The Axumites inhabited an area of eastern Africa lying in what is today Ethiopia. The peoples who settled here around 500 B.C.E. seem to have been a mixture of Semites from Yemen and settlers from the empire of Kush. The main centers of population were the city of Axum and the port of Adulis, both initially recorded in the first century C.E. For the first two centuries C.E., the Axumites controlled the Red Sea coastline and carried on extensive trade with Greek and Egyptian merchants, acting as the outlet for sub-Saharan products such as ebony, ivory, and exotic animals. By the third century, the Axumites were noted throughout the Middle East as a major empire, controlling not only the Horn of Africa but also the southern portion of the Arabian peninsula, from which they collected tribute.

The exploits of the Axumite kings were recorded on stone monuments. The first major conqueror seems to have been Aphilas, who established Axumite dominance in the Yemen area, though it is impossible to tell exactly when that took place. The leader who dominated the expansion of the empire was Ezana in the fourth century. Records show that the Axumites still controlled Yemen, and Ezana campaigned around the borders, defeating harassing tribes and ultimately conquering the faded glory of Kush. Upon securing this conquest, Ezana gave credit to the Christian God, marking the fact that Axum was converted during his reign. At its greatest extent, Axum spread from the Arabian peninsula across the Ethiopian plateau all the way to the Sahara. The last major exploit by an Axumite king took place in 525 when King Kaleb led a force of 30,000 to Nadjran on the Arabian peninsula to avenge a massacre of Christians. He succeeded in this campaign and left behind a garrison of 10,000.

Control of extensive fertile land gave Axum a solid agricultural base for its economy, to which could be added a great amount of international trade. From the third century forward, Axum was well known for its architecture and monolithic monuments. It was also the first African nation to mint coins in gold, silver, and copper. The trade network to which Axum contributed brought travelers from all over the world. Apparently the Axumites were tolerant Christians, as evidence points to Jewish, Kushite, and even Buddhist enclaves. The empire remained important and profitable past the fall of Rome, and kept up good trade relations with the Byzantines, even though the Axumites embraced the monophysite views of the Egyptian church, which the Orthodox church considered heretical.

With the growth of Islam, the power of Axum began to slip, though the Axumites' tolerant religious attitude is shown by the fact that early on, they sheltered persecuted Muslims from Mecca. This action stood them in good stead when Muslim conquerors spread through eastern Africa. Axum remained a Christian island in a sea of Islam and maintained cordial relations with their neighbors, but gradually the political center of the country retreated inland and trade declined. Though not conquered by Islam, Axum would not regain its former influence.

See also Kush, Expansion of.

References: Buxton, David, *The Abyssinians* (New York: Praeger, 1970); Jones, A. H. M., and Elizabeth Monroe, *A History of Ethiopia* (Oxford: Clarendon, 1955); Mokhtar, G., *Ancient Civilizations of Africa* (Paris: UNESCO, 1990).

36   BRITAIN, NORMAN INVASION OF

Norman writers say that King Edward of England had promised the English throne to William, duke of Normandy. While Harold Godwinsson, the earl of Wessex and Edward's brother-in-law, was on embassy to Normandy, he supposedly agreed to Edward's bequest and promised his support. But when Edward died on 5 January 1066, Harold was named king by England's leaders. William decided on war. Only Norman versions of the incidents survive, so it is impossible to determine whether Edward actually promised William the throne. Harold's broken promise, however, was William's argument in gaining papal support for his cause, which allowed him to raise an army fairly quickly. The pope gave his support to William without having any sort of

Scene from the decisive Battle of Hastings
as represented in the Bayeux Tapestry.

input from Harold concerning the truth of William's claims, which was strange considering Harold's consistent loyalty to Rome. The blessing of the Church, coupled with the prospect of some serious pillage and looting in England, was sufficient reason for the aristocracy of northern France to join the expedition.

In May 1066, Tostig, Harold's exiled brother, raided England with the assistance of some Viking allies. In September he invaded the Northumbrian coast with a force provided by Harold III Hardraade, king of Norway. This obliged Harold of England to move many of his troops, which had been awaiting William's attack, away from the south coast. Harold was successful in defeating the Norsemen at the battle of Stamford Bridge, but immediately afterward received word that William's force had landed. He ordered his exhausted troops to march south immediately.

William had concent rated his forces at the mouth of the Dives River in Normandy in August. He probably planned to sail north and land first at the Isle of Wight, where he could establish an offshore base. He was forced to wait for favorable weather and could not sail until September, when a westerly wind allowed him to begin his expedition. The strong wind blew his ships up the English Channel, away from the Isle of Wight, and he had to regroup at Saint-Valery, still on the French coast. He had lost some ships and morale was slipping. Finally, at the end of September, a southerly wind took him to England, where he landed at Pevensey and Hastings.

William organized 4,000–7,000 cavalry and infantry. After ransacking every town in the area, he found himself in a narrow strip of land bounded by the coast on one side and the forest of Andred on the other. On 25 September, word came to William of Harold's victory over his brother near York, along with the news that Harold's army was on the march and would arrive sooner than William had expected.

On 13 October Harold emerged from the thick forest, surprising William. It was too late in the day to continue on to Hastings, so Harold took up a defensive position along a ridge and awaited William's assault the next morning. The Normans repeatedly failed to make headway up the hill against the steadfast line the British maintained. The heavy Norman cavalry could not build up enough speed to break the English line atop the hill, nor could their archers hurt many English behind their interlocked shields. Only when the English broke ranks to pursue a repulsed Norman charge did they lose the protection of their position. In the open field, they fell prey to the Normans. The ensuing melee, and the death of Harold, spelled the end of the English army.

After the battle, William marched his force to London, defeating any resistance he met along the way. He entered the city in December and had himself crowned, like Charlemagne, on Christmas Day. William settled in to sovereignty fairly quickly. There was little resistance at first, and William set about establishing Norman control by constructing forts as centers of power across the country. In early 1068, William moved against risings in the southwest by capturing Exeter and moving into Cornwall. More castles were built in order to maintain control. Trouble in the north took William to Northumbria and York, but he gained the fealty of the northern earls and King Malcolm of Scotland. It was short-lived, for he had to return in the winter of 1069–1070 in a brutal campaign. William destroyed the agricultural production of the northern counties, burning crops and animals to deny the locals any chance of sustaining themselves. An autumn 1069 victory over Scandinavian forces under Swein Estrithson at the Humber River, in addition to a second campaign against Scotland's King Malcolm in 1072, completed William's conquest.

Some Norman influence was present in England prior to 1066, but only after William's conquest did the whole of the British Isles begin to change. The Norman king introduced feudalism into England, and the construction of castles throughout the country, along with the appointment of Normans to own them, created a new ruling class. At first, the conquest was over the aristocracy only, as the predominantly Scandinavian rulers were replaced by continental ones, even though the Normans themselves were not that far from their Scandinavian roots. All of Britain soon felt the Norman presence when William ordered the compilation of the Domesday Book, a census of all the country's people, lands, and possessions for taxation purposes. Much of historians' knowledge of medieval England comes from the minute details recorded in that book. The construction of castles and then churches changed the nature of architecture in Britain, and the new church construction signaled a change in the church hierarchy as well. Not only did the aristocracy change, but local abbots and bishops were replaced by Norman church officials; by the time of William's death in 1090, no high-ranking church official had been born in Britain. The church, being the center of learning on the continent, had a profound effect on the intellectual life of Britain. The country ceased to be part of Scandinavia and began to be part of Europe.

See also France, Viking Invasion of.

References: Freeman, Edward, The *History of the Norman Conquest of England* (Chicago: University of Chicago Press, 1974); Furneaux, Rupert, *The Invasion of 1066* (Englewood Cliffs, NJ: Prentice-Hall, 1974); Howarth, David, *1066: The Year of Conquest* (New York: Viking Penguin, 1977).

37 BULGARS

The Bulgars were another of the nomadic tribes of central Asia who wandered into Europe in the wake of the Roman Empire's fall. Arriving late in the fifth century, at first they were kept at bay by the power of the Byzantine Empire and that of the Avars.

The Bulgar leader Kovrat established a kingdom in 635 recognized by the Byzantines as "Great Bulgaria," but it did not last beyond Kovrat's reign. The Bulgars separated into two groups, one moving northward toward the Volga, and the other establishing itself under Kovrat's son Asparuch (Isperich) on the lower Danube in 680. In 681 Byzantine emperor Constantine IV recognized Asparuch as ruler of the region stretching from the Balkan Mountains to the Dniester.

When Avar power collapsed after defeat by the Frankish leader Charlemagne, the Bulgars moved into the power vacuum left in the eastern Balkans. The Slavs, who had been under Avar domination, fell under the power of the Bulgars; after a few generations, the nomadic Turkic Bulgars were absorbed and transformed by the peasant Slavs. The mixture of the two races created Bulgarians.

Bulgar power grew with the gradual weakening of the Byzantine defensive system in the Balkans. Though Constantinople controlled the area around Greece in the late eighth and early ninth centuries, it could make little headway against the Bulgarians. In 802, the Bulgars came under the leadership of Khan Krum, who challenged both the Byzantines and the Franks. He conquered eastern Pannonia (modern Austria), then turned southward, capturing Sofia in 809, destroying a Byzantine army in 811, marching to the walls of Constantinople in 813, and capturing Adrianople in 814. Krum was succeeded in 814 by Omortag, who followed a more peaceful strategy with Constantinople and exposed his people to Hellenistic influences. The next khan, Boris, allowed Christian missionaries into his realm.

Bulgarian Tsar Simeon (r. 893–927) attacked Constantinople and won a major victory in 896, exacting an annual tribute from the city. When that tribute was discontinued in 912 after the death of Emperor Leo VI, Simeon went to war again. He attacked Constantinople twice, in 913 and 924, but was unable to breach the walls. Though he called himself "Emperor of the Romans and the Bulgars," only his own people recognized the first part of that title. At his death in 927, Simeon's empire stretched from the Adriatic to the Black Sea. His son Peter signed a peace treaty that year and married the granddaughter of a Byzantine emperor; this was the closest to a juncture the two empires ever achieved.

Tsar Simeon's reign marked the height of Bulgarian power. After his time, Byzantine diplomacy brought too many allies into the picture for the Bulgarians to resist. From the 890s the Magyars, a tribe of Scandinavian descent with Turkic blood, had harassed the frontiers of both Constantinople and Bulgaria. In the middle 900s they expanded into the upper Danube plain at Bulgaria's expense. More deadly was the threat from the rising power of Russia, which Constantinople also cultivated. The emperor encouraged the Russian prince of Kiev, Sviatislav, to attack Bulgarian Tsar Peter; in 969 the Russians occupied virtually all Bulgarian lands. When they were forced back to Russia by Emperor John I Tzimisces, the territory once again belonged to Constantinople and the power of the Bulgars was broken.

Bulgaria was influential in eastern Europe in a number of ways. When Christian missionaries were allowed into the territory, the representatives of the church included "the apostles of the Slavs," Cyril and Methodius. These two developed the alphabet that dominates eastern Europe—Cyrillic—and in so doing created Bulgarian literature. The long-term contact with Constantinople was not always hostile, and the culture of the Eastern Roman Empire strongly influenced Bulgar society. The introduction of Orthodox Christianity brought a Bulgarian patriarchate that lasted until the removal of the Russians. The contact with Eastern religions also brought about new interpretations of Christianity, with the incorporation of ancient Manichaean ideas that influenced the Cathar and Albigensian heresies of medieval Europe. Bulgaria was well placed to act as a transition between European and Asiatic views, creating a cultural heritage unique to the Balkans.

See also Avars; Byzantine Empire; Carolingian Dynasty; Magyars.

References: Bury, J. B., *The Invasion of Europe by the Barbarians* (New York: Russell & Russell, 1963); Hosch, Edgar, *The Balkans* (New York: Crane, Russak & Co., 1972); Thompson, E. A., *Romans and Barbarians* (Madison: University of Wisconsin Press, 1982).

BYZANTINE EMPIRE

In the early 300s C.E., Emperor Diocletian came to the conclusion that the Roman Empire was too unwieldy for one man to rule. He therefore appointed himself and Maximian as coemperors, or augusti, and named a subordinate to each, creating two caesars, which effectively divided the empire into quarters. After creating this format, Diocletian resigned. His planned smooth transition of power became chaos, as up to six people scrambled for power. Rising to the top was Constantine, who finally subdued his rivals and established a new capital for the Roman Empire at Byzantium (renamed Constantinople) at the crossroads of east-west trade routes and Black Sea and Mediterranean Sea routes. Though it was not Constantine's intention, this shift of power to the east laid the groundwork for the Byzantine Empire. In 378, the Visigoths defeated Roman troops under Valens at Adrianople and changed the nature of the empire and its military. Valens's successor, Theodosius, made peace with the Goths and ceded them land, hoping they would act as a buffer against other marauding peoples. Upon his death in 395, the empire was divided between his sons and became permanently split into two sections.

The western half soon succumbed to barbarian invasions, but the eastern half prospered. The Byzantines adapted themselves to the new fighting style of the Goths and recruited many of them into their army. They also abandoned the legion style of formation that had long served the Romans so well in favor of smaller, more mobile units. They developed a long-service professional army that rarely numbered above 100,000, but which defended the empire and at times expanded it. The basis of this new army was the cataphract, cavalry that could wield either lances or bows and act as either light or heavy cavalry. Heavy infantry was armed with lances and formed into phalanxes, while the light infantry used bows and javelins. By mixing these various formations in groups of 400, a Byzantine army of 25,000–30,000 had all the necessary units for attack and defense.

With these professional soldiers, Byzantine generals under the direction of Justinian expanded the borders almost to the original boundaries of the Roman Empire, reacquiring northern Africa, Italy, and southern Spain from barbarian conquerors, though they were unable to maintain that far-flung empire when the power of Islam grew. Justinian introduced an updated law code that became the model for the legal system of western Europe, but it proved too oppressive for religious groups who disagreed with Justinian's Orthodox faith. His laws were so resented that many people in the empire saw the religious toleration preached by Muhammad as a better alternative. Muhammad's warmaking, and that of his successors, was effective enough to drive back the borders of the Byzantine Empire in the seventh century and detach the distant provinces of Africa and Spain from Byzantine control.

The homeland of Asia Minor and southeastern Europe was protected by the professional army, occasionally updated and reformed along lines laid out in works like Emperor Maurice's Strategicon and Emperor Leo's Tactica. By holding the Muslim advance at bay until it settled down to consolidation, the Byzantines grew confident in their ability to defend themselves. Over time, that grew into overconfidence. When attacked by the Seljuk Turks in 1063, the Byzantines lost the battle of Manzikert, and with it much of Asia Minor. From this point forward they defended the remains of their territory against increasingly powerful and aggressive enemies on all sides. Still, they managed to survive another 400 years, until the Ottoman Turks became the first and only people to capture

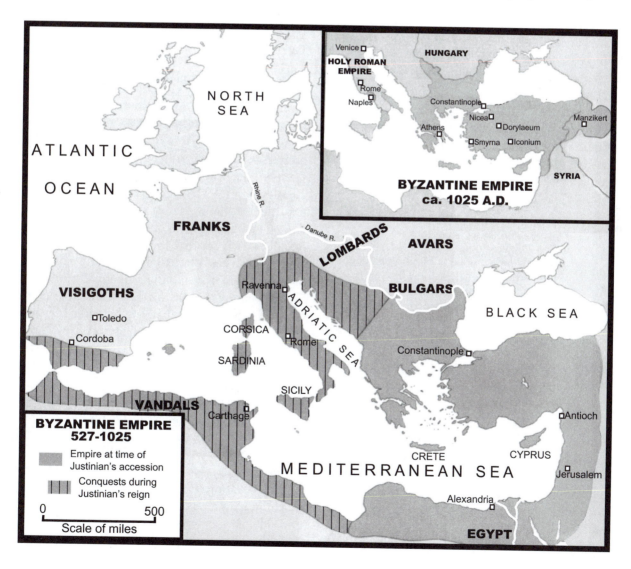

BYZANTINE EMPIRE
ca. 1025 A.D.

BYZANTINE EMPIRE
527-1025

Empire at time of Justinian's accession

Conquests during Justinian's reign

0   500
Scale of miles

Constantinople. The Turks soon controlled almost as much as the Byzantine Empire had at its height.

In 1,100 years of existence, the Byzantine Empire put the stamp of Christian and European culture on the Balkans and the Middle East, while absorbing much of the East's civilization and learning. The empire's longest-lasting influence was in the area of religion: The Eastern Orthodox church was born and survives to this day. Its missionaries spread Christianity from central Europe to Russia to Armenia, surviving onslaughts of Muslims and Mongols in the process. The empire likewise maintained contacts with western Europe, though usually from a position of need. Their call for assistance from Muslim attack in the twelfth and thirteenth centuries brought the Crusades to the Middle East, with a resulting shift in power and trade. The enmity between the Orthodox and Roman churches, however, kept the possible spread of Eastern learning from entering Europe until the Renaissance. The Byzantine Empire lasted long enough to cede control of the Mediterranean to Europe rather than to Islamic countries, and Western naval power ultimately translated itself into worldwide empires in the fifteenth and sixteenth centuries.

See also Constantine, Emperor; Crusades; Justinian; Middle East, Muslim Conquest of the; Turks; Visigoths; Ottoman Empire.

References: Browning, Robert, *The Byzantine Empire* (New York: Scribner, 1980); Byron, Robert, *The Byzantine Achievement* (New York: Russell & Russell, 1964); Franzius, Enno, *History of the Byzantine Empire* (New York: Funk & Wagnalls, 1968).

39   CAROLINGIAN DYNASTY

The Carolingian Empire had its roots in the migrations of the Franks into the frontiers of the Roman Empire in the third century C.E. The Salian Franks, living along the lower stretches of the Rhine, were conquered by the Romans in 358 and became their allies. When the Romans withdrew from the German frontier, the Salian Franks followed them and became the masters of territory above the Loire River in Gaul

(modern France). In the late fifth century, Clovis I established what came to be called the Merovingian dynasty, and he spread Frankish power to the Pyrenees in the south and the Main River in the east. He was responsible for the defeat of barbarian tribes all around his frontiers: the Allemanni, Burgundians, Visigoths, and the Ripaurian Franks of the upper Rhine. Upon his death, however, the empire divided along traditional lines (his four sons each inherited a part), which effectively broke apart a budding empire.

The successive Merovingian kings came to depend more and more on their mayordomo, or mayor of the palace, who acted as a liaison between the king and his nobles and subjects. The position became one of increasing power, and was successively in the hands of the Carolingian family. The Carolingians descended from Pepin the Elder of Landin, mayordomo from Austrasia (now northeastern France), the Low Countries, and western Germany. By the time Pepin of Herstal came to the post in the late seventh century, he virtually ruled the Frankish kingdom in the Merovingians' name. He overthrew the Neustrians and Burgundians, rivals to united Merovingian rule.

The illegitimate son of Pepin of Herstal, Charles Martel ("the Hammer"), became the first high-profile leader of the Carolingian line. Charles invaded and conquered Bavaria, solidified Frankish control in Frisia and Thuringia, and turned his attentions to the south. He harassed Eudo of Aquitaine, taking advantage of his weakness after fighting the Muslims of Spain. Charles defeated Eudo and fought the Muslims at Tours in 732. This Frankish victory proved the high-water mark of Muslim expansion in the West, forcing them to stay in Spain until the fifteenth century. He fought the Muslims again in the latter 730s, and ceded his mayordomo position to his sons Carloman and Pepin the Short.

Carloman resigned his position in 747, and Pepin moved to seize real position as well as power. He overthrew the last of the Merovingians and named himself king of the Franks in 751, thus officially establishing the Carolingian royal line. His action was sanctioned by the Roman Catholic Church when Pepin was crowned by

FRANKISH EXPANSION UNDER CHARLEMAGNE

Frankish Kingdom in 768

Territories acquired by Charlemagne

Tributary states

Byzantine territory

0   300

Scale of miles

Pope Stephen II in 754. This anointing by the pope made Pepin the defender of the Church, and he fulfilled that role in 754 and 756 when he led forces into Italy to fight the Lombards. He also put down a revolt in Bavaria and defeated the Saxons, forcing them to pay tribute, then turned to Aquitaine to quell a revolt there.

Pepin died in 768; following tradition, his sons Carloman and Charles inherited joint control of the throne. Carloman died in 771 and Charles became sole ruler. Through campaigning with his father, Charles had received combat

experience, which he quickly put to use for the defense and expansion of Frankish lands. That experience, coupled with his natural ability, brought him the title Charles the Great, better known as Charlemagne (Carolus Magnus in Latin; Karl der Grosse in German). Charlemagne inherited the position of defender of the Church from his father as well, and he soon had trouble with the Church's main threat, the Lombards of northern Italy. Charlemagne married a Lombard princess in 770, but his repudiation of her, coupled with appeals for aid from Carloman's heirs, brought him into conflict with the Lombards. Pope Adrian I appealed for aid in 772, and Charlemagne marched against the Lombard leader Desiderius, his erstwhile father-in-law. The Franks were victorious in 774, and Charlemagne named himself king of the Franks and the Lombards.

Extending the tradition of fighting the Muslims, Charlemagne invaded Spain in 777. He had mixed success, but finally drove the Muslims south of the River Ebro. He campaigned in southern Italy and Bavaria, putting down revolts, then turned eastward toward the Danube River Valley. In the 790s he defeated and destroyed the Avars and conquered parts of Croatia and Slovenia. On Christmas Day 800, Pope Leo III crowned Charlemagne as emperor of the Romans. That action, and the recognition of his position by the Byzantine Emperor Nicephorus I in 810, created the Holy Roman Empire. Charlemagne spent most of the remainder of his reign establishing an administration for the empire and carrying on regular campaigns against the Saxons, who alternately accepted his suzerainty (and Christianity) and rebelled against him.

Charlemagne's court, built at Aix-la-Chapelle (Aachen), became the first cultural center of western Europe since the fall of the Roman Empire. By promoting widespread literacy and schooling, building monasteries and churches, and advocating and financing art, his reign introduced the Carolingian Renaissance. He created a hierarchy of officials to rule the empire, which expanded from the Pyrenees to the North Sea, France to the Danube Valley, and south into northern Italy. Charlemagne also brought back the concept of a standing army and reintroduced the practices of the Roman Empire in his attention to logistics and transport. He built forts to protect his borders and reintroduced the art of siege warfare. All in all, he proved the best ruler of medieval times from military, cultural, and social points of view.

Tradition served him fairly well at his death, for there was only one son to inherit and thus no division of rule. Louis spent his time maintaining his father's interest in the arts and

scholarship and trying with minimal success to defend his northern borders from increasing pressure by the Vikings. The Carolingian line divided again on Louis' death when his three sons divided the empire into thirds. The three spent an inordinate amount of time fighting among themselves rather than cooperating in the face of Viking attacks. The Holy Roman Empire split into German and French halves; the Saxons took over the western part in 911 and the Capetians took the French territories in 987. Those two territories became the bases of the modern states of France and Germany. The Holy Roman Empire, designed to defend the church of Rome, became more a central European political entity of waxing and waning power over the next several centuries; based more in Austria than in Germany, it came under the control of the Habsburg dynasty.

See also Avars; France, Viking Invasion of; Lombards; Spain, Muslim Conquest of; Visigoths.

References: Barraclough, Geoffrey, *The Crucible of Europe* (Berkeley: University of California Press, 1976); Bullough, Donald, *The Age of Charlemagne* (New York: Putnam, 1965); Holland, Jack, *The Order of Rome* (London: Cassell, 1980).

CHINA, KHITAN INVASION OF

40

During the declining years of the T'ang dynasty, China had little luck resisting nomadic raids from the steppes. The Khitan Mongols had learned the art of farming and iron smelting from refugees of the Han dynasty, thus developing a culture based on agriculture as well as herding. They aided a T'ang warlord in the middle of the tenth century, and for their support were awarded 16 provinces from Peking to the Great Wall, as well as a large annual monetary tribute. The Khitan made Peking their capital, and in the age of first contact with medieval Europe gave the area of northern China the name by which it was then known: Cathay.

They invaded southward when the annual tribute stopped coming, captured the T'ang capital at Kaifeng, and proclaimed themselves the Liao dynasty. Their success was short-lived; the T'ang counterattacked and drove the Khitan northward. In 960 a successful T'ang general started the Sung dynasty, and it was with this new government that the Khitan fought. Fortunately for the Sung, the Khitan were also fighting with the rising power of the Hsia kingdom farther to the west. Still, the Khitan enjoyed occasional success against the Sung. At the beginning of the eleventh century, in response to two unsuccessful Sung campaigns against them, they invaded to the gates of Kaifeng and left only with the promise of tribute totaling 100,000 taels (roughly, more than 8,000 pounds) of silver and 200,000 bolts of silk. In the 1030s the tribute was increased in response to demands and pressure by the Khitan leaders.

Thus, the Sung maintained peace by bribery, not only to the Khitan but also to the Hsia, paying tribute despite the fact that they maintained a massive army of over a million men. History records the development of the first gunpowder weapons, in the form of rockets, during the Sung dynasty. The Sung did not use them effectively enough to establish a military ascendancy, which often accompanies the development of new weaponry. The large amounts of tribute, however, had an unintended effect. The Khitan, already different from other Mongol tribes by their use of agriculture, became increasingly Chinese in their culture and language. This not only robbed them of their fighting edge, but it also provoked the disdain of other Mongol tribes, notably the Juchen Mongols. The Juchen allied themselves with the Sung, and together they defeated the Khitan, destroying the Liao government. Rather than accept payment of the 16 provinces the Khitan had first won, the Juchen continued their invasion of China and forced the Sung dynasty to reestablish itself in the south. The new northern power gave up the name Juchen for the Ch'in (or Kin) dynasty, and set the borders with the Sung at the Hwai and upper Han rivers.

The Khitan invasion had little effect socially on the Chinese, but the huge payment of tribute and the large standing army detailed to protect the population drained the Sung treasury and provoked peasant unrest. The Ch'in became more Sinified than the Sung became Mongolized, but aggressiveness weakened the Sung while giving rise to the growing power of

the Ch'in, which in turn foreshadowed the rise of Mongol power under Genghis Khan.

See also Han Dynasty; Genghis Khan; T'ang Dynasty.

References: Hookham, Hilda, *A Short History of China* (New York: St. Martin's Press, 1970); Kwanten, Luc, *Imperial Nomads* (Philadelphia: University of Pennsylvania Press, 1979); Morgan, David, *The Mongols* (Oxford: Blackwell, 1986).

CHINA, MONGOL CONQUEST OF

41

Genghis Khan was named leader of all the Mongol peoples in 1206, and he set about uniting the tribes and conquering large parts of Asia. One of his main interests was to conquer China, on the southern side of the Great Wall, which had long kept steppe peoples out of "civilized" lands. He first led forces across the wall on raids, stealing livestock and other goods and stockpiling them on the other side. As his army gained experience, he moved farther into China and brought land under his control. He made war against the Hsi-hsia between 1206 and 1209, finally forcing them to acknowledge his position. His war against the Ch'in dynasty was hampered at first by his lack of siegecraft, for his cavalry forces were useless against the Ch'in fortresses and walled cities. Ch'in military men who joined his cause brought with them the knowledge necessary to reduce those fortifications. In 1215 he captured and sacked Peking, forcing recognition of his dominance from the Ch'in emperor.

Mongol forces occupied northern China while Genghis and his army made war farther to the west. In his absence, the Ch'in and Hsia grew restless and allied themselves against the Mongols in 1224—Genghis named his son Ogadai as his successor should death claim the former before the reconquest occurred. Genghis entered the domain of the Hsia in the winter of 1225 with 180,000 men. Across the frozen water of the Yellow River, the Mongols fought a force of some 300,000 Hsia; at the end of the battle, all the khan's enemies were dead. He then divided his army; a third of it to lay siege to the Hsia capital at Ninghsia, a third under Ogadai to drive westward against the

Ch'in, while the remainder Genghis took southeastward to threaten the Ch'in southern border and block any possible reinforcements. In 1227, the Hsia emperor surrendered, but Genghis refused any peace overtures from the Ch'in. With a premonition of death, Genghis returned to Mongolia. He died along the way, after advising his youngest son Tului on the future conquest of China.

Ogadai continued Genghis's expansionary plans, conquering Korea and then returning to deal with the Ch'in. While he and his father's most trusted general, Subotai, pressured the fortified cities of the north, his youngest brother, Tului, took a force of 30,000 southward to the Sung Empire, then swung northward to put the Ch'in armies in a pincer between himself and his brother. He decimated the Ch'in forces by wearing them down in cold mountain fighting, then chased them northward when they retreated to meet the now-attacking Ogadai. Tului died of sickness during the campaign, and Ogadai returned to Mongolia, leaving Subotai to finish off the siege of Kaifeng, the Ch'in capital. The city fell to him in 1233 after a year's siege. The Sung in the south asked for a portion of the Ch'in Empire in return for the safe passage they had granted Tului, but Subotai refused. When the Sung seized Honan, the Mongols prepared to make war on them.

War against the Sung lasted 35 years. Ogadai's nephews Mangu and Kubilai directed the campaigns. Kubilai conquered the province of Yunnan in 1253, and Mangu led the army in a series of campaigns between 1257 and 1259 that defeated Sung armies and captured fortified cities. Mangu succeeded Ogadai as the Great Khan, but his death in 1260 provoked a struggle for the position between Kubilai and his younger brother, Arik-Buka. Kubilai won after a four-year civil war and became the Great Khan, then finished off the Sungs in a campaign designed to be as bloodless as possible. It failed to be totally without killing, but Kubilai spread the news of his benevolent intentions, and many Sung generals turned against their own leaders to join him. When the seven-year-old emperor and his grandmother the dowager empress bowed to him, he declared himself emperor of China,

creating the Yuan dynasty. Sung resistance in the deep south continued until he finally besieged and captured Canton. During his reign, Kubilai Khan unified China as no other emperor, yet he kept his Mongol subjects separate from the mass of Chinese he now ruled. The Mongols ruled China through the existing bureaucracy, and did little to change the country; Kubilai realized that the conquered culture was much more advanced than his own, and that he had much to learn.

The dynasty did not last after his death in 1294. The Mongol conquest, while deadly in its establishment, had little lasting effect other than peaceful times in which to progress. During the Yuan dynasty, drama came to the fore as an art form, but the longest-lasting symbol of the Yuan leadership was the construction of Kubilai's capital at Shangtu, better known in the West as Xanadu. This garden city was Kubilai's home, though he often returned to the steppes to maintain his heritage and pursue the ancient Mongol pastime of hunting.

Kubilai carried on more attempted conquests against Japan and Southeast Asia. Sogatu, one of Kubilai's generals, advanced into the province of Annam in 1257, but he could not overcome the guerrilla war the native Annamese and Chams waged against him. Kubilai tried again to subdue the region in 1287, but it proved costly. After many deaths on both sides, in 1293 the Annamese recognized Kubilai's suzerainty; in return, Kubilai left them alone.

See also Ch'in Dynasty; Genghis Khan; Japan, Mongol Invasions of; Kubilai Khan.

References: Cohen, Daniel, *Conquerors on Horseback* (Garden City, NY: Doubleday, 1970); Kwanten, Luc, *Imperial Nomads* (Philadelphia: University of Pennsylvania Press, 1979); Lamb, Harold, *March of the Barbarians* (New York: Literary Guild, 1940).

42   **CRUSADES**

During the seventh and eighth centuries, the Islamic religion swept out of the Middle East, across northern Africa, and into Spain, where it began to encroach on central Europe. During the tenth century, European Christianity went on the offensive, and by the eleventh century the tide began to turn against Islam. Christian Europe meant not only to overthrow Muslim rule, but to expel it from Europe and recover Jerusalem for Christianity.

Italian city-states exercised naval and commercial dominance, and the German empire was on the rise. Christianity was spreading into northern Europe, and the number of pilgrimages to the Holy Land and other sacred sites was increasing. The desire to spread the gospel was mixed with a desire to open new markets and conquer new territories. Despite the opportunity for war with the Muslims, the feudal barons of central Europe engaged in private wars with one another. The need for peace compelled the pope to declare the Peace of Christ, and later the Truce of Christ, in a vain attempt to limit such conflict.

By 1095, the power and influence of the papacy, as well as the sanctity of the majority of the clergy, were declining, while the power and influence of the German empire were expanding. Pope Urban II, fearing the church would lose what little influence it had, and abhorring the results of continued infighting among the Christian nobility, sought a way to unite Christendom in a common cause. In Clermont, France, he advocated the First Crusade. His plea was a mixture of propaganda concerning the alleged cruelty of Muslims to Christian pilgrims, a request for aid by the Byzantine emperor, a call for a display of righteous action in the recovery of Jerusalem, and an offer of remission of sins for those who participated. The effect was overwhelming. Not only did the nobility—his prime audience—heed his call, but so did many peasants and disreputable people of the cities. Others also took to preaching the crusade, most notably Peter the Hermit, whose call went mostly to peasants and street rabble.

The nobility were led by Godfrey of Bouillon (Rhinelanders), Raymond of Toulouse (Provencals), and Bohemund (Normans of southern Italy). Along with the peasants and rabble, they made up six hosts of 100,000 to 200,000 crudata, or cross-signed, who traveled overland to meet in Constantinople before continuing on to Jerusalem.

The so-called Peasants' Crusade led by Peter the Hermit preceded the main contingents of nobility and men-at-arms, and turned into a binge of pillage, thievery, and eventual widespread murder of innocent Jews. Many of Peter's "army" died at the hands of the Turks, only a few ever reaching Constantinople.

The main forces under command of the nobility reached Constantinople in 1096. The leaders were required to swear allegiance to Alexis, emperor of the Byzantine Empire, in return for immediate gifts and a promise of future help, which never materialized. Alexis's main objective was to get the Crusaders to help him regain territories lost to the Turks, who were seeking to take over his empire. Before they were allowed to leave for Jerusalem, however, the Crusaders were coerced into helping Emperor Alexis capture the city of Nicea in 1097.

The Muslim world was totally unprepared for the Christian invasion; the strength and power of the mounted knights, as well as the bravery of the common foot soldiers, were more than a match for their own cavalry. The march to Palestine was marked by a decisive victory at Doryleum and the conquest of Tarsus by Baldwin and Tancred. The Crusaders and their camp followers were not prepared, however, for the long and arduous march over the Black Mountains toward Antioch. This journey meant the death of many through hunger, thirst, and heat.

Antioch fell to the Crusaders in 1098 after eight months, despite poor provisions and ill health among the besiegers. The Crusaders' confidence in the leadership of their God and the righteousness of their cause helped them to overcome numerous efforts by the inhabitants to break the siege and defeat reinforcements attempting to relieve the city. Antioch finally fell, after betrayal by one of its citizens. The Crusaders spent the next several months in Antioch recuperating, making local conquests, and repelling Turkish attempts to regain the city. Bohemund finally secured Antioch for himself as the others continued on to Jerusalem.

Tales of the seeming invincibility of the

Louis IX of France leading crusaders
attacking Damietta, Egypt.

Christian army preceded it, and the march toward Bethlehem and Jerusalem was without incident. God, it seemed, was surely guiding and protecting them, and no one dared stand in their way.

They reached Jerusalem in 1099 and immediately placed it under siege. It fell to Godfrey and Raymond on 15 July. For several days, any Muslims who could be found were put to death.

After the capture of Jerusalem and the securing of the surrounding territory, most of the Crusaders returned home, feeling that they had done what was required of them by their God and their pope. Only the adventurers stayed on to establish the four states of what would be called the Latin Kingdom. These four states, the kingdom of Jerusalem and the vassal states of Edessa, Antioch, and eventually Tripoli, were islands of Christianity in a hostile sea of Islam. The Muslim world was now much more aware of the Crusaders' presence and purpose, their strengths and weaknesses. The Muslims wasted little time in trying to regain what had been taken from them. Communications among the four Crusader cities was difficult, if not impossible, and the Christians' only hope of survival lay in reinforcements from Europe. In the meantime, however, their strength, bravery, audacity, and faith would have to keep them alive and in possession of the holy sites and the fortified cities.

With the eventual death of the last of the great leaders of the First Crusade, the bravery and piety that had marked it also died. The crusading spirit the soldiers had initiated would wax and wane, but continue unbroken for the next two and a half centuries.

What are commonly referred to as the "Crusades" were actually one long, protracted conflict between Christian Europe and the Islamic Middle East over the land and holy sites of modern-day Palestine. It was the several aggressive endeavors by European nobility, at the behest of successive popes, to reinforce the Latin Kingdom or regain territory lost to Islam that give the illusion of multiple invasions. Battles would continue to be fought, cities would be won and lost, but the great Christian victories of the initial invasion would not be repeated.

The Second Crusade was preached by the pope and St. Bernard of Clairvaux after the fall of Edessa in 1144 to Zangi, governor of Mosul. This crusade was led by Louis VII and Conrad III of Germany (1147–1149). The two armies were unable to cooperate, and were separately defeated in Asia Minor. An attempt to capture Damascus failed, and the Crusaders returned home.

Muslim power was consolidated under Zangi, his son Nur-ed-Din, and later Saladin, who sought a holy war with Christianity. In 1187, Saladin's army overran the Latin Kingdom and captured Jerusalem. This caused the pope to preach a Third Crusade (1189–1192). It was led by Philip Augustus of France, Richard I of England, and Emperor Frederick Barbarossa. Barbarossa drowned in Asia Minor, and Philip and Richard were unable to work together because of jealousy. Philip returned home, leaving Richard in the Holy Land; Richard captured Acre, but was unable to recapture Jerusalem. The best he could manage was a treaty with Saladin to allow safe passage for pilgrims visiting Jerusalem.

In 1198, Pope Innocent III's influence finally brought peace to the feuding nobility of Europe, and he tried to reestablish the Crusade as a holy cause. This Crusade was led mainly by the Venetians, whose only goal was to expand their trading empire by destroying the influence of Constantinople. This they did with the sacking of Constantinople in 1204 by the Crusaders whom the Venetians had starved into compliance after they could not afford their passage to the Holy Land.

In 1215, Innocent III proclaimed the Fifth Crusade (1218–1221). Emperor Frederick of Germany obtained the title of king of Jerusalem by marriage in 1225, but was excommunicated in 1227 for delaying the start of the crusade. In 1228,

Frederick finally went to the Holy Land, gaining Jerusalem, Bethlehem, Nazareth, and a connecting strip of land to Acre—by treaty, not by conquest.

In 1244, Jerusalem fell to the Saracens, and a new Crusade was proclaimed by Innocent IV in 1245 and led by Louis IX of France. Though he invaded Egypt and captured Damietta, Louis was taken prisoner and Damietta was lost. Egypt revolted, and a new Muslim movement called for the recovery of Syria. Within the next few years, all remaining Christian possessions in Syria were captured and the Crusades effectively came to an end.

The major military goals of the Crusades—the driving of the Muslims from the Holy Land and the imposition of Western culture on the captured territory—were never accomplished. On the contrary, the Crusades strengthened and united the Islamic world, and weakened the Byzantine Empire until it was overcome by the Turks in the fifteenth century. The Crusades succeeded, however, in accomplishing Pope Urban II's original goals of returning the papacy to its previous position of power and influence and eventually ending feudal warfare.

The Crusades also had a profound effect on commerce and trade, both inside and outside Europe. Feudalism and serfdom disintegrated. A money economy began to predominate, which stimulated a need for banks. Spheres of influence were set up in port cities of Palestine by the trading powers of Venice, Genoa, and Pisa, providing easier acquisition of goods from both the Middle and Far East. Navigation and shipbuilding improved with the increased need for transportation of people and goods. Many of the developments attributed to the Crusades were merely the end result of changes that had begun before Pope Urban's call to retake the Holy Land. The Crusades served only to facilitate and accelerate them.

In the Middle East, the influence of Europe remained for some time. Italian merchants established trading privileges in the major ports of Acre and Tyre. By controlling the sea lanes of the Mediterranean, they provided Muslim merchants with access to European goods while remaining the sole distributors of Oriental goods to the West. Italian traders moved and worked freely in dedicated districts of these cities, and gained some legal control over citizens and visitors within those districts. Their basic problem was that, though they provided a conduit to the West, they could deal only with Muslim traders who handled Oriental goods, mainly spices. Therefore, the middleman remained, and the local government always got its share of the revenues. Still, there was enough money to go around, and when the trade routes shifted from Alexandria in Egypt to Damascus, Aleppo, and Antioch, the Europeans were able to expand their rights within the area. Political and military conflicts occasionally interfered with trade, but not enough to cut it off completely.

See also Ottoman Empire.

References: Lamb, Harold, *The Crusades, 2 vols.* (Garden City, NY: Doubleday, 1931); Smith, Jonathan Riley, *The Crusades* (New Haven, CT Yale University Press, 1987).

ENGLAND, VIKING CONQUEST OF

43

The Vikings raided and conquered along the coasts of Europe and the British Isles from the late eighth century. They left Scandinavia for a number of reasons, overpopulation being a prime cause, but the drive for trade and/or plunder was almost equally important. The timing was perfect for them because no society other than Charlemagne's Holy Roman Empire could mount any sort of organized resistance, and after Charlemagne's death in 810, his successors had little luck in matching his military prowess. Europe was gaining in wealth, but not in the ability to defend it. Historian Gwen Dyer words this situation well: "Loot is loot in any language, and western Europe was full of it. Ireland, England, France were the vikings' Mexico, with learning, arts, wealth, and a civilization superior to those of their northern conquistadors, and a similar inability to defend themselves from a numerically inferior but mobile and energetic foe."

The Danes first raided England around 789 and 793, even as Swedes pressed eastward into the Baltic and the Norwegians attacked Ireland. The Danes alternated between attacking

England and France, striking both sides of the English Channel at will. In the middle 830s, they probed along the south coast as far as Cornwall, but found the raiding easier along the eastern shore, which they began to assault in 843. Not until 862, however, did large-scale landings take place, with forces numbering perhaps a thousand raiders under Yngvarr, Ubbi, and Halfdan, who attacked to avenge their father Ragnar's death at the hands of King Ella of Northumbria. They defeated an English force under Ella at York in 863, and from that date the Danes began their mastery of northeastern England.

Viking forces quickly expanded into Mercia (central England) and East Anglia, killing King (later Saint) Edmund and occupying his lands. In 870, Halfdan led men into Wessex and won many battles, but at a high enough cost that he made peace and returned to the north to fight the Picts and Scots. That year marked the accession to the Wessex throne of Alfred (later to be titled "the Great"), who would mount the most successful English resistance to the Vikings. Before he could do so, however, the Danes received not only reinforcements but immigrants, and began settling in.

In January 878 the Viking chieftain Guthrum attacked Wessex and drove Alfred southwestward. Outrunning his opponents, Alfred collected a force from Hampshire, Wiltshire, and Somerset. He defeated an army of Vikings in Devon, then marched to fight Guthrum. Guthrum surrendered at Chippenham after a two-week siege, acknowledging Wessex as Alfred's and adopting Christianity as his new religion. The conversion appears to have been successful, because the Christianization of Danes in England began to expand. It did not keep Alfred from attacking southward as far as the Thames in 880, establishing the river as the southern border of Danelaw, that area of England ruled by the Danes. Fourteen years of relative peace followed.

Alfred was greatly assisted by an alliance with Ethelred, who was based in the southeast. United through Ethelred's marriage to Alfred's oldest daughter, the two leaders made progress against Viking pressure. Alfred was recognized as king of England in 886 (of all save Danelaw), and Ethelred was a staunch supporter. In that same year, Alfred negotiated with Guthrum a system of tributes and hostages to maintain the peace between the two peoples. It was an elusive peace at best, for while the Danes may not have made war against Alfred, they had no compunction about assisting any countrymen who cared to try. Thus, when Hastein invaded the mouth of the Thames in 891, the successful English resistance took longer than would have been the case had the population of Danelaw not granted aid. Alfred's improved organization and training of the levies and his construction of forts along the coasts proved invaluable in protecting the country. Further, his construction of ships, though not of the quality of the Vikings, led to some success against them and acted as a deterrent in later Viking planning.

Alfred died in 899, having been the major factor in the Vikings' failure to conquer all of England. He was succeeded by Edward, who carried the English tide northward and regained the land to the Humber River for England by the time of his death in 924. Edward's cousin Ethelwold had con- spired with the Vikings in Danelaw to invade the southern territories, which proved their undoing. Edward and Ethelred were too skillful, and the Viking losses opened Danelaw to English counterattack. After Ethelred's death in 911, he was ably succeeded both politically and militarily by his wife (and Edward's sister) Ethelflaed. She and Edward pressed continually northward, consolidating their gains by constructing numerous fortresses, which Viking tactics had no way to defeat.

Edward attempted to defeat the Danes with as little bloodshed as possible, showing himself to be a merciful victor. He did this both to assure the Christian Danes of retribution and to recruit their aid to fight Norwegian Vikings from Ireland who were beginning to settle on the west coast between Wales and Scotland. After the Norse leader Rognvald captured York in 919, he and Edward made peace; Edward was accepted as king of all England and Scotland—at least for a while.

The deaths of Rognvald in 921 and Edward in 924 laid the groundwork for further conflict between Edward's son Athelstan and Rognvald's grandson Olaf. The Norse Vikings of Ireland joined with the Scots to fight Athelstan's English forces at Brunanburh (actual site unknown) in 937. It was a decisive English victory, but not a lasting one. Athelstan ruled well and in nominal peace with the Danes, but after his death in 939, fighting began again. Until 954, northern England was alternately under English, Danish, or Norwegian rule, but none could rule for more than a year or two because of outside pressure or internal struggles.

England remained English through the reigns of several kings, until the young and weak-willed king Ethelred the Unready (978–1016) had to stand against a second great outpouring of Danish Vikings. Ethelred paid for a peace treaty with the raiding Olaf Tryggvason after the battle of Maldon in 991. Olaf returned a few years later, allied with the king of the Danes, Svein Forkbeard. In 994 the two were paid for peace; Olaf soon converted to Christianity and left England for good, but Svein left only temporarily. His return in 1001 brought another huge ransom. The following year, Ethelred ordered the massacre of all Danes in England. Some killing took place, including that of Svein's sister. Svein invaded in 1003 to avenge her death and succeeded in pillaging as much as he liked; only famine, in 1005, forced his withdrawal. He was back looting the next year and took yet another massive bribe from Ethelred. He finally came to stay in 1012; he was received in the north by the descendants of the first Vikings, and from that base he pillaged the entire country save London, which he could not capture. It did not matter, for the country surrendered to him, and Ethelred went with his family to Normandy.

Svein's victory was short-lived, for he died five weeks later. His son Canute succeeded him and maintained Danish rule over England. This also proved relatively short, for other Viking descendants conquered England under William of Normandy in 1066. The Vikings in England were both conquerors and conquered, as so often happens. They adapted themselves to a countryside that provided much more fertile farmland than the one they had left. The area of Danelaw inherited influences of law, language, personal and place names, and social custom from the invaders. In the long run, however, more change came from the Norman conquest than from the Danes.

See also Britain, Norman Invasion of; Carolingian Dynasty; Ireland, Viking Invasions of; Russia, Establishment and Expansion of.

References: Dyer, Gwen, A History of the Vikings (Oxford: Oxford University Press, 1968; Layn, H. R., The Vikings in Britain (Oxford: Blackwell, 1995); Marsden, John, The Fury of the Northmen (London: Kyle Cathie, 1993).

44 EUROPE, MONGOL INVASION OF

As the middle of the thirteenth century approached, the Mongols had established themselves along the Volga River, assuming the title "the Golden Horde." As they consolidated their hold on Russia, reconnaissance forces penetrated eastern Europe, returning with the news that, like the Russian principalities, the Europeans were divided and quarreling. They reported that the mightiest king, Frederick of the Holy Roman Empire, was feuding with Pope Gregory, so a Mongol advance should meet no consolidated resistance. The leader of the Golden Horde was Batu, son of Genghis Khan's illegitimate son Juchi. He preferred to settle into the steppes of Russia and enjoy his conquest, but Genghis's chief general, Subotai, under orders from Genghis's successor, Ogadai, convinced him that they must invade Europe.

Subotai commanded the invasion force, which went into motion in December 1240. Subotai chose this time because the rivers would be frozen, allowing his horsemen to cross more easily, and the poor weather would hamper the gathering of defensive forces. Their first stop was Kiev, and Subotai offered the citizens peace in return for submission. When the Mongol envoys were slaughtered, so was the population of Kiev, and the most beautiful city east of Europe was destroyed. The remainder of the Slavs inhabiting the area were driven westward until Subotai halted his men before the Carpathian Mountains. They and the nomadic Kipchaks of the south, whom the Mongols had already defeated, spread the news of the Mongols' advance and Kiev's fate. The Kipchaks fled to the court of King Bela of Hungary, offering themselves for baptism in return for his protection. Bela accepted them until Subotai wrote to him that the Kipchaks were Mongol servants who should be returned to him. Bela became convinced that his new converts were spies, so he drove them into the hills, where they became bandits.

On the eastern slopes of the Carpathians, Batu again counseled against entering Europe, and again Subotai overrode him. Subotai ordered his force to divide into four parts. The northernmost, under Kaidu, was to swing around the Carpathians into Poland and then ride southward to Pest on the Danube. A second column was to perform the opposite task, riding southward, then upriver. A third column was detailed to cross the mountain passes on Kaidu's left flank, while Subotai and Batu led the center column through the pass known as the Russian Gates. The four columns were to meet in one month, 17 March, in front of Pest.

Kaidu's column proved fabulously successful. He captured Szydlow, but that was on 18 March; he was well behind schedule. Cracow fell to him on 24 March. He burned the city and marched for Breslau, capturing it a week later. Before Liegnitz, he met a combined force of Moravians, Poles, Silesians, and Teutonic Knights. Kaidu's more mobile cavalry made short work of both the infantry and the heavy cavalry on 9 April. Outmaneuvering a Bohemian force marching to the battlefield, the Mongols captured and burned Moravia. Kaidu was almost a month late, but the northern flank was secure.

The southern column rode through Galicia but was slowed by the heavily wooded terrain, and it failed to reach Pest on the appointed day. Subotai had to force his way past a stout defense in the Russian Gates, but he arrived on 15 March with his advance patrols, while Batu arrived with the bulk of the force two days later. When the second column arrived, notifying Subotai of Kaidu's progress, the Mongol general was prepared to fight with only half his army. King Bela marched his force out of Pest on 4 April. Having collected almost 100,000 men, he was not surprised when the Mongols with-

drew. He followed, not realizing that Subotai was not retreating but leading him on. On 9 April the Mongols turned and attacked, and again their mobility was superior to the Europeans' heavy armor. An opening in their lines allowed the Hungarians to escape, but that too was a ruse. The road back to Pest was five days long, and the retreating men were slaughtered; some reports claim as many as 70,000 died.

The Mongols occupied Pest and sent out more patrols to scout their next operation. Through the summer of 1241, they consolidated their hold on Hungary while sending patrols toward Germany, Austria, and Italy. Europe was horrified. The defeated peoples had run west, spreading the details of the massacres, but the rivalry between Frederick and Pope Gregory was still too intense to overcome, each accusing the other of openly or tacitly supporting the Mongol invasion. Only after Gregory's death in August 1241 did the feud end. In the meantime, the Mongols settled into Hungary, and peace, if not security, returned to the land. Trade flowed once again, and the Mongols proved to be less harsh masters than enemies.

Once winter approached in 1241, however, the Mongols again prepared to move. Following their strategy of a year earlier, Batu crossed frozen rivers with a portion of the army. In late December, they captured and burned the city of Gran, having defeated the force of French and Lombards defending it. Passing Vienna, Batu turned southward and campaigned down the Adriatic coast, pillaging and searching for King Bela, who had escaped the slaughter outside Pest. Batu met little resistance, while Subotai waited on the eastern bank of the Danube for the German attack he was sure would come. Before it could, however, word arrived from Karakorum that Ogadai had died. All Mongol chieftains had to return for the election and installation of a new Great Khan. Subotai marched home, and although now Batu was in favor of staying in Europe, he was obliged to follow.

The death of Ogadai was all that saved Europe from the fate of Hungary. The Europeans had not shown any ability to defeat the tactics of the Mongol horsemen, and there is no reason to believe that any power farther west could have done so. Though the withdrawing Mongols left no doubt that this was a voluntary leave-taking, the Europeans breathed a sigh of relief; they would have time to prepare for the return of the nomads. As it turned out, the Mongols did not return; Batu settled into comfort along the Volga and did not want to leave Russia again. A rivalry among the possible heirs created a division of the Mongol Empire into four khanates, so no concerted effort to return to Europe ever materialized. Other than waste and death, the Mongols left little of their culture behind. The children they fathered went home with them, so no permanent racial infusion resulted. Their campaign had serious effects on the region, however, because the Slavs and Magyars of the region were slain by the invaders or by the resulting famine and disease after the Mongols' withdrawal. The Teutonic peoples, who had not suffered as greatly, therefore filled the power vacuum in eastern Europe. The surviving Bulgars and Magyars were pushed into the Balkan Mountains, to be dominated by Germans and Austrians for centuries.

See also Genghis Khan; Magyars; Russia, Mongol Conquest of.

References: Chambers, James, *The Devil's Horsemen* (New York: Atheneum, 1979); Kwanten, Luc, *Imperial Nomads* (Philadelphia: University of Pennsylvania Press, 1979); Lamb, Harold, *The March of the Barbarians* (New York: Literary Guild, 1940).

FRANCE, VIKING INVASION OF

45

The Vikings sailed their longships throughout the known world between the ninth and eleventh centuries, establishing both a fearsome reputation and a number of colonies. Their conquest of territory in France, however, became a pivotal event in both Scandinavian and European history, for it turned a raiding, seafaring population into a land-based military society affecting Europe and the Middle East.

As long as Charlemagne ruled the Holy Roman Empire, his military prowess kept the Norsemen at bay. After his death, however, his sons had little success in stopping Viking raids. The Vikings captured Paris in 849, holding it

until Charles the Bald ransomed the city. They returned in 885 with 700 ships and 30,000 men, and besieged Paris for 13 months; again they left after receiving a ransom of 700 pounds of silver. Duke Odo and Charles the Simple protected the area around Paris and acted as something of a buffer for the inland provinces, but they did little to actively defend anything other than their own neighborhoods.

Charles the Simple of Paris finally attempted to assuage the Vikings with land of their own, which could then be a buffer between the European interior and the defenseless coastline. In 911 the Treaty of St.-Clair-sur-Epte ceded land at the mouth of the Seine and the city of Rouen to Hrolf (or Rollo), leader of a group of Danish Vikings. Over the next few decades, the Norsemen stretched their borders eastward and westward along the coast, though how much was through conquest and how much through cession by Frankish leaders remains the subject of some debate. Over the next century and a half, Scandinavian and Frankish cultures mixed, with the conquered exerting a mighty influence on the conquerors.

As more emigrants moved to this territory, the Norsemen became Normans and the province Normandy, with French becoming the predominant language. As part of the 911 treaty, the Vikings accepted Christianity. In time, the Norse religions were completely replaced, and the converts became militantly Christian. In viewing the construction of buildings dating from this period, some of the oldest are monasteries and churches because the new Christians set about repairing what their pagan fathers had looted. The Normans soon embraced Christianity with a fervor, not only rebuilding but joining the monasteries in large numbers. When Norman soldiers went out into the world, they went as soldiers of God, often with papal blessing or cooperation.

The sailors soon forsook the ship for the horse; they maintained their warlike heritage, but transformed their naval prowess into cavalry power. The Normans slipped easily into the feudal system of Frankish Europe, and one of the prerequisites of nobility was leadership in battle. The Normans perfected the heavy cavalry of knighthood and developed the code of chivalry surrounding it. This development dominated the military tactics of Europe for three centuries and often ran roughshod over the lightly armed soldiers of Islam and Constantinople.

See also Carolingian Dynasty; Crusades; England, Viking Conquest of; Franks; Ireland, Viking Invasions of; Italy and Sicily, Norman Conquest of; Russia, Establishment and Expansion of.

References: Arbman, Holger, *The Vikings* (New York: Praeger, 1961); Brown, R. Allen, *The Normans* (New York: St. Martin's Press, 1984); Searle, Eleanor, *Predatory Kinship and the Creation of Norman Power* (Berkeley: University of California Press, 1988).

46   FRANKS

This group of tribes living in the Rhine River area was first recorded during the later part of the Roman Empire. The earliest history of the Franks was written by Gregory of Tours, a contemporary of Clovis, one of the early great chieftains. Prior to Clovis's time, the history of the Franks is sketchy. The first recorded leader was Chlodio, who led the tribes into northern Gaul in the early fifth century. Chlodio was succeeded by Merovech, who fought alongside the Roman forces against Attila the Hun at Mauriac Plain in eastern Gaul in 451. The first recorded Frankish dynasty, the Merovingian, was named after Merovech. His son Childeric was on the throne by 457 and apparently remained a friend of the declining Roman Empire; he had perhaps been a captive of the Huns as a child. His Frankish forces again fought alongside Roman soldiers against Visigoths at Orleans in 463 or 464, then kept later Gothic and Saxon invaders away from Roman Gaul.

In 481, Clovis became the Frankish king, though sources indicate that he was merely the chief of other Frankish chieftains, a first among equals. He made war against the remaining Roman leadership under Syagrius, defeating him at Soissons in 486. Soon thereafter, Clovis defeated rival chieftains and claimed supreme authority among the major Frankish tribes, the Salians; Clovis can thus be named as the first real king of the Franks. He extended his authority to the Seine River with his victory at Soissons and later reached the Eoire. A decade later, Clovis went to the aid of the Ripaurian Franks around modern-day Bonn and defeated the Allemanni, thus extending Frankish power into Germany.

Clovis converted to Catholicism, possibly influenced by his wife, Clotilda of Burgundy. Some sources suggest that he was a Christian when he won at Soissons, but many claim that he embraced the faith in 496. He chose Catholicism over the Arian version of Christianity, though both were practiced among the Franks. This choice had profound effects, because it started the Franks on the road to becoming protectors of the Church of Rome.

First, however, there were other lands to capture and other enemies to fight. Clovis's expansion to the Loire River brought him into contact with the Visigoths, who controlled southern France and northern Spain. The Ostrogoth king, Theodoric, an Arian and related to Clovis by marriage, had long striven to maintain peace in southern Gaul, but Clovis went to war as the champion of Catholicism. He defeated the Visigothic forces under Alaric at Poitiers in 507 and sent his son to conquer as far as Burgundy. Frankish authority extended over all of France, with the exception of a southern coastal strip and the Breton peninsula. Clovis moved his capital to Paris and established a church to commemorate his victory over Alaric. Rumor has it that despite his Christianity, Clovis plotted to murder the ruling family of the Ripaurian Franks. The truth remains conjectural, but he was elected their king after his war against Alaric. With his power solidified, Clovis was recognized as king of the Franks by the Byzantine emperor Anastasius. He was made a consul under the emperor's authority and treated as if he ruled in the emperor's name, which was hardly the case.

Clovis's four sons inherited parts of his kingdom and regularly made war against their neighbors. Under the leadership of Theudibert, the Germanic tribes were placed under tribute and the Burgunds were destroyed, which gave the Franks control over the Rhone River valley and the port city of Marseilles. Theudibert's expeditions into Italy weakened the Ostrogothic regime there to the extent that Byzantine forces came to control the peninsula.

The next great leader was Dagobert, who defeated the Avars, a Hunnish tribe threatening to expand past the Danube. He also raided into Spain and received tribute (or bribes) from Constantinople. Dagobert's reign also saw an expansion of Frankish trading power and the widespread coinage of gold and silver. He established a mint at the mouth of the Rhine and carried on extensive trade, mainly in the cloth of Frisia, in modern Belgium. He also supported the Church's efforts to convert the Frisians. Dagobert, the last great king of the Merovingian dynasty, died in 639. His sons fought among themselves, and the eastern (Austrasian) and western (Neustrian) factions of the kingdom struggled for dominance.

The real power in Frankish politics was not the king but the mayor of the palace, who represented the tribal leaders before the king. Pepin II, one of the mayors, gave birth to the next Frankish ruling clan. He led Austrasian forces to victory over the Neustrians at the battle of Tertry in 687, which made him the dominant figure in Frankish politics. He assumed the role of military leader, the defender of the Frankish lands from outside attack. Pepin's conquest of Frisia brought him into close cooperation with the Irish Catholic monks who were trying to convert the Frisians, and the connection between Pepin's family and the Catholic Church began to solidify. Pepin led campaigns against the Allemanni, Franconians, and Bavarians, and the missionaries followed his conquests. Pepin died in 714 as the most powerful man in Frankish politics, but still mayor of the palace.

Pepin's illegitimate son, Charles Martel, inherited the position of mayor. (His Latin name, Carolus, gave his heirs the title Carolingians.) He led campaigns against the Saxons and Bavarians to secure the northern and eastern frontiers. Like his father, he worked closely with the Church to extend Christianity. Charles developed a well-disciplined military based strongly on cavalry; that army won for

him his most recognizable victory. In 732 the Franks defeated a force of marauding Muslims from Spain at Poitiers in a battle widely regarded as saving Europe from Islamic influence. The battle was one of a series in which the Franks forced the Muslims to settle south of the Pyrenees. In 737, the last Merovingian king died, but Charles remained mayor of the palace with no king to whom he could represent the chieftains. He died in 741, dividing his extensive landholdings between his two sons—Carloman, to whom he granted his eastern holdings, and Pepin III, who inherited land in the west.

Carloman became increasingly interested in affairs of the soul, so much so that in 747 he ceded his lands to his brother and went to Monte Cassino to become a monk. With tacit papal approval, Pepin removed the last pretenders to the Merovingian throne and made himself king of the Franks. His successful defense of Rome against Lombard invaders endeared him to the Catholic Church, which named Pepin III "King by the Grace of God." The Franks now became the official defenders of the Catholic Church. Pepin spent the 750s challenging the Muslims in Spain and reasserting Frankish claims on southern France. At his death, the greatest of the Carolingian monarchs, Charlemagne, came to the throne.

To a great extent, Charlemagne's reign ends the story of the Franks. His establishment of the Holy Roman Empire changed the nature of western Europe and laid the groundwork for the nation-states that arose in the following centuries. The greatest effects the Franks had on western Europe were to serve as a stabilizing influence in the wake of the fall of the Roman Empire and to be a force for Christian missionary work in west-central Europe. Though much of this time frame is taken up with warfare, the cooperation of the Frankish tribes, under the leadership of either kings or mayors of the palace, served to facilitate trade in western Europe and the exchange of goods and ideas. Little technological innovation took place, though the development of Frankish cavalry influenced warfare throughout Europe and the Middle East.

See also Avars; Byzantine Empire; Carolingian Dynasty; Huns; Ostrogoths; Visigoths.

References: Gregory of Tours, *History of the Franks*, trans. Ernest Brehaut (New York: Norton, 1969); James, Edward, *The Franks* (New York: Blackwell, 1988); Lasko, Peter, *The Kingdom of the Franks* (New York: McGraw-Hill, 1971).

47   GENGHIS KHAN

Certainly one of the best known and most successful conquerors was Genghis Khan, ruler of the Mongols and founder of the Mongol nation. Son of Yesugai, leader of the Borjigin tribe of Mongols, he was born probably in 1167 (though earlier dates are suspected) and named Temujin (Temuchin). Orphaned at age nine when his father was murdered, Temujin struggled to exist as an outcast in his own tribe. Stories abound as to his charismatic personality even as a youth, and he began to regain his position when an old friend of his father's gave him military support to regather his tribe and avenge himself on those who murdered his father. With the assistance of his childhood friend, Jemuka (now a prince), Temujin was immensely successful in defeating his enemies and from his earliest victories established a pattern for treating his foes: He killed the leaders and brought the commoners into his own tribe. By doing this, he crushed any remaining loyalty to previous clans and required fealty to himself alone.

His early victories were directed against the tribes of the steppes, and he gradually brought them under his control. He began to have some trouble, though, within his own camp when Jemuka started occasionally disagreeing with and gradually challenging Temujin's authority. Jemuka led rival clan leaders in a number of attacks against Temujin, but ultimately Temujin defeated and killed his former ally. By doing so, he brought all the steppe tribes under his control. This was confirmed in 1206 when he was named emperor of the steppes and given the title Genghis Khan, meaning Universal Ruler.

With central Asia in his hands, Genghis began to look outward. With only his sons and his closest advisors for generals, he began to attack China in 1211. He established a base northwest of the Great Wall and moved quickly into Ch'in territory. By 1215, he occupied Peking. At this point, he left the Ch'in conquest in the hands of General Muqali and turned toward the southwest and the Muslim nation of Khwarezm. A dispute over their treatment of a caravan under Mongol protection brought Genghis to this nation east of the Caspian Sea. When representatives from Khwarezm refused to discuss compensation, the Mongols invaded. It is in this campaign in the Oxus River area that the Mongols established their fearsome reputation. Under Genghis's direction, the Mongols began destroying cities, fields, and irrigation systems.

It was also in this campaign that the Mongols began to employ new military methods. Mongol forces were made up totally of cavalry, which were unable to besiege cities. Therefore, Genghis adopted catapults and siege engines from the nations he conquered. He also learned that there was more to empire-building than owning sufficient territory to feed Mongol horses. Cities and towns were necessary to hold territory and establish trade. With this in mind, Genghis began to stop razing cities and only engaged in wholesale slaughter on rare occasions, though often enough to maintain a reputation that he could use as a negotiating tool.

With Khwarezm conquered and under his domination by 1223, Genghis remained relatively passive, though his troops raided far and wide into Russia, southeastern China, and toward India. He died while on campaign in Russia on 18 August 1227, leaving an empire stretching from the Caspian Sea to Peking. This was expanded further by his sons and grandsons, who took the Mongol empire to its heights.

Genghis was equally adept at conquest and administration. While extremely strong-willed, he was able to listen to opposing views and incorporate them into his own if he saw their merit. While believing himself divinely guided, he tolerated every religious belief his subjects practiced. Upon receiving his imperial title, he developed the Great Yasa, a code of civil, military, and economic laws that governed all Mongols, himself included. From his conquered subjects he took not only military tactics and

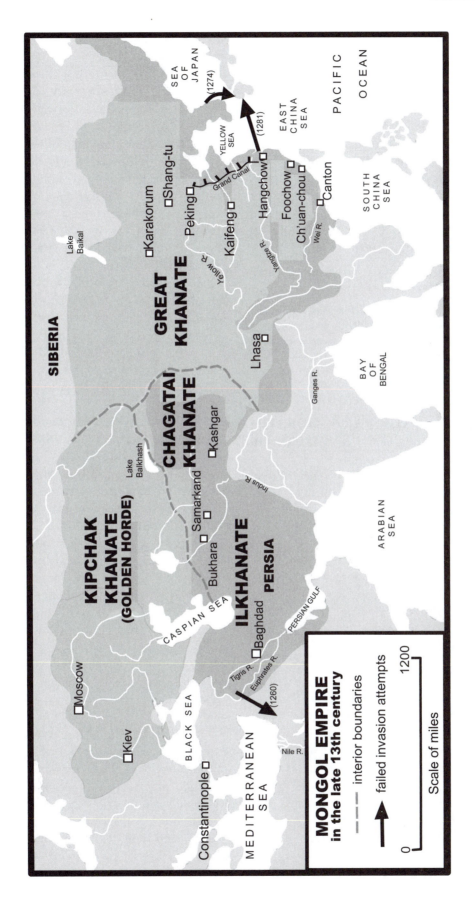

SEA OF JAPAN

(1274)

(1281)

PACIFIC OCEAN

EAST CHINA SEA

YELLOW SEA

SIBERIA

□Karakorum

□Shang-tu

Peking□

Kaifeng□

□Hangchow

Foochow□

Ch'uan-chou□

□Canton

Grand Canal

Yellow R.

Yangtze R.

Wei R.

SOUTH CHINA SEA

GREAT KHANATE

Lake Baikal

□Lhasa

Ganges R.

BAY OF BENGAL

CHAGATAI KHANATE

□Kashgar

Lake Balkhash

Indus R.

ARABIAN SEA

KIPCHAK KHANATE (GOLDEN HORDE)

Samarkand□

Bukhara□

ILKHANATE PERSIA

CASPIAN SEA

Baghdad□

PERSIAN GULF

Tigris R.

Euphrates R.

(1260)

□Moscow

□Kiev

BLACK SEA

Constantinople□

MEDITERRANEAN SEA

Nile R.

MONGOL EMPIRE
in the late 13th century

---- interior boundaries

→ failed invasion attempts

0   1200

Scale of miles

hardware, but also adopted an alphabet, a written language, and whatever cultural accomplishments they could offer. His domination of central Asia initiated a Pax Mongolica that allowed the reopening of the Silk Road, bringing ideas and trade from the Middle East and beyond. Though known for the terror inspired by his soldiers, Genghis used this terror as a psychological weapon more than for its own sake. Unlike later strongmen in the mold of Hitler and Stalin, who practiced genocide and mass murder, Genghis Khan was actually quite an enlightened and tolerant ruler.

See also China, Mongol Conquest of; Kubilai Khan; Russia, Mongol Conquest of.

References: Chambers, James, *The Devil's Horsemen* (New York: Atheneum, 1979); de Hartog, Leo, *Genghis Khan, Conqueror of the World* (New York: St. Martin's Press, 1989); Morgan, David, *The Mongols* (Oxford: Blackwell, 1986).

GHANA, ALMORAVID INVASION OF

48

The nomads of the western Sahara, most notably the Sanhaja tribes, dominated the gold trade between Ghana and the Mediterranean in the eleventh century. This was a profitable pastime until Ghana seized control of the town of Awdaghust, at the southern end of the trade route. Because of internal dissent, the Sanhaja tribes were unable to respond to this loss of power and revenues. The king of the tribes believed something needed to be done to unite his people, and he thought that religion was the key. Islam had spread throughout western Africa since the eighth century, but it was practiced with irregular piety, and among the Sanhaja tribes of the Sahara, the people seemed to be only nominally Muslim. When their king went on his pilgrimage to Mecca, he returned with the desire to increase his people's faithfulness. He brought back a teacher, Ibn Yasin, to motivate his tribes to become better Muslims, a task Ibn Yasin was unable to accomplish.

Disgusted at the intransigence of the nomads, Ibn Yasin went into retreat along the west coast of Africa (some say near the mouth of the Senegal River, while others say Mauritania or an island off the coast). Here he established aribat, a fortified center for the study of religion and warfare, which attracted a following of people pious to the point of fanaticism. These "men of the ribat" came to be known as Almoravids (in Arabic, al-muribatun). When Ibn Yasin had about 1,000 followers, mostly from the Sanhaja tribes, he declared a jihad (holy war). Returning to the territory of the Sanhaja, he told his recruits to either convert their people to a stronger belief, or inspire God's wrath upon them. After a few defeats, the Sanhaja tribes embraced Ibn Yasin's fundamentalist stand and joined his forces, not only for religious reasons, but also for the promise of booty. With enlarged forces, Ibn Yasin moved north to Morocco, defeating the Berber inhabitants in 1054-1055. Here, in Ibn Yasin's homeland, the Almoravid state was established. After Ibn Yasin's death in battle in 1059, the dynasty was founded by Yusuf ibn Tashufin.

While the main Almoravid force was conquering Morocco, a smaller force attacked south with the intent of recapturing Awdaghust. Accomplishing this in 1054, they ultimately attacked deeper into Ghanan territory and captured the capital in 1076. For a while they instituted a strict Muslim rule in the western African state, forcing tribute and the payment of a head tax by non-Muslims. This control lasted only a few years because the Almoravids were more concerned with pillage and profit than local improvement. Even though they controlled both ends of the trans-Saharan trade route, they did not take advantage of it. When the Almoravids withdrew, Ghana remained disrupted, allowing an opportunity for the expansion of Mali into the gold territory.

Meanwhile, the Almoravids in Morocco extended their campaign for Muslim fundamentalism into Spain. They attempted to revive the lethargic practices of the Spaniards and were welcomed as protection against the approaching Christian forces from Europe.

At their height, the Almoravids controlled territory from Spain through western Africa, but that rule was short-lived. They were, in turn, overthrown by another fundamentalist movement, the Almohads, who declared a jihad against them in 1122 and ultimately overthrew them in 1163. That defeat in Morocco, coupled with the inability to make a profit at the southern extreme of their holdings in the gold region of Ghana, brought the Almoravids to a rather abrupt end. The aftereffects of the Almoravid reign are mixed. Though they did not introduce Islam into Ghana, they accelerated the spread of the religion into the interior of western Africa along the Niger River to Mali and the Songhay empires. They also acted as a solidifying influence for the tribes of the Maghrib in northwest Africa; by building their capital at Marrakesh, they laid the foundation for the modern nation of Morocco. Both in Morocco and in the Sahara, the tribes were confirmed in their Islamic faith, but the fundamentalism the Almoravids preached did not last much past their demise.

See also Mali, Expansion of; Songhay, Expansion of; Spain, Muslim Conquest of.

References: Fage, J. D., *A History of West Africa* (London: Cambridge University Press, 1969); Hallett, Robin, *Africa to 1875* (Ann Arbor: University of Michigan Press, 1970); Trimingham, J. S., *Islam in West Africa* (London: Oxford University Press, 1962).

49   GUPTA EMPIRE

Northern India was in a state of flux for a long time after the fall of the Mauryan Empire, coming under the occasional control of the Bactrians and the Scythian Kushans. Their decline in the face of Sassanid Persia, coupled with the decline of the Andhra dynasty in southern India, left a power vacuum that was filled by Chandragupta of Pataliputra. The area of Magadha, around the lower Ganges Valley, had been the base for the Mauryan Empire, and Chandragupta claimed descent from the founder of that dynasty. He campaigned up the Ganges Valley and, having placed it under his authority in 320 C.E., named himself Chandragupta I, King of Kings. He married the daughter of a neighboring king, and their son Samudragupta could claim noble blood

from both parents. After Chandragupta's death in 330, Samudragupta, aiming to reestablish the boundaries of the Mauryan Empire, attacked to the west and southwest, conquering Rajputana and the northern Deccan plateau of central India. His campaign along the eastern coast drove as far as modern Madras, and the remnants of the Andhra territory paid him tribute. He attacked and was able to exact tribute from Assam, Punjab, and Nepal. After Samudragupta's death in 375, his son Chandragupta II maintained the aggressive goals of his forebears. He defeated the Punjabis and gained direct control over their territory in the northwest, then annexed the regions of Malwa, Saurashtra, and Gujarat. The empire reached its greatest extension under his rule, and saw the beginnings of a Golden Age.

Because the empire of the Guptas was not as centralized as that of the Mauryans, much local autonomy was exercised. The environment became peaceful and safe, however, and the main chronicler of the period, the Chinese traveler Fa Hsien, praises the administration for its maintenance of such a quiet land. Poetry and literature were taken to their heights, and in the sciences the value of pi and the exact length of the solar year were calculated. The world's best university at the time was established at Nalanda, near the capital city of Pataliputra, and it attracted students from all over India as well as China and Southeast Asia. By patronizing the cult of Vishnu, the Indian religious climate favored Hinduism and led to a decline in Buddhism. A number of monasteries and temples were also constructed at this time.

The empire did not long survive Chadragupta II, who died in 413. The Ephthalites, or White Huns, drove through modern Afghanistan and through the passes into northwest India. Though kept at bay temporarily by Kumaragupta and Skandagupta, the pressure proved overwhelming by 480, and the Gupta Empire collapsed. The White Huns set up a short-lived kingdom in the northwest, but the subcontinent remained fragmented until the rise of Harsha, the last of the strong native leaders. During his reign (606–647), reunification extended almost as far as the Gupta Empire, but its decentralization guaranteed its collapse into warring factions after his death. Not until the Mongol invasion of India would there again be a centralized administration.

See also Mauryan Empire; India, Kushan Invasion of; Moghul Empire.

References: Allan, John, *The Cambridge Shorter History of India* (Delhi: S. Chand, 1964); Basham, A. L., *The Wonder That Was India* (New York: Taplinger, 1954); Gokhale, Balkrishna, *Ancient India, History and Culture* (Bombay: Asia House, 1959).

50   HUNDRED YEARS' WAR

Rival claims to both land and power were the basis of conflict between Britain and France in the fourteenth century. The death of Charles VI of France in 1328 left a void in the French monarchy. The Capetian dynasty had ruled in France since 987, but there was now no direct male heir. The closest claimant was Edward III of England, grandson of Philip the Fair (1285–1314), but the French nobility had a difficult time conceiving of a foreigner as their king. They chose instead Philip VI Valois, deciding to bring the Capetian dynasty to a close. Edward resisted this choice, not only because he wanted the throne for himself, but also because he was technically a vassal of the French king. Since he controlled some lands in France, he might be called upon to obey his liege lord with actions detrimental to England. The French had also supported the Bruces of Scotland in their struggle for independence from the English. Last, England coveted Flanders, nominally under French control but tied to England via the wool trade. Add to all this the traditional dislike the French and English have always harbored for each other, and war seemed inevitable.

Even though it possessed a larger and wealthier population, France did not have a strong central administration to direct military operations or to collect the necessary taxes to pay for a war. England was better organized, and had more consistent military leadership and superior weaponry in the form of the longbow.

The war was fought in three phases over the space of 116 years. First, Edward provoked trouble in Flanders by instituting an embargo on English wool, placing the merchants and trade guilds in economic jeopardy. The cities of Flanders were obliged to recognize Edward as king of France in order to reopen trade. They signed a treaty of alliance with England, but proved to be unfaithful in following it. With this foothold on the continent, Edward organized an invasion force. He drew first blood with a naval victory over the French at the battle of Sluys in January 1340, a battle which gave him control of the English Channel. Unable to follow this up because of a lack of Flemish support, he was forced to conclude a truce with France.

Edward broke this in 1346 when English forces invaded Normandy and won a series of victories culminating in their triumph at Crécy. He did not want to fight the French at that time, but since his ships had left Calais to evacuate wounded and booty, he could not escape. While on the march for Flanders, he met French forces at Crécy and had to stand and fight. Edward's army of knights and longbowmen faced a French army much superior in numbers of mounted knights and foot soldiers. He won by defense and poor French leadership. Philip attacked late in the afternoon of 26 August, before his entire army had arrived on the scene. The great range and power of the longbows held French crossbowmen at bay and drove back repeated cavalry charges. By midnight the French army was in tatters. Edward retreated to Calais, laid siege to it throughout the winter, and captured it in the spring of 1347. England controlled Calais for the next 200 years, denying the French any opportunity to launch a counterinvasion. Mutual exhaustion and the arrival of the bubonic plague brought the war to a halt for eight years. The second phase of the war came when England won a victory at Poitiers in September 1356. This time, the key English weapon was artillery. By destroying the castle walls at Poitiers, along with the flower of French knighthood at Crécy, England defeated the French army and took King Philip prisoner. Political order in France collapsed and the countryside was vandalized by roving bands of out-of-work soldiers. Scorched earth tactics employed by both armies, coupled with the pillaging of the brigands, brought destruction to all parts of the French countryside. England forced France to sign the Treat of Bretigny in May 1360, freeing Edward from his position as vassal to the French king and forcing France to recognize English control over its territories. Edward renounced his claim to the French throne and received three million gold crowns for King Philip's release.

Owing to domestic problems in England over the next few decades, the country was unable to focus sufficient attention to its possessions in France and the new French King Charles V was able to regain influence over much of France while English kings had to deal with peasant uprisings. After Edward III died in England in 1377, the two countries remained in relative peace. In 1396, Richard II of England married the French king's daughter, sealing a truce. Not until 1415 did the war resume, when King Henry V of England took advantage of a French power struggle and invaded, initiating the third phase of the war. He scored a major triumph at Agincourt in October. Henry's army of 8,000 defeated a French force of 25,000, again doing most of the damage with longbows against a reconstituted French armored nobility on horseback. Unhorsed knights packed into a muddy field fell victim to a swarming English infantry. Enraged by a French attack at his undefended baggage train late in the battle, Henry broke the conventions of the time and ordered his prisoners executed. Half the French nobility died at Agincourt.

Allying himself with the Burgundians, Henry held a commanding position in control of almost all of northern France. He forced the French to sign the Treaty of Troyes, which created a joint monarchy. The deaths of Henry V of England and Charles VI of France in 1422 brought a single king to power, the infant Henry VI. In Paris, he was proclaimed king of both France and England, but most French ignored the treaty and recognized Charles VII Valois.

The two countries were unified in name only. Charles VII soon set about regaining the

The bloody Battle of Agincourt which claimed the lives of half the male French nobility.

throne, but at first had little luck. As his army inside Orleans was being besieged in 1429, a young girl, Joan of Arc, requested an audience with him. She informed him that God had given her the power to lift the siege. As the war had been going so poorly and no French general could succeed, Charles had nothing to lose. Joan was just what the French military needed: a psychological boost. She had no military training, of course, but her arrival at Orleans coincided with a British retreat owing to a lack of supplies. Any French army in this position could have won, but she got the credit. Heartened by this victory and what they believed to be divine guidance, French forces built momentum and scored a series of successes over the English. Charles openly declared himself king as the English forces reeled. The Burgundians saw which way the wind was blowing and, disavowing their English allies, signed an agreement with Charles in 1435. Backed into a corner around Calais, which remained their sole possession in France, the British agreed to peace in 1453. The Hundred Years' War accelerated the pace of change in Europe, especially in France. The defeats of the French nobility at Crécy and Agincourt were important because the feudal system was based on the power of the knights. Without the ability to enforce the system of vassalage, feudalism began to fade. The arrival of the bubonic plague in the midst of this war brought about changes as well. By killing vast numbers of people in the cities, peasants from the countryside, no longer bound to their land by the dead or absent nobles, abandoned an agricultural life for one of business in urban areas. Decreased demand for agricultural products because of the plague, coupled with the lack of farm workers, meant that the nobles on their estates could not maintain an income. This caused political power to shift to where the money was—with the merchants and craftspeople of the cities. Without a strong agricultural nobility, the king became the most important political figure in the nation, and he was supported by the cities, which had no traditional loyalty to one noble as the country peasants had. Feudalism fell, replaced by nationalism. Taxing power from now on lay in the hands of the king, so he used his military power to open and control trade routes and foreign lands, and keep the cities wealthy.

There were changes in England as well. When the war started, Edward III needed money. In order to get it, he needed the approval of Parliament, which he called upon to approve an unprecedented amount of money and supplies. This meant holding regular meetings, which resulted in a steady increase in the power of the House of Commons. Thus, as Edward tried to gain power in France, he was relinquishing it little by little at home.

References: Painter, Sidney, and Brian Tierney, *Western Europe in the Middle Ages* (New York: Knopf, 1983); Palmer, John J. N., *England, France and Christendom: 1377–99* (Chapel Hill: University of North Carolina Press, 1972); Vale, Malcolm, *English Gascony, 1399–1453* (London: Oxford University Press, 1970).

51   HUNS

The Huns are one of a myriad of tribes who rode out of central Asia, but little can be determined of their origin. Probably they were the Huing-nu, who failed in wars against the Chinese and turned (or were forced) westward. Occasional early sources opine that they were the Nebroi mentioned by Herodotus as a semimythical people living on the fringes of territory controlled by the Scythians. Some of the earliest direct references come from clashes with the Goths around the area north of the Black Sea in the mid-fourth century C.E. The first Hun conquest was the Alans; they were then used in the vanguard of Hun attacks against the Goths or emigrated into the Roman Empire.

In 376 the Huns began to harass the Caucasus lands controlled by the Ostrogoths. After fighting around the Crimea, the Ostrogoths were pushed back across the Dnieper to the Dniester River, and began to pressure the Visigoths. The Visigoths had not fared too well against the armies of the Eastern Roman Empire, and their leader, Athanaric, had no wish to see his people defeated by a second enemy. Athanaric established his forces along the Dniester and sent a reconnaissance force east to keep an eye on the advancing Huns. This force was easily destroyed, and the Huns were upon Athanaric's army before the Visigoths could finish their defenses. The Visigoths vanished into the countryside and reformed between the Pruth and Danube rivers, where Athanaric ordered a wall built. A second time the swift Hun army arrived and surprised the Visigoths, who again scattered and retreated toward the Danube. The refugees numbered between 700,000 and one million, and they settled into the forests of Transylvania.

Pressed against the frontiers of the Roman Empire, in 376 the Visigoths begged protection from Emperor Valens. The Visigoths were granted land along the Danube in return for military service. The Ostrogoths, who arrived later, also begged imperial protection, but were denied it; they crossed the Danube anyway. Emperor Theodorus I, crowned in Constantinople in 379, led Roman campaigns against the Huns, who were rampaging through the Balkans, but he could not turn them back.

The two Gothic peoples combined to fight against the Eastern Romans, leaving no strong force to oppose the slowly approaching Huns. The Huns settled into Pannonia along the Adriatic coast.

By 432, the Huns were well established and a force to be reckoned with. Emperor Theodosius II paid tribute to the Hun leader, Ruas, and gave

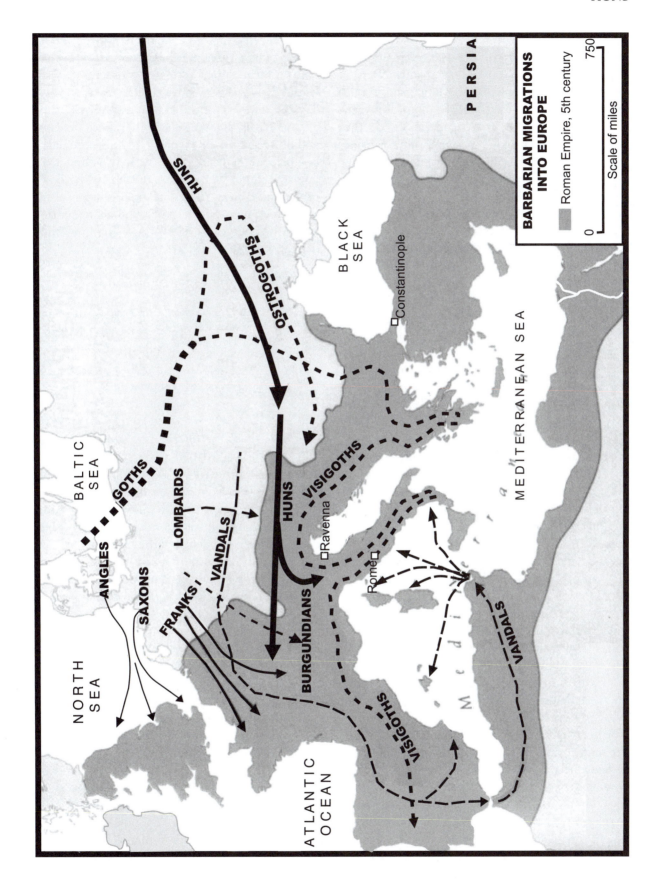

BARBARIAN MIGRATIONS
INTO EUROPE

☐ Roman Empire, 5th century

Scale of miles

0   750

PERSIA

BLACK
SEA

☐ Constantinople

MEDITERRANEAN SEA

HUNS

OSTROGOTHS

BALTIC
SEA

GOTHS

LOMBARDS

ANGLES

SAXONS

VANDALS

FRANKS

NORTH
SEA

ATLANTIC
OCEAN

HUNS

VISIGOTHS

☐ Ravenna

☐ Rome

BURGUNDIANS

M e d i t e r r a n e a n

VISIGOTHS

VANDALS

him a general's commission. Ruas's sons Bleda and Attila renewed the treaty and fought for Constantinople in campaigns against Persia. Growing tired of doing another's fighting, Attila made war against the Eastern Romans. Between 441 and 443, he rampaged through the Balkans and defeated a Roman army outside Constantinople, but could not capture the city. Upon receiving an increase in tribute, he finally stopped. Attila killed his older brother to become sole leader of the Huns, and in 447 reopened his war against the Romans. Though once again turned back from Constantinople, Attila managed to gain a threefold increase in tribute and cession of the eastern bank of the Danube. Theodosius's successor stopped paying the tribute in 450, by which time the Huns were looking westward.

Attila hoped to split the attention of the Western Roman Empire between himself and the Vandal leader Gaiseric, who was laying siege in North Africa. Further, Attila was invited to aid a Frankish chieftain in a succession struggle against his brother, so there seemed to be plenty of reasons to march on Gaul. He crossed the Rhine north of modern-day Mainz with 100,000–500,000 warriors, in addition to their families, who carried supplies. With a variety of auxiliaries, the Huns advanced along a 100-mile-wide front, destroying everything in their path except Paris. The Roman general Aetius formed an army of Franks, Germans, and Alans, but could muster no more than half Attila's strength. In mid-June the two armies fought at the site of modern-day Chalons, and Attila could not prevail. He retreated eastward, and western Europe was saved from Asian domination.

Attila turned south instead and attacked Italy. He had demanded the hand of Honoria, the Western Roman Emperor's sister, and been refused. Northern Italy was ransacked, and refugees fled to the marshlands, creating Venice. Aetius returned to face Attila, but the Huns were having problems. One of Attila's commanders had been defeated in Illyricum (northern Greece), and the Italian countryside proved to be disease-ridden and without supplies. Attila met with Pope Leo I outside Rome and, after an unrecorded discussion, turned the Huns northward and left Italy.

Attila died in 453. His sons fought for his throne while subject tribes revolted. The remnants of the Huns retreated northeast of the Danube, leaving rebelling tribes to their own devices. The last of the Huns, under Irnac, traveled as far as the Volga, but they were defeated and absorbed by the Avars. The Huns proved to be little more than plunderers, traveling from one ripe target to the next, never settling down or building cities. They accomplished nothing more than mass destruction, gaining a reputation as the "scourge of God" punishing a sinful Roman Empire.

See also Avars; Ostrogoths; Scythians; Vandals; Visigoths.

References: Brion, Marcel, *Attila: The Scourge of God* (New York: Robert McBride & Co., 1929); Bury, J. B., *The Invasion of Europe by the Barbarians* (New York: Russell & Russell, 1963); Thompson, E. A., *Romans and Barbarians* (Madison: University of Wisconsin Press, 1982).

INDIA, KUSHAN INVASION OF

52

The arrival of the Yueh Chih, or Kushan, people in India was a result of their defeat at the hands of Shih Huang-ti of the Ch'in dynasty in China. Expelled from their traditional lands, the Kushan migrated west and defeated the Scythians of central Asia, who in turn attacked India at the time of the declining Mauryan Empire. The Scythians, or Sakas, carved out a kingdom of their own in the area around modern Afghanistan, including parts of northern India. They were supplanted, however, by the Kushans, who maintained control over the area of modern Turkistan. Late in the second century B.C.E., the Kushans were at the borders of Bactria, but internecine squabbling divided them into five rival clans. Kujula Kadphises subdued the other four and began to press gradually southward. Around 25 C.E., they gained control of the territory of modern Afghanistan and moved into the Kabul Valley by about 50 C.E. Kujula led his people as far as the Indus River, while his son Wima occupied much of the Punjab. The third ruler, Kanishka, was the greatest of them all. The dates of his reign are a matter of some speculation, but 78–103 is generally accepted. Kanishka drove his armies eastward to capture Palitaputra (modern Patna), the capital city above the delta of the Ganges, then back to the west to occupy Rajputana. At its greatest extent, Kanishka's empire stretched from northern India to Parthian Persia to Turkistan. After his capture of India, he spent much of his time fighting border wars with China.

The Kushans played a key role in international relations in the first two centuries C.E. because their position between the Roman Empire to the west and the Chinese to the east made them valuable middlemen for the beginning of the Silk Road linking the two worlds economically and, to an extent, philosoph-ically. Both Western and Eastern cultures blended in Kushan India, but the Kushans, like most invaders of India, were absorbed by the local society. Kanishka is known as a hero of Buddhism, spreading the faith throughout his empire and introducing it into China. It is also possible that Christianity reached India at this time; legend has it that the apostle Thomas preached there. The perspective of history sees this mingling of cultures as a great age for India and the world, but contemporary accounts (especially those written by Hindus) speak of the dark age of barbarian conquest and the upsetting of traditional values. Still, the Buddhists did well, and the Kushan patronage of the arts produced the greatest era of sculpture, much of which has Hellenistic overtones.

After Kanishka, the Kushan power began to fade. One of the Scythian satraps, Rudradaman, broke away from Kushan dominance and carved out a kingdom of his own in the northeastern portion of India. Other subordinates also broke away. The rising power of the Sassanid dynasty in Persia dealt the Kushans a defeat around 250, in which they lost their hold on their central and southwest Asian lands. Ultimately, the Kushan kings ruled over progressively smaller territories until their total absorption by Indian culture.

See also Ch'in Dynasty; Mauryan Empire; Scythians.

References: Chattopadhyay, Bhaskar, *Kushana State and Indian Society* (Calcutta: Punthi Pustak, 1975); Kumar, Baldev, *The Early Kusanas* (New Delhi: Sterling Publishers, 1973); Mukherjee, Bratindra, *The Rise and Fall of the Kushana Empire* (Calcutta: FirmaKLM, 1988).

INDIA, MUSLIM INVASION OF

As the forces of Islam spread the faith through the Middle East in the 700s, they gained a small foothold in India by establishing a trading community in Sind, where the Indus River empties into the Arabian Sea. Not until about 1000 did Muslim conquerors return in earnest. At first, Afghan Muslims conducted raids into northern India for no other reason than plunder, but they soon added forced conversion to their raiding. Mahmud of Ghazni was the main perpetrator of this rapine, destroying as much Hindu and Buddhist culture as possible while carrying vast wealth out of the country. The cavalry tactics developed over the centuries by Turkic/Mongol peoples served the Afghan invaders well, and few of the Indian kingdoms could resist; only the military culture of Rajasthan gave the Muslims serious competition. Over time, the Muslims stayed in India rather than carrying off their plunder, and by 1200 they were in control of most of the northern part of India. Hindustan and the Punjab were incorporated into a Turco-Afghan Empire, and the invaders established a capital at Delhi, strategically located to confront the few passes giving access to Afghanistan and acting as the gateway to the agricultural lands of the Ganges and Indus river valleys. In 1206 the Delhi sultanate was formally established.

The Muslims continued to raid the countryside to extend their political control, spread Islam, and destroy the Hindu and Buddhist faiths. The population of northern India, though much larger in number than the Muslims, could not find it in their nature to organize under one leader to resist the invasion. The Muslims were successful enough in their attempt to virtually destroy Buddhism in India, the land of its birth, by killing thousands of monks and destroying temples, monasteries, and universities. Hindu temples suffered as well, because the Muslim ban on portraying the human form in artwork meant the destruction of vast amounts of sculpture. As the sultanate grew more secure, however, the later sultans carried on less persecution, and the majority of Indians who practiced Hinduism survived. They lived as second-class citizens in a

Muslim society, forced to pay the head tax all non-Muslims everywhere had to pay. This bought them the right to practice their faith, and once the Muslims looked a bit more closely at the tenets of Hinduism, they found it less objectionable than first thought—its lesser deities could almost be equated with the veneration of saints in some Christian societies. The rise of the bakhti movement, teaching a universal message of divine love, fit neatly into the Sufi teachings of Islam, so the persecution lessened considerably.

Once established, the Delhi sultanate lusted after the southern part of India, but like so many other empires, it failed to make much of a dent in the forbidding Deccan plateau or the warlike Marathas who lived there. Perpetual attempts at subjugation, however, coupled with heavy taxation to pay for the military and a rising disunity in Delhi, brought the sultanate into peril. Palace cabals and discontented peasants kept the leaders from establishing a peaceful empire that could become profitable. Soldiers were often imported Mamluk slave troops, talented at their profession but also eager for power; they fought the wars but also dealt in court intrigues.

The Muslim Empire faced its most severe challenge in the early 1300s when the Mongols made their appearance on the northwest frontier. Sultan Ala-ud-din dealt the Mongols one of their rare defeats and drove them back into Afghanistan.

Ala-ud-din had already made a name for himself as an aggressive leader eager to attack the Deccan, and he had raised an agricultural tax of almost 50 percent to finance his campaigns. This gave him a ready army when the Mongol threat appeared, but it provoked the already oppressed Hindu farmers. When he died on a campaign in 1316, he was little mourned.

Ala-ud-din's successors were the Tughluqs. Muhammed ibn Tughluq came to the throne in 1325 and reintroduced the forced spread of Islam, even though he fell in love with and married a Hindu. He also tried to conquer the Deccan, with only slight success, but his taxes were also heavy; further, from 1335 to 1342, northern India suffered a drought which killed a million people. More people rebelled. Muhammed died fighting a rebellion in Sind, and he was succeeded by his cousin Firuz (1351–1388), who gave up trying to

conquer and focused on internal improvements and construction projects such as hospitals, mosques, universities, dams, and bridges. He eased the tax burdens, but enforced the strict practice of Islam and made the Hindu population know they were second-class citizens. At his death, the sultanate began to break up.

In the midst of internal dissension after Firuz's death, the timing was ripe for another invasion. The Indians seemed to fight among themselves the most bitterly when there was danger on the frontier. Tamurlane invaded with his Turkic-Mongol forces in 1398 and destroyed the city of Delhi. He left behind famine and disorder, and the Delhi sultanate never fully recovered. An attempt at resurrection was made under the leadership of Sikander (1489–1517), and a period of intellectualism flourished. Hindu and Muslim religious thought began to merge in mystic practices. Sikander's successor, Ibrahim, was the last sultan. While attempting to crush a rebellion in the northern territory of the Punjab, the local governor asked an Afghan tribe for assistance; this led to the invasion of Babur "the Tiger" and the establishment of the Moghul Empire.

The role of the Delhi sultanate in the life of the everyday inhabitant of India is difficult to assess, as little primary source material comes from this era. It was difficult for the Hindus and disastrous for the Buddhists, and the oppression did not end with the rule of the sultan. Local autocrats taxed the people for the sultan and then taxed them again for their own courts, and these local rulers gave little decent government in return. The most long-term result of the occupation was the introduction of Islam into India, giving it a hold in some areas it would never relinquish; variations on the faith are seen in groups such as the Sikhs. The Muslim rule engendered no loyalty, and therefore no popular support, when it was needed most—to face another foreign invader.

See also Tamurlane; Moghul Empire.

References: Holt, E M., *The Cambridge History of Islam*, 2 vols. (Cambridge: Cambridge University Press, 1970); Lane-Pool, Stanley, *Medieval India under Muhammadan Rule* (Calcutta: Susil Gupta, 1951); Payne, Pierre, *The Holy Sword* (New York: Harper, 1959).

IRELAND, ENGLISH INVASION OF

54

Around 1159, after hearing reports of corruption and wrongdoing in the Irish Church, Pope Adrian IV gave consent to Henry II, king of England, to invade and conquer Ireland. The Irish Church had been corrupt for some 25 years and, though reform efforts were in place (including the appointment of two new archbishops), Ireland did not have the strong centralized government needed to support a state church. Henry decided against an invasion at that time, however, because of opposition from his mother.

The English invaded Ireland nine years later at the request of Dermot Macmurrough, king of Leinster in Ireland. Macmurrough was having a problem with some Irish princes who had had him removed from his lands by sanction of the high king of Ireland. Macmurrough went to Henry II for help and, with Henry's consent, obtained troops from the Anglo-Norman nobility. The invaders were foot soldiers of an English baron, Richard, earl of Pembroke. In exchange for his military aid, Richard was promised Macmurrough's daughter in marriage and succession to the throne of Leinster.

The invasion began in 1168 and lasted approximately one year. The slings and stones used by the Irish resistance were no match for the armored knights and archers of the Norman-style army. Within the year, Richard's army had seized Dublin. During this time, Richard married Macmurrough's daughter and, at Macmurrough's death, inherited the kingdom of Leinster. After Dublin's fall, Richard continued his campaign deeper into Ireland.

These successes made Henry fear that a power-hungry Richard might use his newfound lands to rise up against England. He also worried that English nobles might divide the conquered territory into individual states independent of English rule. Henry himself had stayed out of the conflict, leaving the fighting to Richard, but now he decided to enter the country and proclaim himself lord of Ireland. He then extended English rule to the territories of Waterford and Wexford, adding them to land Richard had already conquered. In the spring of 1172, Henry returned to England, leaving in charge Hugo de Lacy, the first English viceroy in Ireland. De Lacy was given control over the territories of Waterford and Wexford as well as the province of Meath. Richard maintained control of Leinster.

The immediate effect of the invasion was that the Irish countryside was ransacked by invaders, who built castles and stole land and livestock from Irish chieftains. The Norman-English began to intermarry with the locals, and adopted the Irish language and laws. Distraught by the assimilation, English kings passed laws prohibiting the use of the Irish language, Irish laws, Irish clothing, etc. These efforts proved futile.

Initially the invasion seemed fruitful. The English managed to move into most of Ireland, excluding western and central Ulster. However, from the very beginning, their rule was challenged by Irish landholders, and over time the extent of English rule diminished. Throughout Henry's reign and that of his son John, skirmishes between the Irish and Norman-English were common. By the time Henry died, Norman control existed only in sections of the coast, land along the Shannon River, land in Leinster, and parts of Meath and Ulster. John's reign did nothing to extend that control; in fact, his attitude toward his Irish subjects further angered them and caused more rebellion.

Though Norman-style rule was diminished considerably, long-term effects of the invasion are still visible. During John's reign, the kingdoms under English rule were divided into 12 counties; those counties still exist in modern Ireland. John's main influence, though, was in the introduction of an English style of government and the adoption of English law. Even today, effects of the invasion are evident in the problems between Ireland and England. A rampart used by the invaders still stands. Robert Kee comments, "The rampart sealed off the neck of a promontory which the Normans were to use as a bridgehead. What a bridgehead into Irish history it was to prove. Eight centuries of conflict were to flow from it—a conflict that is still not over."

References: Finnegan, Richard, *Ireland: The Challenge of Conflict* (Boulder: Westview Press, 1983); Kee, Robert, *Ireland: A History* (New York: Little, Brown, & Co., 1982); Orel, Harold, ed., *Irish History and Culture* (Lawrence: University of Kansas Press, 1976).

55 IRELAND, VIKING INVASIONS OF

Viking forays into Ireland began in 795 with the raid on Lambay. Twenty-five raids were recorded between 795 and 840, conducted all along the northern coast of Ireland. These raids centered mostly on churches and monasteries because the church prescribed the use of precious metals, such as gold, for its liturgical vessels. Such places were easy pickings owing to the monks' inability to defend themselves.

In 840 the character of Viking conquests changed. Thorgils, a Norse Viking, invaded and conquered the whole of Ireland. From this point on, Ireland was used primarily as a military base for expeditions to other places. Thorgils founded many garrisons that would become major cities: Dublin, Wexford, Cork, and Limerick. There was no major settling of Ireland by the Vikings, unlike the colonizing taking place in England and on the Continent. Soldiers came, served their time, and returned to Scandinavia. Also, instead of subjugating the people of Ireland, the Vikings ruled in cooperation with the seven Irish kingdoms of Connaught, Munster, Leinster, Meath, Ailech, Ulaidh, and Oriel. The Irish kings stayed kings, some working with their Viking overlords, others opposing them.

Thorgils was drowned in 845 by Mael Sechnaill, king of Meath. The Norse experienced constant conflicts for the next few years, continuing into 850 when the Danes stepped in to take over. Called the Black Strangers, the Danish Vikings raided Dublin and seized the Norse stronghold of Carlingford in 851. In 853, the Norse and Danes were united under Olaf Huiti, the son of the Norse king. In 871 Olaf returned to Norway and was killed in battle, which left Ireland to his brother Ivar, lord of Limerick. Olaf's reign had been rife with petty wars and shifting alliances. Upon assuming leadership, Ivar was dubbed "King of the Norsemen of all Ireland and Britain." This angered the Danish king Halfdan of Northumbria in England, who unsuccessfully declared war on Ivar.

These struggles, along with a reduction in reinforcements because of the settling of Iceland, weakened the Viking hold sufficiently for the Irish

to rise up in 901 and reclaim their land under the leadership of Cearball of Leinster. Ireland experienced peace—until 913, when the Vikings returned. In a four-year expedition, they retook the island and ruled it until 1000, when Brian Boru, king of Munster, defeated Sigtrygg Silkybeard.

The immediate effects of the Viking occupation were both good and bad. The slave trade became widespread throughout Ireland, but the Irish were introduced to the superior boatmaking and seamanship of the Vikings. Contacts with England were also strengthened during this time. Numerous Viking words found their way into the Irish language, including the words for trade, coin, and market. Excavations of parts of Dublin and other sites reveal a wealth of information about the Vikings, and many examples of early Irish art are preserved in Norwegian museums. Despite some holes in our knowledge, we know the Vikings had a long-term effect on the politics, culture, and history of Ireland. Because Ireland was used mainly as a fortress-base for other expeditions, the Viking heritage here was unlike that in England, where widespread colonization occurred.

References: Arbman, Olger, *The Vikings* (New York: Frederick Praeger Publishers, 1961); Jones, Gwyn, *A History of the Vikings* (New York: Oxford University Press, 1968, rev. 1984); Richter, Michael, *Medieval Ireland* (New York: St. Martin's Press, 1988).

56 ITALY AND SICILY, NORMAN CONQUEST OF

Contemporary sources dispute how soon and in what manner the Normans followed up their 999 C.E. foray into Italy. The one common agreement is that they came from Normandy in relatively small groups made up of younger men who stood to inherit little if they stayed home; only by warfare could they increase their fortunes, and fortunes could be made in Italy. The Normans first acted as mercenaries for a variety of local powers, in some cases fighting on opposite sides. Their military prowess proved sufficiently valuable that they were able to obtain lands from their employers and establish a presence that grew stronger until 1042, when southern Italy was divided among them under vassalage to local lords. From this setting, the sons of Tancred de Hauteville—Robert Guiscard and Roger—spread their influence.

By 1061 the Normans were strong enough to extend the will of the Roman church to Sicily, which had been dominated for 200 years by the Muslim Saracens. Internecine squabbling on the island provided a good opportunity for Robert Guiscard and his able brother/lieutenant to ally with one party and insinuate themselves into an influential position. Norman knights landed south of Messina, but their unfamiliarity with maritime operations made the landings a piece-meal effort. However, they arrived in strong enough numbers to seize Messina and, allied with Emir Ibn at-Timnah, marched inland. They failed to seize the enemy stronghold at Enna, in the center of the island, but kept Messina as a base to stage future operations.

The conquest of Sicily took 30 years, mainly under the direction of Roger Hauteville: Palermo fell in 1072, the Saracen strongholds of Trapani and Taormina in 1077 and 1079, respectively, and Syracuse in 1085. The island was considered secure after the capture of Noto on the southeast coast in 1091. The Sicilian conquest was notable for the increasing use of sea power by Normans (both in transport and siege-craft), the aura of a Holy War taken on by the campaign as time went by, and the increasing close cooperation between Norman soldiers and the papacy. By the time Sicily was falling, however, the first great wave of Hauteville conquerors was dying: Richard in 1078, Robert Guiscard in 1085, and Roger, the "Great Count of Sicily," in 1101. From this point forward the Normans consolidated rather than conquered, ruling the Kingdom of the Two Sicilies until its incorporation into the Holy Roman Empire in 1194 under Henry VI.

Some historians regard this conquest as the epitome of Norman accomplishment. The Normans established a feudal society patterned along the lines of western Europe. They introduced a new arm to military affairs: the heavy cavalry. The armored knight on a heavy horse proved overwhelming to the infantry and light cavalry used by their Lombard, Byzantine, and Saracen opponents. This type of warrior domi-

nated warfare throughout the Middle Ages until its demise during the Hundred Years' War. The longest lasting legacy, however, was the spread of Norman architecture, though its description remains a point of conjecture. For a people not far removed from their Viking heritage, surprisingly the Normans seem to have pioneered castle construction. Castles appeared throughout the Mediterranean, wherever the Normans went, but in the construction of churches they adapted styles found in their travels. Churches and monasteries in Sicily and Italy reflect Greek and Muslim tile work and vaulted roof design, and no church building appears to be "typical" Norman style. Indeed, the blending of Latin, Greek, Muslim, and western European cultures shows itself in all Norman artifacts in the Mediterranean. The Norman championship of the Roman church, as well as Norman wars against Byzantine forces and territories, aided in the growing schism between eastern and western Christianity. Finally, their warfare against Muslim Sicily was a foretaste of the Crusades of the twelfth and thirteenth centuries.

See also Crusades; France, Viking Invasion of; Hundred Years' War.

References: Brown, R. Allen, *The Normans* (New York: St. Martin's Press, 1984); Finley, M. I., et al., *A History of Sicily* (New York: Viking Penguin, 1987).

JAPAN, MONGOL INVASIONS OF

57

By the time of the Mongol invasion of Japan, the Mongol leader, Kubilai Khan, was at the height of his power. The Mongol khans had conquered Russia, Poland, Hungary, and Bohemia to the west, as well as China and Korea to the east. In establishing himself in China, Kubilai had subdued his most dangerous adversaries. He could now turn his attention to Japan, the one country that had eluded Mongol domination.

The struggles on the Asian continent had very little effect on Japan. Its contact with the outside world was confined to very limited trade and visits by Buddhist priests. At the time of the Mongol expedition, Japan was under the relatively new rule of the Hojo family. The

Mongol invasion would be the first test of that family's leadership.

In 1266, Kubilai Khan sent envoys to Japan requesting that tribute be paid to the Mongol Empire. The letter to the Japanese government emphasized the fact that the khan held no hostility toward Japan; he merely wanted Japan to be considered a part of his circle of friendly tributaries. The Japanese interpreted this as a Mongol attempt to subjugate them. The government was divided on their course of action; some favored conciliation and delay, while others preferred a policy of contemptuous silence. After six months, the Hojo regent Tokimune sent the Mongol envoys back without a written acknowledgment. Contemptuous silence won out. Undaunted, the khan sent further envoys to Japan, but the results were the same.

Kubilai Khan began to prepare for war in earnest. He ordered the Koreans to step up their agricultural operations in order to supply his army with food. Knowing that his men had no experience as seamen, he enlisted the aid of the Koreans to transport his army across the sea to Japan.

In November 1274, 25,000 Mongol and 15,000 Korean troops left from Korea in 900 ships manned by 8,000 Korean sailors. They began by attacking Tsushima and Iki, two islands situated between Korea and Japan. At Tsushima, a force of no more than 200 samurai held the Mongol forces at bay for a time by fighting to the death. An even smaller force repeated this feat at Iki. On 20 November, when the Mongols reached the shores of northern Kyushu, they were met by the troops of five Kyushu chieftains. The Mongols possessed a superior tactical system. While the Japanese were trained to display their skills by engaging in single combat, the Mongols were trained to work together as a team. If an individual samurai approached a Mongol to do battle, he would be surrounded and killed. The Mongols were excellent horsemen and could easily defeat the Japanese cavalry. Despite this, the Japanese mounted a fierce resistance to the invaders. The final blow to the Mongol army came from a storm, which destroyed many of their ships and inflicted a loss of 13,200 men. They were forced to abandon the operation and return to Korea.

Kubilai Khan did not view the invasion as a defeat; he apparently believed that he had instilled fear into Japanese hearts by displaying the superior tactics of the Mongols. He immediately sent envoys to Japan to summon the emperor of Japan to Peking to surrender to him. The Japanese leaders cut off the heads of the Mongol envoys. Kubilai became more determined than ever to conquer Japan.

A second invasion was delayed for seven years because Kubilai had to subdue the last supporters of the Sung dynasty in southern China. By 1281, having taken care of his problems at home, he was ready to launch a campaign against Japan. This time, however, the Japanese were better prepared to defend themselves. They had built a long defensive wall along the coast of Hakata Bay and had trained in group-combat techniques similar to those employed by the Mongols. As a result, Kubilai's 140,000 troops were unable to penetrate the Japanese defenses and move inland. The Korean and Chinese factions of the Mongol army more than likely had no great desire to fight on, while entire families of Japanese defenders volunteered to fight at the front. The final blow to the Mongol invaders came, once again, from nature. After 53 days of fighting, a typhoon, the "divine wind" (kamikaze), destroyed the Mongol fleet and forced them to withdraw. Kubilai Khan made plans for a third invasion, but abandoned them in 1284 when he began to have problems in Southeast Asia.

Little damage was done to the Mongol Empire by the war. The Chinese contingent of the Mongol army bore the brunt of the loss; 12,000 of them were made slaves by the Japanese. The Mongols lost their share of men and ships, but surprisingly little else. Mongol pride was hurt, of course; Japan held the distinction of being the only state in the Orient that did not pay tribute.

Oddly, the Japanese victory did more harm than good to the Hojo rulers. When the Mongols first arrived, the court in Kyoto appealed to heaven for help. Throughout the empire, prayers were offered, liturgies chanted, and incense burned in the temples. The priests took credit for the Japanese victory over the Mongol invaders, even claiming that they were responsible for the kamikaze, which the Japanese believed was generated by protective kame spirits against its enemies. Many of the priests expected and received huge rewards for their help in the campaign, thus creating resentment among the soldiers who had fought so hard for very small payment. The victory over the Mongols brought no wealth to the victors. The invading forces had left no land as spoils of war to be divided among the Bakufu, the military leaders who were the major landowners, which lowered their prestige. Since the Bakufu had little trust in the Mongols, they did not relax their precautions for many years to come against another invasion, putting a great financial burden on the Japanese government. Eventually these factors led to the downfall of the Hojo family.

The kamikaze legend grew over the centuries, to be called upon again in the 1940s. Hoping for a manmade "divine wind" to save their empire, Japanese pilots used suicide tactics during the U.S. invasion of the Philippines in October 1944, continuing until the final surrender almost a year later.

See also Russia, Mongol Conquest of; Philippines, U.S. Invasion of the.

References: Curtin, Jeremiah, *The Mongols: A History* (Westport, CT): Greenwood Press, 1972); Kwanten, Luc, *Imperial Nomads* (Philadelphia: University of Pennsylvania Press, 1979); Mason, R. H. P., and J. G. Caiger, *History of Japan* (New York: Free Press, 1972).

58   JUSTINIAN

After the Roman Empire split into halves following the reign of Constantine, the western half dealt continually with barbarian invasions of Germanic and Gothic tribes. Ultimately, the area came under the nominal control of the king of the Ostrogoths, Theodoric. He and his successors established a relatively peaceful and prosperous society that practiced the doctrine of Arian Christianity. In the east, however, this doctrine was viewed as a heresy to be destroyed, and became one of the motives for conquest exercised by the emperor Justinian, who came to power in Constantinople in 527.

Justinian was born a commoner, but he had an uncle in the Byzantine army who brought him to the capital and assisted him in his military career. When his uncle Justin achieved the position of emperor, Justinian served as his closest adviser, and later as regent. Upon Justin's death, Justinian acceded to the throne. He named his wife Theodora coemperor, a wise move because of her political acumen and strong faith in her husband and herself. Together they were a powerful team who took the Byzantine Empire to its greatest heights. Though brought up in the military, Justinian's expansion of the empire was directed by two generals, Belisarius and Narses. Justinian and Theodora had the vision, and Belisarius and Narses had the skill to accomplish the expansion.

The first order of business was to defend against Persian attacks from the east. As a junior commander, Belisarius distinguished himself in action against the Persians and thus came to Justinian's notice; he was named to the command of all the armies in the east at age 27. In his first major command, he defeated a Persian army twice the size of his outside the fortress of Daras. During peace talks, he learned of a flanking movement through the desert against Antioch, the richest city in the east. Belisarius quickly moved to block that assault, and the Persians withdrew.

Impressed by his young commander's skills, Justinian ordered him back to Constantinople to lead an invasion of northern Africa. Justinian wanted to return this rich grain-producing area, which had been under the control of the Vandals for the preceding century, to the empire. With only 10,000 infantry and 5,000 cavalry, Belisarius outmaneuvered the Vandals, capturing their capital at Carthage and defeating them in battle outside the city gates at Tricameron. Vandal power was thus destroyed, transferring the province to the Byzantine Empire.

Justinian ordered Belisarius to Sicily and sent a diversionary force along the Adriatic coast to threaten northern Italy, both by their presence and by bribing the Franks to cooperate. With Gothic attention diverted northward, Belisarius easily captured Sicily and invaded the southern end of the peninsula. He quickly captured Naples, but the Gothic king Vitiges was more intent on defeating the Franks, which

Justinian, noted for his codification of the law, ruled a reunited Roman Empire.

allowed Belisarius the opportunity to capture Rome. This caught Vitiges's attention, and he made the Franks a better monetary offer than Justinian had. Vitiges then marched on Rome with 150,000 soldiers, but Belisarius, with a mere 10,000, held the strongly fortified city for a year. When Vitiges withdrew toward his capital at Ravenna, Belisarius followed. He received reinforcements under the command of Narses, an older man with less military experience who nevertheless had Justinian's confidence. The two besieged Vitiges in Ravenna while Belisarius proceeded to consolidate the remainder of Italy. The Franks again intervened on the Goths' behalf, but overplundered the countryside and had to withdraw.

Belisarius was recalled to Constantinople to beat back another Persian threat. Though Belisarius did nothing to give his emperor cause for concern, he became so popular that Justinian began to fear him as a potential rival. Justinian was afraid to give him a large army, and Belisarius had to fight with undermanned forces. He performed more miracles with small forces, bluffing the Persians away from a major assault on Jerusalem and threatening their capital on the Tigris by a series of light-cavalry raids. Belisarius returned to Italy to reconquer the lands that had fallen to newly rebuilt Gothic forces. Again, he did much conquering with few men, and was again recalled because of Justinian's paranoia. Narses was given overall command in Italy, and his victory there succeeded mainly in destroying the country so thoroughly that it was centuries before much of the land was again useful.

Belisarius gave Justinian a reunited Roman Empire, directed from Constantinople rather than Rome. Justinian tried to hold the sundry cultures together as Caesar Augustus had, by codifying laws to promise universal justice. Justinian's Code was a masterpiece of legal order, but it failed to reach the variety of cultures that Augustus's universal law had. By basing much of the law on Orthodox Christian bases, he offended those Christians who practiced other dogmas. Indeed, they considered the law so overbearing that they embraced the rising power of Islam in the 600s because it promised and delivered religious tolerance. The Byzantine Empire soon lost the lands Justinian brought into it, but the professional traditions of the army established in Justinian's time kept it alive for another 800 years.

See also Augustus, Caesar; Constantine, Emperor; Franks; Ostrogoths; Vandals.

References: Barker, John, *Justinian and the Later Roman Empire* (Madison: University of Wisconsin Press, 1966); Browning, Robert, *Justinian and Theodora* (London: Weidenfeld & Nicolson, 1971); Procopius, *The Secret History of Justinian*, trans. Richard Atwater (Ann Arbor: University of Michigan Press, 1961).

59 KHMER KINGDOM

The earliest records, from the first century C.E., of the population of Southeast Asia living in what is now Cambodia are of the Mon-Khmer people. The arrival of an Indian aristocrat and his marriage to the daughter of a local chief mark the beginning of the kingdom of Fu-nan, which the Chinese wrote about a century or so later. The greatest military leader of Fu-nan appears to have been Fan Shih-man, who extended his kingdom's borders east to the South China Sea, south to the Gulf of Siam, and possibly west toward Burma. Contemporary Chinese texts record the conquests and power of Fan Shih-man, who is thought to have died while on expedition to Burma. Control of the coastline along the South China Sea gave Fu-nan domination over the area's maritime trade, and his successor, Fan Chan, entered into diplomatic and economic relations with China and India. These trade contacts continued throughout the third century, gaining value as China came under the Ch'in dynasty after 280. Apparently, Indian cultural influences made regular appearances in Fu-nan over the next two centuries. The kings often had Indian names, their writing is described as resembling northern Indian script, and trade with central Asia and even the Roman Empire was noted. The greatest of the Fu-nan kings was Jayavarman, whose 30-year reign ended in 514; he was recognized by the Chinese as "General of the Pacified South, King of Fu-nan."

Jayavarman's son was probably the last king of Fu-nan, because the Chen-la are believed to have conquered the kingdom after 539. Who the Chen-la were is a matter of some dispute, but they may have been vassals of Fu-nan who deposed their overlord. Rulers of the area at the end of the sixth century still claimed descent from the "universal monarch," presumably the king of Fu-nan, but that may have resulted from Chen-la conquerors intermarrying with the royal family. In the 590s, the Chen-la leader Bhavavarman conquered the Mekong Delta to the Mun River in the north and to the Korat Plateau in the south. He and his brother Chitrasena seized the throne in Fu-nan, but whether as usurpers or restorers of the original royal family is unclear. Chen-la is regarded as the original kingdom of the Khmer people, the inheritors of the land and power of Fu-nan.

Bhavavarman's grandson, Ishanavarman, completed the occupation of Fu-nan to roughly the borders of present-day Cambodia. He established his capital at Ishanapura and pursued a policy of friendship toward his nearest neighbors, the Champa. Consolidation of Khmer power throughout the region continued for another century, through the reign of Jayavarman I (657–681). His death without an heir caused discord and a split in the country; Chinese records speak of a "Land Chen-la" and a "Water Chen-la," corresponding to inland and coastal principalities. The one continuing factor in this time period was the widespread practice of Hinduism, for the Khmers brought the formerly popular practice of Buddhism to an end.

The period of discord attracted outside pressure, notably from the Malay Peninsula and Java. Aggressively pursuing commercial dominance of Indonesia and Southeast Asia, Java seems to have established dominance in the two Chen-las by the late eighth century. The reunification of Chen-la came about in the early ninth century when Jayavarman II ousted the Javanese. His rise to power was confirmed by a religious ceremony naming him "Universal Monarch"; his posthumous title was Parmeshvara, or "Supreme Lord," a title given to the Hindu god Shiva. He built a number of cities and established a capital at whose site Angkor was to be built.

Jayavarman's grandson Indravarman went conquering during his reign (877–889), returning the Korat Plateau to the northwest to Khmer control. He sponsored irrigation projects and built a huge reservoir. Canal and reservoir construction for irrigation, as well as the building of temples and monasteries, remained royal projects for generations. The next several monarchs devoted themselves to public and religious works; not until the reign of Suryavarman (1010–1050) did more expansion take place. During his reign, Khmer power extended into the Menam Valley and to the west of the Great Lake, hitherto a wasteland. Also by his time, a resurgence in Buddhism took place. His sons struggled against internal revolts and attacks from the Cham tribe; the two sons joined the Chinese, however, in an unsuccessful campaign against Dai-Viet.

A new dynasty was established in 1080 by a Brahman who took the throne name of Jayavarman VI. His grandnephew, Suryavarman II, took the Khmer kingdom to its heights. He launched invasions of Dai-Viet in 1128, 1138, and 1150, conquering as far as the Red River delta. He conquered Champa, holding it for four years, and briefly occupied the land of the Mon kingdom. Contemporary Chinese sources state that the Khmer kingdom stretched from Burma to the east coast of the Malay Peninsula. Suryavarman II also constructed Southeast Asia's most notable structures at Angkor Wat, which became his mausoleum, overseen by the Hindu god Vishnu. Rebellions broke out after his death sometime after 1150, but events of the following century and a half are sparsely recorded. Not until the end of the thirteenth century do Chinese accounts describe a fading civilization, though the Khmer again gained control over the Cham territories in the early 1200s. Later that century, a Mongol force entered the area, and records indicate that the Khmers paid tribute to the Chinese emperor Kubilai Khan. After a series of conflicts with the rising power of Siam, the Cambodian capital of Angkor fell to that country in 1431. Though the Khmer recovered much of their strength and territory by the middle of the sixteenth century, the Siamese returned to defeat them. Only the arrival of the Portuguese, who gave military assistance to the Khmer king, enabled them to retain some power. From this point forward, too many internal struggles and outside forces—the influences of Portugal, Holland, and Islam—conspired to allow the Khmer to be powerful again. Finally,

France took control of all of Southeast Asia in the mid-1800s, establishing a protectorate over Cambodia in 1863.

See also Ch'in Dynasty; Kubilai Khan.

References: Audric, John, *Angkor and the Khmer Empire* (London: R. Hale, 1972); Briggs, Lawrence, *The Ancient Khmer Empire* (Philadelphia: The Philosophical Society, 1951); Coedes, G., *The Making of South East Asia*, trans. H. M. Wright (Berkeley: University of California Press, 1966).

KOREA, MONGOL INVASION OF

60

The Mongol armies invaded China and took control of its northern provinces by 1234. As they attacked the remains of the Sung dynasty in the southern part of China, other Mongol forces invaded Korea. The Mongols had been raiding into Korea since 1231, periodically devastating the country. When the capital city of Kaesong was attacked, the ruling family (under King Kojong) and the government (under the leadership of the Ch'oe family) withdrew to an island off the coast, to which the land-bound Mongols could not follow. There, they established a new capital and, with taxes collected from the southern part of the peninsula, constructed palaces and pavilions. The government ignored the conditions on the mainland, where Mongols were killing and enslaving tens of thousands of people.

The government depended on prayers to Buddha to keep them safe on the island, but in 1258 Prime Minister Ch'oe Ui was assassinated, and the royal family decided to make peace with the Mongols. The crown prince traveled to the Mongol capital to apologize for the government's resistance; he returned as vassal to the Mongol government. In 1274, Ch'ungnyol Wang, married to a princess of the Mongol Yuan dynasty, ascended the throne and the two nations were united. The Koreans paid tribute to the Mongols and in return were treated as members of the family, though Yuan officials were posted throughout the country to keep tabs on events. Peace was bought at the price of independence.

The Yuan dynasty enlisted the aid of the Koreans in their attempted forays against the Japanese, and the Korean peasants virtually had to starve themselves to feed the armies preparing for the expedition. When they revolted, a combined Chinese and Korean army suppressed them. Even though the invasions of Japan failed, the relations between Korea and the Mongols grew stronger, which meant that the Mongols' influence increased and the Koreans adopted Mongol forms of government and culture. The peasants continued to suffer, their torment increased by a coincidental wave of raids by Japanese pirates along the entire coastline. The marauders, or Wako, so pillaged the coastal farms and shipping that the peasants withdrew to the interior, and the coasts became wastelands. Throughout the era of Yuan dominance, the peasants suffered continuously, and slavery expanded. A feudal system of sorts was established that kept most people tied to an estate, owned by a Mongol or a Korean supporter of the Yuan dynasty.

The Mongol rule in Korea came to an end when the Mongol rule in China ended. In the 1350s, power struggles within the Mongol ruling family, coupled with rebellions, strained their ability to rule. Bandit uprisings harried the Mongol administration, and the Red Turbans were the most dangerous. Korea was called upon to provide troops to fight the Red Turbans, but they were defeated. The Red Turbans followed up their victory with attacks on Manchuria and Korea in 1359 and 1361. A Red Turban leader declared himself head of a new dynasty, the Ming dynasty, and made war against the Yuan dynasty from the Ming capital at Nanking. Seeing an opportunity, the Korean king, Kongmin Wang, killed the Mongol leaders in his country and sent the army to reoccupy the northern portion of the peninsula. When the Mings established their authority, Korea rushed to recognize it and swear allegiance.

See also China, Mongol Conquest of; Japan, Mongol Invasions of; Ming Dynasty.

References: Charol, Michael, *The Mongol Empire; Its Rise and Legacy* (London: George Allen & Unwyn, 1961); Hatada, Takahashi, *A History of Korea*, trans. Warren Smith and Benjamin Hazard (Santa Barbara, CA: AB.C.E.-Clio, 1969); Henthorn, William, *Korea: The Mongol Invasions* (Leiden: E.J. Brill, 1963).

61 KUBILAI KHAN

In the early thirteenth century, the steppe tribes were united under the dynamic leadership of Genghis Khan, who directed his people to conquests establishing the largest empire in history. That empire, however, was destined to a rather short life. Though Genghis spelled out directions for succession, which his children followed with little trouble, his grandchildren divided the empire beyond the hope of reunification. After the death of Ogadai, one of Genghis's sons, Ogadai's son Mangu ruled as the Great Khan, or Khakhan. Upon Mangu's death, there was a struggle among his brothers. The youngest (designated "Keeper of the Hearth" to rule over the Mongol homeland) was Arik Buka, who had the support of his brother Baiku of the Golden Horde and his nephew Kaidu, who lived on the steppes to the north. However, the next in line for the throne was Kubilai. Arik Buka's supporters rejected Kubilai's leadership because he had become too Chinese and not sufficiently Mongol in his actions, though

Kubilai had been Mongol enough to lead the armies of the steppes into southern China against the Sung Empire. Using the techniques developed by Genghis and the siege engines adapted from Chinese and Muslim forces, Kubilai proved as capable and successful as any Mongol general. He had seen the advantages of Chinese culture—its wealth and scientific accomplishments—and he embraced them as adjuncts to the traditions and military prowess of the Mongols. His interest in Chinese culture seemed a betrayal to the more conservative Mongols in the homelands.

In 1260, Kubilai made a quick truce with the Sungs, then turned his forces northwest toward his younger brother's base at Karakorum. Kubilai captured the city and held it against Arik Buka's counterattacks until, in 1264, the younger brother submitted to the older's leadership. Kubilai forgave him and gave him lands of his own, but punished his brother's advisers for urging the revolt. Kubilai returned to China, never to see the Mongol capital of Karakorum again. His nephew Kaidu refused to submit and spent the next 30 years harassing China's borders.

Kubilai returned to his garden city of Shangtu, better known to Westerners as Xanadu. He also returned to his campaign against the Sung, who had violated the truce in his absence. Kubilai blended traditional Mongol tactics with a new one: He depended on Chinese familiarity with past Mongol cruelties to cities that resisted, then offered peaceful terms to any that would submit willingly. That promise, coupled with benevolent treatment of refugees, won the hearts of most of the Sung people, so that by 1276 the seven-year-old Sung emperor and his dowager empress grandmother surrendered to him. Kubilai had to continue campaigning against Sung supporters in the southeast, capturing Canton and waging a naval war against the final holdouts, but with the submission of the emperor the war was won.

Kubilai's significance lies not in new military developments, but in his political leadership. Many areas of Chinese life improved during the new Yuan dynasty. Public works were of prime importance, and new roads and canals were constantly constructed while he was emperor. Kubilai proved to be a benevolent master to the poverty-ridden peasantry, providing the first public-assistance program in China and introducing the practice of stockpiling surplus supplies in good years for redistribution during lean times. He maintained the Chinese bureaucracy, yet kept the Mongols as a separate class in society. He sponsored intellectual pursuits by ordering the printing of many books and the construction of observatories for updating astronomic observations. The expansion of printing brought Chinese drama to heights never before experienced, and spread its influence widely over the population.

Kubilai was not, however, without his failings. He maintained a large military, the cost of which was a severe burden on the taxpayers. He also sponsored two disastrous invasions of Japan, which cost money and thousands of Chinese lives. In order to maintain the splendor of his palaces, he collected vast sums of silver for his treasury, but introduced printed money to the Chinese economy, overprinting it to the point of high inflation. Though he protected China from the raids of his nephew Kaidu and unified the country into a form it would basically hold to present times, the costs to the peasant taxpayer proved too much of a burden. Though called Kubilai the Wise, he laid the groundwork for the fall of his dynasty. He also oversaw, somewhat by default, the breakup of the Mongol Empire. Birkai of Russia never acknowledged his supremacy and made his portion of the empire independent; Hulagu, Kubilai's brother, established an independent state of the Il-Khans in Persia. Kaidu also maintained his own independence in the northern steppes. Thus, Kubilai was left with China, a nation that reached new heights under his leadership but which quickly overthrew his successors and reestablished Chinese dominance in the Ming dynasty.

See also Genghis Khan; Japan, Mongol Invasions of; Middle East, Mongol Invasion of the; Ming Dynasty; Russia, Mongol Conquest of.

References: Cohen, Daniel, *Conquerors on Horseback* (Garden City, NY: Doubleday, 1970); Lamb, Harold, *The March of the Barbarians* (New York: Literary Guild, 1940); Rossabi, Morris, *Khubilai Khan: His Life and Times* (Berkeley: University of California Press, 1987).

62   LOMBARDS

The Lombards were a tribe of northern Germany who came to recorded history during the later stages of the Roman Empire. The Romans gave them their name: langobard, or "long beard." Though known to fight occasionally against either their neighbors or the Romans, the Lombards tended to be peaceful, pastoral people. Through the fourth and fifth centuries, they began to migrate southward into the Danube River region known as Pannonia (modern Austria). The Lombards fought for Byzantine Emperor Justinian in his campaigns against the Ostrogoths in Italy and received favored status during his rule. His successors, however, favored the Gepids, a neighboring hostile tribe. Fearing a war against the Gepids supported by the Byzantines, the Lombards under King Alboin allied themselves with a tribe newly arrived from central Asia, the Avars. Together they were victorious and split Gepid lands between them.

In the middle of the sixth century, the Lombards established a new tribal organization based on an aristocratic hierarchy. Dukes and counts commanded clans organized into military units (fame), all serving under a king. With this new organization, the Lombards, now in fear of the Avars, decided in the late 560s to migrate farther, to Italy. The long-running war between the Ostrogoths and the Byzantine Empire had left a power vacuum in northern Italy, and the Lombards were able to move in and take over fairly easily. Under Alboin's leadership, by 572 they had conquered the entire northern peninsula to the Po River, and occasional districts in southern and eastern Italy.

Alboin was murdered shortly after the Lombards' arrival in Italy, and for the next few decades the tribe struggled internally while they exploited the Italian people and countryside. The Lombards established themselves as the dominant force in northern Italy, but they adapted readily to the existing agricultural framework in the area, believing that whatever the Romans had organized was the best format for agricultural production. The tribal dukes exercised the most power, with little or no central control. Only when threatened from outside, by the Franks, did the Lombards again form a united front. In 590, when the Lombards elected the duke of Turin, Agiluf, to the kingship, he reconsolidated Lombard power and established a capital at Pavia. King Rothari, who ruled in the mid-600s, issued a legal code for his people along the lines of that produced by Justinian in Constantinople. The leading Lombard king was Liutprand (712–744), who further focused on the internal needs of his kingdom. Later in his reign he reinstituted the campaign against Byzantine power in Italy.

The Lombard incursion into Italy frightened the pope. At first, the Lombards practiced Arian Christianity, which denied the equality of God and Jesus. Their military success, coupled with their heretical views, posed a threat to orthodox Catholicism. Even though they converted to orthodox views in the late seventh century, their power was a source of concern to the pope. When the Lombards under King Aistulf captured Ravenna in 751 and threatened Rome in 754, Pope Stephen II appealed to the Franks for deliverance. Pepin the Short, first of the Carolingian dynasty, marched to Italy and defeated the Lombards in 754 and 756. Pepin recaptured Ravenna and gave land to the Church, creating the Papal States; in return, the pope anointed Pepin as king of the Franks and defender of Rome.

Aistulf remained king of the Lombards, but his successor, Desiderus, was defeated by another Frank, Pepiris grandson Charlemagne, in 773. Charlemagne made himself king of the Lombards and incorporated northern Italy into the Holy Roman Empire, thus bringing to an end the Lombards' existence. Though their rule in Italy was often harsh, the Lombards contributed to the country's heritage. Much of the legal system of the area descends from Lombard practice. King Rothri, who reigned in the mid-600s, issued a law code patterned along the lines of that compiled by Justinian in Constantinople. One of the most important aspects of Rothri's code was the attempt to end the practice of vendetta. The personal feud was to be replaced by monetary payment for damages, known as guidrigild, which appears in later Scandinavian cultures as weregild. The Lombards' greatest effect, however, was indirect, in that they removed once and for all Byzantine power in Italy, thus ending any chance of Eastern Orthodoxy challenging papal authority in western Europe. In the eleventh century, Lombardy played a major role in dominating the trade routes from the Mediterranean into the continent, and the resulting wealth gave them commercial and financial leadership that later translated into political power: They formed the Lombard League, which resisted the invasion of Frederick Barbarossa of Germany in 1176.

See also Avars; Franks; Justinian; Ostrogoths.

References: Bona, Istvan, *The Dawn of the Dark Ages: The Gepids and the Lombards* (Budapest: Corvina Press, 1976); Hallenbeck, Jan, *Pavia and Rome: The Lombard Monarchy and the Papacy in the Eighth Century* (Philadelphia: American Philosophical Society, 1982); Paul the Deacon, *History of the Langobards*, trans. W. D. Foulke (Philadelphia: University of Pennsylvania Press, 1974).

63 MAGYARS

There are two rival claims as to the source of the Magyars. Legend has it that they were descended from Nimrod, a descendant of Noah's son Japheth, who left Babel after the construction of the Tower of Babel. Nimrod had two sons, Hunor and Magyar, who began the two great tribes of the Huns and the Magyars. Following the direction of a magical elk, they moved to the Caucasus, where the two tribes lived in peace. As time passed and the tribes grew, the Magyars remained in the Caucasus and the Huns began a nomadic life that ultimately took them past the Volga into Europe. Under the leadership of Attila, the Huns terrorized Europe. After Attila's defeat and death, his sons returned to the Caucasus and pleaded with the Magyars to return with them to Europe where they could find new lands and opportunity.

Aside from the legend of a Middle Eastern origin, in reality the Magyars seem to have had Finn-Ugaric origins with traces of Turco-Tartar elements. They had long practiced a nomadic lifestyle in central Asia and finally migrated westward past the Ural, Volga, Don, and Dnieper rivers, and at last the Danube. In this movement, they had to successively fight and defeat other nomadic tribes, such as the Bulgars, Khazars, and Petchenegs. The pressure of the Petchenegs and Bulgars finally drove them into Europe. As they entered eastern Europe, they encountered the power of the Byzantine Empire, which hired them as mercenaries and introduced them to Christianity; likewise, German kings hired them to aid in fighting the Slavs.

By the ninth century C.E., the Magyars moved into central Europe under the leadership of Arpad. They entered the Hungarian plain with some 150,000 men, defeated the Slavs and Alans, settled, and used the area as a base for further raiding into German and Italian lands. The Magyars became the permanent occupants of this region, and came to be known as Hungarians. Under Arpad, Magyar soldiers ranged successfully into Italy as far as Milan and Pavia in 899, finally leaving upon receiving sufficient bribes. The Magyars fought in much the same style as the Huns, and were precursors to the Mongol invasion of Europe. Employing mostly light cavalry and archers, they avoided close contact with their enemies, harassing them into exhaustion and then exploiting any openings. The heavy cavalry developed in Europe at this time did not succeed against the Magyars at first, but the Europeans eventually adopted some of the Eastern tactics and began to have more success.

By 907, Magyar interest in Germany forced their rivals into defensive cooperation. Luitpold of Bavaria allied with Ditmar, the archbishop of Salzburg, but their efforts proved futile when the Magyars defeated them at Presburg. In the 920s the Magyars raided as far as the Champagne region of France, again into northern Italy, and as far as the Pyrenees. The Magyars created as much terror as the Vikings from the north, but the Germanic nobles soon began to prevail. Henry the Fowler defeated the Magyars in 933 at Merseburg, inflicting 36,000 casualties. He and his successors began fortifying the frontier, which lessened the frequency of the Magyar raids, and Bavarians began to raid Magyar lands. In 954, up to 100,000 Magyars attacked deep into Germany and France, taking advantage of the revolt of Lorraine against Otto the Great, Henry's son. They made a huge pillaging sweep through France and into northern Italy and back to the Danube Valley, but Otto defeated them the following year at Lechfeld; after that, the Magyars were on the decline.

At home in Hungary, they settled down to a more stable and civilized lifestyle under the leadership of Duke Geyza in the 970s. Christianity replaced their Asiatic animistic and totemic beliefs, and they began showing a toleration and acceptance of other cultures. King Stephen (997–1038) defended his homeland from takeover by the Holy Roman Empire and acquired authority from the pope over a national church. Stephen oversaw the construction of monasteries and cathedrals, and for his efforts and example was later canonized. The Magyar language became, and remains, the official language of Hungary; but for the

Under the leadership of Arpad the Magyars conquered Hungary.

battle at Lechfeld, it might have become the language of much of western Europe. For all their terrorism of the West, the Hungarians nevertheless defended western Europe from the Ottoman Turks as they fought to bring down the Byzantine Empire and expand the Muslim faith into Europe.

See also Bulgars; Byzantine Empire; Carolingian Dynasty; Europe, Mongol Invasion of; Huns; Ottoman Empire.

References: Bartha, Antal, *Hungarian Society in the 9th and 10th Centuries*, trans. K. Baazs (Budapest: Akademiai Kiado, 1975); Macartney, C. A., *The Magyars in the Ninth Century* (Cambridge: Cambridge University Press, 1968); Vambery, Arminius, *Hungary in Ancient, Medieval, and Modern Times* (Hallandale, FL: New World Books, 1972).

64   MALI, EXPANSION OF

By the beginning of the thirteenth century, the large gold-producing nation of Ghana had lost its power. Islamic attack by the nomadic Almoravids from the Sahara had devastated Ghana's main trading centers, and tribes previously under Ghana's dominance began to exert their independence. The Soso tribe was influential for a few decades, but ultimately they fell to the growing power of Mali.

Sundiata, leader of the Malinke clan of Mali, came to power in 1230. The Malinke were originally pagan, but saw the economic potential of Islam. Embracing the faith would not only give them equality with Arabic traders, but it would also lessen the chance of being attacked by aggressive Muslims such as the Almoravids. Thus, Malian traders spread Islam in their travels. Also, Sundiata and his successor mansas, or emperors, attempted to impose military dominance in order to maintain peace on their own terms, a peace that would be beneficial to trade. The empire of Mali claimed descent from Muslim roots, as did most of the West African nations that embraced the religion. Most claimed descent from white forebears, but Mali claimed Negroid descent: Bilali Bunama (Bilal ibn Rabah in Arabic) was Muhammad's first muezzin, and his grandson supposedly settled in the territory that became Mali, establishing power from the Niger to the Sankarani River.

Sundiata was the earliest recorded leader, using military ability to bring area tribes under his direction and establish a capital city at Niani on the Niger River. Niani was well placed for defense and trade, amidst good farmland and iron deposits. As the Mali came to control territory previously dominated by Ghana, they grew in influence and replaced Ghana as the main producer and distributor of gold.

A succession of leaders of irregular quality managed to maintain dominance in the area, but the strongest and best known, Mansa Musa, emerged in 1312. His 25-year tenure was widely reported and praised by contemporary Muslim writers. He became famous for making the pilgrimage to Mecca in 1324 and spending incredible amounts of gold along the way. He also extended the power of the empire by bringing the town of Timbuktu under Mali's control, turning it into the major trade and intellectual center it would remain for generations. Mansa Musa was followed by Mansa Sulayman, who maintained strong contacts with powers as far away as Morocco.

Under the strong leadership of Sundiata and Musa, Mali extended its influence from the Niger River in the east to the Atlantic Ocean in the west. Its power was based on cooperation of vassal kings and chieftains rather than on military control. However, after Mansa Musa's reign,

a series of weaker kings and internal power struggles brought a lack of direction at the top, and former vassals began to break away from the empire. In the 1400s, Berbers from the north conquered the upper reaches of Mali's empire, and the trade centers of Timbuktu and Walata fell under nomadic control. Malian emperors lost their power to internal dissent and the rising power of Songhay to the west.

See also Ghana, Almoravid Invasion of Songhay, Expansion of.

References: Hiskett, M., and Nehemia Levtzion, *Ancient Ghana and Mali* (London: Methuen, 1973); Oliver, Roland, *A Short History of Africa* (New York: New York University Press, 1962); Trimingham, John, *A History of Islam in West Africa* (London: Oxford University Press, 1970).

65 MEXICO, AZTEC CONQUEST OF

Much of Central America was dominated by the Toltec peoples until their dissolution about 1200 C.E. The power vacuum that followed coincided with the arrival of nomadic tribes from the north. One tribe came to be known as Aztecs, or People from Aztlan. They drifted into the valley of central Mexico and became subject to whichever power was able to achieve temporary hegemony. The Aztecs ultimately settled on the western side of Lake Texcoco, where they adapted themselves to the already established practice of building "floating gardens" of built-up silt. They established the city of Tenochtitlan in the mid-fourteenth century; a second city, Tlatelolco, was built by a second Aztec faction. The two cities put themselves under the protection of rival powers: Tenochtitlan under Culhuacan, Tlatelolco under the Tepanecs.

Through the later part of the fourteenth century, the Tepanecs dominated the valley, and expanded their power across the mountains to the west to encompass an area of perhaps 50,000 square kilometers. This consolidation was performed by the Tepanec king Tezozomoc, but after his death in 1423, the various city-states began to rebel. Three powers—one of them the Aztecs of Tenochtitlan—joined in a Triple Alliance to replace the Tepanecs. Despite the occasional disagreement, the three worked fairly well together and dominated central Mexico for 90 years. From 1431 to 1465 they consolidated their hold over the former Tepanec domain, then began a period of expansion. The Aztecs became the dominant partner in the triumvirate, but the three tribes collectively spread the empire from the Atlantic to the Pacific and as far south as the modern-day border between Mexico and Guatemala. Only two tribes remained recalcitrant, and the Aztecs established garrisons along disputed borders. Though they occasionally warred with the Tlaxaltecs and the Tarascans, they never subjugated them.

The Aztecs led the expansion for a number of reasons. Primarily, they wanted to expand their trading routes and incorporate a larger tax base among the conquered peoples. They also fought for religious reasons. The Aztecs worshipped, among others, the god of the sun, Huitzilopochtli. The Aztec religion taught that history moved in cycles, the end of each marked by the destruction of the sun. To keep healthy and shining, the god required sacrifices to eat, and the Aztecs went conquering for sacrificial offerings. The pyramids dominating the city of Tenochtitlan were large altars where prisoners of war were executed daily. On days of special celebration, several thousand would be sacrificed. This need for offerings drove the Aztecs to conquest, but did not encourage loyal subjects.

Once in control of their empire, the Aztecs expanded and beautified Tenochtitlan. The city reached a population of perhaps 200,000, possibly one-fifth of the Aztec population; the total number of subject peoples is estimated to have augmented the empire's population to six million. The capital city was laid out in logical order with straight streets and many canals, along which trade moved by boat. When Montezuma II came to power in 1502, the Aztec empire was well established, and he was responsible for much of the city's lavish architecture and decoration. Their sister-city, Tlatelolco, which they took under their control in 1475, became a commercial center with the largest market in Central America. The Spaniards under Hernan Cortes estimated that 60,000 people attended the market days.

The constant need for sacrificial victims created a resentment among all the subject peoples, however, and when the Spaniards arrived, they easily gained allies to assist in their attacks on the Aztec Empire. Though the Aztecs were in many ways more advanced than the Europeans, they lacked the necessary weaponry and resistance to foreign diseases to defeat their invaders. They had created outstanding works of art and developed an extensive hieroglyphic writing system, but their scientific knowledge was limited. Even without the arrival of the Spaniards, it is questionable how much longer the tribes of Central America would have accepted the military dominance and religious practices of the Aztecs.

See also Cortes, Hernan; Western Hemisphere, Spanish Occupation of.

References: Berdan, Frances, *The Aztecs of Central Mexico* (New York: Holt, Rinehart & Winston, 1981); Canasco, David, *Moctezuma's Mexico* (Niwot: University Press of Colorado, 1992); Henderson, Keith, *The Fall of the Aztec Empire* (Denver: Denver Museum of Natural History, 1993).

MIDDLE EAST, MONGOL INVASION OF THE

66

In 1219, the Mongols under Genghis Khan had spread their influence as far as the Caspian Sea. The shah of Khwarezm offended the Great Khan by declining to extradite one of his governors for the death of two Mongol merchants. His refusal provoked an invasion and the destruction of Khwarezm, and led to the Mongol onslaught of the Middle East. Four Mongol armies engaged in the punishment: Genghis led one army that burned Bokhara, Samarkand, and Balkh; his son Juchi defeated the shah's forces at Jand, reportedly killing 160,000 men in the victory; another son, Jagatai, captured and sacked Otrar; yet another son, Tule, led 70,000 men through Khorasan and pillaged everywhere he went. All the armies proceeded undefeated, capturing and despoiling Merv, Nishapur, Rayy, and Herat.

Genghis returned to Mongolia, but the steppe horsemen stayed. After Genghis's death, his successor, Ogadai, sent 300,000 men to put down a rebellion launched by Jalal ud-Din. Ogadai was victorious at Diarbekr in northern Persia, and in the wake of their victory, the Mongols proceeded to pillage Armenia, Georgia, and Upper Mesopotamia. In 1234, Genghis's grandson Hulagu led a force into Iran to defeat the Assassins at Alamut, then turned his men toward Baghdad. Though Hulagu was a Buddhist, his primary wife was a Christian, and he carried on his grandfather's policy of religious toleration. Therefore, his attack on Baghdad was intent on conquest, not religious persecution.

Hulagu drew on the assistance of troops from the Golden Horde to capture Baghdad. Caliph Al-Mustasim Billah refused to offer allegiance to Hulagu; he also failed to heed his generals' warnings to strengthen the city's weakened walls and military. The caliph depended on his position to draw sufficient defensive manpower, but that prestige had long ago faded. He was forced to choose between the Mongols and the Mamluks, slave-soldiers who had come to power in Egypt and whom he had long scorned. Too late, he looked to his city's defenses; in 1258 the Mongols breached the walls and spent eight days sacking the city. Baghdad lost most of its several hundred thousand inhabitants, as well as its libraries, universities, mosques, and treasures. Never again would it serve as the intellectual capital of Islam.

The destruction of Baghdad had a religious significance Hulagu never intended. On the one hand, his Christian wife urged him to ally himself with the Crusaders based in Syria. On the other hand, his relative Birkai, chief of the Golden Horde, had converted to Islam and refused to aid him any longer; indeed, he offered aid to the Mamluks of Egypt in an Islamic coalition. With Crusader assistance, Hulagu took Aleppo and Damascus and was aiming for Jerusalem when news came to him that changed the fate of the Middle East. The Great Khan Mangku had died, and it was Hulagu's duty to return to Mongolia. Though advised to the contrary by his wife, generals, and the Crusaders, Hulagu left for home. He left behind a contingent under Kit-Boga.

In Egypt, the new sultan, Kotuz, and his brilliant general, Baibars, had been preparing for battle. They took advantage of Hulagu's withdrawal and marched toward Syria. Kit-Boga advanced to meet them and the two forces converged on the Plains of Esdraelon at Ain Jalut (Goliath's Well). The outnumbered Mongols fell to Baibars's Mamluks, who used Mongol tactics to defeat the invaders. Hulagu decided to turn around and avenge Kit-Boga's death, but the Golden Horde now presented a threat to his rear. He marched into Russia instead, surprising his kinsmen at the River Terek in the winter of 1262. The two forces fought each other almost to exhaustion, but neither was able to gain the upper hand. Hulagu retreated to Persia and hoped to rekindle his alliance with the Crusaders, but his death in 1264 ended that plan. His son Abaka marched for Egypt in 1281, but was met in Syria and defeated by Kalawun, Baibars's sucessor, at the battle of Horns. The Mongols retreated across the Euphrates and established the dynasty of the Il-khans.

Hulagu's descendants ruled in Persia and Mesopotamia until 1337. The greatest of his successors was Ghazan Khan, who broke with the Great Khan Kubilai of China. He established the capital of his independent state at Tabriz, where he received envoys from as far away as Spain and England. He ruled wisely and well, stabilizing the currency, protecting the peasants, and building the city into a showpiece that rivaled Baghdad. He built mosques (the Il-khans converted to Islam in 1294), schools, an observatory, a library, and a hospital, then set aside the tax revenue from certain pieces of land to finance these institutions. Travelers passing through Tabriz (including Marco Polo) noted its magnificence, and some estimated its population at one million. Ghazan's brother Uljaitu followed as leader of the Il-khans and patron of the arts and sciences. Literature, art, and architecture reached new heights during his reign. His successor, Abu Sa'id, proved to be the last ruler of a short-lived dynasty. After his death in 1335, factional fighting weakened the regime, making it easy prey for Tamurlane's forces in 1381.

The Mongol invasion of the Middle East was relatively short, the actual fighting taking place over approximately four decades. It proved decisive in confirming the Muslims as the dominant influence in the region, because the Mongols and Crusaders never cooperated as fully as they might have. Kit-Boga's defeat at Goliath's Well, though a relatively small battle, proved to be the Middle Eastern version of the Muslim defeat at Poitiers. Just as Christian Europe had held back the forces of Islam, so Muslim Egypt turned away the forces that could have ended their hold on the Middle East, possibly driving them back to the deserts of Arabia and the Sahara. The Mongols exercised the well-known tactics of destruction and terror, killing hundreds of thousands of people and destroying much of Islam's literature and scientific writings, though the Il-khans strove to renew that intellectual atmosphere during their short dynasty.

See also Genghis Khan; Russia, Mongol Conquest of; Tamurlane.

References: Allsen, Thomas, *Mongol Imperialism* (Berkeley: University of California Press, 1987); Chambers, James, *The Devil's Horsemen* (New York: Atheneum, 1979); Lamb, Harold, *The March of the Barbarians* (New York: Literary Guild, 1940).

MIDDLE EAST, MUSLIM CONQUEST OF THE

67

Muhammad led his followers to control of the cities of Mecca and Medina, which in turn dominated the area known as the Hejaz, along the Red Sea's eastern coast. His charisma held the faithful together, but upon his death, many of the Arab tribes who had followed him proved to be less than faithful. Without a clear successor, the tribes fell back into their independent raiding ways. When Abu-Bakr rose to the position of caliph, the successor to Muhammad's political power, he embarked on a war to force the tribes back under one banner. Abu-Bakr knew that the ways of the Bedouin—raiding and plunder—must be rechanneled because Islam forbade fighting among believers. Therefore, they must find nonbelievers to attack.

Abu-Bakr challenged the authority of the Byzantine Empire in Palestine. He sent his best general, Khalid, on raiding parties that ultimately joined together to defeat a larger Byzantine force at Ajnadain between Jerusalem and Gaza on 30 July 634.

Abu-Bakr's successor, Umar (Omar, 634–644), captured Jerusalem. He then sent forces in all directions to challenge both Constantinople's power and that of the Sassanid dynasty of Persia. Again Khalid was successful, taking Damascus by treachery in 635 and occupying Emesa (modern Horns) by the end of that year. He ceded the city back to a 50,000-man Byzantine army the following spring, then outmaneuvered and annihilated them in August 636. The Byzantine forces, though twice the size of Khalid's, had to deal with a hostile population made angry by years of taxation and religious persecution. Though not Muslim themselves, the people welcomed the invaders as liberators from the repression of Constantinople. This repression, coupled with the fact that the Byzantine Empire had been fighting itself to exhaustion against the Sassanid Persians, made it easy prey.

The Sassanids were just as disliked among their subject peoples, and the Muslim invasion brought about that dynasty's swift downfall. They lost their first battle to Muslim invaders in the autumn of 635, and within two years the Muslim forces controlled the Persian capital at Ctesiphon, then Mesopotamia and Irak. The eastern Muslim forces under Said ibn Wakkas drove farther, taking the ancient Persian capital of Ecbatana in 641, controlling the Persian Gulf by 645, and occupying Khorasanby in 652.

At the same time, a third Muslim force, under Amr ibn al-As, captured Egypt. Amr defeated the Byzantine defenders at Heliopolis in 640 and received Alexandria's surrender to terms in 642. To give themselves a buffer zone, the Muslims spread through Cyrenaica along the Mediterranean coast. Several decades later, they pushed farther along the coast, capturing Carthage in 695 and bringing to an end the last of Roman influence in North Africa. Alliances with the local Berber tribes gave them the impetus to reach the Atlantic and turn north into Europe.

These events occurred during the Umayyid dynasty, which lasted until 750. The ultimate goal of the Muslims was not the plunder of nonbelievers (though they certainly engaged in it), but the capture of Constantinople itself—a dream this dynasty, and others, would not live to see. Umar's successor, Uthman (Oth-man,

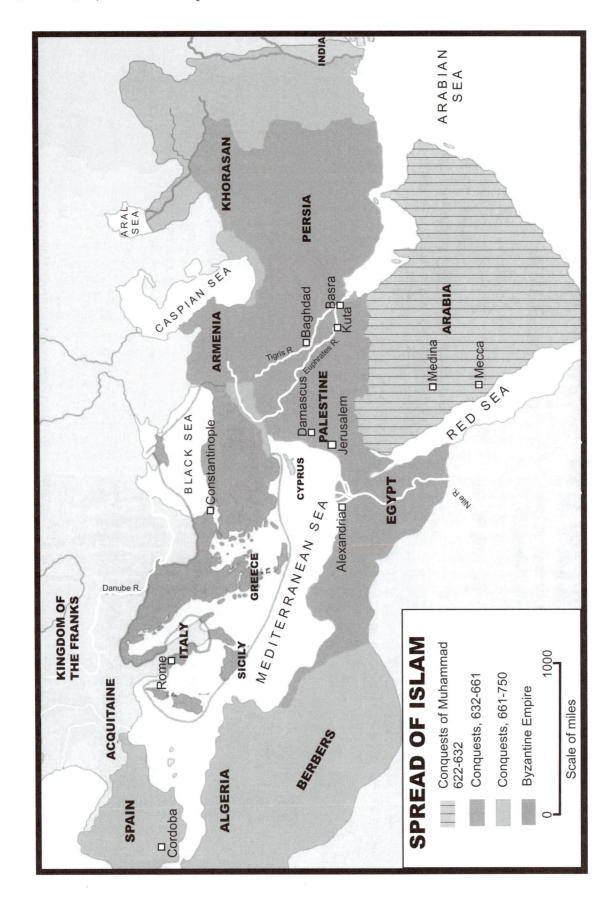

ARABIAN SEA

INDIA

KHORASAN

ARAL SEA

PERSIA

CASPIAN SEA

ARMENIA

Baghdad

Basra

Kuta

ARABIA

Tigris R.

Euphrates R.

Medina

Mecca

BLACK SEA

Damascus

PALESTINE

Constantinople

Jerusalem

RED SEA

CYPRUS

EGYPT

Nile R.

Alexandria

Danube R.

GREECE

MEDITERRANEAN SEA

KINGDOM OF THE FRANKS

ITALY

Rome

SICILY

ACQUITAINE

BERBERS

SPAIN

ALGERIA

Cordoba

SPREAD OF ISLAM

Conquests of Muhammad 622-632

Conquests, 632-661

Conquests, 661-750

Byzantine Empire

Scale of miles

0   1000

644–656), tried it first in 655. His early naval success came to naught when he was assassinated a year later. After some factional struggles among the Muslim leadership, which included an armistice while the question of succession was argued, the Umayyids returned under Muawiya in 668. He crossed into Thrace and attacked from the landward side, but did not lay siege. An attempt to forge the straits and control the Bosporus failed in 677; afterward, Constantinople suffered only intermittent raiding, though the reach of the Byzantine Empire was much diminished. Caliph Walid tried again in 715, by which time Muslim armies had reached India and the borders of China. He died in the attempt, and the next caliph, Suleiman, did not succeed either. After a yearlong siege, the Muslims were defeated by Byzantine naval forces at sea and by Bulgar allies operating in the Balkans. That, and the threat of Franks arriving from farther west, convinced Suleiman to withdraw. A storm wrecked the remains of his fleet, and Muslim sea power was destroyed; their troop losses are estimated at 170,000. The Byzantine Emperor Leo III saved eastern Europe from Muslim domination, and after another victory in 739, regained control of western Asia Minor. This stand, coupled with the defeat of the Muslims at Tours in France in 732, kept Europe Christian.

For a few centuries, the Muslims consolidated their hold rather than extended it, other than the occasional independent actions such as the entry into India. In all their Middle East conquests, they benefited from a weakening of their rivals' military power as well as the aid rendered by disgruntled subjects. The Muslims had a reputation as conquerors of forcing their faith on the defeated, but this happened only occasionally. For the most part, Muslim rulers followed Muhammad's dictates to respect the rights of other faiths. The levying of a tax on nonbelievers, however, encouraged many of the poor to convert and began the long history of Islamic faith in that part of the world. Also, the Arabic language became widely used, replacing the Koine Greek or Aramaic spoken for centuries. The Muslims fought among themselves for centuries over Muhammad's true successor, and to this day various factions, most notably the Shi'ites and Sunnis, claim authority from one or another of the original converts or family members. Occasional conquerors would pass through the Middle East in centuries to come, but none was able to dissuade the inhabitants from their adopted religion. Islam's homeland may not always have been militarily secure, but no one was able to shake the security of their faith.

See also Byzantine Empire; India, Muslim Invasion of; Middle East, Mongol Invasion of the; Spain, Muslim Conquest of; Tamurlane.

References: Armstrong, Karen, *Holy War* (New York: Macmillan, 1988); Koprulu, Mehmed Fuad, *Islam in Turkey after the Turkish Invasion* (Salt Lake City: University of Utah Press, 1993); Serjeant, R. B., *Studies in Arabian History and Civilisation* (London: Variorum Reprints, 1981).

68   MING DYNASTY

Under the Yuan dynasty, the Mongols ruled China and established extensive contacts with the West. Trade along the Silk Road was brisk, and Christian monks traveled to spread their faith. They found a rich culture that the Mongols had appropriated for themselves, but one that they never completely assimilated. After the death of the great Kubilai Khan in 1297, no other leader could match his ability, and the dynasty weakened. In the middle 1300s, a group called the Red Turbans attacked the Mongols. That assault, coupled with decades of mistreatment of the Chinese peasants, led to a peasant rebellion that ultimately overthrew the Mongols. The leader of this rebellion and the first emperor of the newly established Ming dynasty was Chu Yuanchang, a former Buddhist novice.

Chu established the capital of the new dynasty at Nanjing in 1368. Despite his early Buddhist training, Chu was a ruthless emperor who strove to reestablish Chinese traditions in the wake of Mongol rule. He also set about reestablishing China's suzerainty over its neighbors. Within 10 years, the Chinese court was receiving tribute from Okinawa, Borneo, the Malay Peninsula, Java, and the Indian coast, and had set up trade contacts with those countries as well as Japan and the Middle East.

The next Ming emperor of note was Yong Le. He not only maintained China's military position, but extended the empire's strength to include a powerful navy. Between 1405 and 1433, Admiral Zheng He, a eunuch of Muslim descent, led seven expeditions that reached as far as Persia, Arabia, and eastern Africa. With a fleet of 62 ships and as many as 28,000 men, they were a feared organization throughout the China Sea and the Indian Ocean. Their captains demonstrated organiza-tional and navigational skills unmatched until the arrival of the Portuguese in the 1500s.

The Chinese military was used mainly to protect the borders and enforce the will of the emperors upon their subjects. Chu persecuted the remaining Mongols in China and forced them to marry Chinese people rather than their own, for he would not allow purely foreign groups to exist and create trouble from within. After total control was established, arts and

culture once again began to flourish, financed by the income from the far-flung Chinese traders. The famous Ming porcelains were developed in this era, and the construction of palaces in Nanjing, and later Beijing, reflected the Ming desire to reassert Chinese culture. Science and technology had few advances, but literature and philosophy experienced a renaissance.

The later Ming rulers proved less and less capable. The growing power of the Jur-chen and Manchu tribes in the northeast threatened those frontiers, while peasant uprisings in the northwest kept the army busy in that sector. A Japanese invasion of Korea in the 1590s brought Chinese armies into Manchuria, where they were weakened in a victorious war that forced a Japanese withdrawal. The Manchus now had the impetus to conquer Korea and, with their rear protected, make war against the Ming. The cost of war could not be paid because the peasant taxpayers were in revolt, so Ming power slipped. The final Ming emperor hanged himself in 1644, and the invaders established the Ching (Manchu) dynasty.

See also Ching (Manchu) Dynasty; Kubilai Khan.

References: Hucker, Charles, *The Ming Dynasty: Its Origins and Evolving Institutions* (Ann Arbor: University of Michigan Press, 1978); Spence, Jonathan, ed., *From Ming to Ching* (New Haven, CT Yale University Press, 1979); Tong, James, *Disorder under Heaven* (Stanford, CA: Stanford University Press, 1991).

69   OSTROGOTHS

The Goths were a Germanic tribe who possibly came from Sweden in the early centuries C.E. By the third century, they had come into contact with the Roman Empire and often clashed with Roman armies on the northern and northeastern frontiers. They arrived in the region of the lower Danube River, and from there plundered the Balkans and Greece. At the height of their powers, they controlled the lands from the Black Sea to the Baltic Sea. In about 370 C.E., the Goths split into two nations: The eastern Ostrogoths were based in the Black Sea area into modern Ukraine and Byelorussia, while the western Visigoths inhabited the Danube Valley.

The Ostrogoths were among the first in Europe to feel the wrath of the Huns. By force or circumstance, they fought alongside the Huns, especially Attila, during the Hunnish invasion of Gaul in 451. They were obliged to fight their Visigothic kinsmen, who were allied with Rome, but after the Hun defeat at Chalons, the Ostrogoths exerted their independence. They agreed with the Roman Empire to settle into Pannonia, an area roughly equivalent to parts of modern Austria, Hungary, and Slovenia. While settled here, the greatest of the Ostrogothic kings, Theodoric, came to power. He allied his people with the Eastern Roman Empire, especially the emperor Zeno, and with Constantinople's support, the Ostrogoths invaded Italy in 488. The Ostrogoths defeated Odoacer, the first Germanic ruler of Italy, in a number of battles. They finally captured Odoacer's capital at Ravenna, after which Theodoric murdered him and took his place as ruler of Italy.

Though he was not officially given the title of Western Roman Emperor, Theodoric surely exercised the power of an emperor. Under his rule of 33 years, the Gothic kingdom in Italy recovered much of its lost productivity and culture. Raised in captivity in Constantinople, Theodoric appreciated the finer points of Roman culture and brought Roman ways to his people. He practiced Arian Christianity, considered heresy by both the Roman Church and the Eastern Church, but he was tolerant of all beliefs in his realm. Roman law was the basis of the Italian state, but traditional Gothic laws also applied to Goths in Italy. Theodoric's rule was peaceful and progressive, but his death in 526 marked the beginning of the decline of the Ostrogoths. The growing military power, ambition, and religious intolerance of Emperor Justinian in Constantinople spelled doom for Gothic peace. Eastern Empire armies under the command of Belisarius destroyed the Ostrogoths' power, which finally broke apart. They were absorbed by other tribes who established power in northern Italy, mainly the Franks and Burgundians. They absorbed more Roman culture than they imparted characteristics of their own, so little of Gothic society remained after their demise.

See also Huns; Justinian; Visigoths.

References; Cunliffe, Barry, *Rome and Her Empire* (London: Constable, 1994 [1978]); Heather, Peter, *Goths and Romans* (Oxford: Clarendon, 1991); Thompson, E. A., *Romans and Barbarians* (Madison: University of Wisconsin Press, 1982).

70   RUSSIA, ESTABLISHMENT AND EXPANSION OF

Russia's first political foundations lay deep in myth. Vikings, or Varangians, had alternately traded with and plundered the area east of the Baltic coast since the middle 700s, occasionally staying long enough to establish settlements and exact tribute from local tribes. By the middle 800s they were forced out of the area of the upper Volga and Neva rivers by the Slavic tribes they had once subdued. According to the traditions of the Russian Chronicle, the tribes fought among themselves until they jointly agreed to bring in an outside ruler. They asked the Swedish tribe of Rus, or Rhos, to rule over the tribes and protect them from their enemies. The family of Rurik accepted and, with his two brothers, he moved the Rus tribe to the Neva River area. He established himself in Novgorod in 862, placing his brothers in charge of Beloozero and Izborsk. When they died, Rurik took control over the entire area, and his descendants ruled for generations. From them comes the title Russia.

Being Vikings, the Rus continued their practice of trading and plundering, at the same time defending their new subjects from the Bulgars and the Khazars, who lived above the Caspian Sea between the Volga and Dnieper rivers. At times the Russians grew strong or bold enough to approach Constantinople, sometimes in peace and other times as invaders. They made little progress in their military expeditions against the Byzantine Empire, but they succeeded in carrying on a profitable trade in their more peaceful endeavors. They also managed to successfully defend their territory from invaders, both the aggressive Khazars and the raiding Petchenegs, and succeeded in completely driving the Bulgars from their frontiers into eastern Europe. It remains debatable just how well the Russians were organized at this time; some say that they had

established a state, others that they were merely a strong group of warrior chiefs under the leadership of an overlord. The latter seems more likely.

The matter of defense probably took the Rus from their original base at Novgorod to Kiev. The Chronicle relates that two of Rurik's subordinates, Askold and Dir, captured Kiev from Slavic tribes to expand both their defensive perimeter and trade routes. It seems likely that, in the wake of the collapse of the Khazars in the eleventh century and the arrival of the Petchenegs from farther east, the Slavic tribes came together under Rus leadership to provide a more solid defensive stance. For three centuries Kiev played the key role of defensive outpost and vital trading center on the route to Constantinople. Through the 900s the Rus had a trade agreement with Constantinople, but they also sent a number of military expeditions against Constantinople as well, maintaining the seemingly traditional Viking link between trade and plunder. In the meanwhile, the Rus dominated the Slavic tribes, forcing them either into slavery or to the status of tributary, the main tribute being paid in kind or in Arabic coinage. Sometime in the tenth century, the Russians embraced the Eastern Orthodox faith; it was named the state religion by Vladimir I (978–1015), who was later sanctified.

Throughout the tenth century, Kiev was the dominant city-state, if not the capital of a political entity. From there the "Grand Duke" held sway over the other dukes, or governors, who usually were his younger relatives. Thus, what passed for a Russian state was actually a large feudal arrangement based on the oldest male controlling Kiev and the others granting him the highest status.

Early in the eleventh century, feuding among successors brought about the end of Kiev's preeminent position. The Rus split into two more or less equal "states" along either side of the Dnieper, then were rejoined in 1035 under Yaroslav I, who made war against the Finns, Poles, and Petchenegs, and mounted the last (disastrous) expedition against Constantinople. On his deathbed, he willed the land of the Rus to his five sons and a grandson, directing them to aid one another and follow the lead of the eldest son in Kiev. Rather than continue the rule from Kiev as

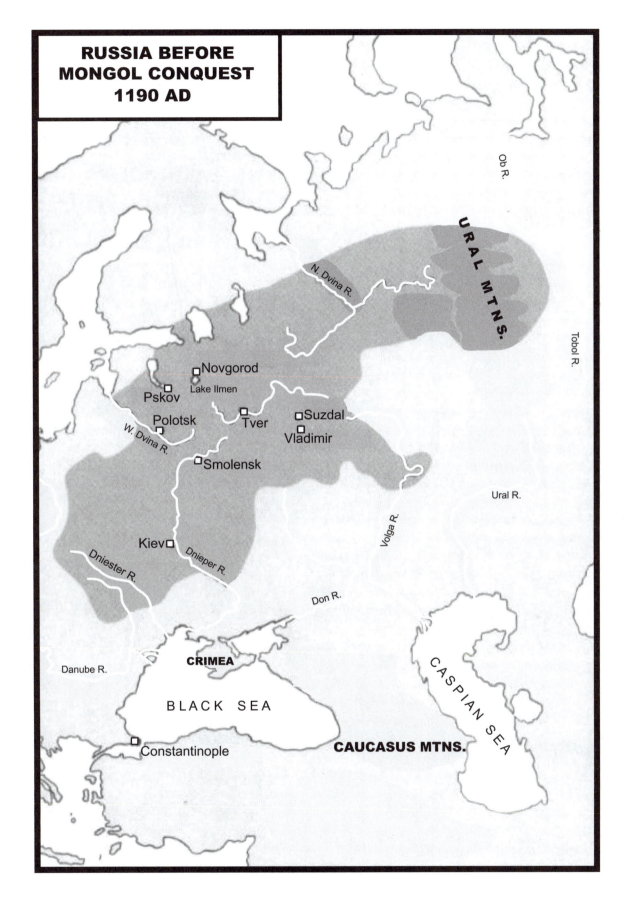

**EARLY MODERN RUSSIA
at accession of
Peter the Great
1689**

Ob. R.

URAL MTNS.

N. Dvina R.

Irtysh R.

Tobol. R.

□Novgorod
Pskov □
Lake Ilmen

□Kazan

W. Dvina R.

□Moscow

LITHUANIA

Ural R.

POLAND

Dniester R.

Kiev □
Dnieper R.

Volga R.

COSSACKS

Don R.

Astrakhan □

CRIMEA

Danube R.

CASPIAN SEA

BLACK SEA

CAUCASUS MTNS.

□Constantinople

Yaroslav had hoped, the brothers took a series of actions to break away from Kiev's domination. Over the next several decades the territories given to the sons became separate entities, often at odds with one another. By 1097, they were held together by a loose confederation bound only by promises to defend their lands from outside threats.

Yaroslav was the last of the strong Russian leaders until the rise of Ivan the Great in the mid-1400s. He was an effective ruler who codified Slavic law, built numerous churches, and sponsored the translation of religious literature from Greek to Slavic. He also established ties with western Europe by giving his daughter in marriage to King Henry I of France. Though the Rus had expanded from a Scandinavian tribe to an important population stretching from the Baltic to the Black seas, Yaroslav's legacy was the destruction of the feudal system, turning the Russians' somewhat unified culture into one of squabbling brothers and cousins who failed to defend their homeland from Petcheneg and Cuman nomadic raiders from the steppes and from the ultimate conquerors from the east, the Mongols.

See also Byzantine Empire; Russia, Mongol Conquest of.

References: Carmichael, Joel, *A History of Russia* (New York: Hippocrene Books, 1990); Chirovsky, Nicholas, *A History of the Russian Empire* (New York: Philosophical Library, 1973); Florinsky, Michael, *Russia: A History and an Interpretation* (New York: Macmillan, 1947).

RUSSIA, MONGOL CONQUEST OF

71

During the time of Genghis Khan, his general Subedai rode westward in a reconnaissance force to scout the steppes of southern Russia. Subedai and Jebe Noyan, another general, roamed over the vast plains west of the Volga, searching for possible invasion routes and testing the mettle of the inhabitants. Their main opponent was the Cumans, Turkic-Mongols who had moved to the area from central Asia some centuries before. The Cumans had established themselves as bandits and pillagers throughout the area north of the Black Sea, making themselves enemies of the Russian principalities. Only after the Cumans had been sorely defeated and forced to retreat into Russian lands did the Russian princes reluctantly join with them to resist the Mongols, or Tartars (Tatars), as the Russians called them. In 1223 the combined Russo-Cuman force was defeated at the Kalka River along the northern shore of the Black Sea, but the Mongols did not follow up on their victory; instead, they joined with Genghis's son Jochi, and returned to report to their leader. The invasion seemed like a bad dream to the Russians, who prayed that the Mongols would prove to be no more than passing raiders.

After attacking and destroying the Bulgars at the junction of the Volga and Kama rivers in 1236, the Mongols returned to the trans-Volga steppes. This time they came not as raiders but as invaders, because the entire tribe of Genghis's heir Batu migrated into the area. It is questionable whether any Russian defensive measures could have halted the Mongol onslaught, but it certainly could not be stopped by the divided, squabbling nobles who inhabited the Russian principalities.

The Mongols crossed the Volga in late 1237 and entered the state of Riazan. They made their way easily across the territory, capturing land and burning cities. By 1239 they had defeated the major noble in the area, Yuri of Vladimir, and seemed to be taking aim at the city of Novgorod. Instead, they turned back onto their invasion path and moved southeast to the territory of the Cumans, whom they again defeated and now drove into Hungary. With a secure flank on the Black Sea, the Mongols drove on to Kiev, capturing the city in December 1240. The Russian princes would not cooperate with each other, even with much of their land under foreign control, so Batu drove his forces into Poland and Hungary. He returned to Russia in 1241, possibly on news of the death of Ogadai, the Great Khan who succeeded Genghis.

Batu settled into Russia, creating what came to be known as the Khanate of the Golden Horde. He established the city of Sarai as his capital, and for the next 200 years the Mongols dominated Russia. The princes of Russia became his vassals, and none could rule without Mongol permission. The settling of the Mongols into one place, however, diminished their traditional warlike manner, and they soon began to act more like the Russian nobles, arguing over succession and wealth. The

Russian princes, bound by their oaths to provide taxes for the Mongol overlords, soon got the job of collecting it themselves; they jockeyed for favor in the Mongol court by promising higher tax revenue in return for political appointments. Of course, this meant more suffering for the peasants paying the taxes to keep their prince in the good graces of the Mongols. The Russians paid nominal service to the Mongols, occasionally revolting but always finding a Mongol army in response. Between 1236 and 1462, the Mongols made 48 military expeditions into Russian lands, either to put down rebellions or to aid one Russian faction vying with another. In all that time, only once did the Russians score a major victory.

In the mid-thirteenth century, the Golden Horde assisted some of its Mongol brethren in an assault on the Islamic Middle East. Genghis's grandson Hulagu led his forces against the Muslims in Mesopotamia, capturing and sacking Baghdad in 1258. He killed most of the city's inhabitants and destroyed its mosques and libraries, bringing to an end Baghdad's reign as the intellectual capital of Islam. His treatment of the caliph, however, offended the Golden Horde's Muslim ruler, Birkai. He withdrew his support and, after Hulagu had allied himself with the Crusader armies, Birkai offered an alliance to the Mamluks defending Syria and Egypt. That threat to Hulagu's rear while facing Muslim forces under the brilliant general Baibars gave Hulagu too many enemies. After the defeat of one of his contingents by the Mamluks, Hulagu retreated across the Euphrates and ended his quest for Egypt and his ties to his cousin in Sarai.

Ultimately bringing the Golden Horde to its demise was the fate suffered by so many conquerors: They lost their fighting edge by easy living and personal greed. They took advantage of their position to profit from the Asian trade with Europe, dealing in silks, carpets, and wine from Persia and China; furs from Russia; jewels from India; and their own horses and leather goods. After the Golden Horde broke from the control of Mongolia in the later part of the fourteenth century, they spent much of their time in court intrigues. Other, more vigorous nomads wreaked havoc on the sedentary Mongols when Tamurlane's invasion in 1395 destroyed the capital city of Sarai. The Golden Horde split into two factions in the middle 1400s, creating the Kazan Mongols along the upper Volga and the Crimean Mongols around the Black Sea. That split so dissipated the military power of the Mongols that Russians under the leadership of Muscovy finally defeated the Mongols and reestablished Russian independence.

See also Genghis Khan; Middle East, Mongol Invasion of the; Tamurlane.

References: Chambers, James, *The Devil's Horsemen* (New York: Atheneum, 1979); Florinsky, Michael, *Russia: A History and an Interpretation, 2 vols.* (Toronto: Collier-Macmillan Canada, 1947); Saunders, J. J., *The History of the Mongol Conquests* (New York: Barnes & Noble, 1971).

SCOTLAND, ENGLISH CONQUEST OF

72

Relations between the northern and southern neighbors of the island of Britain have always been tense. In 1138 and 1149, the king of Scotland tried to gain land at English expense, but in failing to do so, lost the province of Northumbria to the English. The Scots tried to regain the land under William the Lionhearted in 1165 by aiding a rebellion against Henry II. When that failed as well, William was forced to sign the Treaty of Falaise, wherein Scotland swore loyalty to England. The Scots were released from that treaty in the reign of Richard I, who received in return 15,000 marks of silver, roughly equivalent to one-fifth of the annual English royal revenue.

Relative peace reigned for a century, but in the 1280s the Scots began chafing at English dominance. Alexander III of Scotland died in 1286, leaving his daughter as heir to the throne. When she died childless, the line came to an end and various claimants scrambled for the throne. Edward I of England stepped in to support the claim of John de Baliol, who was crowned in 1292. The country became divided: One group of nobles recognized English suzerainty, while another group, supported by the common people, resented English interference. After meeting constant demands to provide soldiers for wars against France, Baliol succumbed to the popular will in 1295 and allied Scotland with France, hoping to gain total Scottish independence. Again the Scots backed the losing side, and England's military occupied Scotland after the battle of Dunbar in 1296, annexing it to their own domain.

Soon Scottish forces under William Wallace rose up against the English, winning at Stirling Bridge in 1297 but losing the following year at Falkirk; Wallace was ultimately betrayed to the enemy. Robert Bruce came to the throne in 1307 and amassed forces to break away from England's power. Edward I died en route to fight him, and Robert was able to consolidate his power throughout Scotland by 1314. In that year, Edward II marched north to defeat at Bannockburn, and Scotland was freed from English overlordship. In 1328 Edward II of England signed the Treaty of Northampton, which recognized Scottish independence and Robert's throne.

Within five years there were challenges to the Scottish throne. John Baliol challenged David Bruce, and defeated David at Halidon Hill with the aid of England's Edward III. Many Scots rejected John for dealing so freely with the English, and two decades of unrest followed, with the French covertly aiding David's supporters. David invaded England in 1346, but lost and was taken captive; he was ransomed in 1357 and ascended the Scottish throne, ruling until 1371.

The Bruce line ran out rather quickly, ending with Robert's grandson, and was followed by the Stuart line. The Scots fought among themselves and against the English for decades. In 1502, the two peoples tried to ease the tensions between them through marriage, when James IV married Henry VII's daughter Margaret the following year. This laid the groundwork for the union of the two nations under one monarch, but not as the English had intended. When Elizabeth I died childless in 1603, James VI of Scotland was the closest blood relative, and he ascended the throne of England, taking the name James I. Relations between the two nations grew somewhat closer, but both operated separate governments. James's son Charles I, however, returned the two peoples to hostility by taking stands more

to the liking of the English than the Scots. Scottish soldiers were ordered into combat in Europe during the Thirty Years' War at Charles's behest. He also alienated Parliament, which overthrew him in a civil war, bringing Oliver Cromwell to power in London. Cromwell exercised a tight rein on both English and Scottish subjects, and he temporarily united Scotland and England under one government. After his death, however, the new monarch, Charles II (another Stuart), could not keep the two countries together.

In 1707 the Scots finally agreed to join with England. They had accepted the kingship of William III of England, who reigned as William II of Scotland, 19 years earlier. For some years Scotland had suffered from severe weather and poor harvests, causing thousands of deaths and perhaps finally breaking the will to independence. The two nations signed the Act of Union, which allowed the Scots to maintain local laws and church policies, as well as have members in both houses in Parliament. The Scots also received equal trading rights. Under one crown since 1603, the two countries now came under one government.

Two fairly serious attempts were later made to exert Scottish dominance. With the aid of France, two Stuarts tried to restore their line. In 1715, the Jacobites failed to provide any successes for James Edward Stuart, and the death of Louis XIV in France ended any chance of worthwhile outside aid. In 1745, Prince Charles ("Bonny Prince Charlie") again tried to raise the Stuart standard and drew a fairly large number of Scottish supporters, but their defeat at Culloden in 1746 ended any further endeavors toward restoring Catholic Scottish rule.

Though it seemed a joining of equals in 1707, the English had almost always enjoyed the dominant position. They had been able to hold Scottish royalty hostage from time to time. For example, the first James Stuart was held by the British and sent to France; when he was later released, he had to pay 40,000 pounds sterling as the "cost of his education." The English also had long drawn on Scottish manpower for foreign wars, which weakened the ability of the northerners to rebel and laid for the London government the foundation of control. Scottish soldiers significantly influenced the history of the British Empire; a longstanding comment was, "There will always be an England (as long as you've got the Scots to do your fighting for you)." Even today, the union has its critics, and a Scottish secessionist movement occasionally tries to return the northern country to its old status.

See also Thirty Years' War.

References: Lee, Maurice, *Road to Revolution: Scotland under Charles I* (Urbana: University of Illinois Press, 1985); Levack, Brian, *The Formation of the British State* (Oxford: Clarendon, 1987); McKenzie, W. M., *Outline of Scottish History* (London: Adam & Charles Black, 1907).

73   SCYTHIANS

Most of the information available on the Scythians comes from the pen of Herodotus (of whom one must often be leery) and from modern archaeology and anthropology. They were an Indo-European tribe who made their way from central Asia into southern Russia in the eighth and seventh centuries B.C.E., though

Scythian horseman depicted on felt artifact.

some elements of their culture can be traced to Siberian tribes of the third millennium B.C.E. Centered in the steppes north of the Black Sea, the Scythians built an empire with an equally strong military and economic base. They inherited the territory from the Cimmerians and ultimately ceded it in the third century B.C.E. to the Sarmatians. All three cultures possibly were related; certainly they had many similarities. The Scythians fought the Cimmerians for 30 years before conquering them and taking their land.

The Scythians were fierce warriors whose organization in some ways presaged that of Genghis Khan. The king was the army's leader, and they were always prepared for battle. Most of their success came from their mastery of the horse, and their enemies usually could not match the Scythian mobility. The king provided only food and clothing; all other pay came in the form of booty, which the Scythian soldier could share in return for the head of an enemy. They wore bronze helmets of a Greek pattern and carried double-curved bows with trefoil arrows.

At their greatest penetration into the Middle East, the Scythians reached Egypt, but mainly they were penned into the steppes by the Persians. They fought the Persian king Darius I in 513 B.C.E., and held off his invasion of southern Russia. However, they could not hold off the Sarmatians in the third century. The two peoples had been clashing for decades along the Asia frontier; the Scythian military finally was defeated, but their economic legacy remained.

Though a minority, the Scythians ruled a vast territory. Their location made them middlemen for trade from Asia into eastern Europe and the Middle East. Apparently they were able businessmen, because the graves of their aristocrats held artwork and weaponry of gold and other precious metals. The graves also held the dead man's wife, household servants, and horses. Two types of artwork were discovered in their tombs: animal subjects, which they made themselves, and Greek objects gained through trade. Steppe art traditionally deals with animal subjects, and the portrayal of two animals fighting was a popular theme. The artwork was rarely large, for their nomadic ways never left them, and their imagery was usually carved into easily transportable items such as jewelry, weapons, and cups. The artwork in gold is regarded as excellent, and they also worked in wood, leather, bone, iron, and silver. The Scythians left a legacy of horsemanship, great warriors, well-stocked tombs, and fine artwork.

See also Genghis Khan.

References: Minns, Ellis, *Scythians and Greeks* (Cambridge: Cambridge University Press, 1913); Rostovtzeff, M., *Iranians and Greeks in Southern Russia* (New York: Russell & Russell, 1969); Tompkins, Stuart, *Russia through the Ages* (New York: Prentice-Hall, 1940).

SONGHAY, EXPANSION OF

74

The Songhay tribe apparently began about 670 C.E. along the eastern banks of the Niger River, where they established the two main population centers of Gao and Koukia. The leading family was of Berber extraction, and their line ruled the Songhay into the 1300s. In 1005, the current king, Kossi, converted to Islam; about the same time, Gao became the capital city and the Songhay became a vassal to Mali. When Mali's Emperor Mansa Musa made his famous pilgrimage to Mecca in the 1320s, his return trip brought him through Gao, where he took two royal sons back to his capital as hostages. One of the boys escaped and returned to Songhay in 1335, taking the name Sonni, or savior. He established a new dynasty and began the resistance to Mali that ultimately brought independence for his people.

The rise of the Sonni dynasty coincided with the decline of Mali. When Mali's power slipped away in the late 1300s, the Songhay threw off their vassalage, but did not come into their own until the latter half of the 1400s. King Sonni Ali, the greatest ruler of his dynasty, brought Songhay to imperial power. He captured Timbuktu from the nomads in 1468 and invaded Mali's old empire with a strong military force based on a river fleet operating on the Niger. The major trading center of Jenne fell to Songhay forces in 1473, but little inland progress was made against the remains of Mali's people. Not until 1492, when Sonni Ali died, did Songhay troops make inroads into Mali's countryside. Under the leadership of Askia Muhammad al-Turi, founder of a new dynasty, an improved infantry became strong enough to break away from the river fleet and strike inland. Askia Muhammad drove along the northern frontier of the old empire, defeating the last of Mali's leaders and gaining vassals for himself. He dominated the old Ghanian empire and took control of the gold trade that had made the area rich and famous. Though kings of Mali remained in control of factions deep in the rugged countryside, they ultimately surrendered to reality and recognized Songhay's control, paying them tribute. After Askia Muhammad was overthrown by his son in 1528, a series of dynastic struggles ensued. Ultimately, his grandsons Ishaq and Dawud ruled successfully from the 1530s to the 1580s.

The Askia dynasty embraced Islam much more strongly than did the Sonnis. Askia Muhammad imported Muslim scholars to Gao, Timbuktu, and Jenne, and he continued to maintain Timbuktu as the intellectual center of western Africa. He used the vast wealth of the empire to support Muslim clerics and build mosques, but the majority of the peoples he dominated remained loyal to their local gods. Under Askia Dawud, the Songhay Empire reached its intellectual and economic zenith. Trade across the Sahara became of greater importance than ever before, and Dawud supported the arts and sciences with royal patronage.

The Songhay ultimately fell to invaders from the north. After fighting upstart tribes in the southern part of the empire as well as sending forces to engage Berbers in Morocco, the empire was defeated by Moroccans with firearms. The empire broke up quickly in the wake of this defeat in 1591. In a matter of just a few years, the Songhay were reduced to their original holdings around Gao.

See also Mali, Expansion of.

References: Levtsion, Nehemia, *Ancient Ghana and Mali* (London: Methuen, 1973); Trimingham, John, *The History of Islam in West Africa* (London: Oxford University Press, 1970).

SPAIN, MUSLIM CONQUEST OF

75

One of the most distinctive invasions of history was that of the Moors upon the Iberian Peninsula. Its unusual aspect lay in the fact that it was a relatively peaceful invasion that permitted three distinct cultures—Christians, Muslims, and Jews—to coexist and flourish. The Arab occupation of Spain was not a preconceived plan of conquest; the Arabs were able to convince the natives of the many local tribes to surrender to attractive offers, which led to Arab control of three-fourths of Iberia for some 700 years.

It began during the seventh century when the Visigoth Empire in Spain suffered through a period of instability and rebellions, instigated by the sons of Visigothic king Witiza. During Witiza's reign (701–709), Arab forces of the caliphate had conquered northern Morocco and laid siege to Ceuta, the last Byzantine possession in the area. Julian, the imperial governor of Ceuta, sent his daughter Florinda to the court of Toledo to be educated. Unfortunately, she caught the eye of Witiza's successor, Don Rodrigo, who dishonored her. In retaliation, Julian ceded his control of the Ceuta to the Arabs and incited the Arab viceroy in North Africa, Musa ibn Nasair, to attack Spain and ally with Witiza's rebellious sons.

The Arab invasion began with a series of excursions by Tarik ibn Zair, the governor of Tangier. Under orders from the viceroy, he attacked across the Straits of Gibraltar in 710 with a force of 7,000 men, mostly Berbers. Reinforced by an additional 5,000 men, Tarik moved to Laguna de la Janda to await the arrival of Spanish forces under Don Rodrigo. On 19 July, Don Rodrigo was defeated and killed. Witiza's sons and supporters, who had withdrawn during the battle, now joined with Tarik and encouraged him to advance northward to seize Toledo and Cordoba. In June 712, Musa crossed from Morocco with an army of 18,000 Arabs and captured Sevilla and Merida. Dispatching his son Abdul Aziz to the southwest, Musa joined forces with Tarik at Talavera, then took up residence in Toledo. In 714 he captured Zaragoza and, with Tarik, made an expedition into Leon and Galicia before returning to Damascus. After occupying Portugal, Abdul Aziz completed the conquest of Granada and Murcia.

On the whole, the invaders met with little opposition. The sons of Witiza and the other great Visigothic families, whether or not they converted to Islam, paid tribute in return for extensive domains. Freed from persecution, the Jews were eager allies, and the serfs gained a measure of freedom. Most of the population converted to Islam, and the converts, known as Muwallads, became active in the general Moorish population. The unconverted, called Mozarabes, suffered little discrimination and formed prosperous communities in the Muslim cities. Too few to colonize the country, the Arabs formed the administrative and military cadres in the Zaragoza region. The Berbers settled mainly in the central and mountainous regions, which resembled their native Atlas Mountains and favored their anarchic tendencies.

Viewed as a whole, the conquest was not a great calamity. In the beginning there was a period of anarchy, but the Arab government soon repressed racial and tribal discord. In many respects the Arab conquest was beneficial. It brought about an important social revolution and put an end to many of the ills that had engulfed the country under the Visigoths. The power of the privileged classes, the clergy, and the nobility was reduced and, by distributing confiscated lands to the population, a peasant proprietorship was established The conquest ameliorated the condition of the peasants; the Moors provided many of the Christian slaves and serfs with an easy path to freedom. They brought Iberia a comparatively advanced culture and new technologies, and introduced economically important crops and new agricultural techniques. Moorish culture influenced architectural styles and native music and dances, while ancient learning, preserved by the Arabs, was reintroduced to this part of Europe.

See also Visigoths.

References: Byng, Edward, *The World of the Arabs* (Plainview, NY: Books for Libraries, 1974); Chejne, Anwar, *Muslim Spain: Its History and Culture* (Minneapolis: University of Minnesota Press, 1974); Click, Thomas, *Islamic and Christian Spain in the early Middle Ages* (Princeton, NJ: Princeton University Press, 1979).

Timur, which translates as "iron," was born 8 April 1336 near the central Asian city of Samarkand, into the Turkic-speaking Muslim tribe of Barulas Mongols. Later, he became known as Timur-i-leng, or Timur the Lame (for an injury to his right leg sustained in a sheep-stealing raid); Tamurlane is the westernized pronunciation. Timur was illiterate, but he had an active interest in history. In later life he kept slaves to read to him and keep accounts of his campaigns.

By the age of 25, Timur had a following of several hundred men, a force with which he began his rise to power. He placed himself and his men under the direction of the ruler of Moghulistan, Tughlug-Timur. For his loyalty, Timur was soon promoted to regional governor of Samarkand. Upon Tughlug-Timur's death, Timur-i-leng took over as ruler of Transoxiana, the area east of the Aral Sea. He made Samarkand his capital, and over the years it benefited from the booty of his conquests.

Timur built a powerful military force of cavalry, infantry, and engineers. His standard tactic was to absorb the enemy's attack with his well-trained infantry, then use his cavalry to exploit the confusion. Like Napoleon in the nineteenth century, he depended on vanguards and flanking units for scouting and for screening his movements. He also had no hesitation in marching his men great distances. He believed that campaigning over a wide area and attacking in random directions kept rivals from having time to establish themselves. He did not really care to absorb the peoples he defeated; he just plundered them. He calculated that a return campaign every few years would give an area time to recover economically without having the opportunity to build up militarily.

In 1381, Timur moved south and west toward Herat in Afghanistan, then advanced into territory covered by modern-day Iraq and Turkey. Having taken his fill of plunder there, he turned northward in 1384 to campaign against the Mongol Golden Horde occupying Russia. For four years he fought against Tokhtamysh, leader of the Golden Horde, defeating him and protecting his own northern frontier. This so weakened the Golden Horde's power that Russia was able to

arise into an independent state. In 1392 he began the "Five Years Campaign," during which he conquered Iran, then Baghdad, and moved northwest into the valley of the Don River north of the Black Sea. Rather than attack the rising nation of Russia, he reattacked the remains of the Golden Horde, capturing and pillaging Sarai and Astrakhan. Timur turned toward India in 1398. Like most of his campaigns, this was for loot rather than conquest. He followed a force led by his grandson, who captured Multan across the Indus River. After Timur joined his forces to his grandson's, they attacked Delhi and razed the city. In 1399 he was out of India and on the campaign trail for his last operation. Covering much of the same ground as he had pillaged at the end of the Five Years Campaign, he drove southward through Georgia into eastern Turkey. He defeated the Ottoman Sultan Bayezid I, after which he invaded Syria and closed out the year 1400 with the capture of Aleppo. The following season, he took Damascus, then once again captured and looted Baghdad, murdering the inhabitants and destroying the city. After taking Smyrna in 1403, he turned for home, where he stayed a short while before deciding to invade China, then under the Ming dynasty. Timur died on the road to China on 18 February 1405. His son and grandson succeeded him, creating the Timurid dynasty, but they lacked Timur's talent and drive, and the clan came to an end within a hundred years.

Timur the Lame goes down in history as a masterful military leader who, unlike his forerunner Genghis Khan, lacked the necessary ability to rule. He is remembered as a cruel conqueror and for little else; hundreds of thousands of people died at his direction. His excesses in mistreating defeated soldiers (beheading, burying alive, etc.) made him a man to be feared, but never one to be respected. Only the expansion and beautification of Samarkand was a positive, lasting contribution to society. His grandson, Ulugh Beg, studied astronomy and oversaw the Timurid period of culture, but it was short-lived.

Timur's conquests had several side effects. His defeat of the Othman Turks in Anatolia hurt them, but did not keep them from rising to power. His campaigns past the Black Sea destroyed the trading centers of the Venetians and Genoese, which spurred them toward maritime rather than overland trade routes, and as a result, they would dominate the Mediterranean as seamen. Because Timur bypassed Moscow, leaving the inhabitants unharmed while he defeated the Mongol Golden Horde that dominated the region, the state of Russia was born.

See also Genghis Khan; Napoleon Buonaparte; Ottoman Empire; Russia, Establishment and Expansion of; Russia, Mongol Conquest of.

References: Lamb, Harold, *Tamurlane, the Earth Shaker* (New York: R. M. McBride, 1928); Manz, Beatrice, *The Rise and Rule of Tamurlane* (Cambridge: Cambridge University Press, 1989).

77   T'ANG DYNASTY

With the dissolution of the Sui dynasty in the early 600s C.E., the T'ang, one of the rival factions struggling for power, finally rose to the top. The first in the T'ang line was Kaotsou. His son Lichiman was his chief general and did most of the conquering for the T'ang. Lichiman captured the capital city of Loyang and destroyed the Sui palace to prove that their dynasty had indeed come to an end; he then pensioned the Sui survivors. Lichiman went on to establish control over all of northern China and defeat a confederation of Turkic tribes on the eastern frontier. So successful was he that Kaotsou abdicated in 620 so Lichiman could rule. On taking the throne from his father, Lichiman took the royal name Taitsong.

Taitsong continued to fight, pacifying the entire Chinese realm by 624. He captured the king of the Tartars, forcing the barbarians to sue for peace. As usual, peace was fleeting, and Taitsong fought the nomads for years. In the first year of his reign, the Tartars attacked with 100,000 men and invaded almost to the capital city. Taitsong turned them away almost singlehandedly. He met with the Tartars accompanied only by a small escort, shaming them, and convinced them to abide by the terms of the previous peace and return home.

Taitsong built a standing army of 900,000, placing one-third of them along the frontier and two-thirds behind them, creating not only a defense in depth, but also a mobile reserve that could react to any crisis. This was China's first standing professional army, and Taitsong became a warrior-king, the first to do so voluntarily. He spent so much time on training and discipline that when his army went on their first campaign, again against the Tartars, the Chinese were so impressive that the nomads gave up without a fight. At this point he named himself khan of the Tartars and took the power to regulate their affairs. This action brought Chinese control into the Gobi Desert and spread its influence even farther.

Taitsong was as good an administrator as he was a military leader. He lowered taxes, instituted a fair civil service, and set the example for his government to follow. As a Confucian, he believed that it was necessary for a leader to promote the harmony of his people by personal excellence. He was assisted in administration by his wife, a woman as dedicated and wise as he. They both lived a simple life, without imperial fanfare. She died in 636, leaving as her legacy a college and the Imperial Library.

Taitsong cultivated Chinese relations with Tibet in 634. After initiating talks, the Sanpou, the Tibetan head of state, requested a Chinese bride to seal their relationship. Taitsong refused, and the Sanpou prepared for war. Taitsong's superior army defeated the Tibetans at the western border. Tibet became China's vassal, and Taitsong rewarded the Sanpou with a Chinese wife—his own daughter. The Tibetans began to adopt Chinese culture and abandon barbarism. That same year, Chinese forces won another victory over Turkic tribes at Kashgar, which extended Chinese authority as far as eastern Turkistan, the greatest limit of national authority until the Mongols' dynasty.

Taitsong's only reverse came in Korea. A usurper in the Korean palace refused to recognize the T'ang line and mistreated Taitsong's ambassadors. The Chinese responded to this insult by invading Korea in 646. The Korean usurper decided he had better pay tribute rather than face the invading army, but Taitsong refused his gifts, deciding to teach the Korean a lesson. The Chinese massed 100,000 men and 500 boats for a combined land-sea operation. Telling the

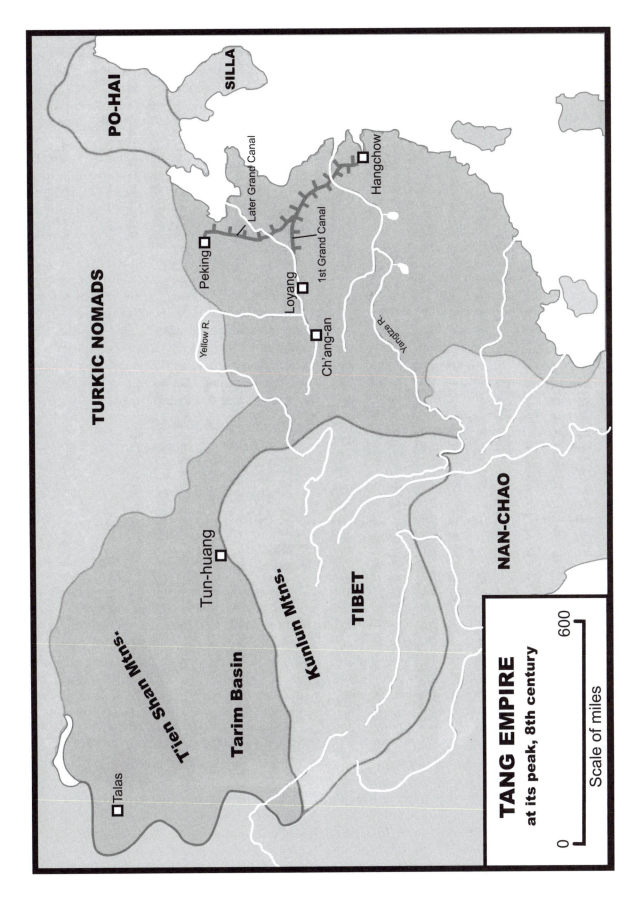

TANG EMPIRE
at its peak, 8th century

Scale of miles

0   600

PO-HAI

SILLA

TURKIC NOMADS

Later Grand Canal

Hangchow

Peking

Loyang

1st Grand Canal

Ch'ang-an

Yellow R.

Yangtze R.

Tun-huang

Kunlun Mtns.

TIBET

NAN-CHAO

T'ien Shan Mtns.

Tarim Basin

Talas

Korean people that he had no quarrel with them, Taitsong proclaimed a war against the king only. However, the Korean people resisted, and after an easy start, the Chinese lost a quarter of their force in a siege at Anshu on the northwest coast, which they were unable to capture. Because winter was coming and Taitsong's forces were short of supplies, he retreated. Taitsong never went back, and died in 649.

When he saw his end approaching, Taitsong wanted to leave a legacy for his successors. He wrote the *Golden Mirror*, a text on statecraft, for his son. Taitsong is regarded as probably the finest of all Chinese emperors of any dynasty, and among the best rulers anywhere and anytime. As is usually the case, his descendants did not measure up, starting with his son, Kaotsong, who married one of his father's concubines, an extremely ambitious woman who came to be known as Empress Wu. She was the power behind the throne, and when Kaotsong died, she seized power openly, one of the only women ever to do so in Chinese history. She ruled with an iron hand and with mixed success in foreign policy. Her armies lost twice to Tibet in 670 and signed a truce to keep the Tibetans out of Chinese territory, then broke the truce and as a result, the army was virtually wiped out. From then on, she could do little more than defend the western frontier from the occasional Tibetan invasion.

Empress Wu had more luck in Korea. Chinese forces fought there for 10 years, ultimately forcing the Koreans to appeal to Japan for aid. Her forces defeated the combined forces in four battles and destroyed the Japanese fleet. Though the Chinese established predominance, they had no long-term advantage. Empress Wu also received appeals from India to assist in repelling invading Muslims, but she wisely refrained from sending her armies so far afield. In 692 she directed her forces to regain preeminence in Tibet, which they did, though they had to continue fighting to maintain their position. Empress Wu's greatest, and last, failure was in dealing with the threat of Khitan Mongols in the north. She allied herself with a Turkic chief, Metcho, in 697, and armed his forces to aid her against the Mongols. Instead, Metcho took the weapons and invaded China himself.

After Empress Wu's death in 705 at age 80, a succession of poor leaders followed. Border wars continued against the Tibetans in the west and the Khitan Mongols in the north. In the middle and later part of the eighth century, the Chinese depended more and more on Turkic mercenaries, who proved able soldiers for the Chinese; at the same time, Turkistan received Chinese aid to keep the Muslims at bay. The constant warfare took its toll on Chinese society. Early in the 700s, the Chinese census numbered 52 million; by 764 the population had dropped to 17 million. The T'ang dynasty stayed in power until 906, when the final emperor conceded power to one of his generals. At the height of the dynasty, the Tangs spread from Korea to Turkistan to the Persian frontier to the borders of Vietnam. They spread Chinese culture, maintained trade relations with the West, and acted as a bulwark against Muslim expansion. The dynasty contained 20 emperors (including one empress), but none as able as Taitsong, who took them to their greatest heights.

See also Vietnam, Chinese Conquest of.

References: Boulger, Demetrius, *The History of China, 2 vols.* (Freeport, NY: Books for Libraries, 1898); Capon, Edmund, *Tang China* (London: Macdonald Orbis, 1989); Wei, Cheng, *Mirror to the Son of Heaven*, ed. and trans. Howard Wechsler (New Haven, CT Yale University Press, 1974).

78   TURKS

The peoples known as Turks originated not in the Turkey of today, but in Turkistan in central Asia. In the middle of the sixth century C.E., they formed themselves into a large tribal confederation, then shortly thereafter split into eastern and western factions. The eastern Turkic tribes interacted strongly with the Chinese, most notably with the T'ang dynasty, and alternately aided or were defeated by Chinese societies. The western Turkic tribes, however, were better known as conquerors for their occupation of territory stretching from the Oxus River to the Mediterranean Sea.

Their first major entry into Western history came through contact with Arabs spreading Islam past Persia and toward central Asia. The pastoral Turks became exposed to the civilizations of Persia and the Byzantine Empire, and began a gradual conversion to Western religions, mainly but not exclusively Islam. Soon Turkic soldiers served in Muslim armies, either as volunteers or as slave-soldiers, forerunners of the Mamluks or the janissaries of the Ottoman Empire. They soon became ghazis, or border warriors, hired by Muslim governments to protect the northeastern frontier. At this point the western Turks also split, the eastern faction becoming the Ghaznavids and the western becoming the Seljuks.

The Ghaznavids

Most of the Turks embraced the more orthodox Sunni branch of Islam, and they spread the faith as well as practiced it. Based in the city of Ghazna (some 150 kilometers southwest of modern Kabul, Afghanistan), in the tenth and eleventh centuries the Ghaznavids spread their power and religion eastward into India. Their original holdings were a land grant given to them as a reward for military services from the Samanid dynasty of Muslims. Under the leadership of Sebuktegin (977–997) and his son Mahmud (998–1030), the Ghaznavids conquered the area today covered by eastern Iran, Afghanistan, the Punjab, and past the Indus River into parts of India. Their most notable achievement was the introduction of Islam into India, but their use of forced conversions often made them more feared than welcomed. They were defeated not by Indian resistance, but by the Seljuks.

The Seljuks

Named for their first major leader, Seljuk or Selchuk, the western Turkic tribes also served Muslim governments. Their position on the Asian frontier attracted growing numbers of Islamicized Turkic tribes, and soon the land grants ceded by the Muslims proved inadequate for the needs of so many pastoral people. Their multiplying numbers gave them an increased military strength as well as a growing need for grazing lands. As the Muslim Buyid dynasty grew weak and the Ghaznavids looked toward India, the Seljuks found conquest of the lands west of Persia relatively simple. They defeated the Ghaznavids in 1040, and occupied Baghdad in 1055. They did not take the city to pillage it, but to return it to Sunni control from the less orthodox Shi'ites. The wedding of the Seljuk chief to the sister of the caliph (religious leader), and the Seljuk's resulting promotion to the position of sultan (temporal leader), established them as the premier military and political force in the Middle East.

Filled with religious zeal, the Seljuks conquered Armenia, the Levant, and moved into Asia Minor. Malik Shah, the most successful Seljuk military leader, scored a major victory over Byzantine forces at Manzikert in 1071. Despite their desire to reestablish the Sunni sect of Islam, they did not undertake the forced conversions practiced by the Ghaznavids in India. Though they made subjects of Christians and Jews, they did not persecute them; the Seljuks followed Muhammad's teachings of religious tolerance. Once established in Asia Minor, they chose as their capital city Konia, a site occupied since the Hittites at the dawn of recorded history, which became a center for culture and learning. The Turks did not create so much as they copied, but their adoption of Persian and Arab knowledge and art was extensive. Seljuk rulers exchanged educators and religious leaders with Constantinople, and seemed for a time to pursue the concept of finding a common belief for both Christian and Muslim to embrace. Such a noble dream of religious cooperation was not to be. The orthodoxy of the Sunni Seljuks frightened Europeans, who rejected peaceful interaction for militant Christianity and mounted the Crusades. The enlightened rulers Ala-ed-din and Jelal-ed-din, promoters of positive religious contact, had no effective counterparts in Europe. Though the Crusades brought about no lasting European presence in the Middle East and the Seljuks remained in power, they were doomed to destruction in the same manner that brought them to power: hordes from central Asia, the Mongols of the thirteenth century. The Seljuks left behind a positive legacy, for the most part. They spread Persian learning and culture, and established universities and religious schools from the Mediterranean to the Caspian. Their occupation of Asia Minor ultimately weakened the Byzantine Empire to the point that it fell to the successors of the Seljuk, the Ottoman Empire.

See also Byzantine Empire; Crusades; Tang Dynasty; Ottoman Empire.

References: Koprulu, Mehmet. *The Seijuks of Anatolia*, trans. Gary Leiser (Salt Lake City: University of Utah Press, 1992); Muller, Herbert, *The Loom of History* (New York: Harper & Brothers, 1958); Rice, Tamara, *The Seljwlcs in Asia Minor* (New York: Praeger, 1961).

79   VANDALS

The Vandals were one of the tribes who migrated from the area below the Baltic Sea during the late Roman Empire. They were of the same racial stock as the Goths, but traveled across Germany more directly than did the Goths, who migrated at the same time but took a more southerly route before moving westward across Europe. Little is known of the Vandals' early history, but they crossed into Germany about the time Rome was loosening its grip on the area in the mid-300s C.E. They were actually the leaders of a group of tribes, and were themselves divided into two groups, the Asdings and the Silings. They led and conquered with the Sueves, another Germanic tribe, and the Alans, who were a non-Germanic people driven into Europe by the advance of the Huns.

The Vandal coalition moved across Germany as the Western Goths (Visigoths) were occupying northern Italy and Dacia, and the two fought each other. The Visigoths had the better of the encounter, and the Vandals seemed to disappear for a time. In 406 they emerged again to lead their forces across the Rhine River. Their passage into western Europe was bloody; the Vandals pillaged through Gaul (areas covered by modern-day Belgium, Holland, and northern France), then turned south and cut a wide swath of destruction to the Pyrenees. This territory officially belonged to the Roman Empire, and the emperor tried to convince his Visigothic allies/mercenaries to save Gaul. By the time they turned to face the Vandal threat in 409, the tribes had moved into northern Spain.

Like the Goths, the Vandals were Arian Christians. The two peoples were of the same heritage and spoke a similar language. The Goths had established themselves in Italy as occasional allies to what remained of the Roman Empire. They therefore went to Spain to regain control of the area for Rome and to carve out whatever good lands they could acquire for themselves, even if it meant making war against people much like themselves. The four Vandalic tribes had spread quickly over much of central and western Iberia, and the Goths operated out of the eastern part of the peninsula. After a failed attempt to cross over to North Africa, the Goths made war against the Vandalic tribes. After a few defeats, the Vandals appealed to Rome for protection; the emperor played one tribe against another by granting or denying favors. Imperial aid went mainly to the Asdings and the Suevians, so the Goths continued to fight the Silings and the Alans. The Silings were virtually exterminated, and the Alans, after losing their king, retreated westward to join the Asdings. The ruler of the remainder came to be called "King of the Vandals and the Alans."

Once the Visigoths went about establishing their own claims, the remaining Vandals were left to themselves. An argument soon arose between the Vandals and the Sueves and, after a battle, they parted company. The Sueves stayed in northwest Iberia, and the Vandals and Alans moved to the south. On the way, they fought and defeated a Roman force, and established themselves in the province of Baetica. The Vandal king Gunderic raided into other areas of Spain and possibly across the Mediterranean into Mauritania. His brother and successor, Gaiseric, saw the potential of the farmland of North Africa, which had long been Rome's primary food source. He was leader of the Vandals when chance called them to Africa.

The general commanding the Roman forces in Africa was Boniface, loyal to Rome and a strong Christian. However, he took a second wife who was an Arian, and this placed him in opposition to the Roman Catholic Church. He refused to return to Rome to answer to the government, and Boniface defeated the first army that came after him. The second one defeated him, however, and Boniface fled to the Vandals. He invited them to come to Africa; if they would fight alongside him, he would reward them with land. Boniface provided shipping, and 80,000 people crossed the Mediterranean, 15,000 of whom were fighting men.

The Vandals proved to be unmerciful in their treatment of the Mauritanian population. They killed and looted towns and churches, caring nothing for Catholic shrines or priests. Gaiseric proved an able military leader and a cunning diplomat. His treatment of Roman citizens encouraged other groups who disliked Rome to join in the fray. Moors and Egyptian Donatists attacked eastward along the Mediterranean shore, and other groups branded as heretics saw a chance to exact vengeance on their Roman oppressors. Attempts to negotiate with Gaiseric proved futile. He not only fought the Roman armies sent against him, but turned on Boniface as well and drove him back into Roman arms. In 430, the Vandals invaded Numidia and besieged the city of Hippo, home to St. Augustine, which held out for a year. When Boniface joined with an army sent from Constantinople in 431, Gaiseric defeated them as well, then turned back and captured Hippo.

In Rome, internal power struggles kept the government from any effective resistance to Gaiseric. Finally the Visigoth General Aetius was able to speak for Rome and convince the Vandals to stop fighting. In 435 they were ceded the Mauritanian provinces and part of Numidia in return for acknowledging the overlordship of the Roman government. Gaiseric consolidated his hold on northwestern Africa, but continued to consider his options. Basing himself in Carthage, Gaiseric built a fleet and began raiding at sea. His forces raided Italy and occupied Sicily and Sardinia. The Vandals did not long survive Gaiseric, however. Roman forces ultimately returned and reconquered the area, bringing the Vandal tribe to an end.

Though Vandal power lasted about a century, the tribe left behind little cultural heritage. Their time in Spain was sufficiently brief that they had no impact there, and even in North Africa, they built and contributed little. The effect of the Vandal migrations and conquests was not small, however. By their very presence in North Africa, controlling the grain-producing lands that had fed Italy for centuries, the power of Rome declined even faster. Without the logistical support of Africa, Roman forces could not aggressively respond to threats in Europe, mostly in Gaul. The advances of the Huns and the Ostrogoths, then of the Franks, came about more easily because Rome could not support enough troops in the field. Roman power fell faster and German influence rose more quickly in Europe because the Vandals, at Rome's back door, split the attention of the fading empire.

See also Huns; Ostrogoths; Visigoths.

References: Bury, J. B., *The Invasion of Europe by the Barbarians* (New York: Russell & Russell, 1963); *Isadore of Seville, The History of the Goths, Vandals and Suevi,* trans. Guido Donini and Gordon Ford (Leiden: E. J. Brill, 1970); Thompson, E. A., *Romans and Barbarians: The Decline of the Western Empire* (Madison: University of Wisconsin Press, 1982).

80   VIETNAM, CHINESE CONQUEST OF

In 221 B.C.E. the Chou dynasty in China was overthrown and replaced by the short-lived Ch'in dynasty. Though this was the first centralized empire in China, it lasted but one generation. However, it was a busy lifetime: All of China was under one rule and Emperor Shih-huang-ti planned an expedition to conquer territory in the far south, called Yueh (pronounced Viet in the south). He began planning the attack in 221 B.C.E., but was not able to launch it until 218. The invasion was both political and economic; Shih-huang-ti hoped to spread Chinese influence and to profit from that spread by accessing the ivory, rhino horn, tortoiseshell, pearls, spices, aromatic woods, and exotic feathers for which Chinese silk had long been traded. The Chinese already had merchants in place in Yueh and were well aware of the area's potential.

The first invasion was fairly easy. The indigenous tribes retreated before the Chinese advance, marshaling their forces until they could outnumber the invaders. Chinese leader Chao T'o (Trieu Da) called for reinforcements, and the lower levels of Chinese society were plumbed for men. The early success was limited to the plains around modern Canton; the Red River delta was left untouched for a while.

Shih-huang-ti's death in 209 B.C.E. brought civil war, ending in the establishment of the Han dynasty in 202. While civil war raged in

China, the governor in the south saw an opportunity to declare independence, but he was unsuccessful. He was replaced by the returning Chao T'o, who executed all officials still loyal to the Ch'in and, in 207 B.C.E., assumed the title King of Nan-yueh (Nam Viet). The Han dynasty recognized him as king in return for his acknowledgment of Chinese suzerainty. In a later trade dispute, Chao T'o declared his independence, and defeated the Chinese force sent against him. He forced the population living farther south, called the Lo (Lac) people, to recognize his position. The Lo lived in a feudal society along the Red River delta and the coastal plains to the south. Even after Chao T'o made peace with China and again recognized their overlordship, this territory continued to recognize his leadership. The area came to be designated a military district called Chiao-chih (Giao-chi).The Lo princes remained vassals to Chao (Trieu) and his successors. When Nan-yueh broke from China in 112 B.C.E., it was invaded by the Han emperor Wu-ti. He was quickly victorious and incorporated Nan-yueh into the Han Empire as a protectorate. He divided it into nine military districts; six of them took up the modern provinces of Kwangtung and Kwangsi in China, and the remainder lay in what is now Vietnam. Despite the incorporation, Wu-ti did not establish a Chinese administration in Nan-yueh, but treated the military districts as colonies with a minority Chinese population. The local lords were confirmed in their positions under Chinese suzerainty, and maritime trade with China opened up.

Not until 1 C.E. did the Chinese begin to impose their culture on the people of Chiao-chih. Through the efforts of Governor Hsi Kuang (Tich Quang), who ruled from 1 to 25 C.E., the Chinese language became more widely used. The influx of Chinese immigrants also aided in the Sinicizing process; many of them were scholars and officials fleeing from the rule of the usurper Wang Mang (9–25 C.E.). Schools were widely established at this time, and Chinese inventions such as the metal plow were introduced to Chiao-chih society. Hsi Kuang also mandated Chinese clothing styles and marriage ceremonies, and trained a militia along Chinese lines and with Chinese weaponry. This

provoked a rebellion in 34 C.E. by the Lo lords, who feared a loss of power, but by 43 it was suppressed through the efforts of one of China's most able generals, Ma Yuan (Ma Vien). This failed rebellion resulted in the further Sinification of the administration in Chiao-chih as the Lo nobles lost their position. From then on, Chiao-chih was treated not as a protectorate, but as a province of the empire.

China dominated the area for the next several centuries, making its culture increasingly Chinese. Under the governorship of Shih Shieh (Si-hiep), traditional

Confucian studies were introduced and Vietnamese students began to go to China to take the civil service exams, which further solidified Chinese culture and administration. Also during this time, the first Buddhist missionaries appeared in Chiao-chih, as did proponents of Taoism and Confucianism.

China ruled the area for almost a thousand years. Those years were mainly peaceful, though plagued by resistance from some of the hill tribes who resented foreign occupation, and by the Champa people farther south who occasionally attempted to spread their influence into Chiao-chih. Periodic revolts of either local chieftains or recalcitrant governors proved unable to dislodge Chinese authority, even when Chinese dynasties changed. The successors to the Han, the T'ang dynasty, reorganized the administration of the area in the 600s, renaming the Chiao military districts An-nan (An-nam), meaning "pacified south." The name survives to the present day as a state in modern Vietnam.

By the 800s, rebellions became more common and the Chinese had to work to keep control. The growing aggressiveness of neighboring peoples like the Champa (in the neighborhood of Hue) and the Laos kept Chinese troops busy, and even seaborne Javanese raiders attacked occasionally. The fall of the T'ang dynasty in 907, however, was the event that eventually brought Chinese control to an end. Local governors and chieftains successively struggled for control in the area while the disruption of politics in China kept any punitive expeditions from being sent. In 968, Dinh Bo Linh proclaimed himself emperor of the territory, which he renamed Dai Co Viet, and in 970 he received recognition from the new Sung dynasty, as long as he would swear to remain a Chinese vassal.

The country that ultimately became Vietnam remained independent from China, though it often had to fight to repel successive Chinese dynasties. Meanwhile the Chinese administrative structure was maintained, giving Vietnam a centralized government stronger than any in Southeast Asia. Strengthened by the nationalism that grew in repeated wars of defense against China, the government served as motivation for Vietnamese expansion southward. By the 1800s, they had conquered the Champa and Khmer peoples along the east coast of Indochina to establish basically the same borders that the country maintains today. Of all the Southeast Asian cultures, only the Vietnamese were strongly affected by the Chinese; the others were more influenced by India. Not long after their consolidation, however, the Vietnamese became the target of French colonization.

See also Ch'in Dynasty; Han Dynasty; T'ang Dynasty; Indochina, French Occupation of.

References: Cannon, Terry, *Vietnam: A Thousand Years of Struggle* (San Francisco: People's Press, 1969); Coedes, G., *The Making of Southeast Asia*, trans. H. M. Wright (Berkeley: University of California Press, 1969); Taylor, Keith, *The Birth of Vietnam* (Berkeley: University of California Press, 1983).

81   VISIGOTHS

The Goths were a Teutonic tribe, probably originating in Scandinavia, who arrived in northeastern Europe in the third century C.E. Coupled with their countrymen, the Ostrogoths, the Visigoths ravaged the lands of eastern Europe as far as Asia Minor and Greece. The first serious conflict between Goths and Romans occurred when a number of Gothic mercenaries aided the usurpation attempt of Procopius in Constantinople in 366. Following Procopius's failed attempt and subsequent execution, the Roman emperor Valens launched an attack on the Goths across the Danube. After an inconclusive war, the two sides agreed on the Danube River as the boundary between their claims. About 370, the two Gothic groups separated, the

Visigoths occupying the land from the Dneister River to the Baltic Sea, the Ostrogoths living east of them to the Black Sea.

In 376 the Goths found themselves threatened by the migration of the Huns from central Asia. The Ostrogoths fled westward to pressure the Visigoths, who appealed to Valens for protection and aid. Valens agreed to allow them across the Danube in return for surrendering their weapons and male children under military age. Under the leadership of Fritigern and Alavius, the Visigoths agreed and gave up their boys, but resisted relinquishing their weapons. The Romans abused the Visigoths and provoked their retaliation after killing Alavius during a parley. Fritigern attacked and defeated Roman forces at Marianopolis (in modern Bulgaria), then called on the Ostrogoths for assistance. Emperor Valens, fighting against the Persians, secured a truce there and moved to protect his northeastern frontier. The Romans and the Ostrogoths fought an indecisive battle at the mouth of the Danube in 377, after which the Goths escaped and raised a general barbarian revolt along the frontier. The Romans finally began to regain control in the province of Thrace by 378, but met defeat while launching an attack on the Gothic forces near Adrianople. Spurning a request for peace talks, Valens attacked the Goths before reinforcements arrived. The Gothic force of perhaps 200,000 warriors (roughly half Visigothic infantry and half mixed barbarian cavalry) badly defeated Valens, who died in the battle along with two-thirds of his 60,000 troops. The Visigothic king Fritigern was in overall command.

Valens's successor, Theodosius I, learned from his countryman's defeat and, after rebuilding an army and restoring order in Thrace, defeated the Goths and then invited them into his army. The Visigoths served Theodosius, but upon his death in 395 they chose their own leader: Alaric. He had earlier raided Roman lands from across the Danube, but was captured and incorporated into the Roman army. Upon his election as king, Alaric led the Visigoths through Thrace and Greece. His only serious enemy was Stilicho, a Vandal general in Roman service who had served Theodosius. The Visigoths remained relatively unbothered, however, because the Eastern Roman Emperor Arcadius ordered Stilicho to remain in Italy. After Alaric spent the mid-390s ravaging Greece, he turned toward Italy.

Visigothic forces marched through Pannonia (along the eastern Adriatic coast) and crossed the Alps in October 401. He overran some of the northern provinces, but Stilicho's delaying actions kept him in the north. During the winter, Stilicho ordered forces from Gaul to Italy and did some personal recruiting among German tribes. The resulting army attacked Alaric's forces, who were besieging Milan. Alaric withdrew and marched south, looking for Stilicho's incompetent emperor, Honorius. After two difficult battles in March and April 402, Alaric asked for negotiations and agreed to leave Italy. Instead, he marched for Gaul, which was left unprotected. Stilicho learned of this maneuver and blocked him, defeating the Visigoths at Verona. Alaric again withdrew and Honorius moved the imperial capital to Ravenna; behind its marshy outskirts, he felt safe from attack. Alaric decided to cooperate with Stilicho and was named master-general of Illyricum. When in 408 Honorius ordered Stilicho murdered, the general's followers appealed to Alaric to invade Italy; he did so gladly. After two attacks on Rome were called off (owing to successful Roman bribery), Alaric marched his forces to Rome. On 24 August 410, Rome fell to foreign invaders for the first time in a thousand years. Alaric marched south to invade Sicily, but died on the way.

Under the leadership of Athaulf, the Visigoths invaded Gaul in 412, supposedly to recover it for Honorius. Athaulf accomplished the conquest by 414 and was rewarded with marriage to Honorius's half-sister. He followed Honorius's direction to reconquer Spain, but died in the process in 415. His successor, Wallia, defeated a number of barbar-ian tribes in Spain and was rewarded with a kingdom of his own in southern Gaul.

The Visigoths settled into lands ranging from the Rhone River into Spain. Their greatest king was Euric, who established a law code based on a mixture of Roman and Germanic legal traditions. The one thing he could not do, however, was establish a hereditary line, for the nobility forbade it. The monarchy was elective, and therefore subject to too much political infighting. This lack of unity laid the Visigothic kingdom open to outside pressure, and in 507, Clovis, the founder of the Merovingian dynasty of the Franks, defeated Alaric II and acquired much of the land north of the Pyrenees. Though the Visigoths managed to maintain their hold on Spain in the face of pressure from the Vandals, they ultimately fell to Muslim invasion. The last Visigothic king, Roderic, was defeated and killed in 711, and the remaining Visigothic tribe was confined to the province of Asturias.

The Visigoths played an important role in the fall of the Roman Empire in the West. Like many of the barbarians who flooded the empire, they converted to the Arian view of Christianity and thus often had troubles with the Roman Catholic Church, which viewed them as heretics. As soldiers, they proved themselves so talented that the Roman army in the East, based in Constantinople, reconfigured itself to adapt to Gothic cavalry. They had little effect on the future course of European history, however, because they spread themselves too thinly—from the Balkans to Spain—and were finally defeated and absorbed by more powerful enemies.

See also Franks; Huns; Ostrogoths.

References: Cunliffe, Barry, *Rome and Her Empire* (London: Constable, 1994 [1978]); Heather, Peter, *Goths and Romans* (Oxford: Clarendon Press, 1991); Thompson, E. A., *The Goths in Spain* (Oxford: Clarendon Press, 1969).

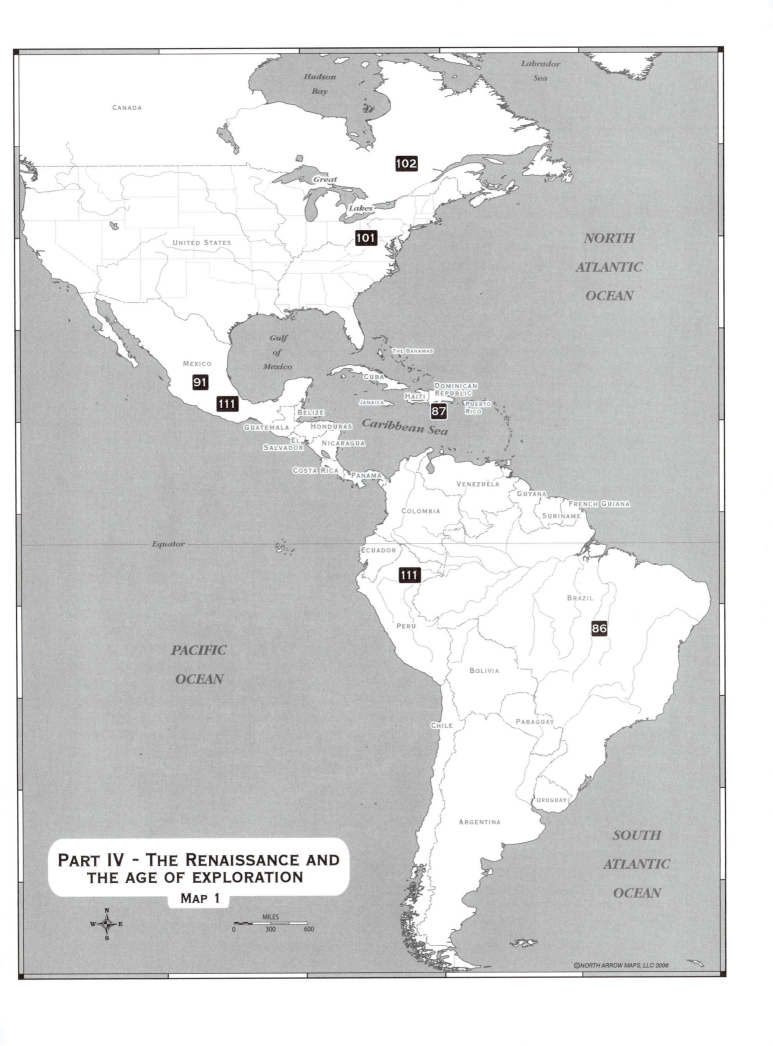

CANADA

Hudson Bay

Labrador Sea

102

Great

Lakes

UNITED STATES

101

NORTH

ATLANTIC

OCEAN

Gulf

of

Mexico

THE BAHAMAS

MEXICO

91

CUBA

DOMINICAN REPUBLIC

HAITI

111

JAMAICA

PUERTO RICO

BELIZE

87

GUATEMALA

HONDURAS

Caribbean Sea

EL SALVADOR

NICARAGUA

COSTA RICA

PANAMA

VENEZUELA

GUYANA

FRENCH GUIANA

COLOMBIA

SURINAME

Equator

ECUADOR

111

PACIFIC

OCEAN

BRAZIL

PERU

86

BOLIVIA

CHILE

PARAGUAY

URUGUAY

ARGENTINA

SOUTH

ATLANTIC

OCEAN

PART IV - THE RENAISSANCE AND THE AGE OF EXPLORATION

MAP 1

N
W E
S

MILES

0   300   600

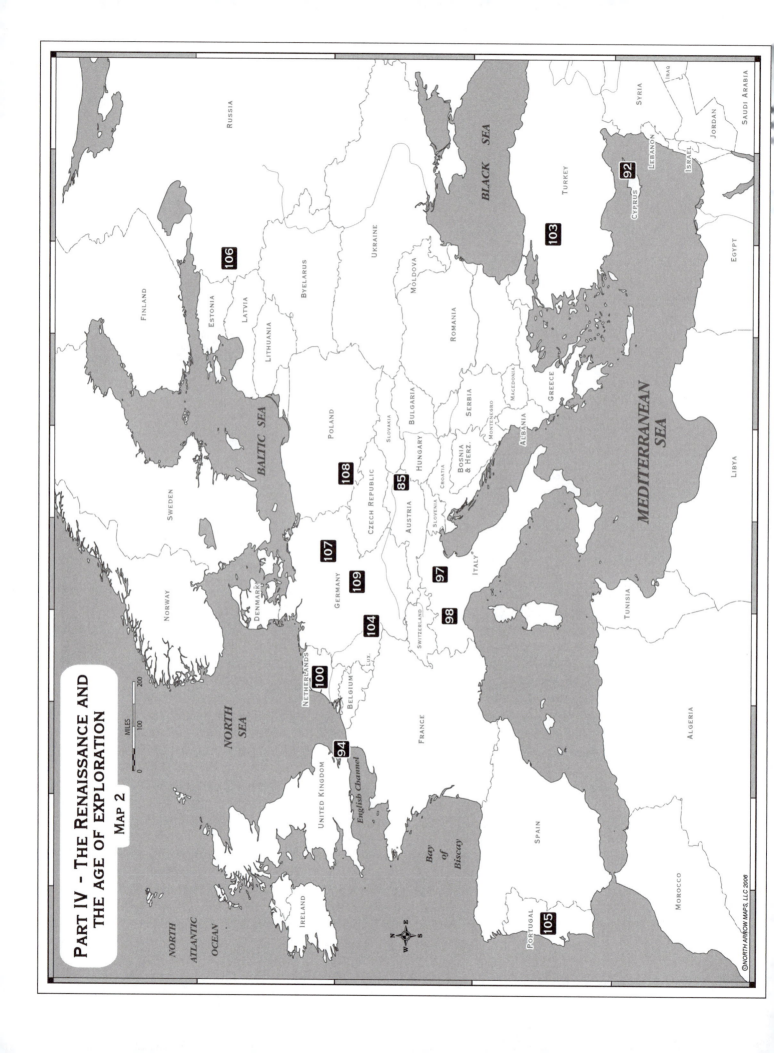

PART IV - THE RENAISSANCE AND THE AGE OF EXPLORATION

MAP 2

MILES
0   100   200

NORTH ATLANTIC OCEAN

NORTH SEA

BALTIC SEA

BLACK SEA

MEDITERRANEAN SEA

English Channel

Bay of Biscay

NORWAY

SWEDEN

FINLAND

RUSSIA

ESTONIA

LATVIA

LITHUANIA

BYELARUS

DENMARK

UNITED KINGDOM

IRELAND

NETHERLANDS

BELGIUM

LUX.

GERMANY

POLAND

UKRAINE

MOLDOVA

ROMANIA

FRANCE

SWITZERLAND

CZECH REPUBLIC

SLOVAKIA

AUSTRIA

HUNGARY

SLOVENIA

CROATIA

BOSNIA & HERZ.

SERBIA

MONTENEGRO

ITALY

MACEDONIA

ALBANIA

BULGARIA

GREECE

TURKEY

CYPRUS

LEBANON

ISRAEL

SYRIA

IRAQ

JORDAN

SAUDI ARABIA

EGYPT

LIBYA

TUNISIA

ALGERIA

MOROCCO

SPAIN

PORTUGAL

92

103

106

108

85

107

109

97

98

104

100

94

105

N
E
S
W

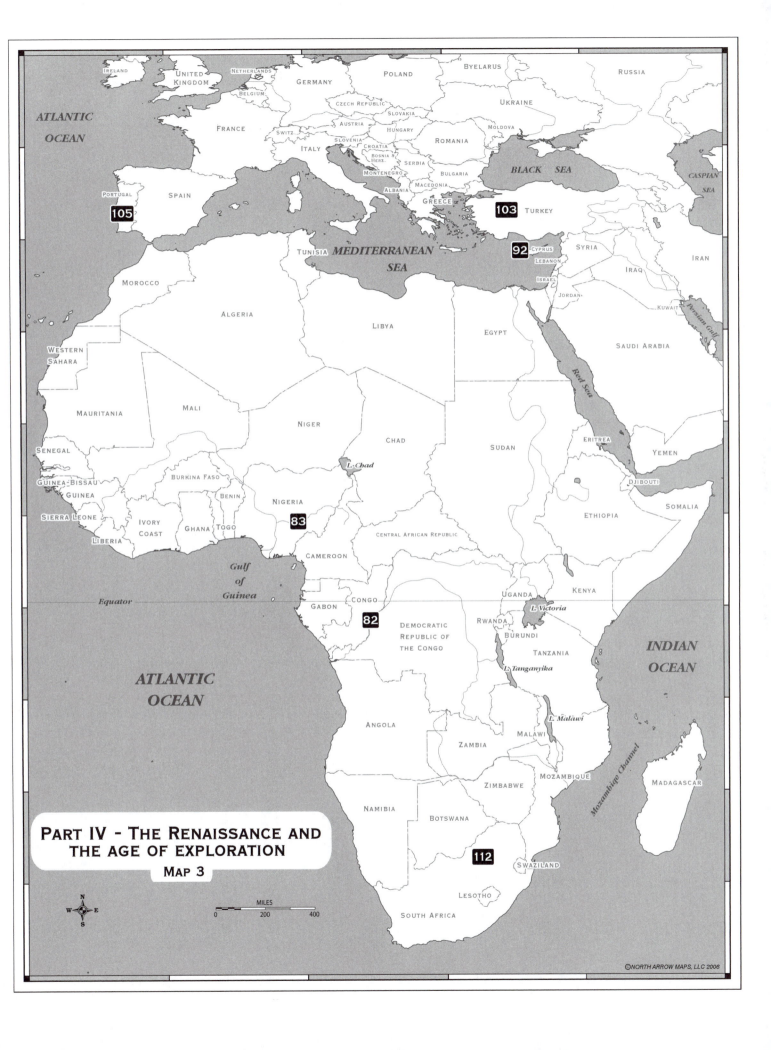

ATLANTIC
OCEAN

IRELAND
UNITED
KINGDOM
NETHERLANDS
BELGIUM
GERMANY
POLAND
BYELARUS
RUSSIA

FRANCE
SWITZ.
CZECH REPUBLIC
SLOVAKIA
AUSTRIA
HUNGARY
SLOVENIA
UKRAINE
MOLDOVA

ITALY
CROATIA
BOSNIA &
HERZ.
SERBIA
ROMANIA

MONTENEGRO
BULGARIA

ALBANIA
MACEDONIA
BLACK SEA

GREECE
103 TURKEY
CASPIAN
SEA

PORTUGAL
SPAIN
105

TUNISIA
MEDITERRANEAN
SEA
92 CYPRUS
SYRIA
IRAN

LEBANON
ISRAEL
IRAQ

MOROCCO
JORDAN
KUWAIT

ALGERIA
LIBYA
EGYPT
SAUDI ARABIA

WESTERN
SAHARA
Red Sea

MAURITANIA
MALI
NIGER
CHAD
SUDAN
ERITREA
YEMEN

SENEGAL
L. Chad
DJIBOUTI

GUINEA-BISSAU
BURKINA FASO
SOMALIA

GUINEA
BENIN
NIGERIA
ETHIOPIA

SIERRA LEONE
IVORY
COAST
GHANA
TOGO
83
CENTRAL AFRICAN REPUBLIC

LIBERIA
CAMEROON

Gulf
of
Guinea
KENYA

Equator
CONGO
UGANDA
L. Victoria

GABON
82
DEMOCRATIC
REPUBLIC OF
THE CONGO
RWANDA
BURUNDI
TANZANIA

INDIAN
OCEAN

ATLANTIC
OCEAN
L. Tanganyika

L. Malawi

ANGOLA
MALAWI

ZAMBIA
MOZAMBIQUE
MADAGASCAR

ZIMBABWE

NAMIBIA
BOTSWANA
Mozambique Channel

PART IV - THE RENAISSANCE AND
THE AGE OF EXPLORATION
MAP 3
112 SWAZILAND

LESOTHO

N
W E
S
MILES
0   200   400
SOUTH AFRICA

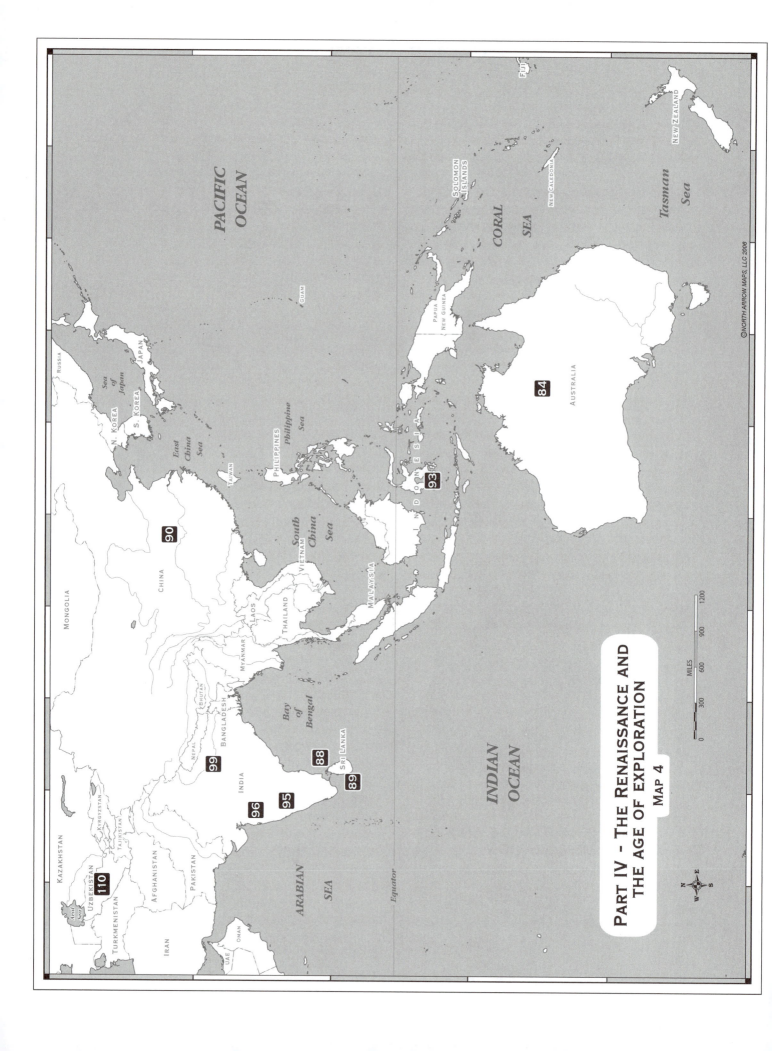

RUSSIA

MONGOLIA

KAZAKHSTAN

KYRGYZSTAN

TAJIKISTAN

UZBEKISTAN

110

Aral Sea

TURKMENISTAN

AFGHANISTAN

IRAN

PAKISTAN

N. KOREA

S. KOREA

JAPAN

Sea of Japan

East China Sea

CHINA

90

TAIWAN

PACIFIC OCEAN

NEPAL

BHUTAN

BANGLADESH

MYANMAR

LAOS

THAILAND

VIETNAM

South China Sea

MALAYSIA

INDIA

96

95

99

Bay of Bengal

88

SRI LANKA

89

OMAN

UAE

ARABIAN SEA

Equator

INDIAN OCEAN

PHILIPPINES

Philippine Sea

GUAM

I N D O N E S I A

93

PAPUA NEW GUINEA

SOLOMON ISLANDS

NEW CALEDONIA

FIJI

CORAL SEA

AUSTRALIA

84

Tasman Sea

NEW ZEALAND

©NORTH ARROW MAPS, LLC 2006

MILES

0   300   600   900   1200

N
W   E
S

PART IV - THE RENAISSANCE AND THE AGE OF EXPLORATION

MAP 4

PART 4
THE RENAISSANCE AND THE AGE OF EXPLORATION

82 AFRICA, DUTCH OCCUPATION IN

The Dutch first considered the idea of establishing trade with Africa even as they were fighting for their lives against their overlord, Philip II of Spain. Their first contact with the maritime routes to Africa came from Jan Huyghen van Linschoten, who for seven years was the servant of the archbishop of Goa, the Portuguese settlement on the western coast of India. Van Linschoten wrote detailed geographical descriptions of his travels for the archbishop and published them as the Itinerario. The information contained in this book proved valuable to the first Dutch sailors to Africa.

In 1595 the Dutch launched their first trading expedition, which went to the Guinea coast near the mouth of the Niger River. They exchanged salt, wine, cloth, copper, flax, timber, and wood products from all over Europe for the gold and ivory for which the area was famous. Within three years, five fleets totaling 22 ships were trading in African harbors. However, their first trading post was not established until 1617, when they concluded a treaty with a local chieftain on the island of Goree, among the Portuguese-held Cape Verde Islands. Twenty years later, the Dutch attacked Portuguese settlements, and by the early 1640s were masters of the Gold Coast.

The major Dutch colonial venture in Africa was not along the Gold Coast but at the continent's southern extreme. After a shipwreck, survivors of the Haarlem discovered the potential of the land that would become South Africa. Their descriptions of the area to the Dutch East India Company convinced the Dutch to establish a base there, for they were in need of a shipping resupply point for carrying on trade with India and the Spice Islands. The company built a fort near the southernmost tip of Africa, around which Cape Town grew up.

The project to found Cape Town and the accompanying fort was directed by Jan van Riebeeck, who arrived on 6 April 1652. Van Riebeeck quickly realized that the fort and town's survival required colonists to exploit the rich agricultural region nearby. Therefore, in 1657 the company began granting land to retiring employees; within a year the colonists were enslaving the local population, but the colony took root. The Castle of Good Hope was constructed between 1666 and 1679, and a second fort was built at Newlands. The nearby mountain was an ideal location for vineyards, receiving the name Wynberg, or Wine Mountain. Through the remainder of the century and into the 1700s, the colony grew slowly, increasing with the immigration of political exiles from the Netherlands and interbreeding with the local population.

The financial fortunes of Cape Town rose and fell with the Dutch competition with Great Britain. Britain had failed to capture the colony during the Seven Years' War, but the defeat of Holland's ally, France, left the colony exposed. When Napoleon conquered the Netherlands, Britain took over the colony to keep it from falling into Napoleon's hands. When Napoleon was defeated in 1815, Britain acquired South Africa (the Cape Colony). Though Britain had political control, the Dutch settlers, or Boers, were slow to cooperate with the new owners, and ultimately warfare between the two broke out.

The strongest heritage of modern-day Cape Town is from the Dutch. The whitewashed walls, spacious and lofty interiors, and massive furniture are all relics of the Dutch era. The Dutch Reformed Church dominated the religious life of the Boer settlers, persuading them that they were a chosen people in a heathen land with divine sanction to do whatever was necessary to master it. The Dutch dialect of Afrikaans remains one of the official languages of the country.

See also East Indies, Dutch Occupation of the; Saxony, Prussian Invasion of (Seven Years' War); South Africa, British Occupation of.

References: Collins, Robert, Europeans in Africa (New York: Knopf, 1971); Heppie, Alexander, South Africa: A Political and Economic History (London: Pall Mall Press, 1966); Israel, Jonathan, Dutch Primacy in World Trade, 1585–1740 (Oxford: Clarendon Press, 1989).

83 AFRICA, PORTUGUESE OCCUPATION IN

The Portuguese did not intend to settle Africa, only to sail around it. The Muslim Middle East controlled the spice trade, and prices were high for European consumers, so in the early 1400s the Portuguese established a new overseas trade route to compete with the Muslims. They also hoped to spread Christianity through the assistance of the legendary Prester John, a Christian king reportedly located somewhere in Africa. An alliance with John would aid both in fighting the Muslims (if necessary) and giving to Portugal sites for trading bases to the Spice Islands and the interior of Africa, where the Muslims also controlled the trans–Saharan gold trade.

The first expeditions down the northwest African coast began in the early 1440s. The Portuguese set up bases at Sao Tome, the Cape Verde Islands, the mouth of the Senegal River, and Guinea. Each expedition traveled a bit farther south and brought back new information for the next voyage. By the 1480s, settlements were set up in Angola. Vasco de Gama's trip in 1497–1498 took the Portuguese around the Cape of Good Hope, and soon afterward Mozambique, on the Indian Ocean coast, was settled. From there Portuguese merchants had access to the spice trade in the Indian Ocean.

The early Portuguese settlements along the western coasts attempted to access the gold and ivory of the region, but the interests of the merchants soon transferred almost exclusively to slaves. The trading posts turned from their original intentions of promoting local agriculture and trading goods to dealing with the already flourishing slave trade from the interior. Native prisoners of war had long been owned as slaves or sold to Arab merchants, but the Portuguese soon cornered the market. Through their bases (each of which was part trading post and part fort), they dealt with local slavers, who provided an almost unlimited supply. It was such a lucrative business that it attracted almost every element of Portuguese colonial society, from the bureaucrats to the clergy. Slaves were taken by the Portuguese administration in exchange for taxes, then sold abroad or used for local agricultural or mining ventures operated by the Portuguese.

The Mozambique colony was originally used as access to the Rhodesian gold fields and as the major stopping point for ships sailing from Europe to India. When the gold revenues did not meet expectations, the Portuguese moved farther inland up the Zambezi River, not to colonize but to get closer to the gold supply. In 1569 Portugal's King Sebastian sent an expedition up the Zambezi to secure control of the gold mines, dislodge the Swahili traders, and gain access for Catholic missionaries. The thousand-man force was almost completely destroyed by disease, and had no luck in establishing permanent control. The missionaries had little success in converting the area's natives, and by the end of the eighteenth century, most missions were abandoned. By 1836, Mozambique shifted its focus to slave trading as well.

The Portuguese rarely controlled extensive landholdings, but their presence along the coastlines had numerous long-term effects. Many of the early settlers were convicts or other undesirables banished from Portugal who intermarried with the locals and became Africanized. They were probably more influential in spreading Catholicism through their marriages than the Church was through its missionaries. Large-scale Jesuit and Dominican missionary ventures had little success in converting the local populations, most of whom remained true to their native religions or found more comfort in Islam. The missionaries involved in the slave trade also did little to promote willing conversions. Still, what little European culture filtered into Africa through the Portuguese came through the efforts of the Church. As the traditional venue for education, the missionaries ran the few European-style schools in the Portuguese colonies. Little attempt was made to educate the mass of Africans; rather, the schools focused on educating those few who were needed to assist the Portuguese in exploiting their property.

The Portuguese had the longest-lasting colonial experience in Africa, but the least effect on the local populations. Because their primary goal was exploitation, the Portuguese disseminated little culture or education. When the last Portuguese colony, Mozambique, gained its independence in 1975, its population was mainly illiterate, diseased, and poverty-stricken. The colony of Angola was no better; though blessed with rich mineral resources, its people lacked the education and dedication necessary to use those resources for the general good. The long-term Portuguese presence proved far more destructive than positive.

See also Ceylon, Portuguese Occupation of.

References: Duffy, James, *Portuguese Africa* (Cambridge, MA: Harvard University Press, 1968); Ferreira, Eduardo, *Portuguese Colonialism in Africa* (Paris: UNESCO Press, 1974); Newitt, Marilyn, *Portugal in Africa* (London: Longman, 1981).

AUSTRALIA, BRITISH OCCUPATION OF

84

The continent of Australia became predominantly British in heritage because the Dutch did not follow up their discovery. The Dutch East India Company did not care to pursue the exploration of the land they called New Holland, despite Governor Anthony van Damien's assurances of the availability of gold and silver. The company preferred to focus on the established spice trade in the Indies, viewing the north and west coasts of Australia (all they had knowledge of) as a barren land.

The English first viewed Australia from the more inviting east coast. In 1688, a shipload of buccaneers landed onshore. Among the crew was William Dampier, who used his descriptive talents to advertise the country when he returned to England, and was able to gain enough backing to charter the *Roebuck* in 1699 for a more intense exploration. It was largely a failure, but he brought back enough information to keep some interest alive in England. That interest was pursued by a tiny band of adventure-minded citizens; the interest of the British government was still three-quarters of a century away.

The Royal Society commissioned another expedition, which sailed on the *Earl of Pembroke* in 1769. The ship carried a group of astronomers interested in viewing Venus as it crossed the face of the sun, an event best viewed deep in the Southern Hemisphere. Captain James Cook was chosen to command the ship, and given leave to explore Australia while the astronomers explored the sky. Cook sailed along the coast in the summer of 1770, mapping it and charting possible landing or colonization sites.

The exploration was well timed, because an upsurge of crime in England, coupled with the impending loss of colonies in North America, meant that the government had to find another location for its criminals. The newly passed Enclosure Laws, which denied public land to

Aboriginies with spears attack Europeans in a touring boat in this 1830 drawing by Joseph Lycett. (National Library of Australia PIC R5688 LoC MS SR)

poor farmers and shepherds, forced a number of countryfolk to the cities, where crime became an even more pressing problem.

"Transportation" as punishment for crime was well established in English law: Some 50,000 people had been sent to North America in the 60 years prior to the revolution. Australia began to look quite appealing as an alternative for the removal of undesirable elements.

At the instigation of Sir Joseph Banks, James Matra, and Sir George Young, the Transportation Act of 1784 officially created the Australian colonies. Matra, who had sailed with Cook, proposed that the government investigate Australia as a site for a penal colony and also as a possible headquarters for trade with the Spice Islands, China, and Japan. Three years later, six vessels sailed from Portsmouth, reaching Botany Bay on 26 January 1789; Captain (then Governor) Arthur Phillip led the expedition. He soon rejected Botany Bay, the primary location indicated by Cook as a colonization site. Instead, the group established Port Jackson at the site that ultimately became Sydney. Over the next 40 years, other settlements would be founded at Norfolk Island, Melbourne, and Hobart. The first convict-settlers were apparently little motivated, and the colony gained few free settlers in its early years. By 1820, the census named only 2,201 colonists as "free immigrants"; the remainder were convicts who had either served their time or were still incarcerated. When land was granted as a retirement bonus to military officers and convict labor was made available free of charge, the country became more attractive. It took some time for the colony to become more than a penal colony, but in the nineteenth century, whaling, sealing, flax and cloth product ion, and sheepherding became important industries. The food supply increased, as did livestock after breeding for the Australian climate was perfected.

The natives of Australia benefited little from their contact with the outside world. The aborigines lived a Stone Age hunter-gatherer lifestyle, and had little interest in the white settlers. Governor Phillip's original orders called for him to establish close and friendly relations with the aborigines, and to punish anyone who harmed them. Unfortunately, the natives had no concept of private property and therefore could not grasp the practice of claiming land or trespass. Thus, less enlightened settlers persecuted them through greed or ignorance, and some historians believe that the 1789 smallpox epidemic among the aborigines was started intentionally. Contact with white society had a major impact on them, and little of it for the better.

By 1850 Australia was a burgeoning colony. There was an expanding economy based on trade and manufacture, and 1851 brought a gold rush. Australia was eventually divided into six colonies, which federated in the 1880s. After many complaints to London concerning its local needs, Australia was granted commonwealth status in 1901. It remains a member of the British Commonwealth of Nations, and its English ties took Australian soldiers to South Africa in the Boer War; Europe and the Middle East in World War I; and North Africa in World War II.

References: Eddy, J. J., *Britain and the Australian Colonies* (Oxford: Clarendon Press, 1969); Frost, Aian, *Convicts and Empire* (Oxford: Oxford University Press, 1980); Shaw, A. G. L., *Convicts and the Colonies* (London: Faber & Faber, 1966).

AUSTRIA, TURKISH INVASION OF

85

After the Ottoman Turks destroyed the remains of the Byzantine Empire by capturing Constantinople in 1453, they had a strong hold on southeastern Europe and wanted to expand their power and their religion farther into Europe. The Turks were turned away after an unsuccessful siege of Belgrade in 1456, but Serbia fell to them in 1459, a year after they captured Athens with no resistance. Bosnia accepted Turkish dominance and Islam in 1463, and Albania fell to them in 1479. Hungary, however, kept the Turks at bay into the sixteenth century. In 1514, Hungary declared a crusade against the Turks and called for troops. Massive numbers of peasants responded; once armed, however, they attacked the nobility instead. The suppression of the revolt forced an even more oppressive dominance over the peasantry and left the country open to possible invasion. The

The Turkish camp surrounding Vienna, 1529. (National Library, Vienna)

Ottoman leader who staged the invasion was Suleiman, called the Wise by his people, the Magnificent by the West. In 1521 he invaded Hungary and captured Szabacs and Belgrade, then turned against the Knights of St. John in Rhodes, whose position threatened Muslim control of the eastern Mediterranean; he secured the island on 1 January 1523. In 1525 Suleiman received a request from Francis I of France, inviting him to invade Hungary in order to weaken the power of Habsburg Emperor Charles V. Turkish forces marched in April 1526, and the pope called for the Christian faithful to resist the Muslim invaders. Martin Luther persuaded his followers not to respond to this call, and even Charles declined to fight. Suleiman's force of some 75,000 scored a difficult victory at Mohacs, and Christianity suffered a moral defeat as well. Suleiman made Hungary a tributary under the control of Transylvanian John Zapolya.

Zapolya consolidated his power in Hungary, but drew the attention of Ferdinand of Habsburg, who defeated him at Tokay. Zapolya appealed for aid, and Suleiman marched in 1529, bringing 80,000 soldiers; Zapolya provided 6,000. Buda fell after a five-day siege and, aided by a flotilla on the Danube, the Turks approached Vienna in late September. They surrounded the city, and for three weeks bombarded and attempted to mine the walls, but failed to breach them. Suleiman withdrew in mid-October to go into winter quarters, but he was pursued by the Austrians, who harassed him constantly and severely damaged his flotilla at Bratislava.

Suleiman returned in force in 1532, but after inconclusive fighting he retreated. Pressed by Persia to his rear, Suleiman decided to make peace in 1533 with Ferdinand of Habsburg, who had to pay tribute to the Turks, but who gained control of about a third of Hungary. Ferdinand was granted, in Suleiman's words, an eternal peace if he would but observe it. He did not. At the urging of Charles V, Ferdinand joined other European forces invading Turkish Hungary in 1537. They were defeated and virtually destroyed during their retreat. Suleiman led his army back into Hungary and annexed it to his empire. Ferdinand attacked at Pest in 1542 but was repulsed, and Suleiman entered Austria, armed with a veteran army and an alliance with France. He pillaged throughout the country until 1544, when France abrogated the treaty. Suleiman again made peace with Ferdinand under the terms of their first agreement.

Ferdinand could not leave well enough alone. He invaded Transylvania in 1551 and was repulsed, but he managed to defeat a Turkish counteroffensive. After desultory fighting, the two leaders renewed their treaty in 1562 at the Peace of Prague. The Austrian Habsburgs were at peace, but Suleiman was still engaged in a war with the Holy Roman Empire. When Emperor Maximilian ordered another attack on Hungary, the 72-year-old Suleiman returned to Austria at the head of a 100,000-man army. The Turks won a month-long siege of Szigeth, but Suleiman died just before the city fell, so the Turks returned home.

Upon Suleiman's death, the Ottoman Empire came under the rule of Selim, known as the Sot. After Selim's navy was defeated at the battle of Lepanto in 1571, Ottoman power began to decline. Fighting with Austrian and Holy Roman Empire forces in the 1590s weakened the Ottoman hold on Hungary and Turkish possessions in the Balkans. The Thirty Years' War diverted European attention away from the Balkans until the 1660s, when the Turks returned to advance on Vienna under the leadership of Fazil Ahmed Koprulu Pasha. They were checked at Neuhause in September 1663 and postponed their attack until the following spring, by which time the Austrians were stronger and better prepared. The battle of St. Gotthard Abbey was fought as peace talks were being held, and the Turks were forced to retreat to Belgrade. The Peace of Vasvar, signed in August 1664, called for a 20-year peace and ceded Transylvania to Turkey. After the 20-year truce, the Turks were back in 1683. Hungary was in the process of rebelling against Austria, so the Austrians were pressed by a number of enemies: the Hungarians, Transylvanians, and Turks. Muhammad IV arrived at Vienna in June with 150,000 men to besiege a city defended by a mere 15,000. The Turks had little siege artillery, but they managed to breach the walls in a few places. They could not break through in strength, however, and

Vienna was spared by the fortuitous arrival of Pole Jan Sobiesky at the same time a German force marched to help. A mixed Austrian-German-Polish force of 70,000 engaged the Turks outside Vienna on 12 September. After a daylong battle, the Turks fled, and the city was saved. When Sobiesky later pursued the Turks, he captured Grau and much of Hungary, which came under Habsburg control over the next five years.

Suleiman II made the last serious threat toward Habsburg territories in 1690, but his defeat at Szalankemen in 1691 and at Zenta in 1697 ended that endeavor. In January 1699 the two powers signed the Treaty of Karlowitz, which ceded Hungary to Austria and left the Turks in control of Serbia.

The defeat of the Turkish invasions served to consolidate Habsburg control in central and southeast Europe, but also stopped Islam from expanding past the Balkans. The Catholics and Protestants had more than their share of struggles, but Christianity in one form or another would remain the religion of most of Europe. Hungary, under Habsburg rule, was later incorporated into the Austro-Hungarian Empire, but the ethnic struggles of the myriad populations of that region simmered under Habsburg control, and to a great extent, continue to this day.

See also Byzantine Empire; Ottoman Empire; Thirty Years' War.

References: Held, Joseph, *Hunyadi: Legend and Reality* (New York: Columbia University Press, 1985); Kinross, Patrick, *The Ottoman Centuries* (New York: Morrow, 1977); Spielman, John, *The City and the Crown: Vienna and the Imperial Court, 1600–1740* (West Lafayette, IN: Purdue University Press, 1993).

BRAZIL, PORTUGUESE COLONIZATION OF

86

When the Portuguese explorer Cabral discovered Brazil in 1500, it was fortuitous that this landmass was dedicated to Portuguese ownership. In 1494, at the direction of the pope, the Spanish and Portuguese signed the Treaty of Tordesillas, in which the world was divided in half for the two signatories to exploit. Spain colonized most of the Western Hemisphere without competition, and the Portuguese dominated trade and exploration along the coasts of Africa and Asia. The only part of the Western Hemisphere ceded to Portugal by the treaty was an area several degrees of longitude from South America's east coast into the interior.

Unlike Central America and Peru, Brazil had little to offer in the way of resources or labor. However, the Portuguese produced agricultural surplus when they introduced sugar cane from the Caribbean and slaves from Africa. With these assets, Brazil grew rich and, as more colonists explored the interior, they discovered valuable metals. Portugal focused its colonization efforts on Brazil because the populations of Africa and Asia resisted Portuguese attempts at settlement, though they gladly engaged in trade. As Portugal's military and economic power ebbed in the African and Asian markets, its interest in the continuing success of Brazil grew.

Portuguese colonists dominated the economic and political life of Brazil, but socially they were open-minded. While it was virtually impossible for a nonwhite to attain high political office, whites, natives, and blacks mingled freely in society and culture. The Brazilian Portuguese were as brutal in their treatment of slaves as any owners anywhere, but they treated free blacks with openness. Mixed-race marriages were common, and children of these unions were accepted without social prejudice. Of all the imperial experiences, only the British in New Zealand approached the racial openness of Brazil. Perhaps this was why Brazil did not chafe at Portuguese control; either they enjoyed the public equality or, by being denied education, had little knowledge of nationalism. Even though large sums left the country for tribute and taxes, the Brazilian upper classes remained loyal.

Brazil gained independence almost by accident. The royal family fled Lisbon for Rio de Janeiro in 1808 when threatened by Napoleon's forces. Not only did they find a country richer and more populous than the one they had left, but they also discovered many of the comforts of home and a society that spoke their language, worshipped in the Catholic Church, and held many of their values. Because of the presence of royalty, Rio de Janeiro became the capital of the

Portuguese Empire. In 1815, Brazil was declared a full sister kingdom, which opened the country to foreign trade previously restricted to Portugal. Brazil grew even more wealthy as it established further contacts with the outside world. This wealth, along with the spectacle of lavish royal spending, the stronger authority of Portuguese courts and officials, and the more direct exploitation of resources (little of which benefited the native population), caused a rebellious attitude. Rio grew more powerful at the expense of outlying provinces, which began rebelling in 1817.

When Britain's Duke of Wellington dislodged French forces in 1811, the royal family was free to return to Lisbon. King Juan VI liked Rio, however, and he stayed until 1820. By then Portugal was chafing at being a virtual colony of Brazil. The Portuguese at home resented the extended presence of the British, the diminution of the international trade they once enjoyed, and the lack of Brazilian income, which stayed with the royal family in Rio. Demands for a liberal constitutional government brought King Juan back to Portugal in 1821, leaving his son Dom Pedro as regent. The Portuguese government demanded a return to the old ways, with Portugal as the center of the empire and Brazil the colony, but the Brazilians had little desire to part with their newly acquired rights and privileges. When Dom Pedro agreed to become king of Brazil and adopt a liberal constitution, the nation declared its independence.

Brazil became officially independent in 1825 when Lisbon recognized its status through the diplomatic efforts of Great Britain. In return, Brazil assumed a large debt that Portugal owed Britain and bought King Juan's estates. Brazil also received British recognition and trade treaties, but at the cost of abolishing the slave trade. Dom Pedro, now Emperor Pedro, tried to maintain family control of both Portugal and Brazil by having his daughter (from Brazil) marry his brother (in Portugal), but he was unable to do so. Brazil remained a constitutional monarchy until the establishment of a republic in 1889.

See also Western Hemisphere, Spanish Occupation of; Napoleon Buonaparte; New Zealand, British Occupation of.

References: Diffie, Bailey, *A History of Colonial Brazil* (Malabar, FL: R. E. Krieger, 1987); Macaulay, Neill, *Dom Pedro* (Durham, NC: Duke University Press, 1986); Prado, Caio, *The Colonial Background of Modern Brazil* (Berkeley: University of California Press, 1967).

87 CARIBBEAN, EUROPEAN OCCUPATION OF

When Christopher Columbus arrived in the Caribbean in October 1492, he was the first European to sight the numerous islands of that sea, and he laid claim to many of them for Spain. The Spanish dominated the area for at least a century, but the islands changed hands periodically through conquest or treaty. Wars in Europe often brought about changes in ownership of Caribbean islands, and the use of these islands as diplomatic bargaining chips did not stop until the nineteenth century.

The Bahamas

The Bahamas were probably the first islands Columbus saw in the Western Hemisphere, but the site of his first landing is the subject of debate. The island Columbus called San Salvador is probably Samana Cay. The first established colony was not Spanish, however, but British. A century and a half after Columbus, the British settled the islands of Eleuthera and New Providence. Though often attacked by the Spanish, they remained under British control. The Bahamas served as a base of operations for buccaneers who struck at the Spanish and any other handy island or ship. At the turn of the eighteenth century, the islands came under the direction of the American colony of Carolina, but the British Crown reassumed direct control in 1717. During the American Revolution, some of the islands were held briefly by foreign powers: The Americans occupied Nassau, and the Spanish were in control at war's end. British rule was restored by the Treaty of Paris, which ended the revolution. The islands suffered economically for decades when slavery was abolished, and again when a cholera epidemic ravaged the population. Proximity to the United States, however, proved profitable when the islands were used by

Confederate blockade runners during the Civil War and by alcohol smugglers during the 1920s era of Prohibition. The British granted local autonomy in 1964 and independence in 1973.

Bermuda

Like the Bahamas, Bermuda was first discovered by a Spaniard but settled by the British. Juan de Bermudez was shipwrecked on the islands in 1503, but no settlement ensued for a century. In 1612, while on his way to Virginia, the British sailor George Somers found himself shipwrecked there as well. The islands bore his name for a time, and were under the direction of the colony of Virginia until 1684, when the Crown took them over. With the introduction of African slaves and the importation of Portuguese laborers from the Azores, the population grew. The Bermuda Islands served as havens for Confederate blockade runners and, at the turn of the twentieth century, as a holding location for prisoners from the Boer War. British warships were based there throughout the nineteenth and twentieth centuries, and the United States received 99-year leases for naval bases under the lend-lease arrangement between the United States and Great Britain.

Cuba

Christopher Columbus made landfall at Cuba on his first voyage and found the island inhabited by the Ciboney, a tribe related to the Arawak. He left some men behind, but the first colony was not established until 1511, when Diego Velazquez founded the settlements of Baracoa, Santiago, and Havana. Cuba was used mainly as a supply base for expeditions to Florida and Mexico. Only after the indigenous population died through disease and abuse did the island become dedicated to agriculture, with labor provided by African slaves. It was often the target of both pirate raids and more organized attacks by the British or Dutch navies, but Cuba remained firmly in Spanish hands until the Seven Years' War, when the British captured Havana. When complete control of the island returned to Spain after the Treaty of Paris of 1763, the Spanish

instituted a liberalized administration encouraging settlement and commerce. By 1817, the population of the island had grown to half a million. Trade laws continued to be liberalized, but the local administration grew more harsh. By the 1830s, the first independence movement formed to rebel against the tyrannical rule of the captain-general, Miguel de Tacon. This revolt and others that followed were suppressed, usually with great loss of life. In the early 1850s, Spanish-American general Narciso Lopez plotted with U.S. officials in Europe to seize Cuba for the United States, but the discovery of the plot and the execution of Lopez ended the scheme.

The United States occasionally offered to buy Cuba, but could never interest Spain in selling the island. Still, whenever the local population rebelled, the United States took an interest and sheltered refugees. In 1873, in the midst of the Ten Years' War, the United States nearly involved itself when some U.S. citizens were executed for gun-running, but a Spanish apology and payment of damages calmed the situation. Not until the revolution of the 1890s, led by Jose Marti, did the United States finally intervene. Spain left a legacy of bitterness in Cuba, but also a culture that is heavily Spanish in its religion, language, and arts.

French West Indies

The French joined the Spanish, English, Dutch, and Danes in the Caribbean colonization game in the seventeenth century, settling colonies on a number of islands. None of these islands had the production capacity of Haiti, or the official notice, but some stayed in French hands much longer. Only Guadaloupe and Martinique (with five small islands nearby) survived as French colonies. Other islands the French had colonized, such as Grenada, St. Kitts, Dominica, St. Martin, and St. Eustatius, were extremely valuable as sugar producers in the eighteenth century and became pawns in European politics. Most were ceded to Great Britain when France lost a number of conflicts on the Continent. Still, they served as profitable markets for American colonists, and played a role in the growing conflict that led to the American Revolution. France made the French West Indies an overseas department in the Fourth Republic in 1946.

Hispaniola

First discovered and settled by the Spanish, the island of Hispaniola was originally populated by an Arawak tribe, the main people (along with the Caribs) of the region. Exploitation under Spanish rule and the introduction of European disease soon made the Arawaks extinct. Thus, the main population of the island came to be slaves imported from Africa. Spain maintained control over the entire island until 1697, when the Peace of Ryswick (ending the War of the League of Augsburg) transferred the western third of the island to the French, who established the colony of Saint-Domingue (now Haiti). The Spanish neighbor on the remainder of the island was Santo Domingo, now the Dominican Republic.

The French invested in their section and it flourished, but Spain's other, more profitable islands kept their portion from growing. In fact, the Spanish cared so little for their share of the island that they ceded it to France in 1795.

The following decade proved tumultuous. Local General Toussaint L'Ouverture first freed the slaves of Haiti, then aided the new French republic in dislodging invading British troops, and established local rule under his leadership. Napoleon sent forces to recapture the island; they took L'Ouverture prisoner but at such a high cost in manpower that Napoleon abandoned the colony. General Jean Jacques Dessalines declared the independence of Saint-Domingue in 1804, and renamed the new nation Haiti.

After Dessalines's assassination in 1806, the island changed leadership regularly, and the eastern section declared itself independent of Haiti. The Spanish reoccupied Santo Domingo and in 1814, after Napoleon's defeat, instituted a harsh government. The abuse provoked a rebellion in 1821 and a declaration of independence, but Santo Domingo was soon invaded and occupied by Haiti. In 1843 Haitian rule was finally overthrown and the independent nation of the Dominican Republic was created. The Dominicans argued among themselves over whether to offer themselves to Spain or the United States; Spain reestablished control in 1861, but left four years later. The incessant political infighting and lack of economic promise kept the Spanish from regretting their decision.

The United States came to the economic rescue of a heavily indebted Dominican Republic in 1906, but rioting forced the establishment of a military government in 1916. Fighting in Haiti also led to U.S. Marines landing there in 1915. After the liberation of Haiti from the French and the Dominican Republic from the Spanish, the United States became the island's major influence. The two sections of the island, particularly the black and mixed-race populations, maintain strong cultural influences from their original colonizers, and the use of the French and Spanish languages is widespread.

Jamaica

The original inhabitants of this island were Arawak, and their word for "isle of springs" gives the island its name. Sighted by Columbus on his second voyage to the hemisphere, Jamaica received its Spanish colonists in 1509. As in Hispaniola, the Arawak population was soon completely wiped out and replaced by African slaves. The island was attacked and captured by British forces under Sir William Penn in 1655; his original assignment from Oliver Cromwell was to capture Santo Domingo, but that effort failed. The middle 1600s was an active time in the Caribbean, with Spanish, English, and Dutch forces attacking one another's possessions, and many islands gaining and losing temporary masters. Jamaica, however, remained British by the Treaty of Madrid in 1670, in which the British promised to halt piracy and the Spanish ceded control of the island.

The British made Jamaica an economically strong island, overseeing the production of cacao, sugar, and timber. Their success brought about an even greater demand for slaves, and Jamaica became one of the world's largest slave-trading markets. For 150 years slavery was an integral part of Jamaican life, but in the

1830s the British government outlawed the practice throughout their empire. Some 310,000 slaves were freed in 1838, and they immediately took over unclaimed land; the production of the past decades dwindled almost to a halt. Increased taxation and discriminatory laws provoked an uprising by the black population in 1865, but it was quickly and brutally suppressed. The local autonomy enjoyed by the island was removed, and Jamaica became a crown colony.

Jamaica is one of the most "British" of Caribbean islands because, even when it was not thriving economically, it was an important military base for the Royal Navy. It has a parliamentary government patterned after Great Britain's, and recognizes as head of state the British monarch, who has a governor-general resident on the island. Power is exercised through a cabinet headed by a prime minister, and the legal code is based on English common law.

Puerto Rico

The island of Puerto Rico was captured in 1509 by Ponce de Leon, who was named its first Spanish governor. The island was populated by the Borinqueno but, as happened so often, they were wiped out by abuse and disease. The Borinqueno were used as forced labor by the Spanish, but after their extermination, the African slave trade brought replacement labor for the plantations and sugar mills. Pirates frequently raided the island, and the Spanish built a number of forts that were stout enough to defeat an attack in 1595 by the famous British pirates Sir Francis Drake and Sir John Hawkins, the latter of whom died of wounds received in the fight. The Dutch attacked the capital city of San Juan and burned it in 1625, and the British sacked Arecibo in 1702.

None of this was sufficient to remove Puerto Rico from Spanish hands, and the island received positive treatment from the homeland: Foreign trade was allowed in 1804, and the Puerto Ricans were granted a seat in the Spanish Parliament in 1808. Nevertheless, the population occasionally rebelled during the nineteenth century. The most serious uprising was the El Grito

de Lares in 1868 but, like all the others, it was suppressed. Spain granted the island local autonomy in 1897, but lost possession to the United States in the Spanish-American War the following year.

The Virgin Islands

Like so many other Caribbean islands, this group, lying east of Puerto Rico, was first located by Columbus, who named them after St. Ursula and other virgin martyrs. They were first settled in 1648 by the Dutch, but one of the islands, St. Thomas, was settled by Denmark, which used it as a base for the Danish West Indies Company. The company controlled the three islands of St. Thomas, St. Croix, and St. John, which were bought by the Danish king in 1755. As on most of the other islands, slavery was practiced, and sugar was the main export.

St. Thomas was occupied by the British during the Napoleonic Wars but restored to Denmark after 1815. Sugar continued as the main crop, but the abolition of slavery in 1848 brought about a decline in production. In 1867 the United States entered into negotiations to buy the Danish West Indies, and an agreement was reached in 1917. The United States continues to govern the islands, but since 1968 the people have been allowed to elect their own governor.

The remaining Virgin Islands belong to Great Britain, which acquired them from the Dutch in 1666. Once a popular pirate haven through the 1600s, today most of its visitors are tourists, from whom the islands draw much of their income. They also have a British-style government, though the governor is appointed from London.

See also Palatinate, French Invasion of the (War of the League of Augsburg); Saxony, Prussian Invasion of (Seven Years' War); Western Hemisphere, Spanish Occupation of; Napoleon Buonaparte; Cuba, U.S. Invasion of; South Africa, British Occupation of; Latin America, U.S. Interventions in.

References: Claypole, William, *Caribbean Story, 2 vols.* (San Juan, PR: Longman Caribbean, 1989); Hamshere, Cyril, *The British in the Caribbean* (Cambridge, MA: Harvard University Press, 1972); Severin, Timothy, *The Golden Antilles* (New York: Knopf, 1970).

88 CEYLON, DUTCH OCCUPATION OF

Portugal's fading mercantile power in the 1600s, coupled with difficulties in cooperating with the local population, provided an opening for the rising power of the Netherlands in the affairs of Ceylon. Unlike the Portuguese, who wanted to spread Catholicism as well as trade, the Dutch were interested in trade only. They allied themselves with the mountain kingdom of Kandy to fight the Portuguese, and in 1656 established themselves as the dominant foreign power on the island. Through the Dutch East India Company, a civil administration was established, directed by a military governor. The Dutch introduced a civil service that, like the Portuguese system, worked with the local government in trade (especially cinnamon) and civil works such as fort and canal construction.

The Dutch soon had troubles with their erstwhile ally, Kandy. The Kandyans were a fiercely independent monarchy, and they raided Dutch forts, for which they suffered Dutch retribution. The Kandyan king Rajasinha II was the major irritant to the Dutch. He hated all whites, and mistreated any with whom he came in contact, whether prisoners or ambassadors. He constantly broke his agreements with the Dutch, and punished any native who cooperated with them. Unable to remove him from his mountain home, the Dutch ultimately left the island's interior to Rajasinha and confined themselves to the coastal areas.

Ceylon was a profitable possession for the Dutch, but eventually the home government grew less interested. When the Netherlands had to deal with the rising power of France in the 1790s, they sold their Ceylonese interests to the British.

During their time on the island, the Dutch established a new law code based on Dutch and Roman law, much of which remains in effect today. They maintained a fair administration, and provided public services to the local population. Other than the law codes, they had little long-term effect on the island. With no distinctive architectural legacy and few remnants of Dutch in the local language, they left behind less of themselves than had the Portuguese.

See also Ceylon, Portuguese Occupation of.

References: Beny, Roloff, *Island Ceylon* (London: Thames & Hudson, 1970); Codrington, Humphrey, *A Short History of Ceylon* (Freeport, NY: Books for Libraries, 1926); Tresidder, Argus, *Ceylon: An Introduction to the Resplendent Land* (Princeton, NJ: Van Nos-trand, 1960).

89 CEYLON, PORTUGUESE OCCUPATION OF

For centuries the Muslims had trade connections with Ceylon, which created some friction when the Portuguese arrived in 1505. The Iberians had been fighting to remove the Muslims from their homeland for several centuries, so there was no love lost between the two cultures. Portugal, the sole European trading power in Asia, did not want economic competition from anyone. When Dom Laurenco de Almeida landed at Colombo, he had to establish a Portuguese power base to protect national interests, so he began construction of a fort at the harbor town. The king of the lowland Sinhalese population, at the capital city of Kotte, welcomed the Portuguese. He was impressed by their guns and armor, and asked their protection in return for an annual tribute to be paid in cinnamon. King Parakrama Bahu VIII hoped to use the Europeans to secure his position against threats from the Tamil peoples in the northern part of the island, the highland king of Kandy, and the Moors.

The Portuguese built forts along the western coast of the island and soon dominated the export market from Ceylon. The island's traders were ruled by a governor-general on the island of Goa, who directed their economic activities throughout Asia. Working with the existing power structure, the Portuguese eventually expanded their trade dominance to political control as well. By allying themselves with the successive kings of Kotte and protecting them against the other powers on the island, they could dictate to the Sinhalese leaders. At one point, the island was divided among three rival Sinhalese brothers. When a secret embassy to Portugal in 1540 asked the government to bless an infant heir to the throne of Kotte, the Portuguese did so, then sent troops and

Franciscans to aid in the young king's rule. This event did much to consolidate Portugal's hold on the economy and the population.

The only serious threat to Portuguese power was King Rajasinha I of the local kingdom of Sitawaka. Learning from the Europeans, Rajasinha built an army furnished with modern weapons, and then defeated Portuguese troops, after which he laid siege to Colombo. He built a navy and harassed Portuguese shipping. He also made war against the other kings on the island and defeated them. At the height of his reign, which lasted from 1554 to 1593, Rajasinha controlled all of Ceylon except Colombo and the kingdom of Jaffna on a small island off Ceylon's north coast. Renouncing the dominant faith of Buddhism and becoming Hindu, he persecuted Buddhist priests on Ceylon. However, he was regarded as a national champion for defending the island from foreign invaders.

During their struggle with Rajasinha, the Portuguese earned the enmity of the Ceylonese by capturing a sacred relic, one of Buddha's teeth. The Tooth Relic was the island's most sacred possession, and losing it to a foreign power was devastating, especially when the Portuguese archbishop at Goa ordered it burned as a heathen talisman. This action, along with the resistance of the islanders under Rajasinha, badly hurt Portuguese chances of recovering their former political or trade position. When the Dutch began to expand their international trade routes, they were able to break into the Ceylon market because of Portuguese weakness.

Surprisingly, 150 years of Portuguese presence in Ceylon produced few lasting results. The main effect was the introduction of Catholicism, a faith followed to this day by a significant minority of Ceylonese. Catholic priests sent to the island by the Portuguese usually acted on behalf of their converts against government persecution, and thus made a favorable impact. Their presence during the Portuguese dominance is regarded as the major reason Islam never took strong hold in southern India or Ceylon. The Portuguese also introduced a number of new food crops, which the Ceylonese turned to the island's benefit.

See also Ceylon, Dutch Occupation of.

References: Beny, Roloff, *Island Ceylon* (London: Thames & Hudson, 1970); Codrington, Humphrey, *A Short History of Ceylon* (Freeport, NY: Books for Libraries, 1926); Tresidder, Argus, *Ceylon: An Introduction to the Resplendent Land* (Princeton, NJ: Van Nostrand, 1960).

90 CHING (MANCHU) DYNASTY

In the early 1600s, the Nuchen tribe was a burgeoning power in Manchuria, to the northeast of the Chinese Ming dynasty. They came to prominence under the leadership of Nurhachi, who united them in 1616 and began to wage war against Ming China. He constructed a strong fortress in his capital, Liaoyang, then began training his soldiers according to the Ming style. He divided them into four commands, or "banners," which later formed the basis of the Manchu political administration. In 1618, Nurhachi led his forces to war, seizing a Ming stronghold at Fushun and defeating the punitive force sent to recapture it. To counter this invasion, the Mings called on their traditional allies in Korea for reinforcements.

Nurhachi drove southwest into China, capturing Mukden in 1621. He could advance little farther, however, because the Ming army introduced artillery provided by European Jesuits, and these weapons were the deciding factor. Nurhachi gave up the assault on China for the moment, and turned west to attack Mongolia. When Nurhachi died in 1626, his son Abahai took over. In 1627, Abahai launched an invasion of Korea to cover their rear for his proposed reinvasion of China. He forced the Koreans to recognize his sovereignty, then returned in 1636 to conquer the peninsula. Repeated raids into China in the early 1630s had proved fruitless, so Abahai began to develop an artillery arm for his forces.

In 1636, Abahai proclaimed the Ching dynasty in Mukden, and the Nuchen-led invaders came to be called the Manchus. Abahai took the regnal name of Ch'ung Teh. The Manchus expanded their power into the Amur River basin in four expeditions lasting through 1644. Ch'ung Teh died in 1643, leaving the

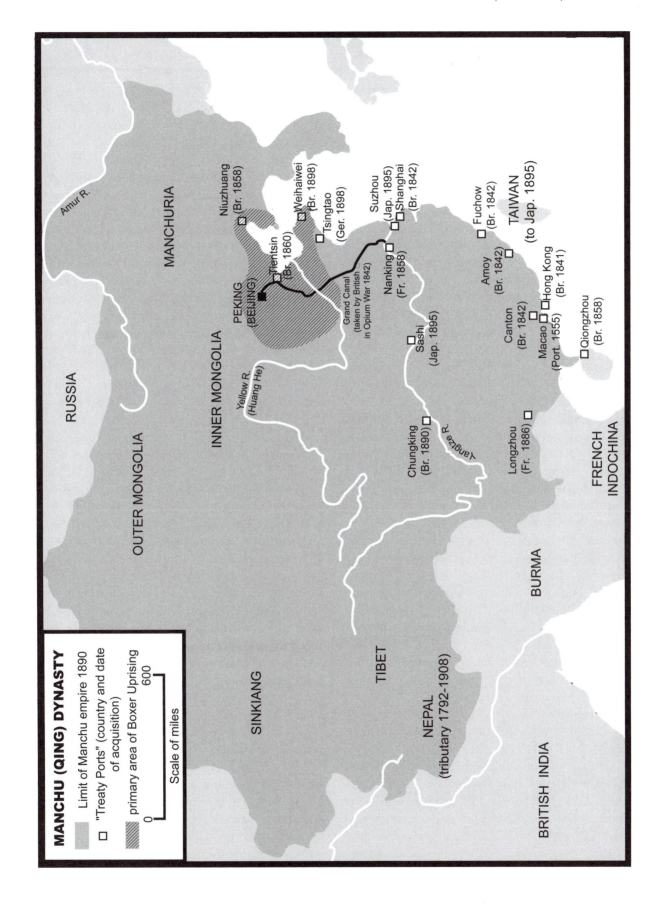

MANCHU (QING) DYNASTY

Limit of Manchu empire 1890

"Treaty Ports" (country and date of acquisition)

primary area of Boxer Uprising

0 — 600

Scale of miles

RUSSIA

Amur R.

MANCHURIA

OUTER MONGOLIA

INNER MONGOLIA

Niuzhuang (Br. 1858)

Weihaiwei (Br. 1898)

Tsingtao (Ger. 1898)

Tientsin (Br. 1860)

PEKING (BEIJING)

Yellow R. (Huang He)

Grand Canal (taken by British in Opium War 1842)

Suzhou (Jap. 1895)

Shanghai (Br. 1842)

Nanking (Fr. 1858)

Sashi (Jap. 1895)

Fuchow (Br. 1842)

TAIWAN (to Jap. 1895)

Amoy (Br. 1842)

Canton (Br. 1842)

Hong Kong (Br. 1841)

Macao (Port. 1555)

Qiongzhou (Br. 1858)

Chungking (Br. 1890)

Yangtze R.

Longzhou (Fr. 1886)

FRENCH INDOCHINA

SINKIANG

TIBET

NEPAL (tributary 1792-1908)

BURMA

BRITISH INDIA

throne to his five-year-old son Shun Chih; the young emperor's uncle Dorgon acted as regent. With the addition of Mongol troops who deserted their own army to join his, and because of the widespread rebellions against Ming authority, Dorgon was able to take advantage of the faltering dynasty. A Ming general asked for cooperation in suppressing a peasant rebellion, and the Manchus aided him. The rebel leader Li Tzu-cheng seized Peking, but lost to the combined Ming-Manchu forces just south of the Great Wall; the Manchurians occupied Peking, then attacked south. The Ming emperor established a capital at Nanking and challenged the advancing Manchus, but lost to Dorgon in a seven-day battle near Yangchow. After slaughtering the defeated army and the inhabitants of the area, Dorgon captured Nanking. From this point, the Ming dynasty began to fade. Though claimants to the throne resisted the Manchus for decades, their internal rivalry allowed the Manchus to defeat them.

Through 1647 the Manchus swept southward, capturing Fukien province and Canton. Dorgon ran into some resistance from the last Ming emperor, Kuei Wang, but defeated him and consolidated control of southern China by 1651. Manchu forces gained control of the southwestern provinces by 1659, but had trouble from the sea. The pirates of Cheng Ch'eng-kung, or Koxinga, championed the Mings and raided along the coast of China, fighting both the Manchus and the Dutch, who had trading posts in the area. The Manchus withdrew their population from the coast and established a barrier 10 miles inland; only Koxinga's death allowed them to regain control. The Manchus later cooperated with the Dutch to defeat the pirates, and the Manchus annexed Taiwan from them in 1683.

Meanwhile, the Russians pressed from the northwest. After a number of campaigns in the 1680s, the Ching emperor signed the Treaty of Nerchinsk, which removed the Russians from the Amur River valley. The Manchus also had to deal with aggressive nomadic tribes in Mongolia. Some tribes resisted the cession of suzerainty granted the Manchus at the Congress of Dolonor in 1689, but Manchu military power ultimately prevailed. With 80,000 men supported by

artillery, the Manchus crushed the main resistance, led by Galdan of the Dzungars, in 1696.

The Manchu expansion to the northwest came under the 60-year reign of Emperor K'ang-hsi (1662–1722). To secure his hold on Mongolia, K'ang-hsi ordered forces to the Tibetan border. A dispute over the Dalai Lama took Manchu troops into Tibet in 1705 to support their candidate against the opposition of most Tibetans. The Dzungars intervened with 6,000 men in 1716, capturing the capital, Lhasa, and imprisoning the Dalai Lama. The Manchu force sent to his rescue was ambushed and destroyed. K'ang-hsi responded with two armies in 1720, one of which reestablished control in Tibet; the other invaded and subdued Dzungar lands. For the first time, the Mongols fought with muskets, but they were no match for the experience of the Manchus. K'ang-hsi installed a more acceptable Dalai Lama, but he also installed a Manchu garrison in Lhasa. Troubles with Tibetans and Dzungars continued through the mid-eighteenth century.

Though successful on the frontiers, an unforeseen source spelled the Manchus' doom. The Ching Dynasty had cooperated with the Dutch and with Portuguese Jesuits, but the increasing presence of Europeans began to diminish their power. The Manchus had incorporated the Ming bureaucracy upon their takeover and embraced the Confucian philosophy upon which the bureaucracy was based. This brought about an ultraconservative view that stagnated progress in China at the same time that growing numbers of Europeans, especially the British in the nineteenth century, brought technology the Chinese could not rival. Demands for trade enforced by military might gave the British a foothold in China that encouraged other Europeans to demand and receive trade and territorial concessions. The conservatism of the imperial court brought about its fall in the early twentieth century.

The Manchus were a foreign invader who established dominance in China, as did the Mongols under the Yuan dynasty. They kept a cultural separation between Manchurians and Chinese, though they adopted most of the Chinese traditions, economy, and technology. The Manchus forced their mode of dress on the

Chinese, but for the most part they absorbed more of Chinese ways than they altered the lives of the common people.

See also China, Mongol Conquest of; Ming Dynasty; China, British Invasion of (Opium War).

References: Hookham, Hilda, *A Short History of China* (New York: St. Martin's Press, 1970); Hsu, Immanuel, *The Rise of Modern China* (New York: Oxford University Press, 1975); Twitchett, Denis, and John Fairbank, eds., *The Cambridge History of China, Vols. 9 and 10* (New York: Cambridge University Press, 1993).

91   CORTES, HERNAN

Hernan Cortes was born in Medellin, Spain. Like many other Spaniards who set sail to the New World in the 1500s, he was a minor noble. Minor Spanish nobles of his era often became conquistadors, for they were wealthy enough to travel to unsettled lands but not rich enough to be assured of the future security of their family fortunes in Spain. The prospect of attaining riches and fame as the first settlers of a newly discovered land recently claimed by the Spanish Crown appealed to many Spaniards of Cortes's generation.

Cortes first distinguished himself in Cuba, where he took part in the Spanish conquest of that island in 1511. At the time of the invasion, he was an officer under the command of Diego Velazquez, who led the military expedition to Cuba and became its governor.

In 1518 Velazquez authorized Cortes to undertake a very important mission. The Spaniards who had studied Columbus's 1492 voyages to America believed there was a kingdom close to Hispaniola that possessed vast quantities of gold. Columbus, who conquered much of the Caribbean and touched on the mainland of America, claimed that the natives of Hispaniola had revealed to him that such a kingdom existed. Cortes was to sail west toward the mainland of the Americas to search for this rich kingdom. As Cortes prepared to sail west with a military expedition, Velazquez, a highly impulsive and temperamental man, abruptly relieved him of his duties. Velazquez's relatives and cronies had pressured him to grant them the privilege of undertaking the voyage, and they persuaded him to issue orders demanding that Cortes relinquish his command. When Cortes heard of Velazquez's change of heart, he hastily ordered his men (who still believed him to be the expedition's authorized commander) to board ship and speedily set sail from Cuba. Cortes's ships landed at Trinidad for provisions, and two messengers from Governor Velazquez brought him orders to return to Cuba under arrest. Having invested virtually all of his personal financial resources in the venture, Cortes resentfully defied the orders and headed for Mexico. His heavy personal investment in the mission, as well as his relationship with the governor of Cuba (he had married Velazquez's niece), perhaps accounts for Cortes's unflinching resolution to complete his voyage and establish himself as ruler wherever he landed. Essentially a fugitive, he had much to gain and little to lose as he headed for the Mexican coast.

When he landed in Mexico on Good Friday in 1519 (in the area where present-day Veracruz is located), he learned that the area was ruled by a vast empire extending throughout Mexico. His own force consisted of only about 600 men. Many were armed with steel swords or bows and arrows,

Hernan Cortés in an engraving by W. Holl.

and only 13 carried guns. Cortes also had 14 cannons and 16 cavalry horses. His soldiers were naturally intimidated at the prospect of invading a vast empire with such a paltry force, so Cortes burned their ships to forestall any desertion.

Cortes bluntly stated his ambition to quickly enrich himself in Mexico, proclaiming, "I have come to win gold, not to plow the fields like a peasant." By 1520 he had his gold, for in the summer of that year he became ruler of an empire with some five million subjects.

Ultimately, the king of Spain richly rewarded him with lands in Spain and ordered him to return. He was granted the title of marquis, and lived quietly in Spain until his death in 1547.

See also Mexico, Aztec Conquest of; Western Hemisphere, Spanish Occupation of.

References: Innes, Hammond, *The Conquistadors* (New York: Knopf, 1969); Marks, Richard, *Cortes: The Great Adventurer and the Fate of Aztec Mexico* (New York: Knopf, 1993); White, John, *Cortez and the Fall of the Aztec Empire* (New York: St. Martin's Press, 1971).

CYPRUS, OTTOMAN INVASION OF

92

The island of Cyprus is perfectly located to be a nexus of trade for the eastern Mediterranean Sea. Unfortunately for its inhabitants, that location has made it a desirable possession for as long as ships have sailed the Mediterranean. The earliest settlements date to 6000 B.C.E., but the origin of the inhabitants is unclear. In the Bronze Age, they were cattle and horse herders, and acquired literacy. The first known conquerors were the Hittites in the middle of the second millennia B.C.E. Like the Greeks, the Cypriots fell into a dark age when overcome by the Dorians, then found themselves occupied by the Assyrians (from 709 B.C.E.), the Egyptians (from 570 B.C.E.), and the Persians (from 545 B.C.E.). During the Persian occupation, two kingdoms on the island, Kition and Salamis, became rivals, struggling for control until 333 B.C.E., when the island was taken over by the successors of Alexander the Great. They ruled for almost three centuries before being expelled by the Roman Empire.

Rome's 350-year reign was a time of peace and prosperity, the only major political upset coming with the division of the Empire into sections and Cyprus coming under the aegis of Constantinople and the Byzantine Empire. During this period (395–649 C.E.) the inhabitants were converted to Orthodox Christianity. This put them once again in the center of warring powers with the rise of Islam in the eighth century. Christian and Muslim forces battled for control of the strategic island, with the Byzantines finally emerging victories in the tenth century. Cyprus, however, began to attract European attention with the start of the Crusades. Starting with the Third Crusade, Cyprus was controlled by European Catholic forces, first those of England's Richard I, then those of the Knights Templar and the Frankish Lusignan Dynasty. The Templars, staunch Catholics that they were, incurred the wrath of the Cypriot Orthodox population, especially as the Templars exacted heavy taxes over and above the religious disputes. After a failed Cypriot rebellion in 1192, the Templars decided that holding Cyprus was too demanding in terms of both money and manpower, so they tried to get Richard of England to take it back. Richard agreed, putting the recently deposed Catholic King of Jerusalem, Guy de Lusignan, on the Cypriot throne.

Whether the island was Catholic or Orthodox made no difference to the Muslims, who established the Ottoman Empire after overthrowing the Byzantine Empire with their capture of Constantinople in 1453. With the Ottoman Turks controlling Anatolia, the eastern Mediterranean coastline, the island of Rhodes, and Egypt, Cyprus was a thorn in their side. Unfortunately for the Cypriots, the European Christians were having a difficult time creating a united front against Islam. Cyprus was attacked by forces from Genoa, which captured the eastern port of Famagusta and held it for almost a century (1372–1464). In 1489, the last of the Lusignan monarchs, Catarina Cornaro, sold her throne to the powerful Renaissance trade center, Venice. As a middleman for trade coming through Muslim territory, the Venetians were very interested in holding Cyprus. Venetian engineers arrived on the island to repair and

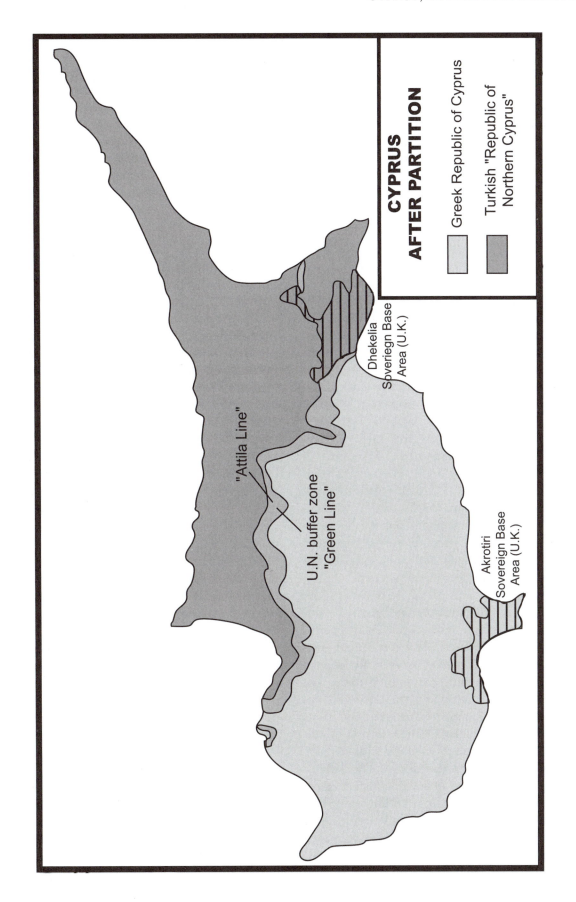

CYPRUS
AFTER PARTITION

Greek Republic of Cyprus

Turkish "Republic of
Northern Cyprus"

Dhekelia
Soveriegn Base
Area (U.K.)

"Attila Line"

U.N. buffer zone
"Green Line"

Akrotiri
Sovereign Base
Area (U.K.)

strengthen the defenses of the major cities of Famagusta and Nicosia. At the same time, they paid Constantinople an annual tribute in order to stay in the Ottoman emperor's good graces.

By 1566, Emperor Selim II found Cyprus too strategically valuable to be in Christian hands. Not only were the island's defenses being strengthened, but the stationing at Crete of a fleet of 200 Spanish, Papal, and Venetian (the Holy League) ships was entirely too threatening. Thus, Turkish troops arrived on the south coast of Cyprus on 1 July 1570. At this point the Catholic-Orthodox hostility came into play. Unhappy with Venetian rule, the Cypriots did nothing to oppose the Turkish landings. The Ottoman army consisted of 50,000 infantry, 2,500 cavalry, and 80 pieces of artillery. The Venetians on the island withdrew into the defenses of Nicosia and Famagusta, but their forces were painfully inadequate, numbering only 5,000 infantry and 500 cavalry. Owing to a disagreement with political leaders in Nicosia, militia commander Astore Baglione abandoned the city for Famagusta, giving his allegiance and manpower to its commander, Marcantonio Bragadin. Rather surprisingly, Nicosia held out until 9 September. After the city's fall, the bulk of the population swore loyalty to the Ottoman commander, Lala Mustapha. That loyalty, however, was not sworn by the defenders of the port city of Famagusta. Lala Mustapha brought his army to the city and began laying siege.

Through the winter of 1570–1571, the Turkish forces dug trenches and awaited reinforcements, which arrived in April. At this point, the siege began in earnest. As was the usual practice in sieges of that period, artillery fire against the walls was constant, but mining under the walls in order to bring about their collapse was also a normal endeavor. In this effort the Turks had some success, but each time a section of wall collapsed, the defenders valiantly pushed back forces attempting to break through. The defenders took a large portion of the decreasing supply of gunpowder and placed it at an important bastion in the city's south wall: If those inside could not hold that key position, they would deny it to the Turks. When Turkish attackers took the position on 9 July, the defenders did, indeed, blow it

up with such force that 1,000 Turkish soldiers were killed. The destruction was so great, and the rubble so high, the Turks withdrew to their siege lines. The standard cannonade and mining continued, and Turkish reinforcements continued to arrive while the Ottoman fleet blockaded Famagusta. Finally, on 1 August, Bragadin asked to negotiate. Although the initial terms were lenient, some dispute arose as to their implementation, whereupon Lala Mustapha, declaring the truce to be over, gave his men free reign to pillage the city and kill the inhabitants.

News of that slaughter finally motivated the European powers who had stayed aloof throughout the siege. The Holy League navy, which was docked in Crete, finally sailed and met the Turkish fleet off the east coat of Greece. In one of the decisive battles of history, Lepanto, the Ottoman fleet was badly beaten and Ottoman naval power was never again projected into the western Mediterranean. It was not viewed as such at the time, however. When the Ottoman and Holy League representatives met to discuss peace terms, "the Grand Vizier told the Venetian ambassador, 'by conquering Cyprus we have cut off one of your arms, but by defeating our fleet you have only shaved our beard. You cannot expect another arm to grow to replace the cut one, whereas the shaven beard always grows again and even more abundantly.'"(Rogerson, *Cyprus*)

However, the defeat at Lepanto, coupled with the 1683 defeat of the Turks at Vienna, meant that Islam would not take a military hold in Europe outside of the Balkans.

The subsequent Ottoman occupation of Cyprus got off to a good start. The Orthodox Church and population were allowed freedom of worship, but the Catholics were forced to either convert to Islam or Orthodoxy, or leave the island. Peasants were given title to the land they had traditionally worked for landlords, and some 30,000 Anatolians moved to the island, as compared to an existing population of some 150,000. The two religious and ethnic groups coexisted peacefully, since they usually had a common cause in opposing corrupt governors sent from Constantinople. The most powerful position in Cyprus came to be that of archbishop, with the political blessing of the sultan. The archbishop ultimately became the tax collector, so the position which had been held by greedy functionaries came to be much more equitable. He also had the power to appoint the head of the civil service (dragoman). Thus, the Muslim Turks technically controlled the island, but the Orthodox Cypriots exercised de facto control.

The peaceful relationship began falling apart in 1818 when Archbishop Kyprianos joined a secret organization, the Philike Heraireia, which was planning a revolt in Greece against Ottoman rule. Kyprianos could not organize a militia to fight the Turkish garrison on the island, so he could only provide moral and financial support to the conspirators. When Greeks across the Ottoman Empire rose in revolt in 1821, Constantinople gave the governor on Cyprus orders to make sure the revolt did not take hold there. Thus, the governor arrested and executed the leading members of the Philike Heraireia, including the archbishop. From that point forward, Greeks and Turks became enemies on Cyprus. The local population not only wanted revenge, but became committed to political union with mainland Greece.

Relations between Greek and Turk settled down somewhat in 1830 when the Greek rebellion ended and Greece achieved independence. The sultan supported some attempts at reform within the empire's administration, but it was not sufficiently widespread to make anyone happy. Trouble simmered beneath the surface and boiled over when Great Britain acquired a major share of the Suez Canal in Egypt in 1875. By then, the Ottoman Empire had already taken on its nickname, the "sick man of Europe." Thus, British Prime Minister Benjamin Disraeli was able to convince Constantinople to cede the island to Britain in 1878. With a military and naval presence on the island, Britain could not only support its position in Egypt, but also have a forward force to intervene to aid the Ottoman Empire from any outside threat (primarily Russia).

Cyprus, therefore, was slowly absorbed into the British Empire and given the status of colony in 1925. However, the old Greco-Turkish rivalries remained. When, in 1960, the British left the island to a newly created Republic of Cyprus, the two groups were soon at each others' throats.

Constitutional rule fell apart in 1963, followed by a coup d'état in 1973 staged by Greek officers. That provoked a Turkish intervention to protect the ethnic Turks on the island and a resulting division of the island into two countries: the Republic of Cyprus in the southern part of the island, and the Turkish-dominated Republic of Northern Cyprus. An attempt at reconciliation and unification came in 2004 when the Greeks applied for membership in the European Union. The vote to unify was passed in the Turkish Republic, but not the Greek section, which joined the EU without Turkish participation.

See also Hittites; Assyrians; Egypt, British occupation of; and Cyprus, Turkish invasion of.

References: "Cyprus History," <www.cypnet.co.uk/-ncyprus/root.html>, 2 January 2006; Rogerson, Barnaby, *Cyprus* (Guilford, Conn.: Globe Pequot Press, 1994); Solstein, Eric, ed., *Cyprus: A Country Study* (Washington, DC: Government Printing Office, 1993).

EAST INDIES, DUTCH OCCUPATION OF THE

93

In the late 1500s, the Dutch acted as middlemen between the Portuguese bringing spices from Asia and the customers of Europe; Portugal handled the importation, Holland handled the distribution. The arrangement was mutually profitable until King Philip II of Spain, in an attempt to crush the power of Protestantism in Holland, closed the port of Lisbon to Dutch shipping and distribution of the spices. Holland had no choice but to bypass Portugal and establish its own contacts in Asia. By 1596, Dutch ships cruised the East Indies, or Spice Islands, looking for markets.

Competition between Holland and Portugal meant increased prices for the Spice Islanders' products. Equally important, the Dutch were uninterested in converting anyone to Catholicism or any other religion. This pleased the Spice Islanders, most of whom were Muslim. The Dutch signed agreements with local sultans and soon began to force the Portuguese out of business. Portugal's resources were stretched thin by maintaining government and trade relations from East Asia to Brazil, so they were unable to mount any serious opposition. They were soon out of the picture when the Dutch, with local assistance from the sultan of Jahore on Sumatra, laid siege in late 1640 to the major Portuguese trading center at Malacca, on the Malay Peninsula. When it fell after six months, the Portuguese ceased being a threat in the area. Though the Dutch had mild competition from England, the English were busy with North America and did not press the Dutch in East Asia.

Soon Holland established a monopoly on spices heading for Europe, and saw the potential for making even more money controlling the trade within Asia. Holland built settlements and forts to protect its interests and carry on trade, but had to stamp out local competition as well if it were to dominate the Asian market. In 1618, the Dutch governor-general, Pieter Coen, established the town of Batavia on the island of Java as the Dutch area headquarters. From here the Dutch controlled the Sunda Straits, the most popular trading route through the islands. Throughout the 1600s, the Dutch spread their contacts through the area, and because of their monopoly, were able once again to lower their buying costs. Because the local producers either had to pay Dutch prices or sell nothing, the Dutch grew very rich. Dutch ships patrolled the waters of the East Indies to keep out foreign ships.

The only trouble the Dutch had for decades came from local powers who did not like the low prices the Dutch paid. Occasionally, the Dutch forced sultans to cooperate at gunpoint rather than sell their wares to other Asian ships that might venture to trade with Europeans. The Dutch wanted to monopolize the tin exports from Perak, on the west coast of the Malay Peninsula. In 1652, when they tried to build a trading post that would control the purchasing in the area, the Perak forces destroyed it. The Dutch built a fort in 1670 to guard access to the country and fought the locals to keep the fort; the sultan of Perak looked for other ways to ship and sell his tin, and the Dutch were never able to establish a monopoly on the product.

Throughout the Dutch tenure as the dominant European power in the area, the local tribes struggled among themselves over matters of local interest. The Dutch had little concern in these relations as long as they could maintain a relatively peaceful atmosphere and keep the trade flowing. Usually, the Dutch did not interfere in the politics of the area unless it directly affected their income. Occasionally, a tribe would challenge Dutch power, as did the Bugis of Celebes in the 1780s. The Bugis were mercenaries whose activities affected the rise and fall of sultanates in the East Indies, and they gradually came to influence the politics of many of the states of the area, much as the Mamluks of Egypt turned from warriors to rulers. The Bugis challenged the Dutch by laying siege to Malacca in 1784, attempting to exert control over the area from Jahore on Sumatra. The six-month siege failed when the Dutch brought in reinforcements and defeated the Bugi naval contingent. After the Bugis were removed from the area, the Dutch signed an agreement with the sultan of Jahore (now freed from Bugi control) that gave Holland dominance on Sumatra.

The cost of European wars in the 1790s caused the most damage to the Dutch in the East Indies, but through the 1700s they had seen the power of the British East India Company rise in Asia. Britain's major enterprise in Asia was Indian and Chinese tea, a market they dominated. By the late 1700s, the British were also looking toward Borneo, an East Indian island the Dutch had ignored as lacking trade potential, considering it merely a haven for pirates. Thus, when Napoleon conquered continental Europe, the British were establishing themselves in the area, and suddenly the Dutch in the Indies had no support from home. They lost Malacca to the British in 1795 through an agreement with the Dutch government-in-exile that Britain would occupy Dutch possessions around the world (to deny them to Napoleon for the duration of hostilities). Though Malacca was returned to Holland in 1815, Britain regained the town in 1824.

The Dutch lost their preeminent trading position in the area, but the political control they had established from Batavia through various treaties with area sultans made them masters of the East Indian islands. Britain came to dominate Southeast Asian trade, but Holland maintained the East Indies as colonies until after World War II.

See also Singapore, British Occupation of; Dutch East Indies, Japanese Invasion of.

References: Hyma, Albert, *A History of the Dutch in the Far East* (Ann Arbor, MI: George Wair Publishing Co., 1953); Ryan, N. J., *A History of Malaysia and Singapore* (London: Oxford University Press, 1976); Vlekke, Bernard, *The Story of the Dutch East Indies* (Cambridge, MA: Harvard University Press, 1945).

ENGLAND, SPANISH INVASION OF (SPANISH ARMADA)

94

The gold and silver of the New World brought untold wealth to Spain, riches that the Spanish kings translated into military power. King Charles I and King Philip II built armies not just for national purposes, but for religious reasons as well. Strong Catholic rulers, they believed their nation was meant to exploit these newfound riches because God smiled on them, and he smiled on them because they were good Catholics. Therefore, they believed it was Spain's duty to do God's work, which meant not only converting the inhabitants of the Americas, but defending in Europe the one true Church from attacks by Protestants, whom the pope viewed as heretics. Philip sent his armies across Europe to smite the heretics, and if Spain should come to control some territory along the way, so much the better. The Protestant nation causing Philip the most grief, however, was not so easy to smite: England.

Since the early 1500s, the Catholic Church in Britain had been in a state of flux. British King Henry VIII rejected the pope's authority and made himself head of the church in England. After his death, his daughter Mary (raised a strong Catholic by her mother) recognized the pope's authority and, to prove herself and her country, married Philip of Spain. The Catholic champion could thus focus on continental heretics and not worry about England—not for five years, at least, for that was how long Mary ruled. Her death brought Elizabeth I to the throne, and Elizabeth was her father's daughter. She not only rejected the pope's power and made herself head of the church, but she also removed

Catholicism altogether and created the Church of England, or Anglican Church. Philip lost the security he had enjoyed regarding England and, to make matters worse, in power was a monarch who supported Protestant movements in Europe. Thus, not only was the Catholic champion challenged, so was the Church itself.

England in the 1500s was not a major power, but Elizabeth dreamed it might become one. Power required a strong navy, which cost money, and most of the real wealth was under Spanish control. Unable to get the money at its source, Elizabeth secretly commissioned privateers to raid Spanish treasure convoys in the Atlantic. It was more than Philip could stand. Not only was this woman challenging his Church, she was stealing his money to do so. Thinking that he could control England as he had done with Mary, Philip proposed marriage to Elizabeth. She declined the offer. Philip considered England to be his because of his earlier marriage into the royal family, so he felt he had no choice but to take direct action against Elizabeth. He would invade England and enforce his will on the country.

In the mid-1580s, Philip began bringing ships together in an invasion fleet. Men and supplies were to be taken by 130 ships up the French coast to Flanders, where a 10,000-man force was currently fighting Dutch Protestants. This force would be ferried to England, and Elizabeth would be overthrown. The British army (such as it was) certainly had no reputation, and no naval force could resist the largest fleet in the world, so Philip saw no reason why the most powerful nation in the world should not be able to defeat a second-rate country such as England. He assembled a force of mixed nationalites: Portuguese, Italian, and even Levantine ships and crews were in the Spanish Armada. The ships were placed under the command of the duke of Medina-Sidonia. The duke had never been to sea, but he was of royal blood, and could command the mixed force with that authority.

The lengthy time required to prepare the armada allowed plenty of time for word to filter to England. The English gathered 102 ships, a mixture of royal and privately owned vessels. Command was given to Lord Howard of Effingham who, like Medina-Sidonia, was not a

The ill-fated Spanish Armada would ultimately lose 64 of its ships and over 10,000 men.

sailor but had sufficient royal authority. Luckily for England, Howard was surrounded by experienced captains such as Francis Drake, Martin Frobisher, and John Hawkins, all of whom had made a name for themselves as privateers and were able to work together.

The armada left Lisbon harbor on 29 May 1588, but bad weather soon drove them into Corunna, on Spain's northwest coast. Three weeks later they sailed for Flanders and rounded the French coast. By 19 July they had entered the English Channel. Most of the English ships were in port at Plymouth, and they rushed to leave the harbor. It was a slow process against adverse winds, but by 21 July they formed up behind the armada and followed, looking for an opportunity. The westerly winds made it impossible for the Spanish to turn and fight, so they continued up the Channel until they reached

Calais, where Medina-Sidonia could resupply and send a message to the duke of Parma's forces in Flanders that he was on his way.

The Spanish ships anchored in a tight crescent formation. In the 1500s, the standard method of fighting at sea was not long-range cannon fire until one ship surrendered or sank. Instead, ships would sail alongside each other, and marines would do battle; whichever force of soldiers prevailed won the battle, and the defeated ship was taken as a prize, virtually undamaged. Therefore, a tight formation was the best method of defense because the interior ships could not be reached by an attacker. This standard defense, however, doomed the Spaniards. Lord Howard took eight of his ships, filled them with gunpowder, armed all the cannon, and set them afire. The prevailing wind carried them directly into the midst of the armada, burning and exploding.

The previously disciplined Spanish fleet broke apart. Each commander was concerned with his own ship as he tried to get away from the other burning ships, for which he had no defense but to maneuver. The massed Spanish force disintegrated and, running for the open sea, ran into the waiting English fleet. The Spanish tried to continue their journey to link up with their army, but Dutch rebels denied them landing and the English continued to harass them. With the way home blocked and the coastline hostile, the Spanish had no choice but to sail home the long way, around Scotland and Ireland. The English chased them until the former's supplies of food and powder ran low, then they abandoned the armada to nature. Heavy weather plagued the Spanish and caused shipwrecks from the Orkneys to the Shetlands, to Ireland and Cornwall. The armada lost 64 ships and 10,000 of its 30,000 men.

Like the Battle of Britain 350 years later, the Spanish invasion attempt is important for its failure. The year 1588 marked the high point of Spanish power. With so many ships destroyed, their stranglehold on the Atlantic began to slip. Though Spain continued to be a power for some time to come, never again were the Spanish as fearsome. At the same time, the battle that cost the English so little brought their fleet into some prominence, and they could now ply the Atlantic with more freedom. England had long lusted after Spain's New World riches and could now freely plant colonies of its own. The British could not go to Central and South America for gold and silver because Spain's power there was still impregnable, but colonies along the North American coast began to sprout in the decades following the armada's defeat. The decrease in Spanish power offset an increase in English strength; the British Empire would soon be in sight. Further, Elizabeth was able to continue her support of Protestant movements in Europe, and the Dutch soon gained their independence from Spain's rule.

To a great extent, the world as it is today dates from 28 July 1588. North America is predominantly British in its heritage rather than Spanish. Had the armada succeeded, Elizabeth's forces could not have withstood Spain's invading army. The well-timed northwesterly breeze—the "Protestant Wind," as it came to be known—that blew the fire ships into the armada saved England. The British Empire, if it ever came to exist, would have been seriously delayed, and the Spanish would have colonized North America as well as the southern part of the hemisphere.

See also North America, British Occupation of; Western Hemisphere, Spanish Occupation of; Britain, Nazi Invasion of (Battle of Britain).

References: Lewis, Michael, *The Spanish Armada* (New York: Thomas Y. Crowell, 1968); Martin, Colin, *The Spanish Armada* (New York: Norton, 1988); Mattingly, Garrett, *The Armada* (Boston: Houghton Mifflin, 1959).

95 INDIA, BRITISH OCCUPATION OF

European sailors reached India in the 1500s, when the Moghul Empire was at its height. The country's riches attracted Portuguese merchants, followed in later years by the Dutch, French, and British. The Portuguese lost the necessary sea power to maintain distant trading posts and the Dutch concentrated more on the spice trade in the islands of Indonesia, which left France and Britain as the main rivals for Indian trade. France's East India Company gained the first foothold, but lost its position on the subcontinent through military defeat in India and diplomatic exchanges of land as the result of wars in Europe. The British became the main European power in India almost by default.

Britain established its first trading post in 1639 when it purchased a harbor from a south Indian ruler; that acquisition, on India's southeastern coast, became the port of Madras. The British built fortifications and began buying up the high-quality Indian cotton textiles. An attempt to enter the north Indian trade ran into the fading power of the Moghuls and the growing power of the Bengalis, both of whom barely tolerated British merchants. With the construction of a fortified base on the Hooghly River, part of the Ganges Delta, the trading

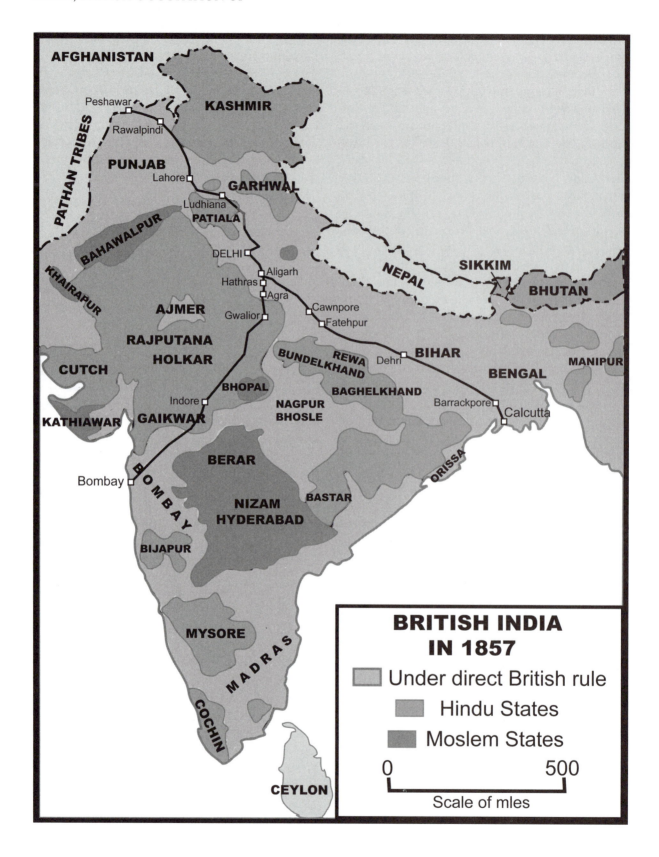

AFGHANISTAN

Peshawar
KASHMIR

PATHAN TRIBES

Rawalpindi

PUNJAB

Lahore
GARHWAL

Ludhiana

PATIALA

BAHAWALPUR

DELHI

KHAIRAPUR

Aligarh

Hathras

Agra

AJMER

Gwalior

RAJPUTANA

HOLKAR

CUTCH

BHOPAL

Indore

KATHIAWAR

GAIKWAR

NEPAL

SIKKIM

BHUTAN

Cawnpore

Fatehpur

REWA

BUNDELKHAND

Dehri

BIHAR

MANIPUR

BAGHELKHAND

BENGAL

NAGPUR

BHOSLE

Barrackpore

Calcutta

BERAR

Bombay

B O M B A Y

ORISSA

NIZAM

HYDERABAD

BASTAR

BIJAPUR

MYSORE

M A D R A S

COCHIN

CEYLON

**BRITISH INDIA
IN 1857**

Under direct British rule

Hindu States

Moslem States

0   500

Scale of mles

center of Calcutta was born in 1690. To attempt entry into western Indian markets, the British gained the defunct Portuguese port of Surat, where the Tapti River empties into the Arabian Sea. All three ports were operated by the British East India Company, which held sole trading rights.

The British solidified their position in the north in a rather odd fashion. The Moghul emperors contracted out tax collection, and the British gained the concession in the areas around Madras and Calcutta. When the Moghul Empire collapsed and factional fighting all over India ensued, the British kept collecting taxes and began to form military units to protect their trading posts and routes. The mixture of European and local troops became the basis of the Indian army, which at first was a business venture rather than a governmental one. Because the British could maintain a measure of stability in an increasingly disrupted Indian society, their trading posts began to attract Indian merchants looking for a secure place to do business. Their soldiers proved their ability to defeat bandits and keep the peace, and various kings began to contract with the company. Military expertise in return for trading rights became standard East India Company procedure, and it aided the British merchants in gaining a major hold on the markets of all parts of India.

With control over Bengal, Madras, and Calcutta, the British settled down to maintaining order in the areas immediately around those cities, which grew rapidly with Indian merchants and artisans looking for a peaceful place to do business. The East India Company gradually began to act like a government, for the warring states offered no justice in their courts or taxation. British control extended in the 1750s via the Seven Years' War, wherein an Anglo-French war in Europe had colonial side effects. The French plotted with local powers to gain a military advantage, but the British defeat of the French and their ally of Hyderabad in the south spelled the beginning of the end of French involvement in the region. The Anglo-French conflict was timely because the Moghul Empire, already on its last legs, was battered even further by invading Afghan armies. The downfall

of the Moghuls encouraged other states to exert their authority. Bengal attacked Calcutta in 1756 and forced the British to evacuate. An avenging force from Madras under the leadership of Robert Clive (who had defeated the Franco-Hyderabad alliance) recaptured the city and defeated the Bengali army at Plassey, giving the company control over Bengal. A victory over a Bengali-led coalition in 1764 removed any serious competition in northern India.

The arrival of Warren Hastings as governor-general in the mid-1770s marked the establishment of Britain and the East India Company as the masters of India. By posing as an Oriental-style absolute monarch, he commanded Indian respect. He enforced just and fair practices in law enforcement, taxation, and the courts that had not been experienced in India since the days of Ashoka. These tactics won him local support, and Hastings intervened in factional squabbles along the frontier, both to extend company power and to divide and conquer the remaining recalcitrant states, notably Maratha in the northwest. Passage of the India Act of 1784 in London cut into his authority, and he resigned.

Hastings was followed by Lord Cornwallis. He furthered the company policy of fair taxation and extended company control to Mysore in the south. His successor, Richard Wellesley, sent British forces up the Ganges from Calcutta to force the cooperation of the state of Oudh, and the British gained control over the main trade route in India. Wellesley also entered into Ceylon, establishing a British presence there to take advantage of the harbor at Trincomalee and to "protect" the Dutch colony from Napoleon's forces. After Napoleon's defeat in Europe, all French influence in India was removed.

Originally interested only in trade, the British implemented fair business practices that attracted many Indians to British settlements. Rejection of the weak and rapacious local rulers left a power vacuum, which the East India Company filled, originally to maintain safe trade routes but ultimately to maintain order for the entire population. The growing bureaucracy solidified British authority and, by attracting Indians to the burgeoning civil service, created a partnership. While the British tradespeople benefited the most, many Indians profited as well. The mass of Indians remained poor, but the opportunity to live in peace and expect justice made the British the favored choice over the local kings, even if that meant outside domination. Along with Hindi and Urdu, English became an accepted language and the path to success in the British civil service and trading circles. For 100 years the Indians lived peacefully under British suzerainty, but in 1857 revolted against the company, which was disbanded. The British government took over its operation. India remained the "jewel in the crown" of the British Empire until India's independence in 1948.

The relationship between the British and the Indians is somewhat strange. Many British were fascinated by Indian culture and studied it in depth. For the most part, the Indians were allowed to continue their cultural practices, but slavery and suttee (the ritual immolation of wives with their dead husbands) were banned. The Indians also took on some British practices. Not only did English become widely spoken, British pastimes like soccer and cricket became Indian passions as well. Still, the British generally did not mingle with the locals, and they tried to recreate some of England in India rather than "go native." The British prejudice against nonwhites showed itself in interpersonal relations, which kept the two races generally distinct, but that did not usually affect the business of running the country. As Kipling described the attitude, the British believed they were "taking up the white man's burden" to assist India. The Indians did not appreciate this viewpoint, but they valued the stability Britain brought, and responded by assisting the British Empire in its wars, sending troops around the world to fight alongside Australians, New Zealanders, South Africans, and others. The British exit in 1948 revived some of the old tribal differences, but a tradition of democracy is well established.

See also Mauryan Empire; East Indies, Dutch Occupation of the; India, French Occupation of; Moghul Empire; Saxony, Prussian Invasion of (Seven Years' War); Southern United States, British Invasion of; Ceylon, British Occupation of.

References: Chamerlain, Muriel, *Britain and India* (Hamden, CT: Archon Books, 1974); Griffiths, P., *The British Impact on India* (Hamden, CT: Archon Books, 1965); Mason, Philip, *A Matter of Honour* (London: Jonathan Cape, 1974).

INDIA, FRENCH OCCUPATION OF

96

As with most of France's international endeavors in the colonial period, the French looked more for trade than empire. In 1664 the Marquis de Colbert formed a government-sponsored company to exploit the Indian trade for French merchants rather than buy from the British and Dutch. Colbert's company inherited few assets from previous private attempts to break into the Eastern trade; only Port Dauphin on the island of Madagascar was a French-controlled port of call. Still, previous merchants had established some contacts upon which the new company was able to expand. The French effort had many of the aspects of a government, most particularly the right to enter into trade agreements and the right to negotiate peace or declare war with non-Europeans. The company had government-appointed directors in Paris, but investment was open to the public, who proved less than enthusiastic: Only about half the shares made available were publicly purchased. The venture ran into hard times because of its inability to compete with the established British and Dutch traders and because of national rivalries being fought out in Europe. By the time of relative peace in 1713, the company was too deep in debt to survive. An attempt to revive it under John Law in 1719 fell apart in four years. The government again stepped in and ran it under the name Compagnie de Indes. The company was granted a monopoly over all international French colonial trade; again, the directors were appointed by the crown and acted as civil servants, which meant that the company did not have to pay them a salary and all trade was profit.

By 1723, the company was able to take advantage of earlier acquisitions, though Madagascar was abandoned in favor of Ile de France (Mauritius) and Bourbon Islands in the

Indian Ocean. Pondicherry was the French trade headquarters in India. The company built "factories" (trading posts) along the Indian coastline, and began to compete more successfully with the British and Dutch. The government provided all necessary naval support, and the company hired soldiers to protect their interests. All went well until 1763, when France and its allies in Europe lost the Seven Years' War. The French governor-general in India, Dupleix, was unable to defeat the forces of the British East India Company and lost some factories as a result. France was able to continue operating in India, and indeed, the profits were considerable, but the losses in ships and the costs of war were too great for trade to overcome. Rather than invest more government money to keep the operation afloat, Paris decided to remove the company's monopoly status and turn the factories into colonies.

Independent merchants were able to profit in India, but not so well that all of France's trade should pass through them. A new company was begun in 1785 with a monopoly on trade, but without the previous powers of government. It survived, but only because it bought through British agents; the French had lost any contacts of their own. The British victory in the Seven Years' War virtually guaranteed that their enterprise, the British East India Company, would dominate the India trade and have the lion's share of the subcontinent's riches. With the political upheaval of the French Revolution, the Compagnie de Indes became a low priority for the Paris government. French trading posts existed, unfortified, through 1815, but in the wake of Napoleon's defeat, the British acquired all the French holdings. In the long run, France had little impact on India; the subcontinent's European influence came almost totally from Great Britain.

See also Saxony, Prussian Invasion of (Seven Years' War); Napoleon Buonaparte.

References: Mason, Philip, *A Matter of Honour* (London: Jonathan Cape, 1974); Miles, William, *Imperial Burdens* (Boulder, CO: L. Rienner Publishers, 1995); Sen, Siba Pada, *The French in India* (Calcutta: University of Calcutta Press, 1947).

ITALY, AUSTRIAN INVASION OF (WAR OF THE SPANISH SUCCESSION)

97

In 1700, Charles II of Spain died childless, having named as heir his somewhat distant relative Philip of Anjou. Normally, the situation would not have created much of a problem, but Philip was the grandson of King Louis XIV of France, an absolute monarch who had made his nation the most powerful in Europe and had dominated European affairs for decades. If his grandson Philip, of the house of Bourbon, did not cede any future claim to the French throne, then the potential for united Franco-Spanish power was too great for the remainder of Europe to contemplate. One of France's traditional rivals, Austria, was ruled by Leopold I, who also held the position of Holy Roman Emperor. He was a Habsburg (as Charles II had been) and believed that his second son, Charles, should inherit the Spanish throne. He therefore planned to fight for his son's rights, and there was no shortage of European countries willing to assist him to restrain French power.

Louis provoked the war, as he had often done in the past, by invading the Netherlands and seizing fortifications along the frontier—moves he claimed were defensive. Leopold claimed the Spanish Netherlands as his own, so the French attack was all the excuse he needed to go to war. Not only did Leopold want his son on the Spanish throne, he hoped to expand Austrian territory in the process. His first move was to commit troops to Italy, much of which was under Spanish control, under his most able commander, Eugene of Savoy. Eugene entered northern Italy in 1701 and faced a superior Franco-Spanish force, which he finally drove back into Mantua.

The other concerned European countries soon entered into an alliance initiated by Great Britain, whose King William III had recently finished a war against Louis. Under William, Parliament raised a large army to counter not only French ambition, but also in response to Louis' recognition of the young James III of the Scottish house of Stuart as king of England and Louis' initiation of

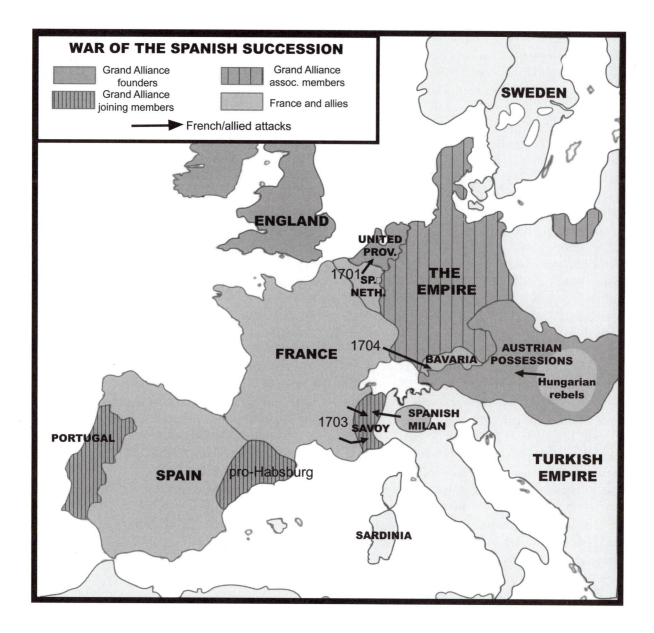

WAR OF THE SPANISH SUCCESSION

- Grand Alliance founders
- Grand Alliance joining members
- Grand Alliance assoc. members
- France and allies
- → French/allied attacks

SWEDEN

ENGLAND

UNITED PROV.

1701 SP. NETH.

THE EMPIRE

1704

FRANCE

BAVARIA

AUSTRIAN POSSESSIONS

Hungarian rebels

SPANISH MILAN

1703 SAVOY

PORTUGAL

pro-Habsburg

SPAIN

TURKISH EMPIRE

SARDINIA

economic warfare against England. William died from an accident in 1701 and was succeeded by his daughter Anne, who continued to support the conflict. The Grand Alliance attracted the membership of England, Austria, Holland, Prussia, and most German principalities. Only Austria had a direct interest in the succession; the others joined to limit French expansion.

The British army was led by John Churchill, the earl (later duke) of Marlborough, one of the finest British generals of all time. He commanded an allied force that invaded the Spanish Netherlands in June 1702; some 12,000 of the 50,000 troops were British, the remainder Dutch and German. His Dutch allies troubled him the most, because their political leaders often overrode his decision to fight when they would not allow him to commit Dutch forces. As he invaded, forces of the empire threatened the French possession of Strasbourg. Marlborough finally convinced the Dutch to allow him to assault fortresses along the Rhine, which he captured by the autumn. He hoped to link up with the Austrians, but the entrance of Bavaria on the French side threatened such a connection. Maximilian, the elector of Bavaria, joined Louis on the promise of the throne of the Holy Roman Empire if

Austria were defeated. He was joined in May 1703 by a French force under General Claude de Villars, who urged an attack on Vienna, but Maximilian preferred to seize the Tyrol and attempt a link with French forces in Italy, a venture that failed. Through the later part of the summer of 1703, Villars enjoyed success against Austrian forces and the German state of Baden, defeating them separately in the Danube Valley. When his second suggestion for an attack on Vienna was refused, Villars resigned. French forces under Tallard also enjoyed success along the middle Rhine.

Meanwhile Marlborough was being frustrated in the Netherlands, either by his hesitant Dutch allies or his French counterpart, Villeroi. The success of the Franco-Bavarian forces drew his attention in 1704, and Marlborough marched to join his army with the forces of Eugene in Austria, who had recently been recalled from Italy. After a series of maneuvers to defeat or baffle the French, Eugene and Marlborough joined forces in August in Bavaria. Together their 56,000 men faced a 60,000-man force of French and Bavarians under French general Tallard and Maximilian. The resulting battle of Blenheim was a smashing allied victory; the defeated Bavarian forces withdrew, and Maximilian's dream of becoming emperor died when his province was annexed by Austria. The battle also destroyed the myth of French invincibility that Louis' armies had held for years.

Despite this turn of events, neither side showed any inclination toward negotiations. The year 1705 brought nothing but stalemate on all fronts. That was broken on the Netherlands front in 1706, when Marlborough scored another victory over French forces at Ramillies, near Namur. This enabled him to consolidate the Spanish Netherlands by October. In 1706 the main theater of war shifted back to Italy, where French general Vendome regained territory lost earlier to Austria. This French success took Eugene back to Italy to lead Austrian forces. In the battle of Turin in September, Eugene defeated Vendome's replacement, the duke of Orleans, and drove the French completely out of Italy. Austrian dominance would be established there for more than a century.

Little happened in 1707, but in 1708 the French once again aimed toward the Netherlands. Vendome had been given command of French forces, and he went on the offensive against Marlborough. The British commander had planned to join Eugene, but before the juncture could take place, Marlborough engaged the French at Oudenarde, winning another victory on 11 July. Vendome turned him back at Ghent shortly afterward, but Marlborough captured the city in a winter campaign, and in January 1709 the French withdrew to defenses along their borders. Louis offered to begin negotiations, but he refused to accept the allied peace terms, which he considered overly harsh, and the war continued. Through the summer of 1709, Marlborough and Eugene tried to break through the French defensive line or force them out into the open field. When they began the siege of Mons, Louis ordered Villars to fight; he marched to Malplaquet to threaten the allied rear. Marlborough turned to meet him there and the resulting battle on 11 September proved inconclusive. The allies lost too many men to follow up, but the French failed to relieve Mons, which fell at the end of October.

In 1711, Marlborough was recalled by a new English government, never to command again. Negotiations began soon thereafter and continued throughout 1712. As talks proceeded, Eugene wanted to continue fighting to gain leverage at the conference, but the Dutch were overly cautious. The French, under Villars, seized the initiative and recaptured some fortresses along the frontier, which gave the French bargaining power. The Treaty of Utrecht was signed 11 April 1713. Louis recognized the Protestant succession in England and ceded some French property in the Americas to England. Philip of Anjou was recognized as King Philip V of Spain, and Louis guaranteed that Spain and France would remain separate. Louis also agreed to cede the Spanish Netherlands as well as Spanish territory in Italy to the Austrian Habsburgs, but the Holy Roman Emperor (now Charles VI) refused to agree. He wanted both Austria and the Spanish throne he had claimed at the beginning of the war, so he continued fighting. His lack of success, however, forced him to sign the Treaty of

Rastatt (as the emperor of Austria) and the Treaty of Baden (as Holy Roman Emperor), making peace with France. He took control of the Netherlands and the ceded Italian provinces, but he refused to recognize Bourbon rule in Spain.

The war accomplished the goal of the Grand Alliance by constraining French expansionism and maintaining a balance of power, although that shifted somewhat. Spain, long a declining power, lost the most: its Netherlands and Italian holdings to Austria, and Gibraltar, Minorca, and its slave trade with the Western Hemisphere to England. France also ceded Newfoundland and the Hudson Bay to England, thus beginning the French expulsion from North America. Though Louis succeeded in keeping his country from being surrounded by Habsburgs again, France had passed its prime. The English were becoming ascendant in the world through their dominance of maritime trade, and future French conflicts with England too often proved futile. The cost of the war severely damaged the French economy, and the cession of overseas possessions did nothing to alleviate that loss. France was perhaps the most grateful for the quarter-century of peace that followed, for they could finally recover from Louis' constant warmaking. Louis XIV died in 1715, and no other monarch was able to exercise his absolute, "divine" rule. Though Louis became the most significant figure of his age, France's power did not long outlast him.

See also North America, French Occupation of; Palatinate, French Invasion of the (War of the League of Augsburg).

References: Hassel, Arthur, *Louis XIV and the Zenith of French Monarchy* (Freeport, NY: Books for Libraries, 1972); Kamen, Henry, *The War of Succession in Spain, 1700–15* (Bloomington: University of Indiana Press, 1969); Lossky, Andrew, *Louis XIV and the French Monarchy* (New Brunswick, NJ: Rutgers University Press, 1994).

ITALY, FRENCH INVASIONS OF

98

It may be impossible to find a more confusing set of political circumstances than that of Renaissance Italy. The peninsula was full of rival city-states with occasional links to European royal houses and an ever-shifting set of alliances among those royal houses and themselves. During the fifteenth and sixteenth centuries, no ruler held particularly strong ties to any other, and the armies of Italy were mercenary condotierri who fought for anyone who paid their price, often shifting sides during battle for a higher offer. The various warring condotierri bands knew one another well enough that the battles were often little more than pantomimes of combat, the mercenary leaders deciding among themselves who should win. Needless bloodshed was avoided, but it created a soldiery that became both more professional and less talented, which did not serve them well when outside armies invaded.

The French under Charles VIII entered Italy a number of times with an unstable set of allies and enemies. Charles had a relatively strong claim to the throne of Naples, but his entrance into Italian politics came by way of an invitation from Ludovico Sforza, the duke of Milan. In 1494, Sforza found the Italian city-states of Naples, Florence, and the Papal States arrayed against him, so he called on Charles for assistance, promising him military aid and access to his throne in Naples. It is a matter of some debate how eager Charles was to claim that throne, but it seems clear that he was eager for adventure, if nothing else. His father, Louis XI, had expanded French territory by conquest and inheritance, making France a strong military power, but he had always remained wary of getting involved in Italian politics. Charles had no such qualms, and he responded to Sforza's invitation.

His army of 25,000 (including some 8,000 Swiss mercenaries) joined with Sforza to conclude a quick and successful campaign. Within a year, Charles had defeated the Florentines and forced them to cede the city of Pisa to him; he occupied the Papal States, and he easily occupied the kingdom of Naples. He considered launching a crusade against the Turks in Constantinople or the Muslims of Jerusalem, but the League of Venice—consisting of Venice, his former ally Milan, the Holy Roman Empire under Maximilian, Spain, England, and Pope Alexander VI—joined together to threaten his line of communications back to France. He marched north in 1495 and engaged a condottieri force under Giovanni Francesco Gonzaga. On 6 July, they fought in the pass at Fornovo, and the French artillery proved too effective and aggressive for the Italians, who retreated after losing almost 10 times as many men as did the French. Charles decided to return to France rather than to Naples.

Naples retained a French army, but its king, Ferrante, had familial ties to the house of Aragon in Spain. Spain sent forces to his aid in 1495, and took advantage of Charles's departure. After an initial loss, the Spanish General Fernandez de Cordoba fought a war of attrition against the French, wearing them out over a three-year period. When he left in 1498, the French had been removed, but a civil war the following year brought them back to Naples.

Charles's son Louis XII returned to claim his throne in 1499. His main ally was Pope Alexander VI, who turned to him to counter the increasing power of Venice. Though Louis entered into an agreement with Ferdinand of Aragon to divide the kingdom of Naples between them, he invaded Naples, thus provoking a war with Spain. Louis easily conquered Milan, and his larger force took over Naples as Spanish ships occupied the harbor at Taranto and blockaded the major French base at Barletta. At the battle of Cerignola on 26 April 1503, Spanish forces under Cordoba defeated a combined Franco-Swiss force by breaking a cavalry charge with harquebusiers, making it the first battle in history decided by gunpowder small arms. Cordoba quickly occupied Naples and spent the remainder of the year harassing French forces. On 29 December 1503, Cordoba launched a surprise attack at the Garigliano River and crushed the French, who were allowed to leave Italy by sea under terms concluded on 1 January. In 1505, Louis ceded his claims in Naples to Ferdinand.

However, France was not through with Italy yet. Louis XII was back in 1508, allied this time with Maximilian, the Papal States, and Spain in the League of Cambrai, formed to resist Venetian power. France scored a major victory at Agnadello in May 1509 and Venice lost much of its territory to Spanish forces, but disunity within the league allowed Venice to recover most of its lands. Yet another combination of combatants was created in 1510 when the Papal States sponsored the Holy League to unite against the French and Maximilian's German troops. Spain joined in the league with Pope Julius II and Venice, but there was little fighting of consequence until 1511, when a new French commander arrived: Gaston de Foix, 21-year-old duke of Nemours. He took the initiative and drove away a besieging force from Bologna, then turned northward against Venetian troops at Brescia, besieging and capturing that city in February 1512. At a fierce battle at Ravenna, Gaston routed a Papal-Spanish force but was killed in the pursuit, robbing the French of a potentially brilliant general.

Just when matters seemed to be going well for France, Maximilian changed sides and withdrew his troops from the French army. Joining with Swiss forces, Maximilian drove the French from Italy. Prince Louis de La Tremoille led the French force back into Milan in 1513, but soon retreated after losing a battle at Novara in June. The French ignored Italy for a while when English forces under Henry VIII invaded France. Switzerland took a French bribe to stay out of the invasion, and Henry VIII and Maximilian quarreled over strategy. All the members of the Holy League made peace with France in 1513 or 1514.

Not content to leave well enough alone, Francis I of France now allied himself with Venice and Henry of England against Spain, Milan, Florence, Switzerland, the pope, and the Holy Roman Empire. Francis's capture of Milan was sufficient to break the alliance against him, and he ended the war in possession of most of northern Italy. Five years later he was at war with Charles I of Spain, soon to become Holy Roman Emperor as well. Francis's invasion through the Pyrenees in 1521 sparked renewed fighting in Italy. France was forced out of Italy by a defeat at Milan, but marched back in 1523. Defeats in the spring of 1524 were followed by an abortive invasion of France in the late summer. French troops came right back in October 1524. Francis's army besieged Pavia, but was defeated by a relieving force in February 1525. Francis was captured by the Spanish and taken to Madrid, where he was forced to buy his freedom with a treaty abandoning all claims in Italy. Francis renounced the treaty as soon as he returned to Paris, and he was soon on the campaign trail again. His war in Italy lasted until 1529, during which time French forces fared poorly. In the Treaty of Cambrai in 1529, he once again surrendered any right to Italian claims. He spent the next seven years reorganizing his army, and invaded Italy in 1536. After a ceasefire, signed in 1538, Francis did the unthinkable for a Christian European: He allied himself with Suleiman the Magnificent, sultan of the Ottoman Empire, who was then threatening the Holy Roman Empire. A Franco-Turkish naval force sacked Nice in 1543, and Francis won the battle of Ceresole, south of Turin, in April 1544. It was a short-lived victory, because French forces were soon home to defend France from invasions by the Holy Roman Empire and England. Emperor Charles soon abandoned the invasion to spend more time on the Turkish threat, but Henry VIII kept French forces tied down until 1546. France tried one more invasion in 1552 under a new king, Henry II, but it failed to restore French power in Italy. Warfare against the Holy Roman Empire until 1559 kept the French so busy that they never returned to the Mediterranean.

It might be said that the Franco-Italian wars brought an end to the Renaissance, because the almost constant warfare for 50 years kept the dukes and princes, who had so strongly supported the arts and sciences, from spending their money on these peaceful and cultural pursuits. The rampaging armies dealt so much destruction to the countryside and the cities, while the rulers taxed the citizens unmercifully, that the peninsula was ruined economically. Every major city saw fighting and destruction to some extent; Rome was sacked for the first time since the Byzantine days. It reconfirmed the political discord of the peninsula, which would not see unity until the end of the nineteenth century. Italy would become a battleground again in the future, but it no longer showed itself to be a leader in any field.

The theorist Machiavelli wrote his discourse, *The Art of War*, in the wake of these invasions, arguing that the centralized power of the French government proved superior to the fragmented power of the Italian city-states. The wars also established a long-lasting hostility between the royal houses of Valois of France and Habsburg in Spain, especially after the Habsburgs succeeded to the throne of the Holy Roman Empire. The Austrian branch of the Habsburgs maintained a hostility with France until World War I, enmity that showed itself in repeated power struggles. From a military point of view, the war was the first postmedieval conflict showing the major use of wheeled artillery and individual firearms in the form of harquebusiers and muskets. Firepower began to replace the shock attack of heavy cavalry, and fieldworks began to make their appearance as protection for those cannon and musketeers.

See also Austria, Turkish Invasion of.

References: Rice, Euguene, *The Foundations of Early Modern Europe, 1460–1559* (New York: Norton, 1970); Taylor, F. L., *The Art of War in Italy, 1494–1529* (Cambridge: Cambridge University Press, 1921); Waley, D., *The Italian City Republics* (New York: Longman, 1988).

99   MOGHUL EMPIRE

After Tamurlane's invasion of northern India in 1398, the area was fragmented among squabbling tribes. A clan of Afghans, the Lodis, captured the capital at Delhi in 1451, but could not extend their rule outside the immediate area of the Punjab in the upper Indus River valley. They persecuted the local Hindus, and provoked rebellions and attacks from all directions. Seeking outside assistance against the Lodis, a Punjabi governor appealed to Babur, the ruler of Afghanistan. A descendant of both Tamurlane and Genghis Khan, Babur "the Tiger" marched his steppe army into northern India. His better trained troops outfought a larger Lodi army at Panipat in 1526. He defeated the warlike Rajputs in 1527, and seized power with his victory over the Delhi sultanate in 1529. At this point he proclaimed the Moghul (or Mughal) Empire (from the Persian word for Mongol).

Babur's reign was short; he died in 1530. His son Humayun was expelled from India in 1540 by one of Babur's Afghan generals, and he went into exile in Iran. He returned to power at the

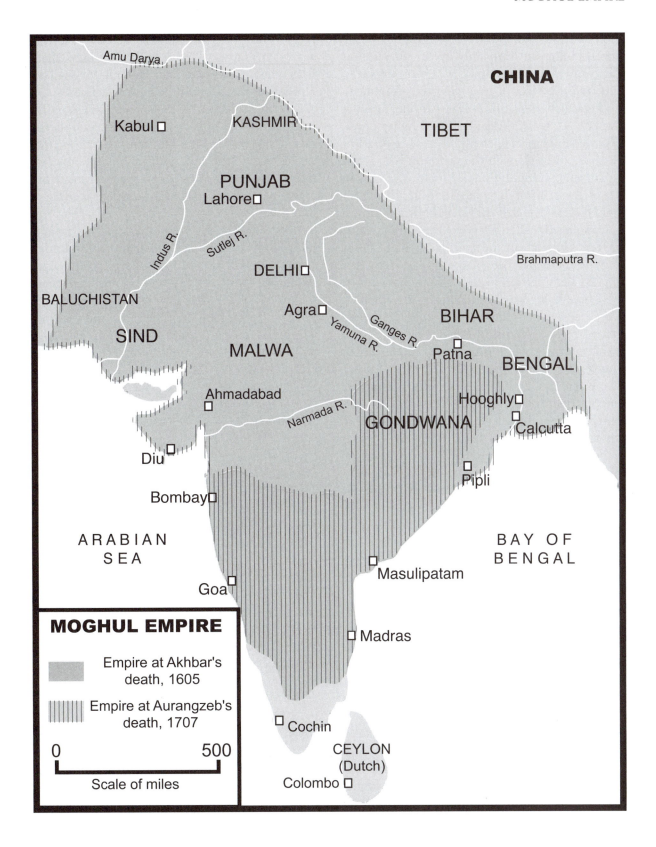

Amu Darya

CHINA

Kabul

KASHMIR

TIBET

PUNJAB

Lahore

Indus R.

Sutlej R.

DELHI

Brahmaputra R.

BALUCHISTAN

Agra

Ganges R.

BIHAR

SIND

Yamuna R.

MALWA

Patna

BENGAL

Ahmadabad

Narmada R.

GONDWANA

Hooghly

Calcutta

Diu

Pipli

Bombay

ARABIAN
SEA

BAY OF
BENGAL

Goa

Masulipatam

MOGHUL EMPIRE

Empire at Akhbar's
death, 1605

Empire at Aurangzeb's
death, 1707

Madras

0   500

Cochin

Scale of miles

CEYLON
(Dutch)

Colombo

head of an avenging army in 1555, but like his father, Humayun lived only a year after taking the throne. His 13-year-old son Akbar succeeded him, and the Moghul army defeated an immediate Hindu challenge to Akbar's throne, again at Panipat. At age 20, Akbar assumed full responsibility as emperor. He spent 20 years extending Moghul power through the northern half of the Indian subcontinent, establishing in the process one of the greatest dynasties in India. By allying himself with defeated tribes, he built an army as he conquered. After his conquest of Rajasthan, he took Gujarat, on the west coast, in 1573; by 1576 he controlled Bengal, on the east coast, and by 1581 he had captured most of Afghanistan.

Though he was born outside the country, Akbar considered himself Indian. He realized that to have a successful empire, he needed to promote loyalty. He was tenacious in battle, but when he defeated a rival tribe he did not punish them, but made them allies. The militaristic Rajput tribe, for example, became the primary source of his military advisers and generals. More important for Indian peace and culture was Akbar's religious tolerance. He was raised Muslim, but he studied and practiced a variety of modes of worship. His four wives were Christian, Muslim, or Hindu. He governed wisely and well, promoting all religions and tribes equally within his administration. He removed taxes that had long been targeted at Hindus, and by bringing peace to a large area of India, he promoted trade. The revenue he collected was dedicated to promoting the arts and building monuments to his empire and his culture. His court became internationally known for its wealth, beauty, and intelligence. Akbar himself wrote and painted, but most of his free time and energy were spent in religious study. He attempted to introduce a new religion that would incorporate aspects of all faiths and unite his country, but the belief did not survive him.

In 1606, Akbar died at the hands of his eldest son, Jahanigir ("World Seizer"), who together with his Persian wife Nur Jahan expanded the Persian influence in the Indian court and spent even more on construction. His dedication to luxury meant that the Moghul Empire did not expand in his reign, which ended in 1627.

Again, the eldest son came to power by plotting against his father. This time it was Shah Jahan, who killed his nearest relatives and removed his mother so there would be no challenges to his throne. He ruled for 30 years and lived as profligate a life as did his father, benefiting neither the people nor the empire. He returned to the practice of heavy taxation, and left behind only two major contributions to India: the Taj Mahal and a new capital city at Delhi modeled on Akbar's Red Fort at Agra.

As usual, Shah Jahan's sons plotted against him. He favored Dara, whose interests followed those of Akbar, but the more ambitious Aurangzeb killed Dara and imprisoned Shah Jahan. Another purge of relatives left Aurangzeb in total control by 1658. Unlike the previous rulers, he turned his back on religious tolerance and restarted the mandatory practice of Islam. His persecution of Hindus caused revolts, as did his increased taxes to pay for the suppression. Aurangzeb took up the expansionist attitude of Akbar and tried to conquer the southern Indian area of the Deccan, but he had only limited success and usually was obliged to surrender whatever gains he had bought at a high cost in money and lives. His army reached the Cauvery River in the south, but could not maintain dominance because of local resistance and the need to suppress rebellions in other parts of the empire. Aurangzeb inspired such hatred that he had to fight virtually every tribe or state in India. The Marathas, Rajputs, and Sikhs—groups that would influence India for centuries—rose to prominence as defenders of India against the Moghul despotism. Aurangzeb's legacy was one of destruction. The heavy taxation, the devastation from the fighting, and the disruption of trade impoverished the country. At his death in 1707, the empire was splintering. The Moghuls remained emperors by title until 1858, but after Aurangzeb, they were little more than figureheads. His persecution of faiths other than Islam divided the country into so many factions that after their common enemy was defeated, they were unable to agree on anything.

The Moghul Empire took India both to its heights and to its depths. At the beginning, Akbar introduced Persian as the official language, which helped create the languages of Hindi and Urdu, the two native languages of India today. Honest and efficient administration made India incredibly wealthy, and the construction he sponsored made it incredibly beautiful. Never before or since has India been as unified in its politics and religious toleration. During his reign, India was the equal or superior of almost any culture on earth. Successive self-indulgent rulers ruined Akbar's accomplishments. Though they added to India's cultural heritage, they did not pursue the sciences, and there were virtually no Indian achievements in technology and agriculture. By the time the Europeans arrived in the 1700s, the country was destitute and divided, and the foreign incursions proved that the rest of the world had passed India by.

See also Genghis Khan; Tamurlane; India, British Occupation of; India, French Occupation of.

References: Harrison, John, *Akhbar and the Mughal Empire* (St. Paul, MN: Greenhaven Press, 1980); Prawdin, Michael, *Builders of the Mogul Empire* (London: Allen & Unwin, 1963); Sharma, G. N., *Mewar and the Mughal Emperors* (Agra, India: Shiva Lal Agarwala, 1962).

NETHERLANDS, FRENCH INVASIONS OF THE

100

The Netherlands of the seventeenth century was a disjointed group of provinces. The northern area was known as the United Provinces and was controlled by the Dutch, whereas the southern provinces (modern Belgium) were under the control of the Spanish Habsburg monarchy, which had ruled all of the Netherlands prior to the successful Dutch rebellion in the sixteenth century. The southern provinces first attracted French interest when King Louis XIV decided to establish a more secure northern border at the expense of the Spanish, who had long been French rivals.

Louis believed that the Scheldt River should serve as a natural northern boundary for France, and in 1667 he set about to make it so.

Louis had an extremely tenuous legal claim to that territory through his marriage to Spanish Princess Maria Theresa, who was the daughter of Philip IV by his first marriage. Though Charles II came to the throne, he was the son of Philip's second marriage. Louis claimed that Maria Theresa's inheritance should outrank that of the progeny of Philip's second marriage and, therefore, the Netherlands were Maria Theresa's by right. It was an incredibly weak claim, but almost no one was in a position to challenge it. Louis had created one of the largest European armies ever, numbering some 120,000 men, and he entered the Spanish Netherlands on 24 May 1667. He enjoyed early success against the unprepared Spanish. By October, Louis' general Turenne captured a vast number of towns and forts and controlled the entire area. Having accomplished such easy victories in the north, Louis turned eastward in 1668 to occupy the Habsburg province of Franche-Comte on the Swiss frontier.

No one was prepared for Louis to launch a winter offensive, but he ordered Conde, the governor of Burgundy, to do just that. Conde's force of 15,000 invaded the province on 3 February 1668 and conquered it in two weeks. Louis rode to Franche-Comte to accept the surrenders of the local leaders; within three weeks the province was in French hands before any other country could react.

Louis had spent the last months of 1667 negotiating with possible rivals, and had threatened or bribed many into submission, or at least cooperation. Most German princes accepted his bribes and stayed clear of his military power. In January he concluded a secret treaty with Leopold, Holy Roman Emperor, in which Louis would cede to him the Spanish throne upon the imminent death of Charles II; he would also give up French claims in the West Indies, Milan, and Tuscany. In return, Louis would receive the Spanish Netherlands, Franche-Comte, Naples, Sicily, and Spanish possessions in Africa and the Philippines. Though the treaty would reward him handsomely and confirm his possession of France's northern frontier, it depended on Charles II's death, and that could not be predicted. Therefore, Louis continued plans for invading deeper into the Netherlands.

Afraid of his aggression, three nations allied themselves to oppose Louis. Holland convinced Sweden and England to join forces, and the alliance proposed a negotiation period through May 1668, beyond which the three nations would make war against France on land and sea. Louis' advisers were divided on the wisdom of continuing the fighting. Spain had been unable to provide troops for the defense of the Netherlands because of problems at home, but the Spanish had made peace with Portugal and might now turn their attention to Louis. The possibility of being surrounded convinced Louis that the secret treaty with Leopold was worth waiting for, so he entered into negotiations with his opponents and signed the Treaty of Aix-la-Chapelle on 29 May 1668. Under this treaty Louis kept only two small pieces of land along the northern French province of Artois.

The invasion Louis launched in the summer of 1667, sometimes called the War of Devolution, was nothing more than a precursor of fighting to come. It proved his ability to handle international diplomacy, and it was the first serious military campaign in which he himself participated; this gave him increased confidence in the ability of his nation and his subordinates, and provided France with a small province that acted as a buffer for possible Austrian or Swiss invasion into northern France. The peace signed in May 1668 proved to be nothing more than a ceasefire, and Louis invaded the Netherlands again in 1672.

Louis realized that to gain control of the Spanish Netherlands as soon as he hoped, he would have to break the Dutch, who feared France as an immediate neighbor. Between the two wars, Louis broke the Triple Alliance of Holland, England, and Sweden. Sweden had long had profitable trade relations with France, and was easily convinced to change sides. Remarkably, England proved almost as easy. Though the two nations had long been at odds, England's King Charles II was a Catholic ruling a predominantly Protestant country, and he had continual troubles with Parliament. Louis offered moral support not only as a fellow Catholic but as a fellow monarch, one who exercised more power in his country than did Charles in England. The thought of gaining personal power at the expense of Parliament (as well as strengthening English naval dominance at Dutch expense) appealed to

Charles, and he fell in with Louis' plans in 1670. The Holy Roman Empire maintained the neutrality it had pledged in the secret 1668 treaty, and most German princes were quiet or cooperative with French bribes. Holland was isolated, and Louis could depend on the British navy to counter the Dutch fleet.

Britain struck first, declaring war on Holland in March 1672. Louis was quick to follow up with an army much strengthened since the end of the last war. Aided by the talented general Turenne, who had trained Louis' army, and the brilliant fortification engineer Vauban, Louis had what seemed to be an unbeatable force. French armies rolled into Holland, and towns fell with remarkable ease. The country seemed helpless before the onslaught, and was saved only by Louis himself, who ignored Turenne's advice for a quick drive on to Amsterdam in favor of laying siege to a number of forts that he could easily have bypassed. The hesitation in attacking Amsterdam saved the Dutch. They sacrificed years of work for their own defense: They broke the dikes and flooded the approaches to the capital city.

No one expected such a radical maneuver, and it brought French operations to a halt. A change of government in Holland brought William of Orange to power, and he proposed to cede Maastrict and the Rhine towns and pay a large indemnity. Louis refused that, and a later, more generous offer. Louis' pride cost him dearly, because he gave up the chance to gain virtually all he wanted for little cost. Instead, he demanded that the Dutch demilitarize their southern border and pay a higher indemnity, which they refused. War was declared, but the flooding ended campaigning in the Netherlands for a while. The following summer, a new coalition formed to oppose Louis; it was made up of the Dutch, the Holy Roman Empire, and the Spanish. They successfully captured cities in German states Louis had previously bribed. Louis' money proved too little an inducement to resist the new coalition; most German states began to join it because they were Protestant and feared Louis' increasingly Catholic viewpoint. Britain also pulled out of the conflict when Parliament forced Charles II to make peace with Holland.

Louis was now isolated but undaunted. He ordered Turenne to invade the Franche-Comte, which he had so easily conquered in 1668. The campaign took six months and provoked a response from the coalition. In August 1674, they drove Turenne back along the Rhine frontier and threatened to invade, held back only by the arrival of winter. Turenne surprised them with another winter offensive just after Christmas and secured the French frontier by a successful campaign in Alsace. After that, the war settled into one of defense. Turenne died in July 1675, and Louis lost his most able general. Conde replaced Turenne, but failing health forced his retirement by the end of the year.

Louis spent his time between the battlefield and Versailles, and in the spring of 1676 was back with his troops. He was in a position to score a significant victory over William's forces near Valenciennes, but hesitated when he received conflicting opinions from his advisers. He returned to his favorite pastime of siege-craft, and the Dutch army remained intact. The French navy was successful in the Mediterranean in 1676, but the lack of progress on land, coupled with a rising discontent among segments of the French population, gave Louis pause. The destruction in the frontier provinces was costly, and he had had to increase taxes and revert to the sale of offices to pay for this war. There was little active campaigning in 1677 other than some successful sieges, but William of Orange married Mary, daughter of England's James II, a union which could presage a closer Anglo-Dutch bond, and this worried Louis. In 1678 he agreed to peace terms at Nijmegen in Holland, then concluded separate treaties with Spain and the Holy Roman Empire. Though required to surrender many Dutch towns, he acquired many more in the Spanish Netherlands and had a belt of fortresses covering his northern frontier reaching from Dunkirk to the Meuse River. The two conflicts against the Netherlands had taken France to the height of its prestige, power not to be seen again until the time of Napoleon. The financial cost had provoked some domestic discontent, but Louis' success solidified his strength as absolute monarch. It also whetted his appetite

for more glory and more secure borders, both of which he pursued in later campaigns: the War of the League of Augsburg and the War of the Spanish Succession.

> See also Italy, Austrian Invasion of (War of the Spanish Succession); Palatinate, French Invasion of the (War of the League of Augsburg); Napoleon Buonaparte.

> References: Hassall, Arthur, *Louis XIV and the Zenith of French Monarchy* (Freeport, NY: Books for Libraries, 1972 [1895]); Israel, Jonathan, *The Dutch Republic: Its Rise, Greatness and Fall, 1477–1806* (Oxford: Oxford University Press, 1995); Sonino, Paul, *Louis XIV and the Origins of the Dutch War* (New York: Cambridge University Press, 1988).

101 NORTH AMERICA, BRITISH OCCUPATION OF

By the time English settlers began arriving on the east coast of North America in the late 1500s, the Native American tribes had already had experience with Europeans in the form of passing Spanish ships. The English settlements along the coast of present-day Virginia were situated in the midst of an Indian confederation led by the local chief, Powhatan. He had domination over a number of tribes and led a population of perhaps 14,000 people, from whom he could draw over 3,000 warriors. He had successfully built a political organization in the neighborhood, and saw the English as little threat—they could either be killed or used for supplies to fight his enemies. Indeed, the earliest attempts at colonization faced extermination both through disease and Indian warfare.

The settlement in 1607 at Jamestown changed the situation. Powhatan continued to believe that these new white people could be used or killed as necessary, and the early experiences of the Jamestown settlers seemed to bear that out. However, under the leadership of John Smith, the English began to practice both military defense and diplomacy. Powhatan traded corn for copper, the metal best known and most valued by the area tribes. Because he commanded a number of tribes, he was able to negotiate with the English through one tribe while attacking them with another. English

The first serious attempt to establish a permanent colony in North America came with the arrival of the Pilgrims as depicted in the "Mayflower in Plymouth Harbor" by William Halsall, 1882.

reinforcements began to change the balance of power, and they actively courted Powhatan's enemies. Powhatan continued to trade with the English even as he persecuted them, but the large supply of English copper deflated its value, and he began to demand weapons (especially muskets) in return for food. By 1610, fighting between the two sides over land and food was common, and the alliances with Powhatan's enemies began to pay off. He refused to pay the exorbitant ransom demand made by his Anglo-Indian foes when they kidnapped his daughter Pocahontas. Instead, after a brief skirmish in 1614, Powhatan accepted Pocahontas's marriage to an English colonist who was investigating the export potential of tobacco. That ended the war.

The English imported more people as the Indians suffered through some bad harvests. Now, they were forced to buy English corn, and the English were beginning to make serious profits with tobacco. More settlers were lured to the New World with promises of free land; that land, however, had to be taken from the Powhatan Confederation. Increased immigration brought English culture, but Powhatan's successor was able to obtain muskets in return for allowing the teaching of Christianity. In 1619 a government was formed, the House of Burgesses, which banned the supplying of muskets to the Indians. Closer ties also brought more death from European diseases. The withdrawal of firearms provoked Opechanecough, Powhatan's successor, to launch a surprise attack against English farms up and down the James River in 1622. The

Indians massacred 342 men, women, and children, and the remaining English withdrew into fortifications, which were soon besieged. The English broke out on occasional sorties to loot the ripe cornfields of the Indians, which forced a food shortage that took warriors out of battle to plant new crops. Slaughter continued on both sides, and the English began underhanded diplomacy: They lured large numbers of Indians into negotiations, then poisoned them. Shortly thereafter, the first reported scalping took place—by the English. The more heavily armed English soon gained the upper hand, killing more Indians in battle and regularly stealing their food. By the early 1630s, the Indians negotiated a truce, which was often violated by both sides. Opechanecough's massacre in 1622 seemed to be all the excuse the English needed to make their settlement heavily militarized and their colonization one of complete domination. The establishment of militia units and their increasingly modern weaponry, coupled with a determination to conquer the land for their own agriculture, made warfare with the Indians a virtually constant pastime.

Relations between colonizing Englishmen and Indians to the north took a somewhat different turn. Early expeditions to fish and trade along the New England coast brought Indians back to England as prisoners. They were taught English and used as interpreters and scouts for later colonists. Only intermittent contact between the two peoples occurred in the first two decades of the seventeenth century, but it was enough to bring about a devastating epidemic in 1616–1618 that wiped out about 90 percent of the local Wampanoag tribe. Their loss of population made them targets for aggressive northern tribes armed by the French or Dutch, so when the English arrived, the Wampanoags hoped to gain an alliance that would aid in protecting their territory.

The first serious attempt to establish a permanent colony came in 1620 with the arrival of the Pilgrims, fundamentalist Calvinists who left England and Holland to escape worldliness and temptation. They came armed and surly, with a professional soldier, Myles Standish, as military adviser. After early aggressive actions against the locals, the Pilgrims made peace with the local Wampanoag chief, Massasoit, through the intermediary Squanto, a captured Indian interpreter. The Pilgrims hoped to use Massasoit as their agent to collect tribute from the area tribes; Massasoit hoped to gain weaponry from them to defend his lands from enemies. Increasing numbers of colonists, not all of them Pilgrims, caused social friction that resulted in a second settlement at Boston. The new arrivals ran afoul of the Massachusett tribe, and relations between Indians and whites became strained. Massasoit used this to convince Standish to attack the Massachusetts, thereby eliminating a Wampanoag rival.

The Pilgrims got into the fur trade as the fastest way to pay off their debts. They began growing corn, then traded the corn for furs. From the Dutch they learned the value of wampum, strings of beads made from seashells. These were a mark of status among area Indians, and because European tools made the production of wampum much easier, wampum soon replaced corn as the medium of exchange. Its increased availability brought about intertribal rivalry in the rush to trade with the Europeans, which also led to increased rivalry between the English and Dutch in the area. A smallpox epidemic killed many members of the Pequod tribe of Connecticut, where the Dutch had established a trading post. The aggressiveness of the Pequods brought about a response by Connecticut settlers in 1637 in what came to be called the Pequod War. An attack on their main settlement, in alliance with some of the area tribes chafing under Pequod dominance, ended in a slaughter of the tribe in May. The tribe's destruction came through fire and genocide, as the English killed men, women, and children in a fashion unknown to the Indians at that time. It set the example for most of the later conflicts in the New England area as the Puritans and other colonists set about to clear the land of whatever stood in the way of European progress.

The English imposed treaties on the defeated Indians throughout their New World colonies, but these usually marked temporary truces rather than lasting peaceful relations. Though the settlers gained from the Indians the

knowledge necessary to survive in North America, whether in agriculture or fur trading, the Europeans gave little in return. The arming of the Indians inflamed preexisting hostilities among tribes and gave later settlers an excuse to make war on armed natives. In the long run, the resources of America benefited only the Europeans; the native people gained little but disease, weaponry with which to kill one another, and exploitation of their land and produce.

References: Stannard, David, *American Holocaust* (New York: Oxford University Press, 1992); Steele, Ian K., *Warpaths: Invasions of North America* (New York: Oxford University Press, 1994); Wright, Ronald, *Stolen Continents* (Boston: Houghton Mifflin, 1992).

NORTH AMERICA, FRENCH OCCUPATION OF
102

Within five years of Columbus's voyage to the Americas, French ships were harvesting cod in the coastal waters off Newfoundland. They competed with other countries doing the same, but in 1524, the explorer Verrazano claimed for the French king the North American coast from Newfoundland to Spanish Florida. In 1534, King Francis I sent Jacques Cartier with two vessels to explore the coast of this new world. Cartier found Indians who attempted to engage in trade with him, which indicated that they had had previous customers for their furs, but other than that, he reported little of value. Cartier took two Iroquois with him to learn French and act as future interpreters; in 1535 he brought them back and sailed up the river now called the St. Lawrence. They wintered at the site of modern-day Quebec and suffered the fate of almost every expedition to New France: scurvy. The French also entered into a practice that would come to dominate their experience in the New World: intervening in the affairs of warring tribes. This immediately brought them into conflict with the Iroquois, a relationship that came to haunt them.

For the remainder of the sixteenth century, the French attempts at colonization suffered from Iroquois hostility, scurvy, and the Spanish. Early in the seventeenth century, King Henry IV tried to establish a colony to maintain the

French claim in the Western Hemisphere, and to do so he authorized Pierre du Gua, sieur de Monts, to form a trading company with monopolistic rights. Europeans were becoming enchanted with beaver fur, and the French wanted to control the trade. The monopoly faced fierce competition from independent traders, but de Monts set up his headquarters at Port Royal on the Newfoundland coast in 1604. De Monts and his associate, Samuel de Champlain, made connections with tribes of the Algonquin peoples, traditional enemies of the Iroquois, and both sides benefited. The French gained suppliers for their furs, while the Algonquin received French weaponry to use in their own intertribal conflicts. The Port Royal settlement was short-lived. De Monts lost his monopoly in 1607 and British settlers from farther south destroyed the village in 1612, marking the beginning of the other major rivalry engaging the French in North America.

Champlain attempted another trading center farther up the St. Lawrence, returning to Cartier's landing site, Quebec. He found fewer Indians, and they were both peaceful and enemies of the Iroquois, so they again entered into a mutually beneficial partnership. Still suffering from scurvy, the French held on to Quebec and promised to aid the local Algonquin tribes in their wars. Champlain's firearms helped make the Huron tribe masters of the area; they also made the French an enemy of the Mohawk tribe, who would plague the French for years to come. Though desirous of trading with the Europeans, the Mohawk had to look elsewhere; they established ties with the Dutch in the area that became upper New York.

Champlain wanted the Hurons to take him farther inland so he could explore new trade possibilities, but they were reluctant. The Hurons dominated the upper St. Lawrence economically as well as militarily; why should they introduce the French to other tribes when they could act as middlemen? Champlain found that he could operate only as freely as his Huron allies would allow. Still, the partnership was profitable, and Champlain was able to advertise his settlement in France. In 1626 he received the assistance of the Catholic Church when eight Jesuit priests arrived, sent by the multifaceted Cardinal Richelieu, King Louis XIII's prime minister. In 1628, Anglo-French fighting in Europe caused the new interest in Quebec to suffer. Over time, British and French possessions in North America and around the world would often change hands at European peace conferences. The French lost possession of their holdings for a few years, but returned in 1632. When the war ended, the Church sent even more priests as well as nuns to minister to the Hurons and establish settlements, including Montreal.

During the French absence from their settlements, the Mohawk returned, eager to assert claim to the St. Lawrence area. An agreement between the Mohawk and some Algonquins over trading privileges brought the Mohawk and French back into conflict. Beginning in 1635, the two parties entered into three decades of intermittent fighting. The Hurons were losing their power as allies, possibly as a result of their contact with the priests, who exposed them to European disease as well as Christianity; epidemics in the late 1630s cut the Huron population by one-third to one-half. Many Hurons embraced Christianity, which divided families along cultural lines that ultimately became political lines. The once powerful tribe began to break apart, and by 1650 had virtually ceased to exist, the remnants drifting off to join other tribes. After years of fighting the Mohawk with minimal success, the French stood by as the Mohawk persecuted their old Huron enemies.

Intertribal warfare nearly destroyed the fur trade, and by the mid-1600s the French were losing money. French soldiers made a futile attempt to take the war to the Mohawk in 1770, but the Mohawk also began to fade because of constant warfare with neighbors and occasional epidemics.

When King Louis XIV came to the throne in 1661, he put the North American venture under royal control. Louis worked closely with his economic adviser Jean-Baptist Colbert in strengthening French colonies around the globe. The king sent over 1,000 soldiers and a military governor, and directed the training of militia units in Canada. Forts were built along major Mohawk trading routes, and the soldiers challenged the Mohawk and the Iroquois directly. By 1665, the Iroquois had negotiated a peace. Sixteen years of peace gave the colony the breathing room it needed to solidify and grow.

Peace also allowed for exploration, and the French began to travel the Great Lakes and beyond. Rene-Robert Cavelier de La Salle oversaw the construction of trading posts from Niagara to the Mississippi River; he navigated that river to its delta in 1682, and claimed all the land drained by it for the king of France, giving the French supposed control over everything from the Rocky Mountains to the upper Ohio River valley.

In general, the French experience in North America differed greatly from the Spanish and British. The Spanish came to conquer and the British came to work the land, but the French seemed to be more financially motivated. Whether it was fish or furs, the primary inducement for French settlement was trade. The alliances facilitated that trade, and the combat in which the French engaged often came about because of arguments over which tribe was going to be the primary middleman. The French did not come to North America in the overwhelming numbers that the British and Spanish did and, especially in the cases of the priests and the independent French trappers, seemed to be less intentionally threatening to the Indians' lifestyles. As did the British and Spanish, they introduced diseases for which the Indians had no natural immunity, but the twin goals of profit and conversion argued against the violent methods of the Spanish or the high-handed style of the British. The French learned that many times, things had to be done the Indians' way, and they came to accept that; the Iroquoian diplomatic rituals became the norm for French negotiations with Indian tribes, and the French often sponsored intertribal councils. The French also discovered that the Indians had learned how to negotiate among themselves economically long before the Europeans arrived, and the Indians' ability to drive a hard bargain forced the French to provide value for value. The Indians often grew wealthy in the eyes of their own kind, and many became powerful warriors, thanks to French goods. The Indians knew the value of fur, and what they could get for it.

The French had the most cooperative European experience with the Indians, but their struggles with the British (in North America, Europe, and India) spelled the end of the French presence. After defeat at the hands of British soldiers and colonists in the French and Indian War (1755–1760), in addition to defeat in Europe during the Seven Years' War (1756–1763), the Treaty of Paris of 1763 took away all French lands east of the Mississippi River and awarded them to the British; a separate agreement ceded the French claims west of the Mississippi to the Spanish. Except for fishing rights off Newfoundland, the French colonial experience was over.

See also North America, British Occupation of; Saxony, Prussian Invasion of (Seven Years' War); Western Hemisphere, Spanish Occupation of.

References: Eccles, W J., *France in America* (East Lansing: Michigan State University Press, 1990); Steele, Ian, *Warpaths: Invasions of North America* (New York: Oxford University Press, 1994); Wrong, George, *The Rise and Fall of New France* (New York: Octagon Books, 1970 [1928]).

103   OTTOMAN EMPIRE

In the wake of the Mongol invasions in 1243 that broke up the Seljuk Turk Empire, Anatolia was filled with small, rival principalities. The group that finally rose to the top was led by Osman, or Othman, who resided in the north-central part of the peninsula at Sogut. According to legend, Sogut's mountaintop location was established by Hannibal, who advised the local rulers at the end of his life. Hence, the great enemy of Rome may have founded the town that brought about the end of the Roman Empire at last: Osman's followers, the Ottomans, delivered the killing blow that finished off the Eastern Roman Empire.

Osman spent his life making war against the Byzantine Empire. His major victory, accomplished as he lay dying in 1326, was the capture of the city of Bursa after a nine-year siege. This city in the northeast part of Anatolia put his son Orkhan in a position to strike across the Dardanelles into Europe. He also spread Ottoman rule eastward to Ankara. Unlike his father, Orkhan sometimes cooperated with the Byzantines, crossing the straits to aid them in beating back European enemies. The third time he did this, he did not go back but began to expand into the Balkans. His son Murad established Ottoman dominion in the Balkans with the defeat of powerful Serbia at the battle of Kosovo in 1389, though Murad died in the battle. Bayezid followed Murad's lead and laid siege to Constantinople in 1395. This provoked a response from Christian Europe, with the king of Hungary leading a coalition of English, French, German, and Balkan forces. They lost to Bayezid at Nicopolis, and the Ottoman Turks became the dominant force in the Balkans, transferring their capital from Bursa to Edina in Thrace.

The unbroken string of successes came to an end when Bayezid turned against traditional policy by attacking eastward, into the strength of Asia. He lost his freedom and his lands when Tamurlane defeated his forces at Ankara in 1402. After a struggle for power among his four sons, Mehmet (Mehmed) came to power in 1421. He reestablished Ottoman power, and his successor, Murad II, reigned for 30 years. Murad extended Ottoman rule farther into Europe, though he had much difficulty with the Hungarians.

Mehmet II came to the throne in 1451, and took the Ottomans to the height of their power. The remnants of the Byzantine Empire, huddled around Constantinople, finally died at Turkish hands.

Mehmet took the city in 1453, but he was not the barbarian the inhabitants had feared. After a mere three days of pillage, Mehmet began rebuilding. He made the city his new capital, and his tolerant policies promoted a quick peace. After centuries of strict Orthodox Christianity, the open-minded Mehmet made the city as cosmopolitan as had any previous ruler. He did not stop with this victory, however. Ottoman forces captured Greece and drove to the banks of the Adriatic; they landed at the tip of Italy, and only Mehmet's death prevented a major invasion. His successor, Bayezid II, did more building than conquering, and his passive nature led to his overthrow by his son Selim, called "the Inexorable." Selim's gunpowder-armed soldiers created the Ottoman Empire, anchoring the east at the head

of the Persian Gulf in 1514 and defeating the Mamluks to occupy Egypt in 1516. Ottoman power stretched to include Mecca, Medina, and Jerusalem. The string of able sultans reached its height—and its end—with Suleiman, known to Europe as "the Magnificent" and to his people as "the Lawgiver." Ruling from 1520 to 1566, he presided over the capture of Rhodes and the North African coast, defeated the Portuguese in the Red Sea and the Hungarians on land, and laid siege to Vienna. Suleiman's devotion to a secondary wife became not only his undoing, but that of the Ottoman Empire. After killing one son and exiling another from a previous marriage, his son Selim II, "the Sot," succeeded him. Ten brilliant leaders were followed by centuries of misrule.

The secret of Ottoman success was in the nature of their soldiers. Like the Seljuks before them, the Ottoman Turks recruited boys and young men from subdued Christian populations. They were called janissaries, raised in isolation and brought up on a mixture of Islamic teaching and strict discipline, learning loyalty to Allah and the sultan. They never left the barracks except to go to war; like the Spartans of ancient Greece, their military unit was their family. Other captive youths were trained in administration skills as well, and they ran the Ottoman bureaucracy. The rulers believed that such trainees would have no loyalty to any faction other than that in power, and therefore would operate the government and the military in a focused and unbiased manner. Through 10 sultans, they performed their tasks well and took the empire to its domination of the eastern Mediterranean world. However, Ottoman strength ultimately became its weakness; weak rulers from Selim II onward became the tools of the talented few who could exercise political and military power. The bureaucracy, rather than the sultans, came to run the empire. The more power the bureaucrats exercised, the more they craved, and they soon turned away from the practices that made the empire strong. Instead of recruiting from the population, they made their sons and nephews janissaries and administrators. The intense discipline and loyalty faded, and show began to replace substance. Weak sultans and military defeat caused the Ottoman Empire to decline from the late 1500s onward.

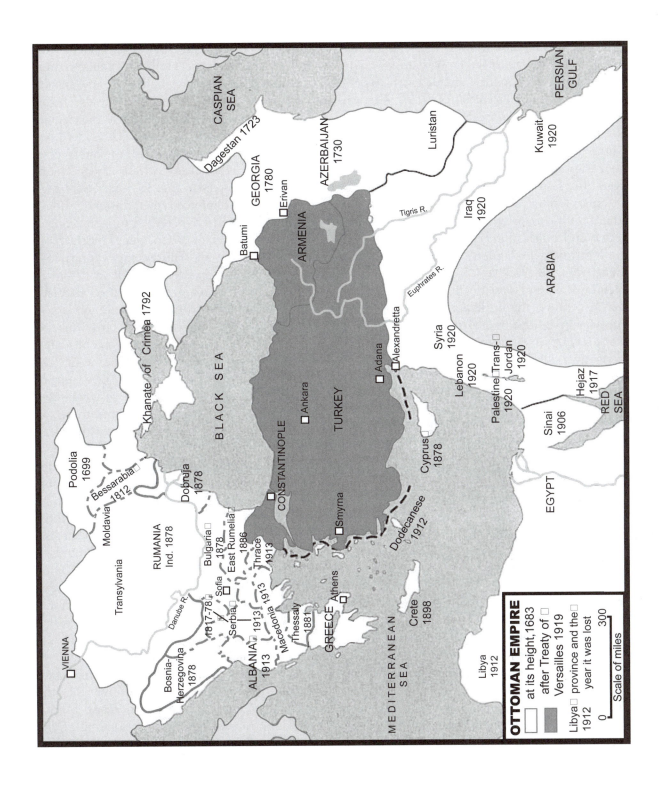

OTTOMAN EMPIRE

at its height, 1683 ☐
after Treaty of ☐
Versailles 1919

Libya ☐ province and the ☐
1912 year it was lost

Scale of miles

0 — 300

CASPIAN SEA

Dagestan 1723

GEORGIA 1780

AZERBAIJAN 1730

Luristan

PERSIAN GULF

Kuwait 1920

Erivan

ARMENIA

Batumi

Tigris R.

Iraq 1920

ARABIA

Euphrates R.

Khanate of Crimea 1792

BLACK SEA

Alexandretta

Syria 1920

Adana

Palestine Trans-
1920 Jordan
1920

Hejaz 1917

RED SEA

Podolia 1699

Bessarabia 1812

Dobruja 1878

Ankara

TURKEY

CONSTANTINOPLE

Lebanon 1920

Sinai 1906

Cyprus 1878

EGYPT

Moldavia

RUMANIA
Ind. 1878

Bulgaria 1878

East Rumelia 1886

Thrace 1913

Smyrna

Dodecanese 1912

Transylvania

Danube R.

1817-78

Sofia

Serbia 1913

Macedonia 1913

Athens

Crete 1898

Bosnia-
Herzegovina 1878

ALBANIA 1913

Thessaly 1881

GREECE

Libya 1912

MEDITERRANEAN SEA

VIENNA

The naval defeat at Lepanto in 1571 marked the turning point of Ottoman fortunes. Expansion ended; instead, the Ottomans defended their gains. By 1699, they began to cede territories in the Balkans, and a century later their empire was "the sick man of Europe." The Ottoman military decline coincided with an economic one. The wealth of the Western Hemisphere and the spread of ocean trade by the Europeans bypassed the traditional overland routes that had made the Middle East wealthy since the time of the Crusades. Political concessions to Europeans living and trading in Ottoman territory—the Capitulations—laid the groundwork for foreign infiltration of the economic and political system. Added to this was the increasing tax burden required to maintain the growing inefficiency of the military. The decline of empire was inevitable. In the nineteenth century, the Turks lost control of their frontiers in Europe and Africa, and by World War I had to pin their hopes on an alliance with Germany to keep up the facade of power.

See also Byzantine Empire; Tamurlane; Turks; Austria, Turkish Invasion of.

References: Kinross, Baron Patrick Balfour, *The Ottoman Centuries* (New York: Morrow, 1977); Shaw, Stanford, *The History of the Ottoman Empire and Turkey* (Cambridge: Cambridge University Press, 1976); Wheatcroft, Andrew, *The Ottomans* (London: Viking, 1993).

PALATINATE, FRENCH INVASION OF THE (WAR OF THE LEAGUE OF AUGSBURG)

104

French forces captured Strasbourg and Luxembourg from the Habsburgs, and King Louis XIV was rewarded with an unchallenged 20-year occupation of them in the Truce of Ratisbone, signed in the summer of 1684. This aided Louis' constant quest for more secure frontiers, but it frightened many Europeans. Hence, the League of Augsburg was formed on 9 July 1686, made up of the Holy Roman Empire, Spain, Sweden, Holland, and various German principalities including Saxony. Pope Innocent XI secretly joined, and Savoy and Bavaria joined openly the following year. Louis responded by demanding

that the Truce of Ratisbone be made a permanent peace and that he be permanently rewarded with his conquests. Louis hoped for the assistance of English King James II, a fellow Catholic and occasional rival of William of Orange, leader of the United Provinces of Holland. Louis wanted Luxembourg as a further buffer for any possible threat from central Europe, and he also hoped that the pope would recognize him as the champion and defender of the Church. The older Louis became, the more he seemed to embrace an aggressive Catholicism, which made many German princes distrustful. In June 1688, their suspicions were reinforced when the archbishop of Cologne died and Louis rushed to install one of his puppets as elector of Cologne; French troops occupied the city, and Furstenburg was named—not elected—elector. Louis immediately followed up this action with a move toward the Palatinate, deeper in German territory. The sole survivor of the ruling family was the wife of the duke of Orleans, and Louis demanded that she be named ruler of the province even though she did not want the position. Louis hoped that by occupying Cologne and the Palatinate, Europe would concede to his demand over the Ratisbone truce.

Louis' invasion of German territory provided a respite from French pressure to William of Orange, who sailed for England and was awarded the throne in the Glorious Revolution of 1688. Although James II had strong suspicions that he was about to be removed, he had rejected Louis' offer of aid as condescending. William's enthronement brought a return to Protestant rule in England and guaranteed Anglo-Dutch cooperation against France. Had Louis invaded the Netherlands rather than the Palatinate, William's accession to the English throne would have been delayed, if not undone; William could never have abandoned his country's defense.

The alliance of two powerful Protestant nations strengthened the resolve of the Protestant German princes to resist French aggression. Further, Louis' revocation of the Edict of Nantes, which had long guaranteed Protestant rights in France, did nothing to allay German fears. Louis seemed unprepared for the strong German response, and also for that of the Holy Roman Empire, which was currently fighting

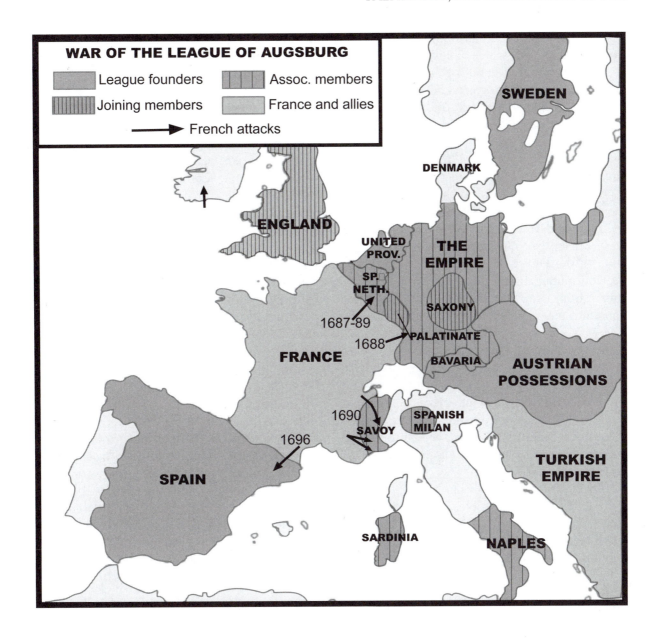

WAR OF THE LEAGUE OF AUGSBURG

League founders
Joining members
French attacks
Assoc. members
France and allies

SWEDEN

DENMARK

ENGLAND

UNITED PROV.

THE EMPIRE

SP. NETH.

SAXONY

1687-89

PALATINATE

1688

FRANCE

BAVARIA

AUSTRIAN POSSESSIONS

1690

SAVOY

SPANISH MILAN

1696

TURKISH EMPIRE

SPAIN

SARDINIA

NAPLES

Turkish aggression. Rather than hold a position too far away from France, Louis decided to abandon the Palatinate—but not before destroying it. French forces burned the countryside and leveled the towns in a manner not seen in Europe since the Thirty Years' War. This wanton destruction also intensified German hostility.

Rather than force Europe to concede to his wishes, Louis had enraged virtually every country. His main problem now was deciding which opponent to face first. He chose the Anglo-Dutch alliance, and launched an invasion of Ireland in an attempt to install James II as king there. A Catholic ally in Ireland would strengthen Louis' strategic position vis-à-vis England, but it was not to be. French troops landed and encouraged anti-English sentiment, but the French defeat at the battle of the Boyne on 1 July 1689 ended any serious chance of success. Two years of sporadic fighting in Ireland confirmed English rule and forced the exile of some 12,000 Irish soldiers who had entered French service. However, France managed to win a costly victory at sea, the battle of Beachy Head on 10 July 1689. It kept their fleet operational in the English Channel, but hurt them sufficiently that ultimate victory against the combined English and Dutch navies would be nearly impossible. Louis maintained the dream of invading England itself and reestablishing Catholic rule, but a naval defeat by English forces off La Hogue in May 1692 reestablished Anglo-Dutch naval dominance.

Meanwhile, Louis had continental enemies to face. In 1690 he made demands on the duke of Savoy; when they were not met, he invaded. He captured Savoy, Nice, and much of the Piedmont; the rest of that province fell to him in October 1693. On the Rhine front, the fighting remained mainly defensive. Louis had no talented general here, so the French showed little initiative, but the continuing struggle against Turkey kept the empire from launching any offensives. The most important action took place in the Netherlands, where Louis engaged in his favorite pastime of laying siege. Aided by Vauban, the master engineer of the time, Louis captured Mons in April 1691. In May 1692 he besieged Namur, one of the strongest fortified cities in Europe, and captured it in June. At that point, Louis could have launched a decisive invasion of Holland, but he was not a talented field commander, and preferred sieges to set-piece battles.

Louis returned to the field for the last time in June 1693 as French forces began the siege of Liège, but they failed to take the city. For the remainder of that year, as well as 1694 and 1695, only sporadic and inconclusive fighting along the Rhine and the Spanish border took place. Louis could make little headway in breaking the league militarily, but he finally did so diplomatically. In 1696 he bribed the duke of Savoy to break with his allies; after returning most of the land he had captured in the southeast to Savoy, Louis had an additional 30,000 troops he could transfer to the Netherlands front. However, he offered to hold peace talks, and the allies agreed rather than face what could be a long conflict in the Netherlands.

Representatives met at Ryswick in May 1697, and in September Louis signed a treaty with Holland, England, and Spain. He withdrew from Luxembourg, allowed the Dutch to fortify their frontier, gave them a favorable trade treaty, and recognized William of Orange as King William III of England, promising not to aid any plots against

his rule. In October, he signed a second treaty with the Holy Roman Empire and the Germans, wherein he withdrew his claims to Cologne and the Palatinate, abandoned all land east of the Rhine (though he fortified the west bank), and abandoned Lorraine. He kept Landau, Strasbourg, and Alsace, much to the indignation of the Germans. He further angered them by demanding that Catholicism remain predominant in whatever territory he ceded.

Louis hoped that he could reestablish friendly relations with the Germans in the face of the rising power of the Holy Roman Empire, but they had had enough of his actions. The destruction of the Palatinate and his aggressive Catholic policies turned them against France permanently; Franco-German hostility reappeared constantly over the following three centuries. Louis failed in his original aim of permanently occupying Luxembourg, but that was his only loss after nine years of war. He broke the league formed to oppose him, kept France well protected and strong, and was in an excellent position to influence events soon to come concerning the rule of the house of Habsburg. Though French pride and power were maintained, Louis' position as the supreme power in Europe declined. The power of divine right and absolute monarchy ended in favor of the democratic, constitutional monarchies of England and Holland.

See also Austria, Turkish Invasion of; Italy, Austrian Invasion of (War of the Spanish Succession); Thirty Years' War.

References: Hassall, Arthur, *Louis XIV and the Zenith of the French Monarchy* (Freeport, NY: Books for Libraries, 1972 [1895]); Lossky, Andrew, *Louis XIV and the French Monarchy* (New Brunswick, NJ: Rutgers University Press, 1994); Treasure, G. R. R., *Seventeenth Century France* (London: Rivingtons, 1966).

105

PORTUGAL, SPANISH OCCUPATION OF

In 1578, King Sebastian of Portugal was killed while fighting Muslim forces in Morocco. Sebastian died without an heir, bringing to an end the house of Aviz. The Portuguese throne was open, and the nearest claimant was Philip II of Spain, whose mother was a Portuguese princess. Spain was in need of the territories that Portugal controlled because, despite the wealth of the Americas, Spanish finances were drained in attempts to suppress revolts in the Low Countries.

Philip's major rival for the throne was Don Antonio de Crato of Beja. He fought Philip for two years, but was finally defeated at the battle of Alcantara on 25 August 1580 by Philip's general, the duke of Alva. Crato fled for France to plan for his return. Philip assured the Portuguese government, the Cortes, that he would not take advantage of the country. He promised to recognize the rights of Portuguese citizens; all civil, military, and judicial offices would remain in Portuguese hands; all the dignities of the Church and orders of knighthood would be respected. He also promised that goods from Portuguese territories would be carried only on their own shipping and that the revenues from the trade with Africa, Persia, and India would remain in the country, kept separate from Spain's revenues. Further, he promised to grant the sum of 3,000 crowns from his own treasury to redeem prisoners, repair cities, and relieve sickness among the people.

Three times Philip had to fight to keep his new possession. Crato attempted to return and seize the throne with both French and British assistance. He tried to capture the Azores with a French fleet in 1582, but was defeated by Spanish Admiral Alvaro de Bazan. He tried the same thing the following year with the same result, confirming the power of the Spanish fleet in the Atlantic. In 1589, the year following the disaster of the Spanish Armada, Philip again turned away Crato's attempt to return to Portugal. Crato landed his forces on the coast with the aid of Sir Francis Drake and Sir John Norris of England; not only did the people fail to rise to his call, but they also turned against the invaders because of English plundering.

Philip kept his promises. The Portuguese held important positions, taxes did not increase, and the laws remained the same. As long as Philip II reigned, things ran smoothly.

The same cannot be said of his sons, however. Philip III and Philip IV saw Portugal as a source of revenue to be tapped and a source of political positions for their associates. Philip II's evenhanded rule collapsed, causing resentment in the country. The Portuguese possessions overseas became the targets of English attacks, and the Spanish did little or nothing to protect them.

The Spanish were experiencing their own problems, with revolts in the Netherlands and in the Spanish province of Catalonia. In 1640, Philip IV asked the Portuguese duke of Braganca to bring troops to Spain. The duke raised troops, but used them to seize the throne with the blessing of the Cortes, the Church, and the people. Braganca tried to establish relations with the Dutch to maintain pressure on Spain from two sides and regain Portuguese possession of territories lost over the past several years, but the Dutch-Portuguese economic rivalry was too great to overcome. They established a 10-year truce, which allowed the Dutch to trade with Brazil, but the peace did not last. Portuguese forces regained some trading posts in Angola and forced the Dutch trade centers in Brazil to shut down. The two countries finally agreed to a trade treaty in 1654. Portugal entered into a mutual-defense alliance with England in 1661 that guaranteed protection in case of renewed Spanish pressure.

Spain was much too busy with revolts to seriously try another occupation. After Portugal repulsed attempts at invasion in 1644 and 1665, the two countries signed a peace treaty in 1668. The "Sixty-Year Occupation" had little effect in Portugal; the only serious result was the loss of overseas trading posts owing to the lack of Spanish defensive measures. Considering the small size of the Portuguese navy in comparison to the growing fleets of England and the Netherlands, the loss of those trading posts may have been inevitable.

References: Marques, A. H. de Olivera, *History of Portugal* (New York: Columbia University Press, 1976); Payne, Stanley, *A History of Spain and Portugal* (Madison: University of Wisconsin Press, 1973); Stephens, Morse, *The Story of Portugal* (New York: AMS Press, 1971).

106 RUSSIA, SWEDISH INVASION OF (GREAT NORTHERN WAR)

In 1655, Sweden's king Charles X took his country to the greatest extent of its power and territorial conquest. His defeat of Denmark and concessions from Poland made Sweden the dominant force in the Baltic region. The First Northern War came to an end with Charles's death in 1660. The Second, or Great Northern War, was much longer and bloodier. Sweden was under the able leadership of Charles XII, only 18 years old. Upon Charles's accession, Poland's King Augustus II saw an opportunity to break away from the domination his nation had suffered since 1660. He led the formation of the Northern Union, made up of Poland, Denmark, and Russia. Russia gave him the greatest support because Tsar Peter, known as the Great, longed to replace Sweden as the major Baltic power.

Instead of letting the Northern Union make the first move, Charles attacked Denmark, his closest and weakest enemy. After the Swedes invaded Zealand and threatened Copenhagen, Denmark sued for peace. In the Treaty of Travedal, signed 28 August 1700, Denmark ended hostilities and promised no further action for the duration of the conflict, but the Danish fleet remained intact and Charles considered it a threat to his lines of communication.

Charles next landed 8,000 troops at Livonia to relieve the city of Riga. However, he learned after debarking that Narva was under siege, the attacking Russians outnumbering the defenders by at least four to one. Taking advantage of a blinding snowstorm on 20 November, Charles surprised the Russians and defeated them, killing or capturing 10,000 men while forcing another 30,000 to retreat and abandon all their artillery and supplies. Charles now made a fateful decision. Instead of advancing on Moscow and taking Russia out of the war, he turned his army around and marched on Poland, which he believed to be the greater threat. The Swedes invaded Poland in 1702 and proceeded to capture both Krakow and Warsaw.

Augustus II was forced to surrender in 1706. The Treaty of Altranstadt on 24 September stated that Poland had to withdraw from the war and Augustus must abdicate the Polish throne in favor of the Swedish puppet Stanislas Leszczynski. The Swedes also gained permission to winter in Saxony and await recruits and equipment for the upcoming campaign against Russia. Meanwhile, Tsar Peter made the most of the time Charles gave him after the defeat at Narva. He had gained control of the Neva River, and had begun work on his new capital city of St. Petersburg at the river's mouth. He also began building a navy on the Baltic Sea while making significant changes in his army, which was now much improved over the force that had performed so poorly at Narva.

Charles led 50,000 men across the Vistula River on 1 January 1708 with the goal of advancing directly on Moscow. He defeated the Russians at Holowczyn on 4 July, but the scorched-earth policy employed by the retreating Russians forced Charles to march south in hopes of acquiring supplies from his new ally, hetman of the Cossacks Ivan Mazepa. This southward move separated Charles from his badly needed supply train and reinforcements, led by General Carl Emil Lewenhaupt. Peter maneuvered his army between Charles and Lewenhaupt, and at the 9 October battle of Lesnaia, he used his four-to-one superiority in troops to defeat Lewenhaupt. The Swedish general was forced to abandon his artillery and burn his supply wagons; of the 11,000 men he had been taking to join Charles, only 6,000 arrived.

These men, along with the Cossacks Mazepa brought, raised Charles's army to around 40,000. A particularly cold Ukrainian winter and constant skirmishing with the Russians diminished the force to about 20,000 by the spring of 1709. Instead of regrouping, in May Charles chose to continue his advance on Moscow. Between his army and Moscow lay the Russian stronghold at Poltava on the Vorskla River. The Swedes laid siege to the city but found themselves surrounded by a force of 50,000 when Peter arrived in mid-June. Short of artillery and gunpowder and cut off from his supply line, Charles had to break out of the encirclement. He launched his attack on 9 July and achieved early success, but the superior number of Russian

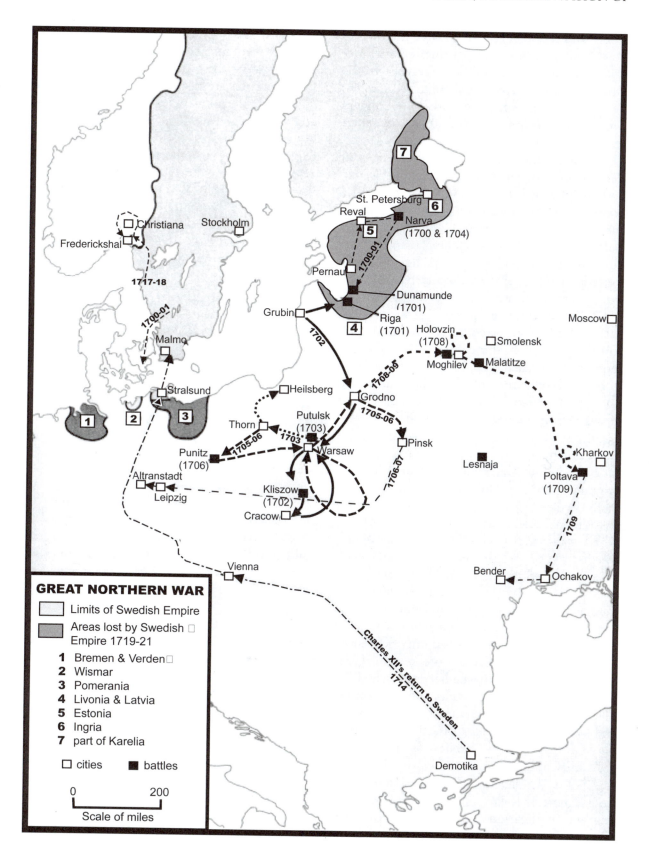

GREAT NORTHERN WAR

☐ Limits of Swedish Empire

■ Areas lost by Swedish ☐
Empire 1719-21

1 Bremen & Verden ☐
2 Wismar
3 Pomerania
4 Livonia & Latvia
5 Estonia
6 Ingria
7 part of Karelia

☐ cities ■ battles

0   200
Scale of miles

Map labels: Christiana, Stockholm, Frederickshal, 1717-18, 1700-01, Malmo, Stralsund, Heilsberg, Thorn, Putulsk (1703), Punitz (1706), Altranstadt, Leipzig, Kliszow (1702), Cracow, Warsaw, 1705-06, 1703, Grodno, 1705-06, Pinsk, 1706-07, 1708-09, Grubin, 1702, Riga (1701), Dunamunde (1701), Pernau, Reval, St. Petersburg, Narva (1700 & 1704), 1700-01, Holovzin (1708), Moghilev, Smolensk, Malatitze, Moscow, Lesnaja, Kharkov, Poltava (1709), 1709, Bender, Ochakov, Vienna, Charles XII's return to Sweden 1714, Demotika troops and cannon (100 to 34) wore the Swedes down. After 18 hours of fighting, Charles was driven from the field and fled southeast to the Dnieper with Mazepa and about 1,500 cavalry; he sought refuge with the Turks. Lewenhaupt was obliged to surrender with 16,900 prisoners at Perevolchna.

Poltava and the subsequent surrender at Perevolchna signaled the demise of Sweden and the rise of Russia. The victory brought a pause in the war as well as a geographic shift in the fighting to northern Germany and the Baltic region. Russia's victory reunited the Northern Union and brought in the additional support of Hanover, Prussia, and Saxony; further, Augustus II was restored as Polish king in 1710. During the five years that Charles spent with the Turks, Peter continued to strengthen Russia's position in the eastern Baltic. Charles returned to Sweden in 1714, but was unable to stop the momentum of the allied armies in northern Germany. Sweden abandoned its last possession in Germany—Stralsund—in 1715. Charles spent the next two years rebuilding his army, which had been at war for almost 20 years. In 1717 he invaded Norway, then a Danish province, and was killed at Fredriksten on 11 December 1718.

With Charles's death, the Great Northern War began winding down. In 1719 and 1720, Sweden signed the Treaties of Stockholm with Poland, Saxony, Denmark, Prussia, and Hanover. Hanover was given Bremen and Verden in return for a large indemnity, Prussia acquired parts of west Pomerania and the city of Stettin, and Denmark retained only Schleswig. Peace with Russia did not occur until 1721, when the remaining two belligerents signed the Treaty of Nystadt on 30 August. Russia acquired Livonia, Estonia, Ingermanland, part of Karelia, and a number of islands in the Baltic. Most of Finland went to the Swedes, as did a large indemnity in payment for the Baltic islands. At this point Russia controlled the Baltic coast from Vyborg to Riga.

The implications of the Great Northern War were enormous. Russia replaced Sweden as the major Baltic power and began a century of expansion southward and westward, finally acquiring its "window to Europe," which allowed economic ties to the West. Peter, who worked desperately to westernize his nation, found the new respect from European powers quite helpful in attracting intellectuals and engineers to Russia. While this contact brought a great degree of advancement for the Russian upper class, the mass of Russian citizens benefited little. All they felt was the tax burden of paying for Peter's ambitions and conscription into the armies fighting for his glory. The Swedish cession of the Baltic provinces laid the foundation for Russian proprietary interest in them to this day.

References: Hatton, R. M., *Charles XII of Sweden* (London: Weidenfeld & Nicolson, 1968); Massie, Robert, *Peter the Great, His Life and World* (New York: Knopf, 1980); Robert, Michael, *Sweden's Age of Greatness, 1632–1718* (New York: St. Martin's Press, 1973).

107 SAXONY, PRUSSIAN INVASION OF (SEVEN YEARS' WAR)

In the wake of the War of the Austrian Succession, the major European powers remained suspicious of one another; indeed, the Treaty of Aix-la-Chapelle was more of a truce than a real peace settlement. Empress Maria Theresa of Austria chafed at the loss of the rich province of Silesia to Prussia's Frederick II, and she directed her chief minister, Count Wenzel von Kaunitz, to feel out possible allies for an attempt to regain her lost lands. Her recent ally, England, had been making overtures to Frederick in hopes of protecting the lands of Hanover, whence came the English royal family. Austria's centuries-old rival, France, was now afraid of Prussia's growing power and desirous of extending its sway into the Netherlands, which Austria controlled and England wanted. Austria also found a sympathetic ear in Russia because Czarina Elizaveta feared Prussian designs on Poland. Even Sweden had a grudge against Prussia for lands lost years earlier. Last, the German elector of Saxony felt more comradeship with Catholic Austria than with Protestant Prussia. Kaunitz's design, ultimately successful, was to draw these powers into line against their common foe. Frederick realized that his hold on Silesia was tenuous, and that Maria Theresa wanted it back. He welcomed England's proposal of friendship, even though England had only a small army with which to assist him should he be pressed on all sides. However, England had an agreement with Russia, which Frederick hoped (in vain, it proved) would keep Russia away from him. Learning of Kaunitz's discussion through his spies, Frederick decided that a preemptive strike was necessary. His English allies were already fighting France over their North American colonies, so an attack by France was certainly plausible. When he asked Maria Theresa for guarantees against aggression, her evasive answers provided all the justification Frederick needed to begin fighting.

Frederick possessed the finest army and possibly the best military mind in Europe. Although his 150,000-man army was no match for the combined forces arrayed against him, it was the equal or better of any of them individually. He attacked Saxony at the end of August 1756, and occupied the territory easily. He acquired and published documents proving Maria Theresa's plot against Prussia. She sent an army from Bohemia to challenge him, and Frederick won the first battle of the war at Lobositz on 1 October. He returned to capture the one remaining Saxon stronghold, at Pirna, then incorporated the 14,000 prisoners into his army, declared Saxony conquered, and drew on its finances to pay for the war. He spent the winter in Dresden.

The European monarchies rallied to Austria, condemning Prussian aggression. Only the English remained at Frederick's side, and then only half-heartedly; William Pitt (Frederick's greatest supporter in England) was removed and later recalled as chief minister. While awaiting England's financial (and token military) support, Frederick's 145,000-man army faced a combined force in excess of a third of a million men. His only hope to survive was to make sure they did not combine. Frederick spent the next six years marching and countermarching to face one foe after another, in the process earning the appellation "the Great." It was a title he did not acquire easily.

Frederick invaded Bohemia in the spring of 1757 and won a narrow victory over the Austrian forces outside Prague, which he was unable to successfully besiege; he had to abandon the effort after a defeat at Kolin at the hands of the great Austrian general Leopold von Daun. Feeling depressed at the military loss as well as the death of his mother, Frederick sent out tentative peace feelers, but they were rejected. The allies saw no reason to negotiate now: A French force defeated a Hanoverian force under English king George II's son at Hastenbeck, Swedish troops arrived in Pomerania, 100,000 Russians overran a 30,000-man force in East Prussia, and a force of Croats attacked Berlin. Frederick contemplated suicide, but at last he turned to face French forces (aided by German principalities) at Rossbach, near Leipzig.

Having left garrisons or forces under other commanders at various spots around his frontiers, Frederick had a mere 21,000 men under his direct command at Rossbach. Nevertheless, he staged one of the great victories of his career. He surprised the German forces with a rapid cavalry assault, then pounded the approaching French with artillery. The Prussians killed 7,700 men and lost only 550. Silesia, however, fell to Austrian forces in November. Frederick raced to recover the province, and met retreating Prussian troops and the Austrian army near Leuthen on the road to Breslau. Though outnumbered almost two to one, Frederick attacked in echelon, a maneuver unheard of in military circles of the time, and which involved the formation of troops in which each unit was positioned to form a steplike line. The maneuver confused the Austrians as to the true focus of his attack, and they were overwhelmed, losing 3,000 men and 116 artillery pieces; 20,000 men were taken prisoner. The twin victories of Rossbach and Leu then etched Frederick's name into the list of masterful generals.

The end of 1757 brought renewed promises of support from England and fresh confidence to the Prussian king. He would need it, for in 1758 he was constantly on the move facing one threat or another, often losing battles. Frederick's rebuilt army had to abandon the siege of Olmiitz to face a Russian army marching toward Berlin, fighting the larger Russian force to a bloody stalemate. Daun again defeated him in Silesia in October,

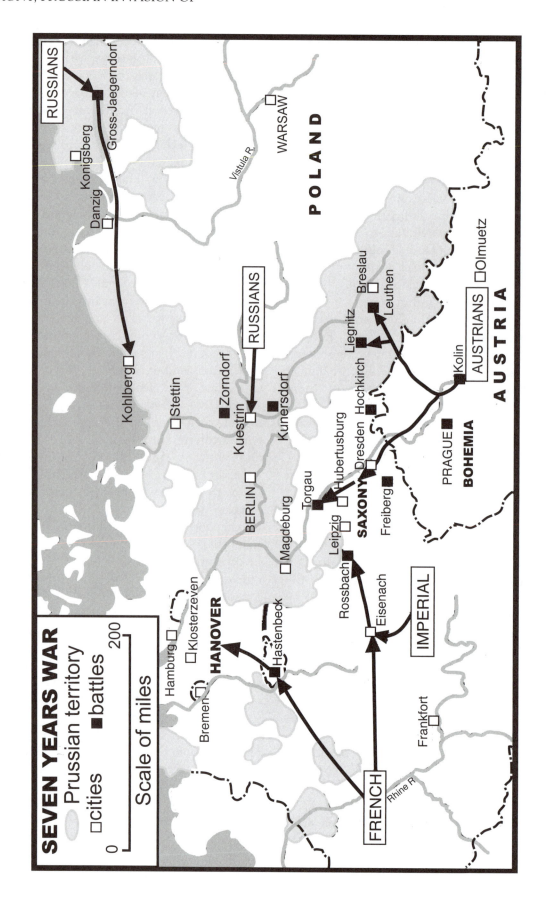

but the winter gave Frederick time to regroup; once again, he considered and rejected suicide.

The Prussians had a hard time of it in 1759. Leaving a holding force near Dresden to keep Daun at bay, Frederick marched to meet a Russian threat to Berlin. After a hard-fought battle at Kunersdorf, the Prussians were at last overwhelmed and routed, but Frederick reformed the survivors and marched back toward Berlin. He found no Russians, because supply problems had forced their retreat, and he turned once again to face Daun. Frederick arrived at Dresden too late to save it from Austrian occupation for the winter of 1759–1760.

He tried to recapture Dresden in the summer of 1760, but had to abandon that siege as well to march to Breslau. He entered the city in triumph after defeating an Austrian force at Leignitz, but at a later battle at Torgau on the Elbe River in November, the best Frederick could manage was a draw and a winter in Breslau. In 1761, much diplomatic maneuvering but little military action took place. The high financial cost of the war wore on every monarch, and peace feelers were extended in every direction. In England, George II died and his successor did not share his passion to defend Hanover; Pitt resigned rather than abandon Frederick, but the English government grew tired of subsidizing Frederick in the wake of their gains in North America at French expense.

Frederick was saved not so much by his endurance and talent as by events beyond his control. The czarina died in 1762, and Peter III replaced her; an ardent admirer of Frederick, he not only signed a peace treaty but allied himself with Prussia. The French could no longer afford to send subsidies to Austria, and the Turks were attacking Austrian territory. Austrian chancellor Kaunitz refused to deal with an English government now hostile to Frederick, and the loss of Russian assistance was too much for Austria to handle. Frederick finally got the best of Daun at Burkersdorf in July, then defeated the Austrians at Schweidnitz in Saxony; in October, a separate Prussian force defeated the Austrians in Saxony, and the war was as good as over.

Reluctantly, the monarchs began to talk peace. The French, no longer in possession of a navy, their North American lands, or very much money, made peace with Britain in return for Caribbean islands. Spain, which had been of slight help to France, gained some concessions, and these settlements left Austria standing alone, facing 100,000 Turks in Hungary. Maria Theresa proposed peace and Frederick agreed, signing a treaty in February 1763. A war begun strictly for political reasons had few direct political results other than a return to the antebellum status quo. Austria lost Silesia for good, and ran up a huge debt. Maria Theresa gave up the title Holy Roman Empress for empress of Austria-Hungary; the German principalities that had for centuries given grudging fealty to the Holy Roman Empire began to drift toward Prussian power. Russia lost 120,000 men, but gained a seat in European councils and laid the groundwork for a partition of Poland. Prussia gained the most in political respect, but lost the most in territorial devastation because the majority of the war was fought across its lands. Frederick claimed some 180,000 soldiers dead through combat or captivity; the total loss to the country was 500,000 people, out of an original population of 4–5 million. Britain came out of the war richer in territory but much poorer in cash; this could have marked the birth of the British Empire, but England's attempts to recoup financial losses via its North American colonies would provoke rebellion in 12 years.

The war brought about a new economic point of view that mass armies needed massive amounts of supplies, so the military-industrial complex was about to be born. The experience of destruction brought about a pessimism that resulted in a renewal of religious faith in the face of earthly futility. Further, the Protestant faith was finally safeguarded in central Europe, as an Austrian victory could have meant a forced return to Catholicism, much as had been seen prior to the Thirty Years' War.

See also Silesia, Prussian Invasion of (War of the Austrian Succession); Thirty Years' War.

References: Duffy, Chris, *The Military Life of Frederick the Great* (New York: Atheneum, 1986); Ritter, Gerhard, *Frederick the Great, a Historical Profile* (Berkeley: University of California Press, 1970).

SILESIA, PRUSSIAN INVASION OF (WAR OF THE AUSTRIAN SUCCESSION)

108

Unlike the War of the Spanish Succession, this conflict did not involve the inheritance of the throne by a foreigner, but by a woman. Emperor Charles VI of Austria had succeeded his sonless brother Joseph in 1711, but Charles also was unable to sire a male child. For 20 years he planned to give his throne to his daughter Maria Theresa, and received the promise of the major European powers to acknowledge the Pragmatic Sanction, a document through which the traditional law of crowning only males on the Habsburg throne was temporarily put aside. It also overrode whatever claim Joseph's daughter may have had to the throne (she had married into the ruling family of Bavaria). When Charles died in 1740, the promises of most European countries proved useless.

The first to react to this female monarch was Frederick of Prussia. He had inherited from his father the best trained army in Europe and, at age 28, was anxious to prove his leadership ability. Frederick offered his services as defender of Austria in return for cession of the province of Silesia, and revived a 200-year-old claim to the land. When Maria Theresa proved unwilling to pay the price for his protection, as he had known she would, Frederick ordered his army into Silesia in December 1740. Maria Theresa immediately appealed to the guarantors of the Pragmatic Sanction, but she found few supporters. Bavaria wanted to push the claim of Joseph's daughter Maria Amalia, France wanted the Austrian Netherlands (modern Belgium) and therefore allied with Bavaria, and Saxony and Savoy saw an opportunity to gain land at Austrian expense. Only the English, whose King George II was also elector of Hanover and had no desire to see that province under Prussian or French dominance, and the Dutch, fearful of French aggression, promised aid to Austria, though their motives were more self-centered than altruistic.

Frederick's first military experience did not prove as glorious as he had hoped. His army met the Austrians at Mollwitz in April 1741, and Frederick fled the field when threatened by Austrian cavalry. Only the steadiness and military acumen of his chief general, Field Marshal Kurt von Schwerin, saved the day; Frederick was 20 miles away when he heard of the Prussian victory. During the summer and fall of 1741, the war widened with a Franco-Bavarian invasion of Bohemia, followed by the capture of Prague and the crowning of Bavarian prince Charles Albert as the new emperor of Austria. His rule was short-lived, because he was quickly forced to return to Bavaria to respond to the Austrian capture of Munich in his absence. A weak French force stayed in the Prague area. The following spring, Frederick threatened Vienna, then withdrew into Silesia. The pursuing Austrians found Frederick waiting for them at Chotusitz, where he defeated them and recovered from the disgrace of the previous year. A few weeks later, Maria Theresa conceded to Frederick's demand for Silesia, and he withdrew his nation from the war.

For two years, Frederick stayed idle while Austrian forces drove back the French. They were so successful that Frederick grew worried about rising Austrian power, and in 1744 he was back in the war. He quickly invaded Bohemia and captured Prague, but withdrew to Silesia just as quickly when superior Austrian numbers marched toward him and spent the winter in Silesia unhindered. Charles Albert died in December; his son and heir decided not to follow in his father's footsteps and rejected any claim to the Austrian throne, for which he was rewarded by the return of all Bavarian possessions captured by Austria.

In January 1745, Maria Theresa created the Quadruple Alliance, entering into a mutual-defense agreement with Saxony, Holland, and England in opposition to Prussia and France. In May the French quickly dealt the English a defeat at Fontenoy, while Frederick defeated an Austro-Saxon force in June at Hohenfriedeberg and at Kesselsdorf in December. Once again Maria Theresa made peace with Frederick, reaffirming his ownership of Silesia in return for his guarantee of the Pragmatic Sanction. The addition of 16,000 square miles of territory and one million subjects earned him the appellation "the Great." The war continued until 1748, with the

Netherlands becoming the main theater of war. France's Louis XV had some success there, but it was offset by naval and colonial losses to the British. The war came to an end with the signing of the Treaty of Aix-la-Chapelle.

Maria Theresa lost Silesia, but gained a large measure of respect; after this war, no one questioned either her right to rule or her ability. The loss of Austria's most productive province, however, spurred Maria Theresa to implement a series of reforms in her empire. Prussia's centralized government had proven more efficient in both command and civil administration, and Maria Theresa learned that her government also needed to move away from feudal aristocracy toward a more enlightened form of government. She reformed the tax codes to her benefit (at the expense of the aristocracy) and broadened legal rights for peasants, making it easier for them to support their families and better able to pay taxes. She was unable to successfully incorporate the Hungarian and Slavic citizens of the empire's bureaucracy, however, and they remained somewhat discontented.

Prussia proved to be the big winner in the war, not only gaining land but establishing itself as a power to be reckoned with and Frederick as a general of no mean talent. The military he perfected became the standard of comparison throughout Europe until Napoleon embarrassed it in the early 1800s. England and France continued their longstanding hostility, but neither came out of the war much richer, because the treaty that ended the fighting called for a return of colonial possessions. American militia fighting in Canada for England resented this because they had scored their first major military success by capturing Louisburg; its return to France created ill feelings, which became one of the many causes of revolution. The peace of Aix-la-Chapelle proved no more than an eight-year armistice, because in 1756 Maria Theresa tried to take Silesia back in what became known as the Seven Years' War.

See also Italy, Austrian Invasion of (War of the Spanish Succession); Saxony, Prussian Invasion of (Seven Years' War); Prussia, Napoleon's Invasion of.

References: Addington, Larry, *Patterns of War through the Eighteenth Century* (Bloomington: Indiana University Press, 1990); Crankshaw, Edward, *Maria Theresa* (New York: Viking, 1969); Duffy, Chris, *The Military Life of Frederick the Great* (New York: Atheneum, 1986).

109 THIRTY YEARS' WAR

In 1555, the Peace of Augsburg became the law of the Holy Roman Empire, which included modern-day Germany, Holland, Belgium, Austria, Switzerland, and the Czech Republic. The ruling Habsburg dynasty was divided into two branches, one in Austria and the other in Spain, each with its own responsibilities and territories. The Augsburg Declaration was an attempt to defuse the rampant religious and political feuding in central Europe, especially in the Germanic principalities. It stated that each prince had the power to decide for his provinces what its official religion would be. Thus, Catholic and Lutheran provinces were officially recognized; the growing Calvinist denomination, however, was not. The Peace worked for several decades, but by the early 1600s, religious alliances became more and more political. A clash between Protestant and Catholic states was inevitable.

In the northern states of the empire, Frederick V, the Calvinist ruler of the Palatine, a province along the Rhine River, organized the Protestant Union. In the south, Archduke Maximilian of Bavaria countered this move with the formation of the Catholic League. Their first encounter took place in Bohemia in 1618. When Ferdinand of Styria (south of Bohemia) became the Bohemian king in 1617, he was determined to impose his strict Catholicism on the province. The Bohemians tolerated a variety of religious views in their country and had little desire to have Ferdinand impose his will on them, so they threw the imperial governors literally out the windows of the castle in Prague. They raised an army and offered the throne to Frederick V, who accepted the crown, bringing the Protestant Union and the Catholic League in conflict.

The war was brief. The Catholics, under the brilliant General Baron von Tilly, defeated

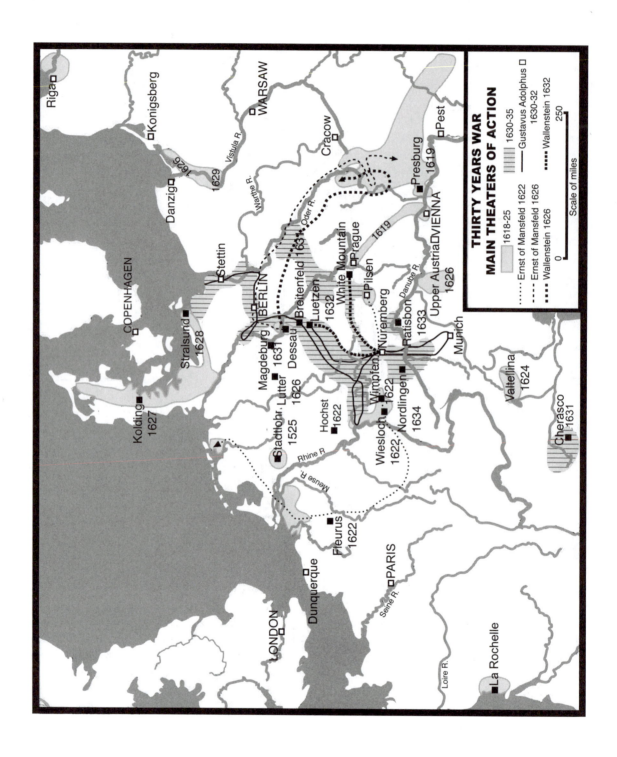

THIRTY YEARS WAR
MAIN THEATERS OF ACTION

1618-25   1630-35   Gustavus Adolphus □
.... Ernst of Mansfeld 1622   1630-32
- - - - Ernst of Mansfeld 1626   ▪▪▪▪ Wallenstein 1632
▪▪▪▪ Wallenstein 1626   Scale of miles

0   250

Frederick's forces in 1620. Ferdinand proceeded to impose Catholicism on Bohemia, and widespread killing and destruction ensued, ruining the nation's economy. The ruling aristocracy was replaced by Ferdinand's supporters, who received large estates. Protestant religious practices disappeared in Bohemia over the next 10 years of persecution, while the Catholic Habsburgs reasserted their authority.

The Protestant Lutherans and Calvinists were so suspicious of each other that the Lutherans actually assisted the Habsburgs in Bohemia. Though the power of Catholic Spain frightened the northern German Protestant states, they could not agree among themselves to present a united opposition. The king of Denmark offered his assistance to the Protestants, but he was motivated more by a desire for north German lands than religious unity; the Spanish under Czech adventurer Baron Albrecht von Wallenstein defeated Danish forces in 1625. Wallenstein led a well-trained force that numbered as many as 125,000, but he had personal ambitions above serving the Habsburgs. He planned to use this army to defeat the Habsburgs' enemies, then carve out a kingdom in central Europe for himself. The Habsburgs came to suspect this, and by the late 1620s, the Catholic forces were beginning to quarrel almost as much as were the Protestants. Still, with Wallenstein's army supreme and the momentum on their side, the Catholic League urged Ferdinand to restore all lost Catholic lands in northern Germany. This decision meant the resumption of war. The loss of their lands as well as their faith finally motivated the Lutherans to action.

At this point, a Protestant champion stepped forward: Gustavus Adolphus, king of Sweden. Gustavus had wisely exploited his country's natural resources of copper and timber to build a strong economy, and he organized the world's first modern professional army based on universal conscription. His army was equipped with the first artillery light enough to maneuver on battlefields, improved muskets, regular pay, uniforms, and discipline. From 1611 through 1629, Gustavus's army had won victories over Poland, Denmark, and Russia, making Sweden the dominant force in the Baltic. It was this dominance

that he wanted to protect from Wallenstein's encroachment. Gustavus committed his forces too late to prevent the destruction of the city of Magdeburg, the cruelest incident in a cruel war, but his forces soundly defeated imperial troops at Breitenfeld in Saxony in the fall of 1631.

That setback obliged the Habsburgs to recall Wallenstein, whom the Catholic League had come to mistrust. His presence was not enough to save the Catholic forces at Luetzen, which proved to be not only Gustavus's greatest victory but his last, for he died during the battle. Without his leadership, the Protestant cause floundered, but with Wallenstein assassinated on Ferdinand's orders, the Catholics had difficulty rallying to take advantage. Imperial armies stopped the Swedes in 1634, but Gustavus had saved Protestant Germany.

With both sides fighting themselves to exhaustion, a new player entered the game: France. France's chief minister Cardinal Richelieu had allied his country with Denmark earlier but, owing to domestic problems, had been unable to directly assist in the war. He now saw an opportunity to strike a blow against the Habsburgs who, by their control of central Europe and Spain, had his country surrounded. Though mostly Catholic, the French made allies of the Protestants, especially the Dutch, who had long suffered under Spanish rule and had been trying for a few decades to confirm their independence. When the Swedish army was defeated in 1634, Richelieu decided France had to intervene directly. The French declared war on Spain and allied themselves with Holland and the German states. The armies on both sides continued to slog through Europe for another 17 years, the war turning into a conflict between the French Bourbon and Spanish Habsburg monarchies. At last Spain, more tired than the others, called it quits. Rebellion in Portugal and Catalonia had weakened the Spanish effort and the allied victory at Roicroi in 1643 crushed the Spanish army. With Swedish forces besieging Prague and approaching Vienna, the two sides sat down in 1644 and began negotiations. The political leaders who had begun the war died off through the late 1630s and early 1640s, and the new generation could no longer sustain the cost of war with their countries devastated and unproductive.

The Congress of Westphalia, which continued until 1648, was Europe's first major, general peace conference. No such international gathering had been held since the Council of Constance had met in the early 1400s to attempt Church reform. The Protestant movements discussed at Constance reached their fruition at Westphalia, for the rival factions were now recognized as legitimate faiths. The status quo established by the Peace of Augsburg, which allowed each nation to choose its own religion, was restored in 1648. This time, Calvinism was accepted as one of the European denominations. The Holy Roman Empire was officially disbanded, and more than 300 German states gained recognition of their independence, as did Switzerland and the Netherlands. The relative positions of Catholic Germans in the south and Protestant Germans in the north was little altered from before the war. The Catholic Church had lost its preeminent position in Europe to the Protestants.

By the time this war was fought, the role of the military had evolved. The widespread introduction of firearms changed the nature of warfare and politics. It established equality on the battlefield, as any peasant with a gun could take the life of a nobleman; it mattered little about their respective training, position, or ability to lead. As equipping large numbers of men with firearms and procuring the newly perfected artillery were both very expensive propositions, only national governments could afford the cost. Hence, nations began to arm and war became an extension of political will and not a moral crusade to fight for the Church, as combat had been for centuries. From this time forward, one sees the rise of standing armies and professional soldiers.

The struggle between rival monarchies of Spain, France, and Sweden wrought its destruction on the people being invaded by so many nations, the Germans. Politically, it caused a major upset in the balance of power. Spain saw its strength seriously reduced and the Peace of Westphalia was a serious military setback for a nation that had lost its naval dominance in the wake of the defeat of the Spanish Armada by the British in 1588. The Dutch Republic was created in the Netherlands, and the Swiss Confederation was formed out of the now-defunct Holy Roman Empire.

The Thirty Years' War was the most destructive Europe had seen up to that time, and it would not see its like again until World War I. The victories usually degenerated into wholesale pillage and plunder by both sides and entire towns disappeared in the process. Cities lost population, agriculture was virtually halted, livestock was wiped out, and the resultant lack of food brought about starvation and disease that killed more people than did the war itself; four (some say as many as eight) million people died out of a central European population of 21 million.

See also England, Spanish Invasion of (Spanish Armada).

References: Parker, Geoffrey, ed., *The Thirty Years War* (London: Routledge and Kegan Paul, 1984); Robb, Theodore, ed., *The Thirty Years War* (Lexington, MA: Heath, 1972); Wedgwood, C. V., *The Thirty Years War* (Gloucester, MA: P Smith, 1969).

110   UZBEKS

A Turco-Mongol tribe, the Uzbeks first appeared as followers of Shayban, who had been allotted land east of the Ural Mountains on the death of his grandfather, Genghis Khan, in 1227. The height of Uzbek conquest came in a short time period. In the fifteenth century, Abu'l-Khair built an empire that stretched from the Ural River to the Syr Darya. He failed to hold the land, but his grandson Muhammad Shaybani conquered land from the collapsing Timurid dynasty between the Syr Darya and the Amu Darya, or Oxus River. Muhammad Shaybani filled the vacuum left by the Timurids, the descendants of Tamurlane, by conquering as far as Herat and Tashkent; by 1503 he was the most powerful figure in central Asia. The Uzbek khans could not make much headway against the Persians and the Khirgiz, but they stabilized control over much of western Turkistan, including Bokhara and Samarkand.

A civil war among the Safavids of Persia in 1526 encouraged the Uzbeks to investigate the potential of acquiring land at Safavid expense. The Uzbeks captured Tus and Astarabad, and moved at will through Khurasan. By 1528, they were laying siege to Herat, in modern Afghanistan. The siege was lifted by a relieving force under Shah Tahmasp, who defeated the Uzbek leader 'Ubayd Allah Khan in a touch-and-go battle. 'Ubayd, though wounded in this battle, returned five times between 1524 and 1538 to invade Khurasan. These invasions, coupled with habitual raiding, gained the Uzbeks plunder, but little territory.

Internal Safavid troubles attracted the Uzbeks again in 1588. Once more, they laid siege to Herat, which they captured in February 1589. With the city in hand, the Uzbeks drove deeper into Safavid territory, conquering half of Khurasan. They exercised nominal control over the area until finally meeting the forces of the greatest of Safavid leaders, Shah 'Abbas, in 1598. The death of the Uzbek leader 'Abd Allah II was the major cause of 'Abbas's success. He marched from Isfahan on 9 April 1598, and the Uzbeks withdrew before him. He advanced on Herat in early August, hoping to bring the Uzbeks, now under Din Muhammad Khan, to battle. 'Abbas showed himself to the defenders at Herat, then withdrew, leaving agents behind to spread the rumor that he had returned to deal with political problems at home. The ruse drew the Uzbek force out of the city to follow him, whereupon he turned and attacked on 9 August. Though his horses were exhausted from a forced march and the Uzbeks outnumbered him 12,000 to 10,000, 'Abbas charged. The charge broke Uzbek ranks and, when Din Muhammad was wounded, the army retreated. 'Abbas's forces chased them until the horses could no longer run, and they killed some 4,000 Uzbek soldiers. This victory, at Rabat-i-Pariyan, regained Herat for the Safavids and secured Khurasan's northwest frontier. A series of treaties ended hostilities between the two peoples.

The Uzbeks began as illiterate nomads, but they improved their society by learning from the cities they captured. They became Sunni Muslims and adopted many Persian elements into their culture. For a time they grew rich by controlling the caravan routes through central Asia, but the rising maritime powers of Europe ultimately took away that overland trade. With less income, the Uzbeks began to quarrel among themselves and lose tribal cohesion. By the nineteenth century, they fell under the control of either the Afghan or Russian government. The last Uzbek emirate to fall was Bokhara in 1868, which accepted protectorate status from Russia. Bokhara came under the control of the Soviet Union in 1920.

The last of the Uzbeks live in either Afghanistan or the former Soviet Union. Though they long ago gave up their nomadic ways, some traces of that lifestyle still exist. Even now, some Uzbeks abandon their houses in the summer for the felt tents of their ancestors.

See also Genghis Khan; Tamurlane.

References: Haidar, Muhammad, *A History of the Moghuls of Central Asia* (New York: Praeger, 1970); Kwanten, Luc, *Imperial Nomads* (Philadelphia: University of Pennsylvania Press, 1979); Savory, Roger, *Iran under the Safavids* (New York: Cambridge University Press, 1980).

111 WESTERN HEMISPHERE, SPANISH OCCUPATION OF

Christopher Columbus's discovery of a "new world" in 1492 led to one of the largest invasions ever undertaken. In this case, it was not merely a neighboring country or region that fell, but an entire hemisphere. Reports of gold led many adventurers across the Atlantic, but they were merely the forerunners of a huge influx of settlers who occupied vast territories at the expense of the native inhabitants.

In 1520, a Spanish conquistador named Hernan Cortes conquered the Aztecs of Mexico. When the Spaniards arrived, the Aztec population was about five million, so Emperor Montezuma II had thousands of warriors at his disposal. Cortes had only 553 soldiers, 13 of whom were armed with relatively crude Renaissance muskets. Most of the rest were armed with steel swords, though Cortes also possessed 10 cannon and 16 horses.

In 1532, another Spaniard by the name of Francisco Pizarro brought down the Inca Empire. The Incas were situated in the area where Peru, Colombia, Ecuador, and Chile are located today, and had come to dominate the region only a few years prior to the Spanish arrival. They established an extensive bureaucracy to control their subjects, and drafted defeated warriors into the Inca military. Only a few weeks before Pizarro's appearance, the Incan emperor Atahualpa came to the throne after a civil war between rival claimants. Although the Incan army is estimated to have comprised between 40,000 and 80,000 men, it were defeated by Pizarro's 200-man force, 62 of whom were cavalry. The cost of defeat to both the Aztecs and the Incas was exceedingly high. The Mexicans and Peruvians of the pre-Columbian era were subject to no one and, indeed, enjoyed mastery over subject peoples, extracting tribute from their neighbors. Their cultural heritages were long and rich, and the Spaniards who conquered them were often envious of the sophistication of the local buildings, the refinement of their culture, and the abundance of goods in vast markets. The Spaniards deliberately and systematically destroyed temples, seized property, and committed acts of violence, theft, and vandalism from the first days they arrived on American soil.

The Aztec and Inca civilizations did not submit willingly to Spanish domination, and both cultures fiercely resisted the invaders. How, then, did so few Spaniards triumph over such a huge population? European racists in the centuries following the conquest, such as the French philosopher Voltaire, would claim that the Aztecs and Incas were docile by nature and otherwise inferior to the Spaniards. In recent decades, such simplistic and naive explanations have yielded to more compelling ones. One of the most important factors in the triumph of Cortes and Pizarro was probably disease. The New World, separated from Europe by a large ocean and from Asia by the frozen Bering Strait, was sealed off from European and Asian diseases for thousands of years. American Indians, who had migrated from Asia in prehistoric times, had never been exposed to such diseases as measles, smallpox, and influenza, and thus had no antibodies to combat them. Unwittingly, the Spaniards created the conditions that led to their victory by simply breathing in the presence of the natives. By some estimates, 90 percent of the population of the Americas died from diseases that Europeans often

experienced as resistant carriers. Particularly rampant among military commanders in the Aztec and Incan ranks were smallpox and measles, both potentially fatal and often debilitating when experienced by adults. Little did Aztec and Incan officers know, as they interrogated Spanish prisoners, that in gathering information they were hastening their own doom.

The Spaniards also had a tactical advantage. Europeans of the 1500s immediately charged upon enemies with swords drawn once they approached the field of battle. Warfare among the Spaniards' opponents was governed by different rules. Aztec and Inca warriors often engaged in preliminary rituals, in which fighting was preceded by confronting the opponent face-to-face unarmed. When Pizarro captured the Inca emperor and massacred his elite guard, which had served him well enough in battles against other American tribes, they were essentially unarmed, anticipating that the actual battle would take place later in the day.

Mexicans and Peruvians suffered yet another disadvantage, one that was truly bizarre. As mysterious diseases raged and mighty armies fell before the strange invaders, Aztecs and Incas looked to their most ancient prophecies. In both cultures, the earliest seers had recorded that white gods across the oceans would emerge one day to signal the end of the world. The legends of Quetzalcoatl in Mexico and Viracocha in Peru thus gave the Spaniards a profound psychological advantage because their opponents were burdened by the necessity of first determining that they were mortal human beings before resolving to combat them.

With dumb luck so uncannily slanted in the Spaniards' favor, it is not surprising that they were triumphant. The societies that existed in modern-day Central and South America were almost completely destroyed, as Europeans brought with them habits and cultures that were imposed on the natives. Today, it is virtually impossible to hear the sounds of Aztec or Incan language or music (though some Andean tribes still speak the Incan Quechua), understand the nuances of their religion, or see the beauty of their artwork because European chauvinism could not appreciate the contributions the peoples of the Americas had made to the world, and could have made to their own cultures. The main purpose of the invasion, to acquire American gold and silver, was so successful that Spain became the dominant political and military power in the world for more than a century, seriously affecting the political situation in Europe.

See also Cortes, Hernan.

References: Diaz del Castillo, Bernal, *The Discovery and Conquest of Moaco* (London: Routledge, 1928); Liss, Peggy K., *Mexico under Spain, 1521–1556* (Chicago: University of Chicago Press, 1975); Means, Philip A., *Fall of the Inca Empire and the Spanish Rule in Peru, 1530–1780* (New York: Gordian Press, 1971).

112   ZULUS, EXPANSION OF

The Zulu nation began in southeastern Africa as a vassal of the neighboring Mtetwa tribe. The Mtetwa first rose to prominence under the direction of Dingiswayo, who became chief in 1795 at the age of 25. Dingiswayo organized his people along regimental lines, establishing a military framework for his tribe. After intensive training, he went on campaign, beginning a series of wars that the area tribesmen came to call the Mfecane. He defeated virtually every neighboring tribe and made them tributaries. The one tribe he failed to bring totally under his sway was the Ndwande, whose chief Zwide would be Dingiswayo's undoing. Dingiswayo refused to allow his warriors to slaughter captives, preferring tribal unification and growth through intermarriage. By this practice he created a –confederation of tribes with the Mtetwa as the leaders. He also established trading contacts with the Portuguese at Delagoa Bay.

Dingiswayo took under his tutelage a young exile from the Zulu tribe who had escaped to the Mtetwa with his mother. Shaka, the illegitimate son of the Zulu chief, had had to leave his homeland to escape persecution from his brothers. He distinguished himself in combat, gaining Dingiswayo's attention, and ultimately rose to the rank of general. Shaka became one of the tribe's leading figures through performance and studying at his chief's side, but he thought that a better strategy in dealing with defeated enemies was destruction and forced integration rather than peaceful absorption. Still, Shaka was devoted to his leader and followed orders.

Word came in 1810 that Shaka's father had died, replaced by one of Shaka's half-brothers. By this time, Shaka was hoping for an independent leadership role, and he wanted the chieftainship of his old tribe. He arranged to have his half-brother assassinated, and persuaded Dingiswayo to appoint him chief instead. Shaka took over the Zulu tribe in 1816 at age 32, though he remained a vassal to Dingiswayo and continued to fight in his campaigns, including three against the Ndwande. All were successful, but Zwide, though openly swearing loyalty, still would not submit. Zwide ultimately captured Dingiswayo in battle and executed him in 1818. By general acclamation, the tribal confederation recognized Shaka as Dingiswayo's successor.

Zwide wanted the position for himself, and two wars ensued between Shaka and the Ndwande tribe. The first began with an invasion of Zululand in April 1818. At the battle of Qokli Hill, a force of some 4,300 Zulus defeated an army more than twice its size, but the remaining Ndwande forces escaped with a large number of Zulu cattle. The second took place 14 months later. Shaka ordered his people to hide all available food, then withdrew his army before a poorly supplied invading force of some 18,000. After leading them deep into Zululand and wearing them down, Shaka attacked the Ndwandes before they could withdraw to their homeland for more supplies. The Zulus scored a solid victory and followed it up with a fast-moving raid on Zwide's royal kraal. Zwide escaped, but caused no more trouble. With the Ndwandes out of the way, Shaka conquered other neighboring tribes while incorporating the tribes he inherited from Dingiswayo into the Zulu nation.

Shaka now became leader of all the tribes in the Natal area of southeast Africa. He built on Dingiswayo's idea of organizing society along military lines, and created one of the most powerful military forces in history. At their height, the Zulu forces numbered 600,000 men, and Shaka's empire covered 11,500 square miles. Shaka established a training program second to none; for example, warriors were barred from wearing sandals in order to toughen their bare

Shaka, the founder of the Zulu nation, in a drawing by James Saunders King. (South African Library)

feet. His men developed the ability to move rapidly over long distances, being able to run 50 miles in a day and go straight into combat. Shaka controlled society by requiring military service of all males and forbidding their marriage until retirement age (in their mid-thirties). At that point, they would be awarded some cattle from the king's herd and could build a homestead. This system made maximum use of the supplies available and produced young warriors who could fight without worrying about family attachments (Shaka awarded a share of the spoils of war to the parents of the slain).

Shaka established a road system to facilitate intertribal communication, a system of unbiased courts to fairly enforce the laws, an equal opportunity for advancement in the military for any male of any tribe who joined him, and an effective intelligence network to keep him informed of potential trouble. This last effort failed him in the end, because his spies did not work within his own capital. Shaka was assassinated by yet another half-brother, Dingane, in 1838.

The Zulus remained the major native power in southern Africa, and their expansion forced the migration of other peoples out of the area that would come to be known as Natal. This depopulation was fatefully timed because Dutch farmers soon arrived in the area, looking for lands to settle. No other tribe could challenge the Zulus, but ultimately they could not stand up to the superior weaponry of the colonizing Europeans.

Like Genghis Khan, Shaka forced his defeated enemies to swear loyalty to him and become members of his tribe, thus creating a nation rather than a confederation as Dingiswayo had done. Similar to the Spartans of ancient Greece, he created a society in which the military was the raison d'etre. He used highly disciplined troops skilled in weapons designed for hand-to-hand combat and motivated by national and regimental pride to defeat every native opponent. While perhaps not quite as enlightened a ruler as Genghis Khan, Shaka's reputation for ferocity was at least the equal of the Mongol leader's, and the Zulu warrior provoked as much fear as any steppe horseman.

See also Genghis Khan; South Africa, British Occupation of; Zululand, British Invasion of.

References: Ritter, E. A., *Shaka Zulu* (London: Longman, 1955); Selby, John, *Shaka's Heirs* (London: George Allen & Unwin, 1971).

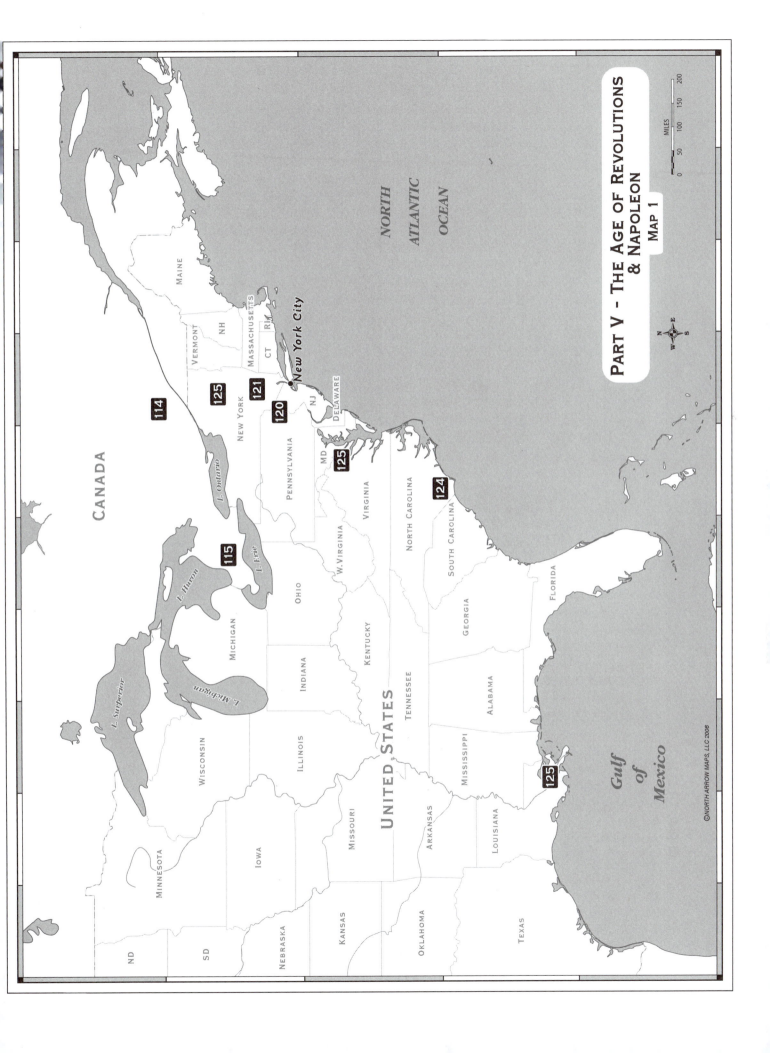

CANADA

L. Superior

L. Michigan

L. Huron

L. Erie

115

L. Ontario

114

MAINE

VERMONT

NH

MASSACHUSETTS

CT RI

New York City

125

121

NEW YORK

120

NJ

DELAWARE

MD

125

PENNSYLVANIA

W. VIRGINIA

VIRGINIA

NORTH CAROLINA

124

SOUTH CAROLINA

FLORIDA

MICHIGAN

OHIO

INDIANA

KENTUCKY

TENNESSEE

GEORGIA

ALABAMA

MINNESOTA

WISCONSIN

ILLINOIS

MISSISSIPPI

IOWA

MISSOURI

ARKANSAS

LOUISIANA

125

ND

SD

NEBRASKA

KANSAS

OKLAHOMA

TEXAS

UNITED STATES

Gulf of Mexico

NORTH ATLANTIC OCEAN

N
W E
S

MILES
0 50 100 150 200

PART V - THE AGE OF REVOLUTIONS & NAPOLEON

MAP 1

©NORTH ARROW MAPS, LLC 2006

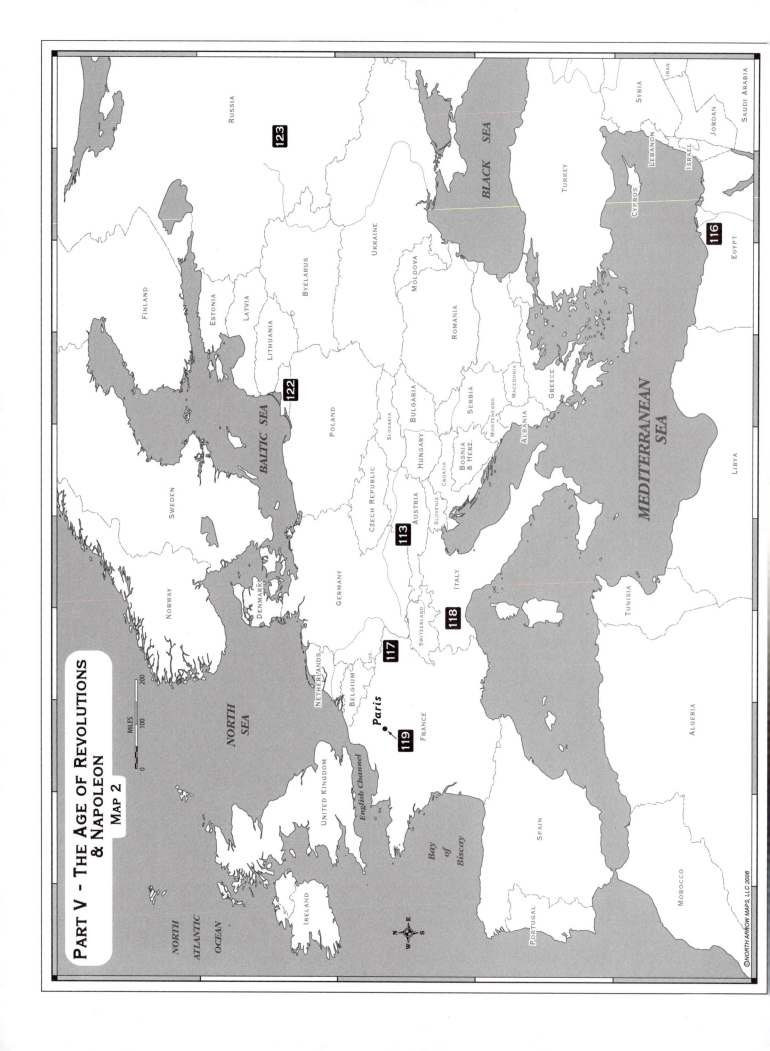

PART V - THE AGE OF REVOLUTIONS & NAPOLEON

MAP 2

MILES
0   100   200

NORTH
ATLANTIC
OCEAN

NORTH
SEA

BALTIC SEA

BLACK SEA

MEDITERRANEAN
SEA

English Channel

Bay
of
Biscay

Paris

N
W   E
S

IRELAND

UNITED KINGDOM

NETHERLANDS

BELGIUM

LUX.

FRANCE

PORTUGAL

SPAIN

MOROCCO

ALGERIA

TUNISIA

LIBYA

NORWAY

SWEDEN

FINLAND

DENMARK

GERMANY

SWITZERLAND

ITALY

CZECH REPUBLIC

SLOVAKIA

AUSTRIA

SLOVENIA

CROATIA

HUNGARY

BOSNIA
& HERZ.

MONTENEGRO

SERBIA

ALBANIA

MACEDONIA

GREECE

BULGARIA

ROMANIA

MOLDOVA

UKRAINE

POLAND

LITHUANIA

LATVIA

ESTONIA

BYELARUS

RUSSIA

TURKEY

CYPRUS

LEBANON

ISRAEL

JORDAN

SYRIA

IRAQ

SAUDI ARABIA

EGYPT

123

122

113

117

118

119

116

PART 5
THE AGE OF REVOLUTIONS AND NAPOLEON

AUSTRIA, NAPOLEON'S CONQUEST OF

113

After his return from the Middle East, Napoleon Buonaparte staged a coup d'état and named himself First Consul of the French government, virtually a dictatorial position. He proposed peace terms to European countries allied against him, but no one accepted his offer. He set about to quickly reconquer Italy, then made plans to amass an invasion force for the conquest of "that nation of shopkeepers," England. As he gathered forces near the Channel coast, he was diverted by the rise in late summer 1805 of an Austrian force that, coupled with an approaching Russian army, planned to attack both Italy and the French positions west of the Rhine. Napoleon put his English expedition on hold and, more quickly than any of his enemies expected, marched his army toward Austria.

Austrian general Baron Karl Mack von Leiberich led 50,000 men to the city of Ulm, near Lake Constance, where he awaited the arrival of 120,000 Russians. He knew nothing of Napoleon's movements until the second week of October, when French cavalry forces appeared out of the Black Forest before his western front. He focused on them, having no idea that the remainder of Napoleon's force was making a massive encirclement of his position. A half-hearted attempt to break out of the encirclement was futile, and Mack was obliged to surrender almost his entire force to Napoleon after one of the most brilliant maneuvers in all military history. After this almost bloodless victory, Napoleon sent several corps to seal off Austrian troops in northern Italy. From there, Napoleon's subordinate Andre Massena drove the Aus-trians through the Tyrol, forming a second French thrust into Austria. The proposed Russo-Austrian junction with Mack's forces never took place; instead, Russian general Mikhail Kutuzov found himself faced with a French army, which drove him backward as Napoleon marched toward Vienna.

Napoleon had moved too swiftly for his enemies to respond, but he had placed himself in a dangerous situation. The Russian army remained formidable; Austrian Archduke Ferdinand commanded another Austrian force at Prague, and two more Austrian archdukes were leading 80,000 men out of Italy toward Austria by way of Hungary. If these armies could join, Napoleon would be outnumbered a long way from his bases in France, Indeed, they saw the opportunity and marched to cut off the French in Vienna from their supply lines to Paris. Napoleon anticipated their move, and lay in wait for them near Austerlitz. He placed his army on low ground and in an extended position, making it an attractive target to the better placed Russo-Austrian force commanded by Kutusov. The bulk of French forces, however, were out of sight. The allied force attacked early on 2 December 1805 and had early success against the French right flank. As they pressed it, however, they extended their own lines so thinly that a French counterattack broke through. With the well-timed arrival of his hidden forces, Napoleon's army divided and encircled the Russo-Austrian force, and by the end of the day, it had virtually ceased to exist. Brilliant as the victory at Ulm had been, it was a triumph of strategic maneuver. The maneuver at Austerlitz was a masterpiece of tactical planning and entrapment, and it went down in history as one of the greatest battles of all time. Two days later, Austrian Emperor Francis agreed to an unconditional surrender as the remains of Russian forces hastily retreated home. The Treaty of Pressburg, signed 26 December 1805, took Austria out of the Third Coalition, and ceded Austrian territory in Italy and Germany to Napoleon. The brilliance of Napoleon's victories was tarnished by the news of his navy's defeat at the hands of British admiral Horatio Nelson at Trafalgar, off the Spanish coast. It doomed his plans for invading England, and allowed the British to obtain mastery of the sea, with which they began a blockade of continental Europe.

Napoleon's victory over Austria placed him in a position to continue his ambition of conquering all of Europe. In the following two years, his armies devastated the forces of both Prussia and Russia. When Napoleon suffered setbacks at the hands of the British in Spain, Austria decided to try its luck again in 1809. Invasion forces marching into Italy and Bavaria had early successes and raised a revolt against the French-supported government of Bavaria. Napoleon's arrival in April immediately reversed French fortunes. In a series of battles from 19 to 23 April, French forces pushed back the Austrians through Abensburg, Landshut, Eggmuhl, and Ratisbon. In a week, Napoleon had undone whatever successes the Austrians had achieved, and in May he was once again in Vienna. Napoleon's forces suffered their first setback along the Danube at the battle of Aspern-Essling, but a reinforced French army of 200,000 prepared to win back the initiative. At the battle of Wagram on 5 and 6 July, Napoleon assembled the largest mass of artillery ever placed in one location and blasted a hole in the Austrian center. His infantry broke through and drove the Austrians from the field. Again, Emperor Francis asked for peace terms. At the Treaty of Schonbrunn, Austria surrendered 32,000 square miles of land and 3.5 million inhabitants to Napoleon and his allies.

The defeat forced Austria to join Napoleon's Continental System, his economic warfare against England. French forces occupied Austria for a relatively peaceful three years, until Napoleon's invasion of Russia and the debacle resulting from that operation once again encouraged Austrian resistance. Their last uprising, aided by a rejuvenated Prussia and a Russian army full of momentum from their victory in 1812-1813, finally brought Napoleon down at the 1813 Battle of the Nations. Austria maintained its empire, and the subject ethnic groups of southeastern Europe did not profit from the philosophy of the French Revolution as had many other occupied populations. Not for another century—in the aftermath of World War I—would they gain liberty from Austrian rule; to this day, egalité and fraternité remain doubtful.

See also Egypt, Napoleon's Invasion of; Napoleon Buonaparte; Prussia, Napoleon's Invasion of; Russia, Napoleon's Invasion of.

References: Arnold, James, *Napoleon Conquers Austria: The 1809 Campaign for Vienna* (Westport, CT Praeger, 1995); Chandler, David, *The Campaigns of Napoleon* (New York: Macmillan, 1966); Connelly, Owen, *Blundering to Glory* (Wilmington, DE: Scholarly Resources, 1987).

CANADA, AMERICAN INVASION OF

When the 13 American colonies sent delegates to the Continental Congress in Philadelphia, Pennsylvania, in September 1774, they made decisions that inevitably led to rebellion against Great Britain. Judging that armed conflict would come soon, the Congress hoped to gain allies in the British colony of Quebec. Because the entire area, from the mouth of the St. Lawrence River to the Great Lakes and beyond, had been a French colony until the Treaty of Paris of 1763, the Americans were sure that the predominantly French population would be glad to take up arms against a traditional enemy. Their delegations to French leaders, however, received no widespread promises of aid. Still, Congress assumed that while the Canadians might not openly support rebellion, they would not hinder American efforts to expel the British.

When Ethan Allen captured Fort Ticonderoga and Crown Point at the southern end of Lake Champlain from the British in early May 1775, a natural invasion route was opened. Two plans were developed to launch the conquest of Quebec. One would drive northward up Lake Champlain into Canadian territory and thence to Montreal. From there, a force could float downstream to the main prize: the city of Quebec. A second attack would move through Maine, up the Kennebec and down the Chaudiere rivers to the St. Lawrence, just opposite the city of Quebec. Both plans were implemented in the fall of 1775, and both were doomed because of timing.

The Continental Congress judged correctly that British forces in Canada were too few to defend both Montreal and the city of Quebec. Hence, with a two-pronged attack, at least one must surely succeed. General Philip Schuyler received directions from Congress to attack Montreal. He spent the summer of 1776 gathering men and arms, both of which were in short supply. A man of irregular temperament, Schuyler did not get his expedition of 1,700 men moving until September, then abandoned it to his second-in-command, Richard Montgomery, when the Americans reached St. John's, some 30 miles east

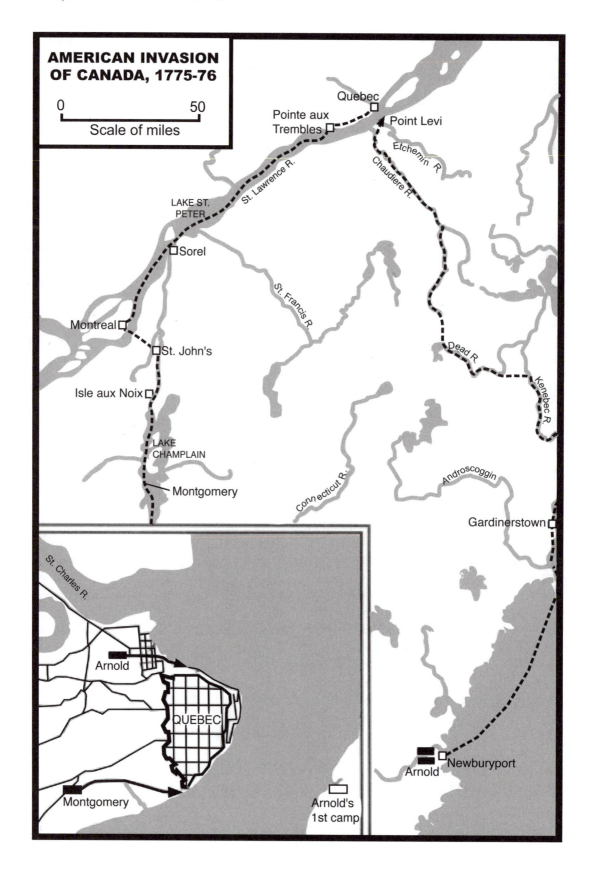

AMERICAN INVASION OF CANADA, 1775-76

Scale of miles
0 — 50

of Montreal. Montgomery had too few men to either storm the British position or leave a detachment behind and bypass it. He therefore was obliged to lay siege. The British held out for 55 days, a delay the Americans could not afford.

Sir Guy Carleton, the governor of Canada and commander of British forces, had spent the summer trying to raise troops amid a disinterested population. He had three infantry regiments and three artillery companies in the entire country; with one regiment and one company assigned to protect Detroit and Niagara, there was precious little left with which to defend Montreal and Quebec. The fort at St. John's held 600 men, all lost when the American siege was successful on 2 November. Meanwhile, Montgomery had been receiving some reinforcements and was partially successful in finding a few Canadians willing to assist. Carleton was obliged to abandon Montreal on 16 November when the inhabitants told him they would not help him fight the Americans. He lost even more of his men, and he himself only narrowly escaped, during the withdrawal down the St. Lawrence toward Quebec.

In the meantime, the second American advance was under way through Maine. Led by Benedict Arnold, these 1,100 men were also too late in getting started; they did not move up the Kennebec River until 25 September. They soon ran into harsh weather, and began to run low on supplies. Arnold pushed his men through the freezing wilderness in October and November, losing many to disease and desertion. Gaining some aid from local Frenchmen, Arnold managed to reach the St. Lawrence opposite Quebec on 10 November, his force reduced to 500 men. A quick assault on the city would have found it undefended because the troops assigned to it were out on patrol. However, Arnold was unable to cross the river for three days, and the defending troops returned in time to hold off an attack on the walled city.

Montgomery and Arnold joined forces on 2 December some 20 miles upriver, their combined army numbering almost 1,000 men. As at St. John's, there were too few men to take the city by storm, so another siege began. It was doomed; the British had more supplies than their besiegers, and the winter weather bothered them much less. The few attacks the Americans made were repulsed (and Montgomery was killed), and Carleton was smart enough not to sally out of his defenses. The Americans suffered through the cold until spring 1776, when reinforcements arrived from Britain. Arnold withdrew to Montreal, but his force was decimated by smallpox, and the Canadian population there would not support him. By June, the Americans had abandoned the invasion.

An earlier beginning to the campaign would almost certainly have made the difference, because Carleton's defensive measures were taking effect just as the Americans arrived. If the revolutionaries had gained control of Quebec and Montreal, the French inhabitants would probably have joined with them. Whether they could have withstood a determined British army and navy in the spring and summer of 1776 is open to question, but an inspired population could have mounted just as effective a guerrilla campaign as the Americans later did in the Carolinas. Instead, Britain maintained control of the country.

A successful invasion in 1775–1776 would have made the war of 1812 unnecessary. The second American invasion of Canada in 1812 again failed to bring Canada into the American union. Hostility between the two countries was ultimately laid to rest with the settlement of border differences in the 1840s, and since then the United States and Canada have become two of the most mutually friendly nations in the world. Indeed, the two countries share the world's longest undefended border. Canada remained a British colony until the 1850s, when it gained dominion status, but it nearly became the fourteenth original American state. What the Americans would do about current Quebecois nationalism, or if it would even exist, must remain a matter of speculation.

See also Southern United States, British Invasion of.

References: Alden, John R., *The American Revolution* (New York: Harper & Row, 1954); Lawson, Philip, *The Imperial Challenge: Quebec and Britain in the Age of the American Revolution* (Montreal: McGill-Queens University Press, 1990); Wrong, George McKinnon, *Canada and the American Revolution* (New York: Macmillan, 1935).

115   CANADA, U.S. INVASION OF

Britain's resistance to Napoleon in Europe had side effects that brought about war with the United States. The Royal Navy's blockade interfered with the Americans' right of free trade, but then so did Napoleon's Berlin and Milan decrees, which forbade neutral trade with Britain. The Royal Navy's need for sailors, however, brought the greatest American outcry. Without government authority to conscript from the public, the Royal Navy was unable to raise more crewmen in Britain. Searching far and wide for sailors to enter into the harsh service at sea, the British began to stop American merchant ships on the high seas. They took away anyone who spoke English; speaking English was proof enough for the British warships that a crewman on an American ship was a British deserter. While this was true in a few cases, most of the men pressed into British service were American citizens, and the United States loudly protested the British government's piracy.

The United States was unable to gain any satisfaction in reference to the trade or the impressment troubles, and in the late spring of 1812, when President James Madison asked for a declaration of war, Congress complied. The American people, though angry at British high-handedness, also had less legitimate reasons for wanting war. Americans living in the western states desired Canada, not only to secure the northern border from possible British interference, but also to expand American farmland northward. Westerners believed that the British authorities in Canada were supplying Indian tribes south of the Great Lakes with weapons. Because of the longstanding antipathy between white and native Americans, white frontiersmen would not accept anyone, especially outsiders, helping their traditional enemies. With Britain busy in Europe in 1812, the time seemed ripe to seize Canada for the United States, a dream many had cherished since the American Revolution.

Even though the forces protecting Canada were small, the United States was unprepared for war against anyone. The standing army had less than 3,000 men. There was no command structure to speak of, no logistical framework for supplying armies, and no staff structure to plan or coordinate operations. The constitution allowed the federal government to call out the militia for domestic use only; many men, called up by their state governments, refused to cross the border into Canada. In order to raise forces for the regular army, volunteer units were needed; these were raised by individuals, some of whom had little military experience, so the quality of both recruits and commanders was irregular.

American Secretary of War William Eustis exercised what little control the military had. He realized that the forces Britain could raise to defend Canada were limited. There were no more than 4,000 British and Canadian regulars, with a varying number of militia and Indian allies of uneven quality. The Canadians could expect little assistance from Britain, but their major advantage lay in the quality of their opponent: Eustis gave them little to worry about. He planned an overly ambitious campaign to seize Canada, and had there been more rapid communications and movement of men and supplies, the plan would have been a good one, but for 1812 it was impossible. Eustis's plan called for a four-pronged offensive to strike simultaneously at Detroit, Niagara, Sackett's Harbor, and Montreal. By spreading the British/Canadian defenses thin, any or all of the thrusts should have broken through. Since the inhabited portion of Canada stretched only some 50 to 100 miles north of the American border—from the Great Lakes to the mouth of the St. Lawrence—there was not all that much of Canada to conquer. It all seemed so easy.

The attacks, when they took place at all, were totally uncoordinated. William Hull gathered a force of more than 2,000 men in northern Ohio and marched for Detroit in May and June 1812. He crossed the Detroit River into Canada and seized the town of Sandwich, which he began to fortify. Hull issued a proclamation calling for Canadians to flock to his banner and throw off British rule; the document also threatened instant death for anyone caught fighting alongside an Indian. Many locals responded to his entreaty, and the British defense forces in the neighborhood found their numbers reduced to

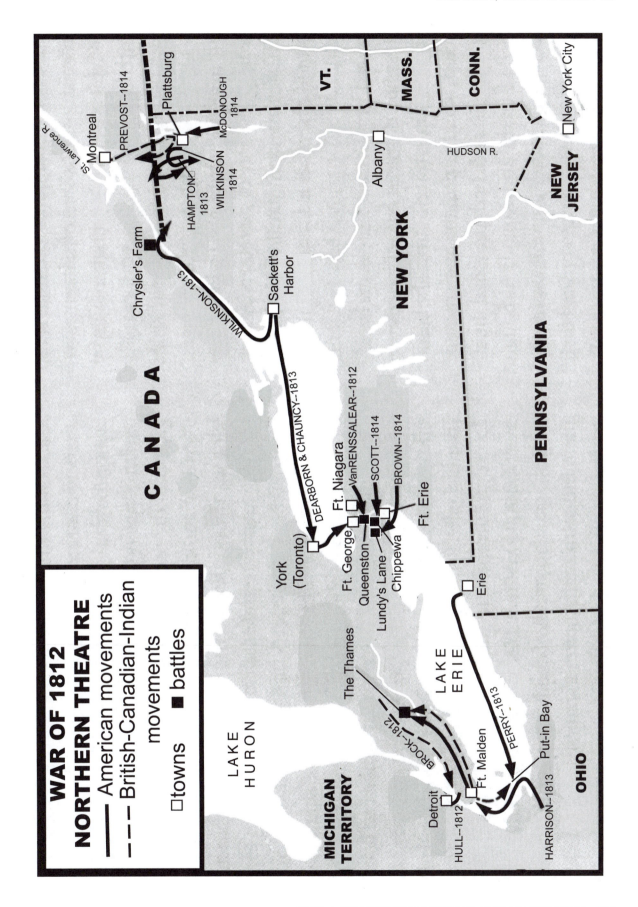

WAR OF 1812
NORTHERN THEATRE
—— American movements
--- British-Canadian-Indian
movements
□towns ■ battles

VT.

MASS.

CONN.

PREVOST--1814

Plattsburg

McDONOUGH
1814

St. Lawrence R.

Montreal

WILKINSON
1814

HAMPTON
1813

Albany

HUDSON R.

New York City

NEW
JERSEY

Chrysler's Farm

Sackett's
Harbor

NEW YORK

WILKINSON--1813

PENNSYLVANIA

C A N A D A

DEARBORN & CHAUNCY--1813

VanRENSSALEAR--1812

SCOTT--1814

BROWN--1814

Ft. Niagara

Ft. George

Ft. Erie

Queenston

Lundy's Lane

Chippewa

Erie

York
(Toronto)

LAKE ERIE

The Thames

BROCK--1812

PERRY--1813

Put-in Bay

LAKE
HURON

MICHIGAN
TERRITORY

Detroit

Ft. Malden

HARRISON--1813

OHIO

HULL--1812

CANADA, U.S. INVASION OF

less than 500. However, this was the best Hull could do. Though a veteran of the revolution, he lacked the dash necessary to seize the moment. While Hull hesitated and worried about his supply lines, the British, under Isaac Brock, governor of upper Canada, reinforced. As more Indians joined with the British and Brock began harassing Hull's supply lines, the American commander lost his nerve. He retreated across the river to Detroit, then gave in to Brock on 16 August. His entire force of almost 2,500 men was surrendered without a fight because Hull was mistakenly convinced that huge numbers of Indians (of whom he had an almost pathological fear) were about to attack. Hull was later tried on charges of cowardice and ordered executed, but President Madison pardoned him. The United States' first invasion attempt gained no more than one mile of Canadian territory, and ended in the loss not only of Detroit but also all of the Michigan territory.

The second attack, at Niagara, was delayed so long that Brock was able to secure Detroit and return to direct the defense of Queenston and Fort George along the Niagara River. A force of 6,000 militia was poised to invade, but because of a mix-up in command and a poor supply situation, it did not go into action until October. It gained an early advantage over the defending forces and captured Fort George. Brock was killed in the battle, and the Americans were on the verge of driving the British from the field and capturing Queenston. Only the refusal of New York militia, held in reserve on the other side of the Niagara River, to cross into Canada and provide the coup de grâce prevented an American victory. The British regrouped and forced the Americans back across the river. The second attempt was close to success, but failed for lack of will.

Meanwhile, the force that was to advance up Lake Champlain and assault Montreal should have been gathering all summer under the main American general, Henry Dearborn. Instead of organizing his force at Albany, he left for Boston, where he did little but inspect coastal defenses and try to convince Massachusetts legislators to increase their aid. When his British opposite learned of the British government's willingness to discuss American demands, he proposed an

armistice, to which Dearborn agreed. However, President Madison rebuffed any peace talks, and Dearborn finally went into action. American troops advanced northward in November to Plattsburgh and met a small Canadian force near the border at the La Colle River. The resultant battle was so confused that Americans fired at one another as often as at the enemy. It seemed the better part of valor to retreat to Plattsburgh for the winter. The forces at Sackett's Harbor, on the eastern end of Lake Ontario, contented themselves with building a small fleet to try to gain control of the lake, and saw no action. The year 1812 ended not with a bang but a whimper.

The year 1813 saw but little improvement in American progress. In April an American force sailed across Lake Erie and captured the Canadian capital at York (modern-day Toronto). Rather than capitalize on this victory, however, the Americans burned the city and withdrew. A second attack against York at the end of July brought the same result. Why they refused to use this city as a base of operations to fight the war in Canada, as opposed to fighting it along the frontiers, remains a mystery. American forces captured the strategic Fort George at Niagara, but they were defeated in attempts to drive inland from there. When the militia's term of enlistment ran out in November and they went home, Fort George could not be held. The neighboring town of Newark was burned, but the fort was not, and the British reoccupied it. At the eastern end of Lake Ontario at Sackett's Harbor, Americans under the command of James Wilkinson (regarded as quite possibly the worst general the country has ever produced) vacillated over how to attack Montreal. Piecemeal troop commitments and arguments among the generals produced only defeat late in the year at Chrysler's Farm just across the Canadian border. Americans went no farther north in this area in 1813 than they had the previous year.

The only real accomplishment occurred in September. American ships under Oliver Hazard Perry defeated a roughly equal number of British ships at Put-in-Bay on the western end of Lake Erie. That victory gave the Americans control of the lake and made it possible to ferry troops across who could cut off the British forces garrisoned at

202   THE AGE OF REVOLUTIONS AND NAPOLEON

Detroit. Before that could happen, the British withdrew from the city; the Americans reoccupied it in October. Kentucky militia led by William Henry Harrison chased the retreating British and Indians, catching up to them along the Thames River. American cavalry made short work of the few hundred British soldiers and, in hand-to-hand combat, American infantry broke the Indian forces by killing their leader, Tecumseh. Again, rather than take advantage of the momentum, Harrison withdrew his men to Detroit for the winter. Whatever successes the Americans accomplished in 1813 they did not exploit.

What had originally appeared to be an easy target defended by few British troops had, at the end of two campaigning seasons, proven too difficult for the disorganized American forces to conquer. The year 1814 would be their last chance. Unfortunately, Wilkinson still held command in the northeast. He led some 4,000 men across the Canadian border and engaged a force of 200 Canadian militia at La Colle Mill. When Wilkinson could not reduce the stone mill by bombardment, he returned home. He was brought up on charges for his incompetence and removed from command. His successor, Jacob Brown, tried to regain the initiative along the Niagara River. His forces, led by young Colonel Winfield Scott, won a resounding victory over quality British troops at Chippewa in June, but failed to make further headway. The British kept their hold on the Niagara forts, and there were no more invasion attempts. Napoleon had been defeated in Europe, and British veterans were on their way, so American forces were soon on the defensive.

The desires of some Americans to remove the British from their northern border and to incorporate Canada into the United States came to naught. Had the American government pursued a strategy of negotiation with disaffected Canadians in 1812, it is possible that a revolution there would have accomplished those goals. By launching invasions, the United States forced Canadians into the arms of the British government so it could defend their lands from aggression. Further, by sacking and burning Toronto, Newark (outside Fort George), and other towns, the Americans caused such resentment among the Canadians that the

two nations remained suspicious of each other for years. Not until the 1840s did Canada and America settle some border disputes and become friends, a relationship that remains to this day. No serious attempt at union between the two countries ever arose again, though there were occasional splinter group activities toward that goal.

See also Canada, American Invasion of; United States, British Invasion of.

References: Berton, Pierre, *The Invasion of Canada* (Boston: Little, Brown, 1980); Coles, Harry L., *The War of 1812* (Chicago: University of Chicago Press, 1965); Mahon, John K., *The War of 1812* (Gainesville: University Presses of Florida, 1972).

116   EGYPT, NAPOLEON'S INVASION OF

By 1798, Napoleon Buonaparte was a national hero in France for his capture of Toulon and his brilliant campaign in Italy. That fame potentially made him a dangerous political rival to the ruling Directory, so he was assigned to a campaign outside the country. The first proposal was an invasion of England, but France lacked the naval power necessary to accomplish that. Thus, the Directory supported Napoleon's plan to invade Egypt, for it would take fewer ships and men. Napoleon hoped by this attack to secure a French colony in Egypt, which would open a path to India, from which the French had been dislodged 30 years earlier. The French government authorized the creation of the Army of the Orient in April 1798, and the force sailed from Toulon in May. The French fleet slipped past the British fleet under the command of Horatio Nelson and made first for Malta. Napoleon secured the island on 12 June from the decrepit Knights of St. John and left a garrison as he sailed for Egypt with 32,000 troops and a large number of scientists.

After a delay for repairs needed because of a storm, the British sailed quickly for Egypt and arrived two days before the French. Thinking he had missed Napoleon, Nelson sailed for Sicily, allowing the French to arrive and debark in Egypt unmolested. The French quickly captured Alexandria on 2 July and marched for Cairo. Along the way they were harassed by bedouins,

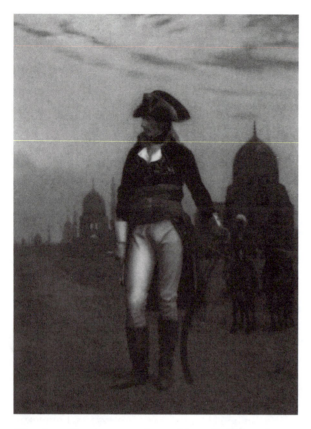

Napoleon Buonaparte, pictured here in Cairo, during his Egyptian expedition of 1798–99.

and then met a force of the ruling Mamluks, the Muslim soldier-leaders of Egypt. Unaccustomed to European-style warfare, the Mamluk cavalry rashly charged the French defensive squares and were slaughtered; the French counterattack destroyed the Mamluk camp. With most of the serious opposition defeated at what came to be called the Battle of the Pyramids, Cairo fell easily on 22 July.

Everything seemed to be going as Napoleon had planned until he learned that Nelson had destroyed the French fleet off Alexandria in Aboukir Bay. This left the coastline in British control and Napoleon's forces without a means of escape. He did not worry, but proceeded to establish a government made up of local religious figures along with a few French commissioners. Napoleon painted his arrival in Egypt not as an invasion but as a liberation from the Mamluks, who resisted the political and religious will of the Ottoman Empire, which the French supported. He mandated that his troops honor Muslim sensibilities, and negotiated a fetwa (directive) from the religious leaders of the Mosque of El Azhar that the French were official allies of Islam. He did everything in his power to allay Egyptian fears that the French were there to persecute them, but he soon admitted that French authority would in the end rest not on good deeds but on military strength.

After escaping the battlefield near the pyramids, the Mamluk General Ibrahim fled to Syria and began raising a force with which to reconquer Egypt. Napoleon struck first, sending a force up the Nile to secure the southern flank while he marched toward Syria with 8,000 men in January 1799. He won the battles of El Arish and Jaffa fairly quickly, which gave him a false sense of security concerning the port city of Acre. He attacked without siege artillery and was thrown back, but he laid siege to the city in mid-March. Though he defeated a Turkish force that marched to relieve Acre, Napoleon was obliged to lift the siege and march away when plague struck the city and began to spread to his own forces. He was constantly harassed on his march back to Cairo, and returned with more than a quarter of his force dead of wounds or disease. The British aided a Turkish invasion force that landed at Aboukir Bay, but the French successfully defeated them in late July. At that point, a British captain sent Napoleon newspapers that updated him on European events showing political upset in Paris and the loss of Italy. A second alliance of nations was forming to threaten France, including Russia and the Ottoman Empire, and Napoleon's military talents would be necessary on the Continent. Needing to look out for his own career as well as gain reinforcements for the expedition in Egypt, Napoleon arranged for a secret escape and returned safely to France.

Napoleon went to Egypt intending to establish a colony and use it as a base for operations against British India. He also played the role of Alexander the Great in this expedition by taking with him a number of leading scientists and intellectuals to investigate the history of Egypt and the potential of constructing a canal linking the Mediterranean with the Red Sea. The discovery of the Rosetta Stone during this expedition, wherein a single message was written in hieroglyphics, Greek, and Latin, made possible the first translation of hieroglyphics and created the field of Egyptology. The administration Napoleon left on the island of Malta was a much more efficient government than had existed under the Knights of St. John, who had ruled the island for more than 100 years. He brought an end to both slavery and the nobility, and gave a number of local students the chance to travel to France to study. In the long run, the invasion of Egypt was little more than an expensive sideshow, but a French success there could have changed the course of the Napoleonic era by obliging the British to reapportion their naval forces away from a blockade of Europe and forcing the European powers to focus more attention on the Ottoman Empire. A French victory over the Ottomans, giving Napoleon control of Constantinople and the access to the Black Sea, could have changed the direction of his aim for empire and altered the balance of power in the Mediterranean for a long time to come.

See also Alexander the Great; Napoleon Buonaparte.

References: Chandler, David, *The Campaigns of Napoleon* (New York: Macmillan, 1966); Connelly, Owen, *Blundering to Glory* (Wilmington, DE: Scholarly Resources, 1987); Markham, Felix, *Napoleon* (New York: New American Library, 1963).

FRANCE, EUROPEAN INVASION OF

117

The success of the French Revolution in July 1789 had an extremely sobering effect on the monarchies of Europe. If the king of France could lose his power so soon after the Americans had removed British King George Ill's power from the American colonies, what might that mean for the remainder of Europe if the idea of successful revolution should spread? Rather than wait for such a subversive philosophy to reach other countries, Prussian King William II joined Emperor Leopold II of Austria in August 1791 to isolate France and attempt to restore the monarchy. Russia and Sweden promised to contribute troops with Spanish subsidies. England did not join, but continental Europe was threatening the French Revolution. At the urging of French

émigrés, Austria and Prussia formed a joint military command in February 1792 and sent troops toward the French frontier; the north Italian kingdom of Savoy joined in soon afterward. The French legislative assembly, having called for the formation of a larger army the previous August, declared war against the Austro-Prussian alliance on 20 April. Patriotic volunteers flocked to the colors, but lacked discipline. The veterans of the army maintained a formal organization, but the removal of pro-monarchy officers somewhat hurt its effectiveness. The invading Austrians had little trouble disposing of the first French forces they met near Lille, and they began a siege of the city.

In July the invading army came under the command of Karl Wilhelm, the duke of Brunswick. He led 80,000 soldiers and, marching from Coblenz, quickly captured the French fortresses of Longwy and Verdun. Because the commander of the French army was the Marquis de Lafayette, his defeat was sufficient for a Paris mob to demand that the French King Louis XVI be stripped of the last vestiges of power. Lafayette was replaced by the more politically acceptable Charles Dumouriez, who joined his new command with that of French General Francois Kellermann to stand in the path of the advancing coalition force. At Valmy, 36,000 French soldiers of irregular quality faced 34,000 veterans under Brunswick. What should have been an easy victory for the invaders proved to be a defeat, thanks to the superior quality of the French artillery. Brunswick withdrew his forces to Germany.

In the meantime, other French forces were enjoying more success; in northern Italy they captured Nice, while other forces captured Mainz and marched toward Frankfurt in western Germany. This helped bring about the formation of the National Convention in September 1792, which formally ended the monarchy in France. Dumouriez scored one more success that year, invading Belgium and defeating an Austrian force near Jemappes, leading to the French capture of Brussels and the besieging of Antwerp. Though the coalition had been thrown on the defensive, Brunswick's recapture of Frankfurt in December ended the year on a positive note for them.

The beheading of Louis XVI in January 1793 provoked the English monarchy to join the coalition against France. In return, France declared war on England, Holland, and Spain. Revolutionary fervor ran high in the wake of the execution and the growing threat to the nation, and the new government declared national conscription. Dumouriez was ordered to invade Holland, but before he could organize the assault, the coalition invaded again. Brunswick attacked Mainz with 60,000 Prussians, while 40,000 Austrians crossed the Meuse River to recover Belgium. More troops formed up along the Rhine River and in Luxembourg. Dumouriez was defeated at Neerwinden in March; when he was accused of treason, he fled to the invading forces. His replacement was killed in action, and more coalition victories resulted in the beheading of defeated revolutionary generals. The success of the invading forces, coupled with the Reign of Terror in Paris during the summer of 1793, nearly brought about the defeat of the revolution. British forces invaded the French coast at Dunkirk and occupied the harbor of Toulon in the south, which, along with Marseilles, had declared itself in favor of a return to the monarchy.

The governing body in Paris, the Committee of Public Safety, ordered the Levee en Masse— the drafting of every adult male.

Fourteen armies numbering almost a million men were soon created, and aided in the recapture of Marseilles. The massive numbers of French recruits proved successful. Even though they had no training and were poorly armed, they overwhelmed enemy forces by their sheer numbers and the nature of their attacks. The soldiers flooded the battlefields, causing coalition generals to withdraw or be surrounded, a battlefield tactic unlike any the generals had ever faced. The English retreated after the battle of Hondschoote in early September; the Dutch ran from the field at Menin a week later. The victory over the Dutch did not lead to a retreat by the Austrians, however, and the French commander found himself a head shorter.

At this point, the military adviser to the Committee of Public Safety, Eazare Carnot, was appointed head of the army. He became known as the "Organizer of Victory" for his ability to create order out of the chaos of the Levee en Masse. By mixing large numbers of the new draftees into existing units manned by a cadre of veterans, the army began to take shape. The veterans set a good example for training and operations, while the recruits provided the ardor and bravery. The new armies turned the tide of battle in the second half of 1793 by recapturing Toulon, invading Alsace, defeating both a Prussian and an Austrian force in successive battles in December, and recapturing Mainz.

In 1794 the new armies continued to grow and overwhelm the forces of Prussia, Austria, and England. French armies completed the occupation of Belgium, drove the English away at Antwerp, and occupied territory up to the west bank of the Rhine. Further victories in Italy and the Pyrenees extended French power past its frontiers. By April 1795, the invaders could stand it no longer. Prussia was the first to make peace at the Treaty of Basel, and the other German principalities of Saxony, Hanover, and Hesse-Cassel followed suit. Some political upheaval followed the overthrow of the Committee of Public Safety and the installation of the five-man Directory in August, but the armies held their own or expanded their successes. By 1796, Carnot's military was able to abandon the defensive and go on the offensive to spread the revolutionary gospel. Archduke Charles of Austria, however, outfought two French armies attempting to invade Bavaria and drove them both back. His transfer to Italy gave the French the opportunity to restart their invasion in the spring of 1797. French successes near the Rhine, coupled with the victories of Napoleon Buonaparte in Italy, forced the Austrians to sue for peace.

By October 1797, France had defeated all its continental rivals, and only England remained at war with the French. The success of the French came partly from the lack of coordination on the part of the coalition forces, and partly from the new style of warfare they introduced. The mass patriotic army proved that in many cases courage could overcome an enemy's discipline, and the burgeoning Industrial Revolution made it possible to arm and equip the massive army France raised. From then on, national armies raised by conscription came to be the norm, and smaller, professional armies became obsolete. The intoxication of the revolution inspired men not only to join the army to defend their new government, but also to take the message of their philosophy to other peoples. That proved to be a two-edged sword, however; as the countries Napoleon occupied learned of the joys of liberté, egalité, and fraternité, they yearned for liberty from French domination. The nationalism inspiring the French success later energized the resistance movements that helped to defeat the armies of Napoleon. From this time forward, wars would be fought not by armies, but by nations.

See also Italy, Napoleon's Invasion of; Napoleon Buonaparte.

References: Best, Geoffrey, *War and Society in Revolutionary Europe, 1770–1870* (New York: St. Martin's Press, 1982); Chandler, David, *The Campaigns of Napoleon* (New York: Macmillan, 1966); Sydenham, M. J., *The First French Republic, 1792–1804* (Berkeley: University of California Press, 1973).

ITALY, NAPOLEON'S INVASION OF

118

By 1796, the European continent had been in constant turmoil for seven years, brought on by the revolution of the French populace against the aristocracy and the Church. With the 1793 execution of King Louis XVI and his Queen Marie Antoinette, and the spread of the ideas of liberté, egalité, and fraternité, the royal courts of Europe mobilized thousands of troops to subdue the French armies and restore the monarchy. They were unsuccessful, and by 1796, only England and Austria remained at war with France. On 27 March 1796, command of the French Army of Italy was given to the little-known Napoleon Bonaparte, setting in motion a series of events that forever changed the face of France and Europe. Napoleon earned the notice of the French rulers by his defense of the governing Directory at Toulon in 1792. The Army of Italy was his first major command.

Napoleon joined the army at its headquarters in Nice. Following a review of the ragged and demoralized troops, he spoke with his divisional officers and outlined his strategy to divide and conquer the opposition—Austria and the Italian state of Piedmont, which was defended by Sardinian forces. By gaining the central position between the two, he planned to quickly eliminate one and then marshal his resources against the second. Though older and more experienced than their new commander, the divisional officers yielded to his domineering attitude and inspirational manner.

Napoleon planned to start his offensive on 15 April, but the Austrians moved first. Their forces, commanded by General Baron Johann Beaulieu, marched on 10 April for the town of Allesandria, northwest of Genoa. A second Austrian force of 20,000 under General de Argenteau marched to Montenotte west of the city, while a Piedmontese force of roughly the same size encamped across a valley at Ceva. Napoleon reacted quickly, dividing his force of 37,000: One force held the Piedmontese to the French left, while Napoleon led the majority of the troops against Argenteau on the right of the valley. At daybreak on 12 April, Argenteau found himself confronted and flanked by Napoleon; the Austrians soon withdrew from an untenable position.

Having driven Argenteau back, Napoleon turned to throw the weight of his forces at the Piedmontese. He drove them from Ceva back to the town of Mondovi, then forced them to run some 50 miles to their nearest base at Turin, abandoning most of their supplies and artillery, both badly needed by the French. The Piedmontese king offered peace terms, which Napoleon immediately accepted without first notifying Paris. This separate peace removed Piedmont from the conflict and gained for France the provinces of Savoy and Nice.

Napoleon had now secured his rear, so he could concentrate on the Austrians. Beaulieu had withdrawn from Allesandria northward to defensive positions behind the Po River. Anticipating French river crossings, he secured the fords and bridges along his front. Napoleon left two divisions across from Beaulieu to keep his attention, while the remainder of his force marched far to the east and crossed the Po at Piacenza on 7 May. This move threatened to sever Beaulieu's communications with Austria, and he was forced to abandon his position and move rapidly to Lodi, north of Piacenza. A quick battle at Lodi forced Beaulieu to withdraw again, this time to the Adige River far to the east past Lake Gardo.

Rather than follow Beaulieu immediately, Napoleon marched northwest to Milan and entered the city on 15 May. He was acclaimed by the public, and arranged treaties with the surrounding duchies. He also received orders from the Directory to surrender half his army to General F.C. Kellermann, commander of the French Army of Germany, and take the remainder south to intimidate the pope. Napoleon threatened to resign his command rather than see his small force made smaller still; his growing popularity with the French public gave weight to his demands, and he kept his army.

Beaulieu meanwhile moved his army south of Lake Gardo to the city of Mantua, where he soon found himself besieged by the French. Suddenly, Napoleon had too many things to do: Maintain a siege, keep an eye on the papal forces to the south in Lombardy, secure his own lines of communication, and keep his army supplied. Without reinforcements or effective action from Kellermann in Germany, Napoleon had to go to an active defense. The Austrians reacted by sending another force under General Count Dagobert Wurmser to deal with the French. Wurmser marched toward Mantua, while secondary forces marched against the French advance post at Verona (to the east of Lake Gardo) and down the west coast of Lake Gardo to cut off any line of French retreat toward Milan.

Napoleon maintained a good intelligence network, and when he learned of the three-pronged attack, he moved to defeat each one separately. He abandoned the siege of Mantua and quickly moved to blunt the thrust along the west coast of the lake. The unsuspecting Austrians found themselves facing a superior French force on 3 August and beat a hasty retreat to the Tyrol. The French wheeled to face Wurmser, defeating him at Lonato the next day, forcing his return to Austria. For a loss of 40,000 casualties, his artillery, and his supplies, Wurmser had managed to get only food to Mantua, which was once again besieged. Leaving a covering force at the city, Napoleon marched northward with the remainder of his army and engaged the newly reinforced Austrians marching south from the Tyrol. Rapid marching once again allowed him to meet the Austrian forces before they could join against him, and Napoleon defeated them at Rovoreno, Primolano, and Bassano in early September. His victorious forces were now placed between the Austrians and their homeland, and less than 40 miles from the Gulf of Venice on Italy's east coast, Wurmser retreated southward toward Mantua.

The Austrian government raised yet another army, and attempted again to drive along Lake Gardo to Verona. Napoleon met the Austrians, led by General Baron Josef Alvintzi at Caldiero, east of Verona. Failing to dislodge them from strong positions, Napoleon withdrew toward Verona, then swung his forces around and behind Alvintzi, attacking his flank and rear at Arcole on 15 November. A three-day battle ensued that forced the Austrians to withdraw yet again. Unwilling to concede defeat, another Austrian force marched to reinforce Alvintzi. Unsure of Napoleon's position or intentions, Alvintzi stretched his forces thin and launched multiple attacks toward Verona, Lognano, and Rivoli. Napoleon massed his strength at Rivoli and drove Alvintzi back yet again after a hotly contested struggle that effectively smashed the Austrian army. These setbacks, when reported to Wurmser in Mantua, compelled his surrender of that city in February 1797.

So impressed was the Directory with Napoleon's victories that they decided to reinforce the French Army of Italy, planning on a triumphant campaign against Vienna itself. With new French troops, plus a number of recruits from the newly conquered Italian provinces, Napoleon crossed the Alps on the way to Vienna in the spring of 1797. Austrian forces under Archduke Karl Ludwig did their best to stem the tide, but the French successively stormed or turned each Austrian position. When the French were 100 miles from Vienna, Karl decided it was time to negotiate. Napoleon's lines of communication were stretched perilously thin, but Karl did not know that; the French commander blustered, and the Austrian commander gave in. The Treaty of Leoben ended the hostilities between France and Austria.

Napoleon rocketed from semiobscurity to national prominence after the Italian campaign. The lightning maneuvers he used to open the campaign stunned the Austrians, leaving them witless. Though his maneuvers were not new, they had not been used in the late eighteenth century. By the rapidity of his marches, his flanking movements to threaten his enemy's rear, and his army's ability to live off the land, Napoleon was able to accomplish much more than expected against superior forces. His personal direction of each offensive and his placement of units for easy mutual support enabled him to bring to bear considerable forces at the most opportune moments. With a superior intelligence service and his own uncanny ability to outguess his opponents, he consistently caught his opponents unaware of his presence, defeating them one at a time.

After a campaign in Egypt, Napoleon was back in Italy in 1800. He staged one of his greatest victories at Marengo, and placed the northern part of the peninsula under French control.

Napoleon brought Italy the first semblance of unity it had had since the Roman Empire. The French attempted to educate the Italians in revolutionary doctrine, but because the mostly illiterate population was more accustomed to repression than political freedom, they were slow to respond. The Italians bridled at the lack of respect shown the pope by the foreigners, but they soon began to work within the bureaucracy installed by the French; thousands acquired hands-on experience in political administration. The French also built schools (even for girls), improved the road system, abolished serfdom, and introduced the Napoleonic Code. Even the British blockade had positive effects, for it forced the start of industrialization and the cultivation of a new variety of crops. When Napoleon was defeated in 1815, much of Italy returned to disunity or Austrian control, but that first taste of national unity would be fulfilled in the 1840s.

See also Napoleon Buonaparte.

References: Britt, Albert Sidney, *The Wars of Napoleon* (Wayne, NJ: Avery Publishing Group, 1985); Chandler, David, *The Campaigns of Napoleon* (New York: Macmillan, 1966); Gibbs, M. B., *Napoleon's Military Career* (Chicago: Werner Co., 1895).

119   NAPOLEON BUONAPARTE

On the small Mediterranean island of Corsica in August 1769, the second surviving son of Carlo and Leticia Buonaparte was born. He was given the name of an obscure saint, Napoleone, a name that in only a few decades would become world-renowned.

Proving his aristocratic Italian bloodline, Carlo was able to enroll his eldest sons in French schools at royal expense. At the school in Brienne, Napoleon immersed himself in his studies, especially mathematics, history, and geography. At military school, he completed his education as an officer in the French army. He graduated earlier than usual, with the rank of first lieutenant, and was posted to an artillery regiment.

The French Revolution's early stages had little effect on Napoleon. However, once the National Assembly had established itself, he was quick to embrace the ideas the revolution professed. He sailed to Corsica to spread the revolution to his homeland, but was unsuccessful in his attempts to bring about Corsican independence. Arousing the anger of Corsica's citizens, the Bonaparte family was forced to flee to France.

Napoleon's career wavered between active and inactive duty during the infancy of Republican France. Not until he was called upon to take command of the artillery at the siege of Toulon was he able to show his talents. The siege's successful outcome elevated Napoleon's status; events would increase or decrease his popularity, once even to the point of a brief prison stay. Nevertheless, political events changed drastically, and brought Napoleon again to the forefront of popularity.

To eliminate any opportunity for a dictatorship, the National Assembly was disbanded in favor of the Directory. Alarmed by the outcry of the Paris mobs, the Directory called upon Napoleon for protection. His "whiff of grapeshot" kept the Directory in firm control and elevated him to second-in-command of the Army of the Interior. In 1796, Napoleon fell in love with and married Rose de Beauharnais, known better as Josephine. With his marriage only days old, Napoleon was dispatched to take

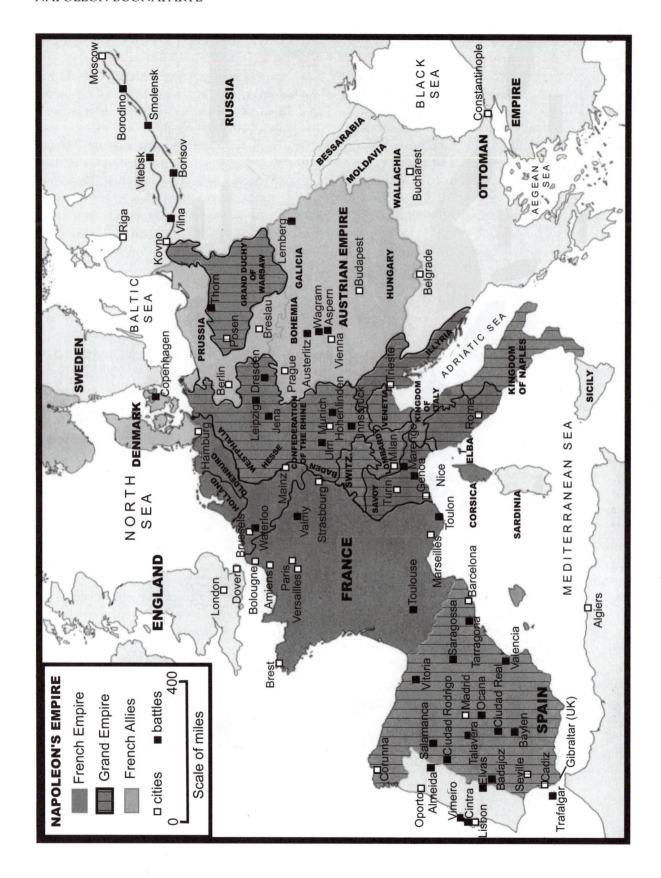

command of the Army of Italy against Austria, one of the two remaining antagonists of Republican France.

In an explosive, masterful campaign across northern Italy to the frontiers of Austria, Napoleon forced a peace treaty in 1797. Returning to Paris to the acclaim of the populace, he began to feel that the future of France and his destiny were intertwined, but the time was not yet right to seize power. Instead, he gladly took the Directory's orders to undertake a campaign in the Middle East. Through another stunning example of generalship, he was successful in subduing Egypt, but the campaign was brought to a halt at the walls of Acre and by the British devastation of the French fleet at Aboukir. In newspapers and letters that filtered through the British blockade of Alexandria, Napoleon learned of the disasters befalling the Republican government. Deciding the time was ripe, he gathered a small group of faithful followers, slipped past the British blockade, and returned to France. Once more in Paris and acclaimed by the population, Napoleon intrigued to become the first consul of the new government.

The consulship was to be a three-person government, but Napoleon soon showed his domineering and persuasive personality, and assumed sole power. He immediately went to work addressing the needs of France. To soothe the populace, he permitted the return of émigrés, the aristocrats who had sought refuge outside France. He reestablished the Catholic Church as the state religion, but provided protection for other faiths as well. He centralized the bureaucracy to better control and oversee district government agencies, and established the Banque de France to regenerate the sagging and disrupted national financial situation.

Napoleon's greatest endeavor was restructuring and establishing a set of civil laws equitable to all citizens. His short prison term during the revolution had given him the opportunity to read the one book available in his cell, Justinian Law. Reworking these ideas into the basis of France's new law, he created what became known as the Civil Code, later the Napoleonic Code. Taking four years to fully codify, the Civil Code would be the greatest achievement of Napoleon's government.

To eliminate the nation's poverty and civil disrepair, Napoleon initiated various public works. Roads were constructed throughout the provinces, while avenues were cleared and widened within major cities to accommodate the movement of commerce and troops. The arts and sciences were patronized so that with their finest work he could transform France, and Paris in particular, into the capital of the European continent.

Compelled by internal and external events, Napoleon spent the majority of 1805–1807 in the position of commander in chief of the newly formed Grande Armée. The genius he brought to military thinking became most evident during this time. Napoleon reworked the French army into a corps system, which maneuvered in an entirely new fashion. Marching with four corps in a loose diamond fashion, the battalion carré, each force could forage for itself and defend itself when attacked, holding an enemy in place until the other units came to its support. Two corps would flank the enemy, while the remaining one would act as a reserve. Thus, any enemy force finding itself with a superiority in numbers soon found itself flanked by the rapidly moving French response. Mobility and speed marked Napoleon's actions, and his enemies usually found themselves defeated by their own ponderous tactics.

In astounding campaigns, he would humble the Austrians, the Prussians, and the Russians. After each one, the sphere of his influence and control spread throughout Europe. With his passion for family ties, he created various realms from the territories he acquired to give to his brothers, sisters, and military/political associates to administer (under his direction). However, he was unable to come to grips with his one major rival, Great Britain. The loss of his fleet, and that of his ally Spain, at the battle of Trafalgar forced Napoleon to devise a means to humble that "nation of shopkeepers." Napoleon established the Continental System: All commerce between the Continent and Britain was to cease and all ports were to close to British shipping, thereby damaging the British economically, since he could not deal with them militarily.

At home, events and emotions over the future of France compelled Napoleon to divorce Josephine. He married Marie Louise of Austria for political reasons, and to produce an heir, which Josephine was unable to provide. For the next two years (1810–1811) Napoleon spent his time on the policies of empire and playing with his son. He soon grew displeased with the constant smuggling of goods through European ports and especially into Russia. Seeking to regain his dominance and influence over the youthful and inexperienced Tsar Alexander, Napoleon called forth over half a million men to invade Russia.

Napoleon left the army during its retreat from Moscow, and returned to Paris to build a new army and forestall a reported coup attempt. During the years 1813–1814, he endeavored to maintain his empire by conducting campaigns against combined enemy forces. Eventually forced back behind the frontiers of France, he conducted a brilliant but futile struggle to keep his throne. The attempt to turn over the reins of empire to his son failed; for the good of France, Napoleon abdicated. Sentenced to exile on the island of Elba in the Mediterranean, he tried to accept the inevitable conclusion of his life. However, the reestablishment of the Bourbons reasserted his belief that his destiny was tied to that of the French people. Escaping from British surveillance, Napoleon returned to French soil and easily regained the throne. His attempts to pacify the European governments so he could maintain his crown failed when the Congress of Vienna outlawed him as a danger to the peace of Europe.

Never one to take the defensive, Napoleon raised an army of 100,000 to take the field against the British and Prussians in the Belgian lowlands. In one of the most famous battles in modern history, Napoleon was beaten at Waterloo and forced once more to abdicate. His punishment for again disrupting Europe was exile to the remote island of St. Helena in the south Atlantic. With little more to do than stroll the limits of his house and grounds, Napoleon spent most of his time dictating his memoirs.

Even though Napoleon attempted to control the vast continent of Europe through his own hands and those of his puppet rulers, today his greatest achievement is considered the Code Napoleon. It has changed little since its institution, and has had an effect on the laws of Italy as well as many other European nations. Napoleon is better remembered as a great military commander, but his compassion for the French people brought about their resurgence in civil works and in the arts and sciences, and a greater belief in the concepts of liberty and equality for all individuals.

See also Egypt, Napoleon's Invasion of; France, European Invasion of; Italy, Napoleon's Invasion of; Prussia, Napoleon's Invasion of; Russia, Napoleon's Invasion of.

References: Abbot, John S. C., *Life of Napoleon, 4 vols.* (New York: Harper Brothers, 1855–1856); Chandler, David, *The Campaigns of Napoleon* (New York: Macmillan, 1966); Markham, Felix, *Napoleon* (New York: New American Library, 1963).

120 NEW YORK, BRITISH INVASION OF (1776)

In March 1776, revolutionary forces under George Washington were successful in forcing a British withdrawal from their main base in Boston, Massachusetts. This effectively curtailed British operations to put down the rebellion until they could reestablish control over a port through which to commit troops and supplies. The next best harbor was at New York City. Washington also understood the British need for a harbor, and guessed correctly that New York would be the target. However, he was handicapped by the forces at his disposal. Even though the revolution was a year old, he was still unable to form a regular army, having a force made up almost entirely of volunteer militia. They were of irregular quality, but fairly well motivated because of the success they had thus far enjoyed. After all, they had inflicted three times as many casualties as they had suffered on the war's opening day at Lexington and Concord in April 1775. They gave a good account of themselves at Breed's (Bunker) Hill the following June; though

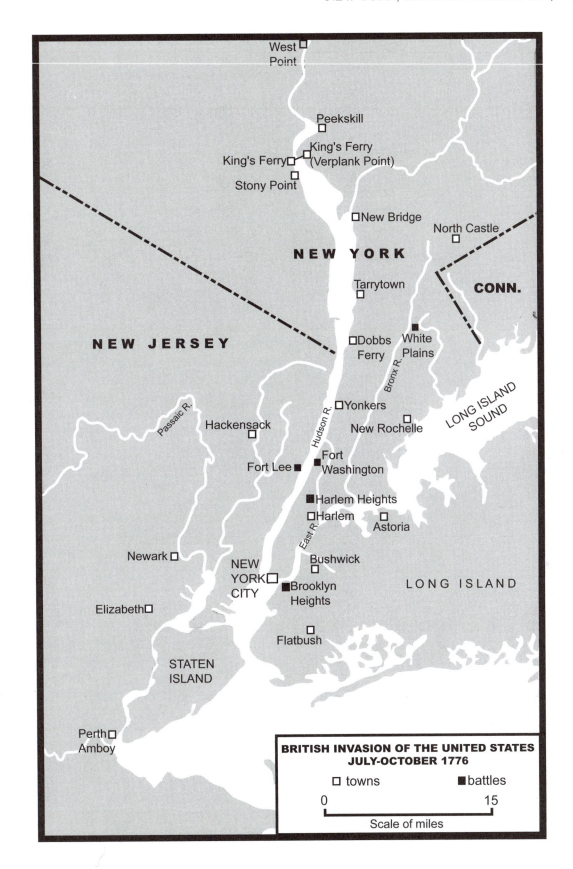

West Point

Peekskill

King's Ferry (Verplank Point)

King's Ferry

Stony Point

New Bridge

North Castle

NEW YORK

Tarrytown

CONN.

NEW JERSEY

Dobbs Ferry

White Plains

Bronx R.

Passaic R.

Yonkers

Hackensack

New Rochelle

LONG ISLAND SOUND

Hudson R.

Fort Lee

Fort Washington

Harlem Heights

Harlem

Astoria

East R.

Newark

NEW YORK CITY

Bushwick

LONG ISLAND

Brooklyn Heights

Elizabeth

Flatbush

STATEN ISLAND

Perth Amboy

**BRITISH INVASION OF THE UNITED STATES
JULY–OCTOBER 1776**

☐ towns   ■ battles

0   15

Scale of miles

they were forced from the field, they inflicted almost 50 percent casualties on the British. The bombardment of Boston, which forced the British almost totally out of the country, capped a year of positive results that ultimately convinced the revolutionary leadership to declare American independence.

Washington knew that ultimate victory would come only with a regular army that could beat the British in the open field, but the supplies and government support he needed to accomplish this were irregular, since the Continental Congress had not been able to establish the authority to collect taxes. Therefore, training and organization were slow. Still, he took what men he had and moved to New York to prepare for the invasion he knew would come.

Washington's next problem was the placement of his troops. He was under orders from the Continental Congress to build defenses to protect the city—almost an impossibility. There were just too many directions from which an invading force could be landed: Staten Island, Long Island, Manhattan, either bank of the Hudson River. Washington tried, but the job was too big for his 20,000 men, of whom more than half were short-term militia. Luckily for him, General William Howe, his British adversary, would be cooperative. The advance guard of the British army under Howe landed on undefended Staten Island on 4 July 1776, but did nothing to slow down Washington's preparations. With the assistance of his older brother, Admiral Richard Howe, General Howe tried to negotiate with the rebels. This occupied about six weeks of his time to no avail, because the revolutionaries stood by their Declaration. Finally, with reinforcements up to a total of 34,000, Howe went into action against Washington's 8,000 men on Long Island on 22 August.

With superior numbers, the British overwhelmed or outmaneuvered the rebels, and Washington was forced to abandon his forward entrenchments and withdraw into prepared defenses on Brooklyn Heights, backed up against the East River. These were untenable should the British navy position itself behind him, so Washington withdrew his army under cover of darkness and heavy weather, extricating his entire force without British knowledge until the operation was completed.

Not terribly aggressive even at the best of times, Howe missed a golden opportunity to crush the rebel army and possibly capture Washington himself. Howe had commanded the forces assaulting the rebel position on Breed's Hill outside Boston the previous summer, and the appalling casualties his force suffered remained in his memory. He often had opportunities to overwhelm the Americans, yet always hesitated at key moments and took the more cautious and careful option, which gave Washington time to react or escape. Though Howe ultimately occupied New York City, his lack of audacity robbed him of the complete victory he might have accomplished.

Howe did not follow Washington's men across the river until 11 September, by which time the rebels were already preparing to withdraw farther north. Washington was chased to Harlem Heights, where his forces stood temporarily and stalled the British pursuit, giving Howe another opportunity to be cautious. Howe began to consolidate his hold on New York City, and did not move toward the rebels again until 9 October. He missed another chance to corner Washington, who retreated to White Plains with his forces reduced to about 14,000. Washington dug in, and the British finally attacked him on 28 October. Again the British were victorious, and again the rebels were allowed to slip away.

In November, the British had New York City well in hand, and Washington was on the run toward Philadelphia. Howe allowed the chase to halt outside New Brunswick, New Jersey, and began the traditional practice of settling into winter quarters. By 1 December, his forces controlled everything from the Delaware River to Newport, Rhode Island, and he put the war on hold until the spring, as was the common procedure of the time. Howe accomplished part of what he had set out to do: He regained a port through which Britain could supply the war. By failing to seize many opportunities to crush the rebellion by destroying its armed force, he allowed Washington to fight another day, and would ultimately live to regret it.

The British held New York City throughout the remainder of the war, but the lack of dash on the part of their commander became a trait of Howe's successors as well. The invasion was a short-term success that for a time disheartened the patriot cause, but in the long run the British were not able to follow up on it.

References: Alden, John R., *The American Revolution* (New York: Harper & Row, 1954); Dupuy, R. E., *An Outline History of the American Revolution* (New York: Harper & Row, 1975); Gruber, Ira, *The Howe Brothers and the American Revolution* (New York: Atheneum, 1972).

121 NEW YORK, BRITISH INVASION OF (1777)

When General William Howe captured New York City in the latter half of 1776, the British believed that they were in a strong position to end the American Revolution. They controlled a wide circle of land surrounding the city, stretching from New Jersey to Rhode Island, and had dealt George Washington a set of serious defeats in the process. Despite the fact that Washington had regained some initiative with victories at Trenton after Christmas and Princeton in the new year, the British authorities did not view the rebels as serious opposition. The only problem the British faced was a lack of direction on how to finish off the rebels. Without a planning staff in London, or one person who exercised total command and control, the generals on the spot were left to develop strategy. This lack of coordination would ultimately spell the doom of the British war effort.

In New York City, Howe proposed attacking Philadelphia. It was the site of the Continental Congress, the capital city, as it were, of the revolutionary movement. Capture the capital and the movement would die, he believed. He sent this plan to London, and received approval from Lord Germain, secretary for America in the British government. However, Germain's approval of an alternate strategy that in some ways contradicted Howe's would ultimately bring about disaster. General John Burgoyne proposed an offensive out of Canada into New York. Burgoyne viewed New York as the linchpin of America, as did Washington himself. By gaining control of the state of New York, the revolution would be physically split, with the heart and soul of the revolutionary spirit in Massachusetts cut off from the supplies of the less ardent southern states.

The idea was a good one, but lacked the key element of coordination, or at least communication. Burgoyne was to lead a major offensive down Lake Champlain to the Hudson River and on to the capital at Albany, which would give him control of upstate New York. Simultaneously, a second and smaller thrust would be led by Barry St. Leger from Lake Ontario eastward down the Mohawk River, thus gaining control of the center of the state. To complete the operation, Howe should march north up the Hudson from New York City and join the other two in Albany, thereby controlling the southern part of the state and dividing the country in two. Burgoyne knew that Howe was dedicated to an attack on Philadelphia, in another direction from his assigned role in this strategy, but the two generals and Germain in London all agreed that Philadelphia would fall quickly enough for Howe to dispatch troops to Albany. Certainly the two strategies should crush the revolution.

Depending on William Howe for speed was a mistake, though in this case the fault was not totally his own. Instead of marching directly for Philadelphia (his forces already controlled most of the route), Howe decided to embark his troops on ships and sail up Chesapeake Bay, where he would debark and attack Philadelphia from the southwest. Not only was this a very roundabout way to reach his objective, but also it depended on cooperation from the Royal Navy, which was not readily forthcoming. There was no overall commander to order the navy's cooperation, and the navy and army rarely got along very well. It took much of the summer for 260 transport ships to be collected to carry Howe's force, and they did not set sail until late July. The troops did not debark until 25 August, and Howe did not contact Washington's defensive force until 10 September. By the time he defeated the rebels at Brandywine Creek and Germantown to take possession of the city, it was October and time to

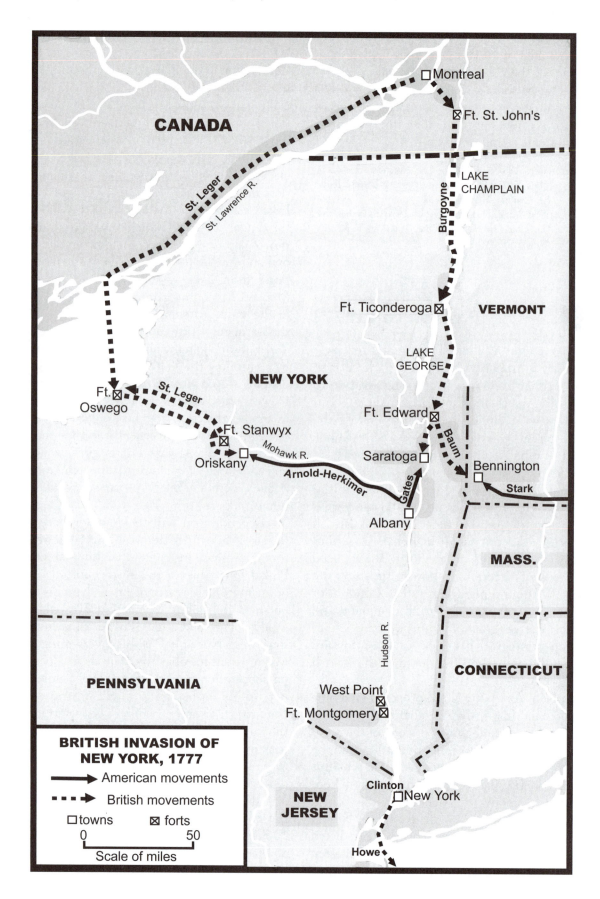

CANADA

Montreal

⊠ Ft. St. John's

St. Leger

St. Lawrence R.

LAKE
CHAMPLAIN

Burgoyne

Ft. Ticonderoga ⊠

VERMONT

LAKE
GEORGE

Ft. ⊠
Oswego

St. Leger

NEW YORK

Ft. Edward ⊠

Baum

Ft. Stanwyx ⊠

Mohawk R.

Saratoga

Bennington

Oriskany

Arnold-Herkimer

Gates

Stark

Albany

MASS.

Hudson R.

CONNECTICUT

PENNSYLVANIA

West Point ⊠

Ft. Montgomery ⊠

**BRITISH INVASION OF
NEW YORK, 1777**

→ American movements

┈► British movements

☐ towns ⊠ forts

0   50

Scale of miles

NEW
JERSEY

Clinton

☐ New York

Howe

settle into winter quarters. He could not possibly dispatch troops to assist Burgoyne at that late date, and the troops left behind to garrison New York City were given no orders to cooperate with Burgoyne's offensive from the north. One-third of the operation would never materialize, but Howe could not quickly communicate that to Burgoyne.

In the meantime, Burgoyne had made good progress. He traveled along Lake Champlain and captured the American Fort Ticonderoga on 6 July. Burgoyne maintained a stable supply line by water most of the way back to Canada, but from Ticonderoga onward he had to move over-land and build a road as he went. This slowed his progress and allowed the American com-mander in the area, Horatio Gates, time to set up a defensive position along the Hudson near the town of Saratoga, halfway from Ticonderoga to Albany. During this slow advance southward, Burgoyne began to run into trouble. A well-known young loyalist, Jane McRae, affianced to an American officer fighting against Burgoyne and awaiting the arrival of the British forces, was murdered and scalped by an Indian guide hired by Burgoyne. Burgoyne wanted to punish the murderer, but he could not afford to alienate his guides so deep into enemy territory, and he let the offender go. Though the victim was a loyalist (and upper New York had many of them), the longstanding enmity between colonist and Indian was aroused. Even those supportive of Britain could not tolerate Burgoyne's decision, and many New Yorkers rose up to either join Gates at Saratoga or harass the British supply line back to Canada. When Burgoyne ordered his mercenary Hessian troops to acquire supplemental supplies from the coun-tryside, they were none too gentle in their treat-ment of the locals, and this further provoked the New Yorkers. Burgoyne found himself in a sud-denly hostile countryside with a growing force of rebels ahead and behind, but he had to push on for Albany. The eastward prong of the attack, from Oswego down the Mohawk Valley, was having even less success. It was slowed by a rebel force of some 850 men behind the strong defenses of Fort Stanwix, at modern-day Rome, New York. Difficult fighting and the arrival of a relief force commanded by rebel General Benedict Arnold disheartened the 1,000 Indians of St. Leger's force. They forced his 800 British, Canadian, and Tory troops to retreat or face the Indians as well as the rebels. St. Leger ordered a withdrawal to Oswego in late August, and Burgoyne was left without the second force he was to meet at Albany. Like Howe in Philadelphia, St. Leger was unable to get word to Burgoyne.

Thus, Burgoyne was alone when he ran into Gates's defenses at Freeman's Farm outside Saratoga in mid-September. Checked by the rebel forces, Burgoyne spent almost a month building defenses and probing the American lines. When he tried again to push through the Americans at nearby Bemis Heights, he was repulsed. The rebels counterattacked under the leadership of Benedict Arnold, recently arrived from the Mohawk Valley. They forced the British back to their defensive lines and sur-rounded them. Cut off from his supplies, Burgoyne soon realized that neither St. Leger nor Howe would arrive to extricate him. He surren-dered his force of 8,000 men on 17 October.

The American victories near Saratoga became the turning point of the revolution. First, they took a large force of British out of the war. Second, they kept the British from controlling New York and splitting the colonies. Third, and most importantly, they impressed the Europeans, whose support the Americans were so desperate-ly courting. The French in particular began to take a serious look at recognizing American inde-pendence. They had refrained from doing so in the past for fear of British retribution, but Burgoyne's defeat convinced the French govern-ment that the revolution had a serious chance to succeed. Loss of its colonies had to weaken the British, and the French could only profit thereby. They recognized the United States, and signed a mutual-defense treaty with the new nation in February 1778. This brought a steady supply of war materiel, which the colonists had to have in order to continue the war and ultimately win it. The French provided arms and ammunition, sup-plies, money, ships, and troops. Their decision also prompted other European nations, notably Spain and the Netherlands, to recognize

American independence as well. Britain now had to guard its interests nearer to home, and could no longer focus its full attention on America. Though the war would continue until 1783, for all intents and purposes the Americans' independence was assured after Saratoga. The very existence of the United States, and what it has meant to the history of the world, was guaranteed in October 1777.

References: Chidsey, Donald B., *The War in the North: An Informal History of the American Revolution in and near Canada* (New York: Crown Publishers, 1967); Furneaux, Rupert, *The Battle of Saratoga* (New York: Stein & Day, 1971); Mintz, Max, *The Generals of Saratoga: John Burgoyne and Horatio Gates* (New Haven, CT Yale University Press, 1990).

PRUSSIA, NAPOLEON'S INVASION OF

122

By 1804, Napoleon was on the road to mastery of Europe. He had proclaimed himself emperor of France in the wake of the French Republic, and with his personal genius and his well-trained, experienced army, he had humbled Austria and taken control of Italy and Spain. The powers of Europe, stymied by Napoleon's devious diplomacy, could not cooperate against him. Prussia was the only power that remained neutral through Napoleon's rise. Prussia was the possessor of a rich military heritage via Frederick the Great, but its victories were 50 years in the past, and its army had lost its quality leadership and training. Prussian King William III lusted after the state of Hanover, home of the English royal family but currently under Napoleon's control. William remained neutral until he could determine whether England or France would be the best ally to satisfy his territorial ambitions. His vacillation provoked Napoleon's contempt.

In May 1804, William got off the fence by joining the Third Coalition, allying Prussia with Austria, Russia, and England. Though Austria went on the offensive into Bavaria in September, William remained a passive partner. He would not commit his troops, even when French troops crossed the Prussian principality of Ansbach. William signed the Convention of Potsdam, wherein the Russian tsar called for the commitment of Prussian troops to the coalition's defense, but still he would not honor the treaty. Napoleon's victory at Austerlitz was therefore gained at the expense of Austrian and Russian troops only.

William sent an envoy to Vienna after Austerlitz to try to convince Napoleon that Prussia had not been a member of the coalition. Napoleon was not fooled, and proposed a treaty in which Prussia would cede some of its territory to France and sever all ties with the former coalition members, allying itself only with France. In return, Hanover would become Prussia's possession, only because Napoleon knew it would act as a point of contention between Prussia and England. As William vacillated over signing this Treaty of Vienna, Napoleon added more conditions: All North Sea ports had to be closed, and all English ships and goods seized. William signed.

Unsatisfied with his humiliation of Prussia thus far, Napoleon established the Confederation of the Rhine, an organization of smaller German states, which threatened traditional Prussian influence in northern Germany. Prussia was further hurt by English actions; England declared war on Prussia over Hanover and seized hundreds of German ships in English ports. When William learned that private peace feelers were extending from London and Moscow toward Paris, his wife Louise convinced him to stand firm and avenge his country's honor.

Prussia's army was in no condition to face Napoleon's Grande Armée. Though it retained its reputation and numbered a quarter million strong, the Prussian army had not been tested in battle for decades. Its weaponry, tactics, and organization were long out-of-date, and its youngest high commanders were in their sixties. They completely failed to grasp any of Napoleon's past strategies, and predicted he would assume a defensive position when they approached him. Their mobilization program was slow and had poor security, so Napoleon learned of their moves and embarked with his traditional speed to beat the Prussians to the punch. On 7 October 1807, Prussia declared war on France, but Napoleon's armies were already on Prussia's frontiers.

The first battle took place the following day, and Napoleon was victorious at Rudolstadt, killing Prussia's Prince Louis in the process. A week later, at Jena, Napoleon scored yet another of his impressive victories. He slaughtered a Prussian corps while his subordinate, Marshal Davout, in a diversionary attack, actually found the bulk of the Prussian army at Auerstadt. Though outnumbered, Davout's aggressive handling of his forces forced a Prussian retreat. By 24 October, Prussia was crushed, and Napoleon was in Berlin. He levied heavy reparations on Prussia but, rather than collect them quickly, Napoleon decided to stay in Prussia and use it as a base for possible operations against Russia.

After the French victory at Friedland in 1807, Tsar Alexander signed the Treaty of Tilsit with Napoleon, promising to make common cause against England. In return, Napoleon forced Prussia to cede its possessions in Poland to Russia. With his eastern flank secured, Napoleon now collected the remainder of Prussian reparations. French humiliation of Prussia caused a groundswell of popular feeling against Napoleon. The Prussians ached for vengeance, and the army learned that it could not rest on the laurels won by Frederick the Great.

Napoleon's occupation of Prussia planted the seeds of his destruction. Though the people came to hate him, Napoleon brought to Prussia the lessons of the French Revolution. The nationalism that saved France from European enemies became the same force that motivated Prussia, which joined with the remainder of Europe to take advantage of Napoleon's weakness in 1813 and was involved with his ultimate defeat at Leipzig in 1814 and Waterloo in 1815. The Prussian General Staff was re-formed to modernize the military and focus on learning the lessons of this and every other war. It became a military organization the world would model in the late nineteenth century. This reconstituted military became the symbol of national power and pride, leading to German unification in 1871 and the German Empire shortly thereafter.

See also Austria, Napoleon's Conquest of; Russia, Napoleon's Invasion of.

References: Chandler, David, *The Campaigns of Napoleon* (New York: Macmillan, 1966); Home, Alistair, *Napoleon, Master of Europe, 1805–1807* (New York: Morrow, 1979); Markham, Felix, *Napoleon and the Awakening of Europe* (London: English Universities Press, 1954).

123 RUSSIA, NAPOLEON'S INVASION OF

By 1807, Napoleon controlled all of Europe, directly or indirectly. Only Britain remained completely free from French control, but Russia had bought some time and security by signing the Treaty of Tilsit. Tsar Alexander agreed to boycott British goods and import mostly French products, but poor Russians could not afford them. Aside from economic sacrifices, Russia looked askance at Napoleon's political desires. Napoleon firmly controlled the duchy of Warsaw, which seemed to Russia a good launch point for an invasion of their country. Further, Napoleon was looking covetously at the Dardanelles, long a strategic goal of Russian foreign policy. He had done little to assure Russia of long-term friendly intentions, and short-term financial woes pressed on the Russian economy. By 1812, Alexander's advisers convinced him to ignore Napoleon's Continental System barring British goods from all of Europe. The Russian government ignored Napoleon's plea to impound a large number of British ships sailing for St. Petersburg, and for Napoleon that was the last straw. He was determined to punish Russia for violating his economic warfare policies, lest other European countries follow suit.

Napoleon's invasion force numbered over half a million men, but included a large percentage of non-French troops whose loyalty and cooperation might prove doubtful. Alexander also had foreign aid; he had been negotiating with Sweden, Poland, Prussia, Turkey, and Britain, and many of the generals Napoleon faced were not Russian. Napoleon's advisers counseled against the invasion, even though French forces outnumbered the Russian foes. The advice went unheeded. Napoleon planned on a relatively easy campaign, because he took few horses and

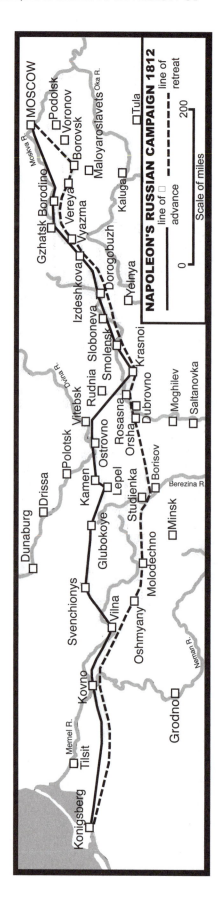

NAPOLEON'S RUSSIAN CAMPAIGN 1812

line of advance

line of retreat

Scale of miles

0   200

ordered the troops to carry only four days' rations. Regularly placed supply depots, in addition to the army's traditional ability to live off the land, would provide for his needs. The long march, however, forced the army to shrink in size: Depots needed garrisons, and forage parties also needed men.

French forces crossed the Nieman River in June 1812. Well aware of Napoleon's prowess, Alexander withdrew his forces before the advance and ordered a scorched-earth policy. Thus, the French could rarely come to grips with a sizable Russian force, and found it virtually impossible to live off the land. The French expected the peasants to welcome them as liberators, but instead they cooperated with the Tsar's orders. Tsar Alexander wanted to lead his forces himself when the two armies would finally meet, but his wife and advisers convinced him to stay in the capital and give command to Baron Barclay de Tolly. The baron followed the plan to avoid confrontation, but was soon criticized and relieved for retreating too quickly. His replacement was the aged General Prince Golinischev-Kutosov, a veteran of earlier encounters with Napoleon.

No battle of import was fought until Kutosov found a good place to stand some 70 miles from Moscow, near the village of Borodino. The battle cost a total of 70,000 lives and could be called little more than a draw, but Kutosov abandoned the field and withdrew toward Moscow. He soon vacated that city as well, as did virtually the entire population. Napoleon sent a messenger to the city to demand its surrender, but no one of any authority remained there. He occupied the empty capital, and claimed an empty victory. The city was soon on fire, the blazes set by retreating soldiers and civilians, and those valuables that could be saved from the flames loaded down the looting French soldiers. After no more than a few days, there was nothing in the city unburned or unplundered.

With cold weather approaching and Moscow unsuitable for spending the winter, Napoleon had little choice but to declare victory and go home. He left on 19 October 1812 and found the road out of Russia as difficult as the one coming in. His army became an easy

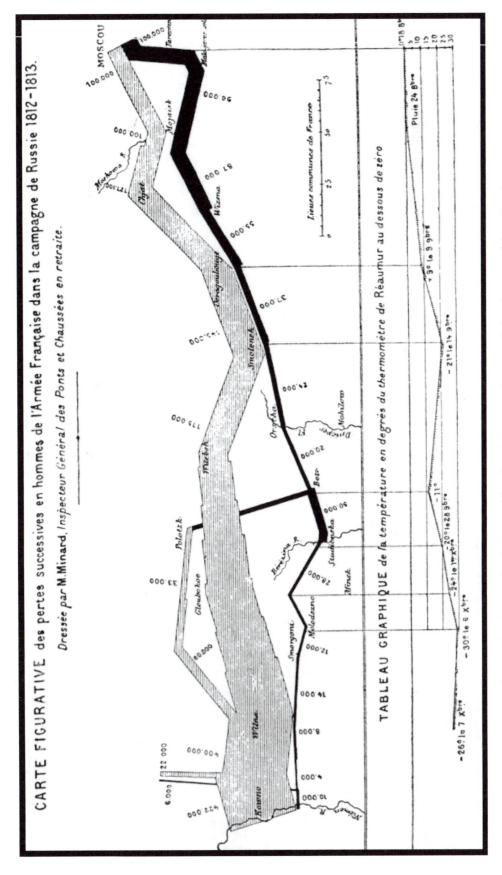

This graphic depicts the decline in Napoleon's forces as they invaded and retreated from Russia. Freezing temperatures and lengthy marches clearly took a heavy toll.

target—slowed by rain and snow, burdened with their loot, and harassed by raiding Russian units. The lack of food and shelter, coupled with the constant sniping, caused many more deaths than did battle. Total casualty counts vary, but of the more than 600,000 men that entered Russia in June, Napoleon led no more than 100,000 out; some sources claim that as few as 10,000 survived. Probably 125,000 of the total were battle deaths.

Napoleon's fortunes dwindled rapidly. Proven to be fallible, the countries he had conquered quickly rose against him. Napoleon reached Paris and raised a new army before news of his disaster reached his country, but his new forces lacked the training and experience of the Grand Armée that had taken him to glory. A coalition of European countries formed and defeated him in 1814 at Leipzig in the so-called Battle of the Nations, and he went to exile in Elba. A short-lived attempt to regain power in 1815 left him defeated again at Waterloo in Belgium; thereafter, he was exiled to St. Helena in the middle of the South Atlantic, too far away to be rescued or exert influence.

The invasion of Russia and Napoleon's defeat serve as landmark events in Russian history. The world enjoys two enduring tributes to these events: Tchaikovsky's 1812 Overture and Tolstoy's *War and Peace*. The Russian tsar's power remained strong, but the peasants who sacrificed for the cause gained no reward for it. Autocratic rule remained in Russia for another hundred years, but to this day the people of that nation depend on Mother Russia and Mother Nature to save them from any invasion.

See also Austria, Napoleon's Conquest of.

References: Gate, Curtis, *The War of Two Emperors* (New York: Random House, 1984); Palmer, Alan, *Napoleon in Russia* (New York: Simon & Schuster, 1967); Tarle, Eugene, *Napoleon's Invasion of Russia in 1812* (New York: Farrar, Straus & Giroux, 1971).

SOUTHERN UNITED STATES, BRITISH INVASION OF

124

After the British failure to split the rebellious American colonies in half by the campaign in New York in 1777, British leaders had to rethink their goals. Possession of New York City and Philadelphia had not brought about neither the collapse of revolutionary resistance nor the expected uprising of loyalist pro-British support among the citizenry. When General William Howe was relieved of his command in the summer of 1778, General Henry Clinton replaced him as head of the British forces in America. In London, American Secretary Lord Germain decided that the wisest course was to move the sphere of action to the American south, where revolutionary feeling was not nearly as intense and loyalist sentiment was supposed to predominate. Building a power base in the south would deprive the rebels of much of their supply source, and the British could pin the revolutionary forces between advancing British troops from the south and the existing British positions around New York City.

Germain ordered Clinton to initiate this southern strategy, and British troops began their campaign in the state of Georgia in December 1778. Savannah fell easily by the end of the month, and by the end of January the entire state was in British hands. The English brought back the former royal governor, who reestablished a British regime for the following three years. With the Georgia operation such an easy victory, the British hurried on toward South Carolina.

The Continental Congress, directing the American military operations, sent Benjamin Lincoln to restore the rebel fortunes, but he was defeated above Savannah and retreated to South Carolina. A second attempt to recapture Savannah, this time with French troops and naval support, failed in late October 1779. Lincoln spent the winter of 1779–1780 reinforcing at Charleston, South Carolina, where he faced a large British force in April. Surrounded by superior numbers and cut off from the sea by the British fleet, Lincoln surrendered the city and its garrison of 5,000 men in mid-May. The loss of such a large number of men, along with 300 cannon, severely hurt revolutionary morale.

In the Carolinas, the British had received reinforcements who came under the command of Lord Cornwallis, with some 8,000 troops at his disposal. The expected enlistment of loyalist forces

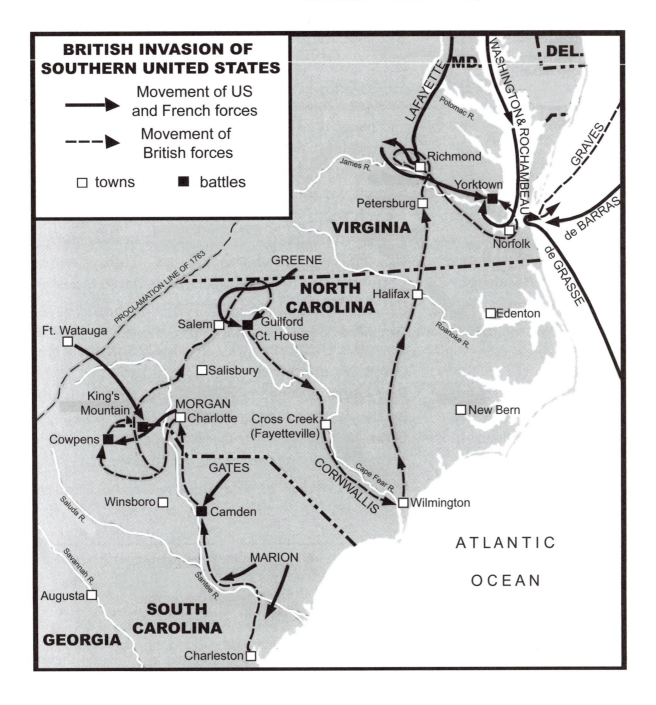

**BRITISH INVASION OF
SOUTHERN UNITED STATES**

→ Movement of US
and French forces

--→ Movement of
British forces

□ towns   ■ battles

finally came as hundreds of locals rushed to join the winning side. Many Americans considered the southern states lost because the British occupied forts all across South Carolina. The Continental Congress sent Horatio Gates, victor of the battle at Saratoga, to mount a defense in the south. The smaller number of men than he had had in upstate New York, his deficiencies as a general, and the fact that he had many more militiamen than trained regulars were his undoing. Cornwallis defeated Gates at Camden in mid-August and followed the retreating rebels into North Carolina.

The only bright spot in the American effort came from small guerrilla groups operating independently in Georgia and South Carolina. They successfully harassed British supply lines and outposts, but their small successes could not make up for Gates's glaring failure; ultimate

British success seemed assured. Only the British could hurt the British, which is exactly what they did. Cornwallis outran his supply lines, and the North Carolina loyalists did not appear in the large numbers for which he had hoped. Cornwallis withdrew his hungry troops back to Camden for the winter of 1780–1781.

Gates's failure caused American Commander in Chief George Washington to plead for a replacement, and Nathaniel Greene got the job. Greene was the best possible choice because he understood the realities of the American military strength. He launched an almost completely guerrilla campaign throughout South Carolina, in which he simultaneously lost most of his battles and hurt the British badly, dancing them around the state, making them tired, hungry, and frustrated, unable to pin him down and destroy him. Greene used his small forces to their best advantage, moving more quickly than the British and denying them control of any territory. They had to chase him, and thus could not occupy any area long enough to establish their authority. In the end, the British controlled the cities and the rebels held sway over the countryside.

Cornwallis chased the American forces into North Carolina in the spring of 1781. Despite a marginal victory at Guilford Court House, Cornwallis again found himself a long way from his supplies, and Greene's force was still intact. Cornwallis marched to the coast to get supplies from the Royal Navy at Wilmington, then marched to Virginia. Greene stayed behind and continued to make life miserable for the British and the loyalist allies in the Carolinas. After marching around central Virginia, and receiving some assistance from a force newly dispatched under Benedict Arnold, Cornwallis marched to the coast to establish a base at Yorktown. He and Clinton still hoped to squeeze the main portion of the revolutionary army between them.

Cornwallis then made a fatal mistake. In July, he began digging defensive positions to protect his base, but he allowed the rebels to operate and concentrate immediately west of him. Cornwallis's position at Yorktown was on the end of a peninsula formed by the York and James rivers, and the

rebel forces commanded by the Frenchman Marquis de Lafayette had him in a corner. Should French ships arrive offshore in Chesapeake Bay, he would be as effectively cut off as Lincoln had been at Charleston. Still, he dug in and awaited word from Clinton on cooperative operations. Without a British force on the loose in Virginia, the revolutionary forces were able to move about freely. Lafayette called for Washington to come from Rhode Island to strengthen the American position against Cornwallis. Leaving a screening force to hold Clinton in place, in late August 1781 Washington marched some 2,000 American and 5,000 French troops unmolested past New York City and through New Jersey and Pennsylvania to Virginia. Simultaneously, the French fleet left Newport to deny Cornwallis succor from the Royal Navy. By mid-September, Cornwallis's 8,000 men were outnumbered two to one by the Franco-American force. Coupled with the 5 September victory by the French navy over a smaller British fleet in Chesapeake Bay, the British position was untenable. French and American troops moved their siege lines gradually closer to the British through September and October. Cornwallis made a vain attempt to escape across the York River, then asked for terms on 17 October. His forces laid down their arms two days later.

If the American victory at Saratoga was the turning point of the American Revolution, Yorktown was the coup de grâce. Six years of futility were more than the British population was willing to accept, and once word of Cornwallis's surrender reached London, the ruling government's days were numbered. Prime Minister Lord North resigned in March 1782, and the new cabinet called for negotiations with the Americans. Talks began in Paris in the summer and dragged on for more than a year. The desires of France and Spain, both of which had contributed significantly to the American victory, were rarely compatible with each other or with those of the United States. Finally, the Treaty of Paris was signed in November 1783, in which Great Britain recognized American independence and established the United States' borders as between the Atlantic and the Mississippi River, and from the Great Lakes down to but not including Florida, which reverted to Spanish ownership. Within the United States there was a large number of loyalists in despair at the outcome of the war, and they could not accept the results. More than 100,000 people left the country, most going to Canada.

The American Revolution, completed after this failed British campaign, changed much of the world. It signaled the first break in the colonial system that Europe had been building, and would continue to build over the next century. Whatever colonies were established in the future, the seeds of discontent were already sown by the Declaration of Independence and the democratic tradition begun by the infant United States in the 1770s and 1780s. Never before had a republican form of government successfully operated in a large nation, but now it became the goal of colonial dreamers worldwide.

See also New York, British Invasion of (1777).

References: Alden, John R., *The American Revolution* (New York: Harper & Row, 1954); Dupuy, R. Ernest, *An Outline History of the American Revolution* (New York: Harper & Row, 1975); Pearson, Michael, *Those Damned Rebels: The American Revolution as Seen through British Eyes* (New York: Putnam, 1972).

UNITED STATES, BRITISH INVASION OF

125

While the British were occupied, along with other European countries, in attempting to defeat Napoleon, the United States declared war on Great Britain. In an attempt to maintain a blockade against Napoleon's European empire, the British had impressed American sailors into the Royal Navy and had kept the Americans from carrying on free trade with Europe. Since the summer of 1812, the United States had attempted to conquer Canada with little or no success, but had not had to worry about fighting many British troops. When Napoleon was defeated at the Battle of Leipzig in 1813 and sent into exile in 1814, the British had plenty of veteran troops to send to the United States to bring a quick end to the war.

In the early summer of 1814, British troops sailed for North America as the British made invasion plans. The United States would be attacked from three directions. First, the British would move from Canada southward down Lake Champlain, a route used by invading armies since the French and Indian Wars of the 1750s. Second, they would attack the American capital at Washington, D.C., to put pressure on the government to surrender. Third, British forces would attack the Gulf Coast in an attempt to carry the war to the western states, where support for war was greatest, and they could also gain control of the Mississippi River. Seeing the Americans' inept manner of fighting displayed thus far, the British (and many Americans) were sure that the veterans of war against Napoleon would walk over any opposition in North America. The route from Montreal down Lake Champlain was much the same path General John Burgoyne had followed in 1777. The British now had 15,000 men to draw on, while the Americans could muster no more than 4,000, mostly militia. The Americans were in a good defensive position, however, with three blockhouses along a narrow front at Plattsburgh, New York. Further, Captain Thomas MacDonough had a force of gunboats ready to fight the British ships sailing along with the advancing British army. The two forces met on 11 September. Though the British army and navy were supposed to launch a simultaneous assault, the navy went into combat virtually alone. Because of headwinds, the British ships could not maneuver past the anchored American vessels, so the two sides faced each other and pounded away. After two hours, the American gunners had the better of the fight, and the remnants of the British fleet, minus their dead commander, retreated to Canada. Seeing his main source of supply sail away, British General George Prevost withdrew his men and followed. His troops outnumbered the Americans at Plattsburgh almost four to one, but Prevost did not care to advance against the blockhouses, and went home. His veterans had little opportunity to prove their superiority, and the first part of the British grand strategy died.

The second plan, to attack the American capital at Washington, proved much easier. British forces under General Robert Ross numbered over 4,000 and had just arrived from France. Since the

American army, such as it was, had been stationed along the Canadian frontier since 1812, the east coast was relatively undefended. The Royal Navy harassed various harbors up and down the coast, but focused their main attention on Chesapeake Bay as the door to Washington. Ross landed his men southeast of the city at Benedict, Maryland, on 22 August without opposition. The American high command had dithered all summer, and produced virtually no plans to defend the capital. Militia units were not called up until British troops had landed, and they had little chance to succeed. Mustering 6,000 men, they attempted to defend their capital by standing at Bladensburg, due east of the city, but they were untrained, disorganized, and poorly commanded. They stood for longer than could be expected when Ross's men advanced against them on 24 August, but retreat soon turned into rout. The British occupied a deserted Washington and set many of the public buildings on fire, paying the Americans back for the burning of the Canadian capital at York the previous year. Finding no one with whom to negotiate, and with a tornado striking the next day, the British returned to their ships on the evening of 25 August. The ships sailed for Baltimore, hoping to find more booty and punish the pirates who had been harassing British shipping throughout the war.

Baltimore proved a tougher nut to crack. The citizens were led by Samuel Smith, senator and Revolutionary War veteran. He was a determined man, and he had some able lieutenants. The city's defenses had been improved through the war, and the gunners at the main bastion, Fort McHenry, were well trained and motivated. On 13 September, Smith placed riflemen along the path the British would have to take to march on the city, and they did a good job of holding back Ross's advance. When Ross was killed, the British went into bivouac; meanwhile, the British fleet attacked Fort McHenry. Some 1,800 shells landed in and around the fort during 25 hours of bombardment, but the defenders would not surrender. Two more sorties against American troops were repulsed, and the British decided the target was too expensive; reboarding their ships, they sailed to Jamaica. The second British offensive also came to naught.

The British had great hopes for their southern thrust. Reinforcing at Jamaica, the British sailed through the Gulf of Mexico. American forces in the south were commanded by Tennesseean Andrew Jackson. Since the summer of 1813, his forces had been fighting the Creek Indians in the Mississippi Territory. Jackson's victories cleared the area of the Indians' presence and gave his men battle experience. The government assigned the defense of the Gulf Coast to Jackson. This area stretched only between Spanish Florida and Spanish Texas; there really was not much to cover. Indeed, only two sites offered themselves as potential targets: Mobile, Alabama, and New Orleans, Louisiana. When Jackson learned that a small British force had occupied Pensacola (in Spanish Florida), he was sure that Mobile was in imminent danger. Jackson arrived at Mobile on 27 August and began organizing the defenses. With reinforcements from Tennessee, he raided into Spanish Florida and destroyed the forts guarding Pensacola, denying the town to the British. This secured his flank and further intimidated Indians aiding the British.

In late November, Jackson left for New Orleans with 2,000 men. He left 1,000 behind in the Mobile defenses and sent another 1,000 to Baton Rouge to act as reserves, ready to support either location should the British attack. In New Orleans, he found local militia units forming and preparing to defend their homes. Jackson set about blocking as many routes to the city as possible, hoping to funnel the British into a trap. The British ships could get no closer than 60 miles because of shallow water, so they needed to control the eastern approaches to assault the city from that direction. On 12 December the British captured the five American gunboats covering the city via Lake Borgne. They brought up men and materiel through Lake Borgne without Jackson's knowledge, but moving through inundated countryside was slow going.

Jackson's one great need was artillery, as he had left most of his cannon back in Mobile. Local pirate leader Jean Lafitte had turned down a British offer to join the attackers, and now he offered his professional gunners and ordnance to Jackson, who accepted them in return for granting Lafitte a pardon for all his crimes.

By 23 December, Jackson was well armed, and just in time; word came of British troops massing just below the city. Jackson led a raid against the British camp that night, setting the British timetable back two weeks. Not until 8 January were they ready to advance on New Orleans. By then, Jackson had 5,000 men behind a defensive wall along a dry canal 1,000 yards wide, stretching from the Mississippi River on his right to an impenetrable swamp on his left.

When the British veterans marched out of the morning fog, they were an impressive sight, but they were being led to slaughter. The massed musket and artillery fire tore huge holes in their ranks and, unable to maneuver in the narrow battleground, they found themselves in a killing field. Of the 6,000 men led by General Edward Pakenham, 2,000 died or were wounded before 8:30 in the morning; American losses totaled 45. Jackson decided against taking his men over to the offensive, and the British decided against another attack. After a truce to bury their dead, on 18 January the British withdrew to their ships and sailed away.

The battle at New Orleans proved to be the one clearcut and overwhelming victory the Americans scored in the entire War of 1812. To an extent, it was also pointless, because American and British diplomats had ended the war with the signing of the Treaty of Ghent on 24 December 1814. Had the British won at New Orleans, however, they could well have kept it and controlled access to the Gulf of Mexico, no matter what may have been agreed to in Ghent.

Though the battle turned out to be a disaster for the British, it became a morale boost for the United States. It turned an otherwise dismal military experience into one that could be viewed, however misguidedly, as another American triumph over Britain. Along with the British failures to punish the Americans at Plattsburgh or Baltimore, the victory at New Orleans brought the American people together in a new sense of nationalism. Though the issues that forced a declaration of war in 1812 were not addressed by the peace treaty, the end of the war against Napoleon brought an end to British violations of American rights on the high seas; Americans convinced themselves that their force of arms had secured the rights for which they originally went to war. Freedom of trade after the war, along with an increased measure of respect from Europe, brought a new financial security, and the United States grew in confidence. The rapprochement between the United States and Britain, showing itself in the settlement of trade and border disputes, allowed the Americans three decades of isolationism to grow economically and physically until the nation established borders on the Pacific Ocean.

See also Canada, U.S. Invasion of; Napoleon Buonaparte; New York, British Invasion of (1777).

References: Coles, Harry, *The War of 1812* (Chicago: University of Chicago Press, 1965); Lord, Walter, *The Dawn's Early Light* (New York: Norton, 1972); Mahon, John, *The War of 1812* (Gainesville: University Presses of Florida, 1972).

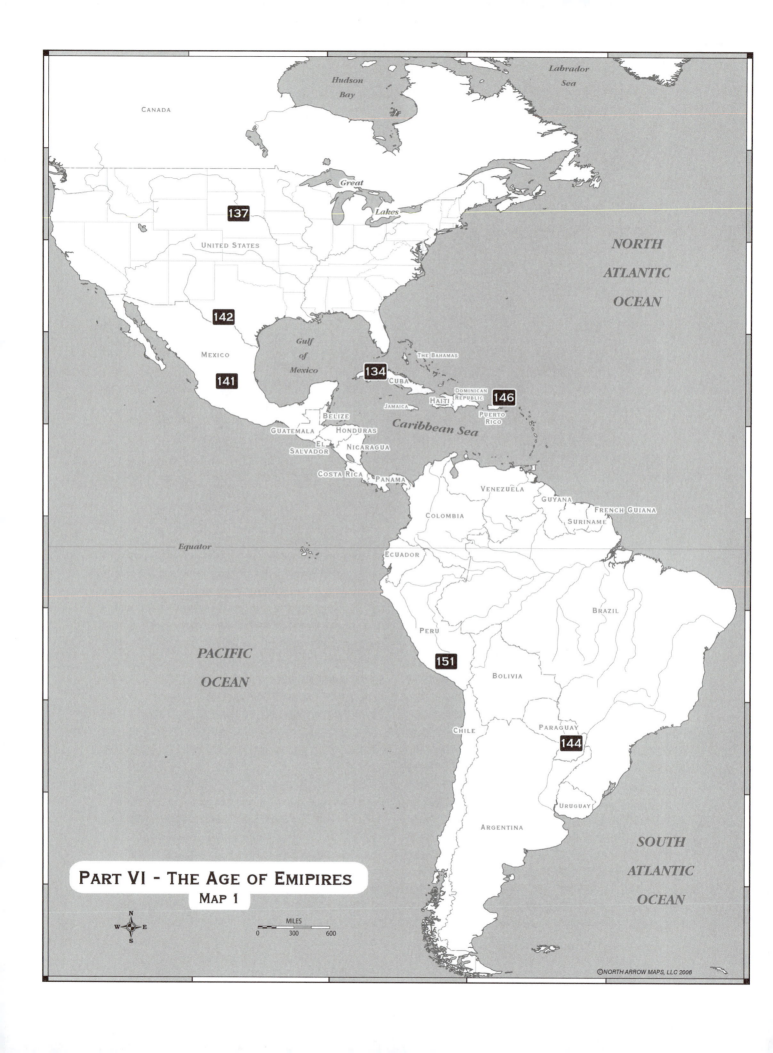

CANADA

Hudson Bay

Labrador Sea

Great Lakes

UNITED STATES

137

142

MEXICO

141

Gulf of Mexico

THE BAHAMAS

134

CUBA

NORTH ATLANTIC OCEAN

DOMINICAN REPUBLIC

HAITI

146

JAMAICA

PUERTO RICO

BELIZE

GUATEMALA

HONDURAS

Caribbean Sea

EL SALVADOR

NICARAGUA

COSTA RICA

PANAMA

VENEZUELA

GUYANA

COLOMBIA

SURINAME

FRENCH GUIANA

Equator

ECUADOR

PERU

BRAZIL

151

BOLIVIA

PACIFIC OCEAN

PARAGUAY

144

CHILE

URUGUAY

ARGENTINA

SOUTH ATLANTIC OCEAN

PART VI - THE AGE OF EMPIRES
MAP 1

N
W E
S

MILES
0   300   600

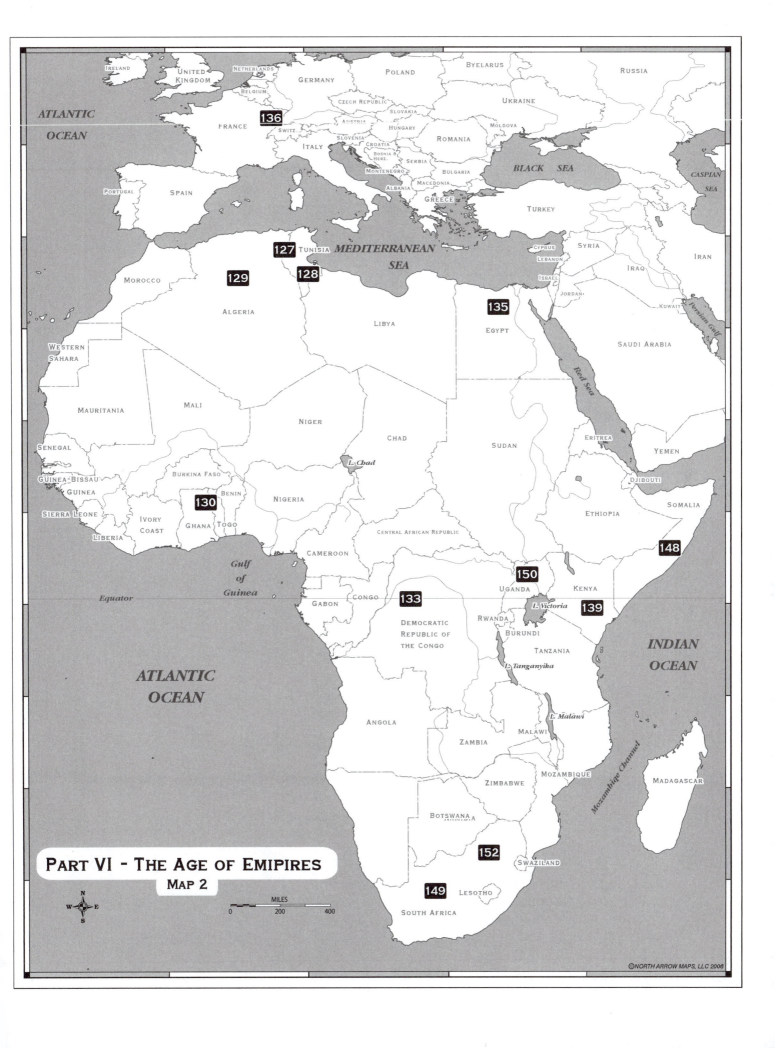

ATLANTIC
OCEAN

136

BLACK SEA

CASPIAN
SEA

127 TUNISIA

MEDITERRANEAN
SEA

129

128

135

ATLANTIC
OCEAN

Equator

Gulf
of
Guinea

130

133

150

148

139

INDIAN
OCEAN

152

149

PART VI - THE AGE OF EMPIRES
MAP 2

MILES
0   200   400

©NORTH ARROW MAPS, LLC 2006

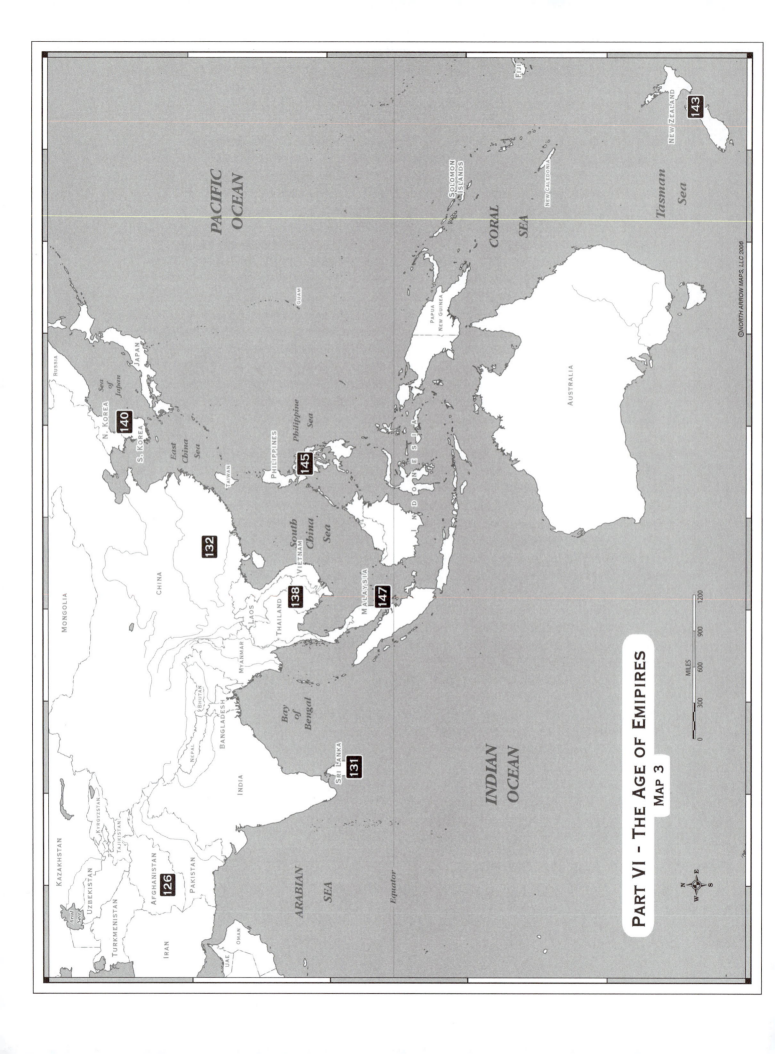

PACIFIC OCEAN

RUSSIA

MONGOLIA

CHINA

Sea of Japan

JAPAN

N. KOREA [140]

S. KOREA

East China Sea

[132]

TAIWAN

Philippine Sea

PHILIPPINES [145]

South China Sea

GUAM

KAZAKHSTAN

UZBEKISTAN

TURKMENISTAN

KYRGYZSTAN

TAJIKISTAN

Aral Sea

IRAN

AFGHANISTAN [126]

PAKISTAN

NEPAL

BHUTAN

BANGLADESH

MYANMAR

INDIA

LAOS

THAILAND

VIETNAM [138]

MALAYSIA [147]

SRI LANKA [131]

Bay of Bengal

ARABIAN SEA

UAE

OMAN

Equator

INDIAN OCEAN

INDONESIA

PAPUA NEW GUINEA

AUSTRALIA

CORAL SEA

SOLOMON ISLANDS

NEW CALEDONIA

FIJI

NEW ZEALAND [143]

Tasman Sea

©NORTH ARROW MAPS, LLC 2006

MILES

0   300   600   900   1200

N
W   E
S

PART VI – THE AGE OF EMIPIRES
MAP 3

PART 6
THE AGE OF EMPIRES

AFGHANISTAN, BRITISH INVASIONS OF

126

The British army and the forces of the British East India Company were regularly successful in India, but they found the inhabitants of Afghanistan more difficult to defeat. Even when the British and Indian forces won clear victories in the field, the political victories were nebulous. The British interfered in Afghan affairs twice in the nineteenth century, and lived to regret both experiences.

The First Afghan War

The mountainous country of Afghanistan had little that the British wanted or needed, but they continually worried that another country would gain influence there and be in a position to attack India. The amir of Afghanistan in the 1830s was Dost Muhammed, who was quite surprised when the British took his courtesy seriously. In a diplomatic letter to Lord Auckland, governor-general of India, he ended by saying, "Consider me and my country as yours." This formal phrase meant nothing more than "I am very truly yours" at the end of a Western letter. Still, it seemed an invitation too good to resist. When a British spy in Afghanistan stumbled into a Russian-led Persian army invading the country, he undisguised himself and offered his services (successfully) to the Afghan army. Rather than bring about closer ties, it led to a British expedition into Afghanistan. If Dost Muhammed could not successfully repel outside incursions, then Britain needed to assist him whether he liked it or not. In fact, it seemed a good idea to bring along a replacement amir more amenable to British intentions: Shah Shuja, who happened to be very unpopular with the Afghan population.

In retrospect, it seems ludicrous that the British would believe the Afghans would welcome another power deposing their leader with a despised lackey for the doubtful purpose of saving them from the Russians or the Persians (neither of whom had proven their ability to invade successfully), and imposing on them this new leader whose troops practiced the Sikh religion, hated in Afghanistan. The British Army of the Indus, formed in late 1838, entered Afghanistan early the next year. The British officers traveled in style through the forbidding country, harassed constantly by small Afghan bands, but met with no resistance they could not overcome. The capture of the fort at Ghazni in July was a major obstacle, but the British marched into the capital city of Kabul in August. Shah Shuja was installed as amir before a sullen populace.

The British attacked pockets of resistance in the area for the next few months. The exiled Dost Muhammed threw himself on the mercy of the khan of Bokhara; for his trouble, he ended up in jail. He was imprisoned with other foreigners as well, including a few British and Russian citizens, so the British decided they needed to deal with the khan and capture Dost Muhammed before the Russians did. Both Russian and British envoys were dismissed, imprisoned, or executed, but the khan received no retribution; when he allowed Dost Muhammed to escape, the political justification for invasion was gone. Besides, trouble in Afghanistan diverted British attention.

The British envoy in Kabul, Sir William Macnaghten, decided to stop tribute payments to hostile tribes who had traditionally controlled the passes into India. Those tribes immediately began to close off British lines of communication, an act which coincided with an uprising in Kabul in 1841. The British and Indian forces quickly found themselves besieged in Kabul, Ghazni, and Kandahar. The Afghans were better armed than the British, and were better marksmen as well; their sniping into the fort at Kabul was deadly. An attempt at negotiation ended in Macnaghten's murder. In early January 1843, the British decided, unwisely, to abandon Kabul for the long march back to India. Some 14,500 men, women, and children (4,500 of them British and Indian) left the city and headed toward the British fort at Jelalabad 60 miles east of Kabul. A week later, a lone horseman staggered into Jelalabad—the sole British survivor of an Afghan attack. A few Indian soldiers and captured wives and children were recovered later.

Jelalabad was surrounded before the defenders could obey orders to withdraw to India. Building and rebuilding walls around the city, they held the Afghans at bay. In April, an attack from the fort drove the Afghans away, and the defenders captured the hastily abandoned enemy camp. A British-Indian force stormed the Khyber Pass, a feat never before accomplished by any army in history, and relieved Jelalabad on 16 April. By September, the defenders of Jelalabad were in Kabul. They freed British prisoners, burned down the Great Bazaar, then marched home. Honor was satisfied, but the original intent of the British government was not accomplished. The First Afghan War was a bitter pill for the British.

The Second Afghan War

The second time the British tried to establish residence in Kabul was in 1879, long enough after the first debacle for the British to have forgotten its lessons. They demanded that the Afghans allow a British diplomatic mission into their capital, as the Afghans had just welcomed one from Russia. The amir was Sher Ali, one of the seven sons of Dost Muhammed, who retook power when the British left in 1842. Sher Ali had as little desire to allow the British into his country as his father had, because he feared that any political concession to Britain was the first step toward annexation. Knowing their demand would fall on deaf ears, the British had an invasion force ready to go: 45,000 men divided into three columns. The major fighting took place in the valley of the Kurram River, which crosses the border 65 miles southeast of Kabul. The smallest column, 6,500 men under General Roberts, fought brilliantly against superior forces in narrow defiles. Wise maneuvering and brave fighting took the British to Kabul. Sher Ali fled for Russia and died on the way, leaving his son Yakub Khan in power. Yakub Khan negotiated the Treaty of Gandemuk in May 1879, in which the British gained everything they wanted: an envoy in Kabul, territorial cessions, freedom of trade for British/Indian merchants, a telegraph line from Kabul to India, and total control over Afghanistan's foreign policy.

It was, as often happens, too good to be true. A British force remained in Kabul, but it was merely a personal guard of some 100 men for the envoy, Major Pierre Louis Napoleon Cavagnari; most of the British forces went home to India. The unpopularity of the treaty and of Yakub Khan for signing it fed local animosity. A mutiny in the Afghan

"Cabul expeditionary force on the march: Quarter Guard of the 3rd Goorkhas. Sketch by Lieutenant C. Pulley, of the 3rd Goorkhas. Nov 30, 1878." An image depicting the fight for Kabul during the Second Afghan War.

army resulting from a demand for back pay led to an attack on the British residency, where the soldiers were sure money could be found. After an all-day battle, the Afghans wiped out the British force in Kabul, losing only 600 men. Roberts, a national hero for his exploits earlier in the war, was ordered to avenge the slaughter, marking the beginning of the second half of the war, sometimes regarded as the Third Afghan War. As Roberts's force moved northwestward up the Karrum Valley, Yakub Khan went there to plead his innocence in Cavagnari's death and hopefully slow down the British advance. Roberts had little time for him, and continued marching his force of 6,600 men toward Kabul. Twelve miles short of the city, the British met their first serious resistance. A sharp engagement on 6 October 1879 at the bridge at Charasia resulted in a British victory and control of Kabul. Roberts followed his orders to find and publicly execute Cavagnari's killers; with this completed and the British installed in Kabul, it seemed a quick end to rebellion.

Roberts bivouacked his men in a well-fortified camp, but did not occupy the major Afghan fortress overlooking Kabul. In the countryside, religious leaders stirred up the tribesmen against the British, and once again lines of communication were harassed or cut. By the end of 1879, several Afghan forces began moving on Kabul, and Roberts's force was besieged on 14 December. He was well supplied and his troops well disciplined, so they held the much larger Afghan army at bay. The siege was short. Failing to overcome British defenses during a major assault on the night of 22 December, the Afghan troops left the city. Still, Roberts was not safe. A British-Indian force under Sir Donald Stewart marched northward from the fort at Kandahar, some 300 miles southwest, to relieve Roberts. Stewart's army of 14,000 secured the British hold on the city when they arrived in May 1880, but word soon arrived that Kandahar was under siege and a British force at Maiwand in southern Afghanistan had been badly beaten. Stewart, the ranking officer in Kabul, sent Roberts to relieve Kandahar. This march was followed closely by the British public and further secured Roberts's reputation. He left Kabul on 9 August with 10,000 men. As he approached Kandahar on 25 August, he received word from the garrison that the besieging forces had left to attack his column. Kandahar was relieved on 31 August, and Roberts's men dealt a severe defeat to the Afghan army the next day. Now seemed like a good time to go home.

The British left Afghanistan, the terms of the treaty now forgotten. They had no representative in Kabul, and did not direct Afghanistan's foreign affairs. The Second Afghan War, like the first, was of no value to the British Empire. Britain continued to fear Russian incursions into the country as late as World War I, but without reason. The Afghans proved too tough a nut for the British to crack; victory on the battlefield did not translate into political victory, and the Afghans remained fiercely independent. In the 1970s, they educated the Russians with the same lessons they had taught the British in 1842 and 1880.

References: Adams, James Truslow, *Building the British Empire* (New York: Scribner's Sons, 1938); Bilgrami, Ashgar, *Afghanistan and British India, 1793–1907* (New Delhi: Sterling Press, 1972); Farwell, Byron, *Queen Victoria's Little Wars* (New York: Harper & Row, 1972).

AFRICA, FRENCH OCCUPATIONS IN
127

After losing its claims in India in the late 1700s, France turned toward Africa and the Far East for colonies. French success in Africa was mixed; along the Mediterranean coast, France gained territory almost by accident, while deeper in the interior, the expansion was gradual and driven mainly by the men on the spot.

Equatorial Africa

France had held trading posts on the far western African coast at Senegal since the late 1700s, and from there the French looked inland. Through the first half of the nineteenth century, European outposts on the west coast had been involved mainly in suppressing the slave trade, but the growing commercial relations with local tribes created European rivalry by the 1860s. In order to gain the dominant share of nuts, palm oil, and other local products, France and Britain began making treaties with as many local chieftains as possible. Between 1854 and 1864, the French carried out a war against the Tukulors, and that fighting took them toward the Niger River. They spent the next 25 years solidifying their hold on the upper Niger area, then fought three wars against the Mandingo of the Ivory Coast, finally claiming that area by 1898. Meanwhile, forces from the French possessions along the Congo River joined with troops invading from Algeria to capture Chad. France was now predominant in the Sahara, and aimed toward a possible transcontinental link reaching from the Atlantic to the Indian Ocean, where France had a colony at Somaliland. French troops reached Fashoda on the upper Nile in 1898, but faced a much larger British force recently arrived from Egypt. After a tense period, the French government ordered a withdrawal, and the British kept alive their own dream of a transcontinental Cape-to-Cairo land link.

Madagascar

During the initial rush in the 1600s for Far East markets, France established a temporary settlement at Fort Dauphin on Madagascar, off Africa's eastern coast. It failed to maintain itself, and for a time France settled for posts on the smaller islands of He de France (Mauritius) and Bourbon. By the 1800s, France had secured treaty rights for protection of French nationals on Madagascar, but the dominant Hova government leaned more toward British than French interests. In 1883,

French warships bombarded the towns of Majunga and Tamatave and landed troops, forcing the acceptance of a French protectorate. The locals resisted the French presence, sometimes under the direction of British officers. The resistance provoked another bombardment of Tamatave in 1894, followed by an invasion the following year. French General Jacques Duchesne landed 15,000 men on the island and began a methodical invasion against violent resistance. By 1896 the island was declared a French colony. A military government deposed the queen and continued to fight the revolts, finally suppressing the locals by 1905.

French colonization was undertaken more for European prestige than for profit or raw materials. Almost none of the colonies made money, and most cost unreasonable amounts to acquire. After the suppression of piracy on the Mediterranean coast, France had no real interests there, and the acquisition of the Saharan colonies gained land but little else. By World War II, French possessions across the upper part of the continent included Mauritania, Senegal, Dahomey, the Ivory Coast, Guinea, French Guinea, French Sudan, Upper Volta, and Niger. Chad, Gabon, and the Middle Congo made up France's equatorial colonies, and the mandates acquired after the Versailles Treaty gave it Togoland and Cameroon. For much of the nineteenth century, France exercised the traditional mercantilist view of colonies—that they should exist for the benefit of the mother country. Exclusive import and export rights were maintained not only to profit the French, but also to keep out other European countries. The population of the colonies remained subject to French rule, with little chance of gaining French citizenship and legal rights. Only Algeria came to be regarded as a department in the French governmental system. Local French administrators attempted to apply French political philosophies, but found the native populations so hostile to their presence that the governors resorted to whatever measures were necessary to maintain order. Only after World War II did France begin to let its colonies go. In 1960, almost all French colonies in Africa became sovereign states, though most maintained some ties with France. Only French Somaliland remained an overseas territory.

North Africa

France first acquired land in Algeria in the north and moved east and west from there. Gaining Algeria was expensive, and further expansion was not politically popular at home, but Tunisia almost begged to be taken over. The ruler of Tunisia, the bey of Tunis, borrowed heavily from France and other European powers to finance an independence movement to break away from the Ottoman Empire. Once accomplished, Tunisia needed more money for modernization. Ultimately, it was too heavily in debt to meet the payments, and in 1869 a multinational European commission entered the country to administer its finances. France was the largest creditor, but had no desire to annex the country. When Italy showed an active interest in taking over, however, French forces crossed the border in 1881 and obliged the bey to sign an agreement making his country a French protectorate. During the expedition, there was a local uprising against the French and the bey, and French forces occupied the entire country. Though the bey remained in nominal control after the revolt, for the most part Tunisia was a French possession.

With such strong control over a stretch of the Mediterranean coast, it is not surprising that the French became interested in Morocco to the west. Italy also showed an interest, but an agreement in 1900 ceded French interests in Morocco in return for Italian interests in Tripoli (Libya). Both were off-limits according to international agreements protecting the property of the Ottoman Empire, but in the rush for African colonies at the turn of the twentieth century, those pacts carried little weight. Owing to their ever-friendlier relationship from 1904, Britain granted France permission to act; when Moroccan bandits raided across the Algerian border, the French responded. France demanded control of the Moroccan police forces to maintain order in the deteriorating political environment; the Moroccan government was under pressure not only from Europe but from popular uprisings in the hinterland. When Germany objected to French actions and began to show interest in the country as well, international hostilities loomed. Only the Algeciras Conference of

1906–1907 kept the peace; France and Spain were given equal rights in Morocco, with an Open Door economic policy for the rest of Europe. The ongoing popular unrest brought French naval bombardment of Casablanca in 1907, followed by occupation of the city; Fez was occupied in 1911 for similar reasons. The Treaty of Fez in 1912 made Morocco a French protectorate, and resident General Louis Lyautey began forging a closer relationship between the two nations.

See also Algeria, French Occupation of; Indochina, French Occupation of.

References: Collins, Robert, *Europeans in Africa* (New York: Knopf, 1971); Fieldhouse, D. K., *The Colonial Empires* (New York: Dell, 1966); Pakenham, Thomas, *The Scramble for Africa* (New York: Random House, 1991).

128   AFRICA, GERMAN OCCUPATIONS IN

Germany first began considering colonization in Africa in the Frankfurt National Assembly of 1848. Acquiring territory in Africa seemed a good way to handle surplus populations displaced by changes in German agriculture, as well as provide a focus for national pride in an active foreign policy. Not until the 1880s, however, did any serious colonization begin. By then, Chancellor Otto von Bismarck had led the new German nation into world affairs, and German economic interests viewed Africa as a good source of raw materials. Besides, foreign control of the coastlines by other powers could prove costly to German trade.

Bismarck had long been leery of the idea of colonies, believing them too expensive to administer and defend, but he finally saw them as a tool of international diplomacy. In 1885 he hosted an international conference in Berlin, where ground rules were laid for African land claims by European powers. At the time, few other European diplomats considered Germany a player in the colonization game. The first colony Germany claimed was Cameroon in 1884. German trading posts had been in the area for some years, and it appeared the British might claim the land first, but Dr. Gustav Nachtigal signed treaties with the two main kings in Cameroon and declared it a German protectorate.

Cameroon was not an economically successful venture, and its acquisition often came under attack by anticolonial factions in Germany. German plantations were successful, but not lucrative enough to pay for the colony's administration. In the 1890s and early 1900s, the colony was newsworthy in Germany for the scandals perpetrated by its governor, Jesco von Puttkamer. He was accused and convicted of financial misadventures and gross mistreatment of natives, both common and royal. He was fined only slightly, however, and recalled from his post.

About the same time the Germans took over Cameroon, they signed agreements with the chiefs in Little Popo, or Togoland. The most successful of the German colonial ventures, Togoland became a model colony, consistently showing a trade surplus and paying for its administration. Local profit meant a looser rein from Berlin, so Togoland also became the scene of scandal and abuse of the native population. Though profitable, Togoland did not hold enough raw materials or profits to be more than a minor success.

The largest of the German colonies was Southwest Africa, stretching from the Portuguese colony of Angola southward 900 miles to the Orange River, beyond which lay the British Cape Colony. The Portuguese originally discovered this territory, but their missionaries had little success there, and it was transferred to the control of the Rhenish Missionary Society of Germany. Bismarck stated that the "missionary and trader must precede the soldier," and within 10 years German clerics had established missions in a number of tribal capitals. The political and military presence was not far behind; German forces intervened in tribal warfare between the Herero and Nama tribes. The Herero signed a protection treaty with the German imperial commissioner in 1885; when the Nama waged guerrilla warfare instead, the Germans led punitive expeditions against them until their surrender in 1894.

There was little source of income in Southwest Africa. The Nama and Herero were cattle herders who did not care to trade their herds to the Germans until 1897, when a plague of rinderpest virtually wiped out their cattle, and they had to sell their lands and possessions to buy vaccinations or new cattle. The German colonists gained the best land available, and the already poor natives were in even direr straits. Many came to the missions for aid and conversion, and German governor Theodor von Leutwein was sure that his administration was maintaining peace and a prosperity of sorts. The German settlers robbed the natives and made them as subservient as possible, which provoked a Herero rebellion in January 1904. Some 200,000 Africans lived in the colony, compared to a German population of about 4,700. The Herero killed every German male who could bear arms, but spared women, children, and non-Germans. They slaughtered inhabitants of isolated farms, but were unable to assault the better-fortified towns.

In February, although Leutwein seemed back in control, Berlin replaced him with General Lothar von Trotha, who had orders to put down the rebellion by any means necessary. The small number of German soldiers in the country could not keep the rebellion down, but with reinforcements from Germany, Trotha attacked the Herero and drove them into the desert, placing guards at every waterhole. With the Herero defeated, Trotha next had to deal with a Nama revolt in October 1904. Guerrilla warfare raged for a year, and both sides suffered badly. Trotha was eventually ordered home in disgrace, but the Nama capitulated in October 1905.

The colony of German East Africa was claimed in the 1880s as well, though German and British traders had long dealt with the sultan of Zanzibar for goods from the interior. In 1885, Carl Peters, the head of the Company for German Colonization, snuck into the region and made with local chiefs a number of suspect treaties, all of which Bismarck supported. In 1888, the sultan of Zanzibar granted Peters's company the administration of the southern coast of East Africa in return for a percentage of the profits. The high-handed German administration insulted Muslim sensibilities and tightened tax collection. German troops and warships enforced their will and challenged the authority of the sultan in his own territory, provoking a revolt among the locals that lasted through the spring of 1889. The British had long supported the sultan, but in this instance they sided with

Germany to "suppress the slave trade" by blockading the coast and allowing the Germans to send in troops. Germany established itself as the dominant European power, but could only hold on to the colony until World War I.

Germany had entered Africa in search of prestige and raw materials, but gained only the former. Though Togoland proved somewhat profitable, none of the other colonies financially justified German efforts. Sending major military support was too costly, so when World War I occurred, the Germans did nothing to save their colonies or take advantage of the raw materials they might have provided. The League of Nations mandated all the German colonies in Africa, mostly to Great Britain. The Germans left behind little but a memory of European abuses.

See also East Africa, British Invasion of.

References: Pakenham, Thomas, *The Scramble for Africa* (New York: Random House, 1991); Smith, Woodruff, *The German Colonial Empire* (Chapel Hill: University of North Carolina Press, 1978); Townsend, Mary Evelyn, *Origins of Modern German Colonialism* (New York: Howard Fertig, 1974).

ALGERIA, FRENCH OCCUPATION OF

129

Long a part of the Ottoman Empire, the regency of Algiers was one of the bases of the notorious Barbary pirates, who harassed or extorted bribes from international shipping passing through the western Mediterranean. Because the country's Ottoman occupiers never numbered more than 15,000, the French had little trouble removing the Turkish janissaries during their 1830 invasion. An insult by the local Ottoman ruler to the French consul after a dispute over debt payment provoked the attack. The French discovered that Ottoman rule was limited merely to coastal and urban areas, while the outlying countryside held only the occasional Turkish garrison cooperating with a few Arab tribes. The Berber population in the rugged terrain was beyond the direct authority of the Turks. The Turks recognized their inability to establish control in the mountains, so did not try.

At first, the French copied Ottoman practices, but they became too ambitious. Presenting themselves as liberators from Ottoman rule, the

French moved into the countryside and found only resistance. The only local groups who would cooperate with them were the urban Jews, long a despised segment of the local population. By allying themselves with the Jews, the Christian French did not endear themselves to the Muslim majority of the country. From the first, the Algerians resented and resisted the French occupation, and organized themselves behind the leadership of Abd al-Kadir, who wanted not only to free his country from outside dominance but also to establish a united Muslim state. Abd al-Kadir took the title of amir and led a jihad, or holy war, against the French. Under his direction, the frontier population organized a Muslim administration that maintained a tax system, a standing army of 10,000, strategically placed forts, and Muslim schools and courts. Initially, the French were willing to recognize Abd al-Kadir as ruler of the interior, but conflict was inevitable. By 1846, more than 100,000 French troops were in the country, and the Arabs could not defeat such superior numbers. In 1847, Abd al-Kadir surrendered and went into exile.

For the first 20 years of their occupation, the French had administered Algeria (so named in 1839) via the Ministry of War, which appointed governors-general to rule. They were later assisted by the establishment of an Arab Bureau, which proved to be more condescending to the locals than helpful to the military. The French solidified their hold on the country by encouraging immigration, and by the time Abd al-Kadir was defeated, the new citizens numbered some 109,000 from all parts of the western Mediterranean. The majority were laborers and craftspeople, but some wealthy French bought large estates. Most of the immigrants had fled France after the revolution in 1848, escaped political upheaval in Alsace and Lorraine after the Franco-Prussian War, or moved to new vineyards when a blight destroyed much of the French wine industry in 1880. The new population tended to settle along the coast, but were protected from the hostile country folk by large numbers of French soldiers.

Uprisings by native tribes were put down through the remainder of the nineteenth century, and French control over the entire country was established in 1900. The most significant resistance to the French government occurred in 1870, when the French military suppressed a revolt in the mountain area of the Kabyles and confiscated most of the land. That same year, the European population rebelled against the rule of Napoleon III, who quieted them by granting local autonomy and reducing the power of the military. Algeria had been declared legally a part of France in 1848, but a French-style government was not installed until 1871.

The country was soon divided into three major areas: the coastal zone, mainly populated by Europeans; the countryside, mostly populated by Muslim Berbers; and the Sahara, which harbored numerous nomadic tribes and was the province of the army. The Europeans dominated the government and the courts. The native Berber population interacted with the French by working for them, occasionally going to French schools, and often moving to France to work. By 1831, the centenary of the invasion, the French occupation appeared to be a rousing success. French writers trumpeted the civilizing influence of the French presence and the economic progress the country had enjoyed.

Underneath the façade, however, was a growing discontent among the Muslim population. Education in French schools had taught them about the ideals of the French Revolution—liberty, equality, fraternity. The Berbers enjoyed none of these rights. The first hint of resistance came in 1912 when native organizations called for equality under the law in return for conscription into the French military. After World War I, during which Algerian soldiers fought and died in the trenches of France, the calls for equality grew louder. In 1920, two native movements began, one calling for equality and assimilation into European Algerian society, and the other demanding independence and a severing of ties with France.

Through the 1930s and 1940s, more organizations sprang up to demand either equal rights or liberation. During World War II, the Algerians again demanded equal rights in return for military service, but the Vichy government suppressed the protest groups, and the Free French under Charles de Gaulle granted only minor concessions. By mid-century, the native population had plenty to complain about. More than one-third of the eight million Muslims in the country were landless, another million were underemployed, 90 percent of the Berber population was illiterate, and a quarter of them spoke only Berber. The French military in Algeria was made up of foreign soldiers, with few Algerians. The European population owned 90 percent of the industry and 40 percent of the best land. After the Europeans rigged the elections of 1948, 1951, and 1953 to maintain their power in the government, violence seemed the only alternative for native resistance groups. Egyptian president Nasser offered military officers to help organize a revolt.

Violent protests broke out under the leadership of the Front de Liberation Nationale, or FLN. The FLN started a campaign of terrorism in November 1954, aimed not at removing its enemies, but at removing the moderates who encouraged assimilation of the two societies. The FLN hoped this would provoke a massive response by the French military that would create hostility on the part of the population. Instead, the government in France installed a new, more liberal governor-general who appointed large numbers of Muslims to positions in the government and civil service, and forbade reprisals by the local gendarmes. The FLN responded by initiating a program of genocide toward the European population, a strategy that provoked the violent government response originally intended. Both the FLN and the government forces engaged in slaughter, with thousands of innocents caught in the middle. In January 1957, the government gave the military carte blanche to deal with the FLN in any manner they desired, legal or not. The murder and torture that resulted provoked a critical response in France, which called for negotiation with the FLN to lead toward Algerian independence.

The French army generals, both in Algeria and France, were loath to lose to the terrorists. When it seemed that the government was going to give in to public opinion, the generals threatened a coup, which brought Charles de Gaulle out of retirement and into the government. The Fifth Republic was established and de Gaulle was elected president in late 1958. Thus, the generals got what they asked for, but not what they bargained for. Because President de Gaulle had long ago realized the futility of continuing colonial rule anywhere, he was determined to remove France from Algeria. Publicly, he continued to support the generals and their policies, but privately he worked to secure his own power base so he could accomplish his goals.

The referendum that created the Fifth Republic also allowed colonies to decide for themselves whether to stay with France or go their own way. De Gaulle began removing the same generals who had brought him to power. He opened negotiations with the FLN in mid-1960, and the Algerians voted for independence in January 1961. The military in Algeria was furious, and rogue generals created the Organization de L'Armee Secrete (OAS) to fight their government's decision. So intent were they on maintaining French power in Algeria that they tried twice to assassinate de Gaulle. They also initiated the same type of terror campaign the FLN had started, and again the innocents suffered. The government approved any measures to destroy the OAS, and once again torture and imprisonment were rife. The vote for independence meant that the European population was in danger from Algerian Muslims, who attacked Jewish businesses and synagogues. In 1962 the Europeans left in large numbers, first destroying many of the things they had created: hospitals, schools, libraries, a university. Some 1.3 million inhabitants left for France, leaving anyone who had cooperated with them at the mercy of the new regime. Thousands of locals who could not afford to leave were murdered by the government created by the FLN.

The departure of the French after 130 years in Algeria left the country in dire straits. The first president of the new government later commented that the only accomplishments during the first 20 years of local rule were negative: Agriculture was destroyed, industry was nonexistent, the government was corrupt, and the leaders were uncooperative with each other. The terrorism brought to the country by the FLN was exported when Algeria became a training base for terrorists of all kinds. The crime and disorder in which the country was born presaged similar conditions in other African countries that gained independence from the 1960s onward.

See also France, German Invasion of; France, Nazi Invasion of.

References: Gordon, David, *The Passing of French Algeria* (London: Oxford University Press, 1966); Henissary, Paul, *Wolves in the City: The Death of French Algeria* (New York: Simon & Schuster, 1970); O'Ballance, Edgar, *The Algerian Insurrection* (Hamden, CT Archon Books, 1967).

ASHANTI, BRITISH CONQUEST OF

130

The people who became the Ashanti migrated into the area of modern Ghana in the seventeenth century, moving into an area bounded by two strong powers, the Denkyra to the north and the Akwamu to the east. For a time they paid tribute to the Denkyra but began to organize against them. The Kumasi tribe led a confederation (Asante) of tribes, and Osei Tuto (r.1680?–1717) became the first leader (Asantehene) of the confederation. He had spent time in both the Denkyra and Akwamu courts and had learned military and political lessons from them. Osei led a "war of liberation" against the Denkyra at the turn of the eighteenth century and many Denkyra tributaries changed sides. Being closer to the coast, the Ashanti had better access to European trade and weapons, so gradually the Ashanti defeated the Denkyra and almost all the neighboring tribes, establishing themselves as the major power in the region by the 1740s. A later Asantehene, Osei Kwadwo (r. 1764–1777), established a bureaucracy, police, and standing army. Kwadwo realized that only a standing army would have the time to develop the discipline necessary to be effective with muskets.

The location of the Ashanti homeland was both a help and a hindrance to their economic relations with the Europeans. The Ashanti controlled the northern trade centers to the markets deep in the interior, but they did not control land all the way to the coast, where the Portuguese (later followed by the Dutch, Danes, and British) had built forts and trading posts. Between the Ashanti and the coast lay the lands of the Fante, a population not known for its bravery but very well known for its fear of the Ashanti. The Fante had supported the Ashanti rivals during their ongoing conflicts, but with

the Ashanti now dominating the region, the Fante began regularly calling for aid from whatever European power was at hand. By the 1820s, the primary European power in the region was Great Britain.

After 1807 Great Britain was strongly involved in suppressing the slave trade, one of the primary Ashanti businesses. Thus, conflict between the two became inevitable. After a number of attacks on the Fante in the early part of the century, the British finally committed troops to combat in early 1824 to avenge the death of a Fante soldier in British service. The result was disastrous. Sir Charles MacCarthy led a 500-man force made up primarily of West Indian troops and local recruits against at least 10,000 Ashanti, and on 22 January, MacCarthy died as his troops were defeated. An Ashanti attack on the main British settlement at Cape Coast Castle in 1826, however, was beaten back. That success, though, did not encourage the London government to reinforce the region. Instead, the British decided the cost-benefit ratio was too unfavorable and sent word to abandon the area and destroy the forts. The local merchants managed to convince the government to turn the forts over to them in September 1828.

With a £4,000 annual subsidy from the government, the merchants hired George Maclean, a man with military experience, to be the local administrator. With his local knowledge he was able to deal peaceably with the Ashanti and secure a treaty with them in 1831 which guaranteed Fante security. He remained in that position until his death in 1847, although the Colonial Office in London had reasserted control in 1843. Starting in 1844, with a new agreement signed with the Ashanti, the British began to slowly expand their influence in the region: They bought out the Danish and Portuguese forts in 1850 and the Portuguese forts and lands in 1871. At about this same time the Ashanti began once again to view the British as a threat, for there now existed no more coastal ports for their slave trading.

The Ashanti had continued their raiding into Fante territory in spite of the treaties, and in 1863 the British government stationed a West Indian regiment along the Pra River at Prahsu.

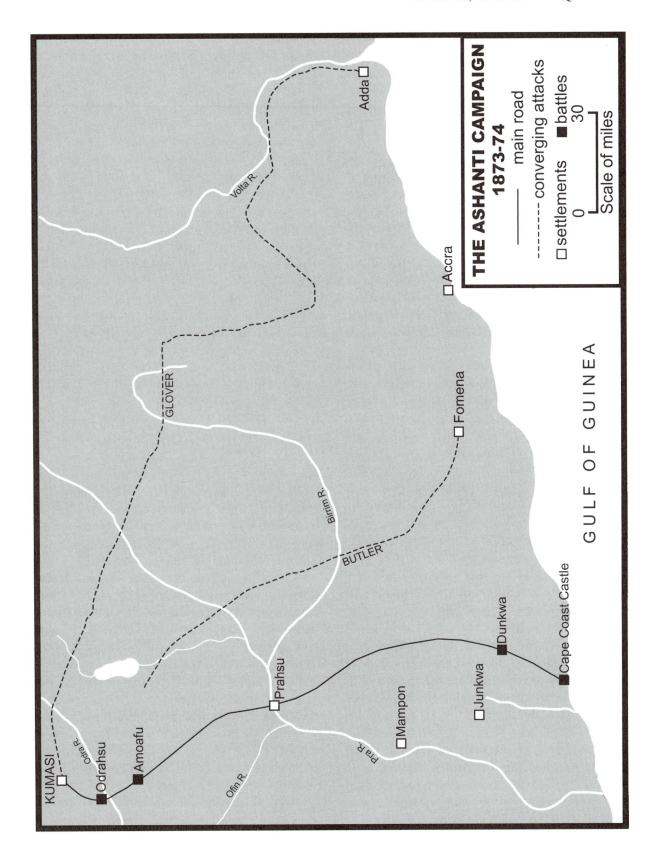

THE ASHANTI CAMPAIGN 1873-74

— main road
------ converging attacks
■ battles
□ settlements

0   30
Scale of miles

GULF OF GUINEA

Adda

Volta R.

Accra

Fomena

GLOVER

Birrim R.

BUTLER

Dunkwa

Cape Coast Castle

Junkwa

Prahsu

Mampon

Pra R.

Ofin R.

KUMASI

Odra R.

Odrahsu

Amoafu

"The operations, badly devised and worse executed," according to Sir Garnet Wolseley's autobiography, "ended in terrible sickness and the loss of life before we made any useful impression on the enemy." This created a political uproar in London, but no reinforcements on site. The Ashanti returned in force in January 1873, occupying much of the Fante land without any response by the British authorities. In June an attack was launched against Elmina, a fort acquired from the Dutch a few miles west of the Cape Coast Castle, but it was beaten back by the garrison of Royal Marines. As there was no follow-up punitive attack, however, "such pusillanimous conduct caused them to believe we were afraid of so great a king and of so great a nation" (Wolseley, *Story*, vol. 2, p. 261). The Ashanti, therefore, continued to harass the Fante while living off their land.

Thus, in August 1873, Secretary of the Colonial Office Lord Kimberly appointed Major General Sir Garnet Wolseley to lead an expedition against the Ashanti, to establish British dominance in the area once and for all. Surrounding himself with a coterie of rising stars in the British officer corps, Wolseley landed in October to find a native population unsuitable for use as troops against the mighty Ashanti. He sent for three battalions from Britain and reinforcements for the West Indian regiment already there. Members of the local Hausa tribe, however, were recruited to man the artillery (with which they had some experience). While awaiting his additional troops, Wolseley and his staff arranged for supplies and recruited local levies for porterage and road building. When the troops arrived, Wolseley kept them in camp for several weeks to try to acclimatize them and to wait for the winter months when the weather was most favorable.

In December 1873 Wolseley had an advanced base constructed at Prahsu, about halfway to the Ashanti capital at Kumasi. Now that the British had indeed arrived in force, and they did not seem to be showing any signs of fear, the Ashanti King Kofi began to see the support of local tribes fade away. By mid-January 1874 Wolseley had 4,000 men at Prahsu supported by seven-pounder guns and rocket launchers.

Wolseley's plan called for other columns (native troops led by British officers) to converge at Kumasi, but in the end only one of them arrived in time for battle. Thus, the bulk of the fighting fell on the regiments of the Black Watch, the Rifle Brigade, and the Welch Fusiliers, along with the West Indian troops, 250 sailors, and some 500 local troops. Wolseley's time prior to the advance had not been wasted, for he had an amazing support system in place. Every 10 miles he had built a station with huts for 700 men, a hospital, water purifiers and storage sheds; at two there were bakeries and at four there were slaughterhouses. Their standard red uniforms were replaced with gray homespun, and one porter was assigned to each three solders to carry their medical gear.

The plan of advance was in an open square formation, but the density of the jungle made it impossible to keep very well organized. Facing the British were some 12,000 Ashanti soldiers armed with muskets, bows, and spears, which could all be used to good effect in the overgrown terrain. The march went well and within five days, on 24 January, the British were within 30 miles of Kumasi. At this point, King Kofi decided it was time to negotiate and offered terms; Wolseley countered with demands he knew could not be met: immense amounts of gold, release of prisoners, and sons of all important chiefs for hostages, as well as surrender of the queen mother and the heir to the throne.

On 31 January combat began with an Ashanti ambush on the British advanced guard. The Black Watch moved forward while the Ashanti attempted a double envelopment. In the heavily wooded terrain there was much confusion, with reports of British units firing on each other at times. Wolseley set up a command post in the center of his square formation. At one point it was attacked and all on hand, including medical personnel, the sick, and war correspondents, were obliged to pick up guns and fight. What came to be called the battle of Amoafu resulted in Ashanti casualties estimated at 2,000.

The British force advanced on toward Kumasi, but the Ashanti continued to harass them from the flanks and rear. Halfway to Kumasi were the Orda River and the village of Ordahsu. On the high ground behind these, the

Ashanti had dug themselves a strong position. While reconnoitering, Wolseley received another message from King Kofi, granting all the previous demands except his heir and the queen mother. Wolseley sent a small force across the Orda to cover the construction of a bridge, which was completed that night in a driving rainstorm. The morning of the fourth proved that Kofi had not acceded to terms, as a two-hour battle for control of Ordahsu took place. Upon its capture, the British had to defend it the rest of the morning from attacks on all sides. By noon it was solidly in British hands and supplies had been brought up. Wolseley ordered the Black Watch to attack the six miles up the road to Kumasi, ignoring their flanks. By that evening, an abandoned Kumasi was in their hands. Wolseley wrote that "as soon as we burst out of Ordahsu and had taken the road to Koomassee [sic], the Ashantee [sic] army collapsed and made no further effort to oppose us."

Wolseley led his force out of Kumasi on 6 February, leaving behind a team of "prize agents" to take away what was valuable, and a team of engineers to blow up and burn the rest. His force had suffered a total of 13 killed and 368 wounded in the battles at Amoafu and Ordahsu. They destroyed every village they passed on their march back to the coast. At Fomena, Wolseley received word from King Kofi that he would sign a peace treaty. On 4 March Wolseley and his staff were on a steamer back to England.

The terms of the treaty were that the Ashanti would pay an indemnity in gold, give up any claim to neighboring provinces and populations, and abandon the practice of human sacrifice. This treaty marked the end of the Ashanti as a military power. Kofi was deposed a year later and the nation broke up into rival factions. Great Britain declared the Gold Coast to be a crown colony, but the Ashanti Empire was not included. In spite of the treaty promises, Ahsanti attacks into Fante territory continued irregularly over the next few decades. In 1894, another punitive expedition in response to Ashanti raids obliged the Ashanti King Prempah to accept protectorate status from the British. The following year, Prempah refused to pay an indemnity and the British once again

invaded and captured Kumasi. Prempah was taken prisoner and exiled to the Seychelles. The British once again declared the region a protectorate, but did not occupy it with troops, although they did build a fort in Kumasi. In 1900, the British tried to gain possession of the Golden Stool, seat of Ashanti kings. Rather than surrender it, the Ashanti laid siege to the fort in Kumasi. Attempts to relieve the garrison proved costly to both sides, but the British finally suppressed the rebellion and on New Year's Day 1902 declared the Ashanti Empire to be a British possession.

After World War I, nationalist movements began to emerge, and by the mid-1930s, the Ashanti were allowed limited autonomy. At the end of the Second World War the British allowed the locals to elect the Ghana Legislative Council. For 10 years a liberation movement grew until, in 1957, the British granted Ghana independence.

131 CEYLON, BRITISH OCCUPATION OF

The Dutch were the dominant European power in Ceylon from the 1650s. They exploited the island's trade goods, but in general treated the natives fairly. Britain wanted the island nation, not so much as a trading center but for its harbors, most particularly Trincomalee on the east coast. When Napoleon took control of Europe, Britain went after the continental countries' colonies to put economic pressure on the French dictator's holdings. At this time, the British moved seriously against Ceylon. In 1796 they worked their way around the island's perimeter, capturing its ports, until the major Dutch base at Colombo fell without a fight. The island was initially controlled by the British East India Company, which replaced the Dutch East India Company as ruling body. Unlike the Dutch and Portuguese, the British refused to cooperate with the local power structure, and England's high-handed manner provoked local revolts. In 1798 the Crown took over the country, installing Frederick North as the governor-general. By dealing with unscrupulous pretenders in Ceylon's royal families, North managed to perpetuate the natives' hostility to the British. The most serious resistance came, as previous foreign powers had learned, from the mountain kingdom of Kandy. Sri Wickrama Rajasinha fought the British until 1815, when he was finally captured and deported to India, ending a 2,300-year-old line of rulers. Having established control, the British tried to make up for their shaky start. They introduced legal and political reforms through a paternal administration, hoping to bring about progress for the native population. They improved the road system, abolished forced labor, and, with the Colebrook Reforms of 1833, broke down the feudal system that had dominated the island since time immemorial. They promoted agriculture (mainly the beginning of coffee plantations), opened schools, and installed the civil service system from India, to which locals could apply after they had learned to speak English.

The power, however, remained with the British, who believed the island was too racially divided to fairly govern itself. They appointed a legislative council to act in an advisory capacity to the governor-general. In time, as the local population pressed for more say in the government, seats were added on the council (some of them elective), but the council stayed in an advisory role. In 1915 open revolt, though quelled, brought attention to the people's need for more voice in the government. The British made the council popularly elected by constitutional change in 1924, but the franchise was so limited by education and property restrictions that only four percent of the people could vote. In 1927, the British government's Donoughmore Commission called for a new constitution, which went into effect in 1931. This document granted universal suffrage in Ceylon, the first Asian country to acquire it.

Some popular resentment, mainly from the Tamils in the northern part of the island, still remained. In 1942, the country pressed for dominion status, which was finally granted in 1947. Ceylon was declared independent in 1948. True to the original British fear, there was enough ethnic division in the country to create trouble. When the dominant Sinhalese made their language the official language of the nation in the 1950s, the Tamils, who were strong in the civil service at that time, protested. Through the next several decades, the Tamils led a violent resistance to the ruling Sinhalese.

See also Ceylon, Dutch Occupation of; Ceylon, Portuguese Occupation of; Napoleon Buonaparte.

References: Beny, Roloff, *Island Ceylon* (London: Thames & Hudson, 1970); Codrington, Humphrey, *A Short History of Ceylon* (Freeport, NY: Books for Libraries, 1926); Tresidder, Argus, *Ceylon: An Introduction to the Resplendent Land* (Princeton, NJ: Van Nostrand, 1960).

CHINA, BRITISH INVASION OF (OPIUM WAR)

132

The British had been trading in Chinese ports in a mutually profitable enterprise from the 1790s, but a wise observer could have foreseen trouble from the start. The two peoples were too much alike, both convinced of the superiority of their culture over all others and unwilling to concede anything to the other. When the first British ambassador refused to kowtow to the emperor in Peking in 1792, the clash of cultures began. The British military action beginning in 1839 came to be known as the Opium War, but that was merely a handy excuse, much like the destruction of tea in Boston leading to the American Revolution.

The illegal importation of opium from India to China was practiced openly and proved lucrative for both parties, but the wide introduction of the drug offended many in Chinese society, who saw it as a foreign attempt to weaken their culture. Chinese officials were easily bribed until January 1839, when an unbribable imperial high commissioner from Peking began a crackdown. He withdrew all Chinese labor from foreign warehouses and laid siege until 20,000 cases of opium were surrendered. It was all handled peacefully, so the British had no excuse for military intervention. Six weeks later, a brawl in Kowloon ended with a Chinese death at the hands of a British or American national, and the Chinese government demanded the culprit's surrender for punishment. The foreign refusal led to another withdrawal of Chinese labor and the exile of British personnel to the rugged island of Hong Kong. Chinese smugglers under the protection of two British frigates supplied the British in Hong Kong. The Chinese government sent 29 war junks to stop the smuggling. Shots were exchanged, and the Chinese suffered losses.

This was excuse enough for action. The British government ordered a siege of Canton until the Chinese signed a treaty guaranteeing British trading rights. The forts around Canton fell fairly easily, and on 20 January 1841, representatives of the two nations signed the Convention of Chuenpi. This agreement ceded Hong Kong to the British, awarded them $6 million in damages, and granted open trading rights in Canton. Both the Chinese and British governments repudiated the agreement. Chinese forces began gathering near Canton, but the British struck first and attacked the city in late May 1841. A naval victory, coupled with the occupation of the heights overlooking the city, convinced the Chinese army to withdraw. The British force of 3,500 prepared to occupy a city of some one million inhabitants. The British government representative, Sir Charles Elliot, stepped in and negotiated another $6 million ransom, which saved the city.

Queen Victoria's government did not care for this arrangement either. Elliot was replaced by Sir Henry Pottinger, and more troops and ships were sent. Major General Sir Hugh Cough's forces marched north, capturing four cities before settling in for the winter. Chinese counterattacks in the spring of 1842 were repulsed, with heavy Chinese losses. The British captured the ports of Hangchow and Shanghai with few losses in the first occupation and none in the second. They soon captured Chinkiang, and were at the gates of Nanking by August. The emperor had had enough. The Treaty of Nanking laid China open to foreign exploitation by guaranteeing trading rights that favored outside interests. It also gave the British $21 million; entitled them to exclusive use of the "treaty ports" of Canton, Amoy, Foochow, Ningpo, and Shanghai; set low tariffs; and gave the British legal jurisdiction over their own nationals. There was no mention of opium.

The British actions in China altered the economic patterns of the world. The practice of granting treaty ports soon extended to other countries, and by the end of the nineteenth century, Britain, France, Russia, Germany, and Japan had staked out the entire Chinese coast in separate economic spheres of influence. In 1899, this began to change when the United States lobbied for an Open Door policy allowing all foreigners equal access to all of China. This arrangement permitted a rapid response in 1900 when a multi-national force entered China to save foreign nationals from the Boxer uprising. The force strengthened the positions of the outside powers and cost China even more indemnities.

The Chinese fear of foreign corruption of their culture also came true. The close trading contacts brought Western ideas and technology into China. This flow of goods and information lasted until the Japanese invaded China in 1937 and the Communists took over the government in 1949. After that, China's isolation lapsed only through one port—Hong Kong. For the British, acquiring Hong Kong was easily the most significant result of the Opium Wars. Its location off the Chinese coastal city of Canton and the island's outstanding harbor turned Hong Kong into an economic treasure for Britain. Though granted ownership of the island in the Convention of Chuenpi, the agreement's repudiation meant Britain and China ultimately had to come to another arrangement. The British lease on the island ended in 1997. Hong Kong is now administered by China under the "one country, two systems" policy, which allows the island considerable autonomy. However, the economic base the British established in the 1840s became, and remains, China's main economic outlet to the world.

See also China, Japanese Invasion of.

References: Farwell, Byron, *Queen Victoria's Little Wars* (New York: Harper & Row, 1985); Owen, David E., *British Opium Policy in China and India* (Hamden, CT Archon Books, 1968); Steeds, David, *China, Japan and Nineteenth Century Britain* (Dublin: Irish University Press, 1977).

CONGO, BELGIAN OCCUPATION OF

Of all the sad stories of European colonization in Africa, few if any can rival that of Belgium's King Leopold II's takeover of the Congo. Like many European rulers of the late nineteenth century, Leopold believed that the path to international greatness and respect was through the acquisition of colonies. His people and his government had no similar desires, so Leopold was forced to embark on a personal quest for colonies. He organized the *Association Internationale Africaine*, disguised as a scientific and philanthropic society, to be the screen behind which he would operate. In 1879, the Association hired famous explorer Henry Stanley to go into the area along the Congo River to establish treaty relations with the tribes there. Stanley, with little respect for the natives anyway, convinced the chiefs that the treaties were of friendship only; in actuality, the treaties were land grants. Thus, Leopold had his colony.

Colonies at the time were not only viewed as marks of status and chips in the great game of diplomacy, but primarily as sources of raw materials. It was the Congo's supply of rubber and ivory that lured Leopold, and whatever profits were made went solely to him, as the Belgian government had never done anything to support this venture. The only way to get the rubber and ivory out of the region was by recruiting local labor. Unfortunately, while acting under the guise of abolitionist, Leopold's agents in the Congo immediately began a peonage that was about as close to slavery as possible. Each region in the colony was to provide a set amount of rubber and ivory per year, as well as a full-time labor force equaling 10 percent of their population and part-time labor equaling 25 percent. The rubber and ivory were paid for, but at a fixed price set by Leopold's people that was far below market value.

Henry Morton Stanley, who while famously locating Dr. Livingstone, also established treaties which laid the groundwork for Belgium's King Leopold II's takeover of the Congo.

Leopold was able to obtain international sanction for his enterprise in an international conference held in Berlin in 1884–1885. Almost the entire continent of Africa was being claimed by one European country or another, often with barely a visit by some European national upon which to stake a claim. Under the chairmanship of German Chancellor Otto von Bismarck, the conference agreed that only a nation exercising effective control over an area could claim it as a colony. Since that was the case with Leopold, he was granted ownership of what was called the Congo Free State. Just what was "free" about it is unknown, but the name stuck until 1908.

Leopold now began to exploit the Congo in earnest. He announced that any uncultivated land belonged to the state, that is, himself. Thus, all rights for what raw materials came from the Congo were his. It wasn't just the forced labor that made Leopold's actions such a crime, but the way in which his rule was carried out. He commissioned a *Force Publique* to maintain both order and production. It was composed of white employees and locally recruited head hunters, both armed with the most modern weapons and with hippo-hide whips called chicottes. It was the actions of the *Force Publique* that made the conditions of the Congolese population so intolerable. The police were told to make sure each tribe produced the necessary rubber and ivory quota, or to terrorize them into obedience by cutting off a hand. Indeed, in order to justify the use of a bullet while on patrol, a policeman had to bring in a hand to show he wasn't just wasting ammunition. Pillage, rape, and looting also were encouraged in order to "maintain order."

The number of people who were worked to death, died for some imagined crime, or died of mutilation, is unknown. The torture and inhumanity did become known to the outside world, which was slow in believing that the supposedly anti-slavery philanthropist could be guilty of anything so heinous. Leopold was good at covering his tracks. Any foreign business interests had to gain permission from him in order to trade and kept such a license only at his discretion; hence, it did not pay to publicize. Although one of the supposed reasons for establishing rule in the Congo in the first place was to bring "civilization," only

Belgian Catholic priests who would do what they were told were allowed to establish missions. Slowly, however, the truth began to leak out.

One of the first to bring tragic tales out of the Congo was English naturalist and writer Mary Kingsley, who wrote about the practices of missionaries in Africa. Her writing inspired E. D. Morel to do in-depth research on the situation in the Congo, resulting in the publication of a series of articles, called *The Congo Scandal*, in 1900. Leopold responded by creating a supposedly independent commission to investigate, but unsurprisingly it turned up no evidence of any wrongdoing. In 1902, Joseph Conrad published *Heart of Darkness*, a novelized account of his travels up the Congo River. In 1903, the British House of Commons called for a real investigation commission. British Consul Sir Robert Casement issued an extremely detailed report in 1904 which confirmed Morel's accusations. Parliament called for another international conference to review violations of the 1885 Berlin Agreement. Leopold denied everything and spat out vast amounts of propaganda, but under international pressure the Belgian Parliament conducted their own investigation, which confirmed Casement's findings. The Belgian population, who had never wanted colonies in the first place and had done their best to ignore Leopold's activities, were finally spurred to react.

The main problem to face in the wake of this furor was who would take over the Congo. The Belgian government was the most logical choice, but they did not want the colony any more than they had before. However, in 1908 they took on the position of mandate power for the colony. It found no profit in the colony, since its primary export, rubber, was being produced much more cheaply in Asia and South America.

Since no census was taken in the Congo until 1924, the number of people who died under Leopold's overlordship varies widely. The initial estimates at the time of his fall (he died in 1909) were three million people; later research has gradually expanded the proposed number to as many as 21 million, perhaps half to two-thirds of the population. These were not all, however, owing to Leopold's rule. Casement's report mentioned four main causes of death:

murder, starvation, decrease in birthrate, and diseases, primarily sleeping sickness.

After 1908, the Belgian administration ended the brutality, but did little to bring relief to the Congolese. Native languages, customs, and cultures were ignored in the face of an educational system that was run completely by Catholic (and a few Protestant) missionaries. There was no local autonomy; the government appointed a governor-general to oversee the colony, renamed the Belgian Congo. Not until after World War II did anything resembling democratic reforms begin, with a resultant nationalistic feeling rising throughout the colony. Unfortunately, tribal rivalries overshadowed the progress made toward independence. Two major factions emerged, both demanding independence but with two different goals. Riots in the capital city of Leopoldville (now Kinshasa) in January 1959 sped the Belgian government's plan to decolonize.

By then, direct government control in many areas of the country was non-existent.

Belgium announced in early 1960 that it would grant independence, and did so on 30 June of that year. It did nothing to end the factional warfare, however, for the two parties were supported by rival superpowers the Soviet Union and the United States. The discovery of uranium in the Congo had once again made it a target for outside interests. A variety of governments have come and gone since the declaration of the First Republic in 1960. Tribal warfare in neighboring countries (primarily Uganda and Rwanda) has kept the Congolese parties divided and the country a center of unrest as of this writing.

References: Fage, J. D., *A History of Africa*, 3rd ed. (New York: Routledge, 1989 [1975]); Hochschild, Adam, *King Leopold's Ghost* (New York: Houghton Miffflin, 1998); Meditz, Sandra W., and Tim Merrill, eds., "Zaire, a Country Study, Federal Research Division, Library of Congress (Washington: GPO, 1994); Pakenham, Thomas. (1991) *The Scramble for Africa* (New York: Random House, 1991).

134   CUBA, U.S. INVASION OF

One of Spain's last remaining colonies in the Western Hemisphere was Cuba, which had no desire to remain so. Throughout the nineteenth century, Cuba staged a series of revolts, all of which were crushed by the Spanish. The United States had always taken an interest in Cuba, even considering purchase or invasion of the island at one time or another. The United States was nearly drawn into one of the revolutions in 1873 when a Spanish warship captured a ship running guns to the rebels and executed the crew, which included eight Americans, for piracy. The Spanish quickly paid damage claims to keep the United States out of the conflict, but the Americans kept a close eye on Cuban affairs.

Another revolution in 1895 directly involved the United States. Thousands of refugees fled to American soil, and told of brutal treatment at the hands of the Spanish military. William Randolph Hearst and Henry Pulitzer, pioneers in "yellow journalism," exploited the stories of the Cuban refugees for their own profit, and demanded that the United States intervene. America was again beginning to view itself as a nation of destiny, fated to "take up the white man's burden," so the public was sympathetic to the idea of protecting its weak neighbor against a European oppressor.

The stories coming out of Cuba were indeed horrible, but slanted in favor of the rebels. The newspapers ignored the guerrillas' tactics of assassination and destruction. The Cubans thought

Wreck of the Spanish Reina Mercedes, Santiago, Cuba., ca. 1898, sunk by the Spanish in an effort to block U.S. entry to Santiago Harbor. (Photograph no. 531117, "Wreck of the Spanish Reina Mercedes, Santiago, Cuba., ca. 1898," Record Group 111: Records of the Office of the Chief Signal Officer, 1860–1982; U.S. National Archives and Records Administration – College Park, MD.)

that by employing a scorched-earth strategy, they could make the island economically useless to the Spanish, and thereby convince them to leave. The Spanish policy to fight the guerrillas became the focus of American press attention. To deny the rebels public support, Spain instituted a policy of reconcentrado, rounding up the civilian population and concentrating them in a number of camps around the island. After this was accomplished, anyone outside the camp was immediately assumed to be a rebel and shot on sight. Unfortunately, because the camps lacked basic sanitary facilities, regular water and food supplies, and decent medical care, 200,000–250,000 people died in them. The American public was informed about the situation by the newspapers, and wanted it stopped. By late 1897, American public opinion was growing stronger in favor of intervention, but the reconcentrado policy had nearly brought the revolution to an end.

Two events in February 1898 finally aroused American action. The first was the publication of a private letter written by the Spanish ambassador to the United States. He had written to a friend in Havana that American President William McKinley was weak and would do nothing to interfere in Cuba. The letter was stolen and given to Hearst, who published it as "the worst insult to the United States in its history." On 15 February, the USS Maine, an American battleship docked in the Havana harbor to evacuate Americans should the need arise, mysteriously exploded. Two investigation commissions, one American and one Spanish, came to two opposite opinions; the Americans announced that the sinking resulted from an external explosion, while the Spanish investigation claimed the blast to have been internal. No one ever determined the true culprit, but the sinking was too well timed not to have had rebel connections.

McKinley had to accede to the public outcry for war. Congress authorized military action, and a blockade of Cuba was begun, provoking a Spanish declaration of war. First blood went to the United States when its Pacific fleet destroyed the Spanish ships based in Manila Bay in the Philippines. U.S. action in Cuba had to wait until volunteer units could be raised because the American army was at its normally small peacetime size. After a tragicomedy of errors getting men, horses, and materiel to Cuba, the fighting was very brief. Once the American forces defeated Spanish troops on the hills outside their main base of Santiago in late June and early July, and the U.S. fleet blockaded the Santiago harbor, the Spanish forces surrendered.

The Treaty of Paris of 1898 that ended the war removed Spain from the Western Hemisphere, bringing to an end a presence the Spanish had maintained since 1492. Because the U.S. Congress pledged not to annex Cuba, but merely to free it from Spanish rule, the treaty stated that the United States would occupy the island only until it was determined that the Cubans could rule themselves. This decision came in 1902. After helping the Cubans write a constitution, the United States agreed to leave under certain conditions. Cuba promised never to contract a debt it could not pay or to sign any treaty that might endanger its independence. Cuba also had to agree to an American-sponsored sanitation program aimed at combating yellow fever. The United States further demanded the purchase or lease of a naval base on the island, reserving the right to intervene in Cuba to protect the country. Intervention was intended only during times of external threat, but American forces intervened in 1906 after the second Cuban presidential election. The outgoing president, refusing to concede defeat, announced that he was rejecting the constitution. American forces removed him from power and oversaw peaceful elections. Over the next three decades, the United States periodically intervened for similar reasons. In 1934, President Franklin Roosevelt allowed the Cubans to give up the promises concerning debts and treaties, though the naval base at Guantanamo Bay remained in American hands.

Even when the American armed forces were not on the scene, the Cubans saw plenty of American influence in their country. American investment dominated the Cuban economy, draining much of the wealth from the island. Cuba endured a string of corrupt leaders as well, almost all of whom enriched themselves at public expense. The average inhabitant lived in poverty with minimal chance for advancement. So, in both war and peace, the United States benefited from its involvement in Cuba. The American victory in this "splendid little war" brought the United States into world power status and solidified the American attitude toward treating Latin America as a little brother it could protect or direct as necessary.

See also Philippines, U.S. Invasion of the.

References: Friedel, Frank, *The Splendid Little War* (New York: Dell, 1962); Millis, Walter, *Martial Spirit* (New York: Literary Guild, 1931); Trask, David F. *The War with Spain in 1898* (New York: Macmillan, 1981).

135 EGYPT, BRITISH OCCUPATION OF

In the later part of the nineteenth century, Egypt was a tributary of the Ottoman Empire. Turkey, the base of the empire, was a fading power, the "sick man of Europe." Still, most European countries preferred even a weak Turkey in control of the Bosporus rather than have a strong country, especially Russia, dominate it. Therefore, whenever Turkey got into trouble (such as the occasional Balkan war, or war with Russia), the rest of Europe, and Great Britain, in particular, stepped in to maintain Turkish independence. Britain was also obliged to act in Ottoman territory if British interests were threatened, since Turkey did not have the power to do so. Because of this, Britain came to dominate Egypt.

The event that brought the British to Egypt concerned the Suez Canal. Built by a French company and completed in 1869, the canal became the most popular sailing route to the Far East, and British shipping made up 80 percent of its traffic. The khedive of Egypt, Ismail Pasha, controlled 44 percent of the canal company's shares. Ismail wanted to improve and modernize Egypt, and he spent lavishly. He also spent handsomely on himself, with money borrowed from foreign investors, mainly British and French. Between 1862 and 1875, Egypt's debt rose from £3 million to £100 million. When the Egyptian government could not pay, Ismail bought some time by selling his shares in the canal company to the British government for a mere £4 million.

The sale staved off his creditors for no more than a few months, and the Egyptian government was declared bankrupt in May 1876.

To recover its lost investments, the French government appointed a debt commission to take over Egypt's finances by administering revenues and collecting taxes fairly. Rather than allow the mostly French commission to have too much authority, Britain decided to play a more active role. However, Ismail removed the foreigners from their governmental duties and replaced them with his son Tewfik, who had little success in restoring Egypt's fortunes. In 1879, the Ottoman sultan removed Ismail as khedive and replaced him, not with someone responsible, but with Tewfik. This situation soon proved too much for the Egyptian military. Disliking Tewfik and foreigners in the government, a colonel named Arabi led a revolt that ousted Tewfik in September 1881.

The British government was not in the practice of using its military to bail out troubled businessmen in foreign countries, but this case was different. As part owner of the canal, the British could not allow any domestic disturbance that could potentially translate into restrictions on trade. At the urging of the French president, Britain agreed in early 1882 to join a Franco-British intervention to maintain both order and income. The arrival of foreign troops provoked an even more violent popular uprising. Rather than reinforce, the French parliament voted to withdraw their forces. Britain remained, and took action against Arabi. In July 1882, the Royal Navy bombarded defensive positions around the harbor at Alexandria, then followed this with an invasion in September. Arabi was quickly defeated, and the British placed Lord Cromer in the position of commissioner to restore financial stability.

The British took control on what they assumed would be a temporary basis, but it lasted until after World War II. They had hoped to place a popular liberal ruler in power, but none could be found except Arabi, who was anti-British. At first, Cromer had no official position, but with the backing of the British army, he stayed 23 years. Despite a lack of cooperation in the Egyptian government and occasional foreign-policy problems (most notably a Muslim uprising in the Sudan), Egypt benefited from Britain's administration. The government's finances were better handled; the Egyptian army grew larger and better trained; irrigation, school, and railroad projects were begun; and taxes were levied and collected more fairly.

Britain remained a dominant factor in Egyptian affairs until after World War II, and continued to maintain its interest in the Suez Canal. The Egyptians nationalized the canal in 1956, and an abortive attempt to overthrow the Egyptian government and retake control proved to be Britain's last gasp in the region.

See also Ottoman Empire.

References: Marlowe, John, *Cromer in Egypt* (London: Elek, 1970); Porter, Bernard, *The Lion's Share* (London: Longman, 1975); Robinson, R. E., and J. A. Gallagher, *Africa and the Victorians* (New York: Macmillan, 1961).

FRANCE, PRUSSIAN INVASION OF (FRANCO-PRUSSIAN WAR)

136

Germany's dominant state in the middle 1800s was Prussia, which had risen to prominence mainly through its military. Ever since its defeat at the hands of Napoleon in 1806–1807, the Prussian military had dedicated itself to becoming the best in the world, both to return to the glory days of Frederick the Great and to ensure that such embarrassment at the hands of the French was never repeated. Prussia developed the world's first General Staff, promoting excellence in all phases of military activity. The system proved itself in 1866 when Prussia easily defeated Austria in a border dispute; that war seemed almost a tune-up for a return match with France. Under the leadership of Chancellor Otto von Bismarck, Prussia gathered the lesser German states around it in a North German Confederation and aimed toward the unification of all Germanic principalities into one state. A war with France would serve as a focus for German nationalism.

After the revolution of 1848, Napoleon III of France reigned as head of state. The Second Empire was a shadow of the First Empire established by Napoleon Buonaparte, but France hoped

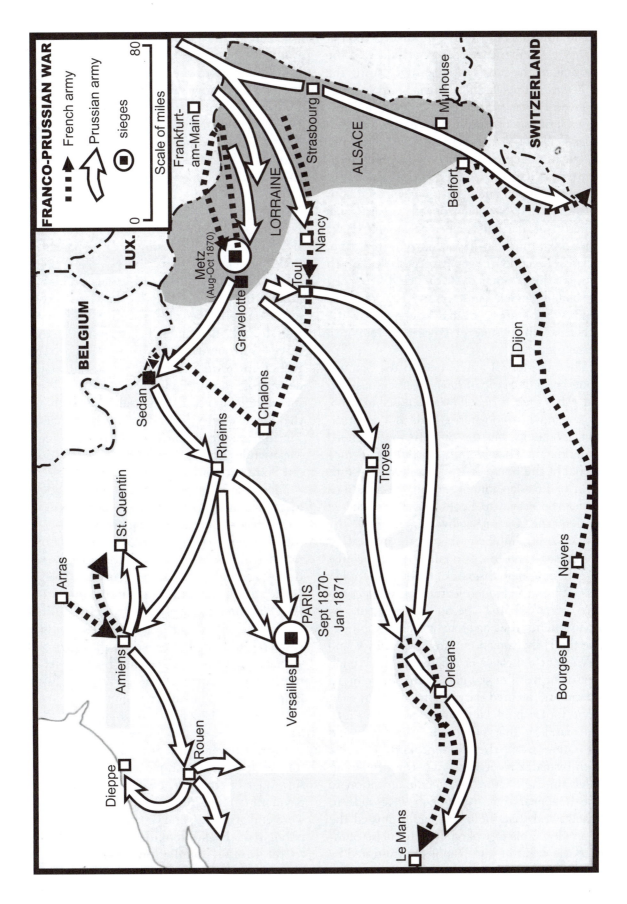

FRANCO-PRUSSIAN WAR

- ▸▸▸ French army
- ⇨ Prussian army
- ⊡ sieges

Scale of miles

0   80

Frankfurt-am-Main

SWITZERLAND

Mullhouse

ALSACE

Strasbourg

LORRAINE

Nancy

Belfort

LUX.

Metz (Aug–Oct 1870)

Toul

Dijon

Gravelotte

BELGIUM

Chalons

Sedan

Rheims

Troyes

Nevers

St. Quentin

Arras

Amiens

PARIS Sept 1870–Jan 1871

Versailles

Orleans

Bourges

Rouen

Dieppe

Le Mans

to maintain a major role in world affairs, even if it could not reach the heights of grandeur of the beginning of the nineteenth century. During the war between Prussia and Austria, Napoleon III had given Prussia tacit support in return for generalized promises of reward. France hoped to gain border lands along the western Rhine after that war, but Bismarck refused to cede any such territory to non-Germans. He then stood in the way of a proposed French purchase of Luxembourg from Holland. When Napoleon hoped to gain some expansion at Belgium's expense through heavy French investment in that country's rail system, Bismarck reminded England of possible French control of the Channel coast, and English opposition halted French aims. In the face of these attempts by France, Bismarck convinced the southern German state of Bavaria to join in a defense pact.

The question of a new heir to the Spanish throne brought Franco-Prussian difficulties to a head. After Queen Isabella was deposed in 1868, the government reorganized itself as a constitutional monarchy, but the Spanish were in need of a monarch. They secretly appealed to Prince Leopold of the house of Hohenzollern, a distant cousin of Prussian king Wilhelm. Negotiations to offer the crown to Leopold were conducted between the Spanish government and the Prussian court. Wilhelm had little interest in the matter, and occasionally spoke against the scheme, but Bismarck pushed Leopold's cause. When the French learned of the negotiations, they feared being surrounded by Hohenzollerns; they had fought such possibilities since the Holy Roman Empire of Charles V and the War of the League of Augsburg. The French ambassador to Prussia met with Wilhelm in Holland and secured the withdrawal of Prussian support for Leopold, but then he pressed his luck by demanding that no future claimant would ever come from the Hohenzollern dynasty. When Bismarck received word of this demand in a telegram, he doctored the communication to make it appear that the French were rude to Wilhelm and that the kaiser had dismissed the ambassador. This provoked French public opinion to the point of war; Napoleon, frustrated by Prussia at every turn, complied.

The French army was not as prepared for war as was French public opinion. Despite minor improvements to the French military over the last two years, it was no match for the Prussians. Under the military leadership of Count Helmuth von Moltke, the German General Staff was prepared for almost every contingency, and they could field an army twice the size of the French. Moltke planned on drawing the French army into a trap, but aggressive action on the part of a Prussian general warned the French of the impending danger. The French slowed their advance to the frontier, but this did little but delay the inevitable. Napoleon divided most of his army into two sections, to be based around the cities of Sedan and Metz. Prussian forces outperformed the French in all phases of warfare, and both French armies found themselves surrounded. On 1 September 1870, French forces in Sedan under Marshal Maurice de MacMahon surrendered some 100,000 men, including Napoleon III himself. A month later, the fortress at Metz, under the command of Marshal Francois Bazaine, also surrendered. Meanwhile, Prussian forces drove across northern France toward Paris.

Hearing of Napoleon's capture, the government in Paris was overthrown; a revolutionary government under Leon Gambetta tried to rally the public to the French colors. The forces they raised could not compete with the crack Prussian troops, and Paris was soon surrounded. The siege of the Paris Commune lasted until January 1871. As Prussian forces besieged the city, Wilhelm was named kaiser, emperor of a united Germany. Bismarck had finally succeeded in unifying the German states, which had not been under one rule since the time of the early Holy Roman Empire under Charlemagne's grandsons.

The French defeat brought an end to the Second Empire, but more importantly for Europe, it brought the French a burning desire for vengeance. The rapid military defeat, the surrender of the head of state, and the forced payment of reparations totaling some $3 billion were embarrassing, and the French military and population began looking for the next war to return the humiliation. France created a General Staff along the lines of Prussia's and laid plans for a decisive attack sometime in the future. Plan XVII was 40 years in the making, and would prove ineffective when the time came for its implementation in August 1914. The French people and government also felt the humiliation, and Franco-German relations, never cordial, remained strained. The two nations struggled with each other diplomatically in the world of empire-building at the end of the nineteenth century, and their rivalry over Morocco almost brought about World War I in 1905. The alliance systems built up by each side laid the groundwork for the Great War of 1914–1918.

See also Carolingian Dynasty; Italy, Austrian Invasion of (War of the Spanish Succession); Palatinate, French Invasion of the (War of the League of Augsburg); Saxony, Prussian Invasion of (Seven Years' War); Napoleon Buonaparte; Prussia, Napoleon's Invasion of; France, German Invasion of.

References: Can; William, *The Origin of the Wars of German Unification* (London: Longman, 1991); Howard, Michael, *The Franco-Prussian War* (New York: Collier, 1961); von Moltke, Graf Helmuth, *The Franco-German War of 1870–71* (New York: Harper Brothers, 1901).

137   INDIANS OF NORTH AMERICA, U.S. CONQUEST OF

From the time Europeans first set foot on the American continent, they attempted to force their will on the native Americans, or American Indians. The major source of these conflicts was land—the Indians had it and the Europeans wanted it. As waves of settlements swept westward, one tribe after another was wiped out. After the United States broke away from the rule of England, the conquest of the Indians accelerated at the hands of the aggressive young nation.

By the 1840s the United States had come up against the Plains Indians, those peoples who lived on the Great Plains of North America, an area that ran from Canada south to the Gulf of Mexico, and from the Mississippi River west to the Rocky Mountains. The Plains Indians tribes included the many nations of the Sioux, Cheyenne, Arapaho, Pawnee, Shoshoni, Crow, Kiowa, Comanche,

and, to a lesser degree, Apache. All these peoples (with the exception of the Apache) shared a common culture—the horse culture, based on the buffalo and the horse.

The buffalo furnished the Plains Indians with all the necessities of life: food, clothing, housing, fuel. With great herds of tens of millions of animals at their disposal, the Indians had a seemingly inexhaustible supply. Horses had been introduced onto the plains by the Spanish around 1550 and instantly adopted by the Indians, who had been following the buffalo herds on foot for thousands of years. The horse gave the Plains Indians a mobility that other North American Indians lacked, and made them into fearsome warriors. They could cover a hundred miles in a day, strike at the weakest, most exposed points in the frontier settlement lines, and be long gone with their spoils before they could be apprehended. Plains Indian societies were intensely militaristic, with advancement in a tribe based on deeds in war and in the hunt. The nearby white settlers, living on isolated farms and ranches, and usually with only themselves for protection, offered opportunities the Indians could not resist. No military force could catch these swift raiders, and no militia could handle them. Armed with lance, shield, rapid-fire bow, and, later, firearms, the Plains Indians easily comprised the finest light cavalry in the nineteenth-century world.

In comparison, the U.S. Army of the post-Civil War period was poorly trained, badly equipped, and subject to a desertion rate sometimes approaching 50 percent in some regiments. From a peak strength of over two million men at the end of the Civil War, the army was reduced by Congress to less than 25,000 by 1870, and only 10 regiments were cavalry. Called upon to build, garrison, and maintain the frontier forts, patrol the settlement lines, protect mail and stage lines, enforce the law, and intercept and punish Indian raiders, the 5,000 or so troops of the U.S. cavalry found themselves badly overtasked. With a single dramatic incident in 1871, all this began to change. General of the Army William Tecumseh Sherman, the highest-ranking officer in the U.S. Army and the man who had helped bring the American South to its knees, came to Texas on an inspection tour. Traveling with only a 16-man escort, Sherman was nearly ambushed by a party of over 200 Plains warriors; he escaped only because the Indians decided to wait for richer prey to come along. After this close brush with death, General Sherman decided to bring the might of the U.S. government to bear on the Plains Indians.

During the American Civil War, Sherman had developed the idea of "Total War," the concept of waging war not just on an enemy's armies but on its people, too, thus breaking their will to resist. Following this notion, Sherman had burned Atlanta and marched across Georgia, burning and destroying everything in a 50-mile-wide path from Atlanta to the sea. This ruthless aggression achieved its purpose, destroying the supply base of the Confederate armies and making the war unpopular with the southern people. Sherman reasoned that this same strategy would work against the Plains Indians.

The first step was to attack the Indians' supply base: the buffalo. Sherman encouraged the New England tanning industry to start using buffalo hides in their manufacturing process; they worked just as well as cowhides and were far cheaper, needing only to be "harvested." The tanning industry hired small armies of buffalo hunters who descended on the plains, shooting hundreds of animals a day merely for their skins, leaving behind a prairie full of rotting carcasses. When the killing began in 1872, there were perhaps 20 million buffalo in the United States; by 1884, there were less than 1,200. General Philip Sheridan reflected the army's position on this slaughter when he told the Texas legislature, "Let them kill, skin, and sell until the buffalo is exterminated, as it is the only way to bring lasting peace and allow civilization to advance."

This government-sanctioned extermination removed the sustenance of the Plains tribes. Sherman next struck at the tribes themselves. Having studied the Indians' lifestyle, he realized that their vaunted mobility was not complete. Indian ponies ate prairie grass, and during the dead of winter when there was no grass, they were too weak to carry riders. Thus, in the cold months, the Plains Indians were almost completely immobile, and passed the winter in box canyons and other remote hidden places. In the spring, almost as soon as the grass was up, the ponies would regain their strength and the Indians would be off again on their epic journeys and raids. Wintertime gave Sherman a window of opportunity to strike at the tribes. Army horses ate grain, which could be carried in wagons, along with infantry reinforcements. In truth, the cavalry was much slower in the winter than they were in the summer, but at least they could operate, which was more than the Indians could do.

Thus, in 1874–1875, Sherman launched a campaign that became known as the Red River War. Thousands of cavalry and infantry crisscrossed the plains of Texas, Oklahoma, and Kansas, looking for hostile Indians in a great search-and-destroy mission. As the Indian encampments were uncovered, the army attacked. Inevitably, the army would drive off the Indian defenders and overrun their camps. At Sherman's order, all captured material was destroyed. Clothing, weapons, food, the irreplaceable hide tepees—all were burned. Indian horses that fell into the army's hands were shot, as many as 1,500 killed at a time; at some places, their bones could still be seen in the twentieth century. Dismounted and devoid of the necessities of life, the dispirited remnants of the southern tribes walked to their reservations and surrendered.

Sherman's tactics, which had worked so well against the southern Plains tribes, faltered against the northern tribes, mostly due to problems in leadership, the most notorious example being Lieutenant Colonel George Armstrong Custer. In 1874, Custer led an expedition into the Black Hills of Dakota, land sacred to the Sioux. The numerous civilian gold miners who accompanied Custer discovered gold in the Black Hills, setting off a rush that violated the Indians' treaty guarantees. The army did nothing to stop these incursions, and when the Sioux attacked the interlopers, the army was ordered to move against the Indians. In June 1876, Custer led his famous Seventh Cavalry regiment in an ill-advised attack on some 5,000 Sioux and Cheyenne warriors under Chiefs Sitting Bull and Crazy Horse along the banks of the Little Big Horn River in the Montana Territory. Custer's entire command of 270 men was wiped out. Sheridan and Colonel Ranald Mackenzie were dispatched to avenge

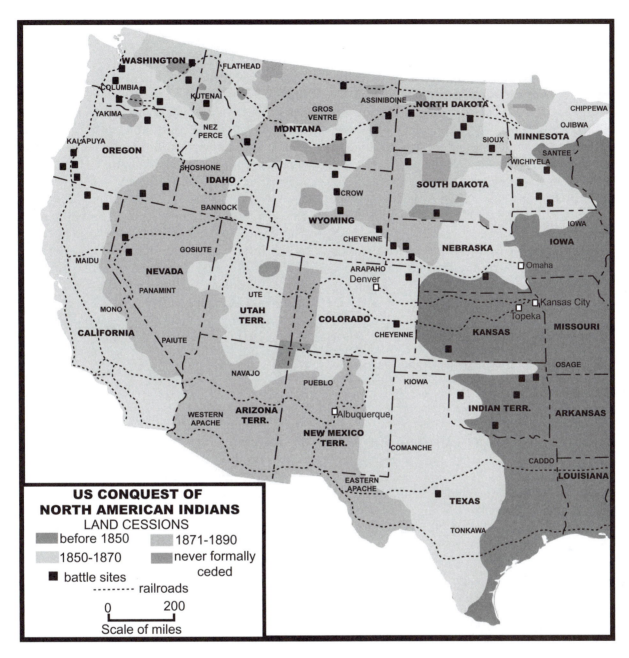

US CONQUEST OF
NORTH AMERICAN INDIANS
LAND CESSIONS
- before 1850
- 1850-1870
- 1871-1890
- never formally ceded
- battle sites
- --------- railroads

0   200
Scale of miles

Custer, and within three years the Sioux and Cheyenne were broken like the southern tribes.

In the mountains of the Southwest, the Apaches fought on under leaders like Cochise and Geronimo until 1886, when their resistance was overwhelmed. The once proud tribes of the plains were now confined to reservations. In the late 1880s a new religion, the Ghost Dance, swept the plains. It promised the return of the buffalo and all the dead warriors, and the destruction of all whites if the living would perform a ceremonial dance at every new moon. The desperate Indians embraced the new religion so strongly that the government became alarmed. In December 1890, during an effort to prevent the dance at the Wounded Knee Agency in South Dakota, hostilities erupted between Sioux tribesmen and elements of the Seventh Cavalry. Some 200 Indian men, women, and children and 25 cavalrymen died in the bloodbath. With Wounded Knee, the period of the Indian wars was officially over. In 25 years, the U.S. Army had fought over a thousand actions, with 932 men killed and 1,061 wounded, and the Plains Indians had suffered an estimated

5,519 killed and wounded. In addition, the culture of the Plains Indians was destroyed. The war between the United States and the Plains Indians had been a guerrilla-type, fast-moving, light-marching war, pitting a brave and savage foe against a modern world power. Though the Indians' struggle had been epic and, in some cases, the stuff of which legends are made, the outcome was inescapable. The days of the lance, bow, and shield were gone forever. The reservation system, developed prior to the Civil War, became the forced habitation of all Native American tribes. Poor funding, corruption, and a lack of national interest virtually guaranteed that the reservation lifestyle would make the Indians overlooked, second-class citizens in a country they once dominated.

References: Hamilton, Allen, *Sentinel of the Southern Plains* (Fort Worth: Texas Christian University Press, 1990); Leckie, William, *The Military Conquest of the Southern Plains* (Norman: University of Oklahoma Press, 1963); Utley, Robert, *Frontier Regulars* (New York: Macmillan, 1973).

138 INDOCHINA, FRENCH OCCUPATION OF

France first became interested in Southeast Asia in the late 1700s when French missionaries began witnessing to the inhabitants. At first the missionaries were protected by the king of Annam, the southeastern portion of the Indochinese peninsula, but after 1820 new monarchs began to persecute the missionaries. This persecution became most extreme under the reign of Tu-Duc (1847–1883), who was determined to stamp out Christianity in his kingdom. The missionaries' appeals to France brought a quick response. Through naval demonstrations off the coast, the French tried to force Tu-Duc to guarantee the missionaries' rights and safety, but without success. Another naval demonstration in 1858 did little better. Rather than allow the French to be harassed, French Emperor Napoleon III sent troops to Annam. They invaded and captured the territory around Saigon and the Mekong River delta.

The success of French troops convinced Tu-Duc in 1862 to grant the guarantees the missionaries demanded, and he also ceded to France the three provinces of Cochin China and the island of Pulo Condore. France's new territory needed a French administration, so bureaucrats were soon installed. Jealous of their land, the civil servants and the newly arrived French merchants pressured the French government to expand its control to create buffer zones around Cochin China. Thus, France expanded its influence deeper into the peninsula: Cochin China was declared a colony in 1874, and Annam was declared a French protectorate. Civil disturbances and the activities of Chinese pirates brought more French troops, and in 1884 they occupied the northern province of Tonking.

In 1887, France created the Union Indochinoise, combining the protectorates of Tonking, Annam, and inner Cambodia with the colony of Cochin China, all under the direction of a governor-general. Two years earlier, France had begun to experience problems in the neighborhood when Britain invaded and occupied Burma; the British believed the French had been secretly supporting Burmese nationalists making trouble along the Indo-Burmese border and harassing British merchants in Burma. The French hoped to extend their economic influence deeper into Southeast Asia, particularly Siam, but this put them into confrontation with Britain. In 1892, France proposed a border between their spheres of influence by claiming everything east of the Mekong River, which would include Laos, then under Siamese control. When Britain hesitated, France invaded; in 1893, they sent an invasion force and a flotilla up the Menam River to Bangkok. At gunpoint they demanded Laos for themselves and a return of Angkor and Battambang to Cambodia. Britain decided not to intervene on Siam's behalf, and France got what it wanted. Siam remained independent, however, because both the British and French realized that a buffer between their territories would be a good idea. These agreements were confirmed by a series of treaties: the Franco-British entente of 1904, a Franco-Siamese treaty in 1907, and an Anglo-Siamese treaty in 1909.

French administration in the area brought French schools and culture, and therein lay the seeds of their own destruction. They taught the French revolutionary principles of liberté, egalité, fraternité, which encouraged the growing intelligentsia to consider their own liberty; the French also favored the Asians who embraced Catholicism over those who remained Buddhist, and this discrimination fostered resentment. By 1919, young intellectuals were considering the benefits of independence. Ho Chi Minh traveled to Versailles after World War I to urge American President Woodrow Wilson to extend his Fourteen Points' tenet of national selfdetermination to all colonies, not just those of the defeated Central Powers. When he failed to accomplish this, he returned home via Moscow and learned the strategies of subversion. In the 1920s he formed the Viet Minh and began the struggle against French imperialism.

When Vichy France turned over Indochina to Japan in September 1940, the Viet Minh fought the Japanese. After the Japanese surrendered to the Allies in 1945, Ho Chi Minh hoped for a breakup of empires that would give his country independence; again, he was disappointed.

The United States did nothing to stand in the way of French desires to reoccupy Indochina, and the Viet Minh resumed fighting the French. The United States initially thought that France should give up its empire, but when the Cold War began and the suspicions of communism increased, President Harry Truman supported France as an obstacle to the spread of communism. American military aid to the French increased through the early 1950s, but the growing numbers of the Viet Minh and the increased support they received from China and the Soviet Union tipped the balance. In 1954, as French and Indochinese representatives met in Geneva to achieve a solution, word arrived that the major French bastion of Dien Bien Phu had fallen to the Viet Minh. The French public was tired of the fighting, and France conceded defeat.

The Geneva Conference declared a timetable for French withdrawal and the independence of the Indochinese countries of Cambodia, Laos, and Vietnam (the former Tonking and Annam). The French were to withdraw in 1956, and elections would be held to determine the new leaders. Though the United States was not a signatory to the Geneva agreement, the Americans did not wish to see Ho Chi Minh elected. Therefore,

President Dwight Eisenhower recognized the regime of Bao Dai, a French functionary who oversaw the French withdrawal from the southern provinces. With American support, the country of South Vietnam was created, and the struggle between North and South Vietnam began.

See also France, Nazi Invasion of.

References: Hammer, Ellen, *The Struggle for Indochina* (Stanford, CA: Stanford University Press, 1955); Randle, Robert, *Geneva 1954* (Princeton, NJ: Princeton University Press, 1969); Thompson, Virginia, *French Indo-China* (New York: Macmillan, 1937).

139 KENYA, BRITISH COLONIZATION OF

Eastern Africa was home to a variety of populations, primarily Cushites and Niloites from the north and Bantus from the south. Local culture and language came from the blending of these populations, which had little contact with the outside world until around 500 C.E. with the arrival of the Arabs, who began colonization and trade, linking local products with markets farther east. They also began trading in slaves. On a more positive note, the blend of the local language and Arabic ultimately emerged as Swahili, which became the dominant language of eastern Africa. Successful trading brought other countries to the area, with the Persians establishing in the fourteenth century what became the modern city of Mombasa. Chinese and Malaysian ships are also known to have docked in regional ports.

European interest in the area began with the Portuguese arrival on 7 April 1498. They sailed into Mombasa briefly, but were driven off by the Arabs who forced them further east. Seeing the ready-made harbors and markets, however, the Portuguese returned in force and began laying siege to the coastal cities. It took almost a century for the Portuguese to establish themselves, since local resistance was fierce, especially in Mombasa, which was besieged three times before finally being conquered in 1588. The Portuguese, however, ruled little other than the coastline and had a minimal impact on the interior except for the introduction of some new crops. Almost immediately upon seizing control, however,

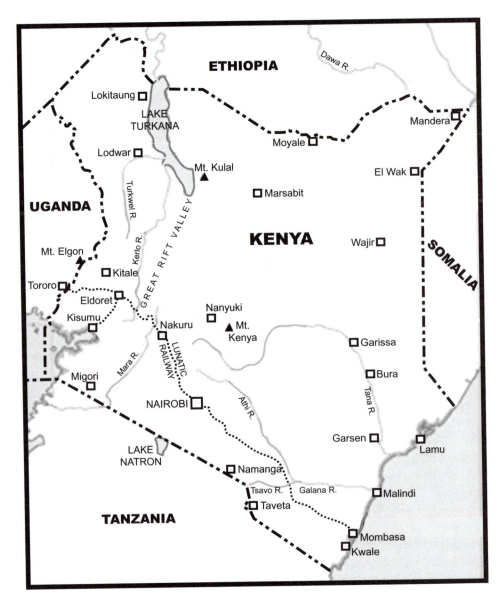

Portugal was challenged by the Ottoman Empire. After some intense fighting and widespread destruction in Mombasa, the Portuguese built a fortress, Fort Jesus. It was the bulwark of Portuguese resistance for more than a century, but ultimately the Sultan of Oman drove the Portuguese out in 1698. The Omanis ruled the region from their home in Muscat until the early 1800s, when the British and French began taking an interest in the region.

After Napoleon's defeat in 1815, however, the British began to spread their dominion over the western Indian Ocean. The Sultan of Oman, Seyyid Said, allied with the British against the French and used that relationship to tighten his grip on eastern Africa. Local forces led by the Mazrui clan launched a rebellion against the Omani and appealed to the British for aid. They refused until 1824, when a Royal Navy captain decided (without authorization) to support the Mazruis in order to establish a British foothold. The London government ultimately withdrew their support, but the Mazrui clan was strengthened by the temporary assistance. Seyyid Said decided to relocate his sultanate to Zanzibar around 1840, from where he began to establish diplomatic ties with most European countries. After his death in 1856, however, a dispute between his heirs ended in a division of the realm, half to Zanzibar and half to Muscat;

Zanzibar kept control over the region that came to be called Kenya.

British interest in the region grew over the next several decades owing to the establishment of a number of Christian missions and the explorations into the interior by notables such as David Livingstone, Richard Stanley, and Richard Burton, discoverer of the source of the Nile. Joseph Thomson, representing the Royal Geographic Society, also explored and mapped the interior in the 1880s, just as European powers were beginning the "scramble for Africa." When German businessmen began staking out spheres of influence in eastern Africa, British merchants were not far behind. William McKinnon began the British East Africa Association in 1887, which gained royal support the following year and became the British East Africa Company. The group wedged itself between the Germans to the south in German East Africa (later Tanganyika, modern Tanzania) and the Italians to the north in Somalia. This was not only to curb the ambitions of other European powers, but also to gain land for a proposed Cape-to-Cairo railroad project of which the imperialists in the British government had long dreamed.

Further, the British were developing a serious interest in Uganda, and Kenya was a necessary possession to secure that colony and to provide an outlet for Ugandan exports to the coast. The British government declared Uganda a protectorate in 1894 and did the same for British East Africa the following year. Soon, work started on a railroad from the interior, across the Great Rift Valley, through swampland to Africa's eastern coast. It was immediately known as the Lunatic Express. "The works progressed quickly, at the expense of the lives of many workers who died from malaria, dysentery, scurvy, cholera, ulcers, and typhus. Tsetse flies decimated the pack animals and camps were always [subject] to raids and attacks from the local tribes. Besides, the workers had to face a danger that became legendary: the man-eating lions of Tsavo" (Kenyalogy). In 1902, the line running from Mombasa to Lake Victoria was completed after seven years of work.

British colonization was slow, but those who emigrated established themselves strongly under the leadership of the largest landowner, Lord Delamere. In 1905, protectorate status was upgraded to that of colony, with a population of about 3,000 whites by 1912. The city which ultimately became the capital, Nairobi, was established in that time period and the English settlers took over lands along the frontier of the two largest local populations, the Masai and the Kikuyu. They soon bought a large portion of land from the Masai, who moved farther south, but the main trouble the settlers faced was a lack of labor for the large farming estates they were founding. The Kikuyu became the targets of exploitation, in a process of forced labor in lieu of taxes. The Kikuyu soon rebelled, but were brutally suppressed by the Third Regiment of the King's African Rifles, a unit established to protect the settlers. This force was all that was available when war broke out in 1914 in Europe; it was too small to face the German forces in German East Africa to the south. British and South African operations in German East Africa kept the forces under General Paul von Lettow-Vorbeck in that colony, although they were unable to suppress his guerrilla operations until war's end. After 1918, Germany lost all its colonies and Britain was in sole possession of East Africa. London's encouragement of settlement in the area took the white population up to 10,000.

In 1920, British East Africa officially became Kenya and the current borders were established. During the postwar era, white rule over Kenya kept the Kikuyu in a subservient and increasingly poverty-stricken condition. Resistance movements began, the first in 1922 under Harry Thuku, leader of the Young Kikuyu. His arrest brought about the first major violence between Kikuyu and whites. Also in this decade came the emergence of the future Kenyan leader Johnstone Kamau Wa Ngengi, better known as Jomo Kenyatta. Political movements sprang up as well, and between the world wars, Kikuyu nationalism grew. When Kenyans were recruited to aid Britain in World War II, they not only saw the vulnerability of the whites but also gained a sense of self-worth, much as occurred in the United States with black troops fighting in the Civil War. During World War II, in 1944, the first black Kenyan was allowed into the government after decades of participation by Arab and Asian citizens.

In the wake of the war, and with the emergence of the Cold War, Britain realized both the strategic necessity of Kenya and the need to promote progress so it could maintain order. As is the nature of reforms, however, they did not appear quickly enough for those awaiting them. Kikuyu activists split into two major groups. The more politically motivated joined the Kenyan African Union (KAU) under Jomo Kenyatta. The Kikuyu Central Association, originally dedicated to civil disobedience, later merged with a failed trade union movement and a secret group of veterans called Forty Group, later known as the Mau Mau. When the British started a local constabulary manned by Kikuyus, the violence which ensued (the Mau Mau Rebellion) was as much or more an internal Kikuyu struggle as it was a rebellion or race war.

In the wake of major strikes in 1950, the white administration engaged in mass arrests and a major show of military force. The less radical KAU called for a greater number of black representatives in the government, but when that was rejected in 1951, they called for independence. Also in that year a radical Central Committee seized control of the resistance movement in Nairobi and began enforcing ritual oath-taking to mold a tightly knit organization. It was from these oaths, sometimes involving animal sacrifice, that the Mau Mau began to gain its horrific reputation among whites. Kenyatta at times spoke out against the Mau Mau, but in the end was suspected by both Mau Mau and the British of collaborating with the other side. In 1953, rumors of an uprising were rife and the newly arrived governor, Sir Evelyn Baring, declared a state of emergency.

What happened in Kenya from 1953 to 1956 was widespread intimidation and depredation by both white and black. The Mau Mau, numbering probably 15,000 guerrillas, operated out of the mountains and forests, attacking farms and killing some white farmers but mostly their black laborers. For many Kikuyu, their choice was forced membership in the local Mau Mau group, or death. The London government, hearing gruesome tales of Mau Mau atrocities, sent in an increasing number of security forces. Some 5,500 guerrillas in the mountains were captured in Operation Hammer

in early 1954. A sweep of eastern Nairobi soon afterward, Operation Anvil, cleaned out most of the rebels in the city. In standard counter-guerrilla strategy, possible supporters of the Mau Mau were rounded up and held in camps, often in deplorable conditions. Recently declassified documents give details of a massive torture campaign by the authorities. The British employed not only the King's African Rifles, but also the Home Guard and (late in the campaign) groups who were little more than gangs of thugs.

The final casualty count in the Mau Mau uprising was indeed large. "Only 32 European settlers died in the subsequent fighting, but more than 1,800 African civilians, over 3,000 African police and soldiers, and 12,000 Mau Mau rebels were killed. Between 1953 and 1956 Britain sent over a thousand Kenyans to the gallows, often on trumped up or nonexistent charges. Meanwhile 70,000 people were imprisoned in camps without trial for between two and six years." (Anderson lecture). Although it was an overwhelming military victory for the British, the final result was the implementation of the reforms that Kenyatta had called for in 1951. With land reform instituted and restrictions on coffee growing relaxed, Kikuyu landowners found themselves rising in economic status. By 1960, the British administration allowed full suffrage and majority rule. In 1963, free elections established a majority black government which received independence from Britain. Kenya's first elected leader was Jomo Kenyatta, who had spent almost 10 years in prison.

In 2003, a reparations commission was created in London to deal with claims presented by the victims of British activities during the rebellion.

See also Africa, German occupation of; German East Africa, British invasion of; and Uganda, British colonization of.

References: Anderson, David, *Histories of the Hanged: The Dirty War in Kenya and the End of Empire* (New York: W. W. Norton, 2005); Anderson, David, lecture at School of Oriental and African Studies, London, 13 January 2005, <www.royalafricansociety.org/reports_publications/recent_meetings/histories _ maumau>, 14 November 2005; "History" at Kenyalogy <www.kenyalogy.com>, 20 December 2005.

KOREA, JAPANESE INVASION OF (SINO-JAPANESE WAR)

140

In the early 1600s, Japan fought and lost a war in Korea; the widespread use of firearms in that war had a lasting effect on Japan's rulers. The samurai warriors who dominated Japanese society could not bear the thought of a peasant having the power to kill one of his betters with a gun. They therefore withdrew from the world rather than allow this technology to upset their culture. Japan remained isolated until 1854, when American Commodore Matthew Perry sailed a fleet of ships into Tokyo Bay and demanded that Japan receive diplomatic representatives. The government bowed before the threat of Perry's artillery; they also saw that the only way to protect themselves was through the adoption of new technology. The samurai lost their political power in the 1868 Meiji Restoration, and Emperor Meiji embarked Japan on an industrial path to modernity.

Japanese society advanced 300 years in four decades. By the 1890s, the country had a modern navy and a well-equipped army, yet maintained the martial spirit that had long dominated Japanese culture. Japan learned from the world how to build modern weaponry, and realized that to be powerful in the late nineteenth century, a country needed colonies. Traditional martial values, coupled with modern weapons and international attitudes, meant that Japan would soon be looking for opportunities outside its borders.

China had exercised suzerainty over Korea for two centuries, but in the early 1880s, Japan attempted to enter the Korean markets. Within the Korean royal family there was an ongoing struggle over the role of foreigners: One side (led by Taewon-gun, the king's father) was xenophobic, while the other (led by Queen Min) wanted progressive reforms and considered recent Japanese reforms to be models. In 1882, the two factions clashed, and China sent in troops to restore order. Japan also sent troops, but they were outnumbered and forced to withdraw. Taewon-gun was captured and removed to China, and the Chinese government began to control Korea through the Min government. A pro-Japanese faction staged a revolution in 1884, seizing power for a short while.

When another Chinese military demonstration compelled the withdrawal of Japanese forces, the Chinese were once again firmly in control. The best the Japanese could gain was the Treaty of Tientsin in 1885, whereby both countries would pull their forces out of Korea and both would send troops into the country in case of internal violence. Japanese status in Korea was low, and economic progress was almost nil.

The "internal violence" appeared in the form of a peasant rebellion in 1894. When the Koreans appealed to China for military assistance to suppress the rebellion, Japan feared the possibility of a Chinese army so close to its shores. Therefore, under the provisions of the Treaty of Tientsin, Japan used the rebellion as an opportunity to establish a dominant position in Korea. Tokyo committed the Japanese First Army to Korea and captured the capital at Seoul in July; war was officially declared on 1 August. Outside observers gave tiny Japan little hope against huge China, but the Chinese military was poorly organized and led, and in Korea it was outnumbered. The larger Chinese fleet failed to move aggressively against the Japanese at the battle of the Yalu River in September and had to concede the naval initiative, which the Japanese never surrendered. Free to move troops across the Tsushima Straits and the Yellow Sea, the Japanese attacked at will. By 15 September they controlled the Korean peninsula and looked to invade China itself.

The First Army continued north and crossed the Yalu River into Manchuria, while the Japanese Second and Third Armies landed on the Liaotung Peninsula. By the end of 1894, Japanese forces had captured the Weihaiwei and Port Arthur, giving themselves a port of entry into China. Though the Chinese manned well-constructed fortifications, they did not mount a serious defense; Japan lost many more men to winter weather and disease than to combat. A second naval battle off Weihaiwei resulted in the destruction of most of the Chinese fleet, while the Japanese army moved deeper into China. By the spring of 1895, Peking was threatened and probably would have fallen had the Chinese not sued for peace. The Treaty of Shimonoseki brought the war to an end.

Japan acquired the Liaotung Peninsula and Formosa, and forced the Chinese to pay a large indemnity, supplanting the Chinese as the dominant power in Korea. The Japanese earned these concessions, but European nations considered them to be too threatening. Russia and France put diplomatic pressure on Japan to return the Liaotung Peninsula, which they did. It soon became a base for the Russian Pacific Fleet, which began a diplomatic feud resulting in the Russo-Japanese War in 1904. By fighting so poorly, the Chinese showed themselves incapable of fielding a disciplined or well-supplied army; central coordination was nonexistent, and corruption among commanders was rampant. European powers were soon making increased demands on China for economic and political concessions.

Once Japanese forces gained control of Korea and the fighting shifted to China, the Japanese launched an ambitious reform program. Among other things, slavery was banned, civil rights were to be granted to certain lower-class professions, feudal rights of the upper classes were removed, family punishment for the deeds of one of its members was banned, political free speech was opened up, tax reform was initiated, and attempts were made to clean up government corruption. These reforms aimed much higher than any the Min faction had ever planned, so much so that later reforms in 1895 banned royal family interference in the government. Most importantly, Japan now exercised the political and economic power that China had possessed for 200 years. Japan began to look past Korea's borders toward Manchuria.

Even though the Japanese and Chinese both fought a "civilized" war with few atrocities, the Japanese destruction of Port Arthur after the discovery of tortured Japanese prisoners was a foretaste of what conquered peoples would experience at Japanese hands in World War II. During this war, however, they treated most of their prisoners and the conquered people with consideration; it was their later administration (after the Russo-Japanese War) and exploitation of the Koreans that dominate the cultural memory. The Western countries paying attention to this war saw little to change their idea that offense was the dominant aspect of military thinking, a view that would haunt them in World War I. Japan, on the other hand, got a taste for imperialism that did not wane until the end of World War II.

Manchuria was under increasing Russian influence, and the Russians had their eyes on Korea. They quickly moved to exercise influence over Queen Min, who had recently taken their side against Japanese influence. The struggle between the two foreign factions in the Korean government effectively halted any implementation of reforms. In October 1895, Queen Min was killed and the pro-Russian ministers were removed from office. The Russians responded by kidnapping the king and killing pro-Japanese officials in February 1896. A pro-Russian government took power while the king ruled from the Russian legation. Japan could only negotiate minor trading concessions to stay in the country.

In 1900, Russia enlarged its army in Manchuria in response to the anti-foreign Boxer Rebellion in China. When Russia refused to remove its troops, a worried Great Britain entered into an alliance with Japan in 1902, setting the stage for a Russo-Japanese showdown. As the war was being fought (1904–1905), the Japanese regained their influence in the Korean government and soon took control. In a series of agreements, Japan took over Korean foreign policy, acquired military bases, and installed a resident-general whose permission was required before the Korean government could act in foreign or domestic affairs. This put Japan in de facto control of Korea, but in August 1910 the country was officially annexed to Japan. Instead of implementing the reforms they had outlined 15 years earlier, the Japanese dominated the entire economy of Korea, using the physical and human resources of the country for their own ends until 1945. Despite resistance from unemployed Korean soldiers, Korean intellectuals, and ex-government ministers, the Japanese held control until their defeat in World War II.

See also Manchuria, Japanese Invasion of (1904) (Russo-Japanese War).

References: Conroy, Hilary, *The Japanese Seizure of Korea, 1869–1910* (Philadelphia: University of Pennsylvania Press, 1960); Dowart, Jeffrey, *The Pigtail War* (Amherst: University of Massachusetts Press, 1975); Lone, Stewart, *Japan's First Modern War* (New York: St. Martin's Press, 1994).

141

MEXICO, FRENCH OCCUPATION OF

Mexico suffered through a civil conflict, the Three Years War, between 1857 and 1860. The ultimate victors—the liberal faction, under the leadership of Benito Juarez—attempted to institute reforms the conservatives had resisted. Rather than accept defeat, the conservatives appealed to Europe for assistance. Great Britain, France, and Spain all responded positively; they had suffered uncompensated economic losses during the war, and foreign bond holders were unable to redeem their investments from a bankrupt Mexican government. With sufficient reasons to intervene, in October 1861 the three European countries agreed to send troops to Mexico in an attempt to recoup their investments by force. The coalition force captured the port of Vera Cruz in January 1862. After receiving assurances from the Mexican government that it was doing all it could to make good the European losses, Britain and Spain decided to withdraw. France, however, remained behind. French Emperor Napoleon III had plans for Mexico. Assured by conservative factions in the country that the Mexican population would welcome the French presence, Napoleon planned to establish dominance over what he hoped would become a Mexican empire, giving him economic and political standing in the Western Hemisphere. He persuaded an unemployed aristocrat, Archduke Ferdinand Maximilian of Habsburg, brother of Austrian Emperor Franz Josef, to rule in Mexico.

Expecting to be welcomed as liberators, French troops marched inland from Vera Cruz westward to Puebla. They found a population far from welcoming. Fierce resistance by poorly equipped Mexican troops in the city forced a French withdrawal on 5 May 1862, but they returned in March 1863 with 30,000 reinforcements and took the city after a two-month siege. Having lost a significant portion of his army at Puebla, President Juarez decided to take his government out of Mexico City, and fled northward into the interior. French forces occupied Mexico City on 10 June and were welcomed by the clergy and conservatives, if not the general population.

By the end of the year, the French occupied the major cities of Monterrey, Saltillo, San Luis Potosi, and Queretaro.

Possession of the cities meant little because the population, mostly loyal to Juarez, controlled the rugged, empty, roadless countryside. Nevertheless, the French thought they were off to a good start. In October 1863, Mexican conservatives offered Maximilian the crown. He responded that he would take it only after consulting with the Mexican people, so a referendum was held. Staged by the French and conservatives, it was not surprising that the results were overwhelmingly in favor of Maximilian, and he accepted the throne in April 1864. Maximilian disappointed the conservative Mexicans, who thought they could easily regain the positions they had held before the Three Years War. Instead, he favored the foreign investment that had come into the country with his accession. Still, he did what he could to keep the conservatives happy while simultaneously courting the liberals. He convinced some of them that he wanted to be fair with all Mexicans—an enlightened monarch—and he gained some converts in the cities. The countryside, however, remained hostile to the foreign invaders.

Trouble hit Maximilian in 1866. Viewing the French occupation as a violation of the Monroe Doctrine, the United States threatened possible military action to liberate Mexico. At the same time, domestic problems in France and an increasingly aggressive Prussia brought Napoleon III to the realization that he needed all his forces at home. As French troops boarded ships for the return home in 1866, the generals begged Maximilian to abdicate and go with them. Instead, he listened to those Mexicans who insisted that he could maintain his hold on power. In early 1867 they convinced Maximilian to go to Queretaro to take command of forces preparing to fight an approaching force loyal to Juarez. Rather than leading his troops to victory, Maximilian was captured on 14 May and soon executed by firing squad.

With all European troops out of his country, Benito Juarez resumed the presidency and attempted to institute the reforms he had tried to begin before the invasion. He started with putting government finances back on a sound footing by cutting expenses, in this case by firing two-thirds of his army. This resulted in a series of revolts he was obliged to suppress. With the remaining budget, he spent heavily on education. Within a few years, Mexico had 8,000 schools with 350,000 students. Juarez also ordered the construction of a railroad line from the port of Vera Cruz through Puebla to Mexico City. In the cities, the first attempts at labor reform and the beginnings of trade unionism began. Juarez's attempts to bring capitalism to agriculture were also successful, but at a high price. He wanted to make farming profitable at the expense of the Indian tribes, who controlled much of the arable land. With government assistance, the landowners brutally put down Indian revolts. The Indians suffered from violence, government confiscation of their lands, and fraud by unscrupulous land speculators.

References: Keen, Benjamin, and Mark Wasserman, *A Short History of Latin America* (Boston: Houghton Mifflin, 1984); Meyer, W. C., and W. L. Sherman, *The Course of Mexican History* (New York: Oxford University Press, 1979); Roeder, Ralph, *Juarez and His Mexico*, 2 vols. (New York: Viking, 1947).

142   MEXICO, U.S. INVASION OF

When Texas successfully secured its independence from Mexico in 1836, the Texans immediately applied for statehood. The U.S. Congress rejected them, so Texas established a republic and operated as an independent nation for nine years. Early in 1845, Congress relented and offered statehood. The only problem lay in the designation of Texas's border with its former owner. Though the Mexican government had never recognized Texas's independence, Mexico had not seriously tried to bring the recalcitrant state back into its union. Upon learning of the state's annexation into the United States, the Mexican government was willing to let Texas go, but only on the condition that the borders follow the land grants Mexico had originally given to American settlers in the 1820s. Those borders stretched from the Nueces River in the south to the Red River in the north, territory that today encompasses central and east Texas. The Texans, however, claimed the Rio Grande as their border with Mexico, and claimed it to its source, which meant Mexico would have to cede about three times as much land, including its main northern settlement at Santa Fe. If the United States accepted the Texas claim to the Rio Grande, Mexico promised war.

American President James Polk sent John Slidell to Mexico to negotiate the purchase of the disputed territory and anything else Mexico might be willing to sell (such as California). The Mexicans not only refused his $15 million offer, they refused to recognize his very presence in their capital. This diplomatic insult, slight though it may have been, was fuel for the expansionist fires burning in American society, fires that Polk stoked in his election campaign. Coupling this incident with Mexico's refusal to pay any damage claims for raids their army had conducted in Texas during the republic period, Polk felt justified in threatening Mexico.

Polk sent troops under General Zachary Taylor from New Orleans to Texas, ordering them to cross the Nueces and establish a presence along the north shore of the Rio Grande. Taylor began building Fort Polk and Fort Brown near the mouth of the river in March 1846. In mid-April, Mexican forces ambushed and captured a cavalry patrol. The Mexicans felt justified because they considered their country invaded as soon as American forces crossed the Nueces. For Polk, however, it was the final justification for war. He sent a message to Congress in early May, saying, "American blood has been shed on American soil" (a view not shared by Mexico). Congress agreed and declared war.

After two fairly easy victories in early May at Palo Alto and Resaca de la Palma, Taylor drove Mexican forces back across the Rio Grande. His forces crossed the river in June and worked their way upstream along the southern bank. In the meantime, the Mexican government had promoted Antonio Lopez de Santa Anna to command their forces. As dictator in 1836, Santa Anna had been defeated at San Jacinto, and it was he who signed the document that the Texans claimed gave them their independence. In 1844, Santa Anna had been removed from power a second time and exiled to Cuba. Some military historians regard him as one of the worst generals

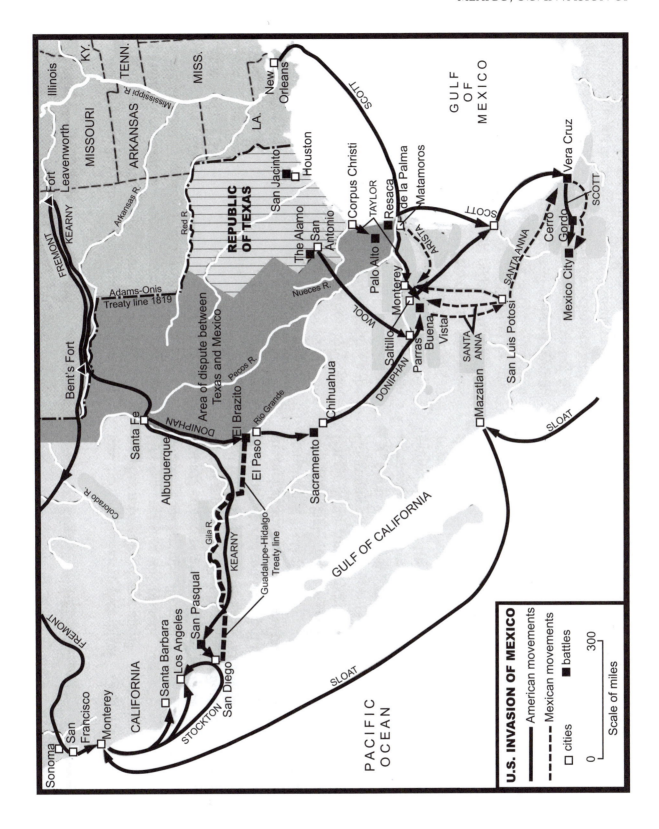

U.S. INVASION OF MEXICO

American movements
Mexican movements
□ cities ■ battles

0   300
Scale of miles

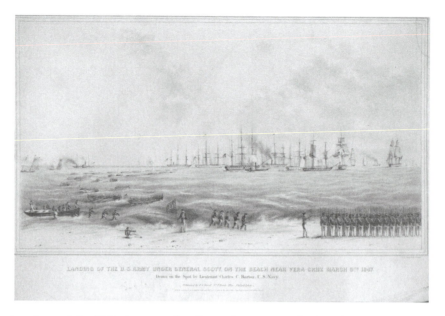

Landing of the U.S. Army, under General Scott, on the beach near Vera Cruz
on 9 March 1847. (Courtesy of the Massachusetts Historical Society)

ever, but he had the ability to rise to leadership positions in Mexico over and over again.

Taylor arrived outside Monterrey with about 6,000 troops in the middle of September. He anticipated little difficulty in capturing the city despite the fact that the Mexicans had fortified the high ground around the city and dug extensive defenses across the more level approaches. The battle for Monterrey took three days, but the defending Mexican general asked for terms after American forces attacking from two directions had captured the high ground and were making their way through the city, which Taylor occupied, allowing the Mexican army to withdraw.

Meanwile, volunteer units were forming in the United States. The largest belonged to Stephen Kearny, a regular army colonel leading 1,500 frontiersmen, who marched westward from Kansas in the summer of 1846. He and his men were assigned to secure the New Mexico Territory, and by mid-August they raised the American flag over Santa Fe, declaring it and the territory to be U.S. possessions. Not a shot was fired on the campaign. In September, Kearny and 300 men marched for California. They arrived in December to find that forces from Oregon under John C. Fremont, along with naval forces under the command of John Sloat, and then Robert

Stockton, had liberated the California Territory but were facing a popular uprising around Los Angeles. Stockton's sailors and marines joined with Kearny's small force to secure Los Angeles by early January. Mexican resistance in the territory ended; the only struggle yet to come was between Kearny and Fremont over who was actually in command in the territory.

As Kearny marched through the Southwest toward California, several hundred men from his original force left Santa Fe and headed south. Alexander Doniphan and his men enjoyed singular success in their expedition. They captured El Paso after a brief fight in late December; after a month of rest and recreation in the city, Doniphan's force marched for the city of Chihuahua. Another brief battle (with two killed and seven wounded while inflicting 800 casualties on the Mexican force) gave them control of that town, followed by another month of rest and relaxation. They next marched for Monterrey to join with Taylor's forces, arriving there too late for Taylor's last major battle, at Buena Vista. They marched to the coast, sailed for New Orleans, were mustered out of service, and went home. They had claimed north-central Mexico for the United States by right of conquest, having accomplished the entire mission without regular army troops, orders, or leadership.

Northern Mexico was coming under American control, but Taylor was having his problems at Monterrey. Even though he was winning his battles, and had extended his hold southward to the town of Saltillo, the government was reining him in. President Polk, a Democrat, feared Taylor's rising popularity, and he wanted to derail any future run Taylor might make toward high office as a Whig. The president ordered him to go on the defensive, but Taylor chafed at these orders. The latter widened his hold on the area around Saltillo, and ran into Mexican forces under Santa Anna. The Mexican force of 20,000 had marched across the desert to reach Buena Vista, south of Saltillo, in late February. After difficult fighting on 23 February 1847, Taylor's forces held their ground, and Santa Anna retreated. It would be the last major battle in the north.

Newly arrived American General Winfield Scott siphoned off some of Taylor's forces and sailed for Vera Cruz. Scott captured the port city fairly easily, and began to march west for Mexico City. Santa Anna had returned to the capital after his defeat at Buena Vista, and began to direct the defense of the city. Scott's advance through difficult terrain was harassed periodically by Mexican guerrillas, but he approached the city by late August. The two sides negotiated a cease-fire to discuss peace terms, but Santa Anna was only buying time to improve his defenses. By early September, the armistice was over and Scott's forces drew nearer to the city.

Unwilling to have Scott negotiate a peace treaty and make him even more popular than his military victories were doing, President Polk sent Nicholas Trist to Mexico to talk with the Mexican government. Congress had returned to Whig dominance after the last election, and the Whigs did not support the war. Polk hoped to secure the original goals of this war: the disputed area of Texas and possibly American possession of California. Certainly Mexico had suffered enough to concede to these demands.

Trist entered Mexico City under a flag of truce and found the government in chaos and unwilling to negotiate. He withdrew and sent word to Polk of his lack of success. The message took six weeks to reach Washington, owing to travel time, and the reply took equally as long.

Trist's original communication had been sent in late July, and the reply did not arrive in Mexico City until November: Forget the negotiations and come home. By then Scott had captured Mexico City, Santa Anna had been deposed, and the new Mexican government was negotiating with him. Still operating under his original orders, Trist was in a quandary. Should he continue to negotiate, or follow the latest directive to go home? He stayed.

In the meantime, Polk learned of the success in Mexico City and saw an opportunity to gain not only Texas and California, but also all of Mexico. He sent a new directive to Trist to forget the original instructions and demand complete capitulation. That message arrived after Trist had negotiated the treaty and left for Washington. Under the terms of the Treaty of Guadalupe-Hidalgo, Mexico ceded the disputed area of Texas and gave up all lands west toward the Pacific. In return, the United States would pay the originally offered $15 million, plus $3.25 million in damage claims held against Mexico by American citizens. The United States had just fought a year and a half to force Mexico to sell land.

When Trist arrived in Washington, unaware of the president's last message, he proudly visited the White House to display the fruits of his labors. Polk was furious, almost murderous. The United States might have taken all of Mexico without paying anything, if only Trist had better understood his president's expansionist attitudes. Had he exercised personal initiative and seized the moment, he could have seized the entire country. Polk did not want the treaty, but knew that congressional opposition would not allow him to continue the war, so he reluctantly signed it and sent it to the Senate for ratification. No one in the Senate liked it, either, thinking that it took too much, or too little, from Mexico; they ratified it as a compromise. The Mexican government were loath to part with any land at any price, but they were in no position to make demands; they ratified it as well.

The Treaty of Guadalupe-Hidalgo is one of the great might-have-beens of history. The future of the United States and all of Latin America would have been radically altered if the United States' southern border had become the Yucatan peninsula. For example, what would have been the policy concerning slavery in this new territory? Could the Southern states have gained power in Congress with new slave states sending representatives and senators to Washington? What would that have meant in 1861? Would the Civil War have been averted if the South had had more say in Congress? Would Mexican states have seceded from the Union and fought for the Confederacy? Further in the future, what problems would the United States have avoided in terms of illegal immigration, or in trade questions like the North American Free Trade Agreement?

Questions aside, there were concrete results from the war. The United States achieved its "manifest destiny" by reaching from sea to shining sea. Within a year of possessing California, gold was discovered and the rush was on. Having two distinct coastlines gave the United States the opportunity to expand overseas trade to the Orient as well as to Europe. The United States benefited greatly from the land gained, despite the fact that the slavery question over this new land almost directly led to civil war. Combat experience gained in Mexico showed itself in just a few years when junior officers under Taylor and Scott became senior officers in Union and Confederate uniforms. In terms of foreign relations, Latin America began to view the United States with increasing suspicion. The nation that had seemed a defender of the region with the Monroe Doctrine in the 1820s came to be viewed as a bully taking what it wanted from a weaker neighbor on trumped-up charges. The United States never lost that reputation, and did little in succeeding years to ameliorate it.

References: Connor, Seymour, *North America Divided* (New York: Oxford University Press, 1971); Eisenhower, John, *So Far from God* (New York: Random House, 1989); Singletary, Otis, *The Mexican War* (Chicago: University of Chicago Press, 1960).

143 NEW ZEALAND, BRITISH OCCUPATION OF

In the wake of the American Revolution, the British needed a new land into which to send their criminals, and chose Australia. The islands east of Australia, known as New Zealand, were used as a British whaling station and remained relatively untouched by civilized hands. After the whalers advertised the beauty and fertility of the islands back in England, land speculators and settlers began to arrive. So many people emigrated that by 1840 the British government annexed the islands in order to save the local population, the Maori.

The Maori had a different view of land ownership than did the English; they believed that the land belonged to everyone and therefore could not be sold. British missionaries helped to muddle things; on the one hand, they defended the natives from aggressive land speculators, and on the other, they themselves were aggressive in their attempts to convert the Maori to Christianity. The Treaty of Waitonga made the Maori British subjects, but allowed them to retain control of the land. This worked for a few years until the formation of the New Zealand Company, which brought in some 30,000 settlers. The original intent of the New Zealand Company was to re-create British culture in a foreign land, and the new arrivals felt that the recognition of Maori rights robbed their own attempts of proper appreciation. The settlers, therefore, had little consideration for the natives. The decision in 1852 to allow local self-government to the settlers foreshadowed conflict, because the Crown was the sole agent allowed to acquire land from the Maori.

In 1860, an individual Maori sold a piece of land to the British government, but the Maori's tribe nullified the sale, saying he had no right to sell property collectively owned. The British took control of the land anyway, and war began. For five years, British troops fought against the Maori. They forced a peace treaty on Maori King Wiremu Kingi, though a violent resistance movement among irreconcilables continued through 1881. The defense of settlers' rights proved too expensive for the British Colonial Office, however, and they withdrew their troops in 1870. The Colonial Office hoped that by shifting the expense to the settlers, they would stop fighting to save money. For the most part, this worked.

The settlers had obtained the right to confiscate land, but surprisingly did not abuse that right. Most New Zealanders established cattle or sheep ranches that provided a good income but did not cover huge areas of land. When the first refrigerated ships arrived in 1881, the New Zealand economy really began to prosper. The export of wool was supplemented by dairy products, and almost all of it went to Britain. The profitable export market, coupled with a gold rush in the early 1870s, gave New Zealanders a high standard of living. These events came at a time in British society when humanitarian impulses were strong, resulting in experiments in social legislation that marked the island nation as truly progressive.

The Maori were able to take advantage of this as well. They maintained control over large tracts of land through the mid-1800s, but in time, European contact brought the same result faced by other native populations: death by disease. By the beginning of the twentieth century, the Maori population had decreased from over 200,000 to just over 40,000, which may account for their absorption into mainstream white society in New Zealand. They did not have sufficient numbers to pose a threat, nor did the whites need large amounts of cheap labor because they kept their landholdings fairly small. The humanitarianism of the time, coupled with the Maoris' ultimate embrace of European culture, created one of the world's few truly interracial societies.

Though the New Zealanders planned in the late 1800s to expand into the southern Pacific region, such dreams never came about. New Zealanders are often considered more British than the British in their rural outlook, but they have far outperformed their role models in the institution of government programs that successfully deal with labor, health, and culture.

See also Australia, British Occupation of.

References: Cain, P. J., *British Imperialism: Innovation and Expansion, 1688–1914* (London: Longman, 1993); Mc-Leod, A. L., *The Pattern of New Zealand Culture* (Ithaca, NY: Cornell University Press, 1968); Thomson, Arthur, *The Story of New Zealand* (New York: Praeger, 1970).

144 PARAGUAYAN WAR

After the removal of Spanish rule in South America in the 1820s, Paraguay resisted Argentine domination by declaring its independence from the previous viceroyalty of Rio de la Plata. Under two successive dictators, Francia and Lopez, Paraguay established a progressive and prosperous nation. The Paraguayans established economic and cultural ties with Europe; phased out slavery, yet had little feudalism or peonage; and had one of the highest literacy rates on the continent. Francisco Solano Lopez came to power in 1862 upon the death of his father.

In 1864, Lopez felt threatened by Brazil's interference in a civil war in neighboring Uruguay, through which landlocked Paraguay had access to the port city of Montevideo at the mouth of the Uruguay River. If a hostile government were to come to power there, Paraguay would have to depend on the goodwill of Argentina to allow sea access through Buenos Aires. Lopez's protests concerning Brazilian interference in Uruguay fell on deaf ears, so he decided to apply direct pressure by attacking the Brazilian province of Mato Grosso. This being a rugged and uninhabited territory, the attack had no effect. Lopez then asked permission of Bartolome Mitre, Argentina's leader, for access through his country to assist Uruguay, a request he refused. Considering this an unfriendly act, Paraguay declared war on Argentina in March 1865 and launched an invasion.

The attack brought about the formation of the Triple Alliance of Brazil, Argentina, and Uruguay on 1 May 1865. A secret clause in the treaty called for the alliance to confiscate about half the Paraguayan territory and divide it between Brazil and Argentina. The coalition of three nations—two of them the largest in South America—seemed overwhelming in its power. Though the well-trained, 70,000-man Paraguayan army outnumbered the combined coalition forces, Lopez was unable to press his invasion of Argentina, and was soon on the defensive. Alliance troops invaded across the Parana River in April 1866 and maintained their momentum. They won a hard-fought victory over a Paraguayan force at Fort Humaita in August 1868, then occupied the capital city of Asuncion in January 1869. Lopez was unable to strengthen his army, but the alliance forces, mainly Brazilian, continued to grow. Lopez's last stand came on 1 May 1870. He was killed in battle after being cornered against the Brazilian border, and his death meant the end of Paraguayan resistance.

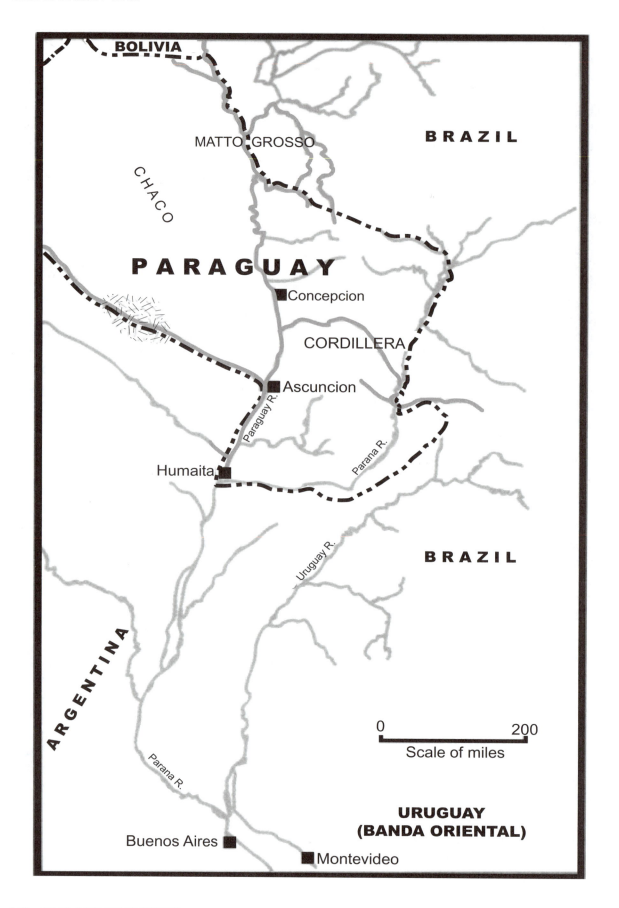

A prosperous and independent Paraguay was no more. The country's population had been devastated by the war, with three-fourths of the 500,000 citizens dying from combat, disease, starvation, or the brutal Brazilian occupation; the adult male population was reduced to only 30,000. As agreed during the formation of the Triple Alliance, Brazil and Argentina annexed about half the country and forced the Paraguayans to pay heavy reparations. Brazil established a puppet government of former Paraguayan generals, and proceeded to dismantle the decades of progress the country had enjoyed. Most of the land was sold to foreign investors at extremely low prices, and the economy came under the control of Brazilian investors.

Paraguay was not the only country affected by the war. Argentina had to raise taxes to pay for its involvement, which provoked a number of provincial uprisings during the conflict. The Argentine government was so busy suppressing these rebellions that by 1867, the Argentinians had virtually withdrawn from the war. Nevertheless, Brazil honored the agreement to give Argentina half the annexed land and half the reparation money.

References: Keen, Benjamin, and Mark Wasserman, A Short History of Latin America (Boston: Houghton Mifflin, 1984); Warren, Harris, Paraguay and the Triple Alliance (Austin, TX: Institute of Latin American Studies, 1978); Williams, John, The Rise and Fall of the Paraguayan Republic (Austin, TX: Institute of Latin American Studies, 1979).

PHILIPPINES, U.S. OCCUPATION OF THE

145

Even though the American declaration of war against Spain in 1898 was brought about by events in Cuba, the United States prepared to make war against Spanish possessions around the world. The first military action the Americans initiated was the U.S. Navy's destruction of the Spanish fleet at Manila Bay on 1 May. While this was an overwhelming victory, it had its drawbacks. Foremost among them was that ships cannot occupy ground, and therefore the Spanish army in the Philippines remained untouched. Because the U.S. Army was rapidly

expanding to fight the war, and the main focus would be on Cuba, troops could not be expected to arrive in the Philippines anytime soon. The actions taken by Admiral George Dewey to secure control of the islands laid the groundwork for a long struggle for American control.

Prior to the outbreak of war, the Filipinos, under the leadership of Emilio Aguinaldo, had engaged in struggles against the Spanish occupation. They failed, and the Spanish deported Aguinaldo to Hong Kong. By sheer luck, the U.S. Pacific Fleet was anchored in Hong Kong when war broke out against Spain. Assistant Secretary of the Navy Theodore Roosevelt cabled Dewey to proceed against the Spanish at Manila, and Dewey took Aguinaldo along with him. What transpired between Hong Kong and Manila is the subject of some debate. Dewey claimed that he asked Aguinaldo to go ashore and rouse his freedom fighters to control the countryside and keep the Spanish army penned in the cities. Aguinaldo claimed that Dewey promised freedom for the Philippines if Aguinaldo would cooperate—a claim which Dewey denied. Whether freedom was guaranteed or implied, the Filipinos believed it was theirs.

When the U.S. Army finally arrived to take possession of the Philippines, the peace negotiations between the United States and Spain were under way in Paris. Officially still at war, the Spanish commander did not want to surrender freely, yet he realized that his forces could not survive extended combat with the Americans. The two forces agreed to stage a mock battle for Spanish home consumption, then hold surrender ceremonies, and honor would be satisfied. This agreement, however, was just between American and Spanish officers. When the firing started, the Filipinos thought it was a real battle and joined in, killing several surprised Spanish soldiers before the Americans could stop the shooting. This exclusion from the official capture of Manila, their own capital, offended the Filipinos and set the stage for strained relations between native and "liberator."

When the Treaty of Paris of 1898 awarded possession of the Philippines to the United States in return for $20 million, the Filipinos assumed that this was a temporary measure, just as the American occupation of Cuba was to last only until the Cubans could govern themselves. After all, the U.S. Senate had stated prior to hostilities that it would not annex Cuba. True, but the declaration did not state that it would not annex anything else. The United States also acquired Guam and Puerto Rico from the Spanish, along with the Philippines, and it planned on keeping them all.

Aguinaldo and his followers felt betrayed, and warfare erupted. The Filipinos had occupied the string of blockhouses outside Manila since the beginning of the occupation, and they now occupied trenches overlooking the city. With their superior training and airpower, the Americans were able to dislodge them in a few days of hard fighting in early February 1899. The Americans pursued Aguinaldo's forces into the interior, where the Filipinos attempted to fight a conventional war, but they were hopelessly outclassed and outgunned. By May the war seemed to be over, and the American commander, Elwell Otis, settled in for the rainy season with bright prospects.

Otis informed Washington that the rebellion was over and that with the return of the dry season, he could begin to impose American will. After all, the Americans viewed themselves as the harbingers of civilization and wanted only to improve the lot of their "little brown brothers." Once civic improvements began, the Americans would be welcomed. There was only one problem: The fighting was not over. The Filipinos had failed to win a conventional war, so they turned to the guerrilla tactics for which their nature and the countryside were much better suited. Simultaneously, most of the American troops, who were volunteers, were coming to the end of their enlistment and were slated to go home. Hence, Otis would be losing much of his force at a time when more intense warfare was about to begin.

When new volunteer forces began to arrive in the fall of 1899, the early action seemed to confirm Otis's views. More of Aguinaldo's forces were defeated, and many of his main lieutenants were captured. With only "scattered resistance" left, Otis began the reform projects: road and bridge construction, increased access to health care and education, railroads, and telephone and telegraph lines. These projects were successful, and illiteracy began to drop, as did infant mortality and deaths from cholera, smallpox, and the

plague. Otis was quite surprised by the ongoing fighting in the countryside.

The countryfolk, long used to dealing with rugged terrain and banditry, became successful guerrillas immediately. Aguinaldo hoped that protracted warfare would disillusion the American public and bring support from Asian weapons suppliers. Hand in hand with guerrilla war against the army was terrorism against those who cooperated with the Americans.

Shadow governments operated in villages and controlled the people when the American forces were not on the scene. Collaborators were punished with either destruction of their property or torture and death. Captured American soldiers suffered similarly grisly fates, provoking equally harsh responses from the U.S. Army. The American soldiers, accustomed to dealing with Indian tribes in the United States, with atrocities committed and received, had little trouble continuing the process in this climate.

Otis was replaced in May 1900 by Arthur MacArthur, who continued Otis's reforms and expanded them, but began a more intensive campaign against the guerrillas. He trained friendly Filipinos to guide and fight alongside American forces, gather intelligence, and protect the villagers. He invoked General Order No. 100, first issued during the Civil War, which stated that war was to be fought between armies; partisans and guerrillas operated outside the law and would not be treated like soldiers, but punished like criminals. MacArthur was able to get more U.S. troops committed to the country, and by early 1901, he commanded 70,000 men. They began sweeping the countryside and harassing the guerrillas, keeping them away from villages that might provide them with supplies. He started a Filipino political party to have input into local administration as an alternative to Aguinaldo's political aspirations. When Aguinaldo was captured in March 1901, the underground leader soon issued a statement calling for an end to hostilities and the start of cooperation with the Americans. For the most part, the guerrillas gave up the fight, but two large bands (more bandit than patriot) continued the struggle.

The final actions against the insurrectos were brutal. Further atrocities provoked the

Americans into corresponding behavior. Field Commander Jacob Smith ordered his troops, "I wish you to kill and burn; the more you kill and burn the better it will please me. I want all persons killed who are capable of bearing arms in actual hostilities against the United States." Any male over 10 years old was to be targeted. While this mandate was not rigorously enforced, burning and destruction were, and they ended the activities of one of the guerrilla groups. The other group, operating in the southern part of the main island of Luzon, saw a different tactic used against them. The Americans rounded up 300,000 citizens in concentration camps, denying any public support to the guerrillas. Though many died of disease in these camps, just as many Cubans had, this tactic served its purpose. By April 1902 the fighting had ended.

After such a difficult experience establishing control, it is somewhat surprising that the Americans ever gained the friendship of the Filipinos. The continued efforts at reform, even in the midst of the brutality, bore fruit. The occupation forces tried to show themselves as helpers who had to deal in unpleasant ways with bandits in order to bring about improvement. The quick assimilation of Aguinaldo and other political figures into the civil administration helped to prove the Americans' desire to cooperate with the locals. Despite the fact that 20,000 Filipino soldiers died and an estimated 200,000 civilians perished from disease or mistreatment, the Americans and Filipinos managed to grow fond of each other. When World War II broke out and the Japanese invaded the islands, American and Filipino troops fought side by side, and then suffered side by side in prison camps. A relationship born in hostility became, through improved administration and cooperation, a close friendship.

See also Cuba, U.S. Invasion of; Philippines, Japanese Invasion of the.

References: Gates, John M., *Schoolbooks and Krags: The United States Army in the Philippines* (New York: Greenwood Press, 1973); Karnow, Stanley, *In Our Image: America's Empire in the Philippines* (New York: Random House, 1989); Miller, Stuart, *"Benevolent Assimilation": The American Conquest of the Philippines* (New Haven, CT Yale University Press, 1982).

PUERTO RICO, U.S. INVASION OF

146

Puerto Rico was one of only two remaining Spanish possessions in the Western Hemisphere when it became the target of American efforts to rid the Caribbean of Spanish influence in the Spanish-American War. Though the main fighting of the war took place in Cuba, which was secured by 17 July 1898, Puerto Rico seemed a tempting target. The Spanish government here was more liberal than in Cuba, allowing the Puerto Ricans a modicum of self-rule, but the Americans were perceived as liberators who would give the island its independence rather than hold it as a colony.

General Nelson Miles commanded the 3,300 troops who landed on the island on 21 July 1898. Fearing a direct attack on the capital of San Juan would prove too costly, they first captured the port of Ponce. The landings went smoothly, against minimal opposition, and reinforcements were soon on hand. The soldiers began to believe the occupation would be bloodless; the only trouble they had was with street vendors and large numbers of welcoming politicians. After a week of easy duty, Miles ordered his force to move across the island along a number of routes, all heading for San Juan. Only the lack of initiative on the part of the Spanish army kept this from being a bloodbath, because the rugged terrain could easily have disguised any number of ambushes. The most difficult engagement turned out to be no more than a skirmish, resulting in six American wounded and six Spanish deaths.

The Americans methodically made their way across the island, capturing town after town against little or no resistance. There was no battle for San Juan, because word came on 13 August that an armistice had been signed. The capture of Puerto Rico seemed ridiculously easy, but Miles's multipronged offensive was designed to outflank any large Spanish force, and the Spaniards rarely stood to fight. Though some writers dismissed the attack as a "picnic," correspondent Richard Harding Davis gave the credit for success to Miles. "The reason the Spanish bull gored our men in Cuba and failed to touch them in Porto Rico [sic] was entirely due to the fact that Miles was an expert matador; so it was hardly fair to the commanding General and the gentlemen under him to send the Porto Rican campaign down into history as a picnic."

The inhabitants of the island were angry that the United States would not grant them independence. Unlike the situation in Cuba, the United States had made no promise about freeing Puerto Rico. Instead, Congress voted to make the island an "unincorporated territory," which meant that the Puerto Ricans became citizens of no nation. Wealthy Americans bought up the best lands for agricultural production, and the locals had to work for them. However, there were benefits for the Puerto Ricans. Prior to the U.S. invasion, only two or three improved roads existed on the island, there were no banks, and only about one-fifth of the land was being farmed. U.S. investment and interest improved sanitation, utilities, and roads, though mainly within or between cities, leaving the peasants in the countryside lagging behind. The education system improved until some 80 percent of the island was literate, much higher than most Caribbean countries. Despite this, most of the profits that accrued from the outside investment resulted in those profits leaving the country. By 1930, the United States controlled 50 percent of the sugar production, 80 percent of the tobacco, 60 percent of the banks, 60 percent of the public utilities, and all of the shipping.

In 1917 Congress finally agreed to grant Puerto Ricans U.S. citizenship, and in 1947 gave them the right to elect their own governor. To this day, the inhabitants remain divided about the island's future, roughly equal numbers wanting independence, statehood, or to keep things as they are.

Spanish troops ready to engage the American forces during the U.S. invasion of Puerto Rico. (Photograph no. 533437; Record Group 165: Records of the War Department General and Special Staffs, 1860–1952; U.S. National Archives and Records Administration, College Park, MD.)

See also Cuba, U.S. Invasion of.

References: Carrion, Arturo Morales, *Puerto Rico, a Political and Cultural History* (New York: Norton, 1983); Friedel, Frank, *The Splendid Little War* (Boston: Little, Brown, 1958); Millis, Walter, *The Martial Spirit* (Boston: Houghton Mifflin, 1931).

147 SINGAPORE, BRITISH OCCUPATION OF

While the Dutch maintained a trade monopoly in the East Indies in the 1700s, the British stayed out of Southeast Asia and concentrated on the tea trade with India and China. By the end of the century, however, Dutch reverses in European wars led to a weakening of Holland's economic strength in the area around Malaysia. The growing power of the British East India Company drew the attention of the British government to the area, and Britain soon saw the need for a naval base on the eastern side of the Bay of Bengal. Francis Light, a trader well connected with Malay leaders, negotiated a British lease on Penang on the west coast of the Malay Peninsula. The base established there proved valuable to Britain's military needs, but the trade port failed to make as much money as Britain had hoped.

During the occupation of Holland by Napoleon, Britain occupied Dutch possessions around the world in an attempt to deny them to the French dictator. Because of this, the British took control of Malacca, farther down the Malay coast. Originally a Portuguese stronghold, the town had been seized by the Dutch in the 1640s. Britain moved into the port in 1795 and was reluctant to return it to the Dutch after Napoleon's defeat in 1815. Stamford Raffles, an active agent for the British East India Company, convinced his superiors of the necessity of dominating Malacca and the peninsula in general if the British were to challenge Dutch trading interests in Southeast Asia. Thus, Raffles was directed to find a suitable site to challenge the Dutch monopoly.

In 1819, Raffles chose Singapore, a small island off the tip of the Malay Peninsula. It had an excellent harbor and was sparsely populated; though the island was in Holland's sphere of influence, the Dutch had no presence there. To gain title to the island, Raffles had to deal with a pretender to the sultanate of Johore, on the island of Sumatra across the Malaccan Straits. By recognizing the pretender, in opposition to the de facto sultan recognized by the Dutch, Raffles placed Britain in a precarious position should the Dutch challenge his occupation of the island. Challenge they did, but the negotiations dragged on from 1820 through 1823, during which time the importance and profits of Singapore grew to the point that the British were not about to abandon their claim. By making Singapore a free port, traders from all over Asia flocked there, away from the Dutch trade center at Batavia. The island's population skyrocketed from 150 when Raffles entered into the lease to 10,000 by the end of 1820. The trade center at Penang, never profitable, slipped even further into mediocrity.

The Dutch finally conceded British occupation of Singapore in the Treaty of London in 1824. Not only did they drop their opposition, but they also received delineated spheres of influence to maintain at least a partial monopoly. Britain could control Singapore and the Malay Peninsula, and Holland would dominate the islands south of the Malaccan Straits. Thus, Britain exchanged its one settlement on Sumatra for the Dutch settlement of Malacca. Trade in Borneo, however, remained contested. The ports of Penang, Malacca, and Singapore collectively became known as the Straits Settlements, and the British government viewed them as protection for trade to China. It would be decades before Britain moved deeply into Malay trade and politics.

By conceding the East Indies to the Dutch, the British abandoned Raffles's idea of creating a British colonial empire in Southeast Asia. The states of the Malay Peninsula were freed from the domination of the sultan of Johore on Sumatra and proceeded on their own course, while Siam dominated the interior for decades. In 1824, the British concluded a new agreement over Singapore. The original pact had given Britain permission to build a settlement; the new one gave Britain the island forever in return for a cash payment and a pension to the local chieftains.

The British may not have established an empire, but Singapore grew to dominate the Southeast Asian trade. By the middle 1800s the city was handling almost as much trade as all of the East Indies. Banks, trading companies, and insurance companies—the extra necessities for commerce—were centered there. The livelihood of most of the population was bound up with shipping, trade, and port labor, and its financial success attracted migration from all over, especially China. From 10,000 people in 1820, the city grew to more than 16,000 by 1830, more than doubled by 1840, and reached almost 60,000 by 1850. By 1860, of the 80,000 inhabitants on the island, 50,000 were Chinese, 13,000 were Indians, and the rest were Malays.

The Chinese dominated trade and the population with their financial success and introduced secret societies to protect their interests. These occasionally caused disturbances when they fought among themselves, and large riots occurred every few years. The fact that British administration for the settlement came from India probably explains the slack control. In 1867, Singapore came under the direction of the Colonial Office in London, but it practiced little direct control. The importance of Singapore as a trading center fluctuated, especially with the establishment of Hong Kong as the major port of egress from China, but with the opening of the Suez Canal and the increase in trade from Australia and New Zealand, the Straits Settlements became profitable enterprises.

Britain controlled the island and its success up to the outbreak of World War II, after which the situation changed.

See also East Indies, Dutch Occupation of the; Singapore and Malaya, Japanese Conquest of.

References: Hahn, Emily, *Raffles of Singapore, a Biography* (Garden City, NY: Doubleday &Co., 1946); Ryan, N.J., *A History of Malaysia and Singapore* (London: Oxford University Press, 1976).

148 SOMALIA, EUROPEAN COLONIZATION OF

The beginnings of a "state" of Somalia happened in the seventh century when the country came under Arab control through the arrival of immigrants from Yemen. In the sixteenth century, Portuguese merchants establishing trade connections in India and points east established a presence in Somalia by gaining control of a number of coastal towns. There was no serious attempt, however, to control territory further inland or to establish a full-fledged colony. When the Portuguese were finally forced out in the early eighteenth century, the sultanate of Zanzibar exercised something resembling control in the southern region, while the sultan of Oman loosely controlled the northern area.

During the widespread European colonization in the latter part of the nineteenth century, Somalia became the target of both British and Italian ambitions. The British arrived much earlier, negotiating treaties for harbor facilities in 1840. By the middle 1880s, the British had negotiated agreements with a number of northern tribes and established a protectorate of sorts. The British wanted to control the local supply of foodstuffs to supply their major port of Aden, just to the north across the Gulf of Aden. They ultimately established the colony of Somaliland and finalized a border with Ethiopia in 1897.

Meanwhile, the Italians were slowly acquiring control over the southern part of the region, also by signing protection agreements. They took control of the lands of two rival sultans in 1889, at which time the Italians informed them that as of the Berlin Conference five years earlier, Italy was now the owner of what came to be called Italian Somaliland. The Italians continued to spread their influence southward at the expense of the sultan of Zanzibar, who finally ceded control of his claims in 1925.

In the interior of the country, however, King Menelik II managed both to keep his country free of European domination and also stake a claim for some Somali territory himself. He did so in a region known as the Ogaden. Unwilling to have the British dominate the Red Sea/Gulf of Aden region, the French also got into the act by claiming a slice of land on the coast between British and Ethiopian claims. This came to be the colony of French Somaliland, today known as Djibouti.

Through the later part of the nineteenth and into the twentieth centuries, the Italians and

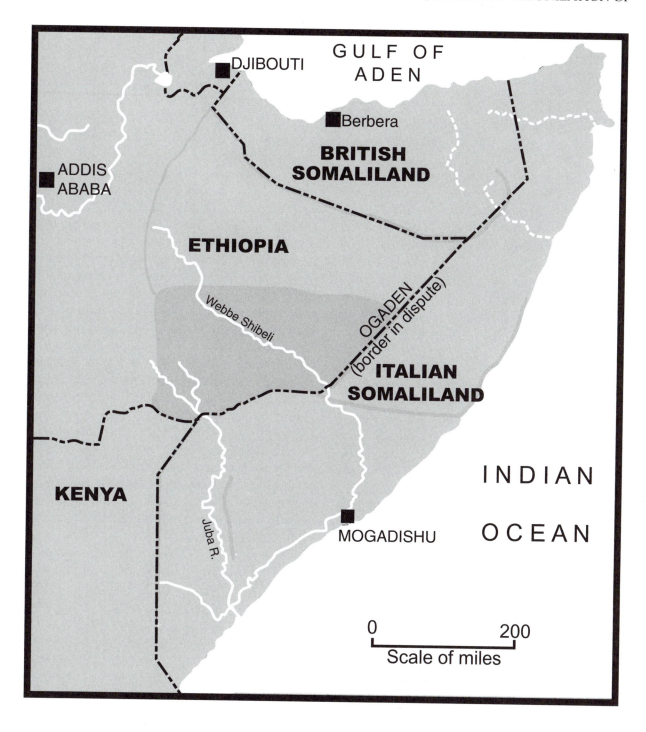

British established colonial administrations funded by taxation of the trade through the harbors
they controlled. In the interior, however,
Ethiopian military forces had no real source of
income and had to live off the land in the
Ogaden, thus alienating the Somalian population. It was this depredation at the hands of the
Ethiopians that began a Somali nationalist

movement. It started in 1899 under the leadership of a radical Muslim cleric, Mahammad
Abdille Hasan. Hasan followed the Salihiyah
order and his followers were the dervishes, the
same order that had resisted Egyptian and British
expansion into the Sudan two decades earlier.
The dervish resistance movement came to target
British as well as Ethiopian interests, and

the British government, after some hesitation, committed troops to fight the "Mad Mullah." In January 1904, Hasan suffered a major defeat which led to his signing a peace agreement in 1905 with both the British and Italian administrations. He honored it only for a couple of years before he was back in British Somaliland staging raids. In the first two decades of the twentieth century, the fighting caused the death of some one-third of the northern Somali population and virtually destroyed the economy. Only Hasan's death in 1920 (killed by British aerial attack on his capital at Taleex) ended the movement.

As in Libya, the Italians became intent on using Somaliland as an outlet for surplus population that would bring European standards to the region. The rise of Benito Mussolini's fascism in the 1920s added further impetus to the plan, as the Italian government was eager to spread its influence wherever possible. Large-scale development projects, primarily agricultural, resulted in a major increase in the colony's economy. In British Somaliland, however, there was less interest in local improvement; instead, the area remained a supply base for Aden as it had always been. The difference in economic growth showed itself when the two colonies merged later.

In 1935, Italy's Mussolini began his aggressive campaign to reestablish the Roman Empire. His assault on Ethiopia was soon followed by a takeover of British Somaliland (1940). This brought, at least temporarily, a unification of the country. During the Italian occupation, the wealth was spread somewhat into the northern region and a barter economy was replaced with a monetary one. More immigrants, both Italian soldiers and civilians from the homeland, moved into Somaliland in order to consolidate Italian control. The Italian takeover also brought further trade with the outside world as well as an increase in public works. For the most part, the Italian occupation was beneficial to the country. Unfortunately, the occupation was brief, as the British established control in 1941 in all Italian-held areas of Africa. After placing Ethiopian King Haile Selassie back on the throne, the British returned the Ogaden region to his authority and placed the former Italian Somaliland under a military administration. The

British goal was primarily peacekeeping. Local forces were raised in northern (Somaliland Scouts) and southern (Somalia Gendarmerie) regions, under British command.

The main long-term result of the occupation during World War II was the influx of weaponry into the country. Coupling that with the encouragement of rebels in the Ogaden to keep the British away from the border caused the population to become better armed and more aggressive. Most of the peacekeeping operations conducted during those years were attempts to disarm Somali bandit groups. Meanwhile, the new British administration began to implement some modernization. Spending more money in the northern region raised its standard of living. Health services and aid to agriculture were increased, as were attempts to expand the water supply for the herders in the countryside. Secular schools were initiated, as was a new judiciary which blended Islamic and British common law. Further, greater local political autonomy was granted as Italian appointees were removed and replaced by governing bodies which advised the British administration. On the other hand, Italian workers and specialists who had begun public improvements were kept on the job as long as they posed no security risk. Also, the Somalis were granted more access to police and civil service jobs.

The roots of Somali independence began with the formation of the Somali Youth Club, a political party formed in Mogadishu in 1943. By 1947, it was renamed the Somali Youth League and began to open party offices around the country. The League openly began to call for Somali unity and independence from both British and Ethiopian rule. Within a few years, a number of parties had formed, most based on a clan foundation, but some trying to unify the country without reference to any family or ethnic basis.

Technically, Italian Somaliland was still an Italian colony, but in 1945 the United Nations Council of Foreign Ministers was assigned the task of determining the nation's future. Britain proposed a single united colony under their control. In January 1948, U.N. representatives arrived to gauge the depth of the Somali independence movement. The Somali Youth League and pro-Italian factions demonstrated to show off their strength, but clashes between the two factions led to violence. Still, the U.N. representatives decided, after talks with a number of parties, that independence was the correct path to follow. However, there was no agreement on how to lead the country to that path. The only solid decision made was to officially give the Ogaden region to Ethiopia, a move which angered Somali nationalists; it did, however, fulfill American and British needs for a military presence in Ethiopia. In 1949, the U.N. General Assembly finally took up the question of Somalia's future. It was decided to allow Italy a 10-year trusteeship over their former colony with independence to be granted in 1960. This further angered the nationalist parties.

In the end, it made little difference. The British voluntarily ceded control of their administration in the north in 1960 so the area could unite with the southern provinces as soon as they became independent. The union took place on 1 July 1960 and the Somali Republic was proclaimed. A constitution was adopted based on the one in place in the southern provinces. Unfortunately, it ended up centering power in the south around the capital of Mogadishu, causing the northerners to feel they were getting less government attention. To keep the pot boiling, there were still active movements trying to reacquire the Ogaden from Ethiopia. Prime Minister Mohamed Ibrahim Egal (1967–1969) announced that Somalia would no longer claim the region, but that angered the Somalis so much that the army, under the leadership of General Mohamed Said Barre, overthrew Egal. That not only ended his career, but also ended party politics in Somalia.

Since 1969, conditions in Somalia have gone from bad to worse. The intermittent border wars over the Ogaden have kept the country in a perpetual state of warfare. The revolutionary council created after the 1969 coup attempted to impose socialism and ally itself with the Soviet Union, but when the Soviets and Cubans sent troops to Ethiopia, Somalia turned to the West for aid. The United States was quick to respond. Barre, however, grew increasingly unpopular with the population and by 1990 controlled little outside Mogadishu. After that, local warlords ran their parts of the country, hijacking international aid for their own influence and profit. Attempts to enforce the delivery of food to the population, primarily Operation Restore Hope under U.S. command, have been miserable failures. Although a transitional government was elected in 2004, conditions within the country remained so chaotic that as of this writing there is no functioning government in Somalia.

See also Ethiopia, Italian invasion of; Libya, Italian occupation of; Kenya, British occupation of.

References: Metz, Helen Chapin, *Somalia: A Country Study* (Washington, DC: Government Printing Office, 1993); "Background Notes: Somalia," Bureau of African Affairs, U.S. Department of State, <www.state.gov/r/pa/ei/bgn/2863.htm>, 18 November 2005; "First Jihad of the 'Mad Mullah'1899-1905," <www.onwar.com/aced/data/mike/madmullah1899.htm>, 10 December 2005.

SOUTH AFRICA, BRITISH OCCUPATION OF

149

The southern portion of the African continent was the last to attract serious attention from Europeans. It is not surprising that the Dutch were the first to settle people there, because they had most of the shipping going around the Cape of Good Hope en route to the East Indies. They established a way station in southern Africa in 1652, from which a colony began to grow. The victualing station needed farmers to provide food and soldiers to provide protection, so a number of Dutch moved in to begin a new life of farming, ranching, or hunting. The inhabitants called themselves Boers, the Dutch word for farmer. Eventually, the Boers expanded their population and moved northward, pressing back the native population with mixed results: The Hottentots became laborers, the Bushmen became targets of genocide, and the numerous Bantu tribes, such as the Zulus and Matabele, became rivals for control of the land.

When French forces occupied the Netherlands in 1795, the British responded by occupying the Dutch colony at the Cape. Increased British trade with India could not be threatened by French forces in southern Africa, though the British saw no economic value in the colony itself. Still, they took it as their own in 1806, and this was confirmed in the peace process in Europe after Napoleon's defeat.

Keeping the colony would not prove nearly as easy as gaining it. When the British began to export settlers to the colony, the Boers resented the intrusion. They had grown accustomed to settling huge ranches, and did not want a foreign population robbing them of what they considered their lands. The British could not abide the relationship the Boers had with the Hottentots, which was one of virtual slavery. When the new British administration began to act in favor of native rights, the Boers decided it was time to move. They pushed northeastward, paralleling the coast, into the area known as Natal, recently left empty because of native wars. When the British would not or could not commit sufficient forces to defend the frontiers expanded by the Boers, the Dutch saw it as "kaffir-loving," a policy of favoring "colored" over white. They decided to move again, this time far enough to get away from British politicians. Thus began the Great Trek.

Beginning in 1835, 14,000 people ultimately migrated into the veld land farther north—lands occupied by native groups who did not want to leave. The Zulu and Ndebele tribes resisted, and their societies, which emphasized military training, were willing to fight the Boers at every turn. The Boer's superior firepower became the deciding factor, and small Boer republics sprang up wherever the Dutch settled to raise their crops and herd their livestock. The Boers became even more conservative in their views: They believed that they were a people chosen by God, the land was theirs to take, and the natives were an inferior race permissible to use or abuse as they saw fit. When the British annexed Natal in 1842, some Boers stayed, while others moved even farther north across the Vaal River, establishing the Transvaal Republic.

The two white communities began to tolerate each other. Then, in 1867, major changes came to the area: Diamonds were discovered just south of the Vaal River. There was a mining rush, mainly British, and the Boers were able to keep few claims. The new wealth created problems. The discoveries were in territory claimed by both Boer trekkers and British; the British bought out the Dutch claims just south of the Vaal. The main labor force in the mines consisted of natives who, though they worked for much less than white miners, still made plenty of money, which they spent on firearms to take back to their tribes. The traditional hostility between native and Boer grew sharper, and British policies were sufficiently irregular to keep the whites hostile to each other as well. The Boers believed the British were too conciliatory to the natives; yet, at the same time, the British occasionally treated the Natal tribes much like the Americans treated the native tribes during their westward expansion, putting them on reservations, then persecuting them when the whites wanted the land. As native labor became more in demand, and therefore more expensive, both the needs of white businessmen and the fears of black power grew.

In 1852 the British recognized the independence of the Transvaal, but the Dutch did not manage their republic too well. Owing to expensive campaigns against local tribes and a defaulted foreign loan, the republic was in dire financial straits. In 1877 the British offered to annex the Transvaal, delivering the Boers from their financial problems and providing protection on the frontiers. The local government reluctantly agreed to temporarily accept the annexation while their representatives traveled to London to get it reversed. The reversal did not happen, but the Boers were in no financial or military state to halt the course of events. Britain wanted the Cape Colony so it could federate all the lands available, much as in Canada, and the Transvaal was necessary for that goal. If the British could establish a united native policy throughout the federation, certainly peace and prosperity would follow. Also necessary was domination over all native lands. The British invaded Zululand in 1878–1879 on trumped-up excuses and established control there; the Pedi were defeated and scattered a few months later, and most other tribes saw the futility of resistance. Momentarily at least, the British had made good on their promise to protect the Boers from hostile natives.

With no native threat, the Boers believed the British presence had become unnecessary, and that the Transvaal should have its independence restored. When the British refused ("As long as the sun shines over South Africa, the British flag will fly over Pretoria"), the Boers began cleaning their rifles. After the British provoked an incident over a Boer who would not pay his taxes, the Boers began organizing. Under the leadership of Paul Kruger (nicknamed "Oom," Dutch for uncle), who had gone to London to protest the annexation, the Boers declared their independence in November 1880. They raised a force of 7,000 men, three times the number the British had in Transvaal, sent men to besiege British garrisons in Transvaal towns, and began to fight a guerrilla war. In November, December, and January they fought three battles, and in each defeated a superior British detachment. The embarrassed British government hastily approved negotiations to give the Boers independence. The general on the spot, Sir George Colley, disagreed with the government's offer and decided to press on. He died, along with the majority of his force of 400 men, at the battle of Majuba Hill in late January 1881. Kruger accepted the offer to negotiate, and in late March the Transvaal was again independent, though the British did retain the right to direct the Boers' foreign policy.

Gold was soon discovered in the Transvaal. In order to exploit the mines, foreign (Uitlander) engineers had to be imported, and they tended to be British. By the late 1890s a large British population had migrated to the Boer republic to work the mines. Despite the wealth they now enjoyed, the Boers remained wary. British expansionists, led by gold and diamond magnate Cecil Rhodes, had acquired land to the north of the Transvaal, effectively seizing the mineral rights, but more importantly denying the Boers room to expand. With British territory above and below them, the Boers felt sure they would soon be obliged to defend their lands. When Rhodes sponsored a raid into the Transvaal, hoping futilely for a British uprising to grab the country and its riches for the empire, the fears of the Dutch farmers were confirmed. They responded by further denying political rights to Uitlanders in their country, keeping them in the position of second-class citizens. The native population, of course, remained beyond the hope of even that lowly status.

This was not a social position the British were prepared to accept. They appealed to the British government to protect them and, desiring not only wealth but the geographic position of Boer lands, the government responded. By controlling Egypt and having a dominant position in countries to the south, a transcontinental Cape-to-Cairo railroad was possible. This would mean wealth and political power for the British Empire if they could build it, but to do so they needed to gain control of the right of way through the Boer republics of the Transvaal and the Orange Free State on Africa's southern border. Additionally, there were soldiers in the British army, still chafing from the defeat the Boers dealt them in 1880–1881, who would truly savor revenge. The British public received a steady diet of anti-Boer propaganda to prepare them for the war that seemed inevitable.

Paul Kruger, now president of the Transvaal, saw the British designs and responded by launching preemptive attacks against British towns in Natal and along the southern and western borders of the Orange Free State. If the Boers could control Natal (which they believed the British stole from them after the Great Trek), the British would have a difficult time bringing in reinforcements. After all, the Cape Colony, even though long under British rule, had a Boer majority among its population.

Britain was confident that the Boers could again be easily overcome. Instead, Boer forces quickly besieged British garrisons and drove 100 miles into the Cape Colony. When the British finally began to arrive in large numbers in November, the Boers stopped to consolidate. When the British attacked in December, the Boers thrashed them three times in one week, and by Christmas, the British had suffered 7,000 casualties. The growing British forces, however, ultimately forced the Boers to resort to guerrilla tactics. As the British made their way into Boer territory, the enemy melted into the hills and harassed them with ambushes. The British responded with the one proven method of dealing with a guerrilla movement. As Mao Tse-tung would later write, "The population is the sea in which the guerrilla fish swims." Take away the population, and the guerrilla has no one to provide food, information, or refuge. The British rounded up the Boer population of women and children and placed them in concentration camps from which they could provide no assistance. Then the British began a slow, expensive process to literally corral the Boers, crisscrossing the countryside with barbed-wire fencing and regularly placed strong points. By building more and more fences, they gradually lessened the area inside which the Boers could operate, and any attempt to break through brought quick responses from the strong points. With a smaller and smaller area in which to operate and gather supplies, the Boers were finally starved into submission.

The fighting went on until May 1902, when the exhausted Boers reached the bitter end and signed a peace treaty. They were promised self-government sometime in the future, plus immediate financial relief for the losses they suffered—and losses there were. Owing to poor initial management of the concentration camps, huge numbers of civilians died from typhoid fever, dysentery, and measles. Casualties numbered some 28,000 white women and children out of a total of just over 111,000, and 14,000 out of almost 44,000 native internees. A total of 7,000 Boer men were killed in combat. The British lost 20,000 men and spent £200 million, but they had control over the land. The Boers and the British ultimately managed a relatively peaceful coexistence. When World War I came in 1914, the South African contingent helping the British was led by Jan Smuts, who had been one of the primary commanders of Boer forces.

The Peace of Vereeniging, which ended the South African War of 1899–1902, had long-lasting aftereffects. The treaty stated that the native population would receive political rights after the nation received its independence, without spelling out exactly when "after" would be. When provincial autonomy was granted in 1906 to the Transvaal and in 1907 to the Orange Free State, the Boer population controlled the government in those provinces, as well as in Natal and the Cape Colony. They also dominated the gold and silver mining, and therein lay a problem. Britain needed the wealth the mines could produce, but the British people had a difficult time with the Boers' policies in regard to their labor, both natives and imported Asians. The Boers kept them in a state of semislavery and allowed them no political rights. The British government tried to protect the rights of the abused, but could not legally do so because they had granted self-government to the provinces. When the provinces united in 1910 to create the Union of South Africa, the descendants of the ultraconservative, God-fearing, self-perceived Chosen People instituted the policy of apartheid that made the country infamous in the latter half of the twentieth century. The country grew to become the wealthiest in Africa, a wealth built on gold and diamonds, but the native population was not included in the spoils.

See also Zulus, Expansion of; Egypt, Napoleon Buonaparte; Indians of North America, U.S. Conquest of; Zululand, British Invasion of.

References: Nuttingham, Anthony, *Scramble for Africa: The Great Trek to the Boer War* (London: Constable, 1970); Pakenham, Thomas, *The Scramble for Africa: White Man's Conquest of the Dark Continent* (New York: Random House, 1991); Porter, Bernard, *The Lion's Share* (London: Longman, 1975).

UGANDA, BRITISH OCCUPATION OF

150

Uganda was settled in the first millennium C.E. by migrations of Bantu-speaking peoples from the south and Nilotic speakers from the north. The northerners, who settled into the grasslands of the northern region, soon established dominance over the more pastoral southerners, who settled in the area around Lake Victoria. As is the nature of herding societies, they tended to be more militarily oriented owing to their need to defend their stock and to acquire new animals from others. That military ability was the primary reason for their dominance, and the first unified government was established circa 1100 C.E. by the Bachwezi (Chwezi) dynasty, which ruled for about 500 years. In the wake of the dynasty's collapse, a number of smaller kingdoms emerged, which eventually centered in Buganda (around Lake Victoria) and Bunyoro in the north, where a new migration of the Bito displaced the Chwezi (who migrated to modern-day Rwanda and Burundi). An exiled Bunyoro pretender to the throne

arrived in Buganda in the 1400s and took control of what was becoming a more organized, less clan-centered society. This exile, Kimera, made himself the first *kabaka*, or king of Buganda.

Over time, the Bugandan kings began a policy of expansion, which ultimately made them the dominant force in the country. By the late nineteenth century, Buganda possessed a huge military. British explorer Henry Stanley, visiting in 1875, described an army of 125,000 leaving for a single campaign, and a navy of hundreds of outriggers controlling Lake Victoria and ferrying troops to suppress rebellions anywhere along the shores. "At Buganda's capital, Stanley found a well-ordered town of about 40,000 surrounding the king's palace, which was situated atop a com-

manding hill. A wall more than four kilometers in circumference surrounded the palace compound, which was filled with grass-roofed houses, meeting halls, and storage buildings. At the entrance to the court burned the royal fire (*gombolola*), which would only be extinguished when the *kabaka* died." (Byrnes, *Uganda*)

It was this powerful kingdom that dealt with a multitude of foreign visitors and merchants. Muslim ivory traders appeared in the 1840s, bringing products from India and (more importantly) gunpowder weapons. They also brought Islam, to which a number of citizens converted, although the king remained more interested in consumer goods. The Bunyoro in the north also traded whatever they had for guns, in an attempt to keep from being overwhelmed. They also had to deal with invaders from the north: Khedive Ismail was trying to expand his Egyptian kingdom further south. Egyptian troops were led by a British officer, Samuel Baker, who barely escaped with his life after an abortive attempt to invade Bunyoro. His account of that event published in Britain prejudiced the country against Bunyoro. That had a great impact when British merchants and missionaries arrived in Buganda, which had been portrayed in a very positive light by J. H. Speke (searching for the source of the Nile in 1862) and by Stanley after his visit in 1875. Indeed, the first British missionaries arrived in 1877 (invited by the kabaka), followed by French Catholic missionaries in 1879. Their success at conversion, coupled with the introduction of Islam 30 years earlier, laid yet another foundation for rivalries among the population.

The increasing influence of Christianity had a negative effect on the kabaka, Mwanga, who found himself being worshiped less and less. When Mwanga moved to ban all foreign religions, the Muslims and Christians joined against him. Then, starting in 1888, that short-lived alliance fell apart in a four-year-long Christian-Muslim civil war. After early successes, the Muslims were finally defeated. Mwanga was reinstated but his position was now little more than figurehead as the Protestant and Catholic citizens had formed themselves into political factions. The Anglo-French religious rivalry, however, was soon overshadowed by an Anglo-German economic competition.

The Imperial East African Company sent F. J. Jackson as their representative to establish firm British influence over Buganda. Unfortunately for him, the German Karl Peters had already arrived and gained the support of the Catholic party and, by extension, Mwanga. Mwanga would not sign a treaty with Jackson, but events in Europe settled the issue. In 1890, Britain traded the island of Heligoland in the North Sea to Germany in exchange for the German withdrawal from Buganda. In response, the Catholics (rather than supporting Britain) urged their party to declare independence. The Catholics gained the upper hand at first, but the arrival of British Captain Frederick Lugard and an early version of

a Maxim machine gun sent the French packing and left the British Protestants in control.

Jackson, the British government representative, aided by Lugard, soon spread British control over the northern and southern regions. In the north, Egypt once again threatened Bunyoro, and the Bunyoro King Kabalega (Kabarega) was buying guns from Charles Stokes, a British missionary turned gun runner. After joining with some Nubian mercenaries left over from the failed Egyptian invasion, Lugard and the Protestant forces finally wrested control of Bunyoro after a five-year struggle. An uprising by those same mercenaries in 1897 took a further two years to suppress. After dealing with a number of minor kingdoms (through diplomacy or military force), the British finally exercised total control over what came to be called the Uganda Protectorate. By the turn of the century, the kingdom of Buganda was granted a large measure of autonomy within the protectorate and also given roughly half of the Bunyoro territory. Still, all was dependent on loyalty to Britain. "The last two provisions [of the treaty] dealt with definitions and the interpretation of the agreement—interpretation in the sense that it was laid down that the English version of the agreement, not the [Ugandan] one, would be binding on both parties and, of course, none of the [Ugandan] signatories understood English." (Karugire, *Political History*)

In 1900, London sent Sir Harry Johnston to oversee the Uganda Protectorate and implement economic reforms. These included distribution of land to private citizens, as opposed to the communal system which had been the norm under royal control. The desire for personal property led to massive internal migration, but the need for land was obvious when the British began instituting taxes. In earlier times the king had collected taxes in kind, but the need to use money to pay taxes was designed to encourage the populace to become productive for the international market. Significant income resulted from the institution of cotton growing, improved by the completion of the railway to the Indian Ocean port of Mombasa in 1902. Education was limited, however, with the missionary schools providing the bulk of the teaching and that being primarily basic literacy, with little or no vocational training. This produced government workers and low-level business employees, but no real middle class.

The first serious stirring of discontent began in the 1920s. Uganda had prospered during World War I, but the younger generation was impatient to move into important government positions held by those who had first taken over with the establishment of British rule. The British government responded by clearing out the old office-holders, who had become quite corrupt, and bringing in younger replacements. There was also an influx of white settlement, though not as extensive as in neighboring Kenya. That, plus the introduction of Asians for import-export workers, began to reduce the native population to lower class status. As the population grew for all races, the prejudice against the black population began to increase. So did the feelings of resentment and movements to remedy the situation. Not until 1947, however, did serious action take place with the formation of the Ugandan African Farmers Union. In 1949, farmers began to demonstrate for a removal of government price controls as well as the breaking up of the Indian-controlled cotton gins. They also demanded a greater say in government, since the powerless kabaka could not speak for them even if he wanted to. The British administration broke up the Farmers Union, but a movement was already in the works in London to grant independence.

In the wake of the British withdrawal from India, the growing African nationalist movements, and a more liberal Colonial Office, the new governor in Uganda began laying the groundwork for independence even before a serious nationalist movement had begun. In 1952, Sir Andrew Cohen began granting all the Farmers Union's demands. The only fly in the ointment came from London, where the idea of an East African federation of countries was proposed. No one in Africa cared for the idea, especially the Ugandans, who feared both a white-dominated government and possible violence like the Mau Mau rising in Kenya. Not only did they oppose the federation, the kabaka began to demand that Buganda be allowed to secede

from the rest of the colony. In response, Kabaka Mutesa was exiled; that created even more resistance to British rule. He was finally allowed to resume his throne in 1955. Throughout the 1950s, political parties began to appear, primarily based on the religious parties of earlier days. In 1958, however, the Uganda Peoples Union was created without a religious foundation. All parties began calling for immediate elections, and finally the British administration scheduled them for 1961. The elections for a constitutional congress were boycotted by the Kabaka Yekka (the party supporting the king), which still wanted an independent Buganda. They soon realized the folly of the boycott and responded to a British proposal for limited autonomy in return for Bugandan support for a federal government. In the end, Milton Obote of the Uganda People's Congress became prime minister of the new, independent Ugandan government, with Kabaka Mutesa granted the ceremonial position of head of state.

Independence did not bring peace, however. The factions that had dominated Ugandan society for decades had not worked together to expel the British, as had happened in so many other colonies. Thus, there was no foundation for cooperation and the longstanding hostilities of north and south, Catholic and Protestant, farmer and herder, all began to reemerge. A mutiny by the army in 1964, although suppressed by British forces, led to a stronger military in its wake. Obote, after secretly aiding rebels in the Congo, faced a no-confidence vote in parliament. He responded by staging a coup d'état under the leadership of his protege, Idi Amin Dada. Obote began to implement a socialist regime and no elections were held again until 1980. Obote, after several failed attempts on his life, was deposed while out of the country. Amin replaced him and established a military dictatorship which began an extremely erratic foreign and domestic policy that ended in the slaughter of thousands of Ugandans and isolation from the outside world. Finally, after declaring war against Tanzania in 1979, Idi Amin was defeated and forced into exile. The 1980 election held after his departure was riddled with corruption, and Uganda remains a country with severe internal problems, as well as ties to the genocide of Rwanda in the 1990s.

References: Byrnes, Rita M., ed., *Uganda: A Country Study* (Washington, DC: Government Printing Office, 1992); Karugire, Samwari, *A Political History of Uganda* (Exeter, NH: Heinemann, 1980); "Political History of Uganda," <www.enteruganda.com>, 27 December 2005.

151   WAR OF THE PACIFIC

From 1874 to 1879, the South American nation of Chile experienced a depression caused by falling copper and wheat prices, a dropping off of exports, and rising unemployment. The only bright spot in the economy was the expanding nitrate business, but its mining eventually caused war between Chile and its neighbors, Peru and Bolivia. Nitrates were mined in the Atacama Desert along the Chile-Bolivia border. Most of the work was done by Anglo-Chilean companies, which operated in the Bolivian province of Antofagasta and the Peruvian province of Tarapaca. An 1866 treaty between Bolivia and Chile set their border at the 24th parallel, with both countries able to mine nitrates between the 23rd and 25th parallels; tax revenue collected by either country along the frontier would be split with the other country. This taxation arrangement was altered in 1874 when Chile agreed to give up its share of Bolivian tax revenue in return for a promise that taxes on Chilean profits in Bolivia would not be raised for 25 years.

Though Chile had no border with Peru, aggressive Chilean miners pushed into the Peruvian desert to mine nitrates. By 1875, some 10,000 people were employed in mining and subsidiary operations in the Peruvian Tarapaca desert region. Peru had thus far said little about the Anglo-Chilean operations in its province, but in 1875 a faltering economy forced the Peruvian government to nationalize the nitrate companies. The Peruvian government paid for the companies with government bonds paying 8 percent, payable in two years. When the bonds came due, the Peruvians were unable to honor their financial commitments and the bonds' value plummeted. The Anglo-Chilean companies were able to absorb the loss of the Peruvian assets, but

when the Bolivians decided in 1878 to raise taxes on the Chileans along the frontier in violation of the 1876 agreement, the loss of profits was too much to take. Chile refused to pay the higher taxes even when Bolivia threatened to nationalize the operations as the Peruvians had done. According to the 1876 agreement, an arbitrator should have been called in to handle the dispute, but Bolivia refused. The Bolivian government felt secure in its ability to back up its threats because of an 1874 secret mutual-defense treaty with Peru, but the Bolivians failed to consult the Peruvians in advance. In February 1879, Bolivia nationalized the mining companies, and Chilean troops went into action. On 14 February, they occupied the port of Antofagasta against no opposition; soon they were in control of the entire province. Not wanting to get involved in the fighting, Peru offered to mediate a peace settlement. Chile then learned of the secret treaty and, accusing the Peruvians of duplicity, declared war on them on 5 April 1879.

The combined Bolivian and Peruvian effort appeared daunting, especially since they had a combined population twice that of Chile, and Peru had a fairly good navy. However, Chile had a stronger and more stable central government, a more motivated population, a well-trained army, and a navy armed with two modern ironclads. Also, the main theater of operations was handier to Chile; the Bolivians had to cross the Andes, and the Peruvians had to cross the desert. All three countries were in economic trouble, but Chile was in the best financial shape and had the assistance of the British because the mining operations were mainly theirs. Both Bolivia and Peru had defaulted on British loans and angered the British by nationalizing the companies, so they had no qualms about supporting Chile.

The key battle of the war took place at sea on 8 October 1879, when the Chilean ironclads captured a Peruvian commerce raider, the *Huascar*, that had been hurting their trade and logistical operations. With control of the sea, Chile could supply its troops more efficiently, and the army was soon marching through Bolivian territory into Peru. Bolivia withdrew from the conflict in mid-1880 when Chilean troops occupied large parts of Peru. After a difficult battle, the Chileans captured the capital city of Lima in January 1881, effectively winning the war. Peruvians continued to fight a guerrilla war for two years, but on 20 October 1883 they gave up and signed the Treaty of Ancon. The treaty gave Chile the province of Tarapaca forever and two other provinces for 10 years, after which a referendum was to be held to determine their nationality. The referendum never took place, but in 1929 the two countries agreed to return the province of Tacna to Peru, while Chile kept the province of Arica.

The Bolivians signed an armistice with Chile in April 1884, in which they ceded the province of Antofagasta to Chile, but cession was not official until 1904, when a treaty was finally signed. That treaty obliged the Chileans to pay an indemnity and build a railroad from the Bolivian capital of La Paz to the coast of Arica. The railroad was completed in 1913.

With their army already mobilized, the Chilean government decided to use it to deal with the Araucanian Indians, a tribe that had been fighting for their land since colonial times. Hopelessly outnumbered and outsupplied, after two years the Indians were forced to sign a treaty in 1883 that placed them on reservations, though they were allowed to maintain tribal government and laws. Chile consolidated the rugged territory that had been the Araucanian homeland. With Peru bankrupt and Bolivia isolated, Chile became the strongest nation on South America's west coast. Control of the area's copper and nitrate meant an improving income, but close ties to Britain kept them from enjoying it totally. Chile decided to honor the Peruvian bonds issued when the Tarapaca mines were nationalized, and British speculators had been buying them up ever since Peru could not fulfill them. Thus, the British were able to control 70 percent of the nitrate production by 1890, as well as profit from their own construction of banks, railroads, and subsidiary businesses. Longstanding ties between Britain and the Chilean upper class made the British acquisition smoother, and some Chileans were able to profit from investments in British concerns.

References: Keen, Benjamin, and Mark Waserman, A Short History of Latin America (Boston: Houghton Mifflin, 1984); Loveman, Brian, The Legacy of Hispanic Capitalism (New York: Oxford University Press, 1979); Sater, William, Chile and the War of the Pacific (Lincoln: University of Nebraska Press, 1986).

ZULULAND, BRITISH INVASION OF

152

Queen Victoria's reign (1837–1901) marked the high point of British expansion and colonialism, with not a single year in which her soldiers were not engaged in combat somewhere in the empire. Of the many tribes the British fought in Africa, none were as feared and respected as the Zulus, the last great native empire on the continent.

The British army was equipped with the latest arms and technology. The officer corps came from Britain's elite, while the enlisted men were the lowest of society, suffering harsh discipline during their long term of service. The rank and file were among the best soldiers of their era, but the quality of the officers varied widely because promotion was a matter of wealth rather than ability, a factor of some consequence in the war against the Zulus. The British were better armed than their enemies and relied on superior firepower to compensate for their inferior numbers. The typical British strategy was to form one large or several small squares, each side two to four ranks deep, to provide virtually continuous fire. The greatest handicap was the British logistical system. Transporting the army's supplies required huge numbers of wagons and animals, often overloaded with officers' personal effects to make the campaign trail more comfortable.

The Zulu army was created by the great chieftain Shaka, who introduced a number of reforms that increased the army's ability. Shaka outlawed the use of hand axes and throwing spears, and introduced as the main weapon the iklwa, a short-shafted stabbing spear with a long, leaf-shaped blade. With the iklwa and a five-foot-high shield, the Zulus became masters of hand-to-hand fighting. Another favorite weapon was the knobkerrie, or iwisa, a club made from ironwood. The Zulu warrior was trained to ignore hunger, cold, and fatigue, and to go barefoot in order to be able to move more

The battle of Ulundi inside the square. (South African Library)

rapidly in battle. The standard battle formation was patterned after the charging buffalo: The central body was the head, followed by reserves immediately behind (the loins), and two flanking units as the horns. The tactic was to hold the enemy with the head while the horns attempted a double envelopment.

The Zulu military system was an integral part of Zulu society and culture, and training started early in life. Boys age 13 to 18 were organized into military kraals where they served three years as cadets, practicing military skills while herding cattle and working in the fields. When their training was over, they went to a regiment assigned to them by the king, where they would await his permission to get married. This would occur around age 35, at which point the warrior would leave the regiment and build a homestead.

The principal reason for war among the Zulus was cattle. Cattle played an important part in Zulu life by providing milk, raw materials, and meat for ceremonies. All cattle captured in battle became the property of the king, who distributed it to men who had reached marrying age and had proved themselves in battle. The importance of putting an age restriction on marriage can now be understood. Had there been none, not enough cattle would have been available for all those who wanted to marry, and Zulu society would have broken down. This cultural practice would become a key factor in the outbreak of hostilities with Britain.

The British goal in 1871 was to form a confederation of the various white colonies in South Africa and create an economy directed to the benefit of England. To accomplish this, the British government sent Sir Henry Bartle Frere, a distinguished colonial officer, to become governor of the Cape Colony. By accepting the position, Frere hoped to advance his personal fortunes and status, but this was not to be. Frere's first attempts to bring about the desired confederation met opposition from the local Dutch/Boer population, who threatened armed resistance. Further, in July 1878 a British

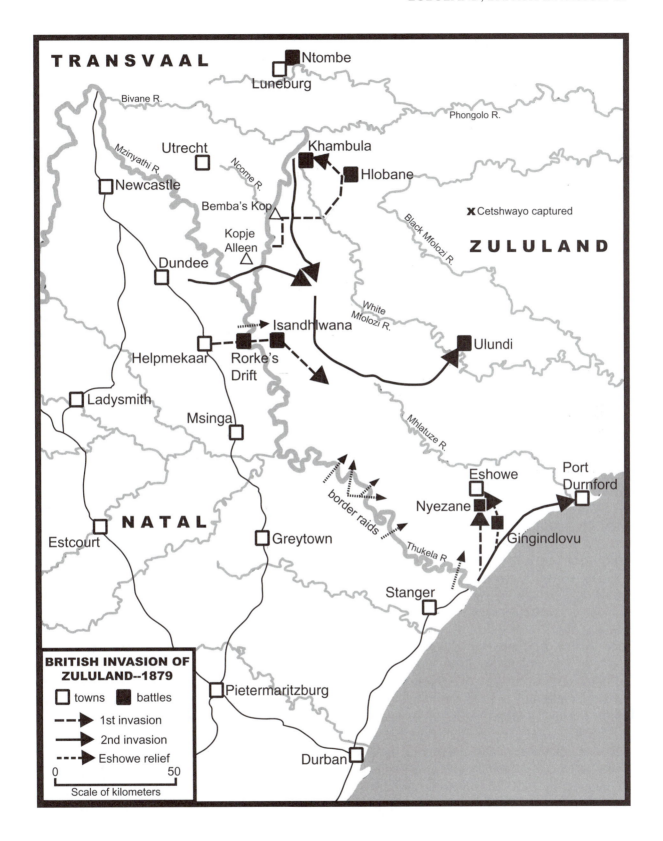

commission that had been appointed to decide a boundary dispute between the Zulus and the Transvaal found in favor of the native population. If Frere enforced this decision, it would increase white resistance and make the Boers even angrier. On top of these factors, many of the conquered African tribes pointed out that the British had failed to conquer the Zulus. Frere felt that in order to control those tribes, Britain must wage a successful war against the Zulus.

On 11 December 1878, Frere issued an intentionally unreasonable communiqué to King Cetshwayo and the Zulu nation. He demanded the complete dismissal of the entire Zulu army, the discontinuation of the Zulu military system, and permission for Zulu males to marry when they desired. Frere demanded an answer in 21 days, knowing it could not be fulfilled. King Cetshwayo was in a difficult position; it was impossible for him to disband the army, as it was not assembled and had not been for 20 years. Unlike European armies, the Zulus did not spend their time in barracks waiting for action. To fulfill Frere's demands would bring about the end of the Zulu social system, as there was not enough cattle to go around and no more could be acquired without going to war. As Cetshwayo put it, he felt like a man "trying to ward off a falling tree." When the ultimatum expired unanswered on 11 January, the British army was immediately on the march.

The British commander, Lord Chelmsford, invaded Zululand along a front of about 200 miles, aiming for the Zulu capital at Ulundi. Three columns invaded at different points, while two more stayed on the border in reserve. The first contact came at Isandlwana. A force of 20,000 Zulus marched to engage Chelmsford's column of 4,700. Chelmsford ordered that their position not be fortified, contrary to the advice of several of his officers. He then split his force, leading half to search out the Zulus and leaving the other half to defend the overly large baggage train. On 22 January, the 1,300 British troops left behind were overrun and slaughtered. The greatest British liability—their arrogance—was exposed.

At Isandlwana they learned a hard lesson, one they would not forget.

By the time Chelmsford returned to find his camp in ruins, the Zulus had already moved on. They attacked a small force of 130 men at a mission station on the Buffalo River called Rorke's Drift. Here the discipline of the British soldiers showed at its best, as they repeatedly beat back attacks over a period of two days. Use of the infantry square and firing in ranks—tactics that had not been used at Isandlwana—proved too much for the Zulus to overcome.

That same firepower and discipline proved decisive on 4 July at Ulundi, the Zulu capital, when the main Zulu army was defeated. Cetshwayo escaped, but his military power was gone. The British victory at Ulundi was credited to Lord Chelmsford, but he was in the process of being superseded by Sir Garnet Wolseley, who presided over the destruction of Zulu independence. Cetshwayo was captured a month after the battle at Ulundi and sent to England, where he met with Queen Victoria. After two years, he was returned to Zululand as king, but without any real power. In 1897, Zululand was annexed into Natal Province; there was a final attempt at freedom in 1906, but the rebellion was quickly suppressed. In the 1970s, some of the historical Zululand was incorporated into the province of KwaZulu, and then remerged to form the province of KwaZulu/Natal for the multiracial elections of 1994.

The Zulus, who had once dominated southern Africa, became just another native tribe under British rule. To this day, they maintain a tribal heritage, and they played a significant role in the Republic of South Africa's first postapartheid elections, but their trademark cowskin shields and short stabbing spears are tourist items now rather than the weapons of war that shocked the British nation in 1879.

See also Zulus, Expansion of.

References: Farwell, Byron, *Queen Victoria's Little Wars* (New York: Harper & Row, 1972); Morris, Donald, *The Washing of the Spears* (New York: Simon & Schuster, 1965).

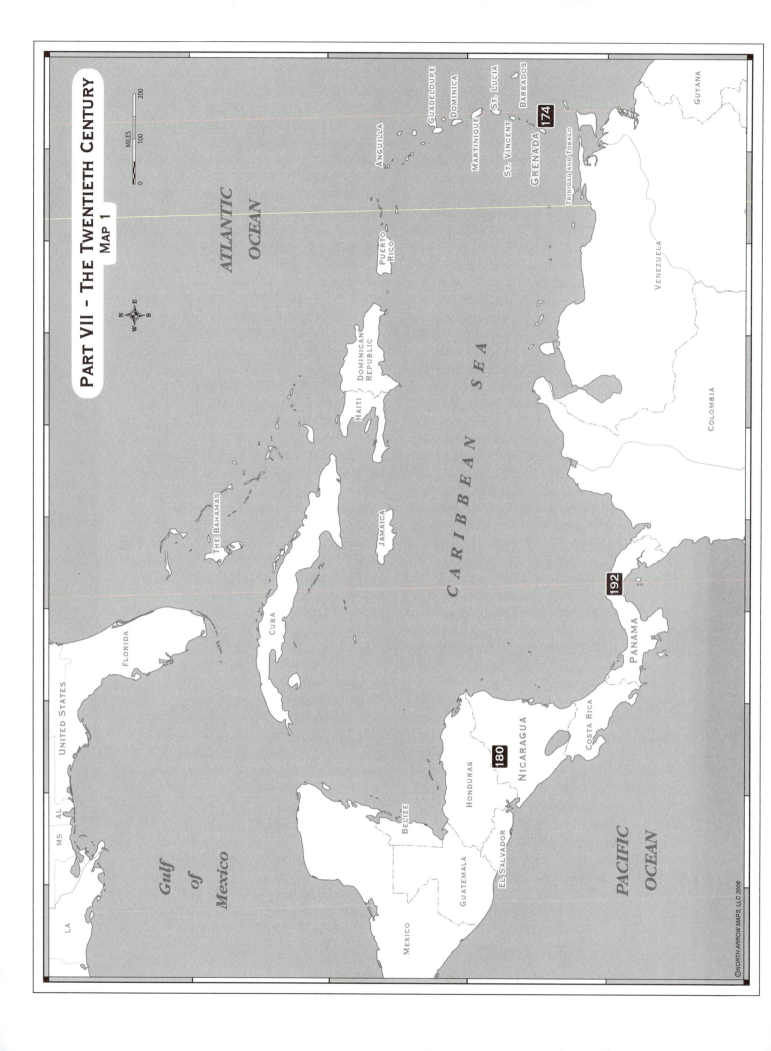

PART VII – THE TWENTIETH CENTURY
MAP 1

MILES
0   100   200

ATLANTIC OCEAN

GUADELOUPE
DOMINICA
St. LUCIA
BARBADOS
ANGUILLA
MARTINIQUE
St. VINCENT
GRENADA **174**
TRINIDAD AND TOBAGO

GUYANA

PUERTO RICO

VENEZUELA

COLOMBIA

DOMINICAN REPUBLIC

HAITI

CARIBBEAN SEA

JAMAICA

THE BAHAMAS

CUBA

FLORIDA

UNITED STATES

LA   MS   AL

Gulf of Mexico

PANAMA **192**

COSTA RICA

NICARAGUA **180**

HONDURAS

BELIZE

GUATEMALA

EL SALVADOR

MEXICO

PACIFIC OCEAN

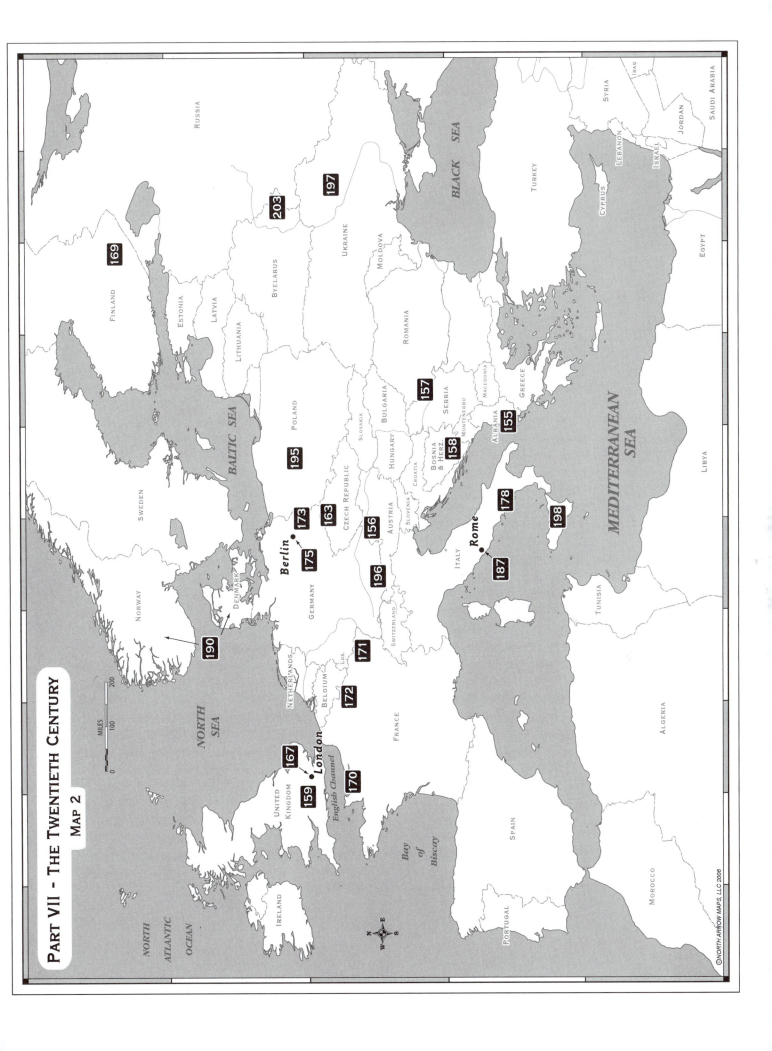

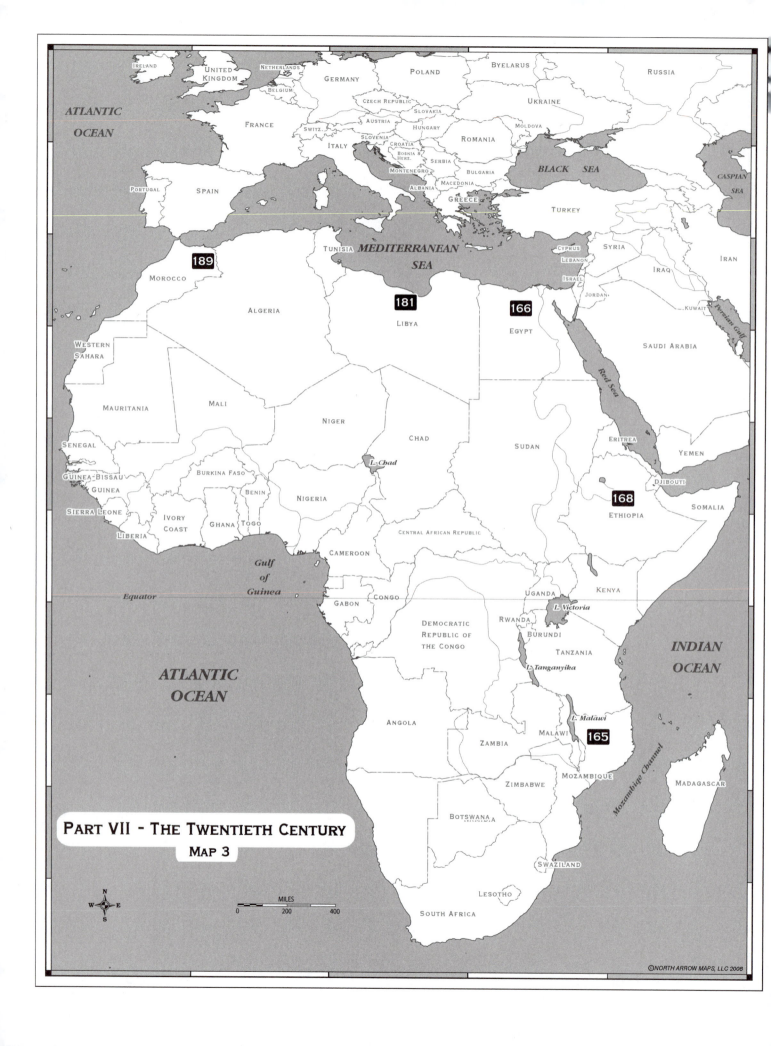

PART VII - THE TWENTIETH CENTURY
MAP 3

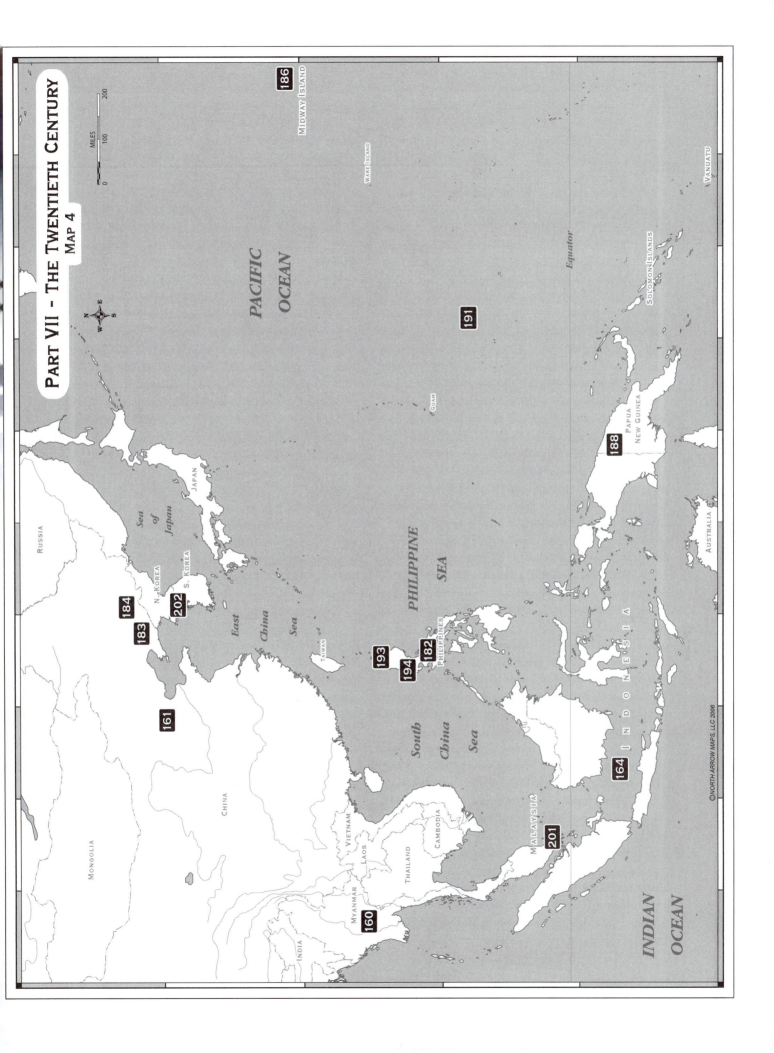

PART VII – THE TWENTIETH CENTURY
MAP 4

MILES
0   100   200

N
W   E
S

PACIFIC OCEAN

MIDWAY ISLAND 186

WAKE ISLAND

Equator

VANUATU

SOLOMON ISLANDS

PAPUA NEW GUINEA 188

191

GUAM

AUSTRALIA

INDONESIA

PHILIPPINE SEA

PHILIPPINES 182

193
194

TAIWAN

East China Sea

JAPAN

Sea of Japan

N. KOREA
S. KOREA 202

184
183

161

RUSSIA

MONGOLIA

CHINA

INDIA

MYANMAR 160
LAOS
THAILAND
CAMBODIA
VIETNAM

South China Sea

MALAYSIA 201

164

INDIAN OCEAN

©NORTH ARROW MAPS, LLC 2006

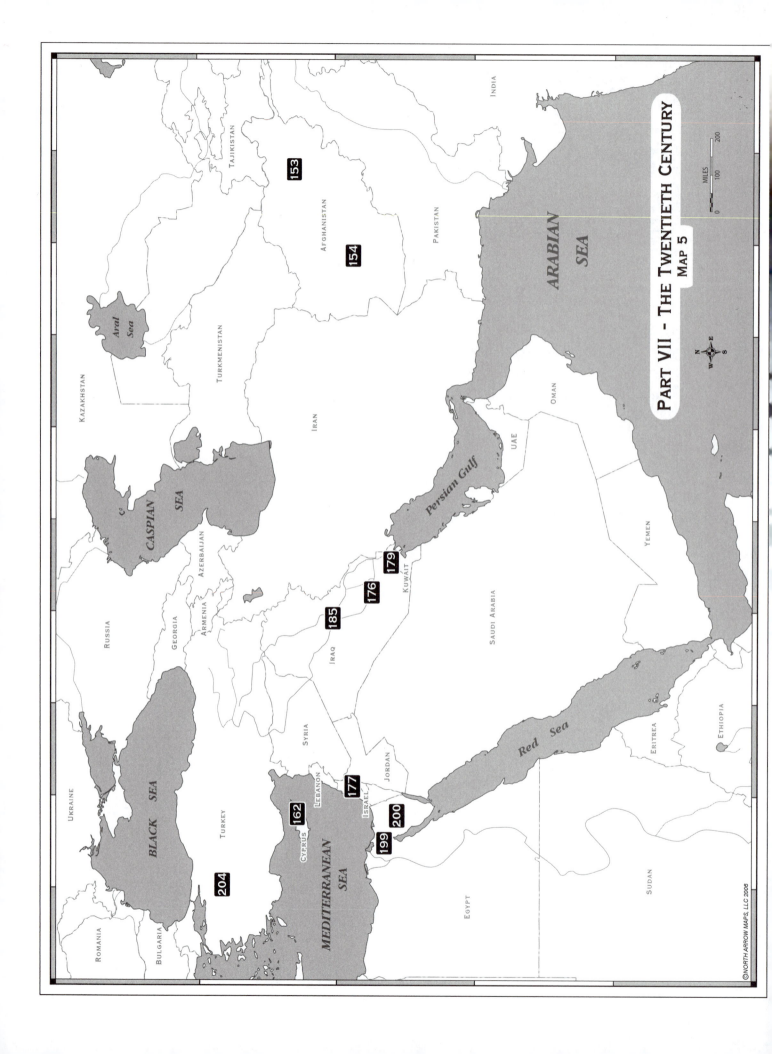

PART VII – THE TWENTIETH CENTURY
MAP 5

MILES
0   100   200

N
W   E
S

ARABIAN
SEA

Persian Gulf

CASPIAN
SEA

Aral
Sea

Red   Sea

BLACK
SEA

MEDITERRANEAN
SEA

INDIA

PAKISTAN

AFGHANISTAN

TAJIKISTAN

TURKMENISTAN

KAZAKHSTAN

IRAN

OMAN

UAE

YEMEN

SAUDI ARABIA

IRAQ

KUWAIT

SYRIA

JORDAN

ISRAEL

LEBANON

CYPRUS

TURKEY

ARMENIA

AZERBAIJAN

GEORGIA

RUSSIA

UKRAINE

ROMANIA

BULGARIA

ERITREA

ETHIOPIA

SUDAN

EGYPT

153

154

185

176

179

162

177

200

199

204

©NORTH ARROW MAPS, LLC 2006

PART 7
THE TWENTIETH CENTURY

AFGHANISTAN, SOVIET INVASION OF

153

The roots of the Soviet invasion of Afghanistan go back to the struggles over influence there in the nineteenth century. British India and Russia jockeyed for influence in Afghanistan and Persia (Iran) for decades, both looking for security on their frontiers. A national border was finally determined by the two powers in 1893. That decision, however, placed a larger number of Pushtuns (one of the largest ethnic groups in Afghanistan) within the northwestern part of India. When India became independent in 1947, so did that northwest territory, now called Pakistan. Many Pushtuns agitated for either autonomous status in Pakistan or a return of the region to Afghan control. Pakistan refused, and did so with the support of major Western powers. Thus, the Afghans began looking to the Soviet Union for assistance.

By the 1970s, the Soviets dominated the Afghan military and economy. Afghan officers were trained in the Soviet Union and Soviet weaponry filled Afghan arsenals. There continued to be a large number of tribal factions in the country, but a fairly strong communist-oriented party, the People's Democratic Party of Afghanistan (PDPA), held sway over the government. Infighting within the party, however, led to a coup in late April 1978. Nur Muhammad Taraki seized power and began implementing radical communist doctrine that challenged Moslem beliefs and created intense resistance among the population. By 1979, armed conflict sprouted across the country as a variety of factions fought the government over its new policies. When Taraki tried to consolidate his hold by weeding out opposition in the military, General Hafizullah Amin acted first and took Taraki prisoner; the latter died soon after. Amin tried to restore some of the pre-communist policies in order to pacify the population, but that provoked a Soviet response.

A variety of factors throughout the region and the world entered into the Soviet decision. In January 1979, the Iranian revolution toppled the pro-Western shah and installed a Moslem theocracy under the Ayatollah Khomeini. The resulting chaos in Iranian politics was reflected in the decision of the Oil Producing and Exporting Countries (OPEC) decision in June to raise crude oil prices 24 percent. That caused an economic recession in the United States. The unsettled economic and political conditions convinced the U.S. Senate to reject ratifying the latest arms limitation treaty, SALT II, with the U.S.S.R. In November 1979, "students" in Teheran stormed and occupied the United States embassy, taking 66 hostages. To further enhance the troubled international political scene, NATO announced that the United States was going to place Pershing II cruise missiles in western Europe. If the United States decided to act aggressively in Iran, the Soviet position in the region could be compromised. Thus, against the advice of senior military leaders in Moscow, the Soviet Politburo decided on 12 December to commit troops to Afghanistan to shore up a friendly regime and prevent the establishment of a government that might resemble that of Iran. Further, the U.S. (through the CIA) had been active in trying to overthrow the Afghan government in the middle of 1979; this is theorized by some to have been an attempt to provoke an invasion in the hopes it would prove destructive to the Soviet Union.

Soviet special forces (*spetznaz*) dressed in Afghan army uniforms started the operation on 27 December 1979. They stormed into the Presidential Palace and killed President Amin. They thought this would lead to a popular acceptance of the communist government. The Soviets installed a new president, Babrak Kamal of the PDPA. After the initial invasion, many Soviet troops were brought in and stationed around Kabul to protect and enforce the new government.

Resistance began almost immediately. Around the country a variety of resistance groups sprang up. These groups varied widely in numbers, popularity, and influence, and had no coordination. That proved a blessing and a curse: There was no central command which the Soviets and the government could wipe out to crush the resistance, but there was no leadership which could plan any sort of national campaign. There were also military advantages and disadvantages for the Afghans. The rebel groups lacked modern weapons (which the government forces had in abundance), but they had centuries of tradition on their side. Afghans had always used the mountainous terrain of their country to keep out invaders, and the resistance fighters, called *mujahideen*, knew the mountains and valleys intimately. The Soviets, on the other hand, had an army that was trained for wide open warfare on massive battlefields, as they expected to fight in Europe or against China. Counter-guerrilla tactics were not part of their training.

The Afghans proceeded to fight a fairly standard guerrilla war. They attacked out of and retreated into the hills. Soviet convoys, no matter how well protected by tanks, were easy prey in the passes. As there were no uniforms for the mujahideen, no one could tell who was friend or foe. Although the Soviets and their client government wanted to protect those people who supported them, citizens being "protected" would randomly shoot at them. This brought about the expected reprisals, in which innocent civilians would die and drive survivors into the resistance. For the first three years, Soviet forces attempted to take the battle to the mujahideen. They could bring in superior firepower, but the dispersed nature of the rebel groups and their ability to melt into the countryside made targeting almost impossible. In the spring of 1985, the Soviets switched tactics. They used Afghan government forces to fight the rebels, providing fire support. The government forces were strengthened by spetznaz troops to help in coordinating ambushes, trying to infiltrate the rebels, and attempting to stop the flow of arms coming from Pakistan.

From the opening invasion, the Soviets had received widespread international condemnation. In the United States, President Jimmy Carter branded the invasion as a threat to peace which could severely impact U.S.-Soviet relations. He also stated that any attempt by the Soviet Union to establish control along the Persian Gulf would be resisted by any means necessary, including nuclear weapons. For all the brave talk, however, the American position was primarily defensive. That changed in January 1981 when Ronald Reagan became president. A long-time opponent of communism, Reagan soon had covert support going to the rebels via the Central Intelligence

Pullout of Soviet troops from Afghanistan, 1988. (Photo by Mikhail Evstafiev from en-Wikipedia.)

Agency. The CIA at first supplied the mujahideen with Soviet-made weaponry acquired from the Israelis, who had captured it from Arab states in their wars. By filtering the weapons through the Pakistani government, the U.S. had deniability. The weapons supply was never in massive amounts for fear the Soviets would retaliate against Pakistan. Money and other support also arrived from Great Britain, France, and Saudi Arabia, while Iranian sources provided weaponry as a duty to fellow Moslems.

By 1985 money and arms were flowing to the mujahideen and the communist government held only major population centers. Also, with some American advisors in-country, there began to be some coordination among rebel groups. Modern communications equipment was also provided. The introduction of shoulder-fired "Stinger" anti-aircraft missiles made helicopter assaults and support much more difficult for the communists. The inability of the communist forces to gain the upper hand created serious morale problems, and desertions from the Afghan army were common. The Soviets tried a new tack by replacing their puppet president Kamal with a more hard-line puppet, Mohammad Najibullah, head of the Afghan secret police. Unsurprisingly, this did nothing to rally popular support.

Finally, the Soviets had had enough. Talks began in Geneva in 1988 and an agreement was signed on 14 April between Pakistan and Afghanistan, since it had been their border dispute that triggered the whole conflict. Both the United States and the Soviet Union signed the agreement as guarantors of the peace, and the Soviets agreed to a timetable for withdrawal of their troops. They promised to remove all of their forces by 15 February 1989. They left behind the last president they had installed, Najibullah, who managed to stay in power until 1992. The primary weakness of the Geneva Accords (as far as Afghanistan was concerned) was that none of the mujahideen were involved. That meant that they did not recognize the agreement, or the Afghan government which signed it. Thus, even though the Soviets did withdraw on schedule, fighting in Afghanistan did not stop.

Three primary factors led to the Soviet defeat and withdrawal in Afghanistan. First, they were unprepared for a guerrilla war, as standard Soviet doctrine and training at the time did not include it. Never did they have success in winning over the population to the communist doctrine, and winning "hearts and minds" is vital to defeating a guerrilla campaign. Second, the casualties proved to be unacceptable. While Soviet forces at any one time numbered from 110,000 to 150,000, the troops were normally rotated through the country in six-month tours of duty. From December 1979 to February 1989, the total number of troops was more than half a million. Officially, Soviet losses numbered almost 14,000 dead, though some Afghan sources claim it to be as high as 50,000. Further, tens of thousands of pieces of equipment, including tanks, trucks, artillery pieces, helicopters, etc., were destroyed or lost. Third, the pressure from the international community, both political and through indirect aid to the rebels, proved to be overwhelming. At home, the Russian public began openly criticizing the government for the war, which marked the first cracks in the collapse of the Soviet Union in 1991. Veterans of the Afghan war were shunned and army morale deteriorated.

Things were even worse for Afghanistan. Perhaps a million people lost their lives during the Soviet occupation, with millions more forced from their homes. The bombings conducted by the communists throughout the operation had destroyed crops and irrigation systems, leaving many people starving. With no strong and unified government to address the problems, tribal factions once again tried to exert control over as much territory as possible. This led, finally, to the Pushtun tribe gaining control of most of the country by the early 1990s and establishing the orthodox theocratic Taliban government. The resistance to the Soviet occupation came to be viewed not as a national struggle but a religious one, which led to Afghanistan becoming a haven for anti-Christian and anti-Western groups such as Al Qaeda.

—Travis Denzer

See also Afghanistan, US invasion of and Afghanistan, British invasions of.

References: Grau, Lester, The Bear Went Over the Mountain: Soviet Combat Tactics in Afghanistan (Washington: National Defense University Press, 1996); Kakar, M. Hassan Afghanistan: The Soviet Invasion and the Afghan Response, 1979–1982. (Berkeley: University of California Press, 1995); Moshref, Rameen, "The Role of Afghanistan in the Fall of the USSR", Afghanistan online, http://www.afghan-web.com/history/articles/ussr.html, 22 November 2005; "The 1978 Revolution and the Soviet Invasion", GlobalSecurity.org, http://www.globalsecurity.org/military/world/afghanistan/cs-invasion.htm, 20 November 2005.

AFGHANISTAN, U.N. INVASION OF

154

On 11 September 2001, members of the terrorist organization Al Qaeda carried out a deadly attack on the United States, crashing hijacked airliners into the World Trade Center in New York City and the Pentagon in Washington, D.C. This marked the beginning of the War on Terrorism, spearheaded by the United States. The first target of that war was Afghanistan. The Moslem theocracy in that country, the Taliban, hosted a number of terrorist training camps under the direction of Al Qaeda leader Osama bin Laden. Al Qaeda had been attacking U.S. targets for some years, including a previous partially successful bombing of the World Trade Center, attacks on American embassies, and a suicide bombing of the USS Cole, a destroyer docked in Yemen. President Bill Clinton had ordered retaliatory cruise missile attacks against terrorist training camps, but they were ineffective.

The United States, with the support of the United Nations, issued to the Taliban government a list of demands which would have to be met or force would be used. President George W. Bush's demands were simple: Turn over all Al Qaeda leaders to the United States, release imprisoned foreign nationals, protect all foreign workers in Afghanistan, close all terrorist training camps, and give the U.S. full access to all training camps to verify their closure. The United Nations seconded these demands in a resolution passed on 18 September 2001. The Taliban refused to carry on direct talks, however, sending their messages through the Pakistani embassy. When the Taliban did nothing to respond positively to the demands, a coalition of forces responded with Operation Enduring Freedom.

Before the aerial bombing began on 7 October, British special forces secretly entered Afghanistan to organize and coordinate local resistance. (For some years, a civil war had been waged in Afghanistan, with a variety of groups attempting to overthrow the Taliban. The largest of these groups was the Northern Alliance.) Late on the night of 7 October, the bombing started, with U.S. and British aircraft striking both Taliban and Al Qaeda targets: power plants, training camps, airports, radar stations, supply depots, and the like came under attack. Following on the heels of the bombings were more flights over the country, but this time they dropped tens of thousands of ration packages on civilian centers. This became a daily occurrence, with as many as 50,000 being dropped per day. During the attacks, the coalition forces did not lose a single plane to enemy fire. The only response by Al Qaeda was in the form of propaganda. Bin Laden released a video tape saying that the United States would fail in Afghanistan and soon thereafter collapse, just as the Soviet Union had in the wake of their invasion of the country in the 1980s.

The primary targets of the air attacks were the cities of Kabul, Kandahar, and Jalalabad. Within a few days, all training camps and local air defenses were destroyed. This allowed coalition aircraft to rove freely, and they destroyed communication centers in order to make coordinated resistance more difficult. Taliban and Al Qaeda troop positions were targeted next. The initial ground fighting was done by Northern Alliance forces with the aid of American and British special forces. The first major battle was for Mazar-e-Sharif in the north-central part of the country. The attack began on 9 November with the bombing of Taliban positions. Northern Alliance forces attacked from the west and south. After taking the airport and the military base, coalition troops were soon clearing the streets of the city and the battle was over in a matter of hours.

With the fall of Mazar-e-Sharif, the next target was the capital city of Kabul in the eastern part of the country. There was no battle; the night before the attack was to take place, almost all the defenders abandoned their positions. Only a small group of devoted Taliban and Al Qaeda fighters stayed and fought. They were all killed in a matter of minutes. With coalition forces now in control of Kabul, Taliban and Al Qaeda forces across the country began to fall apart. Herat, near the Iranian border in the far west, fell within 24 hours of Kabul. Most battles in the wake of the capture of the major cities were small, with pockets of Al Qaeda and Taliban forces holing up and fighting to the death. The last major fighting was for Konduz in the northeast, where some 10,000 Taliban fighters were aided by several foreign volunteers, primarily from Pakistan. Coalition forces attacked the city on 16 November and secured it on 25 November. Most of the surviving defenders fled southwest to the city of Kandahar to make another stand, and the resistance there lasted about two weeks. By this time, more American forces, primarily U.S. Marines, were in the country to supplement the special forces troops that had been operating within the Northern Alliance armies.

As the battle for Kandahar was starting, some of the most intense fighting of the war occurred far to the north at Qala-e-Jangi prison west of Mazar-e-Sharif. A revolt in the prison complex began when some prisoners captured at Konduz attacked a few guards. The revolt lasted three days and in the end, less than 100 of the 600 prisoners survived. About 50 coalition soldiers, primarily Uzbeks, were killed.

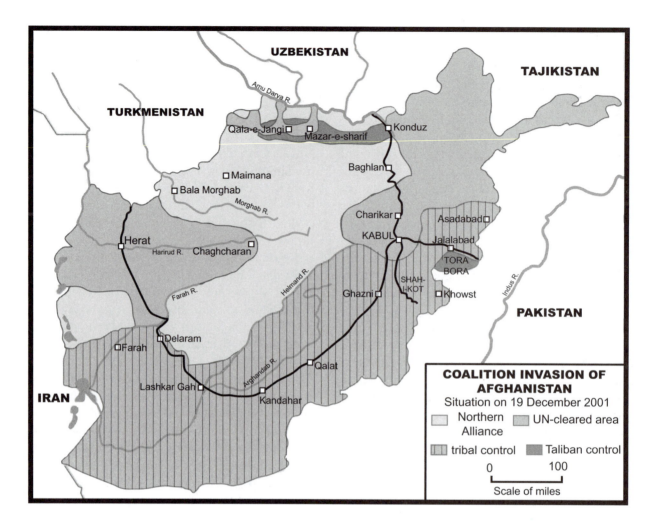

The battle for Kandahar began on 25 November. Taliban leader Mullah Omar vowed on 1 December that the defenders would fight until Judgment Day. That day arrived a week later as the coalition forces took control of the town on the 7th. While Taliban forces fought to the death, Omar and Osama bin Laden were in hiding. The remnants of their followers made their way to the mountains south of Jalalabad, on the Pakistani border. There, during the days of the Soviet occupation, resistance fighters had built a defensive complex of caves in a region called Tora Bora. With winter beginning, fighting in the mountains promised to be extremely difficult. This is where Western technology really began to make its presence felt. Although extremely accurate targeting had been a hallmark of the aerial bombardment so far, more new gadgets made their appearance. Heat sensors discovered which caves were being occupied, and laser and/or video guided missiles sealed them off. Local anti-Taliban warlords, sufficiently bribed by U.S. agents, also helped in locating targets. By 5 December Afghan militia with U.S. support took over parts of the lower mountain region, forcing the defenders into still higher ground. The attacking forces were able to clear out most of the resistance by 18 December. Four days later, a new, provisional Afghan government was established under the leadership of Hamad Kharzai, a member of the Pushtun tribe who had spent years in exile. The Taliban era was officially over.

The country was relatively quiet for the rest of the winter, but on 2 March 2002 operations began in another mountainous region south of Kabul, the Shah-i-kot. As before, the operation, code-named Anaconda, began with intense aerial bombardment before the 1,500 troops went in. In addition to U.S. and Afghan soldiers, special forces from Australia, Canada, Germany,

Denmark, France, and Norway also took part. Intense resistance was met, with American reinforcements being brought in by helicopter—500 more by 4 March, another 300 on the 6th—making the U.S. contingent 1,200 strong. The operation was brought to a successful conclusion on 18 March, with 800 Taliban and Al Qaeda fighters reported killed. Unfortunately, not all resistance was crushed, for some escaped into the mountains. In mid-August, Operation Mountain Sweep sent 2,000 soldiers through the southeastern part of the country, capturing fighters, weapons, and documents.

Coalition forces came to the conclusion that Osama bin Laden had managed to escape into Pakistan. In Afghanistan, however, plans proceeded for elections for a new, permanent government. The U.S. continued to establish bases in the country, the major one being Bagram air base outside Kabul. Smaller bases were set up to continue the hunt for Taliban holdouts and bin Laden. Over time, the number of American soldiers in Afghanistan grew to 10,000. In the meantime, survivors of the fallen regime did what they could to reorganize secretly. They hoped to continue terror attacks, primarily in order to disrupt elections. In that they failed miserably, for when elections were held, the vast majority of adults stood in line for hours to cast their votes.

The invasion of Afghanistan by U.S. and coalition forces killed somewhere between 20,000 and 50,000 people. The goal of bringing down the Taliban and their support of terrorism was successful, although the Afghans will take some time to adapt themselves to a democratic system. Centuries of conflict between isolated tribes, led today by various warlords, keep the country somewhat fragmented. United Nations forces have been in the country since the Taliban's fall, helping to restore infrastructure and encourage unity. It is hoped that by establishing a trained military and police force, the central government will begin to be recognized as the legitimate source of authority. Rebuilding efforts have proceeded well in the cities, but government control is sporadic outside the major population centers.

—Kyle Matheu

References: Boaz, John, ed., *The US Attack on Afghanistan* (Farmington Hills, MI: Greenhaven, 2005); Micheletti, Eric, *Special Forces: War on Terrorism* (Paris: Histoire and Collections, 2003); "Into Afghanistan: Rooting out Terrorists", United States Department of Defense, http://www.defenselink.mil/home/features/1092004a.html (21 November 2005).

ALBANIA, ITALIAN CONQUEST OF

155

In the wake of World War I, Albania came under the leadership of President Ahmed Zogu, who declared himself King Zog. Though he attempted to bring about some modernization and reforms, Zog tied the country to fascist Italy. In 1926, the two countries signed the Pact of Tirane, in which Italy promised to maintain the status quo in Albania. The following year, the two entered into a 20-year defense alliance, which had the effect of binding the weaker Albania to the stronger Italy. The Italians took advantage of this by making themselves indispensable to Albania, giving them no-interest loans and gifts in return for Albanian acceptance of Italian technical aid, military aid and advisers, economic investment, and exploitation of Albanian natural resources. Albania was viewed by most of the world almost as an Italian possession.

As fascism began to spread in the late 1930s, Albania began to fear for its independence, such as it was. When Germany occupied Czechoslovakia in the spring of 1939, Mussolini felt that his ally was overshadowing him and that Italy needed to reassert its aggressive nature. Albania seemed a natural acquisition. When rumors flew in the world press about tensions between the two countries, Mussolini denied it, though plans were already under way for military action. Three Italian warships anchored off the Albanian coast on 6 April, and troops landed the next day.

Fighting was brief. Within a week Italy had installed a puppet government, which offered the crown to Italy's King Victor Emmanuel III. Albania became a part of Italy; foreign ambassadors were sent home, Albanian ambassadors recalled, and the army incorporated into the Italian military.

Because Italy's dominant role in Albanian affairs had long been recognized, most countries had no complaint about Italy's actions, though perceptions varied. Mussolini saw the invasion as yet another step on his road to reestablishing the Roman Empire. Further, he wanted to secure a presence in the Balkans as a counter to Hitler in Czechoslovakia, and he hoped the countries of the region would prefer him to the Nazis. He also hoped to gain British and French recognition of this anti-Nazi move, and possibly establish closer ties. Britain and France refused to see it that way, seemingly rebuffing Mussolini, while Hitler heaped praise on his ally and appeared to be Italy's only friend. Yugoslavia had no qualms about an Italian invasion next door because they hoped to work with the Italians to gain some border concessions. Greece had similar views; once assured that Italy had no designs on the island of Corfu, Greece also hoped to expand at Albania's expense. Within Albania itself, few people missed the exiled King Zog.

Relations among Britain, France, and Italy remained cordial until the Italian invasion of France in May 1940. With relations broken, Britain began to plan possible support of resistance movements in Albania. This proved difficult; even though the population did not care for the elites placed in power by the Italians, they had no leadership to organize resistance. Zog had so little support in the country that Britain refused to recognize him as head of a government-in-exile. Not until Italy attacked Britain's ally, Greece, from Albanian bases did any serious planning take place to begin a guerrilla movement in the country. Albanians themselves were of mixed emotions; some appreciated the opportunity to regain territory in southern Yugoslavia populated by ethnic Albanians. Ultimately, the most effective resistance movement was that of the Communists. A Communist party had existed in Albania since the 1920s, but even they were split into factions. Only after Josip Tito sent agents from Yugoslavia did the Communist resistance become effective. When Mussolini was deposed and Italy resigned from the war in September 1943, German forces occupied Albania. A Soviet military mission arrived in September 1944, and Communist power grew.

As the war progressed, the Communists gained control of the southern part of the country and began to make war against not only fleeing Nazis but also other, more nationalistic resistance groups. By the end of 1944, most of the country was in Communist hands. Ignored by the major powers in wartime conferences, Albania ultimately came under the control of the Communists because no other group had any real organization or ability to challenge them. A Communist government was established in April 1945, and recognized by the major powers. Of those nations falling under Communist dominance in the postwar world, Albania fared more poorly than most. It is regarded as the least advanced, least economically viable country in the Balkans, if not in all of Europe. Even with the fall of the Soviet Union, Albania seems to be the forgotten satellite.

See also Czechoslovakia, Nazi Occupation of.

References: Barker, Elizabeth, *British Policy in Southeast Europe in the Second World War* (New York: Barnes & Noble, 1976); Haines, C. G., and R. J. S. Hoffman, *The Origins and Background of World War II* (New York: Oxford University Press, 1947); Logorici, Anton, *The Albanians* (Boulder, CO: Westview Press, 1977); Lowe, C. J., and F. Marzari, *Italian Foreign Policy, 1870–1940* (London: Routledge & Kegan Paul, 1975).

156 AUSTRIA, NAZI OCCUPATION OF

In his book *Mein Kampf*, Adolf Hitler stated that it was necessary for all German-speaking peoples to be under one government, and this outlook dominated his pre-World War II foreign policy. He was able to slowly extend German power in the middle 1930s despite the fact that the Versailles Treaty, which ended World War I, was designed specifically to keep Germany weak for as long as possible. First, an area known as the Saar, bordering France, returned to Germany. It had been under French occupation since World War I, but in a 1935 plebiscite the population voted 10 to one to return to German control. In March 1936, the Nazis occupied the Rhineland, the area between the French border and the Rhine River. Under the terms of the Versailles Treaty, this area, along with a 50-mile-wide strip of land east of the Rhine, would remain demilitarized. When France and Britain refused to challenge Germany's action, Hitler felt confident he could implement his policy of expansion with no foreign interference.

Austria was Hitler's first target for expansion outside Germany itself. He wanted the land of his birth under German control, and supported the establishment of an Austrian Nazi party to lay the groundwork. In July 1934, Austrian Nazis assassinated the Austrian Chancellor Englebert Dolfuss in an abortive attempt to stage a coup. Italy's dictator, Benito Mussolini, threatened to intervene to protect Austria, and this, coupled with Germany's lack of a strong military, forced Hitler to refrain from grabbing power. Instead, he moved to bring Germany and Italy closer together, a strategy that worked when he was the only world leader to support Italy's invasion of Ethiopia. After the signing of an alliance, Mussolini would not interfere in Hitler's moves against Austria.

Like Dolfuss, new Chancellor Kurt von Schuschnigg was a virtual dictator in Austria. Knowing Hitler's aims and fearing the growing Nazi movement in his country, Schuschnigg tried placating Hitler, making sure nothing happened that Hitler could turn into an excuse for an invasion. He seemed to be worrying over nothing. In May 1935, Hitler publicly stated that he had no desire to violate Austrian sovereignty, and in July 1936, he signed an agreement with Austria, reaffirming that stance. The agreement, however, had some secret clauses stating that the Austrian Nazi party would provide some members to the Austrian Cabinet.

By early 1938, Hitler was ready to bring Austria under his control. He met with Schuschnigg in February and, after accusing Austria of subverting German progress for generations, demanded that Schuschnigg resign and appoint members of the Austrian Nazi party to most of the key positions in the government. After being subjected to a two-hour tirade and a threat of invasion, the Austrian chancellor agreed. He returned to Vienna, but rather than immediately implement Hitler's directives, he called a national plebiscite. This infuriated Hitler, who began to make good on his threat to invade Austria if Schuschnigg did not follow orders. Hitler called in his military commanders and ordered them to mass the army on the Austrian border.

At dawn on 12 March, they were in position. Seeing that the invasion would take place and being unprepared to oppose it, Schuschnigg resigned, and German troops crossed the border to an enthusiastic reception. Hitler entered the country not long after. He spent the night in Linz and visited his mother's grave, then traveled to Vienna, where he spoke to a huge crowd. Hitler announced that Austria was henceforth incorporated into the German Reich, and many Austrians, especially the young, welcomed the idea.

The "invasion" of Austria proved valuable to Hitler and his army. They discovered that their military was not as well organized or supplied as they had assumed, and they set about to address that deficiency. Hitler was reinforced in his assumptions that Britain and France would do nothing to oppose his expansionary dreams, just as they had done nothing substantial when he reacquired the Saar and Rhineland. This lack of action certainly fueled his ambition to bring about the occupation of Czechoslovakia, which occurred six months after the Austrian escapade.

Austria became a German state, giving up its independence, and the new Nazi government set about persecuting anyone who had opposed the Austrian Nazi party prior to the Anschluss, or "joining." Such persons became subject to the whims of the Nazi government and liable for service in the German military, and Austrian Jews received the same fate as the Jews of Germany and the remainder of Europe. Though little, if any, fighting took place in Austria during World War II, Allied soldiers and an Allied administration occupied the country after the war.

See also Czechoslovakia, Nazi Occupation of; Ethiopia, Italian Invasion of; Hitler, Adolf; Rhineland, Nazi Occupation of the.

References: Churchill, Winston, *The Gathering Storm* (Boston: Houghton Mifflin, 1948); Payne, Robert, *The Life and Death of Adolph Hitler* (New York: Praeger, 1973); Shirer, William, *The Rise and Fall of the Third Reich* (New York: Simon & Schuster, 1960).

157

BALKANS, NAZI INVASION OF

After seeing his ally Adolf Hitler triumph easily in both eastern and western Europe, Italian dictator Benito Mussolini decided his country needed some simple glory as well. The German war machine had conquered all its foes from Poland to France, and German diplomacy was reducing Balkan resistance. German troops were "invited" into Rumania after German guarantees against further dismemberment of that nation, and Hitler was pressuring Yugoslavia, Hungary, and Bulgaria into cooperation or alliances. Italy could not let Germany dominate so close to home, so a quick victory was in order. What could be easier, Mussolini thought, than capturing the small nation of Greece? Italy had never had close relations with the country, and was in a good position to launch an invasion from Albania, which Italy had conquered in 1939. In the fall of 1940, Mussolini made demands on the Greek government that he knew they would reject; indeed, he did not even wait for a reply to his final ultimatum of 28 October before sending his troops across the Greco-Albanian border.

The Italian military greatly outnumbered and outgunned the Greek army, but poor discipline, morale, and leadership in the Italian army, coupled with an invasion into the Greek mountains at the beginning of the winter, served to subvert Mussolini's scheme. After early successes, the Italian army was drawn into mountain passes far from their supply depots and ambushed by Greek units. Before the year was out, the Italians were not only defeated, but also had lost a quarter of Albania as well to a Greek counteroffensive. Hitler, as he was concurrently doing in North Africa, sent German forces into the Balkans to bail out his Italian ally.

The German invasion was not just a rescue attempt for a fellow fascist. The Greeks had close ties with Great Britain, and British aircraft had begun to operate out of Greek airfields in support of their war against Italy. Hitler did not want British aircraft in range of his newly acquired oil fields in Rumania, nor did he want a future British offensive out of Greece that would threaten the upcoming Nazi invasion of the Soviet Union. To secure his southern flank, and to put himself in a position to drive into the Middle East if the opportunity presented itself, Hitler sent forces to Greece in the spring of 1941. He concentrated the German Twelfth Army in Bulgaria, and bullied the Yugoslavians into allowing safe transit of German forces through their country. The agreement with Yugoslavia was short-lived; a day after Prince Peter signed the treaty with Germany, his military overthrew him and placed his brother Paul on the throne. Never one to brook resistance, Hitler ordered his army to take Yugoslavia as well.

The German General Staff quickly reorganized their plans, reassigning units to drive for Belgrade from Bulgaria while sending in more troops from Austria. On 6 April, two German invasions took place, both unstoppable. Within 11 days Yugoslavia surrendered, though a strong resistance movement immediately sprang to life. In Greece, the German invasion flanked the main Greek defensive positions and encircled them by driving down the Vardar River valley to Salonika. A second thrust swung eastward through southern Yugoslavia, then southward into northwestern Greece, bypassing the British forces that had come to Greece's aid. Almost 60,000 British Empire troops had left Egypt for Greece in a futile effort to stop the Germans, who outnumbered them almost 10 to one. Outflanked just as the Greek forces had been in the east, the British had to withdraw to avoid encirclement, then withdraw again to the south coast with the Germans hot on their heels. The Royal Navy had to evacuate the army in a second Dunkirk, but this time without air cover, while the German air force pounded them. Still, some 43,000 men got away to Egypt or Crete.

Hitler had taken the rugged country of Greece with the same blitzkrieg tactics that had served the Germans so well in Poland and France. The defenders had been sure that tanks could not operate effectively in the Greek terrain, but they learned differently. Without anti-tank weapons or an air force to speak of, the Greeks were unable to stand up to the onslaught.

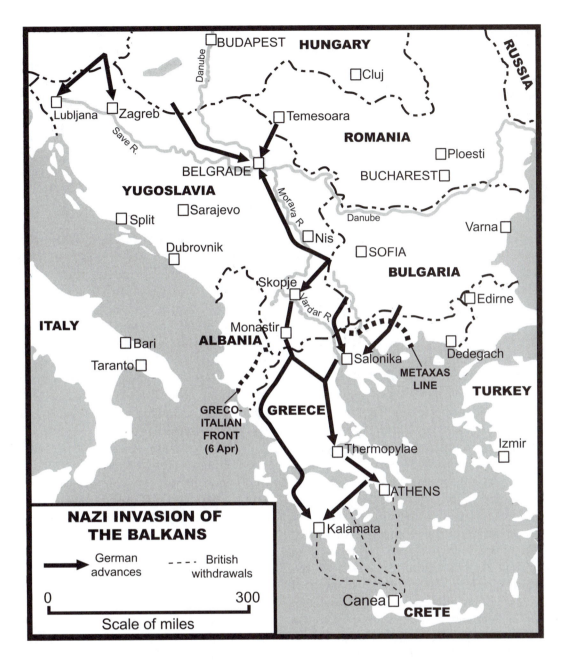

NAZI INVASION OF
THE BALKANS

→ German advances
- - - British withdrawals

0   300
Scale of miles

The hastily assembled British force was little better equipped or prepared. The rapid conquest embarrassed the British and gratified Hitler, but the Germans were not yet finished. With the support of German air force commander Hermann Goering, German General Kurt Student convinced Hitler that it was further necessary to capture the island of Crete. This would give the Germans a strong position in the eastern Mediterranean, and it could be used as a base for possible operations against the Middle East or the Suez Canal.

Student assured Hitler that an amphibious force would not be necessary, that he could do it with parachute troops. German airborne forces had proven their worth in the capture of key positions in Holland in May 1940, but to capture an entire island without follow-up infantry advances had never been done—until then. Crete was full of British troops, some in garrison and some newly arrived from the Greek disaster, but they were poorly supplied and equipped. German paratroopers landed on 20 May and fought to gain control of the island's major airfield. The

Germans lost heavily, but well-timed reinforcements captured the field, and troop transports landed more men, who came out of the planes directly into battle. British morale broke, and the Royal Navy staged yet another evacuation, again harassed unmercifully by German aircraft. The defending force of Greek and British troops numbered more than 40,000, but only 18,000 troops got off the island, and the Royal Navy had nine ships sunk and 13 damaged. The cost to Germany was 6,000 dead and wounded.

The stunning German victories in the Balkans had side effects, and one of the most immediate was in North Africa. Because the British had sent troops to Greece for the campaign against Italy in Cyrenaica, they were unable to deliver the deathblow in North Africa that could have given them control of the African coast before any German troops could show up to stop them. Instead, Erwin Rommel and the Afrika Korps threw the British out of Libya and drove into Egypt. No one believed that the British could stop the Germans in Greece, and the Greeks even asked the British not to help them fight the Italians because they believed it would provoke a German response. Thousands of men died on a fool's errand, and thousands more had to fight and die in North Africa because the campaign was not quickly drawn to a close.

Another result of the German involvement in the Balkans is the subject of some debate: the effect it had on the German invasion of the Soviet Union. The German troops involved in Greece and, more importantly, in Yugoslavia, had been dedicated to Army Group South in the invasion. Hitler had ordered his forces to be prepared by 15 May 1941 for the invasion, but the assault did not begin until 22 June. The strong German armored forces used in the Balkans had to be refitted for the Russian campaign, and that certainly slowed down the timetable. However, late spring rains left Poland and western Russia deep in mud, through which the Germans could not drive their armies. The decision to postpone the invasion, however, came before the effects of the weather were completely known. Whether because of the Balkan campaign or the weather, Hitler sorely missed that extra month of campaigning in Russia.

Another, longer-term result must be discussed: the German occupation of Yugoslavia. Much of the postwar and late-twentieth-century conditions in this area date to the German occupation. Some ethnic groups welcomed the Germans as liberators and fought alongside them against neighboring factions. The underground movement led by Josip Tito hurt the Germans badly, and forced them to keep forces in the country throughout the war. That Tito was supplied and assisted by the Communists more than by the West was to prove a pivotal factor after the war. His leadership role led to political power after the war, and his Communist government ran the country until his death. Tito ruled with such an iron hand that the country's ethnic factions suppressed their hostilities, but after his death the country began to break up. In the mid-1990s, the country divided into numerous groups claiming land and killing other former Yugoslavs. Retribution for actions during the Nazi occupation, for or against the occupying power, was a major factor in the continued fighting.

The Greeks also staged a stout resistance to the Germans. After the war they had to wage another political struggle against Communist groups that, like Tito's, tried to use their wartime actions to lead to political gains. In 1947, American President Harry Truman made economic and military aid available to Greece to stabilize its economy and thus combat Communist influence. It was successful, and led to the Truman Doctrine, that the United States would "support free peoples who are resisting attempted subjugation by armed minorities or outside pressures." That stand became the pillar of American foreign policy for four decades.

See also Albania, Italian Conquest of; Egypt, Italian Invasion of; France, Nazi Invasion of; Hitler, Adolf; Mussolini, Benito; Soviet Union, Nazi Invasion of the.

References: Cervi, Mario, *The Hollow Legions: Mussolini's Blunder in Greece*, trans. Eric Mosbacher (Garden City, NY: Doubleday, 1971); Higham, Robin, *Diary of a Disaster: British Aid to Greece, 1940–41* (Lexington: University of Kentucky Press, 1986); Van Creveld, Martin, *Hitler's Strategy 1940–41: The Balkan Clue* (Cambridge: Cambridge University Press, 1973).

158 BOSNIA-HERZEGOVINA, SERBIAN INVASION OF

"Balkanization" is the concept that an area full of ethnic and religious diversity cannot unite but will constantly seek independence. A look at the region once called Yugoslavia will clearly show why that term originated in southeastern Europe. A crossroads of armies for centuries, the area along the eastern coast of the Adriatic Sea falls into three major religious groups, from which their respective nationalism ultimately arises. The northernmost region (Slovenia and Croatia) was long dominated by Christian Austria-Hungary; the southern and western parts (Kosovo and Montenegro) were controlled by the Muslim Ottoman Empire; and the easternmost part (Serbia) was under the influence of Orthodox Russia. In the middle of this mix was Bosnia and Herzegovina, with a population made up of all three groups. After World War I, with Austria-Hungary and the Ottoman Empire dismantled, the mixed religious and ethnic area was lumped together as Yugoslavia in 1919 at the Versailles Conference. The Orthodox Serbs were the largest group and exercised the most power in the country, dominating the government, army, and police. The other ethnic groups (Croats in the north, Muslims in the south) felt not only left out but also persecuted.

Bad turned to worse during World War II. Many Croats cooperated with invading Nazis, seeing them as their liberators from Serbian rule. The Muslims, being anti-Jewish, tended to side with the Nazi-supporting Croats. The Serbs, with Soviet Communist aid and influence, mounted a resistance movement that fought the Nazis, Croats, and Muslims. All this fighting reinforced the longstanding hostilities among the groups. All was put on hold for a time after World War II, thanks to Josip Broz Tito, a Croat who fought along with the Communist resistance. Although independent of Moscow, Tito was a strong communist who created and ruled over a repressive state that kept all ethnic and religious tensions forcibly suppressed. "Tito hoped this policy would eventually lead his people to forget their differences, but it did not. Stories handed down from parents to children nurtured age-old enmities"

(Kinzer, *Atlas of War and Peace*). Peace lasted as long as he ruled. In 1980, Tito died and so did Yugoslavia as a nation. Although a "collective presidency" tried to hold the country together by having wide representation, with the collapse of the Soviet Union, the final vestiges of communism and socialism were thrown off. The first elections in 1990 showed a rejection of the former system and a desire for the Yugoslav provinces to become independent nations. Nationalism soon became the order of the day.

Before any provinces could secede from the Yugoslav union, however, Slobodan Milosevic (who became president of Serbia in 1989) tried to reestablish Serb-dominated rule over the entire country. Although originally a communist, he turned to nationalism to motivate the Serbs to resume the position of power they had held prior to World War II. His first target was the southern Serbian province of Kosovo, which had been the heart of the Serbian nation in medieval times, but was by the late twentieth century dominated by ethnic Albanians. Using the same strategy Hitler had used in the Sudetenland in 1938, Milosevic claimed to be rescuing persecuted Serbs in Kosovo. His troops conquered the area and replaced all high-ranking Albanians with Serbs. Fearing a repetition of such action across the region, many Yugoslav provinces began to seek independence.

The first to do so was Slovenia, which proclaimed itself a republic in the summer of 1991. Although Milosevic ordered federal troops (dominated by Serbs) to stop the secession, they failed. Lacking a Serbian population in Slovenia, however, Milosevic decided not to press the issue and withdrew Yugoslav troops out of Slovenia into neighboring Croatia. There, however, Croat president Franjo Tudjman was also declaring independence, and Serbs living in Croatia feared for their lives, remembering the hostility between the two factions during World War II. Tudjman did nothing to alleviate those fears, actually reviving some of the old national symbols and anti-Serbian rhetoric. Milosevic sent in the Yugoslav army (based in Serbia and Bosnia-Herzegovina) to keep Croatia in the union. Cooperating with ethnic-Serb militias in Croatia, "savage fighting ensued, marked by the Serbian forces' deliberate targeting

**COUNTRIES AND PROVINCES
OF THE FORMER
YUGOSLAVIA**

— - — - — national borders

- - - - - - provincial borders

of civilians and of cultural landmarks (including the brutal siege of the medieval port city of Dubrovnik and the total destruction of the town of Vukovar, a jewel of Baroque architecture)." (Reidlmayer, *Brief History*)

At this point, foreign intervention may have averted the worst of the slaughter, but the major powers gave mixed signals. The United States pushed for retention of a single Yugoslav state, while European countries, especially Germany, encouraged independence. Thus, Serbs assumed American support for their actions, so they continued the war in Croatia and in 1992 into the newly-seceded Bosnia-Herzegovina. Bosnia had a population numbering some 44 percent

Muslims, 17 percent Croats, and 31 percent Serbs. The Muslims and Croats voted for independence, while the Serbs violently opposed it. As in Croatia, Milosevic made sure that Serb militias were created and supported in Bosnia. On 5 April 1992, many inhabitants of the Bosnia capital of Sarajevo gathered for a peace march. They did not know that Yugoslav forces had already invaded their country.

Meanwhile, declared a Yugoslav Republic on 3 March 1992, although it contained only Serbia and Montenegro. Although was in possession of Kosovo, his brutal treatment of the Albanian majority provoked an independence movement there as well. Needing Kosovo's vast

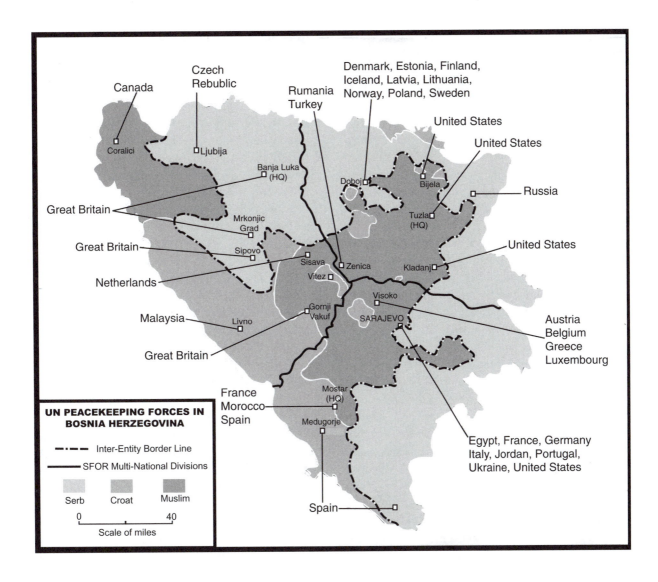

UN PEACEKEEPING FORCES IN BOSNIA HERZEGOVINA

Canada — Coralici

Czech Rebublic — Ljubija

Rumania
Turkey

Denmark, Estonia, Finland,
Iceland, Latvia, Lithuania,
Norway, Poland, Sweden

United States

United States

Banja Luka (HQ)

Doboj

Bijela

Russia

Great Britain

Tuzla (HQ)

Mrkonjic Grad

Great Britain — Sipovo

Sisava

Zenica

Kladanj — United States

Netherlands

Vitez

Malaysia — Livno

Gornji Vakuf

Visoko

SARAJEVO

Austria
Belgium
Greece
Luxembourg

Great Britain

France
Morocco
Spain

Mostar (HQ)

Medugorje

Egypt, France, Germany
Italy, Jordan, Portugal,
Ukraine, United States

Spain

**UN PEACEKEEPING FORCES IN
BOSNIA HERZEGOVINA**

– · – · – Inter-Entity Border Line

———— SFOR Multi-National Divisions

Serb   Croat   Muslim

0   40

Scale of miles

mineral wealth in order to maintain its invasion of Bosnia and Croatia, Serbia began "ethnic cleansing" of the Albanians in order to promote "Serbianization." The practice was repeated in Bosnia. In overall command of the Bosnian Serb militias was Radovan Karadzic, the leader of the Bosnian Serb political party and the Serbian Democratic Party. After Bosnia had declared independence, he began a policy of ethnic cleansing in order to build a better Serbian nation. With direct assistance from the Yugoslav Karadzic formed an army of hand-selected, Bosnian-born Serbs. "By early May the Yugoslav announced that it would withdraw from Bosnia-Herzegovina. In reality, however, some 80,000 men (mostly Bosnian Serbs) simply changed uniforms and, with a powerful arsenal including

tanks and aircraft left behind by the truncated Yugoslav continued prosecuting the war and genocide." ("Summary of the Crisis") Karadzic's ethnic cleansing campaign involved destroying Croat and Muslim villages and towns, driving out the inhabitants, and systematic rape in order to propagate ethnic Serbian children. Concentration camps were created for those forced from their homes, or the inhabitants were simply shot. The justification was to save the Bosnian Serbs from Muslim fundamentalists. By August 1992, some 60 to 70 percent of non-Serbs were forced from Bosnia. Finally, the United Nations decided to intervene through diplomacy by establishing an embargo against Serbia and Montenegro. This created even worse conditions in Kosovo and did nothing to stop the atrocities in Bosnia and Croatia. "Good intentions are worse than useless in the Balkans. Crisscrossed over the centuries by various armies, it is an area that understands force. But through 42 months of war, the United States and its allies tried to use diplomacy unbacked by any credible military threat. The Serbs laughed and continued their bombardments. 'Borders,' the Bosnian Serb general Ratko Mladic noted, 'are drawn in blood'" (Cohen, *Atlas of War and Peace*). Exacerbating the situation was the infighting between Bosnian Croats and Muslims.

From America, only words were forthcoming from the waning presidency of George Bush and the beginning of that of Bill Clinton. Bush's view was that with the Soviet Union gone, issues such as Yugoslavia were Europe's concern. Clinton criticized Bush during the 1992 presidential campaign, but did little himself once elected. "Clinton repeatedly swung between strong proposals and stronger doubts, between guilt over the slaughter and anxiety over the remedy" (Sciolino, *Atlas of War and Peace*). The European Community made threats but sent only nonmilitary aid to the beleaguered Bosnians, Croats, and Kosovars. A United Nations peacekeeping force, primarily made up of French and British troops, made no attempt to force the Serbians away from declared "safe areas." Even when Clinton proposed stronger action, like giving the Bosnian government military aid, the Europeans rejected him. The European Community and the United Nations worked with NATO to threaten air strikes against Serb targets outside the safe areas. The occasional peace plan offered by the U.S. or U.N. was rejected by one party or another, Bosnian or Serb. Not until 1994 was a plan put forward that governments on both sides of the Atlantic could support: Divide Bosnia into two sections, 49 percent Serb and 51 percent Croat and Muslim.

Meanwhile, the highest-profile fighting of the conflict was taking place around the Bosnian capital of Sarajevo. Serb artillery pounded the city continuously. Bosnian Croats and Muslims put their arguments aside to face a common enemy, but without much hope for success as long as the arms embargo stayed in place.

In February 1994, a Serb artillery barrage killed 68 people and wounded another 200. In response, NATO called for a heavy weapons exclusion zone for 12.5 miles around the city and threatened air strikes. For a time, the Sarajevans could evacuate along a NATO-controlled road, but on April 10, 1994, yet another Serbian shelling provoked the first NATO air strikes. They did little to curb the fighting in and around the city.

By March 20, 1995, the Bosnian army had developed into an improved fighting force, activating troops in the northeast. In response, the Serbs subjected Sarajevo to a mass bombing on May 26. This, in turn, set off a second round of NATO air strikes. By August 11, when the conditions in Sarajevo had deteriorated to unlivable conditions, U.S. President Clinton sent a representative, Richard Holbrooke, to help negotiate a peace. Later that month, on August 28, a Serb shell hit the main marketplace in Sarajevo, killing 37 and wounding 85. Two days later, NATO planes and U.N. troops bombed a number of Serb targets in Bosnia in what came to be called Operation Deliberate Force. That finally succeeded in convincing the Bosnian Serbs to withdraw all their weaponry from around Sarajevo on September 14. On October 12, Holbrooke was able to gain an armistice in Dayton, Ohio, between the Croats, Bosnian Muslims, and Serbs. A peace plan was adopted on November 21, 1995. Signing the agreement were Croatian President Franjo Tudjman, Bosnian President Alija Izetbegovic, and Serbia's Slobodan Milosevic.

"The Dayton Accord ended a war that killed 260,000 people and drove 1.8 million from their homes. The accord divided the nation of 3.2 million into two ethnic mini-states with broad autonomy, a shared parliament and government and a three-man presidency" (Klug, AP). Bosnia was divided into three major regions, each occupied by multinational peacekeeping forces. The violence and devastation that took place in the Balkans continues to haunt us today. Mass graves from the concentration camps are still being unearthed and the death toll continues to increase. More and more of the war crimes also continue to be uncovered.

For example, two torture chambers were recently discovered in Pristina, the capital of Kosovo. In Bosnia, tears continue to be shed for the deaths of thousands. Unfortunately for the inhabitants of Kosovo, the Dayton Accord applied only to Bosnia. A guerrilla war between the Albanian population and the Yugoslav army raged until 1999; U.N. forces finally established a ceasefire, but the independence movement as of this writing has yet to succeed in separating Kosovo from Serbia. The practice of ethnic cleansing was declared a crime against humanity, and a special tribunal was created in The Hague to deal with those guilty of the genocide, rape, and torture. As of this writing, some high-ranking officials from the Serbian and Bosnian Serb forces remain at large, including General Ratko Mladic and president of the Serbian region of Bosnia (Republica Srpska), Radovan Karadzic.

Slobadan Milosevic was arrested in 2001 after being indicted for war crimes against the population of Kosovo, Bosnia, and Croatia. His trial dragged on through early 2006, when he was found dead of a reported heart attack in his cell in The Hague. The man primarily responsible for the fighting and genocide in the former Yugoslavia met his fate before the international tribunal could pronounce it.

- Deborah Palacios

References: American Committee to Save Bosnia, "A Summary of the Crisis in Bosnia," MostarOnline, <www.geocities.com/Heartland/19 35/crisis.html>, 19 December 2005; Cohen, Roger, Stephen Kinzer, and Elaine Sciolino, *Macmillan Atlas of War and Peace: Special Reports by Correspondents of the New York Times* (New York: Macmillan, 1996); Klug, Foster, "Leaders to Commemorate the End of Bosnian War," Associated Press News Service, 21 November 1995; Riedlmayer, Andras, "A Brief History of Bosnia-Herzegovina," Mostar online, <www.geocities.com/Heartland/1935/histo ry.html>, 19 December 2005.

BRITAIN, NAZI INVASION OF (BATTLE OF BRITAIN)

159

By June 1940, Hitler had conquered or placed under his control most of Europe. With France in his hands, Hitler was in a position to attack his last remaining opponent, Great Britain.

Luckily, Britain had been able to recover most of its army via the Dunkirk evacuation, but the problem facing Hitler was not with the British army, but with that centuries-old British defensive barrier, the English Channel. He believed he, could defeat the army if only the Channel could be crossed, but the Royal Navy was ready to bar that route. Hence, Hitler had to neutralize the British fleet. Though he lacked the naval power to face the British head-to-head, his battle-tested air force, the Luftwaffe, he felt, should be able to clear the Channel of British warships long enough to complete his planned invasion, Operation Sea Lion. This plan, however, brought up yet another obstacle—the Royal Air Force. The Germans needed air superiority to defeat the Royal Navy in order to cross the Channel, so air operations must precede all else. The Luftwaffe began to prepare for what would become known as the Battle of Britain.

Britain had an air force approximately half the size of Germany's, but the British had a technological advantage. Within the past few months, British scientists had perfected radar, with which they could detect German air attacks in advance. This early warning system would make constant standing patrols over the coast unnecessary, and allow the Royal Air Force sufficient time to assemble defending aircraft over German targets. Learning of radar and its abilities, Luftwaffe chief Hermann Goering attempted first to knock the radar antennas out of action. Though his Stuka dive-bombers had the pinpoint accuracy to accomplish this, their slow speed made them easy targets for British fighters, and the attacks on the towers were rarely successful. Another strategy had to be developed.

Working on the assumption that the Royal Air Force could not resist if their airfields were out of operation, the airfields became the Luftwaffe's next targets. Intensive bombing of the airfields of southeastern England proceeded through the rest of the summer. This strategy was more successful than the radar attacks, and the British ability to maintain their aircraft suffered when hangar facilities were destroyed. However, the airfields had dirt runways, which were easy to repair, and the planes continued to use the fields even if aircraft maintenance was hampered. With the Royal Air Force continuing to operate, German authorities

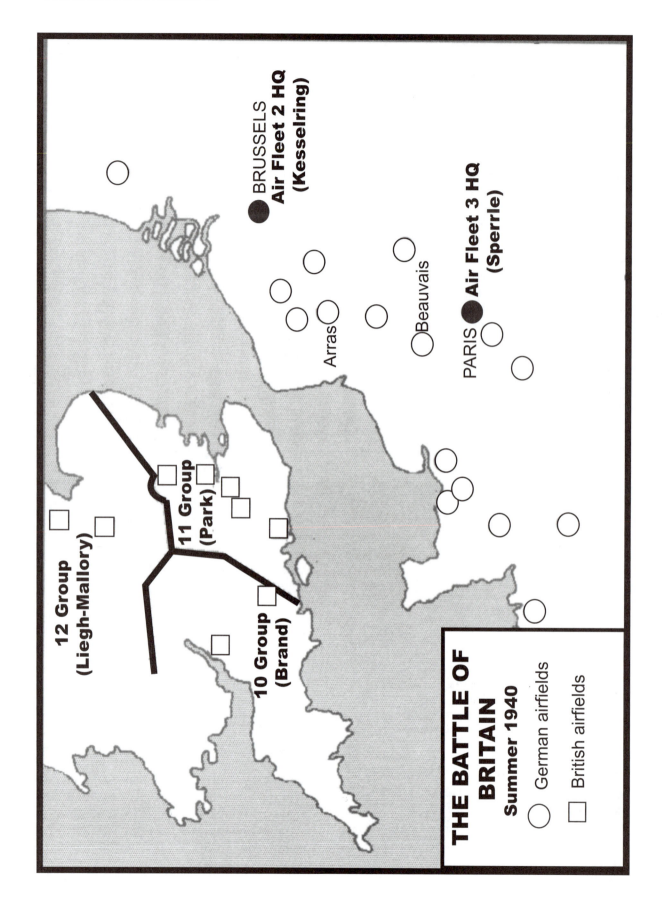

BRUSSELS
Air Fleet 2 HQ
(Kesselring)

Air Fleet 3 HQ
(Sperrle)

Beauvais

Arras

PARIS Air Fleet 3 HQ

12 Group
(Liegh-Mallory)

11 Group
(Park)

10 Group
(Brand)

**THE BATTLE OF
BRITAIN**
Summer 1940

○ German airfields

□ British airfields

decided to target aircraft factories also. If British aircraft could not be replaced, then superior German numbers would soon wear them down. This tactic proved very effective, and soon the British were in desperate straits.

The major change in German strategy that ultimately saved Britain came in response to an air raid on Berlin in August. Enraged that the British would attack civilian targets, Hitler ordered that England be repaid in kind. Attacks on the airfields and factories were called off to focus on British cities. This decision took pressure off the factories and the Royal Air Force, which could now replace their losses and improve aircraft maintenance and repair. Hitler's decision to give up his successful war of attrition with the Royal Air Force in favor of the negligible results of bombing population centers guaranteed that he would not achieve air superiority. Without it, the Germans could not control the Channel, and therefore could not invade. By mid-September, it was too late in the year to attempt a Channel crossing; Operation Sea Lion was postponed, never to be revived. Much like the attempted invasion by the Spanish Armada more than three centuries earlier, the failed invasion attempt in 1940 had long-term effects. As long as the British Isles remained free, they could be used as the staging point for the Allied war effort for the remainder of the war. Had Hitler taken Britain, it would have been difficult if not impossible for the United States to intervene in Europe, and the Third Reich probably would have lasted much longer than 12 years.

See also England, Spanish Invasion of (Spanish Armada); France, Nazi Invasion of.

References: Hough, Richard, and Denis Richards, *The Battle of Britain* (New York: Norton, 1989); Macksey, Kenneth, *Invasion* (New York: Macmillan, 1980); Wood, Derek, and Derek Dempster, *The Narrow Margin* (New York: Coronet, 1969).

160 BURMA, JAPANESE INVASION OF

In the months prior to the outbreak of hostilities in the Pacific, Burma seemed an unlikely arena for fighting. The land was too rugged and jungle-covered to fight through, or so the British

thought. Having only recently become independent from India in 1937, Burma was only just beginning to field an army of its own, so it was unprepared for serious combat. As war became imminent, the Burmese army was placed under the control of the British General Staff, but was still paid for and supported by Burma. When the Japanese finally began the war in early December 1941, total control of the Burmese forces came under the auspices of the Indian army, which had the assignment of defending the country if necessary. The prospects of success against a Japanese attack were minimal: A new and relatively untrained Burmese force, an Indian army weakened by transfers of units to assist Britain in North Africa, and two under-strength British brigades seemed to provide little in the way of a defense force. Still, no one believed the Japanese would come.

Japan began the war in command of Indochina and very quickly seized control of Siam (Thailand) by capturing Bangkok on 8 December. Burma seemed safe, because Japanese forces moved southward down the Malay Peninsula toward Singapore. The British viewed Burma as a giant buffer zone to protect India, but they were unable or unwilling to commit large forces to protect the country, even when they realized the Japanese were coming. To make matters worse, the forces protecting Burma were once again transferred to another command, that of ABDA (American-British-Dutch-Australian), based in Java, and given the task of protecting all of Southeast Asia and Indonesia. The constant shifting of command responsibility made planning virtually impossible.

The Japanese invaded Burma from two sites. On 15 January 1942, a division crossed the border heading north from Victoria Point, the southernmost tip of Burma. Five days later, another division attacked out of Siam west toward Moulmein, a move that would cut off the southern peninsula of Burma. The British-Burmese-Indian forces were stretched too thinly, trying to hold a cordon defense across the entire frontier. At the start of the invasion, one Burmese and one Indian brigade—8,000–10,000 men—were assigned to protect 500–800 miles of frontier. The troops found themselves quickly

Chinese soldiers shortly before their withdrawal at the Salween River, Burma. (Photograph no.196230, Camouflaged and poorly equipped Chinese soldiers repell a charge of 50,000 Japanese along the Salween River near Burma., ca. 06/1943, Collection FDR–PHOCO: Franklin D. Roosevelt Library Public Domain Photographs, 1882–1962; U.S. National Archives and Records Administration–Franklin D. Roosevelt Library (NLFDR), 4079 Albany Post Road, Hyde Park, NY.)

outflanked by more mobile Japanese forces, which forced Allied unit after unit to retreat or face annihilation.

The Japanese air forces bombed the capital city of Rangoon, and brought its harbor operations to a gradual halt. The British air defense consisted of 16 obsolescent fighter aircraft, soon supplemented by the American Volunteer Group (AVG), the "Flying Tigers," on loan from the Chinese. The AVG harassed the air raids, but could not stop them. Luckily for the defenders on the ground, the Japanese close air support was not very successful.

Heavily engaged Allied forces fought the Japanese to a standstill, but at such a cost that they could not hold out indefinitely. By mid-February the commander in the field asked permission to withdraw to more defensible positions behind the Sittang River. When finally permitted to withdraw, the troops had to do it under fire and air attack during hot and dry weather, short on food and water. It was a textbook withdrawal, but the Japanese again staged a flanking attack. Light tanks and newly arrived Gurkha troops were rushed in to assist in the ferocious battle for the one major bridge across the Sittang River. Having barely held the Japanese at bay, the British command ordered the bridge destroyed, even though two-thirds of the Indian 17th Division were on the opposite side. Luckily, the

Japanese committed more troops to the flanking movement, and most of the men were able to escape across the river.

The Allied forces were exhausted, and pulled back from the Japanese attacks. On 8 March, Rangoon fell, though the defenders managed to extricate themselves shortly before the city was surrounded. The Japanese had the initiative, and the Allies were obliged to pull back toward the Indian frontier.

Chiang Kai-shek offered to supply Chinese troops to assist the Allies, but without logistical support of their own, they had to be supplied with whatever meager aid the British could provide. The American General Joseph Stilwell commanded the Chinese forces, and put himself under the direction of the British commander, General Harold Alexander. The two cooperated closely, but the convoluted chain of command sometimes created delays.

The Japanese attacked northward up three rivers—the Irrawaddy, the Sittang, and the Salween—and the Allied forces, including the Chinese, had to withdraw. By mid-April, the retreating Allies were forced to destroy millions of gallons of crude oil stored in tanks at Yenangyaung. With little air power, the British were unable to bring in much reinforcement of supplies, and even the introduction of more Chinese troops in April could not stem the Japanese tide. On 29 April, the Japanese captured Lashio. Lashio was the starting point of the Burma Road, the one roadway to carry supplies overland to China, and its capture spelled an end to direct overland aid to China until January 1945.

The Japanese were unable to destroy the Allied forces, but they pushed them out of Burma. The British-Indian-Burmese forces reached the Indian frontier at the perfect time: the monsoon season. The weather held the Japanese at bay, while the exhausted British and Indian forces reorganized and prepared defensive positions to protect India.

The expected Japanese invasion of India after the monsoon did not materialize. The Japanese seemed content to hold the country and exploit its oil and rubber rather than challenge the mountainous terrain along the Burma-India border. In India, Stilwell and his British counterpart, General Archibald Wavell, trained their men and made plans for reconquest. As they did so, the British tried a new strategy. Orde Wingate, an eccentric British leader, organized and led a guerrilla group into the jungles to harass the Japanese. These "Chindits" survived by air supply, a logistical innovation pioneered by Wingate. The men suffered as they learned how to deal with the jungle and the Japanese, but they succeeded in disrupting Japanese operations. In the meantime, the Americans attempted to keep the flow of supplies into China uninterrupted by flying "over the Hump"—the Himalayas. Until a new overland route could be established starting at the northern Burma town of Ledo, air supply was the only option.

Not until 1944 did the British and Americans feel prepared to go back into Burma. They planned to enter from the north with a mixed Sino-American force, from the northeast with a Chinese force sent by Chiang Kai-shek, and from the west with the British 14th Army. The invasion was thrown off-schedule by a Japanese attack toward the border. The Japanese intended to strike toward the railroad terminal at Ledo, cutting off the attempts to reestablish land communication with China. After early success, they became bogged down around the towns of Imphal and Kohima, where the 14th Army under General William Slim held out through a siege and pushed the Japanese back in the summer of 1944. From then on, the Allied effort went consistently forward. Stilwell and Frank Merrill led the American and Chinese troops southeast from Ledo to Myitkyina, the capture of which gave the Allies a forward air base to bypass the Himalayas into China. By the end of 1944, British forces had captured the port of Akyab on Burma's west coast and crossed the Irawaddy River toward Mandalay, the large rail junction in the center of the country. Too hard-pressed in other theaters to reinforce Burma, the Japanese lost ground consistently. Mandalay fell in April 1945, and Rangoon in May, effectively marking the recapture of the country.

The battle for Burma was one of the most physically trying of the entire war. The battle was fought almost completely in jungle terrain, with which Western soldiers were unfamiliar, and the challenges of terrain, weather, and disease sapped the strength of all soldiers. The necessity of recapturing Burma has since been questioned. The main American reason for the operation was the need to reopen the supply line to China. The United States was convinced that China could tie up masses of Japanese troops, though the British thought that Chiang Kai-shek was more concerned with stockpiling weapons to fight the Communist Chinese than to fight the Japanese. The campaign proved the effectiveness of long-range strike forces such as Wingate's Chindits, and the ability of air forces to provide such operations with supplies and medical evacuation. Certainly the need to deny the Japanese the natural resources of the country was important, but the Allies overestimated Japan's intentions. They did not seriously threaten India's frontiers until 1944, and by then Japan's inability to reinforce meant that no major invasion of India could have taken place even had the British and Commonwealth soldiers not stood fast at Imphal and Kohima.

References: Bidwell, Shelford, *The Chindit War* (New York: Macmillan, 1980); Romanus, Charles, *Time Runs Out in CBI* (Washington, DC: Office of the Chief of Military History, 1958); Slim, William, *Defeat into Victory* (New York: D. McKay, 1961).

161 CHINA, JAPANESE INVASION OF

The onset of the international depression of 1929 led to the seizure of power by militaristic leaders in Japan. Many of these leaders came from a rural background, and the agricultural sector of the economy had been hit particularly hard. The farmers' inclination was to blame politicians and the wealthy for the poor economy; thus, the common people supported the new regime, which stressed honor and devotion to the emperor above all else. The militarists saw themselves as the natural saviors of the downtrodden. Historically, victims of economic woes have often sought solution in military action.

In 1931, the Japanese military flexed its muscles and precipitated a conflict that resulted in their occupation and domination of the Chinese province of Manchuria. With that relatively easy victory, they began to think in terms of the total domination not only of China, but also of Southeast Asia, Australia, and India, creating the Greater East Asia Co-prosperity Sphere.

The military launched the Manchurian campaign without the government's knowledge; presented with a fait accompli, the Cabinet accepted the army's explanation of events and assumed control of the resource-rich province. Events in 1937 followed much the same path, though it is unclear how much actual planning went into the clash of Japanese and Chinese soldiers at the Marco Polo Bridge along the Sino-Manchurian border near Peking in July 1937. Because of the Boxer Protocol of 1901 (forced upon the Manchu government after the abortive Boxer Rebellion), the Japanese military had the right to engage in maneuvers in the area, and the Japanese had been expanding their economic influence into the area for some time. Though the Japanese had the right to protect their interests, the location and timing of the Marco Polo Bridge incident point to deliberate provocation.

The Japanese worked on the assumption that they would be able to take over the five northern provinces of China without large-scale military action. This proved not to be the case, surprisingly so because the Chinese government under Chiang Kai-shek was fragmented and venal, having a power base that included warlords, gangsters, and drug kingpins. Chiang himself rose to power and kept it through the machinations of the Green Gang boss and the strength of the immensely powerful Soong family, which virtually controlled the banking and taxation systems in China. Through his wife, American-educated Soong May-ling, Chiang had access to the highest levels of American government and society, and it was largely through this connection that he was able to get the assistance he needed to fight the Japanese.

China's government was also engaged in a long-running struggle with the Chinese Communists under Mao Tse-tung, and the

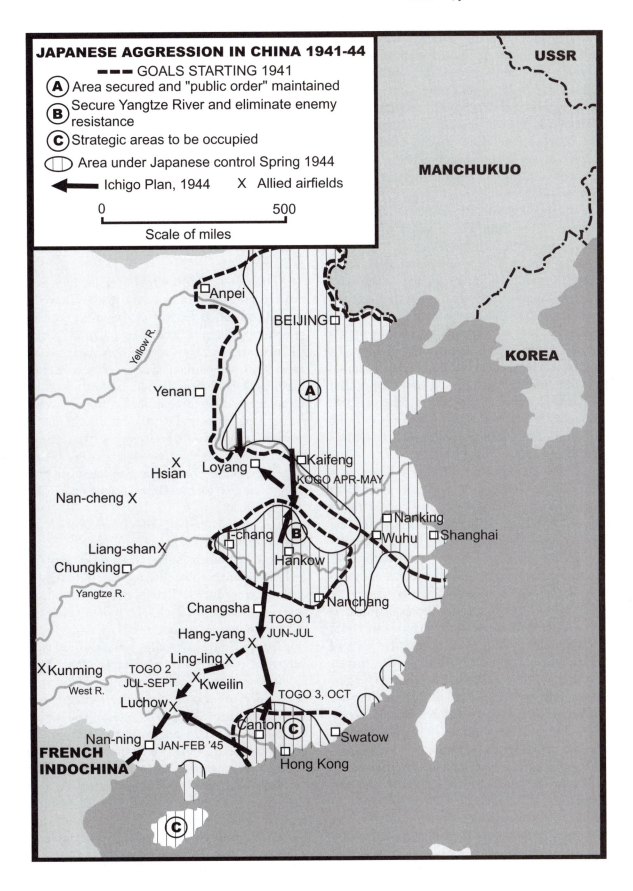

JAPANESE AGGRESSION IN CHINA 1941-44
- - - GOALS STARTING 1941
(A) Area secured and "public order" maintained
(B) Secure Yangtze River and eliminate enemy resistance
(C) Strategic areas to be occupied
Area under Japanese control Spring 1944
⟵ Ichigo Plan, 1944   X Allied airfields

0   500
Scale of miles

USSR

MANCHUKUO

KOREA

Anpei

BEIJING

Yellow R.

Yenan

(A)

X
Hsian

Loyang

Kaifeng

KOGO APR-MAY

Nan-cheng X

Nanking

I-chang   (B)   Wuhu   Shanghai

Liang-shan X

Hankow

Chungking

Yangtze R.

Nanchang

Changsha

TOGO 1
JUN-JUL

Hang-yang X

Ling-ling X

X Kunming

TOGO 2
JUL-SEPT

West R.

X Kweilin

TOGO 3, OCT

Luchow X

Canton (C)

Swatow

Nan-ning JAN-FEB '45

**FRENCH
INDOCHINA**

Hong Kong

(C)

Chinese were unsure of how to fight a war on two fronts when neither had much popular support. The result was that the Nationalists under Chiang fought a war of delay and retreat into the vast interior of the country, relying on what support they could gain from outside the country. For a time Chiang was aided by Prussian military advisers, but they left upon the signing of the Tripartite Pact, which allied Germany and Japan in 1940. Soviet pilots were the mainstay of his air force until Claire Chennault and the American Volunteer Group (the "Flying Tigers") arrived in late 1941 to fight his air battles.

Japan blockaded Chinese ports and poured masses of men and materiel into the fight. Japanese casualties were heavy and they lost the occasional battle, but the losses of manpower on the Chinese side were staggering, and the ferocity and wanton killing of unarmed civilians by Japanese soldiers (highlighted by the infamous Rape of Nanking in 1937) left little doubt that the Japanese would prevail. By the end of 1938, the Japanese realized their goal of capturing north and central China; they had also captured the port of Canton in the south.

Of the unconquered territory remaining, a quarter of it was under Communist control in the northwest. The Communists had as much reason to fear the Japanese as they did the Nationalists, but even though the Communists and the Nationalists stopped fighting each other for a time, there was no united effort or cooperative planning against the common enemy.

By July 1939, the Japanese consolidated and extended the territory they had gained in 1938, including additional ground around the ports of Canton and Nanking. Chiang had been driven back into the interior in a series of major retreats, and he finally established a new capital at Chungking. By the time the Japanese navy attacked Pearl Harbor in late 1941, the Japanese perimeter in China had been extended to control the principal Chinese railroad in the south.

When the United States entered the war, economic and military aid for China increased dramatically. Chennault continued his efforts to strengthen and expand the air war against the Japanese, and General Joseph Stilwell was sent to command ground operations. Stilwell was often at odds with Chiang and Chennault, and he was openly contemptuous of the incompetence, corruption, and internal dissension that made Chinese actions and American support ineffective. After Stilwell was replaced by General A. C. Wedemeyer late in the war, the U.S. government expressed strong interest in giving aid to the Communists as a viable alternative to Chiang's regime. Because of political considerations, however, it was not done, and by the end of the war Wedemeyer had succeeded in reshaping the Nationalist armies to the point where they could go on the offensive against the Japanese.

The initial adventuring of the Japanese militarists on the Chinese mainland may not have had the wholehearted support of the entire Japanese government, but the operations in China provided the military machine with the opportunity to test its skills, train its men, and develop its military hardware for the later execution of its expansionist policies, culminating in the confrontation with the United States and its allies in the Pacific theater of operations. Ineffective as the Chinese armies often were, they forced Japan to maintain a large percentage of its force that could otherwise have been used for operations against the advancing Americans.

As stated earlier, the Nationalists and Communists never cooperated in their war against the Japanese, so the war was not long over in 1945 before the two rival factions were fighting each other again. The United States continued to support Chiang Kai-shek, but that support lessened as time went by, and the Nationalist leadership proved no less corrupt after the war than before or during it. In September 1949, Mao's Communist forces finally forced the Nationalists to abandon the country and set up a government-in-exile on the island of Formosa. The United States continued to recognize the Nationalists' claim as the legitimate government of all the Chinese, even though many countries extended recognition to the Communists as the de facto government on the mainland. This difference in recognition has provided some interesting times in the United Nations, because China has a pe manent seat on the Security Council. Mao Tse-tung established himself as not only the leader of China, but also virtually its god, and his personal policies or whims affected tens of millions of individuals through economic policies, purges of political rivals, and the occasional foreign military venture. Japan's invasion may have postponed Mao's seizure of power in China, but the years of struggle endured by the common Chinese citizen certainly aided his consolidation of power, if for no other reason than as an end to years of fighting and destruction.

See also Manchuria, Japanese Invasion of (1931); South Korea, North Korean Invasion of (Korean War).

References: Hi, Hsi-sheng, *Nationalist China at War* (Ann Arbor: University of Michigan Press, 1982); Liu, F. E., *A Military History of Modern China* (Princeton, NJ: Princeton University Press, 1956); Tuchman, Barbara, *Stilwell and the American Experience in China* (New York: Macmillan, 1970).

CYPRUS, TURKISH INVASION OF

162

Enosis. It is a Greek word meaning "union." That one word has been the source of conflict and bloodshed in Cyprus since 1923.

After acquiring Cyprus through conquest in 1571, the Ottoman Empire oversaw an island that had few ethnic problems. The native population, overwhelmingly Greek in heritage and numbering some 150,000, had little problem peacefully coexisting with an influx of about 30,000 Turks from Anatolia. The newly arrived Turks settled across the island and the two cultures lived side by side with no significant problems. That changed, however, in 1821 when a revolution broke out in Greece attempting to break away from Ottoman control. The Archbishop (and virtual ruler) of Cyprus was Kyprianos, who belonged to a secret organization (Philike Heraireia) which had been plotting the revolution. Although no serious hint of revolt came from Cyprus itself, the Ottoman government directed its governor there to maintain order. He did so by rounding up all suspected members of Philike Heraireia, including the archbishop, and executing them. Two hundred and fifty years of cooperation vanished overnight.

The Greeks did gain their independence, but that was only on the mainland, and many Greek Cypriots wanted union with what they say is their mother country. Nothing drastic happened on the island, however, until 1878 when the British acquired it. The Ottoman Empire was a shadow of its former self by that time and the British needed an eastern Mediterranean base to support its new acquisition, the Suez Canal. While not overwhelmingly popular, the British administration was accepted by the Cypriot population. When World War I broke out, the second phase of Greco-Turkish violence began. In order to gain Greek support against the Central Powers in World War I (which included the Ottoman Empire), the British government offered to give Cyprus to Greece. Although the Greek Prime Minister Venizelos was in favor of the idea, it was vetoed by the Greek king. Thus, the Greek government missed a golden opportunity.

After the war ended, the terms of the Versailles Treaty called for the dismemberment of the German, Austro-Hungarian, and Ottoman Empires. The Ottoman Empire was broken up into the nations of Turkey, Syria, Trans-Jordan, Palestine, Iraq, Lebanon, and Saudi Arabia (along with some Persian Gulf sheikhdoms). In the 1923 Treaty of Lausanne, Turkey ceded to Great Britain all claims to Cyprus; Britain declared the island a Crown Colony in 1925. With the coming of the Great Depression of the 1930s, the British imposed higher taxes to pay for their administration and provoked massive rioting. Some 2,000 people were convicted for being connected with the violence, and two bishops were sent into exile. Laws were imposed limiting the Church's power and banning nationalist movements. Still, Greek and Turkish Cypriots aided Britain and the Allies during World War II. In the wake of the war, Britain could no longer afford to maintain its empire and it began granting independence to many colonies, such as India, and ceding its position as peacekeeper in the eastern Mediterranean, as seen in its withdrawal from Palestine in 1948. The United States stepped up to take over Britain's role, especially when communist movements began

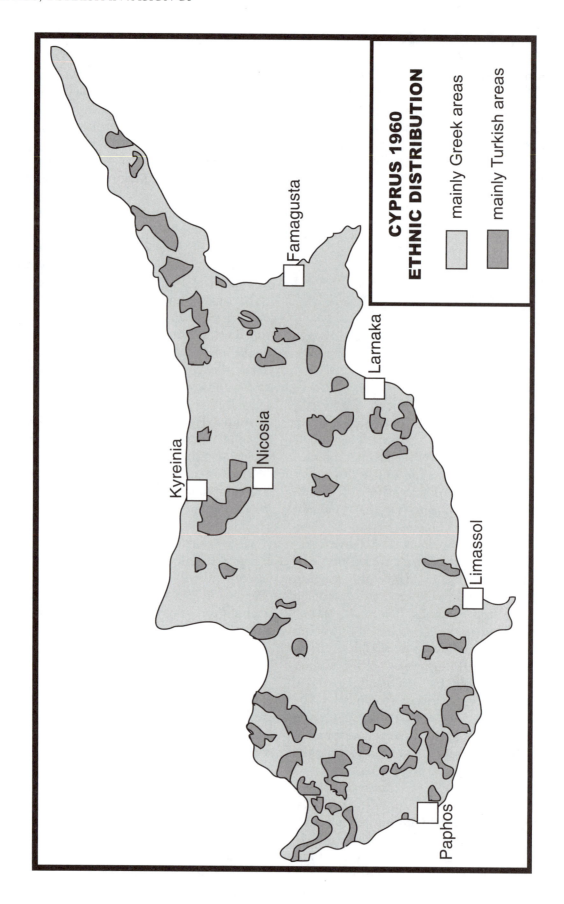

CYPRUS 1960
ETHNIC DISTRIBUTION

mainly Greek areas

mainly Turkish areas

Famagusta

Larnaka

Kyreinia

Nicosia

Limassol

Paphos

to emerge in both Greece and Turkey. With American aid given to both governments, the communist movements were suppressed. A Greek resistance fighter named George Grivas returned to his native Cyprus and began pushing the concept of enosis, union with Greece. He became a reluctant ally of Archbishop Mikarios III, who at first hoped for a political solution for union. In 1953, the British Colonial Secretary Henry Hopkinson dealt a blow to the concept of a peaceful solution when he announced that some colonies, however, could never leave the British fold. Cyprus was just too strategically placed to be abandoned by Western powers.

When Britain used its position in the Security Council to overrule a United Nations debate on the Greek-Cyprus union question, the Cypriots responded: Mikarios and Grivas in 1955 agreed to work together and founded the National Organization of Cypriot Fighters (Ethniki Organosis Kyprion Agoniston, better known as EOKA. EOKA began a series of attacks against British facilities on the island. London responded by sending a new governor, Chief of the Imperial General Staff Field Marshall John Harding. Harding proposed to Mikarios that Britain would supply large amounts of aid to the island if it would accept limited self-government and postpone any movement toward enosis. Talks proceeded in fits and starts until March 1956 when Mikarios was deported after being accused of connections with EOKA violence. Thus, the militant George Grivas rose to head the EOKA and immediately stepped up the violence. The Turkish Cypriots, meanwhile, introduced the concept of partitioning the island into Greek and Turkish territories. Finally, in 1958, talks began in London with the intent of giving Cyprus independence, thereby sidestepping the question of enosis. Multiparty talks finally emerged with three treaties: the Treaty of Establishment, the Treaty of Guarantee, and the Treaty of Alliance.

The Treaty of Establishment brought about a power-sharing constitution with a Greek Cypriot president and a Turkish Cypriot vice president, as well as a set number of seats in a parliament.

Both ethnic groups formally forswore their goals of enosis or partition. The Treaty of Guarantee placed Greece, Turkey, and Great Britain in the position of guarantors of the peace. The Treaty of Alliance called for mutual cooperation among Cyprus, Turkey, and Greece in matters of island defense. Turkish Cypriots greatly preferred independence to partition, but many Greek Cypriots still wanted enosis. Mikarios, elected first president, decided it was the best solution the island could hope for.

The solution lasted three years. In 1963, Mikarios proposed 13 amendments to the constitution which would severely limit Turkish rights. This created increased tension that exploded in December when an arrest-gone-wrong provoked widespread ethnic violence. Fighting continued for months, even with the intervention of a U.N. peacekeeping force. When it finally began to settle down in the summer of 1964, Turkish Cypriots began to leave their homes for Turkish enclaves, primarily in the city of Nicosia. During the crisis, Turkish members of parliament had boycotted the government and marked the end of constitutional rule. In the wake of the violence, the government called for creation of a National Guard, with all Cypriot males ages 18–59 being liable for duty. George Grivas came home from exile to command the organization. Not surprisingly, it soon took an anti-Turkish turn. Violence against Turks provoked a threat from the Turkish government that it would intervene if Grivas was not expelled and Greek forces not removed from the island. Turkish forces began mobilizing along the Greek border and ships for an invasion were readied. U.S. Representative Cyrus Vance was able to broker a truce and most Turkish demands were met in 1967. The National Guard, however, was not disbanded, even though Grivas was exiled.

Through the next several years the Turkish enclaves across the island began developing a plan for self-government, but since they were isolated in many locations, it was impossible to act in concert to establish their own government. Rifts appeared in the Greek Cypriot ranks as the enosis faction began to receive encouragement from a group of Greek officers who had seized the government in Athens in September 1973. Mikarios tried to stay in the middle ground between the unionists and partitionists, but that path came to an end in 1974. Grivas had returned to Cyprus a few years earlier and started another underground movement, EOKA-B, aimed at removing Mikarios in order to achieve enosis. Grivas's death in January 1974 did not end the movement; it was taken over by Nicos Sampson. Calling himself "hammer of the Turks," Sampson staged a coup d'état in July 1974 and removed Mikarios from power. His planned assassination by the National Guard failed when Mikarios managed to escape to a British base and flee the island. Assuming the coup was supported by Athens, the Turkish Prime Minister Bulent Ecevit called on British assistance to enforce the Treaty of Guarantee. The Greek Cypriot population had assumed that the treaty had lapsed when the U.N. sent in peacekeepers in 1964, and the British (while not taking that view) did not show much interest in upholding their part of the bargain. Hence, the Turkish government decided to send in troops on the basis of the Treaty of Guarantee.

What happened afterwards is widely debated, depending on if one is viewing Greek or Turkish sources. To the Turks, this was intervention to keep the peace as they were obliged to do. To the Greeks, this was invasion. Last-minute talks conducted by U.S. envoy Joseph Sisco failed to gain Greek agreement for Turkish demands, which looked much like those they had made after the fighting in 1964. The Turkish army landed in Cyprus on 20 July 1974. Within days the military junta in Athens was removed from power and Sampson resigned as head of the Cypriot government. Thus, a major Greco-Turkish war seemed to have been averted, but with Turkish troops on the ground in Cyprus, matters there were far from settled. "Prime Minister Ecevit publicly welcomed the change of government in Greece and seemed genuinely interested in eliminating the tensions that had brought the two countries so close to war. Nevertheless, during the truce that was arranged, Turkish forces continued to take territory, to improve their positions, and to build up their supplies of war matériel." (Solstein, *Country Study*)

For a time things remained relatively calm as talks in Geneva began, with representatives exploring the plans for partitioning the island. In August, the Turks proposed a split in which Turkish Cypriots would control 34 percent of the island, even though they comprised less than 20 percent of the population. When the Turkish representatives came to believe the Greeks were stalling, the Ankara government ordered the Turkish troops forward. At this point, the Turks violated the Treaty of Guarantee under which they claimed to be operating. The treaty states that the signatory powers "undertake to prohibit, as far as concern them, any activity aimed at promoting, directly or indirectly, either union of Cyprus with any other State or partition of the Island." The Turkish army seized 37 percent of the island and established on August 14 what they called the Attila Line as a border between Turkish and Greek populations. Thousands of people were killed in the few days the Turkish army was operating, and tens of thousands were displaced. In 1975, the Turkish Cypriots proclaimed the Turkish Federated State of Cyprus; they declared themselves an independent nation in 1983. Over the next several years, talks were conducted about the possibility of reunification, but they have shown no success.

Human rights organizations have condemned the Turkish occupation. A European Commission of Human Rights investigated the situation in 1976 and claimed Turkey had violated human rights conventions. Human Rights International comments, "Turkey's analysis of conduct in terms of Article II of the 1948 Convention on the Prevention and Punishment of the Crime of Genocide makes it clear that Turkey committed a species of genocide as respects the Greek Cypriot community. Turkey intended to destroy the Greek Cypriots as an ethnic and religious group in the occupied area by deliberately inflicting on it conditions of life calculated to bring about its physical destruction in part and its total and permanent displacement from the occupied part of Cyprus. Unfortunately no international judicial machinery is available to arraign Turkey as she has not recognized yet the jurisdiction of the International Court of Justice." (hri.org)

Turkish economic aid keeps the northern part of the island at a respectable standard of living, but the Turkish Republic's economy has suffered since the intervention/invasion and has not entirely recovered. That of the Greek Cypriot Republic, however, has rebounded well and is on a par with that of western Europe.

See also Cyprus, Ottoman invasion of.

References: Hitchens, Christopher, *Hostage to History: Cyprus from the Ottomans to Kissinger* (London: Verso, 1997 [1984]); Solstein, Eric, ed., *Cyprus: A Country Study* (Washington, DC: Government Printing Office, 1993); "History," <www.cypnet.co.uk/ncyprus/history/index.html>, 2 January 2005; Onwar.com, "Turkish Invasion of Cyprus, 1974," <www.onwar.com/aced/data/tango/turkeycyprus1974.htm>.

163 CZECHOSLOVAKIA, NAZI OCCUPATION OF

After the successful Nazi occupation of Austria in March 1938, Hitler focused his attention on Czechoslovakia in accordance with his policy, spelled out in his book *Mein Kampf,* of bringing all German-speaking people under one government. The far western area of Czechoslovakia, the Sudetenland, had a large German minority, and Hitler claimed they were being treated unequally by the Czech government. Within a few weeks of the Austrian Anschluss, Hitler had his generals working on invasion plans; meanwhile, his agents in the Sudetenland were engaged in a propaganda campaign to blow out of proportion any slights the Czechs may have inflicted on Germans.

The Czech government followed two strategies: Negotiate with Germans in the province, and make sure the defense treaty with France would be honored. The German spokesman, Czech Nazi leader Konrad Henlein, proposed a plan that would give German communities in the Sudetenland local autonomy, a scheme to which the Czech government had little opposition. Despite Czech willingness to cooperate, rumors persisted of a German military buildup along the border. Nevertheless, Czech president Edvard Benes twice received assurances from the French government that their defense commitments to Czechoslovakia would be honored.

With a British mediator on hand in Prague, Czech officials entered into negotiations with Henlein on 3 August 1938. After several days, talks stalled. France continued to assure the Czechs, but the French also quietly asked Britain what support they would supply if France mobilized against Germany. The British replied that they would defend French security, but could not give an assurance in advance concerning any other country without first consulting with the dominions of the empire. Talks continued in Prague through September, but finally broke down on 12 September.

The Nazis in the Sudetenland began rioting, provoking the intervention of Czech troops and the declaration of martial law. German intervention seemed inevitable, and Britain's prime minister, Neville Chamberlain, asked to meet with Hitler. At Hitler's private estate at Berchtesgaden on 15 September, Chamberlain offered an agreement to "far-reaching German proposals" in order to avoid war, including support for a referendum in the Sudetenland and its cession to Germany. Though Hitler demanded "the return" of the three million Czechs of German descent, in reality this area had never been under German control, but that of Austria. Hitler agreed to postpone any action until Chamberlain spoke with the French. Over the next several days, Chamberlain convinced the French to agree to cession of the territory, and the Czech government saw their foreign support slipping away.

Unknown to Western sources until after the war was the resistance to Hitler's actions within Germany. The German military was convinced that the French and British would never allow an invasion of the Sudetenland but would mobilize and invade Germany, which did not have the necessary defensive works constructed along the French frontier. Within the high command, several generals plotted to overthrow Hitler if he gave the order to invade. Since they had to plot in secret, they made no attempt to inform Britain or France of their intentions. Such information surely would have stiffened the British and French resolve and avoided another world war.

In Chamberlain's second meeting with Hitler on 22 September, the prime minister informed Hitler that France had agreed to support the cession of the Sudetenland. Pleased that he had averted war, Chamberlain was shocked when Hitler added another demand: immediate German military occupation of the area. When Chamberlain could not guarantee French or Czech acceptance, he was met with yet another demand: total Czech withdrawal from the Sudetenland beginning on 26 September, to be completed by 28 September. By coincidence, immediately after this demand was made, word came that the Czechs had ordered the mobilization of their armed forces. Chamberlain knew he certainly could not convince the Czechs to withdraw in so short a time period, if at all. Hitler granted a concession: He would wait until 1 October. Chamberlain jumped at it, not knowing that 1 October had been the German target date all along. Unfortunately, neither the British Cabinet nor the French government would agree to Germany's latest demands. France ordered a partial mobilization.

Czechoslovakia had much to fight for. Though it was a new country, formed by the Versailles conference out of the old Austro-Hungarian empire, the Czechs had a strong nationalist feeling. Further, loss of the Sudetenland would not be merely the cession of a piece of land, but of the defensive fortifications that protected the country, located in the nation's most rugged terrain. Giving up that land would mean giving up their one natural defense. They had an army of some 800,000 men, equal to what Hitler could mobilize, but they believed Hitler's bluff that his military was much larger. Without the defenses of the Sudetenland, without the assurances of aid from France, the Czech government was not sure its army could defeat Germany. An existing defense agreement with the Soviet Union was useless, because the Soviets were denied access through Poland or Rumania to give assistance.

A last attempt to avert war came when Mussolini invited Chamberlain and French president Edouard Daladier to meet with him and Hitler at Munich on 29 September. Czech representatives were not invited. In this conference, Britain and France gave in to Hitler's demand that his army begin entering the Sudetenland on 1 October, finishing the occupation by 10 October.

The Czech government was informed that if they did not agree to this arrangement, they could face Germany alone. The agreement signed by Hitler, Chamberlain, Mussolini, and Daladier gave the Germans control of the Sudetenland, but guaranteed the remainder of Czechoslovakia. Hitler stated, "I have no more territorial demands in Europe. I want no more Czechs." With this agreement in hand, Prime Minister Chamberlain told the British public, "We have peace in our time."

The Czech government gave in and ceded the territory. Within a matter of months, the country ceased to exist. A German-backed Slovak independence movement removed the Slovakian segment of the country from Czech control. Because the borders that had been guaranteed by the Munich agreement no longer existed, Britain did not lift a finger to stop the German occupation and annexation of the remainder of the country in March 1939. Neither did the Czech government ask its population to resist. As with the occupation of Austria, the Germans had added another conquest to their list without a shot being fired. All Czech provinces became German protectorates, including Slovakia. Acquisition of Czechoslovakia put Germany into a commanding strategic position in relation to Poland, putting Nazi forces on both the western and southern borders. Later that same year, Germany would quickly invade and subjugate Poland as well.

Some historians argue that the Munich agreement bought time for England and France to prepare their respective armed forces for the war they knew would be coming. If that argument is accepted, they did not spend their time wisely. The best summation of the actions of Britain and France was given by Jan Masaryk, Czech minister to Britain. He told Chamberlain and Foreign Minister Halifax, "If you have sacrificed my nation to preserve the peace of the world, I will be the first to applaud you. But if not, gentlemen, God help your souls."

See also Austria, Nazi Occupation of; Poland, Nazi Conquest of.

References: Churchill, Winston, *The Gathering Storm* (New York: Houghton Mifflin, 1948; Shirer, William, *The Nightmare Years* (New York: Little, Brown, 1984); Shirer, William, *The Rise and Fall of the Third Reich* (New York: Simon & Schuster, 1960).

DUTCH EAST INDIES, JAPANESE INVASION OF

164

As Japanese forces fought against Chinese Communist and Nationalist forces, they needed more and more oil to fuel their war machine. At the same time, the United States, their major supplier, began to negotiate with the Japanese to halt their war with China and even withdraw from the territories they had already occupied. The Japanese goal of dominating Asia economically as well as militarily would not allow them to withdraw, so negotiations dragged. When Japan joined Germany and Italy as one of the Axis powers in September 1940, Japan received free access to the French colony of Indochina, ceded to the Japanese by the French Vichy government.

Japanese troops in Indochina and the strong coastal position the Japanese held in China frightened the United States. Japan seemed to be slowly working its way around the Philippine Islands, controlled by the United States since 1898. American President Franklin Roosevelt decided to begin an embargo of oil and scrap iron to Japan, hoping to pressure the Japanese into more serious negotiations over China. Denied their primary supplier, the Japanese had to make a decision: Give in to American demands, which would weaken their plans to dominate Asia and entail a great loss of face, or continue their expansion and find a new source of oil. The only source near at hand was in the Dutch East Indies. The United States knew that as well, and U.S. Secretary of State Cordell Hull warned Japan that if it invaded those islands, the United States would go to war, even though the Americans had no direct interest there.

Japan and the United States continued to negotiate through 1941, but the talks served only to drive the two sides further apart. By late summer, the Japanese government decided to continue conferring with the Americans but simultaneously prepare for war in case the talks failed. By late November, Tokyo bowed to the inevitable—war against the United States—because Japan had to have oil. As naval forces secretly left Japan to launch the strike against Pearl Harbor, other Japanese forces embarked for attacks against American possessions in the Pacific, the British base at Singapore, and the British colony of North Borneo. On 7 December 1941 (8 December on the other side of the international date line, Japanese troops were seemingly everywhere at once.

Within a month, Japanese forces controlled most of the Philippines, and the southern island of Mindanao became their base of operations for the invasion of the Dutch East Indies. Allied forces in the area knew the invasion was imminent and tried to mount an effective defense, forming the ABDA (American-British-Dutch-Australian) Command under the direction of British General Archibald Wavell. Naval and air forces were under subordinate American command, and land forces were commanded by the Dutch. Even though the Dutch had the most intimate knowledge of the sea lanes in the area, they were rarely consulted on naval matters.

The Japanese planned three separate invasion forces. The Western Force assembled at Cam Ranh Bay in Indochina to attack southern Sumatra and Java. The Central Force left the base of Davao, on Mindanao, for attacks along the eastern coast of Borneo, to be followed by aiding the attack on Java. The Eastern Force also left Davao, heading for the islands of Celebes, Ambon, and Timor. The ABDA forces could do little to stop these onslaughts, for none of the countries represented could commit large forces to the area. Holland was under German occupation, Britain was fighting in North Africa, and the United States was still trying to get its military organized and operating in the wake of Pearl Harbor.

Japan began the operation on 7 January 1942 when elements of the Eastern and Central Forces left the Philippines. The Eastern Force landed on 10 January on Celebes's northeastern coast at Manado, and in three days was in control. On 24 January they captured the new airfield near Kendari on the southeast coast. From here, Japanese aircraft could harass shipping throughout the area and attack targets in Java. The island of Ambon was secured on 5 February; Timor was attacked by amphibious and airborne forces on 17 February and secured a few days later.

The Central Force was just as successful. The main Dutch oil and coal sources were on Borneo, and its towns fell with frightening rapidity: Tarakan on 13 January, Balikpapan on 24 January, Bandjermasin on 10 February. Borneo's oil production and refining were now in Japanese hands, and the Dutch had only one remaining oil field, Palembang on the island of Sumatra. The Japanese prepared to assault this spot with the Western Force, which began by securing the island of Banka on Sumatra's east coast on 14 February. When amphibious forces sailed up the Musi River toward Palembang, resistance by ABDA naval forces proved futile, both because of a lack of Allied coordination and because of Japanese air superiority. Palembang fell on 16 February, one day after the British surrender of Singapore. Though reinforcing the Allies was impossible, planning for the area's defense proceeded, for political if no other reasons.

The Japanese juggernaut moved on. On 18 February it struck Bali. The Allies attempted to stop the landings, but failed. A mixed Dutch-American naval force sustained much more damage than they inflicted, and they withdrew to try again later. On 27 February the naval forces tried to forestall the invasion of Java, and the resulting Battle of Java Sea became an Allied disaster. The two sides had roughly equal numbers, but the Japanese were more experienced and had practiced working as a unit. The American, Dutch, and British ships had never worked together in combat, and they had difficulty communicating. After an early exchange of shots that caused light damage on both sides, the Japanese began to register deadly hits with torpedoes and shell fire. Three Dutch ships and a British ship were sunk, and the damaged American and British ships had to withdraw. The invasion of Java was delayed but one day. By 9 March the Japanese were in a position to demand, and receive, unconditional surrender from the remaining Dutch forces. The entire operation to control the Dutch East Indies took three months, half the expected time.

The Japanese occupation of the islands got off to a good beginning. So disliked were the Dutch that the Japanese were welcomed as liberators, particularly by the Javanese. The Japanese encouraged anti-Western feeling by allowing the display of the Indonesian flag and the playing of the national anthem, both of which the Dutch had outlawed. Within six months, all Dutch and Eurasian inhabitants still on the islands were rounded up and committed to camps. This caused a major loss of civil servants, but the Japanese replaced them with Indonesians, a policy that both ensured a loyal following in the islands and gave the locals experience in running the bureaucracy. Japan promised that they would soon allow the Indonesians a self-governing state, and they promoted Indonesian nationalism through the creation of a home guard of 120,000 men and the support of Sukarno, the leading prewar advocate of independence from Holland. Japan tried to use Sukarno to encourage local support for Japanese war aims, created an Islamic forum to obtain religious support, and opened the educational system to all, regardless of ethnicity.

All these programs bought the Japanese the goodwill of the people, but they also gave the Indonesians a taste for education and political advancement that could only be satisfied through independence from all outside domination, whether Dutch or Japanese. Further, by creating a national guard, the population became armed, as well as ambitious. The political leaders who trained in Japanese schools graduated not as supporters of Japan, but as Marxists, which did not spell good news for a Japanese occupation. As the war turned against the Japanese, they gave more and more promises to the Indonesians concerning independence, which they finally awarded in March 1945. Rather than bind the locals to Japan with friendly feelings of gratitude, it made them more anxious than ever to rid themselves of the Japanese.

On 6 August 1945, the day the first atomic bomb was dropped, the Japanese were prepared to cede all political power to the Indonesian Nationalists; on 17 August, Sukarno declared independence, and the following day the nation of Indonesia was organized. With the war over, the Dutch assumed they would reoccupy the islands and pick up where they had left off in 1942, but the British were assigned occupation duties. The Allied political leader in Southeast Asia was Britain's Lord Mountbatten, and the military leader of occupation forces was

American General Douglas MacArthur. They both decided to recognize Sukarno's government, and did nothing to reestablish Dutch authority. Thus, Indonesia benefited from Japan's conquest more than any other country, because it brought them independence, if somewhat by default.

See also China, Japanese Invasion of; Egypt, Italian Invasion of; France, Nazi Invasion of; Philippines, U.S. Invasion of the.

References: Collier, Basil, *Japan at War: An Illustrated History of the War in the Far East* (London: Sidgwick & Jackson, 1975); Hyma, Albert, *The Dutch in the Far East* (Ann Arbor, MI: George Wahr Publishing, 1953); Ryan, N. J., *A History of Malaysia and Singapore* (London: Oxford University Press, 1976).

165 EAST AFRICA, BRITISH INVASION OF

When World War I broke out in August 1914, German colonies around the world became targets. Germany had entered the empire-building race late in the 1800s and was not as successful in claiming productive territories as its European rivals. The main location for action during the war was the colony of East Africa, which was surrounded by other colonies controlled by or allied to the British. Though the German colony was enclosed, it would give Germany the opportunity to strike in several directions while maintaining interior lines of communication. As soon as war was declared, the German officer in charge, Paul von Lettow-Vorbeck, began doing just that.

Lettow-Vorbeck could draw on a force of about 1,800 active-duty soldiers and 5,000 reservists, backed by several thousand askaris (native troops). He had been an observer with the Boers during their war with Britain and had learned their impressive guerrilla commando tactics. The Germans used this hit-and-run fighting style to keep the British Ugandan Railway in a constant state of disrepair.

The British responded by creating Force B of 8,000 soldiers from the Indian army and Force C of 4,000 Indian army soldiers stationed in British East Africa. Force B was to land on the Indian Ocean coast, then drive inland to link up with Force C. It never happened. On 4 November 1914, the invasion was first held at bay by a lone German machine gun, then by hastily dispatched German reinforcements. Street fighting in the town of Tanga the next day was fierce enough to cause 2,000 British-Indian casualties and force their withdrawal. The British spent the next year training local units to handle the fighting; Lettow-Vorbeck spent the time continuing his raids against the Ugandan Railway.

Another conflict was going on simultaneously that had more prestige than military value. The Germans armed several boats to control Lake Tanganyika, and the British and Belgians responded. In a series of clashes reminiscent of the movie *The African Queen*, the Allied force ultimately prevailed with the assistance of aircraft sent from Britain. By midsummer 1916, the lake was in Allied hands. The other naval aspect of this theater was the appearance of a German cruiser, the *Koenigsberg*, which had been harassing Allied shipping in the Indian Ocean. British warships chased the cruiser into the delta of the Rufiji River, but the deeper draft British ships could not follow. Nevertheless, they pounded the cruiser with their big guns until the *Koenigsberg* settled into the mud. Lettow-Vorbeck salvaged some 4.1-inch guns and some sailors to handle them, and used them in his campaign.

In January 1916, 30,000 newly trained African troops were ready to take the offensive. They came under the command of South African Jan Smuts, one of the Boers who had given the British fits almost 20 years earlier. Smuts planned a two-pronged offensive around the north and south sides of Mount Kilimanjaro to catch the Germans in a pincer. Poor communications and extremely difficult terrain argued against a well-coordinated effort, and the Germans were able to hobble the attacks and then fall back southward. A large battle in March pitted Lettow-Vorbeck's small force against an entire division under Smuts. The Germans and askaris took the most casualties, but were again able to slip away. The British forces had to give up the chase because of a lack of food and water as well as a growing casualty list from disease. Still, one of the main objectives was achieved: The Germans were never again in a position to cut the Ugandan Railway.

The British attempts to flank the Germans and cut them off came to grief owing to the terrain and the weather, both of which exhausted the supply animals as well as the men. In September, however, the British occupied the port city and capital, Dar es Salaam. After the fall of the city, Lettow-Vorbeck's force was down to 1,100 Germans and 7,300 askaris when he received news that the Portuguese were committing 7,000 men from the Congo to aid the British. Nevertheless, the British were still unable to catch the Germans. By the end of 1916, the white British and South African forces were relieved by West Indian and Nigerian units better acquainted with the tropical climate; 15,000 British soldiers were discharged and sent home as medically unfit.

The Allied forces finally came to grips with the Germans in October 1917. Their 4,000 men outnumbered Lettow-Vorbeck's force two to one, most of his men being askaris. The two armies fought hard, often hand to hand, in a four-day battle. Once again, Lettow-Vorbeck was able to withdraw and continue his movement south. In late November he ordered all his sick and wounded to surrender to the British, while he took his remaining men into Portuguese East Africa. The British forces gave chase, and through most of 1918 the two forces circled each other, but with little contact. Lettow-Vorbeck crossed back into German territory in early November and fought his last battle on 12 November, one day after the armistice was signed in Europe.

Lettow-Vorbeck and his remaining 200 German troops were taken back to Germany, where they were treated as heroes in Berlin. He remained in the army for two years and aided in suppressing rebellions in the chaotic postwar German society. He served in the government throughout the 1920s, but gave it up rather than work with the Nazis. He kept in contact with his old enemy Smuts, who sent him food parcels and suggested to German conspirators in 1944 that Lettow-Vorbeck be named head of a new government should the Nazis be overthrown.

In East Africa, the Germans left behind a country that had flourished before the war. They had built railroads, schools, and hospitals, and established a profitable trade in sisal. The League of Nations decided that all German colonies in Africa should be assigned as mandated territories, which European powers would administer under the general direction of the League. The British were assigned German East Africa, which they renamed Tanganyika. They inherited a rail system badly damaged by the Germans during the war and a number of plantations left derelict for four years; the native population suffered from hunger and influenza. The most economically rich areas of the country, Rwanda and Burundi, were detached as nations of their own. The British administration was slow to act, but finally in the 1920s the country began a slow climb back to normality.

See also South Africa, British Occupation of [144]; France, German Invasion of [160].

References: Harlow, Vincent, ed., *History of East Africa, 2 vols.* (Oxford: Clarendon Press, 1965); Hoyt, Edwin, Guerilla (New York: Macmillan, 1981); Lineberry, William, *East Africa* (New York: Wilson, 1968).

166 EGYPT, ITALIAN INVASION OF

Since the Italian peninsula became unified into one country in the 1870s, they had harbored the desire to dominate the Mediterranean. When Benito Mussolini came to power in the early 1920s, he set about preparing the Italian military to accomplish this dream. It seemed logical to extend Italian power from its existing location in Sicily through to Tunisia, thus controlling the central Mediterranean. France, however, had a protectorate in Tunisia. That fact had driven the Italians into an alliance with Germany prior to World War I (which they withdrew from early in the war) and was the main motivating factor in Mussolini's support of Hitler's invasion of France in May 1940. Italian troops also invaded southern Italy, but the Germans were so successful in overrunning the country that Italy gained little control and could thus demand little in the way of spoils. The German-controlled Vichy government in the south of France maintained a tenuous hold on French colonies, in Africa and elsewhere.

Unable to take advantage of his Axis alliance to gain a stronger position in Africa, Mussolini turned toward Egypt, long protected by Great Britain. Using the Italian colony of Libya for a base, plus the southern position of Ethiopia that Italy had conquered in 1937, Mussolini had troops sufficient (he thought) to defeat the British. Early success against the badly outnumbered British in Somaliland confirmed this notion. Control of Egypt would not only give Italy dominance in the Mediterranean, it would give the Axis powers possession of the Suez Canal, a vital seaway for British supplies. Unfortunately for Italy, Mussolini was looking at Eastern Europe as well as Africa, and this split focus cost him in both regions.

Mussolini had some 200,000 troops in Libya, as opposed to only 63,000 British Commonwealth forces in Egypt, Palestine, and East Africa. Field Marshal Graziani's invasion in September 1940 seemed destined for success. British General Archibald Wavell was a long way from the strategic or logistic decision center in London, so he had to make do with what he had on hand. It was enough. The Italian attack drove 60 miles into Egypt, reaching Sidi Barani. It was at this point Mussolini hurt himself. He launched an invasion of Greece at the same time as the Egyptian campaign opened. On the one hand, that forced a division in British interests which had long-range results, but it hurt the Italians more. Early November saw a series of Italian disasters. The British Royal Navy dealt a punishing blow to Italian naval forces at Taranto, the invasion of Greece bogged down in the face of the rugged Greek resistance and terrain, and Wavell launched a counterattack in Egypt.

Although Wavell's attack was merely meant to recapture Sidi Barani, it was so successful he decided to exploit his advantage. The Italians lost 38,000 prisoners in this one engagement, and soon lost more. By February 1941, Wavell had captured the Libyan port of Tobruk and surrounded and captured the majority of the Italian army at Beda Fromm. Two months' of campaigning netted the British 130,000 prisoners plus the destruction of 500 Italian tanks and the damage or capture of almost all their trucks and heavy guns. British losses totaled 2,000 men. Wavell

proposed to march west and capture all of Libya, but this was not to be. With attacks on so many fronts, Prime Minister Winston Churchill could not spare any men or materiel. Instead, he ordered Wavell to set up a defensive position and send some of his forces to assist the Greeks. When Mussolini had suffered his reverses there, Hitler drove through Yugoslavia to aid him, and the Greeks were sorely pressed. That British diversion of men to a lost cause cost the Allies dearly in the African desert.

Not only did Hitler bail Mussolini out in Greece, he diverted two divisions under Erwin Rommel to assist in Libya. Rommel had proven himself to be an audacious leader of armored forces in the invasion of France, and he reinforced that reputation in Africa. Like Wavell, Rommel was ordered to hold a strong defensive position; also like Wavell, he took the opportunity to exploit a small victory. In March 1941, he quickly overran Wavell's holding force and, forced to leave a besieging force at Tobruk, drove for Egypt. For the next year and a half, British and German forces drove back and forth along the coast of Cyrenaica, limited by the length of supply lines and what the respective governments deigned to send for supplies. They were also limited by the range of air cover: Halfway into Egypt the British could dominate from bases in Cairo and Alexandria, but halfway into Libya the Germans could dominate from Benghazi or Tripoli. Reaching those limits, usually timed with an arrival of reinforcements for the enemy, forced advances and withdrawals over the same ground in what came to be known as the "Benghazi Handicap."

Wavell was removed from command, although it was the lack of support from home that hurt him, not his generalship. British forces continued to be pushed back, although their new commander, Sir Claude Auchinlek, received better support from Britain. Still, Rommel was on the offensive through most of 1941. In November, Auchinlek counterattacked an overextended Rommel and drove back into Libya, but a large German supply convoy in January 1942 stiffened the Axis forces and Rommel was back on the offensive immediately. Again the British spent the summer months going backward, and again Rommel reached the limits of his supply lines by the fall. The Nazi invasion of Russia drew so much attention, and therefore supplies, that Rommel was unable to maintain himself, though he was ordered never to retreat.

Churchill's new commander in Egypt, Sir Bernard Montgomery, was in command when the climactic battle at El Alamein took place in September and October 1942. Rommel could not break through to Alexandria and was forced to withdraw in the face of a British counteroffensive.

This was the last leg of the Benghazi Handicap. Logistical superiority for the British, as well as the American invasion of North Africa in early November, put the Axis in the middle of a vise. By May 1943, the Allies controlled all of North Africa and used it as a base for further invasions to Sicily in July 1943 and Italy in September. The failed Italian invasion in September 1940 led to the country's ultimate removal from Africa and the loss of its colonies. Never again could Italy mount offensive actions, and within six months of their defeat in Africa, they surrendered unconditionally to the Allies. Even though the British did not lose Egypt militarily, they did abandon it as a protectorate after the war. Only French Algeria remained a European colony, but it was only a matter of time before that country, too, became independent. Egypt has undergone a number of political changes since, flirting with communism, pan-Arabism, and finally peaceful cooperation and attempts at national internal improvement. One of the longest-lasting legacies, however, is a byproduct of the nature of the war in the desert. Both the Axis and the Allies liberally used land mines, and as late as the 1970s an average of one person a day was still being hurt or killed by them.

See also Ethiopia, Italian Invasion of; France, Nazi Invasion of; Italy, Allied Invasion of; Mussolini, Benito; North Africa, U.S. Invasion of; Sicily, Allied Invasion of; Soviet Union, Nazi Invasion of the.

References: Barnett, Corelli, *The Desert Generals* (London: Viking Press, 1960); Heckman, Wolf, *Rommel's War in Africa* (Garden City, NY: Doubleday, 1981); Jewell, Derek, ed., *Alamein and the Desert War* (London: Times Newspapers, 1967).

167 EISENHOWER, DWIGHT DAVID

Dwight Eisenhower was born in 1890 in Denison, Texas, but raised in Abilene, Kansas. He entered West Point at age 21 and graduated in 1915, going into the infantry as a second lieutenant. His World War I experience was completely in training and he saw no combat, but he rose to the wartime rank of lieutenant colonel commanding a tank battalion at the army's first tank training center at Camp Colt, Pennsylvania. After the war, he met Colonel George S. Patton and, together with other tank advocates, developed armored warfare doctrine. They produced tactics calling for speed, mass deployment, and surprise; such ideas would be adopted by the beginning of World War II.

Eisenhower reverted to a peacetime rank of major in 1920 and spent the next decade working his way through the necessary slots for advancement, graduating at the top of his class at the Command and General Staff School in 1926, then from the Army War College in 1928. The following year he was assigned to the office of the secretary of war, where he served as executive assistant for four years, participating in plans for the nation's industrial mobilization in time of war. In February 1933 he became personal assistant to Army Chief of Staff General Douglas MacArthur. For the remainder of the decade, he worked directly under MacArthur, writing speeches, lobbying Congress, and drafting annual reports. He followed MacArthur to the Philippines in 1935 when the general took the position of President Quezon's military adviser. Eisenhower was pessimistic concerning the abilities of the Filipino army, but MacArthur forced him to write a more optimistic assessment to go to Quezon. The stress of working for MacArthur and the Filipinos made him glad to leave the country in late 1939.

In the United States, Eisenhower was made chief of staff of the Third Division, then of the IX Corps. In late 1941 he received his first promotion in 16 years, to the temporary rank of colonel. He was next assigned to become chief of staff at Third Army headquarters at Fort Sam Houston in San Antonio, Texas. During this tour of duty he participated in the Louisiana maneuvers, the largest war games yet held by the U.S. Army. During these exercises he learned the problems of dealing with logistics, training, communications, equipment, and junior officers.

A week after the Japanese attack at Pearl Harbor, Eisenhower was assigned to Washington, D.C. He was directed by the Army Chief of Staff General George Marshall to the War Plans Division as chief planner. They agreed on a "Europe First" strategy, whereby the major American effort would be directed toward the war against Adolf Hitler, while a defensive posture would be taken in the Pacific. In June 1942, Eisenhower, now a major general, arrived in London as commander of American forces in Europe. He and Marshall favored an immediate attack on France, but Prime Minister Winston Churchill and the British chiefs of staff convinced them that Allied forces were not yet strong enough or sufficiently trained to undertake such an operation. Instead, they would strike the Germans where they were weaker—in North Africa and the Mediterranean. In July, Eisenhower was promoted to lieutenant general and named commander of Allied forces for the U.S. invasion of North Africa. During the operation in North Africa, he commanded U.S., British, and Free French air, sea, and land forces. His first experience with coalition warfare was successful.

Eisenhower received his fourth star in February 1943, and by May the Axis forces were driven from North Africa. He directed the operations to invade Sicily in July and Italy in September. In December he was named commander of Operation Overlord, the Allied invasion of France, the largest combined operation undertaken up to that time. Eisenhower decided to launch the invasion during a break in bad weather on 6 June 1944. The diversions and disinformation the Allies had fed to the Germans were successful in keeping enemy forces away from the landing areas, and the beaches were secured in short order. The fighting through the hedgerow country of Normandy was slow, but on 1 August the Allied forces broke through and raced across France.

Eisenhower took direct command of the ground forces on 1 September. He now had to

U.S. President Dwight D. Eisenhower, with his wife Mamie Eisenhower. (Photograph no. 199122; "Photograph of General Dwight D. Eisenhower and Mrs. Eisenhower, smiling in the back of a limousine., 06/18/1945," collection HST-AVC: Audiovisual Collection, ca. 1850 – ca. 1990; U.S. National Archives and Records Administration – Harry S. Truman Library (NLHST), 500 West U.S. Highway 24, Independence, MO).

make a hard decision on the manner of assaulting German territory. Limited supplies forced him to choose between the options of a narrow front with more impact and a broad front for more widespread pressure. He decided on the broad front as a more conservative and less costly strategy; German offensives would be less apt to succeed, shorter supply lines could be used, and a stronger reserve could be built up. The decision was also politically correct, in that both Americans and British would share more equally in the final victory. However, the British favored a single thrust, using their forces under the command of Field Marshal Bernard Montgomery; they felt that the broad front would lengthen the war and its ensuing financial burden.

Eisenhower's decision stood. After a brief scare in December 1944 when Hitler launched an offensive through the Ardennes Forest, the wide front proceeded forward. American forces secured a bridgehead across the Rhine in March 1945; a week later, Allied forces all along the front had crossed. Again, Eisenhower resisted

British pressure for a drive on Berlin because the territory that would be gained at the cost of British and American lives would have to be turned over to the Soviets according to agreements made by the political leaders at the Yalta Conference in February. Allied forces under Eisenhower's command cleared out pockets of resistance in the western part of the country and captured as many prisoners, cities, and factories as possible.

After the war, Elsenhower commanded the occupation forces in Germany, then became army chief of staff in November 1945, a position he kept until his retirement in 1948. As chief of staff, he oversaw the demobilization of the American armed forces. He spent a short time in retirement before returning to command NATO forces in Europe in 1950; he stayed in that post until mid-1952, when he retired to run for president. As president he favored peace, a balanced budget, and a strong deterrent force to combat the growing arms race with the Soviet Union. He proposed the "New Look" military: army and navy budget and manpower cuts, with priority being shifted to the air force, nuclear weapons, and delivery systems.

Though Eisenhower was never a battlefield commander, he was an efficient, outstanding general/statesman, as well as an able strategist, a conciliator and compromiser between divergent national interests and goals, and a commander with the ability to draw the best from his subordinates.

See also France, Allied Invasion of; Hitler, Adolf; MacArthur, Douglas; North Africa, U.S. Invasion of.

References: Ambrose, Stephen, *Eisenhower: Soldier and Statesman* (New York: Simon & Schuster, 1990); Carver, Sir Michael, *The War Lords: Military Commanders of the Twentieth Century* (Boston: Little, Brown, 1976); Eisenhower, Dwight, *Crusade in Europe* (Garden City, NY: Doubleday, 1948).

ETHIOPIA, ITALIAN INVASION OF

168

Italy established a trading post at the Red Sea port of Assab, along the coast of Eritrea, in 1882. Three years later, the Italians occupied Massawa, Ethiopia's outlet on the Red Sea. In 1888, Italy claimed a protectorate over the area now known as Somalia. In the 1890s, Italy demanded the right to annex large parts of Eritrea, a region that Ethiopia had always claimed. When the Ethiopians resisted Italian demands, war followed in 1896. Lacking maps and good communications among the three attacking columns, Italian failure was inevitable. At Adowa, Italy lost over 4,000 men, and the remainder of their force was captured. The greatest disaster in European colonial history, it would play a major psychological role in Italy's future goals in the area.

When Benito Mussolini came to power in Italy in 1922, he dreamed of reestablishing the Roman Empire, and Ethiopia looked like an easy conquest. Though Mussolini sponsored Ethiopia's membership in the League of Nations and concluded a friendship treaty with the country in 1928, he continued to stockpile arms and build up troop concentrations in Eritrea and Somalia. Inside Ethiopia, the domestic situation was unstable. Emperor Haile Selassie had succeeded to the throne after a series of factional battles and the mysterious death of the previous empress. In the mid-1930s, Mussolini suggested to the League of Nations that Ethiopia be expelled because of the lack of unity within the country. Italy seemed primed for intervention, and the other European powers did not care to stop the Italians. Britain and France rebuffed U.S. President Roosevelt's attempt at mediation, hoping to court Italy's support against the rising power of Adolf Hitler in Germany.

Before Italy could begin a war with Ethiopia, it was necessary to create an "incident." This took place at Walwal, an oasis of a few dozen acres in the middle of a scrub-covered desert. Contemporary maps were sketchy concerning the borders in this area, but all agreed that it was well within Ethiopian territory. When an Anglo-Ethiopian commission studying grazing rights found Italian troops at the oasis in December 1934, the Ethiopian government demanded Italian withdrawal and ordered up their own army. Shots were fired on 5 December; more than 200 Ethiopians died, while the Italians and

Somalis lost 30. Mussolini's invasion came before the end of the month; tanks and aircraft were ordered into action to halt an Ethiopian "counterattack." Selassie appealed to the League, which debated into the following year.

The Italian expeditionary force numbered over 200,000 officers and men armed with thousands of machine guns, 700 artillery pieces, 150 tanks, and an air force of 150 bombers and fighters. The Ethiopian army was basically a tribal assemblage with personal loyalty to a chief. The regular army numbered about 100,000 men, but only the Imperial Guard, a few thousand strong, was well trained. They were armed with a mixture of old and new rifles, a few hundred old machine guns, and an air force of 12 planes, all transports. Local levies were often armed with little more than spears, and female soldiers carrying swords were seen riding mules into combat.

Wanting to prove that Italy was the aggressor, Haile Selassie ordered his people not to resist. Some League sanctions were imposed on Italy, but none were seriously enforced. The League failed to embargo oil, which Italy was obliged to ship via the Suez Canal to fuel its military. Since members of the League were split over how to respond, little happened, except that they managed to offend Italy by allowing Haile Selassie to address the League in Geneva, an action that, coupled with the mild embargo, provoked Italy's resignation.

Gaining no support from the international community, Ethiopia went on the offensive. They were occasionally successful, using their superior knowledge of the terrain to ambush Italian forces. Ultimately, however, Italy's modern weaponry, including poison gas, was too much to overcome. Ethiopian generals lost too many troops trying to fight the Italians directly. Though successful at ambush, whenever large numbers of Ethiopian troops gathered to fight, they were badly hurt by Italian airpower. After losing a series of hard-fought battles, Haile Selassie was forced to admit defeat and flee from the capital at Addis Ababa in early May 1936. Organized resistance was broken, but local leaders continued to operate independently with guerrilla tactics. Ethiopians often controlled the countryside, allowing the Italians to own the cities.

Italian success was short-lived, not lasting much longer than the outbreak of World War II. When Mussolini declared war on Britain and France in June 1940, he had 91,000 troops in East Africa, along with 200,000 local troops. With these forces, Italy went on the offensive against the British in the Sudan, Kenya, and British Somaliland. After a poor beginning under General William Slim, British forces under General Archibald Wavell prepared to remove Italy from the Horn of Africa. Three columns, including one comprising Ethiopian troops under British officers, invaded in November 1940. By January 1941, Haile Selassie was back in his own country, and by 5 May, the fifth anniversary of the fall of Addis Ababa to Italian forces, he was back in the capital. British forces were able to occupy the country fairly easily; the Italian forces surrendered quickly upon hearing reports of atrocities committed on Italian women by Ethiopian irregulars. Ultimately, the British took 230,000 Italian and Somali prisoners.

Italy occupied Ethiopia for five years and left behind a positive legacy. Despite the bloodshed inflicted in the invasion and consolidation, Italian authorities began a program of internal improvements the likes of which the natives had never seen. Roads, bridges, buildings, hospitals, and schools were built all over the country, though the Italians did not have enough time to institute a broad educational program. The country was unified and developed at a faster pace than ever before, and the people began to gain a respect for law and order. The Italians laid the physical foundations for Haile Selassie's modern Ethiopia, but the people did not embrace the negative aspects of the occupation, such as fascism or racism.

References: Barker, A. J., *The Civilizing Mission* (New York: Dial Press, 1968); Schwab, Peter, *Haile Selassie: Ethiopia's Lion of Judah* (Chicago: Nelson-Hall, 1979).

FINLAND, SOVIET INVASION OF

For almost as long as there have been Finns and Russians, there have been disputes over their borders. It was not surprising, then, that the

Soviet Union took advantage of a passive Nazi Germany to annex territory at Finland's expense in the winter of 1939–1940. A secret clause in the German-Soviet Nonaggression Pact of August 1939 allowed the Soviet Union a free hand in the Baltic States and Finland, in return for its assistance in Poland and the cession of the western half of Poland to Germany. Within two months of Poland's surrender, the Soviets were preparing to attack Finland.

The Soviet government staged an incident on 26 November to justify their invasion. After three days of diplomatic arguing, the Soviets launched their attack on 30 November. Why they wanted to make war in the depths of winter remains a mystery; the only justification appears to be their confidence that they could crush their opponents in less than two weeks. The Soviets had every reason for that surety: The Soviet military was overwhelming in its size, while the Finnish army was without heavy weapons; large numbers of aircraft and ammunition; training; or discipline. The Finns' only advantages were the bitterly cold weather, to which they adapted more readily than did the Soviet military, and the brilliance of their commander, 72-year-old Marshal Gustav Mannerheim. Mannerheim had thoroughly familiarized himself with Soviet training manuals, and knew their tendencies and tactics. He believed that their dependence on frontal, steamroller attacks could be negated by defenses in depth, coupled with the actions of small guerrilla units that knew the countryside better than did the invaders.

The Soviets attacked Finland at five points, stretching from the Arctic seaport of Petsamo to the southern Karelian Isthmus, which held the Soviet-Finnish border just northwest of Leningrad. The Soviets launched their heaviest offensive across the isthmus, exactly where the Finns were best prepared behind the Mannerheim line of entrenchments, antitank ditches, and open fields of fire. The Finns beat back repeated Soviet attempts to cross the isthmus, slaughtering huge numbers of Soviet troops in the process. In the north, the Finns engaged in scorched-earth tactics, which denied the Soviets any shelter in the increasingly harsh weather,

and they quickly developed masterful abilities at setting booby traps. The swarming guerrilla units operating on skis chopped up formation after formation of Soviet infantry, while mines and Molotov cocktails took care of Soviet armor. In the air, the Finnish pilots, terribly outclassed in their obsolete aircraft, used nothing more than courage to down large numbers of Soviet planes, at a terrible cost to themselves.

The easy conquest was an illusion. The huge Soviet army was being embarrassed by a tiny force, and Soviet Premier Joseph Stalin was furious. He removed the top commanders, either by retirement or execution, and appointed Marshal Semyon Timoshenko to take over the campaign. Timoshenko halted the offensive and regrouped his forces, quickly training and disciplining his men for their task. In January 1940, he harassed the Finns in the Mannerheim line with small attacks and large artillery barrages while he prepared his forces. On 1 February he sent Soviet aircraft to bomb reserve positions behind the Mannerheim line and ordered a huge artillery barrage that shot some 300,000 shells into Finnish positions. Under a smoke screen, he sent in six divisions to rush the dazed defenders; he kept up the pressure with assault after assault for days. Soviet lives were still wasted at an appalling rate, but the Finns were quickly running out of ammunition. Timoshenko's continuing pressure proved too much, and on 14 February, Mannerheim ordered his men to withdraw to a second line of defenses a few miles to the rear.

The withdrawal did little more than delay the inevitable. By early March, Soviet forces were breaking through everywhere along the isthmus, while pockets of Finns fought to the last man. When the Swedes refused to allow a force of 100,000 British and French soldiers to cross their territory, any chance of continued Finnish resistance collapsed. On 6 March, the Finnish government opened negotiations. The treaty of 12 March cost the Finns one-tenth of their territory—25,000 square miles of land, including all the Karelian Isthmus and their access to the Arctic Ocean. It also cost Finland almost 25,000 dead and over 43,000 wounded; Soviet casualty estimates range from 200,000 to one million.

The chance for revenge was not long in coming. When the Nazis invaded the Soviet Union in June 1941, the Finns saw an opportunity to recover their lost territory. Though the Finns never allied themselves with Germany, and only occasionally cooperated with them directly, they took advantage of the Soviet retreat to reoccupy their lost territory. This "Continuation War" lasted until 1945, when the defeat of Germany brought a stronger and better-trained Soviet military to Finland's borders. Again the Finns were obliged to accept the loss of the Karelian Isthmus and all claims to Lake Ladoga on their north shore.

The Finnish resistance provided the world with a heroic story of an underdog fighting against overwhelming odds, but it also exposed the illusion of Soviet military might. If a tiny and unprepared country such as Finland could deal the Soviets a disastrous beating, then certainly, Adolf Hitler thought, Nazi Germany could crush the Soviets with little trouble. Hitler went to war against the Soviet Union with the same overconfidence the Soviets had displayed in November 1939, and the persistence of a determined population and the ravages of the Russian winter cost the Germans just as dearly.

See also Hitler, Adolf; Poland, Nazi Conquest of; Soviet Union, Nazi Invasion of the.

References: Erfurth, Waldemar, *Warfare in the Far North* (Washington, DC: Center for Military History, 1987); Lundin, Charles, *Finland in the Second World War* (Bloomington: Indiana University Press, 1957); Wuorinen, John, ed., *Finland and World War II, 1939–1944* (Westport, CT Greenwood Press, 1983).

FRANCE, ALLIED INVASION OF

170

By November 1943, the Allied forces of the United States, Great Britain, and the Soviet Union seized the initiative from Nazi Germany and began to take the offensive on all fronts. That month, the three nations' leaders—Franklin Roosevelt, Winston Churchill, and Joseph Stalin—met in Teheran, Iran, to discuss future strategy. This was the first time Stalin had met with the other two leaders, and he was eager to have input into the planning against Germany. Stalin felt that his country had borne the brunt of Nazi aggression because of American and British hesitation about launching major offensives, and he was determined to force the two countries to strike hard at Germany.

Roosevelt and Churchill were agreeable to a major offensive, but the three leaders had difficulty deciding where such an assault should take place. Churchill favored an attack into the Balkans. Britain had been forced to abandon an ally when the Nazis invaded Greece in 1941, and Churchill felt obligated to liberate the area. He advocated an offensive against the "soft underbelly" of Europe, where German forces and defenses were weak. This would put American and British forces directly on the German flank and provide the Soviets with the most direct assistance. Stalin would have none of it. He argued in favor of an Anglo-American landing on the coast of France. By striking the German rear, this would force Hitler to fight a two-front war rather than concentrate his troops only in the east.

Both plans had facets in their favor, but certainly Stalin and Churchill were also looking ahead at a postwar world. Having been invaded by Germany in 1914 and again in 1941, Stalin surely wanted to acquire as large a buffer zone as possible against any future aggression. If British and American forces occupied the Balkans, this would deny the Soviets that buffer zone and put a new potential enemy—the United States—and Great Britain, a nation long at odds with Russia, on his doorstep. Churchill apparently saw Stalin's plan also, and he did not like it. Britain had no aggressive designs on the Balkans or the Soviet Union, but Churchill did not want to see Communist power extended past the Soviet Union's borders. He tried to get Roosevelt to see this as well.

The question was, which plan would Roosevelt support? Roosevelt also saw into the political future, but his focus was elsewhere. In November 1943, U.S. Marines were just beginning their island-hopping campaign in the Central Pacific and had met fierce resistance wherever they fought the Japanese. The presi-

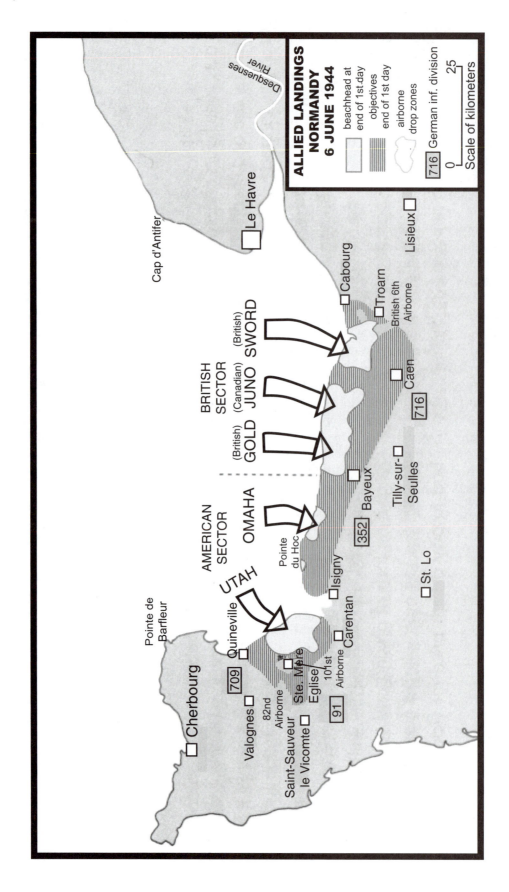

ALLIED LANDINGS
NORMANDY
6 JUNE 1944

beachhead at
end of 1st-day

objectives
end of 1st day

airborne
drop zones

716 German inf. division

Scale of kilometers
0   25

Desquesnes River

Le Havre

Cap d'Antifer

Cabourg

Lisieux

Troarn

British 6th
Airborne

(British) SWORD

BRITISH
SECTOR

(Canadian) JUNO

Caen

716

(British) GOLD

Bayeux

Tilly-sur-
Seulles

352

AMERICAN
SECTOR

OMAHA

Pointe
du Hoc

Isigny

St. Lo

UTAH

Carentan

Pointe de
Barfleur

Quineville

101st
Airborne

Ste. Mère
Eglise

91

709

Valognes

82nd
Airborne

Saint-Sauveur
le Vicomte

Cherbourg

dent's advisers had estimated an extremely costly campaign to capture the Japanese homeland, and Roosevelt wanted help. He reasoned that if he cooperated with Stalin on this strategy, he could get Stalin to provide troops to fight Japan when the war in Europe was completed. This hope influenced his thinking more than Churchill's views, so Roosevelt supported Stalin's demand for an invasion of France.

The United States had been massing forces in Great Britain for months. Though many of them had gone on to fight in North Africa or Italy, many more were on British bases waiting for the big attack. American and British air forces had begun strategic bombing of industrial sites on the Continent, and in the first months of 1944 began hitting targets in France as well. Dwight Eisenhower, designated overall Allied commander in Europe, oversaw the largest armada ever assembled. Warships and landing craft gathered off England's shores in preparation for the invasion. First scheduled for early May, poor weather postponed the operation until the first week in June.

The Germans were aware that something was afoot. They had brought one of their most skillful generals, Erwin Rommel, to supervise the construction of defenses along the English Channel coast. Concrete bunkers and gun positions covered the beaches from Calais to Cherbourg, with most of the works concentrated near Calais, where the Channel is narrowest and therefore the easiest location for bringing in supplies and reinforcements. The Allies went to great lengths to convince the Germans that they were defending the correct place. A huge disinformation campaign, attempting to confirm the German belief in the Pas-de-Calais as the invasion site, used false radio traffic, troop movements, and even inflatable tanks and trucks all over southeastern England to give the impression of an Allied buildup there. The landing site in Normandy, farther southwest, was successfully hidden until the landings actually took place.

Despite threatening weather, Eisenhower ordered the forces to invade on 6 June. American and British airborne forces landed in the dark,

with mixed success, to seize bridges and roadway junctions to slow or halt German reinforcement. When the naval bombardment opened at dawn, the Germans were completely surprised. Two American, two British, and one Canadian army landed at five beaches. Some were easily secured; others were not. The American forces landing at the beach farthest west (designated "Omaha") met the most resistance and suffered the greatest casualties: one man killed or wounded per square yard of beach. But by the end of the day, all the armies had men into the nearby countryside and had secured a beachhead. On Hitler's orders, German reinforcements were not allowed to move from the Calais area to counter this invasion because the Nazi leader was convinced that the landing was a diversion. By the time German forces were released to counterattack two weeks later, it was too late.

Still, getting into France was not easy. Though the beachhead was secure and supplies began to flow in through artificial harbors created by the Allies, German resistance in the farm country of Normandy was intense. Each small field was surrounded by an impenetrable hedgerow, very easy to defend and extremely difficult to capture. Bulldozers and tanks had to break through the hedges one at a time, and the invasion was almost two months old before the Allies were able to break through. On 1 August, a massive carpet of bombs from a huge air assault paralyzed the Germans, and an Allied armored attack broke through. The race was on.

The blitzkrieg with which the Germans had terrorized Europe was now used against them. Fast-moving American armored columns drove across France and took hundreds of thousands of prisoners. Paris was liberated in late August, by which time a second invasion had occurred along the French Riviera, and American forces were racing northward to link up with troops of the first invasion. By September they had outrun their supply lines and had to halt along the German frontier.

Eisenhower ordered the Allied armies to consolidate their positions and dig in for the winter; once fully supplied in the spring, they would drive into Germany. The Allies' only setbacks were a defeat at the Dutch city of Arnhem in September 1944, and Hitler's Ardennes offensive from mid-December 1944 through mid-January—the famous Battle of the Bulge. American forces crossed the Rhine in early March, but stopped at the Elbe River rather than drive on to Berlin, which had been promised to the Soviets at another three-power conference in the Russian resort city of Yalta in February 1945.

As Winston Churchill had foreseen, after the war, the Communists established dominion over eastern and southeastern Europe. Churchill was unable to remind Roosevelt of this, because the president died in April 1945. Thus, the liberation of France had results far beyond that nation's borders. Within France, the people had to face a postwar political reality that was hard to accept. Regarded as a major power for centuries, it had been reduced to no more than a second-rate country. France's poor showing during the Nazi invasion in 1940 left them with too small a force to be a factor in the liberation of their own country, though Charles de Gaulle, leader of the French government-in-exile and Free French forces, exerted what influence he could. France was not as physically devastated as it had been after World War I, but in 1948 the French had to accept aid through the American Marshall Plan to rebuild their economy. De Gaulle, as president of France, tried to give the illusion of independent strength with the development of a French nuclear bomb and limited cooperation with the North Atlantic Treaty Organization. He also attempted to maintain a French empire, but defeat in Indochina and resistance in Algeria robbed France even of that.

> See also Algeria, French Occupation of; Indochina, French Occupation of; Eisenhower, Dwight David; France, Nazi Invasion of; Greece, Nazi Invasion of; Italy, Allied Invasion of; North Africa, U.S. Invasion of; Pacific Islands, U.S. Conquest of; Russia, German Invasion of; Soviet Union, Nazi Invasion of the.

References: Ambrose, Stephen, *D-Day, June 6, 1944* (New York: Simon & Schuster, 1994); Carrel, Paul, *Invasion: They're Coming*, trans. E. Osers (New York: Dutton, 1960); Keegan, John, *Six Armies in Normandy* (New York: Viking, 1982).

FRANCE, GERMAN INVASION OF

171

After the Franco-Prussian War of 1870–1871, France burned to avenge itself after the poor performance of its armies, the humiliation of paying reparations to Germany, and the loss of the provinces of Alsace and Lorraine. France soon began reforming its military by imitating the German General Staff concept of command. The French government also set about looking for allies. France signed an agreement with Russia, creating enemies for Germany in both the east and west in the event of war, and in 1905 allied itself with Great Britain, whose navy could effectively isolate Germany not only from its colonies, but also from the rest of the world. This Triple Entente seemed an effective grouping of nations to defeat Germany. With Plan XVII, France prepared to position its forces along the German frontier and thrust immediately into its neighbor's territory. Germany was not idle while France was making these preparations. If France could create allies around Germany, the latter could strengthen itself in the middle by allying first with the Austro-Hungarian Empire and then with Italy, creating the Triple Alliance. The Germans also hoped to gain stature vis-à-vis the rest of the major powers by engaging in empire building; Germany claimed colonies in Africa and the Pacific Ocean, but they were not prime locations for raw materials or trading purposes. Germany began looking to build an inland empire—what came to be called Mitteleuropa, or the Central European Customs Union. By working on the alliance with Austria-Hungary and strengthening ties with the aggressive new Committee of Union and Progress in the Ottoman Empire, Germany could stretch its economic power from the North Sea to the Persian Gulf. With German money and engineering, the Balkans' labor and raw materials, and the Middle East's oil, Germany could control everything it needed to create a powerful economy and have ocean access at northwestern and southeastern extremes. All of it could be tied together by the Berlin-Baghdad Railway, along which supplies and goods could be shipped in peacetime, and men and materiel could be shipped in

wartime. Mitteleuropa would make overseas colonies extraneous.

There was one major problem in this plan: the oil of the Middle East. Though Germany was bidding on drilling sites in the Ottoman Empire, the only oil currently flowing in significant amounts was in Persia. The Anglo-Persian Oil Company made that oil available mainly to Great Britain, but Russia regarded Persia as being within its sphere of influence. Any German move toward Persia could provoke war with Russia, and that meant war with France because of the Triple Entente. Thus, by 1912, Germany saw that war with France was inevitable if Persian oil was to come under German control.

The German General Staff had been working on plans for a war with France. The plan was authored by Alfred von Schlieffen, who had been formulating it since the 1890s. He envisioned a massive sweep past the left flank of the French forces poised on the frontier, a maneuver that would bypass most French resistance and put German armies in Paris even more quickly than in 1870. The Triple Entente made it necessary to place a number of German forces in the east to oppose Russia, but a holding action there would allow sufficient time for the German armies to knock France out of the war. Germany could then deal with Russia at leisure, and Persian oil would soon follow Russia's defeat. Since Great Britain and Russia had no great love for each other, the Germans assumed that Britain would do nothing if France was quickly disabled. Though the French plan called for a quick thrust into Germany, the ground on which France planned to attack was rugged and wooded; a German holding force there could keep them pinned down while the "right hook" swung down on Paris. The Schlieffen plan seemed unbeatable, but by 1914 there were problems. First, von Schlieffen had died in 1905 and left the plan to the General Staff under Helmuth von Moltke the Younger, son of the main strategist of the Franco-Prussian War. He saw the potential for problems, and began to weaken the main assault in order to strengthen the holding forces in the east and along the French frontier. There were also diplomatic problems. To sweep around the French left flank, German armies would have to pass through Belgium, a neutral country. Violating a country's neutrality was not an action to be taken lightly, but there was no other way to drive quickly into France. Everything depended on speed, because France had to be neutralized before the Russians could mobilize their military. By 1914 both Germany and France seemed to be waiting for an excuse to go to war, one for power and the other for revenge.

The assassination of Austrian Archduke Franz Ferdinand on 28 June 1914 became the excuse. Germany supported severe Austrian demands on Serbia, which they believed knew of or participated in the assassination. If Serbia went to war, its main supporter would be Russia; Germany would honor treaty commitments to Austria-Hungary through the Triple Alliance. Thus, Germany would have the excuse to fight Russia. When the Serbians did not give in to Austrian demands by 28 July,

Austria declared war and the dominoes started to fall. Russia began mobilizing its army immediately. On 1 August, Germany declared war on Russia; on 3 August, Germany declared war on France; on 4 August the Schlieffen plan went into action. The attack through Belgium precipitated British reaction, because Britain had a longstanding defense treaty with Belgium. Only Italy remained out of the fray, for it had a nonaggression pact with Great Britain. (Italy changed sides in 1915; the Ottoman Empire joined with Germany and Austria in November 1914.)

At first, all seemed to be going according to German projections. French armies along the frontier attacked but made little headway, while German forces raced for Paris. The one thing the Germans could not overcome, however, was the lack of roads with which to keep its forces supplied. German troops made rapid headway against relatively ineffective British resistance, but by the time Paris was in sight, the German offensive ran out of steam. The soldiers were exhausted, and supplies were slow in getting to the front. The French General Staff, realizing that Plan XVII was useless, attempted to reverse its armies from the frontier to defend the capital. General Joseph Joffre called on Parisians to rally, and France had its proudest moment. Ferried to the Marne River in Paris taxicabs, the hastily formed units threw together a defensive line just as the German onslaught was faltering. Once the German forces overcame their exhaustion and were resupplied, they staged another flanking move, but to no avail. The rapidly arriving British forces in the north blunted moves to the German right, while moves to their left met French armies returning to their capital.

The attempts by each side to outflank the other, or keep from being outflanked, ultimately spread the offense and defense into lines stretching from the English Channel to Switzerland. Unable to move, the two sides began to dig in, and the Western Front was created. Most of World War I was fought in the trench lines of northern France, where neither German nor French planners ever expected the war to be. What was to have been a quick war became the least mobile and deadliest war ever. Germany was forced to fight on two fronts. In France, four years of mud, barbed wire, poison gas, and millions of casualties were the results. Not until the Russians withdrew from the war in 1918, and the American forces arrived at the same time, did the deadlock break. The war devastated not only the French countryside, but the psyches of a generation of French, British, Germans, and Americans. The French were able to wreak some vengeance on Germany via the Versailles Treaty of 1919, but the result was exactly the same as the harsh peace of 1871: a desire for revenge—this time on the part of the Germans—that would provoke yet another war. The peace gained in 1919 lasted but two decades, and the memories of the horrors of war in the trenches of France paralyzed the British and French populations and governments when Germany rose again to prominence under the leadership of Adolf Hitler.

See also France, Prussian Invasion of (Franco-Prussian War); Hitler, Adolf; Russia, German Invasion of.

References: Fischer, Fritz, *War of Illusions* (London: Chatto & Windus, 1975); Koch, H. W., ed., *The Origins of the First World War* (London: Macmillan, 1972); Tuchman, Barbara, *The Guns of August* (New York: Macmillan, 1962).

FRANCE, NAZI INVASION OF

172

While still fighting in Norway, the Nazis directed their attention to Germany's traditional enemy, France, in the spring of 1940. Since the breakup of Charlemagne's Holy Roman Empire, the rulers of the principalities of north-central Europe had been at odds with the rulers of France. This situation was at its worst in the 1870 Prussian invasion of France when German forces embarrassed the French army and imposed a harsh peace with severe reparations. It repeated itself in the 1914 German invasion of France, in which France came within a hair's breadth of another humiliation. The Germans provoked the wrath of the world at that time for violating Belgian neutrality at the start of their assault, but they had found it necessary to break international law in order to gain a strategic advantage over the French defensive plans.

Ultimate French victory in World War I brought about a resolve to be fully prepared for any future German aggression, and this manifested itself in the construction of the Maginot Line, a string of fortresses guarding the Franco-German frontier. This defense, coupled with a large air force and an army equipped with almost as many tanks as its opponents could muster, made France feel secure despite the diplomatic victories and military successes scored by Hitler through the late 1930s.

There were shortcomings in the French strategy. First, though the Maginot Line was universally regarded as impregnable, the string of forts did not stretch all the way across the French border, and thus failed to protect France completely. These gaps occurred not only because of the prohibitive cost of construction, but because a fortress line all the way to the English Channel would necessitate building forts that pointed not at Germany but at neutral Belgium, hardly a favorable public relations move. The French tried to include the Belgians in the construction effort, but with no success. In addition, though the French army was large on paper, it was neither well motivated nor well led. Many units dedicated to manning defensive works were unable to operate in the fast-moving warfare that eventually took place. Late-developing defensive plans worked out by the French high command were not communicated to lower-ranking officers, and therefore failed to be properly implemented. Even as German forces were massing for the assault in early May, much of the French army was on leave. Further, France's equipment was no better than, and in many cases inferior to, that of the Germans, especially in the air force.

Therefore, when Germany launched its invasion on the morning of 10 May 1940, France and its allies were only partially prepared. They were also surprised by the German decision to disregard the neutrality not only of Belgium but also of Holland. Hitler wanted to control the coastline completely, so the Dutch became victims as well. The first attacks were launched against Dutch airfields, where the Germans repeated the successes they had scored early in the Polish invasion, destroying most of the aircraft on the ground. They advanced against little organized resistance

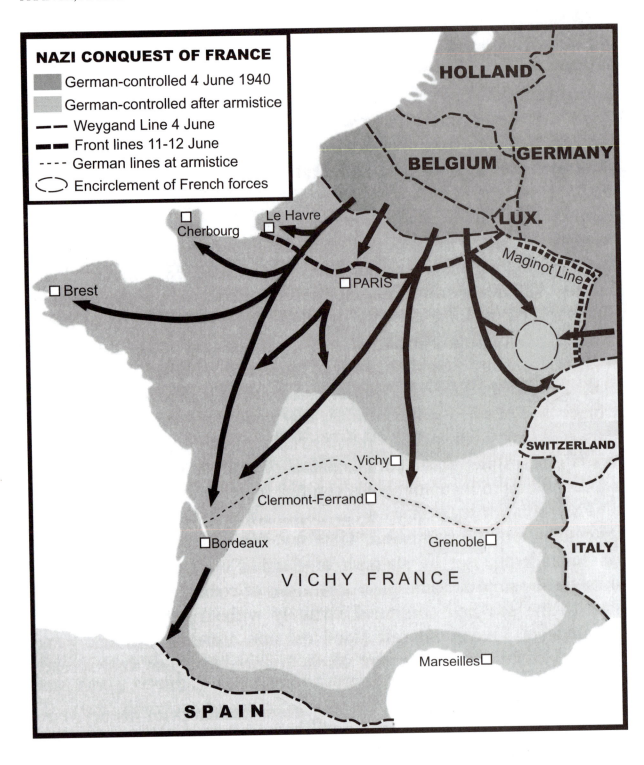

NAZI CONQUEST OF FRANCE

- German-controlled 4 June 1940
- German-controlled after armistice
- ⎯ ⎯ Weygand Line 4 June
- ▬ ▬ Front lines 11-12 June
- - - - German lines at armistice
- ⬭ Encirclement of French forces

and achieved a major victory by securing the huge fortress at Eben Emael along the Dutch-Belgian border by the first-ever use of glider troops. As the Dutch retreated before the onslaught, the German air force began pounding the port city of Rotterdam. When the Germans continued their advances and also threatened aerial destruction of Amsterdam, the Dutch had had enough. They laid down their arms after four days of battle.

By this time, the Germans were making their way into Belgium and beginning to meet some French resistance. Allied defensive plans began to be implemented, and in some cases showed effectiveness, but the effort suffered because of a lack of coordination among French, Belgian, and British troops who had arrived to assist their allies during the "phony war" period (October 1939–April 1940). The Germans were able to take advantage of the confusion and exploit the capture of a few intact bridges across the Albert Canal and the Meuse River. As more French forces were sent to assist, they unknowingly fell into a German trap. The Nazi plan called for an attack through Holland into the flat coastal plain of Belgium, which would draw the bulk of the Allied forces. When these had been committed, the Germans would launch an armored thrust through the town of Sedan, site of the major French defeat in 1870. The French were unprepared for this, believing the wooded terrain too difficult for armor to negotiate. The Germans knew better, and aimed their thrust through the Ardennes forest, just north of the final Maginot Line defenses in an area held only by poor-quality reservists. By 12 May the Germans had reached Sedan with only light resistance and, after a devastating aerial attack, they captured the high ground west of the Meuse River late the following day. With the bulk of the French and all of the British and Belgian armies to the north, the pathway was open for the armored blitzkrieg to show its effectiveness.

The cumbersome French chain of command suffered from a shake-up at headquarters in the midst of the campaign and the accidental death of the general commanding the French First Army in Belgium. The Germans moved too quickly for the French to react; even if France could have reacted, there would not have been enough time for the Allied forces to respond cooperatively. At one point, French forces were ordered to withdraw from Belgium, and the British and Belgian generals learned of it only by accident. The one overwhelming aspect of the German invasion was its speed, and the Allied forces were never able to adapt to it, steeped as they were in the lessons of defense learned in World War I. Once past the Ardennes, German tank units raced northwestward for the Channel. They reached St. Quentin, the halfway point, on

18 May; the same day, the Belgian city of Antwerp fell. The French government had already been considering the consequences. On 16 May, the French met with Winston Churchill, who had taken control of the British government six days earlier, and admitted they had no strategic reserve and could no longer mount an active defense. The French begged Churchill for as many troops and aircraft as he could spare, a request he ultimately denied. He could see that France was falling, and a further commitment of British resources would make the defense of his own country that much more difficult. On 19 May the French government replaced their commander in chief, Maurice Gamelin, with General Weygand, a 73-year-old veteran of the command structure that had saved France in 1914. He promised nothing when he took the job, which was a wise decision because the next day, news arrived that German tanks had reached the Channel at Abbeville. The French First Army, along with the British Expeditionary Force and the remnants of the Belgian army, was now isolated.

The rapid armored movement had succeeded in splitting the French military, as expected, but it put the Germans in a precarious position because their infantry had not been able to keep up and consolidate the ground. British and French attempts to seize the opportunity failed because their counterattacks were too slow or too weak, and they scored only occasional, moderate successes. During the remainder of May, the Allied forces in Belgium slowly crumbled under the weight of the German advance. The Belgians and British staged a hard-fought withdrawal, but they could only withdraw toward either the German armored columns or the Channel. By 26 May the British had been forced to the coastal city of Dunkirk, where they began a miraculous withdrawal across the ocean under the noses of German troops. They were assisted in this operation by Hitler himself. Already overly worried about the condition of his tanks, he responded favorably to a suggestion from the chief of Germany's air force, Hermann Goering. The air force, or Luftwaffe, could bomb the British into submission, Goering claimed, and there would be no need to risk the armor.

Hitler agreed, and ordered the assault on Dunkirk to halt.

The British had been throwing together Operation Dynamo over the previous few days and had to draft every available boat to assist. When the port cities of Boulogne and Calais fell to the Germans, the harbor facilities at Dunkirk were damaged, and only shallow-draft boats could get right up to the coast and take soldiers onboard. Every yacht, pleasure craft, and ferry boat along the southeast coast of England was pressed into service to aid in the evacuation. Under cover of occasional bad weather and the effective action of the Royal Air Force, the operation continued around the clock for nine days, by which time more than a third of a million men left France for England. The operation had to be called off with some 40,000 men left behind, but the bulk of the British army, as well as refugees from the French and Belgian armies, lived to fight another day.

After an unbroken string of successes, Hitler had finally committed a grave error. Had he allowed the German army to finish off the troops in the ever-shrinking pocket around Dunkirk, which they certainly could have, Britain would have had to build a new army virtually from the ground up. As it was, the British now had a large force of veterans around which to expand their numbers and continue the fight.

Hitler did not see that at the time; he was too busy celebrating the victory on the Continent. Belgium unconditionally surrendered on 28 May, and though the French fought on, they were doomed. German forces attacked southward along a broad front and overcame or bypassed most of the French opposition. To compound the French problems, Mussolini brought Italy into the war on 10 June, although Italy did not invade until 20 June. Threatened by imminent encirclement, on 11 June, the commander of French forces in Paris declared it an open city, and the Germans entered it three days later. On 16 June, a new French government was formed at Bordeaux under the leadership of World War I hero Marshal Philippe Petain, and the next day he ordered the French to stop fighting. An armistice was signed on 22 June, and 400,000 French soldiers surrendered.

The French expected the worst, but it did not occur. The Germans offered lenient terms, which the French were glad to accept, especially when they remembered the cost of defeat at German hands in 1870–1871. Many blamed Britain for having abandoned France at Dunkirk and used the British as a scapegoat for the defeat. German occupation forces did little pillaging or looting, and even left the southern half of France apparently unoccupied.

The "unoccupied" section was under the authority of a French government in Vichy led by Petain, a role into which the Germans forced him. Actually a puppet government, the Vichy regime gave the impression of independence for the sake of France's overseas possessions. The Germans hoped that the French possessions would continue to take orders from home, orders that would actually come from Germany. The only resistance to this action came from a young French general named Charles de Gaulle. He had escaped France when the British left, and in London announced that he was forming a French government-in-exile. He would lead the French resistance that would ultimately free his country, he claimed, and he ordered French possessions around the world to ignore the Vichy government and resist their orders. Most French people, both inside and outside France, had no idea who de Gaulle was, whereas everyone knew who Petain was: the hero of the great battle of Verdun in World War I. This set the stage for a number of problems that Allied forces would have to face in the future. Whenever French-owned territory was attacked, such as Algeria was in November 1942, would the inhabitants listen to Petain or de Gaulle? Would they resist or cooperate? It varied. Under the direction of the Vichy government, the French administration in Indochina gave up control of that province to the Japanese in 1940 when Germany and Italy brought Japan into the Axis fold. Those who responded to de Gaulle's leadership and resisted, in France and in the colonies, became the first French people to support the man who would dominate French politics and society for two decades after the war ended.

Other than the normal lack of amenities that exists in any occupied country, the French did not suffer extensively until the Allied invasion in the summer of 1944 obliged the Germans to seriously enforce their will on the population. Only French Jews felt the wrath of Nazi policies on a regular basis. Still, an underground movement, the Maquis, did creditable work in harassing the German forces in France and offered considerable assistance during the Normandy invasion.

Postwar France, like postwar Britain, found itself a second-rate power. Without an empire, with only the memory of a humiliating defeat and a long occupation, France had little but faded glory to fall back on. Only de Gaulle's obstinacy maintained French prestige in international relations, and the chauvinism he practiced can still be seen to an extent in the French attitude toward their neighbors on the Continent and in their relations with the United States.

See also Carolingian Dynasty; France, Prussian Invasion of (Franco-Prussian War); France, Allied Invasion of; France, German Invasion of; Norway and Denmark, Nazi Invasion of; Poland, Nazi Conquest of.

References: Home, Alistair, *To Lose a Battle: France, 1940* (Boston: Little, Brown, 1969); Jackson, Robert, *Dunkirk: The British Evacuation, 1940* (New York: St. Martin's Press, 1976); Sweets, John, *Choices in Vichy France* (New York: Oxford University Press, 1986).

GERMANY, SOVIET INVASION OF

173

Besides being the largest armor battle ever fought, the Battle of Kursk in July 1943 symbolized the changing fortunes of war for both Nazi Germany and the Soviet Union. The battle marked the beginning of the end for Nazi Germany, since it was the last time that the once mighty German Wehrmacht mounted a major offensive in the East. The Soviets, on the other hand, learned many bitter lessons over the two previous bloody years and now possessed a well-trained, well-equipped, and well-led army. The Red Army never relinquished the initiative in the East after Kursk and launched an almost continuous series of offensives that pulverized what

remained of the Wehrmacht. In fact, the offensives forced the Germans into the vicious cycle of committing newly trained replacements and refurbished panzer (armored) units into battle with progressively less training. This cycle ended with mere boys defending Berlin in May 1945. Following the Battle of Kursk, the Soviets almost immediately launched their Summer Offensive, which lasted from 12 July to 26 November 1943. Utilizing massed armor, the Soviets attacked along a front from Smolensk to the Black Sea. German Field Marshal Erich von Manstein conducted a well-executed mobile defense until Adolf Hitler on 2 August ordered him to retreat no farther. Hitler's intervention deprived the Germans of their last advantage over the Soviets: the ability to conduct effective maneuver warfare at the tactical level. The Soviets broke through Manstein's lines the next day and threatened to destroy his army. In order to avoid this disaster, Manstein ignored Hitler's orders and abandoned the city of Kharkov on 23 August. Despite this loss, Manstein was able to keep his army intact as he fell back to the Dnieper River.

By the end of the Summer Offensive of 1943, the Red Army had advanced along their entire front. In the northern sector of the offensive, the Russians had pushed the German Army Group Center back to the Pripet Marshes, liberated Smolensk on 25 September, and recaptured Kiev on 6 November. In the south, the Red Army had forced a bridgehead across the Dnieper River and had cut off 210,000 soldiers of the German Seventeenth Army in the Crimea. Hitler had refused to allow the peninsula's evacuation.

The Soviet Winter Offensive of 1943–1944 began almost where the Summer Offensive had left off. Only the unseasonably mild weather of December, which left the small lakes and waterways above the Pripet Marshes unfrozen, gave the German army any respite. The main thrust of the Soviet Winter Offensive ran the entire length of the front from the Pripet Marshes to the Dnieper River. From 29 January to the end of March 1944, the newly renamed Soviet First Ukrainian Front (under Marshall Georgi Zhukov) and the Second Ukrainian Front (under General Ivan Konev) continually

Russian soldiers fly their flag over the Reichstag following the fall of Berlin, 2 May 1945.

battered Manstein. By mid-February the two Soviet fronts had encircled two German army corps near Cherkassy, inflicting over 100,000 casualties. By 1 March, Zhukov's First Front had crossed the 1939 frontier of Poland and was threatening Lvov.

The Germans also suffered defeats in the north around Leningrad and in the south in the Crimea during this time. In Leningrad, the forces broke through the German Eighteenth Army and lifted the 900-day siege on 26 January. The three Soviet fronts continued to attack until they were stopped on 1 March at the line of Narva-Pskov-Polotsk by a combination of spring thaws and Field Marshal Walter Model's hard-pressed Army Group North. In the Crimea, the Soviet Fourth Ukrainian Front attacked across the widened Crimean Kerch peninsula on 8 April and soon trapped the German

Seventeenth Army in Sevastopol, which was evacuated from 4 to 8 May 1944.

In a little over four months, the Soviets had broken the siege of Leningrad, liberated the Ukraine and the Crimea, destroyed 16 German divisions of at least 50,000 soldiers, and reduced a further 60 divisions to skeletal strength. In addition, the Germans had weakened the only stable sector of their line, Army Group Center, by siphoning off troops to the collapsing flanks. As a result, the weakened Army Group was positioned in a huge salient without a large reserve. It was at this spot that the Soviets launched their next offensive.

The Summer Offensive of 1944 opened on 22 July, three years to the day after Hitler's invasion of the Soviet Union. The Soviet First, Second, and Third White Russian fronts attacked along a line 350 miles wide, stretching from

Smolensk to Minsk to Warsaw. Since the German air force had been sent west to protect the homeland from Allied bombing, the Soviets gained complete air superiority, with which they were able to mass their artillery and soon open a 250-mile-wide gap in the German lines. Soviet formations quickly liberated the cities of Vitebsk (25 June), Bobruisk (27 June), and Minsk (3 July). By 10 July, Zhukov had enlarged the gap and was advancing toward Warsaw. His right flank attacked northward and began to trap German Army Group North against the Baltic Sea. The Germans were able to slow the First White Russian Front just short of Warsaw, but were unable to halt the First Ukrainian Front's drive in the south. It captured Lvov on 27 July and reached the upper Vistula River at Baranov on 7 August. The 450-mile Soviet advance only halted when the fronts outran their supply lines. The Germans lost over 450,000 men (including 300,000 in one 12-day period), 2,000 tanks, 10,000 artillery pieces, and 57,000 motor vehicles. The heart of the once-mighty Wehrmacht was torn out.

For the remainder of 1944 and into early 1945, Soviet forces continued to advance, especially in the north, where they trapped over half a million Germans in Courland, and in the south, where they pushed into the Balkans and removed Nazi satellite countries from German influence. This set the stage for the final act of the war, the attack on Berlin. Over a third of the USSR's 6,461,000 soldiers were committed for the advance on Berlin; the Germans had less than 2,000,000 soldiers left in the East, of which 500,000 were trapped in Courland.

The Soviet attack on Berlin began on 16 April, when Zhukov's and Konev's fronts crossed the Oder River. They faced stiff, desperate German resistance, but by 19 April, both were ready to assault Berlin itself. On 20 April the guns of the Sixth Breakthrough Artillery Division shelled the streets of Berlin, and on the next day Zhukov's tanks entered the city's northern suburbs. Despite fierce German opposition and the efforts of the German Twelfth and Ninth Armies to try to rescue the city, the Soviets surrounded Berlin on 25 April and prepared for the coup de grâce. The Soviets continued to advance house by house into Berlin, while the Germans, by 27 April, held only a salient three by 10 miles.

Hitler, fearing that he would be captured alive, committed suicide on 30 April. That evening, just after 10 o'clock, two Red Army soldiers planed the Red Victory banner over the dome of the Reichstag, the German Parliament building; that signaled the end of the battle, although mopping-up operations continued through 2 May. Germany's unconditional surrender was announced on 8 May.

Nazi Germany's defeat left the country shattered physically, emotionally, and financially. The Allied leaders had met at the Russian resort city of Yalta in February 1945 to discuss postwar Germany. At that time President Franklin Roosevelt, Prime Minister Winston Churchill, and Premier Joseph Stalin drew lines on the map designating areas that the forces of each nation should occupy. Decisions at Yalta profoundly affected the postwar world, for the eastern portion of Germany and the nations of Eastern Europe were captured and occupied by Soviet troops. Decisions made at Potsdam, in July and August 1945, gave the occupied areas to the capturing nation until each country was prepared to embark on an independent course.

That meant, for eastern Germany and Eastern Europe, Soviet occupation and domination for 45 years. Believing that they had suffered the most of any nation during the war, the Soviets felt justified in looting the remaining assets of the occupied countries for the reconstruction of their homeland. They also launched a campaign to convince the people of those occupied nations that Soviet communism was the ideal system of government. That need to convince the population doomed the people of East Germany, Poland, Bulgaria, Hungary, Czechoslovakia, and the Baltic States to decades of privation and hopelessness, cut off from the outside world. The USSR refused to allow any of its occupied countries to accept money from the United States offered under the Marshall Plan of 1948. Thus, industrialization in those countries was extremely slow and the factories never matched the quality of those in the West.

The East Germans might well have suffered the most, for in their midst the city of Berlin was divided into four occupation zones, and three of them were managed and aided by France, Great Britain, and the United States. As those three sections rebuilt and progressed, they proved the value of a capitalist economy over a communist one and were a constant reminder to the inhabitants of the East of the oppression of Soviet rule. Soviet forces occasionally intervened when subject nations believed they had reached the point of independence: Czechoslovakia was invaded in 1948, Hungary in 1956, and Czechoslovakia again in 1968. Only the collapse of communism in the Soviet Union freed the people of Eastern Europe, and they faced the mixed blessings and problems of capitalism and democracy for the first time since World War II.

See also Hitler, Adolf; Soviet Union, Nazi Invasion of the.

References: Duffy, Christopher, *Red Storm on the Reich: The Soviet March on Germany, 1945* (New York: Atheneum, 1991); Glantz, David, and Jonathan House, *When Titans Clashed* (Lawrence: University of Kansas Press, 1995); Ziemke, Earl, *Stalingrad to Berlin: The German Defeat in the East* (Washington, DC: Center for Military History, 1968).

174   GRENADA, U.S. INVASION OF

Grenada, a tiny island in the Caribbean at the southern tip of the Windward Islands, was long a British possession. It became independent in 1974, but from 1979 was ruled by a Marxist party under the leadership of Maurice Bishop. The United States is traditionally leery of any Communist-leaning government, especially in the Western Hemisphere, and Grenada's close ties to Castro's Cuba and anti-American votes in the United Nations worried Presidents Jimmy Carter and Ronald Reagan. Bad matters worsened in 1983, when Bishop was overthrown and the coup installed an even more communistic government.

President Reagan became convinced that Grenada held the potential to become another Soviet satellite like Cuba. To forestall that possibility, he ordered American forces to invade the island, arguing the need to protect American medical students attending school there and to rid the island of Cuban soldiers. Early on the morning of 25 October 1983, the United States launched Operation Urgent Fury. For some unknown reason, 1,250 Marines and two Army Ranger battalions landed on opposite ends of the island, far from the main city and U.S. objectives. Nevertheless, they were backed with an impressive array of Navy, Marine, and Army airpower, as well as armored vehicles.

The invasion was a case of overkill. A mere 43 Cuban soldiers were garrisoned on Grenada, in addition to almost 600 construction workers, and they had no air support or heavy weapons. Despite this almost nonexistent defense force, three days were needed to declare the island secured. The invasion showed a marked lack of interservice coordination and planning, factors addressed by congressional action within a matter of months. The reforms instituted in response to this action were showcased in 1991 during the U.S. invasion of Panama.

In the wake of the American invasion, the people of Grenada were able to hold elections for a parliamentary-style government, which has operated without mishap since 1984.

See also Panama, U.S. Invasion of.

References: Adkin, Mark, *Urgent Fury: The Battle for Grenada* (Lexington, MA: D. C. Heath, 1989); Bolger, Daniel, *Americans at War, 1975–1986: An Era of Violent Peace* (Novato, CA: Presidio Press, 1988).

175   HITLER, ADOLF

The most important figure of the twentieth century was born in Braunau-am-Inn, Austria, on 20 April 1889. His upbringing is the subject of some debate. Hitler claimed to be the impoverished son of a minor bureaucrat, but later research suggests that his father was fairly well-to-do and that Hitler was actually raised in middle-class surroundings. As the first surviving son, he was spoiled by his mother, and any poverty in which he lived would have come after his father's death, because he freely spent his mother's inheritance. Harboring desires for an artistic career, he moved to Vienna, where he was an irregular student. The surviving artwork shows a talent that was more technically than aesthetically good. Some historians argue that when Hitler was rejected for admission to an art school in Vienna, he blamed the Jewish directors of the school, beginning or reinforcing his anti-Semitic stance.

He lived in Vienna in poor housing on the income from selling paintings; the story that he hung wallpaper for a living is a myth. He left his home country for Germany in 1913 when called up for the Austrian draft. In Munich, he lived much as he had in Vienna, though a deep, long-felt love for Germany raised his spirits. When World War I broke out in August 1914, he volunteered for a Bavarian unit and went to fight in France. Four years in the trenches brought a mixture of success and failure. He had the duty of messenger, running communications from the front to the rear headquarters when telephone lines were out, which was often. It was a dangerous job that carried a life expectancy of about two weeks, and he did it throughout the war. He was wounded in battle, decorated, and received quite positive reports from his superiors. Nevertheless, he rose only to the rank of corporal. Merely by surviving the deaths of so many around him should have made him an officer, one would think, but those same superiors who wrote good reports about him also noted that he lacked leadership ability.

After the armistice was signed in November 1918, Hitler remained in the army for a while. He spoke for the army to demobilized soldiers, encouraging them not to get involved in the political chaos that ran through Germany in the months after the war, but to wait for calmer times when Germany could reassert itself. Hitler showed some speaking talent in this position, and was later asked by the army to do some spying. The army kept watch on the growing number of political parties in postwar Germany, placing agents in each to watch for signs of danger should a political group prove threatening. Hitler was assigned to join the Socialist Workers Party, an extremely small group operating in Munich. He found their political philosophy interesting and, when he was released from the army in the wake of the Versailles Treaty, he decided to go into politics. He quickly took control of the party, renaming it the National Socialist German Workers Party. Under his

direction, the Nazi party (so called because the opening word, National, is pronounced Naht-see-o-nal in German) slowly grew.

In late 1922 and throughout 1923, Germany suffered the worst inflation in history. Lack of hard currency, owing to the damage payments imposed by the Versailles Treaty, forced the German government to print money, and print they did. By November 1923 it took 40 billion marks to buy one dollar. Millions of Germans had their savings wiped out and faced poverty or starvation. Believing that desperate times called for desperate measures, Hitler decided to overthrow the government of the state of Bavaria and place himself in charge. In the Beer Hall Putsch of November 1923, Hitler stormed into a rival political party meeting, and at gunpoint coerced a promise from the city mayor and the state governor to give him power. When his forces marched on the capitol building the next day, they found soldiers waiting for them. Shots were fired and Hitler was wounded, then taken captive.

History could have changed at this point, but unluckily for the world, the trial judge favored Hitler's political views and allowed him to use his trial as a forum. He was found guilty of treason, but was sentenced to only nine months of minimum-security confinement. During this time, he dictated *Mein Kampf* (*My Struggle*), the book in which he told the story of his upbringing and laid out his plans to return Germany to respect and its rightful position in the world.

This rambling, difficult work boils down to a few points. First, Germany did not lose World War I, but was forced into surrender when the government could no longer get loans to finance the war from Jewish bankers. So, getting rid of the Jews was a top priority. Second, all German-speaking people needed to be under one government. Third, Germany needed *lebensraum* (living space). The land they had captured in the east in World War I—most of European Russia—was rightfully German, and Germany should use this land to settle its hardworking people. Fourth, the people who lived in this area were *untermensch* (subhumans), who would be killed or used for slave labor for the superior German race. He spelled out his racial views and his plans for expansion for all to see. Why, then, was all that happened later a surprise to the world? Because *Mein Kampf* was so bad, nobody read it. It was not widely read in Germany until after Hitler came to power in 1933, and not read outside Germany until much too late.

After his release from prison, Hitler decided that force was not the way to gain power He spent the remainder of the 1920s building his party, gaining the support of business contributors who liked the idea of Germany being great again. The Nazi role in the government grew with each election, though Hitler himself held no office. After the election of 1932, Hitler was approached by the Social Democratic party to form a coalition government. He agreed, as long as he could hold the number two position, chancellor. Because the Social Democrat president—and that would be World War I Field Marshal Paul von Hindenburg—would retain most of the power, Hitler could be kept under control, so the agreement was made. Hitler became chancellor at the end of January 1933.

Within a few months, he announced that Germany would no longer pay the reparations demanded by the Versailles Treaty. When Britain and France refused to go to war to force payment, Hitler knew that the Versailles Treaty was "a scrap of paper." After Hindenburg's death in August 1934, Hitler forced bills through a Nazi-dominated special session of Parliament that achieved two important things: The positions of president and chancellor were combined, and all political parties but the National Socialists were banned. Political resistance was brief because vocal opponents soon found themselves in prison. With dictatorial power, Hitler began wholesale violations of the Versailles Treaty. He expanded the army past the prescribed 100,000 men, he built an air force, and he constructed warships. No one outside Germany resisted him, because public opinion would not allow more war so soon after the horrors of the last one.

He began to follow the plan laid out in *Mein Kampf*. Jews were soon restricted in their rights, then openly persecuted. He used the army to reoccupy the industrial area of the Rhineland in 1936. Later that year, he lent his air force to Francisco Franco, who used it to begin the Spanish Civil War. German pilots received on-the-job training fighting with Franco through 1939. Hitler supported, then allied himself with, Benito Mussolini, dictator of Italy. In March 1938, Hitler threatened Austria with war if the government would not give itself up to him; it did, and Austria became a German state. In September 1938, he threatened war over the Sudetenland, the western province of Czechoslovakia, which held a large German population. France and Britain would not honor defense treaty commitments to the Czechs, and the land was conceded without a fight. Hitler occupied the remainder of the country in May 1939. The threat to use force over access to Danzig in Poland finally brought outside resistance. In Europe, World War II began 1 September 1939.

Hitler's political intuition had brought him the prewar gains, but that same intuition began to fail him in wartime. Bad decisions cost him strategic victories during the Battle of France and the Battle of Britain, while his support of Mussolini's failures diverted valuable men and materiel from more important ventures. His determination to destroy European Jewry brought about the concentration and death camps, and transport dedicated to that use was siphoned from desperately needed military use later in the war. His decision to fight a two-front war and his declaration of war on the United States proved his ultimate undoing. Germany was overwhelmed by manpower and weaponry that negated the German army's advantages of training and experience. Hitler grew more paranoid and more self-assured as the war progressed. He was convinced that no one could accomplish what he could, and no one had his vision, so he trusted fewer and fewer people. He ended the war in an underground bunker as Soviet and German troops destroyed Berlin over his head. Until the last, he directed the movements of units long since destroyed, but which he would not believe had ceased to exist. He committed suicide on 29 April 1945 rather than be humiliated by his captors.

Hitler came to power by sheer force of will, and that will destroyed not only himself and his country, but altered the entire world. The long-expected death of the British Empire, the rise of two superpowers, the passing of French influence, and the Cold War with all its repression and confrontation since 1945 can be directly traced to World War II, which was Hitler's war. He is remembered for his cynical political actions, his naked aggression, and, of course, for the Holocaust. Like Tamurlane, Attila the Hun, and Genghis Khan, his name became synonymous with terror and destruction. The German people have yet to emerge from his shadow, and he still has the ability to frighten the modern world, for his views live on in a lunatic fringe that revere his name and his dreams.

See also Genghis Khan; Tamurlane; Austria, Nazi Occupation of; Britain, Nazi Invasion of (Battle of Britain); Czechoslovakia, Nazi Occupation of; Egypt, Italian Invasion of; France, Nazi Invasion of; Greece, Nazi Invasion of; Mussolini, Benito; Poland, Nazi Conquest of; Soviet Union, Nazi Invasion of the.

References: Bullock, Alan, *Hitler: A Study in Tyranny* (New York: Harper, 1953); Payne, Robert, *The Life and Death of Adolph Hitler* (New York: Praeger, 1973); Shirer, William, *The Rise and Fall of the Third Reich* (New York: Simon & Schuster, 1960).

IRAQ, US/COALITION INVASION OF

176

Following the terrorist attacks on New York City and the Pentagon on September 11, 2001, the United States launched itself into a war on terror. Any nation which participated in terrorism or gave aid to terrorists would face retribution. As the United States began confronting this terrorist threat, it became cognizant that involvement in overseas operations would be necessary. First, American and allied forces invaded Afghanistan and overthrew the oppressive, ultra-conservative Muslim Taliban government, which harbored Al-Qaeda terrorist training camps and leaders like Osama bin Laden. The next move in the war on terror was against Iraq, which was known to have ties to international terrorist organizations and to harbor terrorists. Further, it was widely reported that the regime of Saddam Hussein had been developing chemical, biological, and perhaps nuclear weapons.

With the assistance of the United Nations and the International Atomic Energy Agency, inspectors went into Iraq to search for weapons of mass destruction. For months, the Hussein regime played a game of cat-and-mouse with inspectors, giving the very strong impression that it had something to hide. However, only indirect evidence could be discovered. Without concrete confirmation, the United Nations Security Council would not sanction military operations. France and Germany led European critics of any Western military intervention. It has been suspected that illicit trade from those countries had been rampant during the United Nations embargo imposed on Iraq after the 1991 Gulf War. Receiving neither approval nor assistance from the United Nations, the United States began building a coalition force to invade Iraq. The stated goal was to make the region (and perhaps the world) safe from weapons of mass destruction in the hands of Saddam Hussein, who had already used poison gas in contravention of international agreements during his war against Iran in the 1980s. Further, Iraq's ties to terrorism allowed for the possibility of such weapons being used anywhere in the world, as Al-Qaeda had already shown in their willingness on 9/11 to mass-murder innocents.

American President George W. Bush's first action was to deliver an ultimatum to Saddam Hussein. He was given the opportunity to leave Iraq, along with his two sons Uday and Qusay, or the United States and its allies were prepared to take offensive action against the country. Meanwhile, America had been gathering allies for the operation, primarily Britain, Australia, Poland, Italy, and Spain, which came to be called the "Coalition of the Willing." They assembled troops along the Iraqi border in Saudi Arabia and Kuwait. American troops numbered 100,000 and the British contingent was 45,000. They would later be bolstered by an additional 50,000 Kurds, the population of northern Iraq that had long been persecuted by Hussein but had enjoyed something of a political resurgence in the post-Gulf War era. The United States requested permission to base troops in Turkey, but that was denied by the Turkish government, which hesitated to fight a fellow Muslim nation. Eventually, however, Turkey did allow free use of its airspace for launching attacks and delivering supplies and personnel into northern Iraq.

Coalition Invasion of Iraq, Initial Operations

U.S. forces called the invasion Operation Iraqi Freedom; to the British it was Operation Telic, and to the Australians it was Operation Falconer. The invasion began around 05:30 Baghdad time on March 20, 2003, some 90 minutes after the passing of the deadline for Hussein to resign. The initial invasion troops were of the Australian Special Air Service which crossed over into southern Iraq from Kuwait. At 22:15 Eastern Standard Time in Washington, D.C., President Bush declared that he had ordered coalition troops to launch an "attack of opportunity" against significant targets in Iraq. The plan deemed most promising by U.S. commanders was a continuation of the "shock and awe" strategy originally developed in Afghanistan.

According to this strategy, coalition forces would use superior mobility, firepower, and speed to overcome Iraqi defenses before they could be brought to bear against an invasion force. It was hoped that this mobility and coordination would lead to a rapid collapse of the Iraqi command structure and, thus, a victory with minimum casualties. The plan also resembled the "island-hopping" strategy of World War II in that coalition forces avoided major troop concentrations in large cities. This limited major combat saved many lives that would have been lost in house-to-house fighting. Commanders also hoped they would gain local support once the leadership of the army and government had fallen.

As coalition troops advanced deeper into the heart of Iraq, one of their objectives was to secure the country's oil infrastructure. The oil was considered a vital objective for strategic as well as economic reasons. On March 20, troops of the British Royal Marines 3 Commando Brigade launched an evening air and amphibious assault against the Al-Faw peninsula to secure the oil facilities there. Frigates of the Royal Navy and Royal Australian Navy supported the operation. As this was taking place, the British Fifteenth Marine Expeditionary Unit took the port of Umm Qasr, while the Sixteenth Air Assault Brigade secured the area's oil fields. Once Umm Qasr was secured, it was opened to shipping that brought in more troops as well as humanitarian aid for the local population.

As British troops fought for control of southern Iraq's oil supply, the American Third Infantry Division moved northward through the desert toward the capital city of Baghdad. The U.S. First Marine Expeditionary Force and British First Armoured Division slogged through thick marshland that considerably slowed their progress. At this point, it became impossible to avoid entering the cities any longer, as it was necessary to capture strategic bridges over the Tigris and Euphrates rivers. In the largest tank battle fought by British troops since World War II, the Royal Scots Dragoon Guards knocked out 14 Iraqi tanks on 27 March. On April 6, the British Seventh Armoured Brigade (the famed "Desert Rats" of World War II) entered Iraq's second-largest city, Basra, where they encountered heavy resistance from Iraqi army forces and irregulars called *fedayeen*. On April 9, lead elements of the British First Armoured Division linked up with U.S. forces around Al Amarah.

At this point, with the imminent collapse of the Iraqi government, electrical and water shortages became a major problem for coalition troops, as did the start of looting and other civil disturbances. The coalition soldiers found themselves playing the role of police while trying to maintain order and distribute humanitarian aid. Once U.S. troops reached the area around Hillah and Karbala, the offensive came to a temporary halt owing to heavy resistance and blinding sandstorms. The troops rested for several days and, after resupplying, were able to continue the attack.

Operation Iraqi Freedom also employed Special Forces troops in wider roles and in larger numbers than they had been since the Vietnam War. The Soldiers of Special Operations Command (SOCOM) were vital to the success of the invasion and occupation of Iraq. The Second Battalion Fifth Special Forces Group (the Green Berets) conducted reconnaissance and raids throughout southern Iraq, as well as providing support for conventional invasion forces. In northern Iraq, elements of the Tenth SFG aided Kurdish militia factions such as the Union of Kurdistan and the Democratic Party of Kurdistan. After heavy fighting in the north, Special Forces troops and their Kurdish allies were able to rout the Thirteenth Iraqi Armored and Infantry Division. The American 173rd Airborne Brigade parachuted into H3, an Iraqi airfield, and secured it for coalition use.

Three weeks into the invasion, U.S. forces entered the streets of Baghdad. The original plan to capture the city had been to surround it with armored forces and have airborne troops move in and engage in street fighting. The plan was changed, however, in favor of a "thunder run" of about 30 M1 Abrams main battle tanks through the city streets. The tanks met some resistance, including suicide attacks. Another such assault took place two days later and succeeded in capturing Saddam Hussein's palace. On April 9, Baghdad was declared "secured" and the Hussein regime officially ended. Difficult fighting continued for a few weeks in Basra and An Nasiriyeh.

Although the bulk of the Iraqi army was defeated, some isolated units held out and, worse for the allies, guerrillas began operating in both cities and the countryside, while looting became so widespread that little could be done to stop it. Not only were government offices looted by those who had been terrorized by them for so long, but those with a more professional eye soon removed many treasures from the National Museum of Iraq. So many buildings and facilities had to be protected that not everything could be watched. Many believe that the best pieces were taken by members of the Hussein regime before the city fell.

On May 1, 2003, President Bush declared major combat operations to be at an end. On May

22, 2003, the United Nations voted to end the embargo against Iraq and support the U.S.-led government that was being planned. As far as the Iraqi field forces were concerned, the war was indeed over, but thousands of die-hard Hussein supporters as well as terrorists from outside Iraq began a classic urban guerrilla war. Areas dominated by Sunnis (the minority group that had dominated the government) were bases for rocket and mortar attacks, as well as sniping and the new weapon of choice, hidden roadside bombs called improvised explosive devices, or IEDs. Although those leading the war called for expulsion of the infidels occupying their country, the bulk of the population of the Shia faith were more than happy to see Hussein and his cronies removed and grateful to the soldiers who made it happen. As the guerrillas began to find that they received far greater casualties than they inflicted when fighting coalition troops, they altered their targets to Shia civilians in hopes of provoking a religious civil war. Although tensions remained high between Sunni and Shia factions, no mass uprising took place.

In what became the highest-profile media event, the U.S. government issued a deck of playing cards that had pictures of the most wanted figures from the collapsed regime. Saddam Hussein, as most important, was Ace of Spades, with his family and high officials further down the line. Hussein's sons Uday and Qusay were killed in a firefight in Mosul on July 2003, and on December 14, Saddam himself was found hiding in a "spider hole" in a village outside his hometown of Tikrit.

Since then, the war has been one of hit-and-run. The coalition forces have had some successes in cleaning out nests of guerrillas, as in the capture of the city of Fallujah in April 2004. Reconstruction of Iraqi infrastructure has been an ongoing project for the coalition forces and the new Iraqi government, which officially took power on June 28, 2004. Also, Iraqi police and military forces have been organized and continue (as of this writing) to train and expand, taking a greater role in suppression of guerrilla forces. On January 30, 2005, the first free elections were held for a 275-seat Iraqi National Assembly. Scores of attacks took place against polling places and the Sunnis boycotted it, but 58 percent of the eligible population

voted. Government officials were named in early April, and in August a constitution was proposed, which was voted on in mid-October and approved by 79 percent of the voters. On December 16, the first elections under the new constitution were held, and even the Sunnis, who had boycotted earlier voting, came out for this one.

Resistance to the war among the American public has been loud, and many accusations of bias in the media against the war have been leveled. Should the U.S. have invaded? how long should the coalition forces stay? is it all worth it? are questions asked across the country and the world. The suicide bombers continue their attacks and IED's continue to explode at the end of 2005, but the Iraqi nation seems to have turned the corner and is playing a greater role in its own government, administration, and defense. How long coalition forces might stay in Iraq is the subject of heated debate both inside and outside Washington, but as Saddam Hussein is tried by an Iraqi court for crimes against humanity, a new government in Iraq has been established and a new road has been taken. How long the country will stay on that road is unknown.

- Michael Barden

See also Kuwait, Iraqi invasion of.

References: Fontenot, Gregory, *On Point: The United States Army in Operation Iraqi Freedom* (Annapolis: Naval Institute Press, 2005); Keegan, John, *The Iraq War* (New York: Knopf, 2004); Knights, Michael, *Operation Iraqi Freedom and the New Iraq* (Washington, DC: Institute for Near East Policy, 2004); "Iraq," www.npr.org, 28 December 2005.

ISRAEL, ARAB INVASION OF (YOM KIPPUR WAR)

177

After the 1967 Six-Day War, Israel occupied the entire Sinai Peninsula (previously Egyptian), the Golan Heights (previously Syrian), and the West Bank territory between Jerusalem and the Jordan River (previously Jordanian). The added territory gave the country some buffer zones to protect its population centers, but at the cost of administering large numbers of hostile Palestinian residents. On the defensive ever since its independence in 1948, Israel became

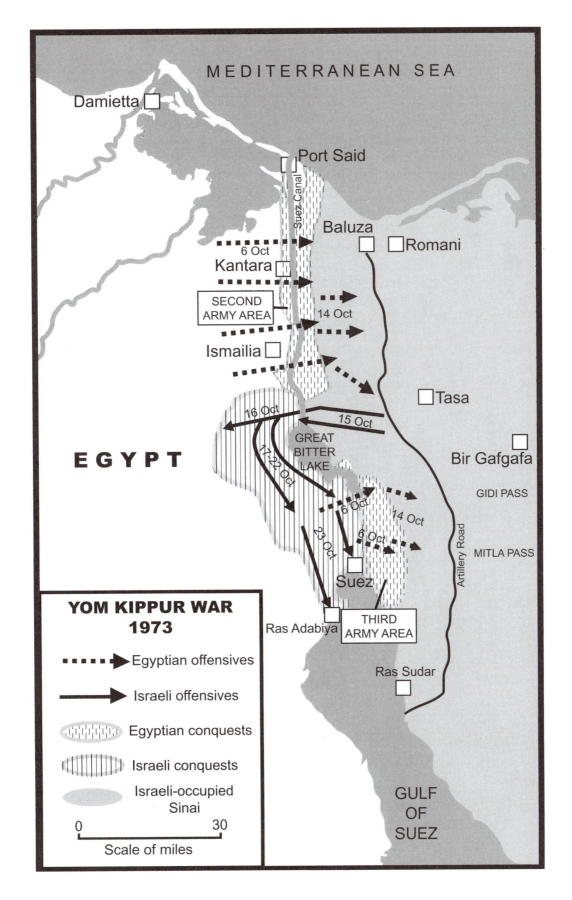

MEDITERRANEAN SEA

Damietta

Port Said

Suez Canal

Baluza

Romani

6 Oct

Kantara

SECOND
ARMY AREA

14 Oct

Ismailia

Tasa

16 Oct

15 Oct

EGYPT

GREAT
BITTER
LAKE

Bir Gafgafa

17-22 Oct

GIDI PASS

6 Oct

14 Oct

Artillery Road

MITLA PASS

23 Oct

6 Oct

Suez

Ras Adabiya

THIRD
ARMY AREA

Ras Sudar

GULF
OF
SUEZ

**YOM KIPPUR WAR
1973**

▪▪▪▪▶ Egyptian offensives

──▶ Israeli offensives

Egyptian conquests

Israeli conquests

Israeli-occupied
Sinai

0   30

Scale of miles

even more of an armed camp. Combat against the Arabs in 1948, 1956, and 1967 convinced the Israelis of their superior military abilities.

Ever since the Six-Day War, the Arab states had been carrying on a terrorist campaign against Israel, waiting for the best time to recover their lost territories. Rearmed with Soviet weapons and better trained by Soviet advisers, Egypt led the Arab states in plotting revenge. After Gamal Abdel Nasser's death in 1970, the new Egyptian president, Anwar Sadat, directed the Arab coalition with as much determination, if not the bluster, of his predecessor. By October 1973, he thought they were ready.

Israeli intelligence warned the government of the impending Arab assault, and Defense Minister Moshe Dayan had to make the decision whether to strike first, as they had done in 1967, or absorb the first blow and take the moral high ground with the international community. Against the wishes of many of the generals, the government decided to wait. The Arabs timed their attack for the Sabbath day that began Yom Kippur, 6 October. Though the generals and the government knew of the coming attack, the population did not. The government thought that mobilization would be interpreted by the international community as provocative, so there was none. The decision to accept the first blow almost caused Israeli defeat.

Israel was attacked from two sides simultaneously: The Egyptians crossed the Suez Canal to regain the Suez Peninsula and the Syrians swept down on the Golan Heights. Syrian forces numbered almost 1,000 tanks in the assault, with another 500 in reserve, and the early attacks overran some Israeli positions. An airborne assault by helicopter forces quickly captured the main Israeli post on Mount Hermon, robbing them of the highest ground. Israel had no more than 200 tanks on-site to defend themselves, but they were well positioned and did the Syrians a great deal of damage. Israeli forces gave ground slowly and at great cost for four days, but by 10 October had regained the upper hand and began a counteroffensive.

In the meantime, Egyptian forces enjoyed great success. The Israelis had built a series of guardposts along the canal, but the Egyptians cleverly avoided them by using high-pressure water hoses to destroy the embankments between the outposts, then building pontoon bridges to cross over. The lightly held outposts were soon cut off by two Egyptian armies swarming between and behind them. The Egyptians prepared for the expected counterattack by building 130-foot-high antitank positions on the western bank to fire down and past the lower embankments on the eastern side. Israeli casualties in men and tanks were high because of this Egyptian tactic, in addition to the fact that almost the entire Israeli air force was dedicated to the Syrian front. Israeli generals held the three key passes (Mitla, Gidi, and Khatmia) into the peninsula while they concentrated forces for the counteroffensive. Successes against Syria allowed Israel to transfer some air support to the Sinai, and they began probing attacks on 10 October.

On the Syrian front, the Israelis also built up their forces behind the tenacious defense which the garrison forces had been conducting since the outbreak of the war. With hundreds of Syrian tanks and armored vehicles charred and smoking along the frontier, the Israelis drove through them toward the Syrian capital of Damascus. A force of Iraqi tanks attempting to join the battle by striking the Israeli flank found themselves trapped in an ambush and destroyed in a night battle illuminated by a full moon. The Israelis drove to within 20 miles of Damascus when they received word of the Syrian acceptance of the U.N.-sponsored ceasefire. The cessation of hostilities on the northeastern front allowed the Israelis to focus on the Sinai.

With massive Egyptian forces across the canal, the defending Israeli units were extremely hard-pressed. On 14 October, the Egyptians launched a massive assault to gain the passes. The two sides engaged in a tank battle on a scale not seen since Kursk in 1943, with some 2,000 tanks engaged. In their defensive positions the Israelis held off the assaults and shocked the Egyptians with their gunnery. By the end of the day, the Israelis had lost only six tanks while destroying 264. With their forces gathered and with increased air support, the Israelis decided to cross the canal themselves and get behind the Egyptian thrust, cutting it off from its supplies. While some forces fought desperate battles against the Egyptian beachheads on the eastern shore, one Israeli thrust drove to the canal at the north end of the Great Bitter Lake. During a night of hard fighting on 15–16 October at Chinese Farm on the eastern shore, the Israelis managed to build a bridge across the canal. No Egyptian forces were to be found on the western bank, and the Israelis ran amok.

Armored forces swiftly drove south along the Great Bitter Lake and secured the western shore of the canal beyond it, cutting off the Egyptian Third Army on the Sinai. Egypt soon called for a ceasefire as well.

The United States, the Soviet Union, and the United Nations had been proposing ceasefire plans for some days, but the Arabs rejected them early in the conflict and the Israelis rejected them later. Not until Israeli units were well in control of the situation did the Israeli government agree to stop fighting. The Soviets, who had been aiding the Arabs since the 1950s, saw their clients losing materiel at a fantastically high rate, and within a few days of the war's start the Soviet government began resupplying them. The United States saw the same thing happen on the Israeli side, and responded with tanks and aircraft. These actions strained the relationship between the two great powers at a time when they had begun to thaw, but neither side wanted to intervene directly and expand the war. Eventually, pressure from the United States and the USSR was the primary factor in bringing the fighting to a halt, though a U.N. peacekeeping force was formed (without their participation) to stand between the two armies during disengagement.

The Yom Kippur War taught lessons for many nations. The United States and the Soviet Union were able to see their respective weapons systems in action and judge their effectiveness against their major rival. The American equipment tended to dominate, but the Egyptians and Syrians badly hurt the Israeli air forces with Soviet surface-to-air missiles. The two superpowers also learned what modern war does to soldiers and materiel: It eats them up in huge amounts, needing rapid repair and/or replacement.

The Israelis learned that the Arabs could fight much more effectively than the former had suspected. The air of invincibility the Israelis had built around themselves proved false. Even though

the Israelis won handily in the end, they were sorely pressed at the beginning and surprised by the skill and tenacity of Arab forces. They also realized the need for territory; had they not held the Sinai, the Golan Heights, and the West Bank, the Arab forces would have overrun Jerusalem and Tel Aviv. The closeness of the conflict hardened Israeli resolve not to return any captured lands.

The Arabs learned that fighting with Israel was perhaps too expensive a proposition. Soon after the war, Egypt began to make tentative moves toward a reconciliation. Through the efforts of U.S. Secretary of State Henry Kissinger, tensions began to ease somewhat through the mid-1970s, and Israel slowly began to consider the return of Arab land in return for guarantees of safety. In 1977, Egypt recognized Israel as an independent nation, the first Arab country to do so. In return, the Egyptians got the Sinai Peninsula back, beginning a long process that by the early 1990s brought about similar Arab actions. Israel, a nation born in battle, seemed by the middle 1990s to be more secure in its borders and cooperative, if not overly friendly, with its Arab neighbors. Some radical Arabs, however, continue the old campaign to bring Israel's existence to an end.

See also Germany, Soviet Invasion of; Sinai, Israeli Invasion of, 1967 (Six-Day War).

References: Badri, Hasan, *The Ramadan War, 1973* (Boulder, CO: Westview Press, 1978); Dupuy, Trevor, *Elusive Victory: The Arab-Israeli Wars, 1947–1974* (New York: Harper & Row, 1978); Herzog, Chaim, *War of Atonement, October 1973* (Boston: Little, Brown, 1975).

ITALY, ALLIED INVASION OF

178

In World War II, the British and Americans invaded Italy almost by accident. After clearing North Africa of Axis forces and securing the island of Sicily at Italy's southern extremity to control Mediterranean shipping, the veteran troops had little to do other than wait several months for the invasion of France. Because the fall of Sicily had occasioned Benito Mussolini's downfall, the Italians were eager to withdraw from the war. Their new prime minister, Pietro Badoglio, had no desire to see his homeland become a battleground, so he covertly contacted the Allies through agents in Portugal, even as he publicly assured the Italians and the Germans that Italy would fight on. Italy secretly signed surrender papers on 2 September 1943, and several days passed before the news was made public. Upon learning of the withdrawal, German forces disarmed the Italian troops with them and prepared to fight for the country.

The German commander in Italy, Field Marshal Albert Kesselring, was one of the few Germans who wanted to fight in Italy. Even as he withdrew forces from the southern tip of Italy in accordance with orders from Berlin, he prepared defensive positions to slow or stop the Allied advance. With the Appenine Range running down the peninsula's spine and often reaching all the way to either coast, the terrain presented Kesselring with a multitude of opportunities to achieve his desire. He persistently lobbied Hitler to allow him to fight south of Rome, which all other German military authorities counseled against. When Hitler finally gave him that permission, Kesselring was ready to act. He had to do so in a hurry.

British forces crossed the Straits of Messina into Italy on 2 September, and made rapid headway against the withdrawing Germans. On 9 September, British and American forces landed at the port city of Salerno, 200 miles down the coast from Rome. The landings went smoothly at first, but Kesselring's retreating forces joined with reserves rushed down from Rome and quickly counterattacked. For a few days, it looked as if the Allies were going to suffer another Dunkirk, but they managed to solidify their beachhead by 14 September. Made cautious by the German resistance, the Allies moved slowly inland, giving the Germans time to man their mountain defenses, called the Gustav Line, which ended any chance that Italy would fall quickly.

Kesselring used not only the mountains, but also the swift-flowing rivers cutting through them as defensive strongholds. His men dug into the hillsides overlooking successive rivers, and were able to pound any attacker who tried to cross. As the American and Commonwealth troops tried to break through along both coasts, they had to face withering fire expertly directed from hidden observation posts in the mountains.

The Sangro, Rapido, Garigliano, and Liri rivers stopped the Allied advances and made them sitting ducks for German artillery. Throughout the autumn and into the winter of 1943–1944, troops of multiple nationalities pounded against the German lines and were repulsed. American, Free French, French colonial, British, New Zealand, South African, Australian, and Polish soldiers each took turns dying in the Italian mountains.

The most difficult of the battles was along the Rapido River, which was overlooked by Monte Cassino, site of the original Benedictine monastery. Convinced that the Germans were occupying it for observation purposes, the Allies debated whether to attack it. The decision to bomb the historic shrine went all the way to Supreme Commander of Allied Forces Dwight Eisenhower, who reluctantly approved the attack at the urging of the New Zealand force commander whose troops were slated to attack the mountain. The air attack took place on 15 February 1944 and the monastery was leveled. Subsequently, the Allies learned that the Germans had not occupied it, but had been using observation posts camouflaged on the mountainside. After the bombing, however, reluctance to violate the sanctity of the monastery was moot, and the Germans turned the rubble into a much more difficult objective than the hilltop would have been otherwise.

As Eisenhower pondered the fate of Cassino, American forces staged another amphibious landing. The need for shipping for the upcoming Allied invasion of France robbed the Italian campaign of necessary transport and landing craft, so the landings at Anzio were a somewhat haphazard affair. General John Lucas commanded the 50,000-man force that went ashore on 22 January 1944 against an undefended beach. The Germans were unprepared for the landing, but Lucas gave them time to regroup. He spent a few days digging in and making sure his beachhead was secure; by the time that was done, Kesselring had shifted reserves to Anzio and launched his own attack. Though the Allies were once again on the verge of being pushed into the sea, they held on. They could not make a relatively quick move off the beaches as they had after the Salerno attacks, because this time the Germans were not in the

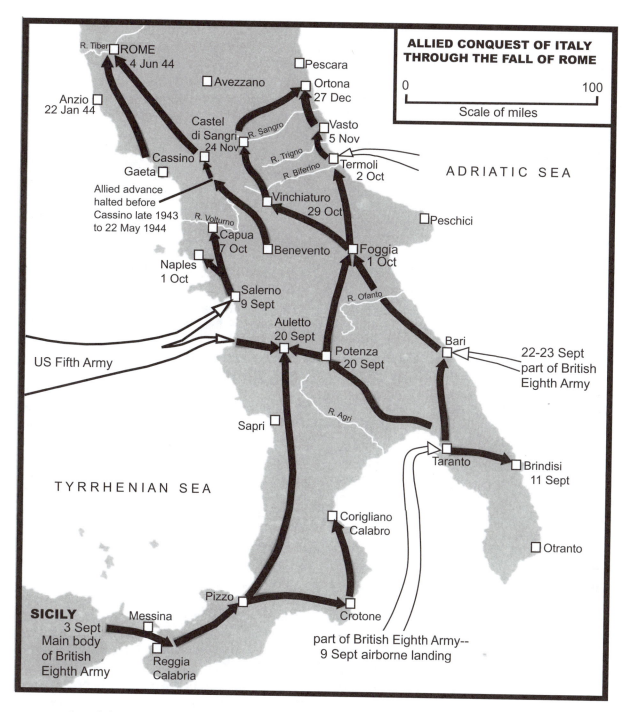

ALLIED CONQUEST OF ITALY THROUGH THE FALL OF ROME

0   100
Scale of miles

R. Tiber
ROME
4 Jun 44

Pescara

Anzio
22 Jan 44

Avezzano

Ortona
27 Dec

Castel
di Sangri
24 Nov
R. Sangro

Vasto
5 Nov

ADRIATIC SEA

Cassino

R. Trigno

Termoli
2 Oct

Gaeta

R. Biferino

Allied advance
halted before
Cassino late 1943
to 22 May 1944

R. Volturno

Vinchiaturo
29 Oct

Peschici

Capua
7 Oct

Benevento

Foggia
1 Oct

Naples
1 Oct

Salerno
9 Sept

R. Ofanto

US Fifth Army

Auletto
20 Sept

Potenza
20 Sept

Bari

22-23 Sept
part of British
Eighth Army

R. Agri

Sapri

TYRRHENIAN SEA

Taranto

Brindisi
11 Sept

Corigliano
Calabro

Otranto

Pizzo

Crotone

part of British Eighth Army--
9 Sept airborne landing

SICILY
3 Sept
Main body
of British
Eighth Army

Messina

Reggia
Calabria

process of withdrawing, but had come to stay. The Anzio beachhead went nowhere for four months, and any assistance it may have rendered to the troops in the south was minimal.

The Allies finally broke through the Gustav Line in the spring of 1944. The British Eighth Army attacked up the eastern coast, drawing the German reserves to that end of the line. A few days later, the American Fifth Army again chal-lenged the Rapido River and Monte Cassino, while French Moroccan forces fought through the mountains in between. The Moroccans and the Poles scored the first breakthroughs, and the race was on. With the Germans finally dislodged and pulling back, General Lucian Truscott (now in command of the forces at Anzio) attacked eastward, hoping to block the fleeing Germans and hold them as the advancing Allies pushed north. It almost worked. As Truscott's men were about to reach the Liri River valley and cut off the German line of retreat, he was ordered to turn northward instead and take Rome before British troops could reach the city. Rome, declared an open city by the Germans, fell without a fight on 4 June; the German army slipped away to a new defensive line in the north.

The Allies captured all of central Italy in a matter of weeks, then ran into the Hitler and Gothic lines, where the Germans again stopped them cold. Another fall and winter passed with Allied forces struggling against mountain strongpoints, and they were doing it with fewer and fewer men because many troops were drained off for operations in France. Only because the German government collapsed in the spring of 1945 did the German resistance break in Italy, but it had forced the Allies into a much costlier campaign than had ever been anticipated. Much debate has ensued about just how vital the campaign was. True, it forced Italy from the war, but after Sicily the Italians were on the verge of giving up anyway. The fighting gave the Allies air bases from which to attack targets in southern France and the Balkans, which assisted in the invasion of France in the summer of 1944 and also hurt German oil refining in Rumania. Germany was obliged to shift men from the Balkans, France, and Germany to aid their effort in Italy, which could have had a significant effect because they were then unavailable to counter the Normandy invasion. It was a murderous campaign that resembled the fighting experienced in World War I in the slow progress of advances and the numbers of men lost for the amount of ground gained. Italy did not suffer as much as many other countries because most of the fighting was in limited areas in the mountains, but in some cases the destruction was significant. Rome saw no fighting at all, and the treasures of the city were saved. The same can be said for most of the major historic cities, but historic treasures such as Monte Cassino can never be replaced. Italy's losses were more economic than physical, and the democratic government that replaced the fascists after the war has provided Europe with the most varied of political arenas.

See also Egypt, Italian Invasion of; Eisenhower, Dwight David; France, Allied Invasion of; France, Nazi Invasion of; Mussolini, Benito; North Africa, U.S. Invasion of; Sicily, Allied Invasion of.

References: Clark, Mark, *Calculated Risk* (New York: Harper, 1950); Majdalany, Fred, *The Battle of Cassino* (Boston: Houghton Mifflin, 1958); Morris, Eric, *Circles of Hell* (London: Hutchinson, 1993).

KUWAIT, IRAQI INVASION OF

179

In 1990, Iraqi leader Saddam Hussein invaded his neighbor, Kuwait, on the Persian Gulf. He claimed that in Ottoman times, Kuwait had been part of territory controlled by Baghdad, so it should return to Baghdad's control as the nineteenth province of Iraq. Actually, this had not been the case; Kuwait was a separate sheikhdom under the Ottoman Empire, and Baghdad had merely served as the district capital for the Ottoman governor. It seems likely that Hussein's real reason for invasion was control of the Kuwaiti oil fields, and he was intent on being the major factor in the pricing of Middle Eastern oil. Kuwait appeared to be the first target of his expansion, and the United States in particular did not want to see other, more friendly oil producers come under Hussein's control. Hussein had made threatening gestures toward Kuwait for weeks, but the United States thought it was nothing more than saber-rattling.

Earlier, when Hussein waged war against Iran, the United States had opened its military largesse to him. In addition, when Iraq first complained about Kuwait's oil-pricing policies, the United States told Hussein that any Middle East "border dispute" was none of America's business. Once the invasion took place, however, American President George Bush became the leader of an international coalition not only to resist further Iraqi expansion, but also to restore Kuwait's independence. In response to calls for aid from other Arab countries, notably Saudi Arabia, Bush sent American troops and cajoled the United Nations into aiding him in dealing with Hussein. European allies joined in with troops, but other nations dependent on Middle East oil, such as Japan and Germany, were barred by their post-World War II constitutions

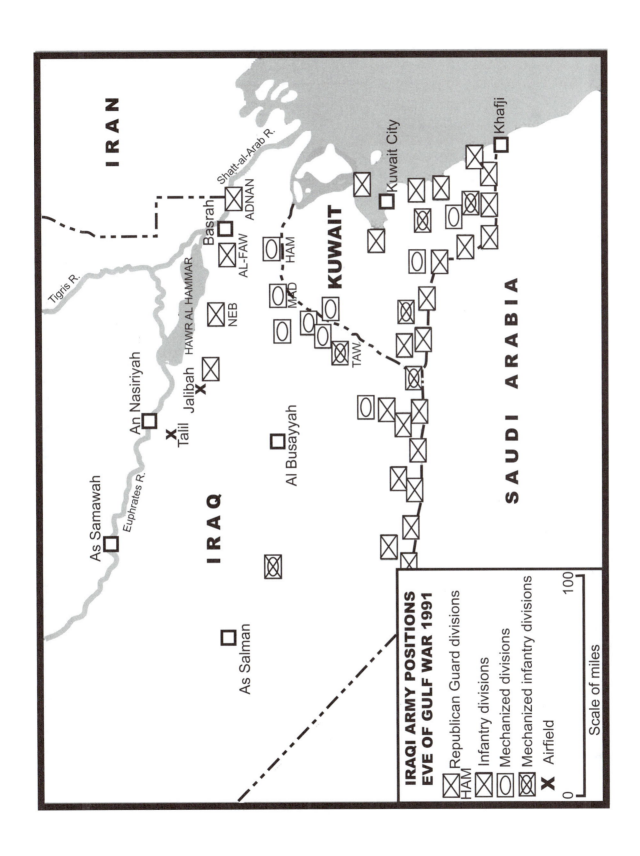

**IRAQI ARMY POSITIONS
EVE OF GULF WAR 1991**

Republican Guard divisions HAM

Infantry divisions

Mechanized divisions

Mechanized infantry divisions

X Airfield

Scale of miles

0   100

IRAN

IRAQ

KUWAIT

SAUDI ARABIA

Kuwait City

Khafji

Basrah

Shatt-al-Arab R.

ADNAN

AL-FAW

HAM

MAD

TAW.

NEB

HAWR AL HAMMAR

Tigris R.

An Nasiriyah

Talil Jalibah

Euphrates R.

As Samawah

Al Busayyah

As Salman

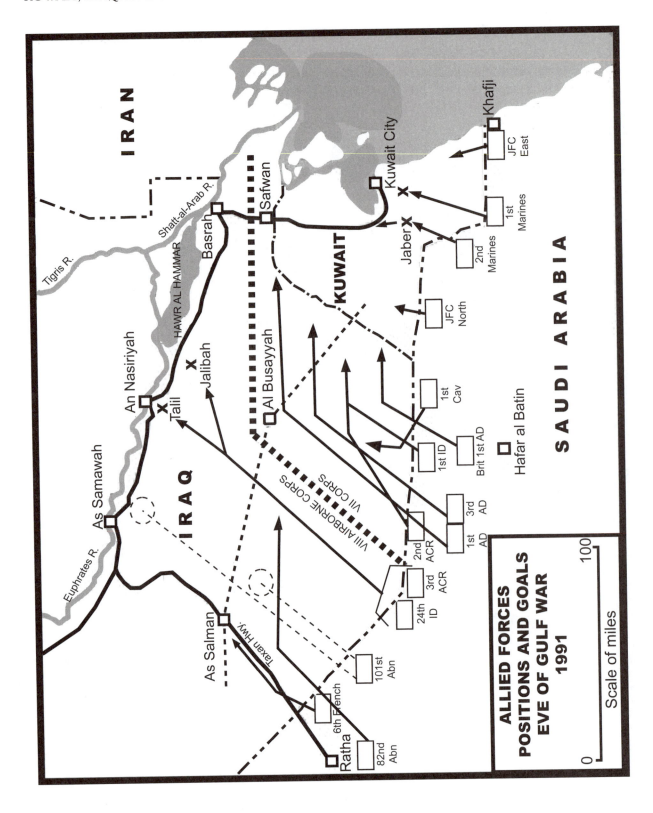

ALLIED FORCES
POSITIONS AND GOALS
EVE OF GULF WAR
1991

Scale of miles

0   100

from sending troops outside their borders; they instead offered financial aid. Operation Desert Shield, organized under the command of American general Norman Schwarzkopf, put almost half a million men along the Saudi-Iraqi border by January 1991.

Much has been made of Bush's motives for Desert Shield and its successor, Operation Desert Storm. Certainly American and world dependence on a stable Middle East oil supply was a factor. As a member of the generation that had fought in World War II, Bush saw Saddam Hussein as a latter-day Adolf Hitler who needed to be stopped rather than appeased. Stories of Iraqi brutality in Kuwait further increased his resolve to resist totalitarian aggression. Also, because communism was collapsing in the Soviet Union and Eastern Europe, Bush saw an opportunity for what he called a "New World Order," where peace-loving nations would cooperate to maintain sovereign borders against flagrant expansionism. The international response to Bush's pleas was remarkable. Even such hostile nations as Cuba and Libya voted to condemn Iraqi aggression. Hussein tried to court Arab assistance by attacking Israel, but only the Palestinians gave him any support.

Throughout the second half of 1990, the coalition forces massed along the Iraqi and Kuwaiti borders. Rather than launch a preemptive strike, Hussein allowed the forces to grow while he began building a defensive line along the border, and dared the coalition to attack it. Schwarzkopf gave the impression that he would do just that, then planned a major turning movement through the desert along the Iraqi right flank. Economic attempts to pressure Hussein to leave proved futile, and by the end of December, President Bush gave Iraq a 15 January deadline to withdraw from Kuwait. Last-minute negotiations proved fruitless, and Schwarzkopf received word to turn Desert Shield into Desert Storm.

Shortly after 3:00 a.m. local time on 17 January, a massive air assault struck the Iraqi capital and key locations across the country. Cruise missiles, Stealth fighters, and laser-guided "smart" bombs took out military installations with pinpoint precision. Iraqi command, communication, and control were paralyzed and then destroyed by 38 days of air attack. Hussein

responded by launching "Scud" missiles against Israel, hoping to provoke an Israeli response that would attract Arab support to his side. Israel took relatively light damage, and did not respond militarily. That restraint effectively isolated Iraq, as did the Scud attacks on Saudi Arabia.

Hussein still refused to accede to international demands, so the land war finally began. It lasted a mere 100 hours until President Bush called it to a halt. The Iraqi army displayed what was possibly the poorest performance in all of military history. Anecdotes are told of soldiers surrendering to drone observation aircraft and news correspondents. Thousands died, and tens of thousands surrendered; coalition casualties numbered less than 800 dead and wounded. Kuwait was liberated in hours, and the massive defenses the Iraqis had spent months constructing were first outflanked and then easily pierced when the defenders gave up.

Many around the world believed that Bush stopped the war too soon, that the coalition should have completely destroyed the Iraqi military, driven to Baghdad, and removed Hussein from power. Because none of those things happened, the defeat of the Iraqi army accomplished little. Saddam Hussein retained power and the core of his military, and soon he was persecuting Arabs around Basra and Kurds in the north. Hussein had ordered oil spilled into the Persian Gulf to thwart an amphibious attack, and retreating Iraqi forces set fire to most of the Kuwaiti oil wells. The environmental damage was huge, but quick response by fire-fighting teams put the fires out sooner than expected. An international embargo remained for years as the United Nations awaited the extremely slow revelation of Iraq's atomic and chemical warfare capabilities. Through the middle 1990s, Hussein retained power, while the people of Iraq suffered extreme economic hardship because minimal imports were allowed and no Iraqi oil was exported.

In Kuwait, the political administration of the emir suffered some discontent from Kuwaitis who had remained in the country during the occupation and conducted resistance action. They demanded some representation in the government, which came about by 1994. The large resident population of Palestinians, who had worked as laborers in Kuwait, was persecuted because the Palestine Liberation Organization had supported Iraq. Almost all were driven from the country in a matter of months.

See also Hitler, Adolf.

References: Blackwell, James, *Thunder in the Desert* (New York: Bantam Books, 1991); Friedman, Norman, *Desert Victory* (Annapolis, MD: Naval Institute Press, 1991); Woodward, Bob, *The Commanders* (New York: Simon & Schuster, 1991).

LATIN AMERICA, U.S. INTERVENTIONS IN

180

Since the 1820s, the United States has viewed itself as something of a Western Hemispheric police officer. In response to the possible reconquest of Spanish colonies in Latin America, President James Monroe and Secretary of State John Quincy Adams formulated the Monroe Doctrine. This stated that the Western Hemisphere was closed to colonization, that any attempt to interfere in the internal affairs of a Western Hemisphere country would be viewed as an unfriendly act, and that the United States would not meddle in European affairs. No European power made good on the threat of reconquest (more because of British threats than those of America), so the United States considered itself the protector of the Americas. What began as basically a defensive stance became, over time, more interventionist. President Theodore Roosevelt added the Roosevelt Corollary, stating that the United States would act preemptively to keep Europeans out of Latin America. In 1934, President Franklin Roosevelt created the Good Neighbor Policy, wherein the United States promised retaliation against any invasion and also reserved the right to intervene when local disturbances threatened American lives or interests. With and without that reservation, the United States has often sent forces into Latin American countries to protect its interests (strategic or economic) or to support friendly governments from internal resistance.

American naval forces were sent to Chile in 1891 to enforce payment of damages demanded by the U.S. government from the Chileans when American sailors were killed in a riot. To many

Latin American nations, it seemed like extortion, but no country was in a position to challenge the action. The United States made itself a mediator in a Venezuela-British Guiana border dispute in the middle 1890s; at first, Venezuela invited the United States to protect them from British claims to gold fields, but when the American mediators sided with British claims, the Venezuelans refused to abide by the decision.

Cuba

The United States removed Spanish control from Cuba in 1898, and in 1901 a democratic government was established and the first president elected. After losing the following election, the president refused to cede power, so American troops entered and oversaw new elections. This oversight became an ongoing exercise until 1934, when President Franklin Roosevelt instituted the Good Neighbor Policy and withdrew from the Cuban political scene. The result was the establishment of a dictatorship in Cuba, put in place by Fulgencio Batista (with U.S. military and economic aid). Batista oversaw a regime as corrupt as any in Latin America, and established close ties to organized crime (through casinos) and American businesses, which exploited most of the island's agriculture and raw materials. In the 1950s, Fidel Castro led a revolution, and in 1959, he succeeded in overthrowing Batista. Castro turned to the United States for economic assistance, but was rebuffed by President Eisenhower. On the advice of some left-leaning lieutenants, Castro turned to the Soviets, who were more than happy to establish influence so close to the United States.

Castro, rejected by the Americans, now became their number one enemy. His expulsion of organized-crime figures and those who had profited under Batista created a group of disgruntled Cubans in exile in the United States. They appealed to Eisenhower for help, and he ordered the CIA to aid them in returning to Cuba, where they promised a popular uprising against Castro. President John Kennedy inherited the operation, but gave it inconsistent support. When the Cubans landed at the Bay of Pigs on Cuba's south coast in April 1961, the invasion was a fiasco. Though Kennedy ransomed the 1,100 prisoners,

Cuban exiles were convinced he had not done enough to aid them in their attempt to reestablish control. An embargo on Cuba, long tied to the American economy, hurt them even more than did the invasion.

The Soviet Union's 1962 attempt to install in Cuba offensive missiles capable of carrying nuclear warheads brought the island once again to Kennedy's attention. Plans were considered for bombing targets in Cuba or perhaps an invasion, but Kennedy instituted a "quarantine" around Cuba to stop Soviet ships. Soviet Premier Nikita Khrushchev publicly announced his intention to break the quarantine, and nuclear war seemed imminent. It is not overly dramatic to say that the world held its breath until, at the last minute, Khrushchev decided not to push his luck. The Soviets agreed to remove the missiles if the United States promised not to invade Cuba.

The Dominican Republic

The United States has sent forces to the Dominican Republic several times. In 1907, the two countries signed a treaty giving the U.S. the right to collect Dominican taxes and customs. President William Taft sent troops to the island to dislodge a corrupt leader and oversee new elections. A few years later, American troops were back, protecting the island from a possible German attempt to establish a naval base there during World War I. More importantly, however, President Woodrow Wilson sent troops into the Dominican Republic to maintain internal security. While Cuba and the Philippines seemed to be progressing along democratic lines, Caribbean island nations remained politically unstable. Although Wilson said he wanted to "teach the South American republics to elect good men," he established a military occupation that oversaw no elections.

When Warren Harding became president, he began the withdrawal of American forces from the Dominican Republic in 1922. Supervised elections were held in 1924 and the Marines left, although the Americans retained control over customs revenue to relieve the republic's debt. A civil war soon broke out, however, and the Marines went back in 1927. They stayed until President Franklin Roosevelt announced his Good Neighbor Policy in 1934, in which the U.S. agreed with the Montevideo Conference resolution against intervention. The realization that the Americans were militarily supreme in this hemisphere ended the traditional argument that control over Caribbean nations guarded access to the Panama Canal.

The Dominican Republic came under the dictatorship of Raphael Trujillo, who was succeeded after his assassination in the early 1960s by Juan Bosch. When Bosch was overthrown in 1963, President John Kennedy withdrew American diplomatic recognition and financial support, which he had made available through his Alliance for Progress, a Latin American Marshall Plan to stabilize the economies of Latin American countries. Another civil war in 1965 saw the arrival of 21,000 American Marines and airborne troops, sent by President Lyndon Johnson. This met with a negative response by the Organization of American States, which Johnson finally convinced to agree to an Inter-American Peace Force. The Americans, who provided the largest part of that force, favored a military junta with an openly anti-communist stance, although the group was not democratically elected. Finally, through the efforts of the Organization of American States, fair elections were held in 1965 and 1966 and the troops were removed. American economic aid returned and the communist threat, real or imagined, receded.

El Salvador

The United States showed little interest in El Salvador prior to the 1970s, when reform movements rebelled against a coalition of the upper class and the military. When the military began using death squads to suppress the revolt, President Carter cut off U.S. aid. Moderate military officers attempted to institute some reforms by staging a coup in 1979, but they failed. In 1980, Jose Napoleon Duarte returned from exile to the presidency and tried to quiet both the extreme right and left. However, in time he had to lean more heavily on the military, and soon the repression returned. Carter again cut off aid to Duarte, then reinstated it because of a strong revolutionary offensive. The struggle turned into a long, low-intensity fight that killed thousands on both sides and ruined what had been one of Central America's strongest economies. President Reagan sent in forces to aid Duarte in putting down the rebellion, but succeeded only in pushing more people into the rebels' camp. After a nullified election in 1982, Duarte was finally reelected president in 1984. He seemed to have widespread support, but he could not institute the land reforms so desperately needed. The military resumed the death squads, and the right wing took power in the elections of 1989, continuing the death and destruction.

Guatemala

By the 1940s, the United Fruit Company of Boston owned 42 percent of the land in Guatemala. In 1944, a reform-minded revolt overthrew the government, and in 1951 Jacobo Arbenz Guzman was elected to the presidency. He and his wife Maria set out to improve the educational and health conditions of the country's poor. Arbenz planned to confiscate a quarter-million acres of land from United Fruit, though he offered to pay for it. The administration of President Dwight Eisenhower, however, became convinced that this was a pro-communist action. No proof of communist collaboration existed, but in 1954 the Eisenhower administration acted (without the cooperation of the Organization of American States) by ordering the Central Intelligence Agency (CIA) to train a group of disaffected Guatemalans. Arbenz turned to the Soviet Union for arms, and that proved to Eisenhower that communism was in the neighborhood. The CIA-trained force invaded and overthrew Arbenz, executed his followers, and stopped the reform movements. The leader of the coup, Carlos Castillo Armas, made himself dictator and established a three-decade string of strongmen in power.

Hispaniola

The island of Hispaniola, site of Spain's first colony in the New World, was later divided into two nations: Haiti in the west and the Dominican Republic in the east. Both nations have had their share of internal troubles, and no other nation has been occupied by the United States as much as these two.

Haiti became an independent nation in 1803 under the leadership of Toussaint L'Ouverture. It remained independent throughout the nineteenth century, but with a long string of increasingly corrupt leaders. Haiti was unable to repay foreign loans, and U.S. President Woodrow Wilson was forced to intervene to forestall possible European intervention. When negotiations failed and President Guillaume Sam was assassinated in July 1915, U.S. Marines landed and occupied Port-au-Prince. The United States impounded tax revenues, and demanded the right to appoint tax officials and policemen. The Haitians rather reluctantly agreed, and the United States kept troops in the country for 19 years. A constitution was adopted in 1918, but it provided for little more than an American-backed dictator. More dictators followed, further impoverishing the country for their own benefit. In the early 1990s a president was elected, but the military forced his exile. In 1994, American troops were once again in Haiti to maintain order, break up a corrupt police force and military, and oversee new elections.

The Dominican Republic, established after a revolution against Haiti in 1844, was also the site of many dictators and much corruption. Almost constant revolution had indebted the nation to many European countries, and President Theodore Roosevelt intervened to forestall the arrival of European forces. Roosevelt entered into an agreement with Dominican President Morales whereby American officials would collect customs duties and take the responsibility of distributing them to the country's creditors. By 1911, the country was financially solvent and public works were being constructed. It was too good to last; in 1911 the president was assassinated, and the country returned to factional infighting. When the Dominican government rejected President Wilson's attempt to return to the original peaceful era, Wilson sent in troops and ordered the establishment of a military government, run by an American navy captain. For six years, the navy ran the government, with no hint of Dominican involvement.

President Coolidge removed American forces, and Franklin Roosevelt's Good Neighbor Policy, along with the formation of the Organization of American States (OAS), established freedom of action in Latin American countries. In 1965, however, President Lyndon Johnson sent American forces back into the Dominican Republic, claiming a possible Communist takeover in the wake of a 1963 revolution. With minimal OAS support, a compromise government was installed and the 21,000 U.S. forces were withdrawn.

Nicaragua

Nicaragua has probably seen more American intervention than any other Latin American country. When the United States learned that Britain had acquired possible rights to a canal site in the 1840s, the former acted to gain an equal share. Cornelius Vanderbilt convinced the Nicaraguan government in 1848 to cede transportation rights to the country's waters to the United States. When one of Vanderbilt's employees killed a Nicaraguan, a local protest was sparked, ending in an American bombardment of the port of Greytown. The arrival in 1855 of William Walker, an idealist American reformer, again brought American attention to the Nicaragua. In an attempt to bring democracy to the country, Walker worked with some of the local political factions and Vanderbilt to conquer Nicaragua. Foolishly, he ceded mineral and land rights to American business interests, who in turn aided in his overthrow in 1857. In 1912, the United States supported the assumption of power by Adolfo Diaz, who offered his country as an American protectorate. When the Nicaraguans rebelled at this decision, American troops landed to protect his regime. American banks and business interests owned much of Nicaragua, including 51 percent of the railroads, and they advanced Diaz more loans in 1913 in return for the rest of the rail system. Secretary of State William Jennings Bryan negotiated the Bryan-Chomorro Treaty (ratified in 1916), which gave the United States the rights to build a canal through Nicaragua (rights that are still retained). By this time, the country was almost exclusively under American control.

U.S. Marines stayed in Nicaragua through the middle 1920s, until President Calvin Coolidge ordered their return. Within a few weeks, fighting flared up, and the Marines were back. The major opponent to a negotiated settlement was Augusto Sandino, who led a guerrilla operation out of the mountains for years. American forces were harassed continually by the Sandinistas, costing hundreds of lives on both sides. American public opinion finally demanded the Marines' withdrawal in 1933, at which point Sandino laid down his arms and negotiated with the Nicaraguan government. Its American-trained national guard, under the direction of American-educated Anastasio Samoza, immediately took Sandino prisoner and executed him. The military now in his power, Samoza seized control of the government in 1936; with American assistance, he stayed in power until the 1970s, when his corruption and greed proved too much for the people. A guerrilla movement fashioned after the Sandinistas of the 1920s and 1930s was reborn and carried on a brutal resistance to Samoza. In 1979 he was forced from power and into exile. While the American Congress debated an aid package to the bankrupt nation, the revolutionaries appealed to Cuba, and the promised elections were postponed. Under President Ronald Reagan, the United States openly and later covertly supported the "Contra" movement against the Sandinistas, but with little positive outcome. Finally, Oscar Arias Sanchez of Costa Rica offered a peace plan, which began to have good results. The American-backed Contras, unable to win in the field, finally won in the peace talks and elections of the late 1980s.

Panama

American relations with Panama have usually been close, but sometimes stormy throughout the twentieth century. Theodore Roosevelt was active in assisting the Panamanians in winning their independence from Colombia in 1903, using a timely naval and marine force to bar the reinforcement of Colombian troops. Within hours of its independence, the United States recognized the new country, and within days had arranged to build a canal through the country at a price less than that demanded by Colombia. The negotiator for Panama was Phillipe Bunau-Varilla, a Frenchman who had a financial stake in the canal and who had secretly financed the revolution. He named himself ambassador to the United States and negotiated a treaty before any Panamanian representatives arrived in Washington. This treaty gave the United States sovereign rights in the canal zone, a strip of land 10 miles wide from Atlantic to Pacific. In the administration of President Jimmy Carter, new treaties were negotiated to return the zone to Panama in 1999, but even now, disagreement over control remains. In President Ronald Reagan's administration, the United States sent troops into Panama to unseat dictator Manuel Noriega, who was accused of trafficking in illegal drugs.

After the establishment of formal relations with Latin American countries upon their declarations of independence in the early 1800s, American relations with the rest of the hemisphere steadily deteriorated. The Monroe Doctrine, formulated to meet a onetime potential threat, by accident became the dominant feature in hemispheric relations. The United States often tried to assist Latin American countries, but usually wound up aiding the more corrupt factions (with which U.S. companies cooperated) to the detriment of the majority of the population. U.S. companies have consistently dominated Latin American economies, and through this, their governments. Intentions that often began as beneficial turned into local corruption and massive poverty. The American determination to resist communist expansion in the post-World War II era often made bad matters worse: The United States would aid any corrupt dictator who took an anti-communist stance. The vast majority of people in the affected countries suffered privation, persecution, and death, while a small number of powerful people benefited from the close relations with the power of the U.S. military and businesses.

See also Caribbean, European Occupation of; Panama, U.S. Invasion of.

References: Collins, John, *America's Small Wars* (Washington, DC: Brassey's, 1991); LaFeber, Walter, *The American Age* (New York: Norton, 1989); Smith, Gaddis, *The Last Years of the Monroe Doctrine, 1945-1993* (New York: Hill & Wang, 1994).

181

LIBYA, ITALIAN OCCUPATION OF

The region that encompasses modern Libya has rarely been independent throughout recorded history. In early historic times, the region comprised two provinces, Cyrenaica to the east and Tripolitania to the west, both stretching along the southern Mediterranean coastline. Tripolitania was originally settled by the Phoenicians and later dominated by Carthage until the Third Punic War, after which it came under Roman control. Cyrenaica, however, started out under Greek influence (thanks to Alexander's conquest) before falling under Roman sway. The migration of the Vandals out of northeastern Europe via Spain in the fifth century provided the next occupation, followed by their defeat at the hands of the Byzantine general Belisarius a century later. The region was then conquered by Moslem Arab armies in the seventh century, becoming a tributary of either Constantinople or Damascus. Sicilian Normans conquered Tripoli in 1146 but lost it to another Moslem force in 1321. The Knights of St. John occupied Tripoli in the first half of the sixteenth century, then lost it to corsair leaders from the Ottoman Empire in 1553. From that point, although the Barbary Pirates based at Tripoli exercised great independence, they were officially subject to the Ottoman Empire and its government in Constantinople.

The Turks exercised a loose suzerainty over the provinces until 1911, when they had to face an interested European power, Italy. Only recently unified, Italy, therefore, was late getting into the colonization game in which Europeans had been engaged for some years. Frustrated by France in an early attempt to dominate Tunisia (the nearest African land to the Italian peninsula), Libya seemed the next most logical target. Picking Libya was a clever move, since by 1911 the Ottoman Empire based in Turkey was the weakest power in Europe and heavily committed to crises elsewhere, primarily in the Balkans. Italy, through the turn of the twentieth century, had been claiming a greater share of Libya's international trade and was granted a *pro forma* sphere of influence which other European powers assumed would someday lead to political and military intervention.

In 1911, Italy trumped up the charge that the Ottomans had been arming the Libyan tribesmen. Demanding the right to commit troops to protect her interests, Italy received no answer from the Ottoman government. Italy, therefore, declared war, sent its navy to bombard Tripoli, and landed 35,000 troops. Against little resistance, the Italians occupied not only Tripoli but the coastal cities of Tobruk, Al Kumns, Darnah, and Benghazi. The 5,000 Turkish troops withdrew inland in the face of these attacks. In the countryside, Ottoman officers Enver Pasha and Mustafa Kemal rallied the interior tribes around a religious focus. Unfortunately, the flare-up of another Balkan war obliged the Turks to make a quick peace with Italy in order to deal with more pressing problems. In the Treaty of Lausanne of October 1912, the Ottoman Empire recognized Tripolitania and Cyrenaica as independent. Italy at once announced its annexation of both provinces.

Starting in the 1840s, the Libya region had been home to a growing religious sect, the Sanussi, which blended some of the conservative Whahabi teachings with some Sufi mysticism.

The Sanussi became the dominant population in Cyrenaica (and to a lesser extent in Tripolitania and the southern province of Fezzan). They were theoretically under the religious direction of the caliph in Constantinople, who retained jurisdiction in the Libyan religious *shahira* courts after the Ottoman withdrawal. Unfortunately for the Italians, the religious courts and the civic courts often intertwined, and Italian attempts to separate the two brought about intense religious resistance, led by the Sanussi. Further confusing the mix were the bedouins, who recognized no government and wanted none.

The Sanussi got off to a successful start by expelling the initial Italian troops in the Fezzan and southern Cyrenaica. A victory in April 1915 over an Italian column along the coast near Sirt netted them a large stock of weaponry. A follow-up invasion of Tripolitania failed owing to bedouin resistance to any nationalist movement. The conflict increased when, in 1915, Italy joined the Allied powers against Germany, Austria, and Turkey. The Sanussi leadership decided to support the Central powers in order to hurt the Italians. Aided by Turkish guns and advisors, the Sanussi movement strengthened, but was badly beaten during an abortive attack on Egypt in April 1916. Control of the Sanussi movement fell to Idris, grandson of the founder of the sect and a supporter of the Allies. A cease-fire resulted which changed neither the Italian claims nor those of the local population. Still, Idris was recognized as amir of interior Cyrenaica, at least until war's end.

The Allied leaders in the Versailles Conference recognized Italian sovereignty over the region. The Italian government took a more peaceful tack in the postwar era, perhaps because its army controlled only the coastal strip. Tripolitania and Cyrenaica were treated as separate provinces and the Fezzan was declared a military district. Recognizing Idris's strength in the interior, Italy confirmed him as amir of Cyrenaica with virtual freedom of action in the interior. The next few years were peaceful enough, although the Italian authorities had little idea of what their goals for the colony were. With Idris being cooperative in the east and there being no coherent resistance movement in the west, the Italians had no real pressure to be either repressive or progressive.

Some western cohesion began to form, thanks to an outside influence, the Arab nationalist Abdar Rahman Azzam of Egypt. He convinced the two leading Tripolitanian leaders, Baruni and Ramadan as Suwaythi, to demand an independent state to be called Mistata. Negotiations bogged down over how much land was to be included in this country, but the resistance movement did call for a National Congress to meet and formulate goals. No one course of action could be formulated, and a number of factions traveled to Rome to appeal to the home government. In the meantime, a new Italian governor, Count Giuseppe Volpi, took office in Libya with a much more hard-line attitude. He took direct military action against the various nationalist factions, all of which collapsed. With no clear leader to oppose Italy in the west, the leftover rebels appealed to Idris in Cyrenaica, offering him the position of amir in Tripolitania. As the Sanussi sect had never been very strong in the west and Idris was smart enough to know that any aggression on his part would spoil the peace his people had been enjoying, he did not reply to the offer. Over time, however, he apparently thought it best that someone stand up for the faith, resist the infidel occupiers, and attain freedom for the entire region. He accepted the offer in November 1922 and immediately left for Egypt to avoid Italian reprisal.

Idris's decision coincided with a major change in Italy: Benito Mussolini's accession to power. Although not in favor of colonies in his younger days, he was of a different mind now that he was in power. He developed a goal to restore Italian glory by reoccupying the old Roman Empire, of which Cyrenaica and Tripolitania were part. He continued to support Volpi's military actions against any resistance and the Italians fairly quickly subdued Tripolitania and the Fezzan. Cyrenaica, however, resisted.

With Idris in Egypt, command of Sanussi forces fell to an aging warrior named Umar al Mukhtar. Never commanding more than a few thousand men, Mukhtar headed for the hills to conduct a guerrilla campaign against the Italians. In this he was spectacularly successful. Italian forces were largely recruited from the Italian colony of Eritrea in the horn of Africa, but were commanded by Italian officers. After 1929, an officer appeared who could fight Mukhtar the only way possible. Rudolfo Graziani implemented the tactics the British had developed in their successful suppression of the Boer guerrilla movement in South Africa: Round up the population into camps, slaughter livestock, and harass the guerrillas with fast-moving columns and airpower (an addition to the British weaponry against the Boers). He also constructed a barbed wire barrier, extending 320 kilometers southward from the coast, to deny Mukhtar access to supplies or manpower from Egypt. Graziani's campaign lasted two years and came to a successful conclusion in 1931 with the fall of the last Sanussi stronghold in the Al Kufrah region and the capture and execution of Mukhtar.

Once pacified, Italy merged all Tripolitania, Cyrenaica, and the Fezzan into one colony, Libya, the name it had been called under Diocletian's reign during the Roman Empire. The colony was divided into four provinces, each under the control of an Italian-appointed governor and all under the direction of a governor-general. A lot of money flowed into the colony in order to modernize the coastal region. Roads, railroads, public works, port expansion, and irrigation all became part of the Italian plan to modernize the colony and make it a home for Italian immigrants, called "the Fourth Shore." Mussolini began in 1938 with an initial shipment of 20,000 people to settlements along the coast, with more in 1939 and 1940, until over 110,000 people had been settled, making up some 12 percent of the population. While most were intended to be olive growers, Mussolini hoped to have a half-million immigrants in Libya by the 1960s, to exploit the natural resources of the colony. Medical care and an upgrade in sanitary conditions benefited much of the Libyan population, but once away from the coastal strip, there were few improvements. People in the interior were virtually ignored, except to crush out any last vestige of the Sanussi.

As World War II approached, nationalists hoped for an Italian defeat which would pave the way for independence. The futile League of Nations' response to Mussolini's invasion of Ethiopia in 1935 did nothing to bring hope from that quarter. When war finally broke out in Europe in September 1939, the Libyan nationalists met in Alexandria, Egypt, to see if they could overcome their differences. Other than agreeing on Idris as the representative for all of them, the Cyrenaicans and Tripolitanians could cooperate on little else. When Italy committed troops to the European conflict in June 1940, another meeting of Libyans in Cairo confirmed Idris as the one national leader and authorized him to negotiate with the British on how to assist the war effort against Italy. The provision that a Sanussi government would be acting with the British did not set well with the Tripolitanians, who preferred the term "Libyan" rather than "Sanussi." The British would make no promises about the postwar peace settlement, but Idris linked onto them as the best hope for liberation. Five Libyan battalions were raised and fought well under British command.

With German and Italian troops expelled from North Africa in May 1943, the British set up a caretaker administration and began training civil servants. Free French forces occupied the Fezzan, leading to fears that the French colony of Chad might try to incorporate the province. No final decision on the status of Libya was reached until the end of the war. The United Nations proposed a national trusteeship, while the Soviet Union proposed dividing the country into three trusteeships to be overseen by the Soviets (Tripolitania), the French (Fezzan), and the British (Cyrenaica). When the French proposed that the country be given back to Italy (in spite of an Allied agreement made at the Potsdam Conference), Britain suggested immediate independence. The UN finally appointed a four-power commission to consider the situation. They found Libyans wanted independence but remained very tied to their provinces rather than to a single nation. The Commission decided that the Libyans were not ready for independence yet; Idris declared Cyrenaica an independent amirate in 1949. After much debate and no agreement over a multi-power trusteeship, the UN finally called for a single government for the country, to be given national status in 1952. "In the final analysis, indecision on the part of the major powers had precipitated the creation of an independent state and forced the union of provinces hitherto divided by geography and history" (State Department).

The UN appointed Dutch diplomat Adrian Pelt to try to bring order out of chaos. He appointed a Council of Twenty-one, made up of seven members from each province. They finally created a National Constituent Assembly to comprise equal representation from the three provinces. The Assembly met for the first time in November 1950 and agreed to create a constitutional monarchy, with Idris as the first king. By the time the constitution was finished in October 1951, the French and British administrators in the Fezzan and Cyrenaica had already withdrawn and turned their duties over to local personnel.

The country struggled economically at first, but the discovery of oil in 1959 changed that. However, disagreements over the distribution of wealth and a growing pan-Arabic movement created enough internal unrest to make foreigners wary. During the 1967 Arab-Israeli War, oil company offices were looted and the small Libyan Jewish population was forced into exile. Although not a major player in the Arab coalition, Libya did contribute oil wealth to the reconstruction of those states hurt in the war against Israel. Idris tried throughout his tenure to foster a more nationalistic feeling, but never succeeded. In 1969, the monarchy was overthrown in a military coup led by Colonel Muammar al-Qaddafi, who took a much more anti-Western stance for his country and remains in power as of this writing.

References: Metz, Helen Chapin, *Libya, A Country Study* (Washington, DC: Government Printing Office, 1989); Shaw, Stanford J., and Ezel Kural Shaw, *History of the Ottoman Empire and Modern Turkey*, vol. II (Cambridge: University Press, 1977); Wright, John L., *Libya: A Modern History* (London: Croom Helm, 1982).

182   MacArthur, Douglas

Douglas MacArthur was born into a military family in Little Rock, Arkansas, on 26 January 1880. His father, Arthur, had distinguished himself as a Union general in the Civil War. MacArthur attended the U.S. Military Academy at West Point, where he graduated first in his class (with the highest marks ever received by any student) in 1903. He was commissioned as a second lieutenant of engineers, and spent the years prior to World War I in a number of teaching and staff positions, including one in Asia with his father and another with President Theodore Roosevelt. He was attached to the General Staff in 1913, and participated in the Vera Cruz expedition the following year.

When the United States entered World War I in April 1917, MacArthur was with the General Staff. He assisted in organizing the multistate National Guard "Rainbow" Division and was its chief of staff when it was assigned to France in October 1917. He served as a general during the Aisne-Marne campaign, commanding the Eighty-fourth Brigade at Saint-Mihiel (September 1918) and the Meuse-Argonne offensive (October-November). MacArthur was one of the last commanders who believed in leading from the front, and he received 10 medals for valor and two Purple Hearts. He stayed with the occupation forces until his return home in April 1919.

He became one of the youngest superintendents of the Military Academy in June 1919, and initiated a number of reforms: codification of the Honor Code, revitalization of the curriculum, emphasis on the humanities and social sciences in addition to the "hard" sciences, and an attempt to end hazing. With these reforms, MacArthur tried to reflect the citizen-soldier nature of the cadets. His term ended in 1922, when he received orders for the Philippines. Three years later, he returned to the United States to command the Third and Fourth Corps areas in Baltimore and Atlanta, respectively. He faced the problems of a shrinking military budget, obsolescent equipment, decrepit facilities, and a low reenlistment rate. Three years later, in 1928, he was again in the Pacific as commander of the Department of the Philippines.

MacArthur held the position for two years; in November 1930 he was back home as army chief of staff. His experience in the Corps commands served him well in dealing with the even more stringent military budgets of the Great Depression. Though he focused on plans for industrial mobilization and manpower procurement, he became involved in political affairs as well. In 1932 he convinced President Herbert Hoover to send in troops to dislodge from Washington, D.C., the Bonus Army, a group of

General Douglas MacArthur wades ashore in the Philippine Islands 1944. (photograph no. 531424; "General Douglas MacArthur wades ashore during initial landings at Leyte, Philippine Islands, 10/1944," Record Group 111: Records of the Office of the Chief Signal Officer, 1860–1982; U.S. National Archives and Records Administration, College Park, MD).

World War I veterans attempting to gain promised compensation from the government.

He was again in the Philippines in 1935, preparing that colony's military for independence. When he was ordered home in 1937, before the job was completed, he chose instead to retire and stay in Manila. He was appointed field marshal in the Philippine Commonwealth Army. When war against Japan seemed imminent in 1941, MacArthur was recalled to active duty and appointed commander of U.S. Army Forces in the Far East (USAFFE). As Philippine field marshal, MacArthur seemed to overestimate the abilities of his adopted army, while underestimating those of the Japanese. He learned the difference on 8 December 1941 when most of his air forces were destroyed on the ground by surprise Japanese attacks. He ordered a fighting withdrawal from Japanese forces landing on the island of Luzon,

and spent the next months preparing defensive positions on the peninsula of Bataan and the island of Corregidor. He begged the U.S. government for reinforcements and supplies, but the decision in Washington was to write off the Philippines and defend Australia. MacArthur was ordered by President Franklin Roosevelt to evacuate the islands with his family and staff, which he did on 11 March 1942. U.S. and Filipino forces held out another month before their surrender to the Japanese.

In Australia, MacArthur was named supreme commander of the Southwest Pacific area. He secured the lines of communication by denying the Japanese a base at Port Moresby. With limited troops and support craft, he repulsed the southward Japanese advance across the island in the summer of 1942. He and Admiral Chester Nimitz, commander in chief, Pacific Fleet (CINCPAC), worked on strategy to carry the war to Japan's home islands. With army troops and naval support, MacArthur would stage leapfrogging amphibious landings along the western Pacific islands to bypass or cut off large Japanese fortifications or troop concentrations. The strategy proved successful as American forces worked their way northwest up the Solomon Island chain, New Guinea, and to the Philippines. Nimitz meanwhile used Marines and naval forces to "island hop" across the Central Pacific while bypassing major Japanese strong points. Both commanders used the growing American superiority in aircraft and warships to neutralize Japanese bases.

MacArthur argued for an early invasion of the Philippines to fulfill his promise to the population that he would return. He overcame the Washington leaders who preferred an assault on Formosa, and ultimately Roosevelt and the Joint Chiefs of Staff agreed. MacArthur and Nimitz carried out a joint operation in October 1944 against the island of Leyte. It was a daring plan, attacking the central section of the archipelago to split the defenders occupying the islands and prevent them from unifying. MacArthur was then able to separately defeat both Japanese forces. He spent the remainder of the war organizing the redeployment of his troops to areas outside his command and launching cleanup operations against the bypassed Philippine islands. On 2 September 1945 he presided over the Japanese surrender aboard the USS *Missouri*.

Now a five-star general, MacArthur was appointed military governor of occupied Japan. He transferred his headquarters to Tokyo on 8 September and began his oversight of the political and economic reconstruction of Japan. As supreme commander of Allied Powers, he directed the writing of a new Japanese constitution. His term as governor can be described as one of the most efficient, honest, and fair of all military occupations in history. Much of Japan's condition today can be attributed to the foundations MacArthur laid in the late 1940s.

On 25 June 1950, North Korean forces attacked across the 38th parallel into South Korea. The weak nature of the South Korean military and the inability to provide sufficient reinforcements left only the southeastern corner of the country around the port city of Pusan uncaptured. MacArthur was named supreme commander of United Nations forces on 8 July. Because his immediate goal was to prevent the fall of Pusan, he brought in as many American troops as were available from occupation duty in Japan, and ordered American airpower to support the forces trapped in what came to be called the Pusan Perimeter. While the area was being held by General Walton Walker's Eighth Army, MacArthur argued for newly arriving forces to be committed to a daring assault of Inchon, the harbor city serving the South Korean capital of Seoul on the peninsula's west coast. Again, MacArthur's influence and persuasiveness overcame Pentagon objections, and the landings on 15 September were an overwhelming success.

The United Nations expanded the scope of the conflict by permitting South Korean forces (closely supported by U.N. forces) to invade North Korea. The Communist Chinese government threatened intervention if their border was threatened, but MacArthur was certain they were bluffing; at Wake Island in mid-October, he assured President Harry Truman that the Chinese would not get involved. On 25–26 November 1950, the Chinese launched a massive assault that pushed U.N. forces south of the 38th parallel. Just as he had underestimated the Japanese in the late 1930s, he repeated his mistake in 1950. From the beginning, MacArthur and Truman could not agree on a strategy. Truman feared an escalating conflict that could become World War III, while MacArthur continued to believe in the goal of liberating North Korea. In addition to their personal differences, MacArthur began to publicly criticize Truman's foreign policy; he felt his hands were tied because the president would not let him increase air operations, blockade Chinese ports, deploy Nationalist Chinese forces from Formosa, or possibly use nuclear weapons. Truman began to depend on the advice of Field Commander General Matthew Ridgeway, and MacArthur's continuing critical tone and public statements released against orders proved too much for the president. MacArthur was relieved of his command on charges of insubordination on 11 April 1951. He returned to an adoring public and talk of the presidency in 1952, but his increasingly aggressive statements soon turned the public against him. He retired to West Point where (as he informed Congress of an old ballad common at the academy) he, like other old soldiers, faded away.

See also New Guinea, Japanese Invasion of; Pacific Islands, U.S. Conquest of; Philippines, Japanese Invasion of the; Philippines, U.S. Invasion of the; South Korea, North Korean Invasion of (Korean War).

References: Carver, Michael, ed., The War Lords: Military Commanders of the Twentieth Century (Boston: Little, Brown, 1976); Costello, John, The Pacific War, 1941–1945 (New York: Quill, 1982); Manchester, William, American Caesar (Boston: Little, Brown, 1978).

MANCHURIA, JAPANESE INVASION OF (1904) (RUSSO-JAPANESE WAR)

183

In the late nineteenth century, the major powers of the world divided the coast of China into spheres of economic influence. Great Britain, France, Germany, Holland, Russia, and Japan had exclusive rights to trade within their spheres. In 1899 the United States convinced these countries to cooperate, rather than compete, by the adoption of the Open Door policy. Under this plan, the whole of China would be open for free trade, and the spheres of influence would gradually fade away.

The Russians held sway in Manchuria, and had laid claim to Vladivostok as the base for its Pacific fleet since the 1860s. After the Sino-Japanese War ended in 1895, Russia, France, and Germany put diplomatic pressure on Japan to withdraw from Korea, which the Japanese did under protest in what seemed to them a humiliating concession. Therefore, Russia and Japan were already unfriendly when in 1903, Russia failed to give up its rights in Manchuria, in which Japan was intensely interested. Russia promised to leave within six months, but instead reinforced its army, strengthened fortifications, and sent additional warships. This buildup not only contradicted their Open Door promises, but also gave the impression of threatening Korea, where Japan was keeping its pledges to open trade. Anticipating that Russia might prove recalcitrant, in 1902, Japan had entered into a defense agreement with Great Britain stating that either country would come to the aid of the other if one of the countries were fighting two enemies. The Japanese estimate seemed accurate, because the Russians refused to negotiate in good faith and continued their military buildup. By January 1904 the Japanese were convinced that further negotiation was futile, so military action seemed the only alternative.

On 8 February, the Japanese navy struck the Russian fleet based at Port Arthur. Torpedo boats sneaked into the harbor, flashing Russian signal lights, then torpedoed two battleships and a cruiser. The next day the Japanese fleet stood outside the harbor and shelled the ships and facilities inside. The Russian ships that survived did little to challenge the Japanese. The Russian fleet commander realized his sailors were not well trained in fleet maneuvers, so he decided not to challenge the Japanese in open water. Leery of the coastal defenses around Port Arthur, the Japanese hesitated to draw close enough to the harbor to destroy the Russians. Both sides kept a close eye on each other for some months.

The Japanese army was in action as well, landing on 8 February at Inchon, Korea, then moving slowly up the peninsula over bad roads. Russian resistance was minimal, and the Japanese worked their way northward toward the Yalu River, the border between Korea and Manchuria. The Japanese staged a brilliant river crossing in April, which established them in Manchuria and forced the Russians to withdraw into the mountains. With bridges under their control, the Japanese were prepared to invade Manchuria from Korea as well as from the south. Japanese forces landed on the peninsula above Port Arthur on 5 May and rapidly sealed off the city from reinforcements. Japan hoped to capture Port Arthur easily, as it had done in the war against China 10 years earlier, but the Russians mounted a much stouter defense. More and more men were committed to breaking through the well-prepared Russian defenses, and the siege lasted months longer than anticipated. Trench networks, massed artillery barrages, machine guns in defensive positions—all brought about massive loss of life on both sides in a preview of France in World War I.

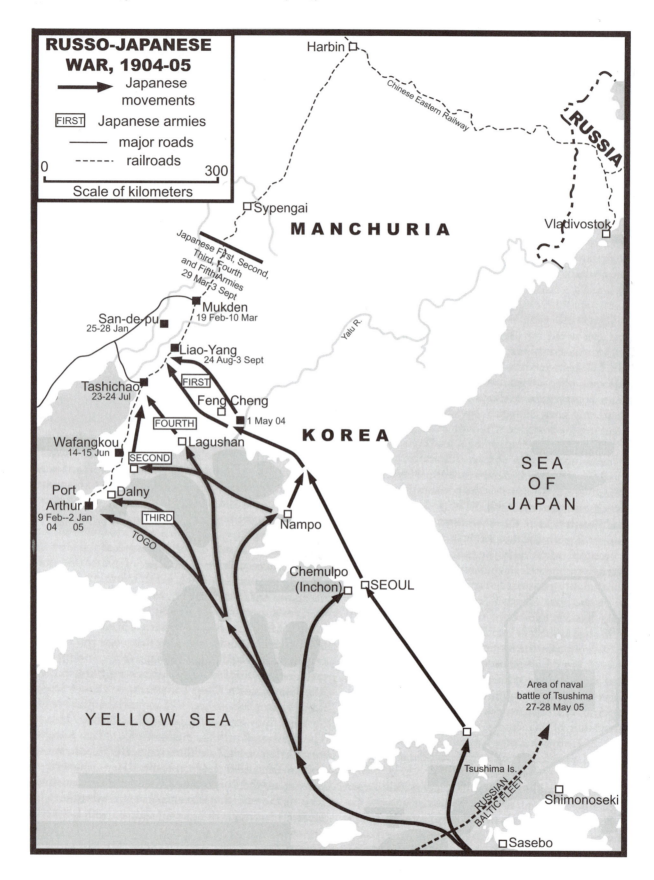

RUSSO-JAPANESE WAR, 1904-05

→ Japanese movements

FIRST Japanese armies

── major roads

╌╌ railroads

0 ──────── 300

Scale of kilometers

Harbin

Chinese Eastern Railway

RUSSIA

Sypengai

MANCHURIA

Vladivostok

Japanese First, Second, Third, Fourth and Fifth Armies 29 Mar-3 Sept

Mukden
19 Feb-10 Mar

San-de-pu
25-28 Jan

Liao-Yang
24 Aug-3 Sept

Yalu R.

Tashichao
23-24 Jul

FIRST

Feng Cheng
1 May 04

FOURTH

KOREA

SEA
OF
JAPAN

Wafangkou
14-15 Jun

Lagushan

SECOND

Port Arthur
9 Feb-2 Jan
04   05

Dalny

THIRD

TOGO

Nampo

Chemulpo
(Inchon)

SEOUL

Area of naval battle of Tsushima
27-28 May 05

YELLOW SEA

Tsushima Is.

RUSSIAN BALTIC FLEET

Shimonoseki

Sasebo

In Port Arthur the Russians were in deep trouble. The fleet attempted to attack the Japanese in August but failed, leaving the navy demoralized. The Russians anchored their ships and moved the sailors to man the defenses on land. Through the fall of 1904, the Japanese continued their assaults on the city, inflicting and receiving huge casualties but edging ever closer. By December the highest point overlooking the city was in Japanese hands, and artillery placed there finished off the Russian fleet. The defenders, though killing more men than they themselves were losing, realized that there was no hope of relieving forces from the north. The Russian commander surrendered the city on New Year's Day 1905. The Japanese fleet could now go home for repairs, and the Japanese army marched north to aid their comrades near Mukden.

In late February, the largest battle started. Just over 200,000 Japanese attacked almost 300,000 Russians in a double envelopment at Mukden. It was a long, slowly developing battle with poor leadership decisions and hesitant generalship on both sides. On 9 March the Russians withdrew the bulk of their forces before being surrounded, leaving behind 90,000 casualties. More aggressive action on the part of the Japanese would have captured the entire force, but the Russians re-formed 40 miles northward. It made little difference, as no more major land fighting took place.

The final major battle of the war took place at sea. In October the Russian government had dispatched the Baltic fleet to sail to Vladivostok and engage the Japanese fleet. It finally arrived in late May 1905 and ran into the Japanese in the narrows between Japan and Korea at Tsushima Strait. The Russian fleet was old and manned by inexperienced crews, and the battle was no contest. The more modern Japanese ships pounded the Russians in a day-long battle that cost the Russians 34 of their 40 ships, either sunk or captured. The Japanese capital ships all took heavy damage, but only three destroyers were sunk. After the devastation at Port Arthur and Tsushima, the Russian navy virtually ceased to exist.

The Japanese were winning every battle, but financially they were unable to continue fighting. Though the Russians lost every battle, they continued to send men and supplies 5,000 miles down the Trans-Siberian Railway to keep the war going. The news of the losses, however, fomented discontent in Moscow, and the Russian government had to deal with revolutionary rumblings. Since the outbreak of the war, American President Theodore Roosevelt had offered to mediate, but both sides refused. After Tsushima, the Japanese secretly informed him that if he would again offer his services, the Japanese would agree to talk. The Russians agreed to Roosevelt's new proposal on the condition that the Japanese publicly agree first, and that only representatives of the belligerents conduct negotiations. Roosevelt provided a venue for talks in Washington, D.C., in August 1905, but after no progress was made he moved them to the more comfortable site of Portsmouth, New Hampshire. Though not allowed into the conferences, Roosevelt worked behind the scenes to assist the negotiations, and he was able to bring them to a successful conclusion. The Portsmouth Treaty recognized Japan as the premier power in Manchuria, but the Japanese had to return captured Russian ships and not demand reparations payments from Russia. For his efforts Roosevelt received the 1905 Nobel Peace Prize.

The Japanese people were not happy with the treaty. They felt that they deserved more spoils of war, and blamed Roosevelt for the shortfall. Coupled with anti-Japanese legislation passed in California, relations between the two countries became strained. Roosevelt's personal influence in both California and Tokyo defused the situation, but he saw that Japan was a new power to be reckoned with. His dispatch of the American battleship fleet on an around-the-world cruise in 1907 was aimed primarily at flexing American muscles in the Pacific while concluding the Root-Takahira Agreement, which spelled out American and Japanese spheres of influence in the Pacific region. The two nations remained fairly friendly until the 1930s.

The war itself was an omen for any soldier who would see it. Observers in Manchuria, especially German General Staff members, saw the devastating effects of machine guns, and incorporated the knowledge into their military views. What almost everyone failed to see, however, was that the improved defensive capabilities called for new offensive doctrine. Many of the elements of destruction the Europeans inflicted on one another in World War I made their appearance in Manchuria.

In Russia, the czarist government's days were numbered. The poor handling of the war by both generals and governmental leaders, plus the cost in money and men, encouraged the radicals in Moscow and St. Petersburg to preach revolution. The 1905 uprising, which the government suppressed, laid the groundwork for the revolution of 1917, again brought on by military disasters. In Japan, the people and government reluctantly accepted the peace, but they savored a taste of victory that encouraged future military ventures. Their success in 1904–1905 over the heavily favored Russians reinforced the longstanding traditions and training of the Japanese military and established a tradition for their navy. Their introduction to the modern industrialized world a mere 50 years earlier made the Japanese realize they needed raw materials that their country did not possess and, whether it was in Manchuria or elsewhere, military action was a proven method of gaining them. Participation in World War I to obtain German possessions in the Pacific, as well as aggression in the 1930s in China, can both be traced to the successes of 1904–1905.

See also Korea, Japanese Invasion of (Sino-Japanese War); China, Japanese Invasion of.

References: Coonaughton, R. M., *The War of the Rising Sun and the Tumbling Bear* (London: Routledge, 1991); Walder, David, *The Short Victorious War* (London: Hutchinson, 1973); Warner, Denis, *The Tide at Sunrise* (New York: Charterhouse, 1974).

184 MANCHURIA, JAPANESE INVASION OF (1931)

The Open Door policy had been the economic rule in China since 1899: All nations had equal access to China's markets. When the Russians would not cooperate in Manchuria, Japan went to war with them in 1904, and from 1905, Japan held a predominant economic position in Manchuria, within the Open Door framework. In 1914, Japanese forces captured the Shantung Peninsula, which the Germans had leased from the Chinese. With Japanese troops on Chinese soil, Japan attempted to press its advantage by making demands of the Chinese government that would give the Japanese virtually exclusive economic and political rights in China. Their Twenty-one Demands were withdrawn under American pressure, but the Japanese focus was now on China as its future. Poor in natural resources but rich in population, Japan saw its huge neighbor to the west as a source to be controlled and tapped.

This idea faded a bit in 1922. In Washington, D.C., Japan signed the Nine-Power Agreement, which recognized the Open Door policy and guaranteed Chinese territorial integrity. The Japanese government was dominated by moderates, but the moderates were increasingly in conflict with army leaders, who demanded expansion. The uneasy relations between government and army strained to the breaking point in 1930 when the prime minister was assassinated, and in 1931 when a group of officers narrowly failed in staging a coup d'état.

In China, the disorganized governmental situation brought on by revolution finally solidified in 1926 under the leadership of Chiang Kai-shek and his Nationalist Party, the Kuomintang. Chiang began moves designed to assert more Chinese control over Manchuria, which was, after all, Chinese territory. When the warlord in control of Manchuria was assassinated in 1928, his son took power and openly allied himself with Chiang. Growing Chinese influence in the area would certainly be detrimental to Japanese plans for growth.

To further complicate matters, Japan was also having trouble with the United States, which had initiated the Open Door policy, and since then had friendly relations with China. Should hostilities begin, a potential Japanese-American rivalry would ensue. Further, a longstanding Japanese agreement to unilaterally restrict emigration to the United States was overturned by the U.S. Congress in 1924, when an immigration policy was established specifically excluding all Asian immigration. The Japanese took that as an insult. Negotiations over the next few years eased tensions somewhat, but the growing strength of the military in Japan at the expense of moderates in the government kept the wound from healing.

In September 1931 the Japanese army decided to act independently of their government before more international concessions might be negotiated. On the night of 18 September, an explosion on the Japanese-owned and operated South Manchurian Railway destroyed a mere 31 inches of track. The culprits have never been identified, but most authorities assume the Japanese did it, perhaps through the agency of Chinese radicals. Whoever was responsible, Japan blamed the Chinese; the Japanese immediately moved on the Manchurian capital at Mukden, seizing the city and its 10,000-man garrison. Japanese troops soon captured other strong points along the railroad right-of-way.

Chiang's government in Nanking appealed to the United States and the League of Nations for assistance, but found little. The powerless League called for Japanese withdrawal, but had no ability to force such a move. The U.S. secretary of State Henry Stimson hoped to deal with the moderates in the government and not provoke the Japanese military, but the government was losing or had already lost control over the army. The League sent an investigation commission to look into rival Japanese and Chinese claims, but the Japanese were already seizing all of Manchuria, which they accomplished by February 1932. In that month the state of Manchukuo declared its independence from China and was soon recognized by Japan as a sovereign state. It was, in fact, a puppet government full of Japanese.

In October 1932, the Lytton Commission presented to the League its report stating that the people of Manchuria did not want the new Manchukuo government and calling for Japanese troop withdrawal. The report did not call for complete Japanese withdrawal, however, but for a Sino-Japanese treaty to address the interests of the two nations and an outside peacekeeping force to maintain order. When the League accepted the report and voted that none of its members should recognize the independence of Manchukuo, Japan resigned from the international organization. Shortly afterward, Henry Stimson announced the Hoover-Stimson Doctrine, which declared that the United States would not recognize any political act that came about as the result of aggression.

Japan ignored both the League and the United States, and proceeded to launch attacks into China past the Great Wall. Japan also invaded Shanghai to force China to withdraw its boycott of Japanese goods. Both acts of aggression ended with Japanese withdrawal, but all of Manchukuo and the eastern provinces of Mongolia were under Japan's thumb. China lost large numbers of soldiers during the fighting, but proved too difficult for the Japanese to completely overpower. Chinese resistance so angered the Japanese that they engaged in widespread looting, rapine, and destruction. Condemnation of Japan for violations of the Nine-Power Treaty or the 1928 Kellogg-Briand Pact, which outlawed the use of force as national policy, fell on deaf ears.

Japan exploited the coal, iron, copper, lead, and other natural resources of Manchuria/Manchukuo and used the territory as a release valve for population pressures, but the new country did not prove as economically stimulating as Japan had hoped. To feed its growing nationalist and militarist desires, Japan needed to conquer all of China, and attempting that goal was not long in coming.

See also China, Japanese Invasion of; Manchuria, Japanese Invasion of (1904) (Russo-Japanese War).

References: Nish, Ian, *Japan's Struggle with Internationalism* (New York: K. Paul International, 1993); Tuchman, Barbara, *Stilwell and the American Experience in China* (New York: Macmillan, 1971); Yoshihashi, Takehiko, *Conspiracy at Mukden* (New Haven, CT Yale University Press, 1963).

185   MESOPOTAMIA, BRITISH INVASION OF

When the Ottoman Empire joined the Central Powers in November 1914, British interests in the Persian Gulf were threatened. For decades, Great Britain had had close ties with the sheikhs of the area, maintained extensive economic interests, and controlled piracy in the gulf. The gulf sheikhs had little love for the Ottoman government and welcomed British forces who landed at Bahrain late in October. British oil interests in Persian Arabistan have been traditionally viewed as the main reason the British went into

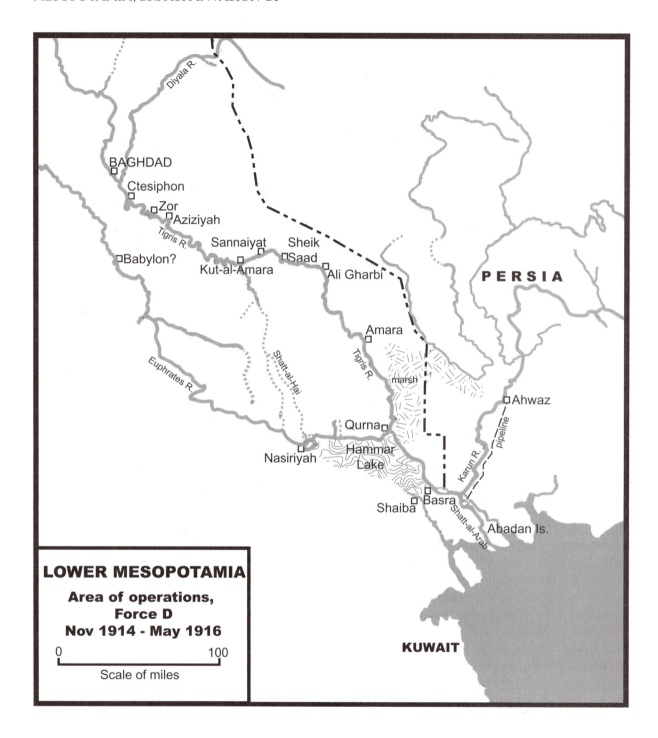

LOWER MESOPOTAMIA

**Area of operations,
Force D
Nov 1914 - May 1916**

0   100

Scale of miles

action in Mesopotamia, but economic invest-ments and a fear that the Turks would raise a holy war that would spread to India were equal, if not greater, motivations for making war against the Turks.

British forces landed at the mouth of the Shatt-al-Arab on 6 November, and quickly made their way to the port city of Basra. Few Turkish troops were stationed in the region, and within a few weeks British and Indian troops consolidated the river and approached Kurna, where the Tigris and Euphrates meet to form the Shatt-al-Arab. By March 1915, Indian Expeditionary Force D occupied Shaiba (south of Basra), Kurna, and Ahwaz in Persian Arabistan, where the oil pipeline to Basra originated. These actions were really all that was necessary to maintain a secure British hold, but the government in India, abetted by an aggressive new commander in Mesopotamia, General Sir John Nixon, could not leave well enough alone. Using the British government's fear of a holy war, Viceroy Hardinge and General Sir Beauchamp Duff, the commander in chief in India, urged an expansion of the campaign so that the local Arabs would not rise up, thinking the British were afraid to advance. This rationale moved the secretary of state for India in London to authorize advances up both the Tigris and Euphrates. These actions took place in the heat of summer, and the British and Indian troops suffered immensely, but that mattered little to Nixon, the commander in Mesopotamia. When the Sixth Division captured Amara, 450 miles up the Tigris from Basra, the lure of Baghdad, another hundred miles upriver, was too much for India and London to resist.

There was a problem, however. The Force D troops moved ever farther up the rivers, but received supplies less often because their transport craft had farther and farther to go, and they were given no additional river craft. With less materiel, both military and medical, to sustain themselves, their ability to hold the territory they had captured became increasingly tenuous. Both General Nixon in Mesopotamia and the government in India later claimed to be aware of the need for more transport, but no one informed London. In October 1915, the British Cabinet decided that the capture of Baghdad would be immensely prestigious and would help to erase the disappointment of the recent failure at Gallipoli. The British government, therefore, approved an attack on Baghdad, not knowing that Nixon had grossly overestimated the ability of his own forces and underestimated those of the Turks.

In November, the Sixth Division attacked Ctesiphon, just outside Baghdad, and was unable to break the Turkish defensive lines. The resultant retreat, with greater-than-expected casualties and too little transport, forced incredible suffering on the troops involved. Within a week they were surrounded by Turkish forces at Kut-al-Amara. The Turks penned the Sixth Division inside the town, dug into extensive defensive positions astride the Tigris, and succeeded in stopping British attempts

to break the siege. General Charles Townshend, Sixth Division commander in Kut-al-Amara, maintained a solid defense through April 1916, but was ultimately forced to surrender because of a lack of food. At 149 days, Kut marked the longest siege in British history.

The British government took control of the campaign away from India and began to provide the necessary materiel to maintain a defensive position for the rest of the war. Reports on the suffering of the troops led to a Parliamentary Commission, which condemned the Indian leaders but punished no one. Conditions improved in Mesopotamia, but defense was the order of the day until the new commanding general, Sir Stanley Maude, convinced the General Staff to let him advance. Sure of his supplies and transport, Maude retook Kut in February 1917, then captured Baghdad in early March. After resting his troops through the summer, Maude secured the area around Baghdad in the fall, but a bout of cholera took his life in November. His replacement, General W. R. Marshall, completed Maude's consolidation and reached the Mosul oil fields as the war ended in November 1918.

The British had hoped throughout the war to incorporate Mesopotamia into their empire, either directly or as a sphere of influence. Secret negotiations in 1915 with the French and Russians had divided the Ottoman Empire among the three countries. The early publication of that agreement by the Soviets, when they left the war in November 1917, showed that British and French claims in the secret negotiations did not match promises made to the Arabs to secure their support against the Turks; thus, Britain was forced to deny any claims to the area. However, the British received Mesopotamia as a mandate in the Treaty of Versailles at the end of the war, so they maintained a presence in the country afterward, and in the 1930s presided over its change into modern-day Iraq. Britain left the country to its own devices after World War II.

See also Turkey, British Invasion of.

References: Barker, A. J., *The Neglected War* (London: Cassel 6k Co., 1967); Davis, Paul, *Ends and Means: The British Mesopotamia Campaign and Commission* (Rutherford, NJ: Fairleigh Dickinson University Press, 1994).

MIDWAY, JAPANESE INVASION OF

186

Like the Spanish Armada in 1588 and the Battle of Britain in 1940, the battle for Midway resulted in the repulse of an attempted invasion, the failure of which was significant. By early June 1942, the Japanese seemed virtually invincible, having invaded and conquered targets throughout the South Pacific in the hectic seven months following the bombing of Pearl Harbor. Only a setback at the Coral Sea, northeast of Australia, in early May 1942 marred an otherwise perfect record. The thrust to Midway was designed to set up a base in the Central Pacific from which the Japanese could invade Hawaii, thus denying the United States its most strategic anchorage and its forward base of operations against Japan. If Hawaii fell, the U.S. Navy would have to operate out of San Diego on the West Coast, adding almost 2,000 miles to any Pacific action. Indeed, Hawaii's fall might be the blow necessary to convince the United States to make peace with Japan.

In order to mount an invasion of the Hawaiian Islands, however, Japan needed Midway. An invasion fleet escorted by a large naval force, including four of Japan's largest aircraft carriers, seemed sufficient for the job. The Americans had only one significant advantage: They had just succeeded in breaking the Japanese military code and knew exactly what their intentions were. Admiral Chester Nimitz concentrated his forces to meet the threat. He could muster three aircraft carriers and their support ships, hoping that surprise and the broken code would give him the edge. On 3 June, American scouting aircraft based at Midway located the Japanese fleet and launched an attack of heavy bombers and torpedo bombers, neither of which inflicted any damage. The following day proved to be the day of decision, marked by a series of missed opportunities that could have tipped the balance to either side. The Japanese struck first by launching an air attack on the facilities at Midway. When the bombers returned to rearm for another attack, Japanese commander Chuichi Nagumo learned of the presence of the American aircraft carriers. Most

of the bombers were ready for the next attack on the island when the crews were ordered to rearm with torpedoes in order to attack the American fleet. While the changeover was taking place, American carrier-based aircraft arrived. American torpedo bombers attacked from several directions, but failed to score any hits and lost a majority of its force to antiaircraft fire and swarming Japanese fighter planes. An apparent disaster for the Americans proved to be just the break they needed. By forcing the Japanese fighter cover to low altitudes to deal with the torpedo bombers attacking at wave-top heights, the Americans coerced the Japanese to leave the skies above their fleet unprotected when American dive bombers arrived. They were able to strike the Japanese virtually unhindered, and succeeded where every other assault had failed. Within a matter of minutes, three of Japan's four aircraft carriers were hit and sinking. The fate of the Japanese operation was sealed; unable to launch the aircraft necessary to destroy the American fleet or to recover all the fighter planes that had been airborne, their strike force was crippled. Bombers from the remaining carrier launched a strike against the American fleet and badly damaged the USS *Yorktown*, but it was too late. American follow-up attacks on 5 June finished off the last Japanese carrier and inflicted damage on other capital ships. Without the strength of its airpower, Japan could not hope to launch a successful landing on Midway, so the fleet was ordered home.

The Japanese scored the final success in this battle when one of their submarines finished off the *Yorktoum*, but it was small consolation. The destruction of four of Japan's best aircraft carriers and, just as importantly, the death of so many of their most experienced pilots were losses they would not overcome. The battle for Midway became the turning point of World War II in the Pacific. Japan was now unable to mount major offensives, obliged instead to consolidate its gains. The United States, on the other hand, could go on the offensive and keep Japan reeling. Two months after Midway, U.S. Marines would land on Guadalcanal and begin the strategy of island-hopping that ultimately brought them to a position from which they could invade Japan itself.

Had Japanese timing been a little better concerning their ability to locate the American fleet, vital time would not have been lost rearming their aircraft and exposing themselves to American attack. If they had been able to launch the first strike instead of receiving it, the battle almost certainly would have gone the other way, and the U.S. Navy would have been crippled to the point of impotence. Japan would have easily captured Midway because the garrison there could not have put up a significant defense, and Hawaii would have followed within a matter of months. One can only conjecture what the United States would have done in this situation, but the outcome of the war and the shape of the postwar world would almost certainly have been radically altered.

See also England, Spanish Invasion of (Spanish Armada); Britain, Nazi Invasion of (Battle of Britain); New Guinea, Japanese Invasion of; Pacific Islands, U.S. Conquest of.

References: Layton, Edwin, *"And I Was There": Pearl Harbor and Midway—Breaking the Secrets* (New York: Morrow, 1985); Lord, Walter, *Incredible Victory* (New York: Harper & Row, 1967); Prange, Gordon, *Miracle at Midway* (New York: McGraw-Hill, 1982).

187   MUSSOLINI, BENITO

The man who would lead Italy into World War II was certainly a product of his time. Born in 1883, Benito Mussolini was raised by a socialist father and a schoolteacher mother in a time when Italy was virtually stagnant while the rest of Europe was progressing. While Britain, France, and Germany built or expanded empires and also enjoyed industrial growth, Italy remained a poor agricultural community with few resources. It also had little luck in trying to gain resources in futile expeditions against African nations like Ethiopia. Class struggles within Italy did nothing to promote progress, and a frustrated nation looked for answers.

Mussolini followed in both his parents' footsteps, becoming an elementary schoolteacher and a socialist. He spoke and wrote forcefully about Italy's needs, but could not do much himself until World War I started. Although officially allied to Germany, Italy remained neutral at the war's outset. Indeed, Italy's main quarrel was with Germany's chief ally, Austria-Hungary. Italy had long desired the cities of Trento and Trieste at the head of the Adriatic Sea and, as Austria was busy fighting a war with Serbia, it seemed an opportune time to grab some land. Mussolini loudly argued for Italian involvement in the war on the Allied side, and it alienated his socialist comrades. He was fired from his job of editing the socialist newspaper *Avanti*, so he started his own paper and pushed for Italian expansion. When the Allies convinced Italy to unite with them in 1915, Mussolini joined the army and fought until 1917, when he was wounded.

Although the war brought Italy territorial concessions, it also brought a huge loss of life and continued political controversy. In March 1919, Mussolini started the Fascist party, blending conservative nationalist desires with socialistic government control of the economy. The Fascists promised all things to all people: a tradition of greatness, a change from disordered politics, yet protection from the radical change of communism, opportunity for the poor, wealth for the nation, justice for the oppressed, and, above all, order. His party grew rapidly until, in October 1922, his supporters marched on Rome and demanded control of the government. While this march may not have been the reason for the change, King Victor Emmanuel asked Mussolini to organize a new government.

Calling himself "Il Duce" (the Leader), Mussolini used a growing military to maintain himself in power and crush opposition. He seemed to the outside world to be good for Italy. The economy improved and unemployment was low, but at a cost of freedom. The law and order he promised appeared, as did the decline in political corruption, since there was only one political party. He was recognized in the United States by *Time* magazine as Man of the Year and will forever be remembered for the tribute: "He made the trains run on time." He also urged Italian women to have more children, for he needed soldiers to rebuild the Roman Empire.

Empire-building lay at the heart of his dream to bring about Italian greatness, and he focused on the Mediterranean area as his bailiwick.

In 1935, he flaunted international condemnation by invading Ethiopia, a fellow member of the League of Nations. The only supporter for this expedition was Adolf Hitler in Germany, and the two concluded an alliance in November 1936, after which Mussolini stated that from that time forward, "the world would revolve around a Rome-Berlin axis" (hence, the Axis powers of World War II). The two countries cooperated in aiding Francisco Franco in the Spanish Civil War, and Mussolini stood by while Hitler occupied Austria and Czechoslovakia. He did, however, feel that Italy was losing some of the limelight, so he invaded Albania to remind the world that Italy was not to be ignored, and to try to influence Balkan politics.

It was Italy's role in World War II, and Mussolini's continuing attempts to gain territory for his empire, that brought about his downfall. Mussolini ordered the invasion of Greece and Egypt, but had to beg Hitler for assistance when his armies were defeated in both arenas. Mussolini, the senior dictator, became the alliance's junior partner once the war started. He watched his troops do little more than support German armies in North Africa and then in Sicily. When the Allied forces captured Sicily in August 1943, Mussolini's days were numbered. The British invasion of the toe of Italy in early September brought about Mussolini's forced abdication, then imprisonment. Hitler ordered Otto Skorzeny, his commando leader, to rescue his Italian partner from prison, then set him up in a puppet government in the north of Italy until the war's end. In the spring of 1945 Mussolini fled for Switzerland, but did not reach the border before he was captured by Italian resistance fighters, who assassinated him and his mistress, then took the bodies to Milan for public display.

Mussolini was somewhat of an aberration in Italian politics, a ruthless strongman who dominated a nation that seems to revel in provincial differences and rivalries. No one before or since has exercised such power in Italy, but neither has anyone brought about such shame and despair. The Italian countryside and economy were badly damaged by World War II, and Mussolini was the man who took Italy into that war. Unlike Hitler, he had no racial policies to condemn him, but like his German partner, he left behind a legacy that some in Italy to this day would like to see restored.

See also Albania, Italian Conquest of; Hitler, Adolf.

References: Collier, Richard, *Duce!* (New York: Viking, 1971); Dabrowski, Roman, *Mussolini: Twilight and Fall* (New York: Roy Publishers, 1956); Gallo, Max, *Mussolini's Italy*, trans. Charles Markmann (New York: Macmillan, 1973).

188 NEW GUINEA, JAPANESE INVASION OF

Because the island of New Guinea lies due north of Australia, its location, rather than any inherent value, made it a target for Japanese aggression at the opening of World War II. The Japanese military spread across the western Pacific, and forces under the command of Major General Horii landed on the north shore of the island early on 23 January 1942. As they had experienced elsewhere, the invaders had little serious opposition from the defenders—in this case, badly outnumbered Australian troops. The Australians withdrew inland, closely pursued by Japanese troops. At the same time, the Japanese secured the major port of Rabaul on the island of New Britain, the real prize in the area. New Guinea was to serve mainly as a guard for the bastion soon created at Rabaul. Japanese control of Rabaul made Allied possession of New Guinea vital as well, and brought the immediate attention of Douglas MacArthur, commander of Allied military forces in the Southwest Pacific.

The Japanese quickly secured the northern half of the island and established bases at Hollandia, Wewak, Madang, and Lae. Their next target was Port Moresby, on the southern shore of the peninsula forming the eastern part of the island. It was lightly defended and would have provided little difficulty for the invaders, but they never arrived. The Japanese force sailing around the eastern tip of the island met a combined American and Australian naval force in early May in the Coral Sea. The battle was unique at the time: It was the first naval battle in which ships never engaged one another. Instead, the battle was fought totally between carrierborne aircraft and enemy ships. For three days, opposing bombers and fighters fought it out over enemy shipping, and both sides lost roughly equal numbers of ships, including one aircraft carrier each. The battle was a tactical draw but a strategic victory for the Allies; it was the first time the Japanese failed to accomplish a mission. The Japanese fleet turned back and the tide of war began to turn.

Despite the naval reverse, the Japanese continued their victories on land, driving into the Owen Stanley mountain range that forms the spine of the island. They drove the Australians back across the range and to within a day's march of Port Moresby, but could go no farther. Reinforcements of Australian and American troops massed along the southeastern part of the island, and the jungle through which the forces fought took its toll on the ill-supplied Japanese army. American aircraft arrived and achieved air superiority, which meant that Allied troops could get supplies into the mountains without the need of "humping" it through the extremely rugged terrain. The Australians fought their way back up the mountains via the Kokoda Trail, entering the town of Kokoda along the ridge line on 2 November 1942. The large numbers of dead attested to the Japanese inability to survive the jungle on meager supplies, and the Allied offensive picked up some steam heading down the northern slope. By January 1943, the Australian and American troops owned the northern shore of Papua, thereby controlling the eastern half of the island.

Through 1943 the U.S. Navy and Air Force dominated the area. The battle of the Bismarck Sea in March 1943 was a victory of American airpower over Japanese attempts to bring in large numbers of reinforcements. As Rabaul was sealed off by American sea power, MacArthur made plans to work his way west along the New Guinea coast. With the use of large landing craft, MacArthur's forces made a series of landings along the coastline, capturing Japanese-held towns and airfields. They captured or bypassed all four Japanese strongholds, and established a bomber base on the island of Biak, just off New Guinea's northwest corner. This not only gave them complete aerial domination over New Guinea, but also provided a major base for MacArthur's

ultimate goal, the U.S. invasion of the Philippines. By the autumn of 1944, the focus of the war shifted to the Philippines and farther north, but New Guinea was not completely quiet. Japanese forces fought on even after the war was over; not until mid-September 1945 did they receive word of the atomic bomb drops and their government's surrender. The Japanese left behind a somewhat positive legacy with the construction of good roads and airfields, which remain in use even now. Though thousands of Japanese, Australian, and American soldiers were killed in fighting on the island, relatively few natives were directly involved. Over 50,000 were conscripted as laborers for the Allies, but very few engaged in fighting. However, they suffered from Japanese atrocities and sustained collateral damages from the fighting. The lack of men in native villages forced some hardships on those who remained, but the increased contact with the outside world had some positive side effects on the hitherto isolated island. Tribal enmity, already on the wane as more Europeans came to the islands in the first part of the century, diminished even more. The discovery of manufactured goods changed the lives of many in the mountains, for good or ill. In some remote areas, the first arrival of parachute-borne equipment seemed heavensent, and the rise of what came to be known as the "cargo cults" lasted for some years after the war (some natives became convinced that certain rituals would bring back the largesse provided from the sky).

See also MacArthur, Douglas; Philippines, U.S. Invasion of the.

References: Mayo, Linda, *Bloody Buna* (Garden City, NY: Doubleday, 1974); Robinson, Neville, *Villagers at War* (Canberra: Australian National University, 1981); Vader, John, *New Guinea: The Tide Is Stemmed* (New York: Ballantine, 1971).

NORTH AFRICA, U.S. INVASION OF

189

Once the United States entered World War II in the wake of the 7 December 1941 Japanese bombing of Pearl Harbor, Hawaii, and the German declaration of war on 10 December, President Franklin Roosevelt was anxious to begin operations against the Axis powers. At the Atlantic Conference the previous August, he and British Prime Minister Winston Churchill agreed that if and when the United States became engaged in the war, Hitler's Germany would be the primary enemy, no matter who else became involved. Soviet foreign minister Molotov also urged rapid American action, hoping to get early relief from the Nazi invasion of his country. Roosevelt was anxious to commit troops before the end of 1942, but could not agree with the British on the target. Britain balked at the idea of an early invasion of France, afraid of the consequences if it failed. They preferred an assault on northwestern Africa to aid their campaign against German and Italian troops. Most American planners disagreed with the idea, but when an invasion of France was definitely rejected, they reluctantly accepted. The operation was code-named Torch.

Before the invasion could begin, two major questions had to be answered. The first: Where should the landings take place? British planners wanted landings that would quickly seize Tunis and Bizerta, the major German supply points in Tunisia; therefore, landings should take place as far east along the Algerian coast as possible. The Americans thought that idea too risky. Without a strong hold on the area around Gibraltar, Spanish air forces or Italian shipping might block that supply route and leave the landing forces cut off. An invasion on the Atlantic coast around Casablanca would provide the safest supply situation, the Americans argued. The main problem with that idea was that Tunis was more than a thousand miles away.

The second question: Would the defending French troops accept the orders of Marshal Petain in Vichy or aid the Free French movement led by Charles de Gaulle in London? The Allied planners did not want to kill French troops if they were going to cooperate, but they did not want to send troops ashore into stiff resistance if they were not. The American diplomatic representative in Algeria sounded out some friendly French officers, who asked for a meeting with a ranking American. General Mark Clark, second in command of the landing operation, went ashore in late September to assist the French with their decision. They would not totally commit to aiding the landings, partly because Clark would give them little or no solid information on when and where they would take place. Thus, when the troops went ashore, they were still unsure of their reception.

The Anglo-American planning staff finally chose to land at multiple sites, ranging from Casablanca on the Atlantic coast to Oran and Algiers along the Mediterranean coast. The French commanders onshore had been told that General Giraud, a well-known officer close to Petain but anti-German, would take command of French forces once the Americans landed. The units that landed on 8 November were either totally American or an Anglo-American mix, as the appearance of British units alone might not be acceptable to the French. The landings met sporadic resistance, but most of it was either token fighting to ensure the safety of officers' families in France, due to slow communications concerning the landings, or because of the occasional pro-Vichy officer who wanted to fight. The ranking French officer in North Africa, Admiral Darlan, ordered all resistance to cease on 10 November. Darlan was given overall political command of the French forces and Giraud was to command the military, but Giraud took over complete control when Darlan was assassinated on Christmas Eve by an anti-Vichy gunman.

The landings were a complete success. Against scattered opposition, the Americans lost less than 2,000 men killed and wounded, and were in a strong position to begin advancing eastward to support the British, who were now driving German commander Erwin Rommel before them through Libya. The British forces involved in Operation Torch, the First Army, moved along the coast road while the Americans basically paralleled them to the south. Within three days after the original landings, the British captured Bougie (120 miles east of Algiers) and Bone (270 miles east of Algiers). On 17 November the British ran into serious German opposition at Tabarka, halfway from Bone to Tunis. Meanwhile, Rommel was in full retreat from Montgomery's advance, but that actually helped the Germans by placing them closer to their supply bases, while the British moved farther away from theirs. In January heavy rains fell, which halted the British advance and gave Rommel time to reorganize. Pressed from east and west, he was able to use his interior lines of communication to quickly transfer troops from one front to the other, holding the British at the defensive lines he had built at Mareth while striking a devastating blow to the Americans at Kasserine Pass in mid-February.

It was not enough. The Americans recovered and won a clear victory at El Guettar, and the British flanked the Mareth Line at the end of March. Rommel became ill and left in March for Germany; he did not return. General von Armin, left in command, could do little more than delay the inevitable, and the British capture of Tunis and Bizerta in early May sealed the Germans' and Italians' fate. Many of them were able to withdraw from those ports before they fell, but some 250,000 Germans and Italians were taken prisoner, making the total North African loss to the Axis almost one million men over two years.

With all of North Africa in Allied hands, the next step was to decide where to go next. When Prime Minister Churchill and President Roosevelt met in Casablanca in January 1943, they agreed on two things: The Allies would accept only unconditional surrender from the Axis powers, and the next offensive should be the invasion of Sicily. North Africa served only as a supply base for the rest of the war, and reverted to its prewar situation after 1945. France returned to Algeria and tried to reassert its authority after the fiasco with the Vichy government, but the seeds had long since been sown for an independence movement.

See also Algeria, French Occupation of; Egypt, Italian Invasion of; France, Nazi Invasion of; Sicily, Allied Invasion of.

References: Brewer, William B., *Operation Torch* (New York: St. Martin's Press, 1985); Gelb, Norman, *Desperate Venture: The Story of Operation Torch* (London: Hodder & Staughton, 1992); Howe, George E., *Northwest Africa: Seizing the Initiative in the West* (Washington, DC: Office of the Chief of Military History, 1957).

NORWAY AND DENMARK, NAZI INVASION OF

190

In the immediate wake of the Nazi conquest of Poland, very little happened. The fall and winter of 1939-1940 were known as the sitzkrieg, or phony war; although war had been declared, little fighting took place. The only major military action was the Soviet invasion of Finland from November 1939 through March 1940. Germany and the Soviet Union had signed a nonaggression pact in August, so the Germans did nothing when the Soviets occupied the Baltic states of Lithuania, Latvia, and Estonia, and attacked Finland. However, the aggression provoked British interest in the Finns. Britain's attention to Scandinavia, along with the German need for iron ore from Sweden, made war over Norway inevitable, and war over Norway ushered in the German occupation of Denmark.

Germany imported some 10 million tons of iron ore from Sweden, 90 percent of which was shipped through the Norwegian port of Narvik. At first, Germany felt that a neutral Norway was sufficient to maintain the flow of ore, but when Britain approached Norway about the possibility of traversing its territory in order to aid Finland, Germany saw the potential for trouble. There was also the problem of the German navy. In World War I they had been bottled up by a very effective British blockade of Germany. If, in 1940, the Germans could gain control of Norway, this would give them an extended coastline and make a British blockade much more difficult. The final motivation came from a visit to Berlin in December 1939 from Major Vidkun Quisling, former minister of defense in Norway. Fearful of a Communist victory in Finland and a possible Communist spread through Scandinavia, Quisling told Hitler that he headed up the Norwegian National Socialist Party and would do what he could to assist the Germans protecting his country from the Soviets. Though Quisling was somewhat mentally unbalanced and his claims imaginary, the idea piqued Hitler's interest. He ordered the German High Command to begin studying the possibility of invading Norway.

In February 1940 the British gave Hitler a potential reason for mounting the assault. A

German heavy cruiser Blucher which was sunk during the German assault on Oslo, 9 April 1940.

German ship, the *Altmark*, was in Norwegian waters carrying British POWs captured from British ships destroyed in the South Atlantic by the German pocket battleship *Graf Spee*. A British cruiser and two destroyers stopped the *Altmark* in a fjord along the south Norwegian coast on 16 February and demanded to board and search it. When the *Altmark* grounded in an attempt to get away, the British boarded it and released 299 prisoners. This was not only a violation of Norwegian neutrality, but an illegal boarding under international law. It provided the provocation Hitler needed to decide finally on the invasion.

The Germans were not depending on Quisling's questionable aid. They planned to assault Norway in five places, from Oslo in the southeast to Narvik in the far north. A combination of landings along the coast and paratroop operations against airfields would seize the key cities. Norwegian defenses were few and not well directed. Even when informed of the imminent German invasion, the Norwegian government refused to mobilize, thinking it would be provocative. When Norway finally decided to mobilize on 8 April, the government directed it to be done secretly; the forces were informed by letter to report for duty. Since the invasion was scheduled for 9 April, this was of little use. Other than a few coastal defense vessels and a handful of fighter, bomber, and scout aircraft, Norway had little in the way of heavy weapons for their defense. A nation that had been at peace since the days of Napoleon was in no way prepared for a modern war.

The invasion took place just before dawn on 9 April 1940. The Germans met little or no resistance in four of their attacks; only the assault on Oslo experienced trouble. Coast artillery sank the German heavy cruiser *Blucher*; this convinced the troop ships to withdraw. Only when a handful of paratroopers landed against orders and captured the Oslo airport did the assault continue. It was successful by the first afternoon.

The Norwegian government fled before the German advance, and the newly appointed minister of defense attempted to mobilize Norwegian forces to resist from the interior of the country. They had little chance of holding out for long against a much larger and better equipped army. Still, they fought hard, and got some assistance from Britain and France. The British Royal Navy was successful in sinking and damaging a number of German ships and landing troops along the coast. The British chose to concentrate their efforts at the northern port city of Narvik, though they also attempted to capture the central coastal city of Trondheim. They were not prepared for the weather conditions (still snowy in much of the country) or the large numbers of German troops. Without tanks or much artillery, the British could do little more than the Norwegians. Nevertheless, the early fighting on land and the British successes at sea gave Hitler a scare; he considered withdrawing from the country within a week of the invasion. However, German forces gained control of the road network and linked up to provide a more concerted effort than the British could muster. By 1 May, British troops around Trondheim were withdrawn.

Near Narvik, British troops supported by forces from the French Foreign Legion and French and Polish chasseurs lasted a bit longer. Through May, the Allied forces in cooperation with the Norwegians managed to push German troops back. Foreign Legion amphibious landings surprised the Germans and gained some successes. British aircraft were beginning to arrive and operate from fields around Narvik. The city was captured by French and Norwegian troops on 28 May, but even as it fell, the Allies were making plans to evacuate. The Germans had launched their invasions of Holland and France on 10 May, and all military strength available had to meet this threat. The last British and French soldiers sailed away on 8 June, along with Norwegian King Haakon and the Norwegian government. A ceasefire went into effect the next day, and the Norwegian soldiers were allowed to go home.

Hitler set up a puppet government in Norway under the direction of Vidkun Quisling.

This action made his name synonymous with the word traitor in Europe, much as Benedict Arnold is viewed in the United States, and he did not long survive the defeat of Germany in 1945. With Norway under his control, Hitler could count on the iron ore shipments that Sweden continued to provide; the Swedes saved themselves from invasion by maintaining the trade. Their neutrality worked to the advantage of the Allies as well. The crews of many American bombers damaged during raids over Germany flew their aircraft to Sweden to be interned for the duration of the war.

Denmark had little role in the Norwegian operation. Knowing the Danes had absolutely no chance of putting up any sort of defense against Germany, the Danish king announced the surrender of his country almost as soon as German forces entered it on 9 April. Germany needed the country as an air base to assist the invasion of Norway, and occupied the country in a matter of hours. The ease of conquest belied the nature of the occupation, however. The Danes mounted one of the most effective underground resistance movements of any occupied country, and provided the Germans with a major headache in attempting to control it.

See also Napoleon Buonaparte; Finland, Soviet Invasion of; France, Nazi Invasion of; Poland, Nazi Conquest of.

References: Churchill, Winston, *The Gathering Storm* (Boston: Houghton Mifflin, 1948); Nissen, Henrik, *Scandinavia during the Second World War*, trans. Thomas Munch-Petersen (Minneapolis: University of Minnesota Press, 1983); Petrow, Richard, *Bitter Years: The Invasion and Occupation of Denmark and Norway* (New York: Morrow, 1974).

191 PACIFIC ISLANDS, U.S. CONQUEST OF

Even before the United States entered World War II, American President Franklin Roosevelt met with British Prime Minister Winston Churchill in August 1941 at a secret conference off the coast of Canada. At this Atlantic Conference, the two decided that no matter who should join the Axis powers, the primary enemy was Germany and all planning should take place

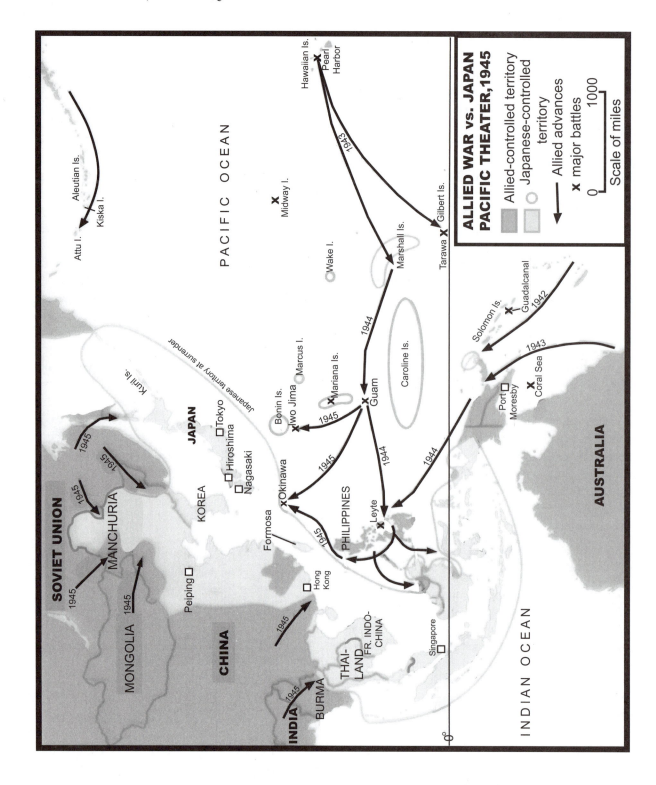

ALLIED WAR vs. JAPAN
PACIFIC THEATER, 1945

Allied-controlled territory
Japanese-controlled territory
Allied advances
x major battles

0   1000
Scale of miles

PACIFIC OCEAN

Aleutian Is.
Attu I.
Kiska I.

Midway I.

Wake I.

Gilbert Is.
Tarawa x

Hawaiian Is.
Pearl Harbor

1943

Marshall Is.

1944

Caroline Is.

Solomon Is.
Guadalcanal
1942

1943
Coral Sea

Port Moresby

Japanese territory at surrender

Kuril Is.

JAPAN
Tokyo
Hiroshima
Nagasaki

KOREA

Formosa

Bonin Is.
Iwo Jima
Marcus I.
Mariana Is.
Guam

1945
1945

1944

1944

Okinawa

PHILIPPINES
Leyte

SOVIET UNION
1945
MANCHURIA
1945
1945
1945
MONGOLIA 1945

Peiping

CHINA

Hong Kong

1945

BURMA
INDIA
1945

THAI-
LAND
FR. INDO-
CHINA

Singapore

AUSTRALIA

INDIAN OCEAN

0°

with that in mind. The policy of "Germany first" would be sorely tested when Japanese aircraft bombed Pearl Harbor in December 1941 and the United States became a full participant in the war.

As Japanese forces expanded through Southeast Asia and the Central and South Pacific, American planners began to call for more and more supplies and manpower to be diverted to the war against Japan. The postponement of a proposed invasion of France from 1943 to 1944 allowed the redistribution of American forces to the Pacific. In Washington and in the Pacific theater, however, there was little agreement on how those forces should be deployed. American General Douglas MacArthur was based in Australia after the successful Japanese invasion of the Philippines. He had promised the people of the Philippines that he would return to liberate them, and his plans were designed toward that end. But U.S. Navy leaders did not want to turn their ships over to army command or risk them in the distant waters of the Southwest Pacific. Admiral Chester Nimitz, commanding the Pacific Fleet, with the support of Chief of Naval Operations Admiral Ernest King, preferred a plan that had been developed prior to the war. Plan Orange called for action across the Central Pacific toward the Philippines. Neither King nor MacArthur seemed to concede much to the "Germany first" plan and, in planning conferences held with the Americans, the British continued to press for fewer troops to the Pacific in favor of operations in Europe.

MacArthur had a prestigious career and many friends in Washington, but he could not directly influence decisions there as long as he stayed in Australia. Thus, he had to demand as much as he could and hope for the best. Because of the navy's resistance to the idea of committing too many valuable aircraft carriers to support army operations, someone had to make the decision, and it fell to the Joint Chiefs of Staff in Washington. With a modicum of navy support, MacArthur would direct the operations of American, Australian, and New Zealand forces in the Southwest Pacific with the primary aim of regaining control of New Guinea and the Japanese-held Solomon Islands to the east. The U.S. Navy, with its Marine Corps, would go through the Central Pacific.

Before the war and after their conquests in the first six months of the war, the Japanese had fortified islands virtually too numerous to mention. Recapturing every island would be an overwhelming task, so the navy planners decided that many could be bypassed and cut off, saving valuable time and manpower. By this strategy, some of Japan's most powerful bases would prove utterly useless to them. American forces would need only to capture key islands with good airfields or anchorages in order to control an area. With the expanding U.S. submarine fleet and air superiority established with carrier-based and then island-based planes, Japanese strongholds would be denied reinforcements or supplies. Regular bombing would destroy their air forces and runways, so the strongholds would be neutralized and unable to impede American progress or assist the Japanese war effort.

The Solomon Islands

The first American offensive operation against Japan was against the island of Guadalcanal in the Solomons on 7 August 1942. The Japanese were unprepared for the landings, and U.S. Marines gained a quick beachhead. The Japanese responded with a vengeance, and the Americans learned for the first time of the tenacity and aggressiveness of the Japanese soldier. Whatever lessons army forces may have learned when the Philippines fell went unheeded, so the Marines had to deal with an enemy of unexpected ferocity. The Japanese military were trained under a strict code of conduct, the ancient Bushido warrior's code, which taught that victory was everything and surrender was not an option. Unlike troops of virtually every nation in the world, Japanese forces would not admit defeat, and fought to the death in every engagement. Prisoners were few and far between.

The struggle for Guadalcanal was one of the longest in the Pacific war. The Japanese scored an early naval victory, which forced the United States to withdraw its support of the Marines on the island. The Japanese regularly brought in reinforcements from bases farther up the

Solomon chain, and used their navy to pound American positions. Ultimately, the Americans won with a stubborn air defense and an even more stubborn force of Marines, and the island was declared secure in February 1943. Fighting in jungle conditions was a new experience for Americans, but it continued in the other battles in the Solomons. In July 1943, Marines assaulted New Georgia, northwestward up the chain, and on 1 November, the largest island, Bougainville. By Christmas, most of the airfields were captured, and by mid-January 1943, the invading marine forces were relieved by army occupation forces to finish the job. Christmas landings also took place on New Britain, home of the largest Japanese base in the Southwest Pacific, Rabaul. Three months of fighting in the jungles brought American conquest of only a third of the island, but with airfields in hand they could pound Japanese defenses and isolate the garrison. MacArthur continued his offensive by securing New Guinea, which put him in a position to plan for his return to the Philippines.

The Gilbert and Marshall Islands

As the Marines moved up the Solomons, Admiral Nimitz got his Central Pacific campaign under way. The first target was Tarawa Atoll in the Gilbert Islands, northeast of the Solomons. The landing would be unlike anything the Americans had ever attempted, since this was a small collection of coral islets surrounded by reef. The Japanese had approximately 4,800 men defending Betio, three miles long and no more than 600 yards wide. Betio was the site of the airfield, so this was the target. The Japanese had spent a year building bunkers of concrete, palm logs, and sand so well constructed that only a direct hit by the largest naval shells could harm them. Every square foot of the beaches had been zeroed in by mortars and artillery.

The landing was preceded by a three-day naval bombardment, and the Marines were in trouble from the start. Most of the landing craft could not get past the reef, and the men had to wade 700 yards across a lagoon in water up to their necks under crisscrossing machine-gun fire. Those who managed to reach the beach found themselves under intense mortar fire and unable to advance because of a seawall. For most of the first day, 20 November 1943, they were pinned down, unable to advance or retreat. Once they broke through the seawall, the Marines had to reduce each bunker, one at a time, with explosive charges placed against the concrete and through the gunports. The interlocking Japanese fields of fire made each assault extremely difficult. Within 76 hours the Americans secured the island, though the short time period belies the adversity. Only 146 prisoners were taken, most of them Korean laborers. Virtually the entire Japanese garrison had to be killed, at a cost to the Marines of 1,000 dead and 2,000 wounded. Nearby Makin Island, another atoll in the Gilbert group, was easier to capture, costing the lives of another 66 soldiers while defeating more than 400 Japanese defenders.

The Tarawa landing became a proving ground for future amphibious operations. From now on, longer preinvasion bombardments would take place. The Marines who fought here, already veterans of jungle warfare at Guadalcanal, learned how to fight on coral sand with no cover, lessons that were put to good use shortly. A mixed marine and army force landed at Majuro and Kwajalein atolls in the Marshall Islands, north of the Gilberts. The Japanese had not been able to reinforce this island group because of heavy losses in other areas, and the Americans made fairly short work of this island chain. Landings began on 30 January 1944, and the largest island, Kwajalein (site of the world's largest lagoon), was declared secured by 4 February. The Americans attacked Eniwetok, the westernmost atoll in the Marshalls, on 18 February, and the islands of the atoll were declared secured by 23 February. Control over the Gilberts and Marshalls gave the United States secure bases for the most difficult of operations to come: the Caroline Islands and the huge Japanese base at Truk. As it turned out, that invasion proved unnecessary. An American carrier raid against the harbor in February destroyed so many Japanese aircraft and ships that the bulk of the fleet stationed there was withdrawn farther west to the Palau Islands. Truk—indeed, the entire Caroline group—was bypassed.

The Mariana Islands

With the outer rim of Japanese defenses pierced or controlled, the inner ring came under attack in the summer of 1944. The Marianas contained fine harbors and airfields, and included Guam, an American possession since 1898 that was lost to the Japanese at the start of the war. Possession of islands here would put the U.S. Air Force within range of the Japanese home islands. Also, the connection between Japan and its bases in the Southwest Pacific would be severed. To avoid this, the Japanese prepared for a huge naval battle, which they were confident they could win if they could bring their capital ships into contact with the American fleet. The naval battle took place, but the tradition of Tsushima in the Russo-Japanese War, or even the surface victories off Guadalcanal, was not to be repeated. The aircraft carrier was the dominant player and, since Midway, the United States owned the advantage in these ships.

To avoid tipping his hand as to the location of the next strike, Nimitz used 15 aircraft carriers to strike everywhere at once. They supported MacArthur's landings on the north coast of New Guinea, struck Truk again, and then struck the Palaus. The carriers hit targets at Saipan and Guam in the Marianas and made a side trip to Iwo Jima, halfway to Japan, to interdict any reinforcements from the home islands. Saipan was a target of the first landings on 15 June 1944. When the landings began, the Japanese imperial navy knew just where the American fleet was, and they gathered their strength for the major clash they envisioned.

What ensued—later called the Battle of the Philippine Sea—became more popularly known as the "Marianas Turkey Shoot." Rather than leave the landing force unprotected, U.S. Admiral Raymond Spruance stayed near Saipan and waited for the Japanese fleet to come to him. With advance warning provided by submarines, the Americans were prepared to protect their ships with swarms of fighter aircraft when Japanese bombers and fighters arrived on 19 June. Of the 430 planes onboard his five heavy and four light carriers, Japanese Admiral Oiawa lost 328 on the first day and 75 on the second. Two Japanese carriers were sunk by American submarines; another was sunk and two damaged by American aircraft. These losses, plus the damaging of a battleship and cruiser, forced the Japanese to withdraw. The Japanese navy was now in tatters.

Meanwhile, the Marines and soldiers on Saipan were victorious as well. The island was declared secured on 7 July, and the island of Tinian, just south of it, was invaded 24 July and secured on 1 August. Landings on Guam, at the southern end of the island chain, took place on 21 July, and the island was totally in American hands by 10 August. Now the long-range B-29 bombers had a base from which to begin the strategic bombing of Japanese cities.

Iwo Jima and Okinawa

MacArthur returned to the Philippines in October 1944 after the Marines had occupied Peleliu, the main island in the Palau group southwest of Guam and due east of the Philippines. These islands acted as a staging area for MacArthur. As American forces fought to regain the Philippines through the end of 1944 and the first months of 1945, Nimitz and the navy prepared plans for another offensive.

The air force had been losing a significant number of damaged aircraft returning from raids on Japan, and the high command decided that possession of Iwo Jima, due south of Japan, would allow the crippled bombers to land and save large numbers of aircrew. Accordingly, the invasion began in February 1945. Iwo Jima was a volcanic island covered with sulfurous ash. The Japanese had had years to dig in, and their time had not been wasted. More than 20,000 Japanese who garrisoned the island were often entrenched in caves where naval gunfire could not reach. When the Marines landed to light resistance, they hoped for an easy time, but instead they saw a replay of Tarawa in the accurate, predetermined targeting by Japanese artillery. The rugged terrain and entrenched enemy conspired to make this the Marines' most deadly operation to date. It took five weeks to secure the island and months to flush out the last Japanese defenders. Ultimately, it took more than 6,000 dead and 18,000 American wounded to defeat the

Japanese garrison, who fought as ardently as their comrades on every other island. More than 2,400 damaged B-29s landed here, saving many thousands more lives than were lost in the battle.

The invasion of Okinawa, scheduled for 1 April 1945, was a preview of the invasion of Japan itself. Okinawa had long been a Japanese province, and its inhabitants were officially Japanese citizens. Fighting here would give the Allied high command a taste of what it would be like to fight Japanese civilian resistance. Further, they expected a hard-fought struggle for the first territory of Japan proper.

They got what they were looking for. Many civilians either fought the Americans or committed suicide rather than become prisoners, believing the propaganda they had heard concerning American atrocities. Most of the fighting took place on the southern half of the island, a honeycomb of caves that had to be cleared one at a time. The Japanese garrison of 117,000 fought to the finish, the resistance lasting through July. The Japanese tactic of kamikazes, suicide aircraft attacks against American shipping, which had been introduced in the Philippines, proved to be a major headache for the U.S. Navy. They lost 34 ships sunk and more than 350 damaged, but it was not sufficient to turn them away.

The capture of Okinawa put the United States (plus the Allied forces of Britain and the Soviet Union once Germany was defeated in May) in a position to invade Japan. Plans were under way for a November invasion, but it never came about. President Harry Truman's decision to use newly developed nuclear weapons brought the war to an abrupt end. The island-hopping campaign demonstrated the ability of amphibious troops to land and overcome any prepared defenses, provided reinforcements and naval support were sufficient. Lessons learned here would be repeated again in just five years, when MacArthur again ordered Marines to go ashore at Inchon during the Korean War.

See also MacArthur, Douglas; Manchuria, Japanese Invasion of (1904) (Russo-Japanese War); Midway, Japanese Invasion of; New Guinea, Japanese Invasion of; Philippines, Japanese Invasion of the; Philippines, U.S. Invasion of the; South Korea, North Korean Invasion of (Korean War).

References: Dunnigan, James, and Albert Nofi, *Victory at Sea* (New York: Morrow, 1995); Leckie, Robert, *Strong Men Armed* (New York: Random House, 1962); Morrison, Samuel E., *The Two-Ocean War* (New York: Little, Brown, 1963).

192 PANAMA, U.S. INVASION OF

The United States' long and intimate relationship with Panama was the main factor in bringing about Panamanian independence from Colombia in 1903. That action, necessary in President Theodore Roosevelt's eyes, brought about a treaty that gave the United States generous terms for the construction of an isthmian canal: permanent lease on a strip of land 10 miles wide stretching from the Atlantic to the Pacific for $10 million down and $250,000 a year. By 1914, the canal was completed, and U.S. forces were stationed on-site to protect it.

The American forces occupying Panamanian bases since that time brought the small nation security and income. Not enough income, apparently, because the population began agitating for cession of the canal to Panama. In 1978, American President Jimmy Carter negotiated a new treaty with Panama, promising to give them control of the canal in the year 2000. Until then, the United States would increase its yearly payments and maintain a military presence.

Ten years after the Carter treaty, political troubles in Panama changed American attitudes. The Panamanian president tried to remove the head of the Panamanian military, General Manuel Noriega, and for his efforts was overthrown in a coup. Noriega consolidated his power by authorizing the activity of personal, secret military enforcers. To pay for this increase in the military, he allied himself with international drug traffickers. Though he conceded to international demands for a supervised election in 1989, he refused to recognize its legitimacy when he was voted out of office.

A year earlier, U.S. courts had indicted Noriega for his involvement in international drug dealing. When he refused to seat the duly elected officials in May 1989, the United States froze Panamanian assets held in U.S. banks. President George Bush increased the American military presence in Panama and encouraged the

Panamanian citizenry to oust Noriega, but too many people feared the consequences of trying. Tensions remained high throughout 1989 and reached a crisis point with the death of an American soldier in December, in addition to the arrest and abuse of a navy lieutenant and his wife. Noriega announced that he had been named "maximum leader for national liberation," waved a machete, and declared that a state of war existed with the United States, apparently believing that the Americans would not strike directly at his country. It was an assumption soon proven wrong.

A well-coordinated land-air assault, Operation Just Cause, struck Panama City, and Noriega's support soon evaporated. Though only 24 American servicemen were killed in action, the United States received severe criticism for the relatively high number of civilian casualties, many of whom were innocent bystanders and not Noriega's troops. Despite that, most Panamanians approved of the American action. Noriega ran for asylum to the Vatican Embassy while the officials elected several months previously were installed in office. After a few days, he surrendered to American authorities and was taken to Florida, where he stood trial on the charges brought against him in 1988. He was convicted in 1992.

Panama returned to peaceful conditions under elected officials who had sworn to uphold the country's constitution. This invasion followed much the same pattern the United States had often shown in Latin America, wherein American forces intervened to overthrow a ruler hostile to American interests. This time, it was a much more widely accepted intervention because it was short, effective, and fulfilled the needs not only of the United States (often the only motivation in the past) but also of the local population. The Organization of American States leveled some criticism at the United States for this unilateral action, but it was not condemned.

See also Latin America, U.S. Interventions in.

References: Donnelly, Thomas, Margaret Roth, and Caleb Baker, *Operation Just Cause: The Storming of Panama* (New York: Lexington Books, 1991); Flanagan, Edward, *The Battle for Panama: Inside Operation Just Cause* (McLean, VA: Brassey's, 1993); Woodward, Bob, *The Commanders* (New York: Simon & Schuster, 1991).

PHILIPPINES, JAPANESE INVASION OF THE

193

When Japan received permission from the Nazi-controlled French Vichy government in July 1941 to occupy French Indochina, the United States began to worry even more seriously about Japanese intentions.

The Americans had been trying to negotiate with the Japanese to stop their aggression in China, but without success. With Japanese troops along the southern Chinese coast and then in Indochina, the Philippine Islands, controlled by the United States since 1898, appeared to be in the process of being surrounded. The Filipino army, recently under the training command of American General Douglas MacArthur, was incorporated into the U.S. Army, and MacArthur was given command of USAFFE; U.S. Army Forces in the Far East. The combined Filipino-American forces were primarily concentrated on the main Philippine island of Luzon at the north end of the archipelago, mostly along the western coast between Manila and Lingayen Gulf. USAFFE was made up of 10 infantry divisions, five coastal and two field artillery units, and a scout force of cavalry and scout cars. All together, they numbered (at least on paper) some 150,000 men.

When the news reached Manila early on the morning of 8 December 1941 of the attack on Pearl Harbor, the USAFFE in the Philippines was only partially prepared. Though American intelligence analysts considered the Philippines the most likely American target of Japanese aggression, the islands were not well fortified. Indeed, there being so many islands with such long and winding coasts, choosing a possible landing site to defend was difficult. Thus, when Japanese forces under General Masaharu Homma made ready to land, there was little resistance on the many beaches where his troops came ashore.

The Japanese assault was at once masterful and lucky. The planned surprise air attack against naval and air facilities around Manila was delayed by fog, which grounded the aircraft operating from Formosa. Thus, USAFFE commanders knew that war had started, and would not be caught unaware. They immediately launched aircraft to search for oncoming Japanese, then recalled those aircraft to refuel and arm for an attack on the Japanese base at Formosa. The timing could not have been worse for the USAFFE. Just as American aircraft were completely fueled and armed and preparing for takeoff, the fog-delayed Japanese air attack took place. The destruction of the American air forces, designed to be accomplished by surprise early in the morning, was just as completely achieved by a quirk of the weather. The Japanese bombers and fighters wreaked havoc at the main air base at Clark Field, north of Manila, destroying B-17 bombers and P-40 fighters on the ground and setting most of the hangar and repair facilities on fire. Never during the invasion would the Japanese air superiority be seriously threatened.

Subsequent air attacks in the next two days finished off most of the remaining defending airplanes, while the last of the B-17s were ordered to withdraw to Darwin, Australia. The navy also feared for its capital ships, and ordered the cruisers and destroyers based at Cavite on Manila Bay to flee the area. On 10 December, the first Japanese troops landed on the northern and northwestern beaches of Luzon against virtually no resistance. They quickly captured two airfields, which made their air operations even simpler since they no longer had to fly down from Formosa. The Japanese advanced easily through northern Luzon against sporadic defenses, while the bulk of the USAFFE military remained around and north of Manila. With U.S. attention focused on the north, MacArthur was unable to mount any serious opposition to more landings, neither on 12 December at the southern end of Luzon, nor on 20 December to Japanese forces coming ashore at Davao on Mindanao, the southernmost Philippine island.

All the early Japanese landings were carried out by relatively small units, with General Homma betting that MacArthur would not try to be everywhere at once. He gambled correctly, and was able to grab beaches and airfields with little troop expenditure, while conserving the bulk of his force for the major invasion that landed on 22 December at Lingayen Gulf. The landings were slowed by rough seas more than by gunfire; only one machine gun was on-site, and

only two large artillery pieces shot at the oncoming landing craft. Where the Japanese ran into Filipino or American troops, they were slowed, but they were able to establish and expand beachheads with little problem. Despite the fact that Homma's forces totaled just two divisions, their brilliant placement in multiple landings kept the USAFFE commanders guessing and unable to commit overwhelming forces anywhere. When yet another landing took place on 24 December at Lamon Bay south of Manila in the center of Luzon, MacArthur decided to pull his forces back to a central location and make the Japanese come to him. On Christmas Day he announced he was abandoning Manila, declaring it an open city. He began massing his forces across Manila Bay on the peninsula called Bataan.

MacArthur pleaded for reinforcements, but none were coming. The U.S. Navy was still reeling from the shock of Pearl Harbor, and few troops were ready to depart from the United States even if transport was ready and willing. Japan had total air and naval command of the Southwest Pacific, and nothing could get through from the United States. MacArthur's forces far outnumbered the Japanese, but they were outfought or outmaneuvered and had no air or naval support. The smaller Japanese forces could easily outflank American and Filipino units and force their withdrawal. Therefore, MacArthur took his men on to Bataan, where outflanking was impossible. Unfortunately, so was retreat.

On 2 January 1942, the Japanese began to follow the retreating defenders onto the peninsula. Whatever success the Japanese had over the infantry was usually negated by outstanding American and Filipino artillery fire. Bataan is extremely rugged and easy to defend, and the Japanese assault soon bogged down. Some 80,000 troops and 26,000 civilians were on the peninsula, but with six-month provisions for only 40,000, food and fuel were soon in short supply. USAFFE forces held the high ground, and their artillery dealt the Japanese severe damage, but the defenders soon learned the nature of the Japanese military code of conduct: Surrender was not an option; victory was more important than life. The Japanese kept coming.

It took four months for the Japanese to secure Bataan, a finger of land some 20 by 30 miles. Difficult as the constant combat was, the worst enemies were hunger and disease. Food and medicine were unavailable for the thousands of defenders. American forces surrendered on 9 April, but that did not end the resistance. About 13,000 troops had been stationed on Corregidor, a fortified island in Manila Bay, and about 2,000 soldiers, nurses, and civilians managed to escape there as Bataan fell.

Douglas MacArthur was no longer there to direct the defense. On 12 March, at the direction of American President Franklin Roosevelt, MacArthur was spirited away via torpedo boat and aircraft, accompanied by his wife and son and 17 staff members. General Jonathan Wainwright was left in command. Upon reaching Australia, MacArthur stated in a radio broadcast to the Filipinos, "I came through and I will return."

Through the early fighting on Luzon, the garrison on Corregidor was untouched. The Officer's Club operated, and soldiers kept themselves inspection-ready. On 29 December they came under Japanese fire. General Homma began an air campaign against Corregidor and the three other fortified islands in Manila Bay. Planes bombed the targets at irregular intervals, depending on the need for air support over Bataan. When that peninsula fell, Homma could focus his entire attention on the Americans' last retreat. He brought up every artillery piece that could reach the island and began pounding it. The American artillery returned fire and dealt some serious blows to the Japanese, but they could not replace their spent shells. Just like on Bataan, the defenders of the Manila Bay islands could expect no resupply of ammunition, food, or medicine. The artillery duel that lasted through the month of April gradually became more one-sided, and with total air superiority, Japanese bombers joined in the destruction. Even though Corregidor boasted extensive underground hospitals, barracks, storehouses, and magazines, the guns had to be on the surface and they numbered fewer every day.

By early May, the defenders knew their days were numbered. Heavily fortified ammunition dumps finally gave in under the pounding and exploded. Intense artillery and air bombardment removed virtually every American cannon. On 5 May, Homma ordered his Fourth Division to land on Corregidor. Stiff currents blew the landing craft farther down the coast than intended and, as they drifted, the last few Americans guns blasted them. More than half the landing craft were sunk, but enough Japanese got ashore to begin the maneuvering and outflanking tactics that had served them earlier. Even though the final count of invaders was only 1,000 men against almost 15,000 defenders, the lack of coordination and communication, coupled with the weakened state of the sick and starving soldiers and Marines, spelled disaster. With too few boats to bring in substantial reinforcements, Homma could only hope for the best. The Japanese who got ashore proved sufficient because General Wainwright broadcast a message the second day, 6 May, signaling the surrender of his forces. The American soldiers destroyed their weapons and remaining ammunition. Corregidor, the "Gibraltar of the East," believed invincible by everyone except General Homma, did not survive the onslaught of months of explosives.

The Japanese occupation of the Philippines proved horrific. The first disaster for the defeated Filipino and American forces was the removal of those forces who surrendered on Bataan. Without food or water, under intense heat, they were forced to walk miles to prisoner camps in what became known as the Bataan Death March. The Japanese, whose code would not condone surrender for their own men, could not conceive that anyone who surrendered was worthy of the least consideration. Hundreds died of exhaustion or execution along the way. American civilians taken prisoner were not as badly treated, and life assumed something like normality during the occupation. The men were separated from their wives and children, but in their respective camps they did the best they could with schools, musical and theater groups, and other imitations of peacetime pieced together from what little the Japanese allowed them to salvage or collect. Filipino civilians became laborers for the army of occupation, and suffered from overwork and abuse. Filipino and American soldiers who managed to avoid capture went into the hills and began guerrilla activities that lasted until the U.S. invasion of the Philippines in the autumn of 1944.

See also MacArthur, Douglas; Philippines, U.S. Invasion of the.

References: Hartendorp, A. V. H., *The Japanese Occupation of the Philippines* (Manila: Bookmark, 1967); Toland, John, *But Not in Shame* (New York: Random House, 1961); Young, Donald, *The Battle of Bataan* (Jefferson, NC: McFarland, 1992).

PHILIPPINES, U.S. INVASION OF THE

194

After the American surrender to Japanese forces in 1942, General Douglas MacArthur dedicated himself to fulfilling his pledge to the country that he would return. Since the fall of the Philippines, he had been based in Australia and was in command of U.S. Army forces in the Southwest Pacific, forces trying to regain control of New Guinea and fighting in the Solomon Islands northeast of Australia. By the late summer of 1944, MacArthur's naval counterpart, Admiral Chester Nimitz, had used the U.S. Navy and Marines to capture Japanese-held islands across the Central Pacific. With the Mariana Islands under attack in September 1944, and their bases about to be used for air attacks on Japan itself, American forces were in a position to attack the Philippines as well. Historians have debated the need for recapturing the Philippines, but by doing so, Japan would be cut off from whatever raw materials it had been able to access in the East Indies.

Before the invasion could take place, however, the Americans had to secure the Palau Islands to control sea access from the Marianas to the Philippines. A combined force of 20,000 soldiers and Marines had to dig Japanese soldiers out of caves honeycombing the mountain that dominated the island. For a loss of 7,900 dead and wounded, the Japanese defense force of more than 13,000 was killed; they gave up only 400 prisoners. This was the highest percentage casualty rate of any American amphibious assault in history.

The American invasion of the Philippines was remarkable for its similarity to the Japanese invasion in 1941. This time, however, the roles were reversed, with the United States having command of the sea and air around the islands. MacArthur decided to assault the island of Leyte first to give the United States a central position in the archipelago from which to base its airpower. Accordingly, amphibious landings took place on 20 October. Though the Japanese could muster 350,000 men to defend the islands, they knew they could not repel the Americans without control of the sea. Therefore, the Japanese imperial navy planned to stop the invasion by destroying the transports near the beach. The Japanese sent a force of aircraft carriers southward from Japan to draw the American carriers and surface fleet away from the landing zones. They planned to strike the unprotected transports in two thrusts, from north and south, with ships sent from Singapore and the East Indies. However, American submarines sighted one of the Japanese fleets sailing from the Indies to the west of the Philippines. They sank and damaged a number of cruisers, and alerted the invasion force to the coming attack. The bulk of the U.S. Navy under Admiral William Halsey had swallowed the northern bait and sailed to strike the diversionary force, leaving the transports protected only by escort aircraft carriers and aging battleships (some resurrected from the bottom of Pearl Harbor). The battleships parked themselves at the end of Surigao Strait and waited until one of the Japanese fleets sailed into their guns and was destroyed. The second was able to get through the islands and into the area where the landings were taking place. They dealt some damage to the escort carriers, but turned back before attacking the defenseless transports; Halsey's ships to the north had destroyed much of the diversionary force with aircraft and then turned south to try to catch the retreating Japanese. Though Halsey was much criticized for chasing the diversionary force with the majority of his ships, his forces dealt extensive punishment to the empty Japanese aircraft carriers and returned south in time to seriously damage the retreating Japanese. The Battle of Leyte Gulf, actually three separate battles, destroyed the Japanese imperial navy as

An armada of U.S. ships prepares to take Leyte Island, Philippines. (photograph no. 513206,
"The liberators move against the Philippines. An armada of American power steams in
impressive array along the coast of Leyte Island in the Philippines as dawn of A–Day bathes
the Pacific in golden glory, 10/1944," Record Group 26: Records of the U.S. Coast Guard,
1785 – 1992, U.S. National Archives and Records Administration, College Park, MD.)

an effective fighting force: Three battleships, four aircraft carriers, 10 cruisers, and nine destroyers were sunk for the American loss of three destroyers and two escort carriers.

From this point forward, the Americans controlled the sea and air. The only way the Japanese could challenge the U.S. Navy was through the introduction of kamikazes, suicide pilots flying bomb-laden airplanes into American shipping. Translated as "divine wind," kamikaze referred to the storms that twice destroyed Mongol invasion fleets attacking Japan in the 1300s. The Japanese hoped that this storm of dedicated flyers would perform the same task. More of a psychological weapon than an effective means of destruction, the tactic would be used by Japanese air forces for the remainder of the war in every succeeding

American invasion. In this case, the kamikazes managed to sink a few ships, but not enough to deter the invaders, and it used up the last of Japanese aircraft in the islands.

Japanese General Tbmoyuki Yamashita wanted to abandon Leyte after the naval defeat, but was overruled from Tokyo. He reinforced as best he could with the few transports he could get past American air cover, and the Japanese troops fought as hard there as everywhere else. With no air cover and inadequate transport, the Japanese were obliged to fight from a series of defensive lines, which took the Americans two months to overcome. Not until late December was Leyte declared secure; the mopping up of isolated pockets of resistance went on four months longer.

In mid-December, American forces landed on the small island of Mindoro, off the main island of Luzon, in order to establish closer airfields for the main battle. On 9 January they came ashore on Luzon from Lingayen Gulf, just as the Japanese had in 1941. The Americans drove across the central plains toward the capital at Manila, both to recapture the city and to free the large numbers of civilians who had been held in prisoner camps. The undernourished and abused civilians steeled American resolve to fight to the finish. Unlike in 1942, when MacArthur had declared Manila an open city, Yamashita fought for it street by street. The Americans finally captured a city in ruins in March 1945. During this battle, Japanese soldiers committed a number of atrocities for which Yamashita was held responsible; after the war, he was executed as a war criminal. By the middle of March, Luzon was in American hands, but the rugged nature of the terrain allowed the Japanese to continue fighting from the hills and jungles, and the fighting in the Philippines did not end until the Japanese government surrendered in August 1945. The Americans lost 14,000 dead and another 48,000 wounded, while the Japanese lost all 350,000 to death or capture.

See also Dutch East Indies, Japanese Invasion of; New Guinea, Japanese Invasion of; Pacific Islands, U.S. Conquest of; Philippines, Japanese Invasion of the; Singapore and Malaya, Japanese Conquest of.

References: Breuei, William, *Retaking the Philippines* (New York: St. Martin's Press, 1986); Friend, Theodore, *The Blue-Eyed Enemy: Japan against the West in Java and Luzon, 1942–1945* (Princeton, NJ: Princeton University Press, 1988); Smith, Robert, *Triumph in the Philippines* (Washington, DC: Office of the Chief of Military History, 1963).

195 POLAND, NAZI CONQUEST OF

Hitler's armies occupied the remainder of Czechoslovakia in the spring of 1939, in the wake of a promise that he had no more territorial ambitions in Europe after acquiring the Czech province of the Sudetenland. European leaders finally stiffened their resolve to resist further German expansion. Hitler, of course, assured them that he wanted nothing else after he gained the small Baltic port of Memel in late March from the Lithuanians, who had received the city as part of the Versailles Treaty. Control of Memel extended the coast of East Prussia farther north and gave Germany a port on the Baltic.

Both Britain and France alerted Poland in April 1939 that they would honor their defense treaty, unlike their actions concerning Czechoslovakia. This guarantee of Polish sovereignty created a huge amount of tension through the spring and summer of 1939, because to protect Poland, the Western democracies had to have the support of the Soviet Union; what form that support would take was the overriding question. Britain wanted Soviet leader Joseph Stalin to announce a similar guarantee of Polish sovereignty, but Stalin wanted more: an alliance with the West—a 10-year mutual-defense agreement. The British government thought this would be too provocative to Germany, making war more likely, and the British still wanted to deal with Hitler through diplomacy. The Soviets saw Britain's hesitation as a rejection of their country as a serious power. Further, Britain and France sought to guarantee the sovereignty of Rumania as well, and Stalin saw this as a Western ploy to gain control over eastern Europe, which Stalin considered his sphere of influence. When he could not gain the agreement he desired from the Western powers, Stalin began to look to Germany for common ground.

In the 1920s Germany had fairly close ties to the new Soviet Union. The German military had trained at Russian bases and cooperated in producing poison gas. That relationship had come to an end when Hitler came to power in 1933 and signed a nonaggression pact with Poland. By the spring of 1939, however, it looked as if those ties might be renewed. If the Western powers would not guarantee Soviet dominance over eastern Europe, perhaps Hitler would. After all, Germany's military alliance with Italy, the "Pact of Steel" signed in late May, was clearly directed against Britain and France; certainly Hitler would not be interested in eastern Europe anytime soon. As Soviet relations with the Western powers deteriorated, relations with Germany reopened.

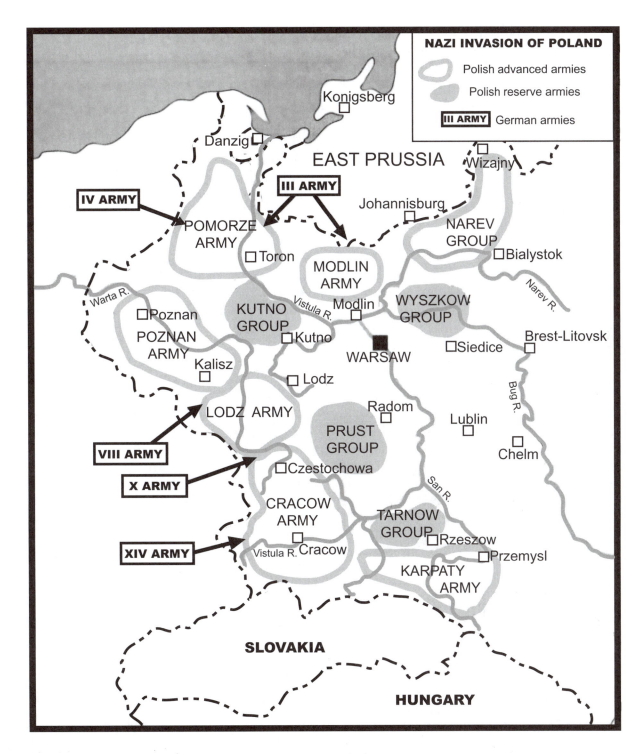

NAZI INVASION OF POLAND

Polish advanced armies
Polish reserve armies
III ARMY German armies

Konigsberg

Danzig

EAST PRUSSIA

Wizajny

IV ARMY

III ARMY

Johannisburg

POMORZE ARMY

Toron

MODLIN ARMY

NAREV GROUP

Bialystok

Narev R.

Warta R.

KUTNO GROUP

Vistula R.

Modlin

WYSZKOW GROUP

Brest-Litovsk

Poznan

POZNAN ARMY

Kutno

WARSAW

Siedice

Bug R.

Kalisz

Lodz

Radom

Lublin

Chelm

LODZ ARMY

PRUST GROUP

VIII ARMY

Czestochowa

San R.

X ARMY

CRACOW ARMY

TARNOW GROUP

Rzeszow

XIV ARMY

Vistula R. Cracow

Przemysl

KARPATY ARMY

SLOVAKIA

HUNGARY

If Hitler had to fight Britain and France, the last thing he wanted was a two-front war. Therefore, Germany started the process by having Foreign Minister Ribbentrop send out feelers to new Soviet Foreign Minister Molotov. The two conducted secret negotiations throughout the summer as Anglo-Soviet relations deteriorated.

In the meantime, Hitler prepared for aggression against Poland. In creating an independent Poland, the Versailles Treaty gave the country a seaport on the Baltic at Danzig. While termed a "free city," Danzig was totally German in its population. Further, Poland was granted land on either side of the city, the so-called Danzig

Corridor, an action that created a detached German state, East Prussia. Using the same rationale he had used in overtaking Austria and the Sudetenland, Hitler began agitating for all German-speaking people to be under one government. In this case, that meant Danzig and the corridor. If Poland would merely cede the city and area to Germany, Hitler claimed that he had no more territorial demands in Europe. Such an action would make Poland landlocked.

This demand brought the British and French guarantees to Poland; they had no desire to look the fools again after the Sudetenland debacle. The only problems were: Hitler did not believe the Western democracies now any more than he had earlier; and Poland was so isolated that direct British and French intervention would be nearly impossible. Hence, Soviet aid was vital, but the Western powers would not give Stalin what he wanted. The Soviets continued to play both ends against the middle, waiting for the best offer from either side. They finally signed a nonaggression pact with Germany on 23 August, an agreement that shocked the world. Ever since Hitler had entered politics, he had been virulently anti-Communist, and Stalin had never expressed any love for Nazism. The Polish government was in a state of panic; it had assumed that Stalin would never allow Nazis on his doorstep, and now Poland was stuck in the middle of these strange bedfellows. With this agreement in hand, Hitler ordered Nazis in Danzig to provoke an incident with Poland.

There was no formal declaration of war. Early on the morning of 1 September, German aircraft flew into Polish airspace and attacked airfields, road junctions, troop concentrations, and command centers. Fast-moving armored columns with close infantry support crossed the border just before dawn. The Poles were the first to be on the receiving end of the blitzkrieg, or lightning war. This strategy of using rapid thrusts to surround and cut off troop formations or defensive strong points, then letting them starve or be mopped up by infantry, had been theorized by British military thinkers between wars, but German theorists perfected it. The close air support, which assisted the attacking columns once the strategic targets were destroyed, was highly successful because most German air crews had had on-the-job training in close support operations while assisting Franco's forces in the Spanish Civil War.

The Polish army, though three million strong, was unprepared for this style of warfare. Because the Polish forces were called to protect the capital city of Warsaw, the defenseless countryside gave Soviet troops an easy opening to come pouring in from the east on 17 September. Unknown until that moment was a secret clause in the nonaggression pact Hitler and Stalin had just signed that called for Poland to be divided between the two countries so that each could have a buffer zone from the other. Attacked from two sides and hopelessly outclassed, Polish authorities were obliged to surrender. Warsaw fell on 28 September, and all fighting ended by 1 October.

Britain reluctantly fulfilled its obligations to Poland, in a manner of speaking. The British government declared war on 3 September, with the French government following suit soon thereafter, but did nothing to help the Poles. The Poles did not see one British or French soldier, aircraft, or ship. All they got from the alliance was the knowledge that the world was going to war over them.

The German occupation was a harsh one because Hitler soon began implementing his "final solution" for European Jews. Occupied Poland was the site of most of the Nazi death camps, including the infamous Auschwitz and Treblinka camps. Poland was also the staging ground for later German aggression. When Hitler decided to invade the Soviet Union in the summer of 1941, Poland provided the base for German army groups heading for Leningrad, Moscow, Kiev, and the Caucasus. When the tide turned and Soviet troops entered Poland in 1944, the German occupation forces in Warsaw put down a massive uprising in the Jewish ghetto by destroying virtually every building and killing every person in that area. Classed as untermensch (subhumans), according to Hitler's racial theories, all Poles, Jewish or not, suffered simply because of their heritage. A nation crisscrossed by armies since the time of the Roman Empire endured yet another brutal experience at the hands of foreign soldiers.

See also Czechoslovakia, Nazi Occupation of; Germany, Soviet Invasion of.

See also Czechoslovakia, Nazi Occupation of; Germany, Soviet Invasion of.

References: Guderian, Heinz, *Pander Leader* (New York: Dutton, 1957); Liddell Hart, Basil, *History of the Second World War* (New York: Putnam, 1970); Shirer, William, *Rise and Fall of the Third Reich* (New York: Simon & Schuster, 1960).

196 RHINELAND, NAZI OCCUPATION OF THE

One of the results of the Versailles Treaty, which brought about the end of World War I, was that the territory known as the Rhineland was to be occupied by Allied troops for a period of time and demilitarized indefinitely. No German troops, military installations, or fortifications were to be located in the demilitarized zone, which included all German territory west of the Rhine, along with the territory on the east side of the Rhine River to a depth of 50 kilometers. Though the Germans were forced to accept these terms in 1919, in 1925 they willingly agreed to a demilitarized Rhineland when they signed the Locarno Pact.

As early as May 1935, Adolf Hitler ordered the German High Command to create a plan for the reoccupation of the Rhineland. During this period, the French government received reports that the Germans were constructing barracks, ammunition depots, airfields, rail lines, and roads in the demilitarized zone, but failed to do anything about these warnings. By the beginning of 1936, Hitler believed the time was nearing for a German move into the Rhineland. Hitler watched closely how the League of Nations dealt with Mussolini's aggressions in Ethiopia. He rightly concluded that if the League could not get together on this problem, it would lack the resolve needed to confront Germany for its violations of the Versailles Treaty and the Locarno Pact.

On Hitler's command, the Minister of War and Commander in Chief of the Armed Forces General Blomberg issued on 2 March 1936 the preparatory orders for the reoccupation, code-named Winterubung (Winter Exercise). Three days later, on 5 March, the date for Z-Day (D-Day) was set for Saturday, 7 March. Historians believe that Hitler purposely planned many of his important actions to begin on Saturdays to take advantage of the long weekends enjoyed by many European diplomats.

The military leaders, including Army Chief of Staff General von Fritsch, did not believe the army was ready for such a move, and that the French and British would easily force the German troops out of the Rhineland. At this time, the German army was inferior to the those of the Allies in numbers, equipment, and training, and a German defeat would be a severe blow to Germany's rearmament program and growing political strength. On the day of and immediately after the invasion, the German generals urged Hitler to recall the troops west of the Rhine for fear of French reprisals. This was the first open conflict between Hitler and the army, and after the success of the German reoccupation, Hitler placed less value on his generals' opinions and more on his own intuition.

At dawn on 7 March, elements of the German army moved into the Rhineland, supported by two squadrons of fighter aircraft. These soldiers entered the zone undeployed for battle. Only three battalions of infantry crossed the Rhine River, and German panzers never entered the demilitarized zone. The total number of German troops was 36,000, which included 14,000 local police organized as infantry.

The consequences of the reoccupation were enormous. First, many historians believe that France and England could have easily prevented Germany from fortifying the Rhineland. If France alone or in conjunction with England had used force against the Germans, the German army would have been forced to retreat. In fact, the soldiers on the west side of the Rhine had orders to conduct a fighting withdrawal if they encountered French troops. However, the only response from the Allies was a formal protest to the League of Nations. A number of important consequences occurred by allowing Germany to regain control of the Rhineland. The Allies failed to strike a crucial blow against the rising power of Nazi Germany and Hitler's influence at home by neglecting to act against Hitler's aggression. After the reoccupation of the Rhineland, a plebiscite was conducted in Germany that showed a 98.8 percent approval rate for Hitler and his actions. The German fortification of the

Rhineland allowed Germany's western frontier to be protected with only a minimum number of soldiers, and provided cover for Germany's industries and mineral deposits located in the Ruhr, thus providing security for Germany's rearmament program. With Germany firmly entrenched in the Rhineland, France could no longer come to the aid of its allies in central and eastern Europe. Now, with the remilitarization and reoccupation a fait accompli, Hitler would be able to begin expansion in the east to achieve *lebensraum* (living space) for the German people with little interference from the Western allies.

See also Ethiopia, Italian Invasion of; Hitler, Adolf.

References: Kagan, Donald, *On the Origins of War* (New York: Doubleday, 1995); Shirer, William, *The Collapse of the Third Republic* (New York: Simon & Schuster, 1969); Taylor, Telford, *Munich: The Price of Peace* (Garden City, NY: Doubleday, 1979).

197 RUSSIA, GERMAN INVASION OF

Germany went into World War I planning to quickly defeat France through its long-anticipated Schlieffen Plan, finishing off Russia at its leisure. This would give the Germans, with assistance from the Ottoman Empire, access to oil in Persia, a country under Russia's economic dominance. Coupled with the raw materials of central and eastern Europe and German financial and management abilities, Persian oil would be the final necessary addition for an empire under German dominance stretching from the North Sea to the Persian Gulf. When Archduke Franz Ferdinand, heir to the throne of Germany's ally Austria-Hungary, was assassinated in June 1914, a chain of events was set into motion that brought the world into war.

Germany urged Austria to blame the Serbian government for the act of terrorists and to demand concessions so intense that Serbia could not comply. When Austria declared war on Serbia on 28 July, Russia rallied to the aid of its fellow Slavic country. Germany declared war on Russia on 1 August; this was followed by another declaration on Russia's ally France on 3 August. The following morning, German troops violated Belgian neutrality on their way around the French army's flank, and by doing so brought Great Britain to Belgium's assistance.

Most of Germany's forces were dedicated to the offensive in France; the German Eighth Army remained in the east to maintain an active defense for a predictably slow Russian mobilization. When Russian forces scored a small early success in Poland, two infantry corps and a cavalry division were transferred from France to East Prussia. A new commander was also brought in: Paul von Hindenburg, a veteran of the Franco-Prussian War. He was assisted by a very able chief of staff, Erich Ludendorff, and inherited the talents of Chief of Operations Max Hoffman. The Eighth Army faced the Russian First and Second armies in Poland and had just retreated from the more northerly enemy, the First. Hindenburg and Ludendorff took control just as the Eighth was repositioning itself to attack the Russian Second Army to the south. The result was a huge German victory at Tannenberg at the end of August. Within two weeks the Germans had pivoted northward and destroyed the Russian First Army at the battle of Masurian Lakes. These victories did not result in momentum, for the exhausted German troops soon found more Russians in their path and retreated to East Prussia.

In the meantime, the Austrians had not had good luck against Russia. They attacked northeast into Galicia, and at first made good headway against the Russians, but the overconfident Austrian commander, Count Conrad von Hotzendorff, attacked Russian forces who were not as broken and demoralized as he had believed. By the end of August, as the Germans were winning at Tannenberg, the Austrians were in full retreat and did not stop until they reached the Carpathian Mountains in mid-September. Against Russian casualties of 250,000, the Austrians lost 450,000, virtually half the army with which they had started the war.

German forces attempted to capture Warsaw in October, but ran into fierce Russian resistance, which forced Hindenburg's men back to their starting point. Though he continually faced superior numbers, Hindenburg had the advantage of a superior intelligence staff who regularly intercepted Russian wireless transmissions. Using this knowledge of Russian plans and troop disposi-

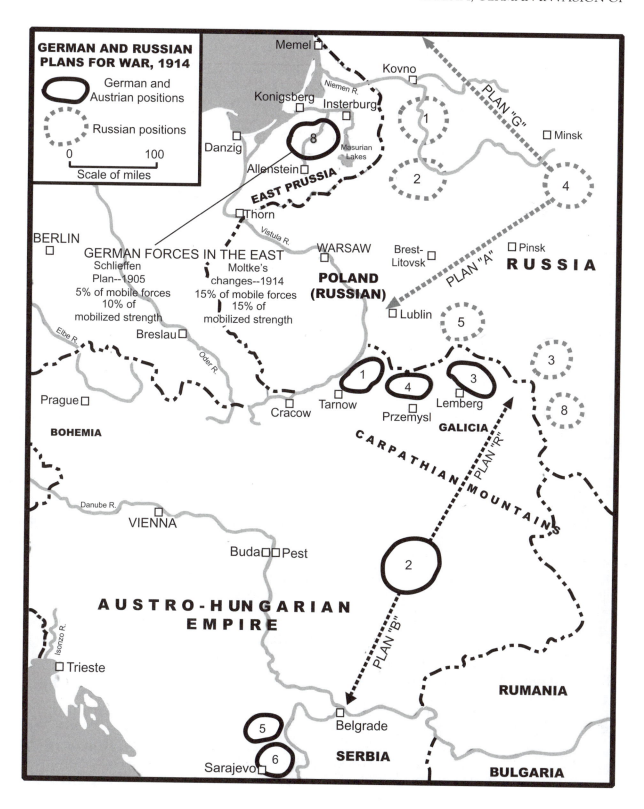

GERMAN AND RUSSIAN PLANS FOR WAR, 1914

German and Austrian positions

Russian positions

0   100
Scale of miles

Memel

Kovno

Niemen R.

Konigsberg

Insterburg

PLAN "G"

Minsk

8

Danzig

Masurian Lakes

Allenstein

EAST PRUSSIA

1

2

4

Thorn

BERLIN

Vistula R.

WARSAW

Brest-Litovsk

Pinsk

GERMAN FORCES IN THE EAST

Schlieffen Plan--1905
5% of mobile forces
10% of mobilized strength

Moltke's changes--1914
15% of mobile forces
15% of mobilized strength

POLAND (RUSSIAN)

PLAN "A"

RUSSIA

Lublin

5

Elbe R.

Breslau

Oder R.

3

8

Prague

1

4

3

Tarnow

Przemysl

Lemberg

GALICIA

Cracow

BOHEMIA

PLAN "R"

CARPATHIAN MOUNTAINS

Danube R.

VIENNA

Buda Pest

2

AUSTRO-HUNGARIAN EMPIRE

RUMANIA

Isonzo R.

Trieste

PLAN "B"

Belgrade

5

SERBIA

6

Sarajevo

BULGARIA

tions, Hindenburg shifted forces to attack Lodz, which the Germans captured after difficult fighting in December. Throughout the last months of 1914, Hindenburg begged for more men, but could get few from Erich von Falkenhayn, army chief of staff, who was dedicated to the Western Front. For the most part, the Eastern Front got reserve divisions, but enough new troops arrived to make up three armies (the Eighth, Ninth, and Tenth) by he end of the year, with Hindenburg in overall command.

In 1915, the Germans scored their greatest successes. In late January, Austrian forces attacked in terrible weather, and after early success, ground to a halt in the snow. In a second battle east of the Masurian Lakes in mid-February, the German Ninth and Tenth armies captured 55,000 Russians and drove off the remainder of the Russian Tenth Army, though the Russians did not have the ability to press farther. The German successes could not convince the High Command to send more troops, but the Austrian difficulties brought a new army to the east. Falkenhayn sent the newly formed Eleventh Army to aid the Austrians, and together (with massed artillery preparations), they broke through the Russian defensive positions in Galicia in May. The Russians fought bravely but lacked the necessary ammunition; Russian transport was woefully inadequate. By 22 June, the Germans and Austrians were at the Bug River. Hindenburg favored a huge pincer operation with his forces, idle in the north, swinging around to meet the Austro-German force and capturing the Russian army. Falkenhayn and Kaiser Wilhelm settled instead for a smaller pincer that won battles but failed to surround the Russians. Even with the addition of a fourth army, the Twelfth, to Hindenburg's eastern force, the Germans were unable to destroy their enemy. By the autumn of 1915, the Russians had extracted themselves from any encirclement and saved their army, though they were forced to take up new positions deep in their own territory. The Germans had captured vast tracts of land, but Falkenhayn refused to maintain the momentum and withdrew several divisions from the east to return to France. Hindenburg was told to go on the defensive.

The Russians conducted a scorched-earth withdrawal and forced the residents of the abandoned countryside to flee with them. This actually aided the Germans, who did not have to worry about feeding or keeping an eye on a hostile population. It hurt the Russians by burdening their overtaxed supply system, and the waves of refugees spread defeatism. Despite this negative development, the Russians had time to recover their strength when the Germans went on the defensive. New but short-term Minister of War Aleksai Polivanov raised and trained two million conscripts and got Russian industry up to the task of producing weapons and ammunition. He reorganized the Russian army into three fronts, but the commanders of two of them were incompetent. Only Aleksei Brusilov, commanding the Southwest Front against the Austrians, was an inspired choice. He saw the potential for success in the south and exploited it.

The Austrians, Brusilov believed, were a broken reed. They had recently removed many of their Slavic troops to fight their new enemy, Italy, which meant that the hold on their section of the front would be weakened. A Russian offensive in the north in mid-March 1916 had come to naught, and the front commanders there never again mounted serious attacks against the well-entrenched Germans. Nevertheless, German attention was focused in the north, and that meant that Brusilov was able to prepare his offensive more easily. After a 24-hour bombardment, the Russians attacked five Austrian armies on 5 June. They were unstoppable. The Austrian armies on the flanks broke, and the Russians took 200,000 prisoners in the first week. Brusilov called a halt to regroup. Had the commanders of the two northern Russian fronts launched attacks at this time, the German force, which had been spread thin by the transfers to France, would have been unable to hold on. After the failure in March, however, they would not move until too late. Hindenburg was able to shift men to the south to stiffen the Austrians just in time to stave off disaster. By October, Brusilov had reached the Carpathians and overlooked the Hungarian plains, but he could go no farther. The well-trained men with whom he had begun the offensive were now dead, and their replacements were too green.

Brusilov's offensive had far-reaching effects. The Habsburg monarchy in Austria-Hungary was faced with increasing ethnic tension that affected the army as well as the civilians. Emperor Franz Josef died in November 1916, and his successor, Charles, began secret negotiations to take Austria out of the war, but the Germans would not allow it. There were negative side effects in Russia as well. The loss of one million men in the offensive, on top of the quarter-million casualties per month the Russians had lost in the first year and a half of the war, was causing unrest on the home front. The addition of Rumania as an ally 'had no positive results; their army was useless and their country overrun in four months. Russia was ripe for revolution.

On the German side there were changes as well. The setback with Austria brought an end to Falkenhayn's tenure as chief of staff, and he was replaced in August 1916 by Hindenburg and Ludendorff. Max Hoffman became the commander of German forces in the east. After pleading so long for increased attention to the Russian front, the two new leaders shifted their attention to France. They finally learned just what had been occurring for two years in the west, and they had to deal with British and French offensives that kept men away from Russia. It looked as if the Eastern Front would become inactive while both sides tried to recover.

Russia broke first. Bad news from the front, coupled with food shortages, brought riots in March 1917. The troops ordered to quell the riots joined them instead, and Czar Nicholas was obliged to abdicate in favor of a democratic government under the leadership of Alexander Kerensky. He tried to keep the war effort going, but proved no more successful than the czarist government. The German foreign office tried to negotiate a separate peace with Kerensky, but the lack of German military activity gave hope to the new Russian leader. He kept the army going for another few months, long enough for the new commander in chief, Brusilov, to launch a new offensive in the south in the summer of 1917. It soon petered out, and Hoffman counterattacked in mid-July, making strong gains in Galicia. He ordered his forces in the north to attack the Russian flank at Riga, and captured that city easily in September.

The German successes caused friction between Kerensky and his new commander in chief, Lavr Kornilov. Kerensky believed that Kornilov was plotting against him, so Kerensky was forced to ally himself with the Bolshevik leaders he had kept in jail. They turned against him and overthrew him in six weeks. The Bolshevik leader, Vladimir Lenin, called for immediate peace talks, but balked at Ludendorff's demands for huge territorial concessions. A new offensive in February 1918 changed Lenin's mind, and the Treaty of Brest-Litovsk removed Russia from the war. Germany transferred hundreds of thousands of men to France for the spring offensive of 1918, but the timely arrival of American forces blunted Germany's last great hope in the west. If the occupation forces kept in the east had also been shifted, it may have had a decisive effect, but that can never be known.

Ultimately, the German invasion was successful only until November 1918, when Germany was forced to sign an armistice. The Versailles Treaty that was forced on the Germans in the summer of 1919 took away all their eastern conquests as well as their overseas possessions. The greatest effect of their offensive was not on Germany but on Russia, because the war hastened the downfall of the Romanov dynasty and brought the Communists to power. Their reoccupation of the Ukraine caused such hostility that the local population would ever after chafe at Communist control and yearn for the day they could be free of it. The Treaty also left the Germans with a grudge—the land they had won was taken from them. Hitler's dreams to reconquer that land would bring on another world war.

See also France, Prussian Invasion of (Franco-Prussian War); France, German Invasion of.

References: Rutherford, Ward, *The Russian Army in World War I* (London: Gordon Cremones, 1975); Showalter, Dennis, *Tannenberg: Clash of Empires* (Hamden, CT Archon Books, 1991).

198   SICILY, ALLIED INVASION OF

Having successfully completed the occupation of North Africa, British and American leaders pondered the next target in their campaign against the Axis. American President Franklin Roosevelt and British Prime Minister Winston Churchill met in Casablanca, Morocco, in January 1943 to discuss this and other strategic matters. Two options presented themselves for a continued campaign in the Mediterranean area: Corsica or Sardinia, to set up an invasion of southern France; or Sicily, to set up an invasion of Italy. The two leaders decided to feint at Sardinia and plan the operation for Sicily. Occupation of the island would open up the sea-lanes of the Mediterranean to the Suez Canal and save time over the Cape of Good Hope route then in use. Hopefully, it would also force Germany to divert troops from the Russian front to counter the southern threat.

More than 400,000 German and Italian troops defended the island, which was known for its rugged terrain. The British Eighth Army under General Sir Bernard Montgomery was to land on the southeastern corner of the triangular island and drive up the coast to Messina, cutting off any Axis retreat into Italy. The American Seventh Army under General George Patton was to land in the central part of the south coast and clear the middle and western parts of the island of the enemy as well as drive north parallel to the British attack.

Early on the morning of 10 June 1943, American airborne troops landed for their first-ever combat operation. Their mission was to seize road junctions and delay any reinforcements that came up the few roads available on the island. The Germans had decided to hold back most of their troops from the beaches and respond to the Allied initiatives as though there were too much seacoast to defend. The initial landings went smoothly, but a German armored counterattack the next day put severe pressure on the American positions. It was ultimately driven back, and by the fourth day of the invasion, the Allies had a secure beachhead.

As Montgomery's forces encountered severe resistance along the coast road, they gradually had to move farther and farther inland, pushing American forces farther west. Patton took it upon himself to send his forces northwest to capture Palermo, then drive eastward along the north coast road, thus putting pressure on the retreating Axis troops from two directions. By the end of

June, the Germans had decided to abandon the island, and began a fighting withdrawal toward the port of Messina. Despite constant pressure from the British attacking overland and Patton staging amphibious flanking moves, the Germans managed to extricate themselves according to plan. When Allied forces entered Messina on 17 August, they found the city empty; the Germans had evacuated 100,000 men and 10,000 vehicles.

While not the stunning victory for which the Allies had hoped, the capture of Sicily had major results. It accomplished its primary mission of securing the sea-lanes through the Mediterranean. More importantly, it put such a strain on Italian morale that Mussolini was overthrown, and the new Italian government secretly approached the Allies to talk peace, ultimately agreeing to the demand for unconditional surrender called for by the Allies at the Casablanca Conference. This action was no surprise to Hitler; he had been sending German troops into the country for some months in anticipation of the Italian defection. Though the Italian army was no longer a factor in the war effort, the Germans did not abandon the countryside. The defense the Germans mounted after the landing of British troops in September 1943 continued until the end of the war. The Germans fought a slow and costly (for both sides) withdrawal up the entire peninsula, and were still fighting hard in the far north of the country when the surrender was signed in Germany in May 1945.

The invasion of Sicily caused a large amount of destruction, particularly around the cities of Palermo and Messina. The island's inhabitants were glad to see both the war and the fascists go. The Allies were welcomed, if for no other reason than that they brought food and medicines. The lack of a fascist government structure left a power vacuum behind, which was filled by leaders of the local Mafia families. They backed a popular separatist movement until 1946, when Italy granted the island a large measure of local autonomy. The new relationship with Italy was further strengthened by the inclusion in the new Italian constitution of a clause instituting land reform; the largest landowners had to break up their holdings or be subject to government intervention. With land to work and universal suffrage, the Sicilians found their postwar condition much improved.

See also North Africa, U.S. Invasion of.

References: Birtle, A. J., *Sicily* (Washington, DC: U.S. Army Center of Military History, 1993); Garland, Albert, *Sicily and the Surrender of Italy* (Washington, DC: U.S. Army Center of Military History, 1965); Smith, Denis Mack, *A History of Sicily* (New York: Viking, 1968).

199 SINAI, ISRAELI INVASION OF (1956) (SUEZ CRISIS)

In 1954, Egypt came under the control of Gamal Abdel Nasser, who dreamed great dreams for his nation: He wanted to modernize his country and make it the leader of the Arab world. To modernize Egypt, he proposed the construction of a dam on the Nile to bring hydroelectric power to his people and improve their living standards. To lead the Arab world, he proposed to make life difficult for Israel. In 1956 he set about accomplishing both these tasks.

The United States and Britain were interested in making money available to Egypt for the dam project, and worked with the World Bank to secure funds for Nasser. American President Dwight Eisenhower reconsidered the offer when he learned that Egypt had just contracted with Czechoslovakia, a communist state, to buy arms. Nasser had been sponsoring terrorist activity in Israel, and hoped with increased weaponry to have an army sufficient to defeat Israel. But if Nasser wanted to deal with communists, Eisenhower reasoned, he could not have American money for his dam. The United States withdrew its support for the project without first notifying the other party involved, Great Britain, which was also obliged to back out. Nasser responded quickly and shockingly. Was there not a ready source of income in Egypt already—the Suez Canal? Why should the British and French stockholders be making money on this waterway when it was within Egyptian territory? Nasser announced that Egypt would nationalize the canal.

Britain and France did not care to lose income on a company they had owned since the 1870s, and they did not want to lose control of such a strategic waterway. If Egypt leaned toward the Soviet Union, Egyptian control of the canal could badly hurt European trade and troop movement. Moreover, France was upset with Nasser because of his support of revolutionaries in Algeria. On top of all of this, however, was the humiliation of being outdone by a Third World leader. The British and French wanted their canal back, and just when they needed a handy ally, one appeared: Israel.

The Israelis had long wanted to do something to stop the Egyptian harassment of their country, and they feared what Nasser might do with the new supply of weapons he had just acquired. Egypt had been blockading the Straits of Tiran at the mouth of the Gulf of Aqaba, the branch of the Red Sea that reaches Israel's southern border. Since all three countries wanted to hurt Nasser, they made common cause. If Israel would invade the Sinai Peninsula and drive for the Suez Canal, the British and French would give them aid. Once the invading Israelis approached the canal, the Europeans would recommend a United Nations resolution to keep both Israeli and Egyptian troops 10 miles from the canal. Then, Britain and France would volunteer to provide a peacekeeping force to guarantee that the canal stayed open. By coincidence, that would also put them in control again. If the United Nations or Egypt rejected the offer, the Europeans would invade and enforce their will. All of this planning was done in secret in Paris.

On 29 October 1956, Israeli troops went into action. They quickly drove down the west coast of the Gulf of Aqaba to seize the Egyptian post at Sharm al-Sheikh. They also landed parachute forces at Mitla Pass in preparation for an advance on the southern end of the Suez Canal, while an armored force was prepared to drive down the Mediterranean coast road to seize the northern end. When Egypt rejected Britain and France's offer of a peacekeeping force and a halt of belligerents 10 miles on either side of the canal (which the Israelis were not yet near), the second phase of the plan went into operation. British and French aircraft bombed Egyptian airfields, and ships were en route with an amphibious force, which landed at Port Said on 5 November. In the meantime, Israeli troops overran Egyptian defenses along the coast road, though Egyptian forces put up a much stiffer resistance deeper in the Sinai.

The United Nations condemned the invasions but could do little to stop them; both

Britain and France were able to veto any Security Council resolutions. The real pressure came from the United States and the Soviet Union. President Eisenhower privately and publicly accused the British and French of colonialism, and suggested an embargo of Latin American oil to slow the invaders down. The Soviet threat was more to the point: They were willing to commit "volunteers" to aid Egypt, and possibly target Paris and London with nuclear missiles. That the Soviets would start World War III over Egypt was hard to believe, but neither the British nor the French were willing to call their bluff. They withdrew. That left the Israeli army deep in Egyptian territory without the promised support, but they were loath to give up their gains. The United Nations committed a peacekeeping force to the Sinai Peninsula to protect Israel from further Egyptian incursions, and the Israelis achieved the security they wanted—at least until 1967, when the peacekeeping force was withdrawn. The British and the French got nothing but embarrassment and governments voted out of office. Nasser lost almost all his newly purchased weapons and saw his army badly handled by the Israelis, but he kept the canal and got Soviet money to build his dam. Because he seemed to have humbled the British and French, he was the big winner; he gained higher status in the Arab world, and was encouraged to keep planning actions against Israel. Relations between the United States and its allies were strained for some time, but Eisenhower's refusal to support them in what could possibly have turned into nuclear holocaust was a wise move. The worst aspect for the Americans was their seeming cooperation with their archrival, especially since, concurrently with the Suez crisis, the Soviets were brutally suppressing a revolt in Hungary. To an extent, what this incident really proved was that Britain and France were not the powers they once were.

See also Algeria, French Occupation of; Eisenhower, Dwight David.

References: Beaufre, Andre, *The Suez Expedition, 1956*, trans. Richard Barry (New York: Praeger, 1969); Bowie, Robert, *Suez, 1956* (London: Oxford University Press, 1974); Ovendale, Ritchie, *Origins of the Arab-Israeli Wars* (London: Longman, 1984).

200 SINAI, ISRAELI INVASION OF (1967) (SIX-DAY WAR)

For 10 years after the Suez crisis, the Middle East remained relatively peaceful. The United Nations emergency force kept the Egyptians and the Israelis at a distance, but they could not interfere in the diplomatic connections maintained by the Arab nations. Egypt's President Nasser still wanted to make his country the leader of the Arab world and, after 10 years of Soviet military and economic assistance, he was establishing contacts with the other Arab nations to bring pressure on Israel. Nasser had helped bring into existence the Palestinian Liberation Organization, which was carrying out guerrilla and terrorist raids into Israel that Egypt could no longer mount. The nations of Syria, Jordan, Lebanon, and Iraq supported the Palestinians to one extent or another, so Israel was under increasing pressure from all sides. When Nasser demanded and received the removal of the U.N. forces from the Sinai in May 1967, he occupied Sharm al-Sheikh and closed the Straits of Tiran (Israel's access through the Gulf of Aqaba to the Red Sea). Israel knew that a more serious attack was imminent. Israeli Prime Minister Levi Eshkol gave in to pressure and appointed Moshe Dayan to the post of defense minister. Dayan had been one of the heroes of the 1956 conflict and was well known for his aggressive views of Israeli security. On 3 June, Dayan publicly announced Israel's intentions to carry on diplomatic efforts at peace, but he was secretly mobilizing the military and making plans. Increasing terrorist activity and threatening statements from its Arab neighbors gave Israel sufficient cause to strike first, Dayan believed. He did not think the United States would condemn him, or that the Soviet Union would directly interfere. The official alliance of Jordan with Egypt on 1 June and the passage of an Iraqi division through Jordan were the last straw for Israel.

Just after 8:00 a.m. in Cairo on 5 June, Israeli aircraft flew in low over the Mediterranean and attacked Egyptian airfields, destroying the vast majority of their combat aircraft on the ground. (The Egyptian pilots thought it terribly unfair to be attacked during breakfast.) Within a few hours, Israel had air superiority over the Sinai Peninsula, and its army was on the move. Three columns attacked Egyptian positions in and south of the Gaza Strip, meeting occasionally heavy resistance, but moving deep into the Sinai by the end of the first day. The Egyptian army fought hard at almost every defensive position, but was beaten or outflanked at every one. The Egyptian commander ordered his forces to withdraw to a line 50 miles east of the Suez Canal to defend the three passes covering the approach to the canal.

On Israel's western flank, operations were equally successful. The Iraqi and Jordanian forces were no match for Israeli armor, and soon the Arab forces that withdrew to the east bank of the Jordan River gave the Israelis control of the entire city of Jerusalem for the first time. Again, Israeli air forces were dominant in this area, and won air battles by destroying most Arab aircraft on the ground. The quick Israeli success, coupled with air superiority, convinced the Syrians not to mount an invasion, but to remain in defensive positions on the Golan Heights, from which they could lob artillery fire into the area of Galilee.

By 8 June, the fourth day of the war, Israeli forces were within striking distance of the Suez Canal. Stubborn Arab resistance at the Mitla and Khatmia passes slowed them down, but outstanding Israeli tank gunnery and close air support made all the difference. That evening, the Egyptian government issued a call for a ceasefire, so Israeli commanders ordered a mad dash for the canal to establish the best strategic and tactical position possible before the fighting ended. Israeli forces managed to reach the canal and control the entire western bank, including Port Tewfik, dominating the southern end.

Syria's acceptance of a proposed ceasefire, to go into effect early on 9 June, motivated the Israeli defense minister. Though Israel had not been invaded from the north, Dayan ordered his army to capture the Golan Heights before the ceasefire went into effect. Throughout 8 June, after the armistice was supposed to have begun, Israeli troops fought for the high ground. That night, they dug in and waited for counterattacks that did not come. On the morning of 9 June, they heard explosions; the Syrians were destroying their fortifications and withdrawing. Dayan managed to get the ceasefire time extended long enough to secure vital road junctions to hold the Golan Heights.

The Israeli victory was overwhelming. At a cost of some 800 killed, Israel extended its borders across the Sinai Peninsula (making control of the Gulf of Aqaba a certainty), secured land up to the west bank of the Jordan River (including the whole of Jerusalem), and gained the strong defensive position of the Golan Heights. Militarily, it was as impressive as any operation in history. Politically, it had its drawbacks. Though the war was halted, the fighting did not stop. No Arab nation made peace with Israel, and terrorist attacks intensified, both inside and outside the country. The United Nations, the United States, and the Soviet Union all tried their luck at assisting the peace process, and all failed. The Soviets replaced the lost Arab military equipment and argued that no negotiation could take place until Israel withdrew from its conquered territories. The United States supported Israel, calling for guarantees of Israeli rights before withdrawal. Both Arabs and Israelis carried on a war of attrition that lasted until 1972.

Israel's new lands held almost 1.4 million Arabs, who chafed at the control of their new overlords. The Israeli government had a huge refugee problem, as well as the task of administering territory three times the size of its land area prior to the war. The longstanding hostility against the Jews, intensified by the army of occupation governing them, was a recipe for civil unrest and terrorism. No Arab nation would recognize Israel's right to exist, and after 1967 Israel was in too strong a position to negotiate without solid guarantees to its rights.

See also Israel, Arab Invasion of (Yom Kippur War); Sinai, Israeli Invasion of (1956) (Suez Crisis).

References: Byford-Jones, W., *The Lightning War* (Indianapolis, IN: Bobbs-Merrill, 1968); Dupuy, Trevor, *Elusive Victory: The Arab-Israeli Wars, 1947–1974* (New York: Harper 6k Row, 1978); Gruber, Ruth, *Israel on the Seventh Day* (New York: Hill & Wang, 1968).

201 SINGAPORE AND MALAYA, JAPANESE CONQUEST OF

Singapore was the pride of the British Empire in Southeast Asia, its fortifications bringing it the nickname "the Gibraltar of the East." The British had controlled the island since the early 1800s

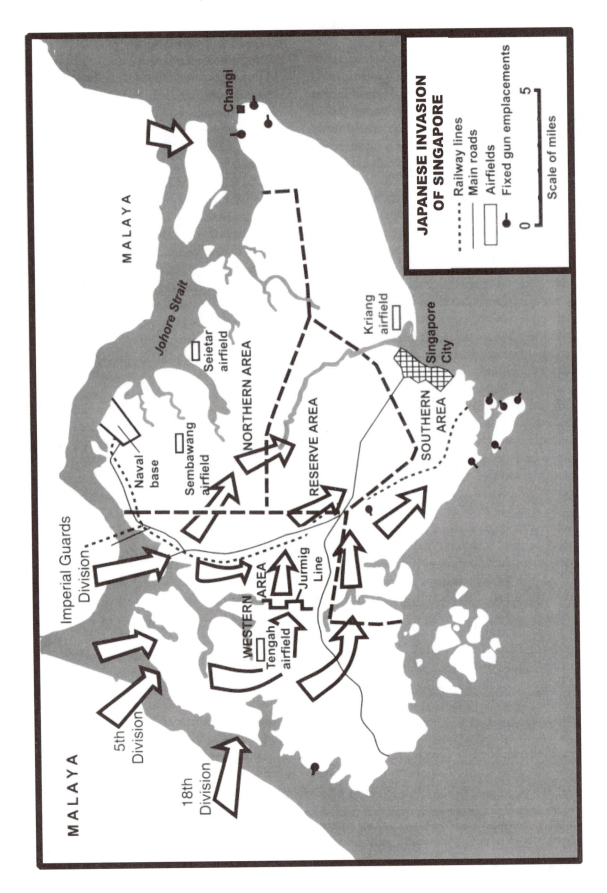

JAPANESE INVASION
OF SINGAPORE

Railway lines
Main roads
Airfields
Fixed gun emplacements

0   5
Scale of miles

MALAYA

Changi

Johore Strait

Seietar airfield

NORTHERN AREA

Kriang airfield

Singapore City

Naval base

Sembawang airfield

RESERVE AREA

SOUTHERN AREA

Imperial Guards Division

WESTERN AREA

Jurmig Line

Tengah airfield

MALAYA

5th Division

18th Division

and had protectorate rights over the remainder of Malaya south of Thailand. Singapore served as the major British port for trade and defense, and the huge artillery protecting the island from invasion made the defenders feel impregnable. The Japanese had other ideas. Certainly, the big guns were daunting, but they had one serious drawback: They pointed to the sea. If the Japanese could invade down the Malay Peninsula, the back door to Singapore should be easy to enter. The British had little concern over this possibility, for there were only two roads down the peninsula, and the remainder was impenetrable jungle and swamp. To Japanese planners on the island of Formosa prior to World War II, the jungle could be penetrated and the British beaten. Specialists in jungle warfare developed tactics to move men through the rough terrain, and by the end of 1941 the Japanese had trained in Formosan jungles and had become the finest jungle fighters anywhere.

As war approached in late 1941, the British commanders in Singapore begged London for an increase in men and aircraft. As only a few ships could be spared to the Indian Ocean, the British thought that air power was their best defense from invasion. However, because of the demands of British forces in Europe and Prime Minister Winston Churchill's focus on that theater, little could be spared for Singapore and Malaya. Some Indian army troops were sent to bulk up the defense forces, but they were not well trained or equipped. Australian troops were the primary defense forces in Malaya.

The British commanders in Singapore were sure that when war came to their area, the Japanese based in Indochina would be sending men their way. There were only three likely points of invasion along the eastern shore of the Malay Peninsula, and two of those sites were in Thailand. Plans were prepared for British forces to move first and seize the towns of Patani and Singora before the Japanese could land there, but London decided that any move prior to Japanese action would be provocative, so the preemptive strike never happened. The three Japanese divisions detailed for the invasion, under the leadership of General Tomoyuki Yamashita, landed in Thailand to no resistance, and only limited defenses at the Malay port of Kota Bharu.

Japanese landing craft went ashore just after midnight on 8 December through waters that were almost too rough in which to operate. They overcame the resistance of Indian army forces at Kota Bharu, and moved inland. At Patani and Singora, the Japanese quickly established themselves and moved south across the peninsula along the two roads that led to the western shore. The only serious British defense was mounted at Jitra by the Eleventh Indian Division, but they were amazed to find the enemy moving through the jungle and outflanking them. On 12 December, the British withdrew, and from that day forward the Japanese were unstoppable. The Commonwealth forces were insufficiently prepared for the attack, and soon their spirit broke. The demoralized forces often withdrew even against inferior numbers, and they took casualties far out of proportion to those they inflicted.

The British withdrew rapidly down the peninsula, stopping to fight at each river crossing, then destroying the bridge and pulling back. Anticipating this tactic, the Japanese had brought more than the usual number of engineers and bridge-building units who quickly built bridges and continued the pursuit. The British were never able to stand at one spot long enough to dig in and stage a serious firefight. When the terrain became too difficult even for the specially trained Japanese, they staged amphibious landings to outflank the British and keep them on the run. By 31 January 1942, the Japanese occupied the entire peninsula, and the British, Indian, and Australian forces withdrew to the island of Singapore.

Yamashita had staged an impressive march, but he was still dissatisfied. His superiors disliked him for political reasons, and did not provide him with the support he deemed necessary. One of his three divisions was commanded by a general who was continually insubordinate. His entire command had never trained together, and his staff had been created only a few weeks prior to the invasion. Those factors made his success even more phenomenal, but he still had to take Singapore. He spent four days reconnoitering before launching his assault. He ordered one division to feint across the eastern end of the strait and draw the British reserves to that end of the island. He sent the other two divisions in landing craft against Singapore's western shore.

The heavy artillery on the island's southern shore did the best it could, but not all the guns could be traversed to meet the attack from the north, and even those that could had difficulty doing significant damage, because the range of 15 miles or more made observing and targeting almost impossible. The units assigned to beach defense tried to fight the landing craft in the dark, but the Japanese units came in along such a wide front that they were again able to penetrate and outflank the defenders. Orders came from Churchill to fight to the last man in the rubble of a destroyed city, but the fighting did not go on that long. A lack of water, caused by the aerial destruction of the pumping machinery, brought the defenders to a rapid crisis. Yamashita also faced a crisis: He was running out of ammunition. He decided to keep fighting as hard as possible, rather than scale back his attack and give the British an indication of his problem. His ruse worked; the British raised the white flag on 15 February and surrendered unconditionally.

The 73-day campaign cost the Commonwealth 9,000 dead and wounded and 130,000 prisoners. The Japanese lost a mere 3,000 killed and 7,000 wounded in the entire campaign. The British commander, Lieutenant General A. E. Percival, had asked for and received promises from Yamashita that the civilian population would remain unharmed, but the Japanese occupation was not pleasant. Food was scarce and the currency became worthless; the locals, especially those of Chinese descent, were treated harshly and forced into labor gangs for the Japanese. One source mentions that 70,000 Chinese were arrested, then executed—by being tied together and thrown into the sea. Anyone suspected of or caught in the act of espionage was tortured and beheaded. The British had left some men behind Japanese lines, somewhat by design, and they organized resistance groups that operated out of the jungle throughout the war. They did not do much damage, but they trained the locals for action when the Allied reinvasion took place. These units did not coordinate their activities too well, but they were in contact with British authorities in India, who kept them supplied with weapons and equipment through air drops. Along with these British-sponsored units was a Communist organization, the Malayan People's Anti-Japanese Army (MPAJA).

By June 1945, Australian forces were working their way through the East Indies toward Singapore and Malaya, and plans for the invasion of the peninsula were well advanced. The atomic bomb drops in early August made the invasion unnecessary. The Australians were not prepared to immediately come in and take over, so the MPAJA came in from the jungles and tried to establish control, using the time of disorganization to execute those whom they suspected of collaboration. The Japanese favoritism toward the Malays during the occupation, coupled with their persecution of the Chinese, led many guerrillas to believe that collaboration was widespread. The British military administration set up in September, and for some months ran Singapore in the absence of a civil government. The Colonial Office in London had plans to offer Malaya independence by 1946.

It took many months before production of goods and services could be reestablished. Even though the Japanese had invaded the peninsula to take advantage of its natural resources of tin and rubber, they had produced virtually none of either. The economic disorganization was matched by political disarray. Prior to the war, the peninsula was called the Unfederated Malay States, and for years the London government had planned on independence for this area based on states' rights. However, the constitution they imposed in 1946, the Malay Union, created a strong central government, which the factions in Malaya were unwilling to support. The union did not include Singapore because it remained vital to British strategic needs, and its dominant Chinese population would not fit well with the peninsular groups. Resistance to this government was widespread and even criticized in Parliament, so in 1948 a conference was held to fine-tune the document. The strong central government would be replaced by a confederation in which Malays held the dominant citizenship privileges. The state governments would exercise major power, while participating in a central legislature. The new Malay government came from the efforts of political moderates after left-wing groups were banned. By 1951, Malay and Chinese banded together in political parties.

First, however, the Communists had a try at taking over. Since they had operated out of the jungles throughout the war, they were accustomed to the terrain, and used it well. British antiterrorist units were brought in; by relocating the population away from the guerrillas and treating them well in relocation camps, the Communist movement was crushed. A state of emergency lasted from 1948 through 1955. By 1957, the citizens of the peninsula had drafted a constitution, and independence was granted in August.

The British were hesitant to grant independence to Singapore because of the former's strategic interests. A city council was granted, which formed the first political parties on the island. The Communists, though not as violent as on the mainland, agitated through labor unions and Chinese schools. Not until 1958 did the island acquire self-rule and control over its economy and trade; Britain retains only defense rights. Singapore has developed into the fourth largest port in the world and one of the world's premier banking centers.

See also Singapore, British Occupation of.

References: Caffrey, Kate, *Out in the Midday Sun: Singapore 1941–1945* (New York: Stein & Day, 1973); Ienaga, Saburo, *The Pacific War, 1931–1945* (New York: Random House, 1978); Ryan, N. J., *A History of Malaysia and Singapore* (Oxford: Oxford University Press, 1976).

SOUTH KOREA, NORTH KOREAN INVASION OF (KOREAN WAR)

Numerous foreign powers occupied Korea throughout its history, but the peninsula had always been the home of one nation. This changed for the first time at the end of World War II. At the Yalta Conference in February 1945, American President Franklin Roosevelt, British Prime Minister Winston Churchill, and Soviet Premier Joseph Stalin agreed on zones of occupation for their forces at war's end. On the Korean peninsula, a line was drawn at 38 degrees north latitude to designate which forces would accept the surrender of Japanese troops: the Soviets above the line, and the Americans below it. Soviet forces entered Korea in early August 1945 and soon announced that the inhabitants requested their assistance in creating a Communist government. Koreans below that line, oddly enough, made no such request. The matter was sent to the new United Nations, which decided, in August 1947, that internationally supervised elections should be held throughout the country to determine the will of the people. The Soviet-occupied northern half of the country refused to cooperate, and announced the formation of the Democratic People's Republic of Korea. The inhabitants of the south formed a democratic government, the Republic of Korea.

Thus, a nation that had never been divided was split in half. The Soviets provided the North Koreans with military training and heavy weapons, while the Americans assisted the South Koreans in creating a lightly armed defense force. For almost three years there was unrest along the border. The critical point in relations between the two Koreas came in January 1950. U.S. Secretary of State Dean Acheson announced the creation of a "defense perimeter," areas of the world the United States considered vital to its security and therefore would quickly defend. Areas outside that perimeter, which included South Korea, were told to appeal to the United Nations if threatened by outside forces. Coupled with a gradual withdrawal of American occupation forces, the North Koreans saw this as an admission that South Korea was not important to the United States. North Korean leader Kim Il Sung traveled to Moscow to ask Stalin for permission and assistance in attacking the south, and plans were made for an invasion.

On 25 June 1950, 175,000 heavily armed North Koreans invaded the south. Within a few days, the republic's capital at Seoul was captured, and South Korean forces, along with the few remaining American troops, were in retreat. South Korean President Syngman Rhee appealed to the United Nations for assistance.

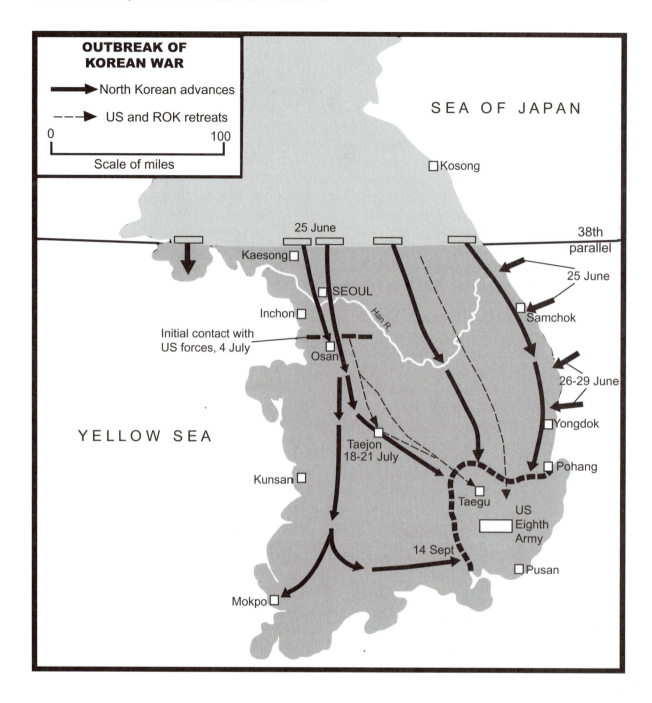

OUTBREAK OF KOREAN WAR

→ North Korean advances

⇢ US and ROK retreats

0   100

Scale of miles

SEA OF JAPAN

☐Kosong

25 June

Kaesong☐

☐SEOUL

Inchon☐

Han R.

Initial contact with
US forces, 4 July

☐
Osan

YELLOW SEA

Taejon
18-21 July

Kunsan ☐

Taegu ☐

38th
parallel

25 June

☐
Samchok

26-29 June

☐Yongdok

☐ Pohang

US
Eighth
Army

14 Sept

☐Pusan

Mokpo☐

At American urging and in the absence of a Soviet delegate boycotting the organization, the United Nations voted to ask for world nations to volunteer forces to aid the Republic of Korea. Sixteen countries ultimately offered aid in one form or another, but the vast majority of troops came from the United States.

American President Harry Truman ordered American forces in Japan under the command of General Douglas MacArthur to assist South Korea. MacArthur immediately had U.S. aircraft based in Japan giving direct support to retreating Allied forces and attacking North Korean troops and supply lines. U.S. forces in Japan were ferried to the south coast port of Pusan, where they began to set up a defensive line along the Naktong River while troops were being mobilized in the United States. From late July to mid-September, American and South Korean troops fought a tenacious defense against almost constant Communist North Korean attacks in what came to be known as the Pusan perimeter.

What was needed was an attack in the North Korean rear to isolate their forces and cut off their supply lines. MacArthur proposed landing U.S. Marines at the port of Inchon, just west of Seoul. Because most of the North Korean effort was concentrated along the Pusan perimeter, few troops would be in the rear to fend off such an assault. The problem with this idea was the target city itself. Inchon is the site of the largest tidal swell in the world—30 feet between high and low tides. Ships would have to unload very quickly during high tide to avoid being stranded in the mud and exposed to hostile fire at low tide. MacArthur overcame Washington's resistance to the idea and staged the landing on 15 September. It was a huge success. Within two weeks, U.S. forces had crossed the peninsula and cut off virtually the entire North Korean army. Coupled with an offensive out of the Pusan perimeter, the invading troops were almost completely captured between the two forces.

At this point, the U.N. mission had been accomplished. By the first week in October, South Korea was again free. President Truman decided to fulfill the U.N. mandate of 1947 to hold supervised elections all across the country. On his own, with the immediate approval of Syngman Rhee and the hesitant approval of the United Nations, Truman ordered MacArthur to lead U.N. forces into the north. On 7 October, South Korean troops backed by U.N. forces entered the north on a mission of reunion. This action led to a dangerous response. China, which was traditionally xenophobic, did not like the idea of foreign troops approaching its borders. The Communist Chinese government, in power for only a year, warned the United Nations that if China felt threatened, its government could not stop "volunteers" from crossing the Yalu River into North Korea to assist their Communist brethren. MacArthur assured Truman that this was a bluff; the Chinese could not possibly commit enough troops to make any difference. With this assurance, Truman ordered the advance into the north to proceed.

By late November the operation seemed nearly complete. Because of a mountain range running north-south through the peninsula, the forces advanced in two columns that were not in direct contact with each other. U.N. forces on both sides of the mountains had almost reached the North Korean border with China at the Yalu River.

The presence of Chinese troops was minimal, and the advance halted so the troops could enjoy a Thanksgiving dinner in the field on 25 November; MacArthur guaranteed the men that they would be home by Christmas. The next day, 180,000 Chinese Communist forces swarmed down from the mountains, surrounding and decimating large numbers of U.N. troops. To make matters worse, extremely cold weather struck. Allied troops had to make a fighting withdrawal in subfreezing temperatures against Chinese troops that were everywhere at once. By early 1951, U.N. forces, in full retreat, had crossed the 38th parallel heading south. Seoul was again captured by Communist forces. MacArthur denied any responsibility, and blamed Washington for not allowing him to use air power to interdict Chinese men and materiel at or beyond the Yalu River. Truman refused to sanction any attacks on Chinese soil, so MacArthur was not allowed to attack anything unless it was already in Korea. When he complained to the press about the restrictions put on his decisions, and did so contrary to orders from Washington, President Truman relieved him of his command in April 1951 and replaced him with General Matthew Ridgeway.

In the spring of 1951, Ridgeway was able to solidify the U.N. resistance some 50 miles south of Seoul. He counterattacked, and by June had recrossed the 38th parallel going north, but could go no farther. Trench warfare ensued, looking more like World War I than the fast-moving fighting of the previous year. When both sides failed to make headway against each other, they began considering peace talks. The first attempt at negotiations bogged down in July, and the fighting continued. By November, the two sides were talking at the border village of Panmunjom as the killing went on. Negotiations stalled on the question of prisoner exchange. Most of the prisoners captured by U.N. forces, both North Korean and Chinese, expressed the desire to remain in the south rather than go back to their forces or their country. When the United Nations promised them that they would not be forcibly repatriated, the Communists demanded the return of all the prisoners, not believing the U.N. claim that so many did not want to be returned. No agreement could be made, so the fighting went on until June 1953, when Joseph Stalin died in Moscow. He had been the major supporter of the North Korean effort and, in the ensuing struggle for power in the Soviet Union, the Korean War fell low on the list of priorities. At this point, the Communists in Panmunjom agreed to take back only those prisoners who wanted to return, and an armistice was signed. Negotiations continued on a treaty to bring about peace and an official end to the conflict. Those negotiations were still going on 40 years later, with no end in sight.

The Republic of Korea maintained its democracy and reestablished close ties with the United States. By the 1990s, it had become an economically expanding nation with a growing export market in the mold of Japan: electronics and automobiles. The people enjoy a high standard of living and are active in Asian affairs. North Korea, on the other hand, has not enjoyed the same success. Tied to the Soviet Union throughout the Cold War era, its people lived under the iron hand of Kim Il Sung, who established a personality cult dominating every part of their society. The North Koreans continued to harass the border along the ceasefire line, and attempted to make life generally miserable for the south. Their hard-core Communist government remains one of the last such regimes in the wake of the collapse of the Soviet Union and the downfall of communism throughout most of the world. An isolated nation, cut off from most of the world's trade and political relations, the country has advanced very little since the end of the conflict.

References: Fehrenbach, T. R., *This Kind of War* (New York: Macmillan, 1963); Langley, Michael, *Inchon Landing* (New York: New York Times Books, 1979); Stokesbury, James, *A Short History of the Korean War* (New York: Morrow, 1988).

SOVIET UNION, NAZI INVASION OF THE

203

Early in his political career, Adolf Hitler wrote *Mein Kampf*, spelling out his ideas on how to make Germany great again after the disaster of World War I. One of the necessities was to regain land that the Germans had captured from Russia in that war, but which had been taken away from them by the Treaty of Versailles. This land was rightfully theirs by conquest, Hitler argued, and Germany needed that land as *lebensraum*, or living space. Since the Germans had conquered almost all of of European Russia, and been ceded that territory by the Communists through the Treaty of Brest-Litovsk in early 1918, their invading Russia would simply be a reoccupation of land legally belonging to Germany. Of course, this was the best land the Soviet Union owned: the great farm country of the Ukraine, the industrial and economic centers of Kiev and Minsk, and the Baltic ports.

Hitler successfully hid his intentions from the Soviets. Though he openly attacked communism in his speeches and backed Franco's forces in the Spanish Civil War while the Soviets supported the government cause, he made no open threats against the Soviet Union. He was quick to exploit the hesitancy of the British and French in the summer of 1939 when they would not treat the Soviet Union as an equal partner. Soviet Premier Joseph Stalin had not expected this rebuff, and it resulted in the signing of the German-Soviet Nonaggression Pact, or Molotov-Ribbentrop Treaty, in August 1939, just days before Hitler invaded Poland. That agreement amazed the world because the Soviets seemed to be just as violently anti-Nazi as Hitler was anti-Communist. Even more shocking, the world soon learned that a secret clause of the nonaggression pact was an agreement to cooperate in Poland's dismemberment. The Soviet invasion of Poland in mid-September 1939, just as the entire Polish military was focused on the defense of Warsaw, was one of the most blatant stabs in the back in all of history. Stalin and Hitler, the strangest of bedfellows, each had half of Poland to act as a buffer zone against the other. Further, Hitler promised Stalin that

NAZI INVASION OF THE SOVIET UNION

Nazi lines of advance
Front lines 1 Sept 1941
Front lines 5 Dec 1941
Territory reoccuppied by Soviets 6 Dec 1941-Apr 1942
Front lines 18 Nov 1942

0   500

Scale of miles

Germany would not interfere with the Soviet Union's attacks on the Baltic States or Finland, which the Soviets undertook in November 1939. This diplomatic marriage of convenience was off to an auspicious start.

With his rear covered, Hitler made war against the West in the spring and summer of 1940, invading Norway, Denmark, the Low Countries, and France; he then spent the next few months in a fruitless attempt to bring Britain into the Nazi fold. Only after September 1940, when he postponed indefinitely the invasion of Britain, did Hitler turn back toward the East and his dream of *lebensraum*. From the fall of 1940 through the spring of 1941, he made preparations for the invasion, all the while dealing with unexpected sideshows such as aiding Italy in North Africa and Greece. These diversions, which included an airborne attack on Crete, served to delay the invasion of the Soviet Union. A one-month suspension of the start, until 22 June 1941, was quite possibly the reason Hitler's attempt on Mother Russia failed.

Stalin remained blissfully unaware of Hitler's intentions, even though there were attempts to warn him. Britain's code-breaking machine, ULTRA, gave the Western allies a look at Germany's plans. Britain was officially at war with the Soviet Union, but British Prime Minister Winston Churchill nevertheless tried to alert Stalin to Hitler's intentions—to no avail. Stalin was busy purging his own military and had no time to worry about anyone else's. Certainly, Stalin thought, Churchill was just trying to sow some discontent between allies.

Thus, Hitler's generals were able to amass three army groups for the invasion eastward. Army Group North was directed to drive through the Baltic States to secure the port city of Leningrad. Army Group Center's target was the Soviet capital city of Moscow. Army Group South was to drive for the Caucasus and its oil fields. All three got off to outstanding beginnings. The unprepared Soviet government watched in horror as entire Soviet armies were surrounded and captured in a matter of days. The German blitzkrieg, perfected in Poland and France, proved itself once again on the plains of Byelorussia and the Ukraine. The initial attacks were so successful that Hitler spurned an opportunity that arose early in the invasion. He found that many Byelorussians and Ukrainians so despised the Communist regime that they would assist the Germans in deposing it. Some people viewed the Germans more as liberators than invaders. "The Baltic countries, Ukraine, and Byelorussa all welcomed Nazi invasion in June, 1941, as a potential means of liberation from Soviet rule. Although the Slavs were considered to be of subhuman status according to Nazi ideology, nationalists hoped that by participating in brutality against the Jews, they would ingratiate themselves with the Germans." (secretlives.org)

The German forces thus had the opportunity not only to gain ground, but to gain size; as they drove deeper into enemy territory, they could actually build a larger army—an army augmented by motivated soldiers familiar with the Soviet military.

Instead, Hitler was married to the racial policies spelled out in *Mein Kampf*. The *lebensraum* was to be for Germans only, so the *untermensch*, or subhumans, who lived there were to be removed. Therefore, the would-be volunteers were either killed, rounded up for slave labor, or—if they were Jewish—shipped to extermination camps. "Those same communities were sorely disappointed as the German military, the Gestapo, and other fascist security forces deemed the Ukrainian nation–like all Slavs–as nothing more than slave labor to be exploited" Lavelle, Commentary). Those who managed to escape those fates headed for the hills and forests to organize guerrilla partisan movements, which made a great difference to Hitler's ultimate fate in the East. At the height of the German advance, when they were engaged heavily at Leningrad, Moscow, and Stalingrad, they were obliged to maintain almost half their army in the rear to guard their supply lines. Instead of building his army as he went, Hitler was forced to cut in half the army he had in order to deal with the Ukrainians and Byelorussians he had rejected.

Perhaps Hitler's grasp on reality was beginning to fade, or perhaps it was the overwhelming success of his invasion that dictated his attitude toward the people he conquered, because his opening successes were phenomenal. German armies raced over vast tracts of land; the only defense the Soviets could mount because of their huge losses in manpower was a scorched-earth policy. By denying the Germans the ability to live off the land, and by partisans harassing the ever-lengthening supply lines, the Soviets finally forced the German army to move not as it wished, but as its dwindling logistics dictated. Still, by September the port city of Leningrad was being surrounded and besieged, Moscow was virtually within German artillery range, and German armies were in the Crimea and poised to move into the oil-rich Caucasus. Another month of good weather, denied them because of the delay in starting the invasion, might have put the German army in warm cities when the winter came. By using rather than abusing the local volunteers, the Germans would have had easier transport and supply lines to put them in those same cities. Instead, German soldiers had to face Mother Russia's oldest ally, Mother Nature.

Virtually every invader over the centuries has learned to his dismay that few winters can match those found in Russia. When Napoleon invaded Russia in 1812, he found himself in weather reaching -32 degrees Celsius, and 1941 proved to be 1812's rival. German forces had to survive in their summer uniforms because Hitler had been positive their goals would be reached before winter uniforms were necessary. Warm clothing was available in Germany, of course, but the increasing difficulty of moving materiel over guerrilla-infested supply lines kept most of that clothing out of German hands. Military activity basically ground to a halt until the following spring. Though the Germans suffered, so did the Russians. The two million people besieged in Leningrad (and another million in outlying areas) had to survive two successive winters with virtually no contact with the outside world. But survive they did, in one of history's most heroic defenses. Just over half a million people were in the city when it was liberated in January 1944.

The spring of 1942 brought the return of German successes in the south, but Hitler's maddening habit of withdrawing units from the south to reinforce the other army groups, especially around Moscow, limited Army Group South's effectiveness. Advance German units reportedly saw the Caucasus oil fields in the distance, but the Nazis never reached them. Instead, the major portion of the force went to capture Stalingrad, on the Volga River. Because the city was named for the leader of his enemy, Hitler demanded that there be no withdrawal until Stalingrad was captured. Stalin, equally prideful, demanded his forces fight just as hard and long.

The German Sixth Army went into Stalingrad in late summer 1942, and never returned. Some 350,000 German soldiers fought to capture the city, and only 5,000 ever saw Germany again. Combat was street by street, house by house, room by room, mostly in the dead of winter. Russian tank factories rolled tanks off the assembly line, put a crew inside, and sent them around the corner or down the street directly into combat. Desperate to save his city, Stalin decided to withdraw forces from the Far East, where he had been awaiting a possible Japanese offensive. Those troops, transported across the breadth of Russia, finally surrounded and destroyed the Sixth Army and blunted Germany's thrust toward Russian oil. Hitler ordered his forces in the city not to break out: "Where the German soldier has once set foot, there he remains." He promoted the army's commander, Frederick von Paulus, to field marshal, since no German field marshal had ever been taken prisoner. The orders doomed the Germans, because a tactical withdrawal might have linked up with forces fighting to relieve the Sixth Army and made a later capture of the city possible.

By the spring of 1943, German forces had driven almost as far as they ever would. They had made little headway against Leningrad or Moscow and, after Stalingrad, they were forced onto the defensive in the south. Hitler's dream of *lebensraum* died in the light of military realities: insufficient logistics, a hostile civilian population, inconsistent command from Berlin. The one overriding factor, however, was one that Hitler had preached against after the German experience of World War I: fighting a two-front war. Trying to supply men and materiel to both the Eastern Front and to North Africa, then Sicily and Italy, and finally to France after June 1944, proved impossible, just as it had in 1917–1918. Too many enemies at once, both from abroad and among the conquered territories, proved to be more than any country could handle.

The fighting in the Soviet Union created long-term results for the people defending the country and ultimately for the world. In the Soviet Union, this conflict was referred to not as World War II, but as the Great Patriotic War. People who hated Stalin and communism ultimately fought for them—not out of ideology, but out of love for their country. There is an almost mystical tie between the Russian people and their land, and Stalin played on that throughout the war and afterward. From the time he met with President Franklin Roosevelt and Prime Minister Churchill in Teheran in November 1943, Stalin accused the West of delaying a major European invasion so that the Nazis and Communists would kill each other. That accusation became the justification for almost all his actions through the end of the war and into the postwar period. Russia had suffered, so Russians should benefit by capturing Berlin, taking control of Eastern Europe, and exploiting the German people and territory they had captured. Stalin's appeal to patriotism saved the country in 1942 and 1943, but it set up a confrontational attitude throughout the Cold War.

See also Russia, Napoleon's Invasion of; Britain, Nazi Invasion of (Battle of Britain); Egypt, Italian Invasion of; Finland, Soviet Invasion of; France, Nazi Invasion of; Greece, Nazi Invasion of; Hitler, Adolf; Norway and Denmark, Nazi Invasion of; Poland, Nazi Conquest of; Russia, German Invasion of.

References: Carrell, Paul, *Hitler Moves East, 1941–1943* (Boston: Little, Brown, 1965); Clark, Alan, *Barbarossa* (New York: Morrow, 1965); Guderian, Heinz, *Panzer Leader* (New York: Dutton, 1957); Lavelle, Peter, "Did Russia Defeat Hitler?", United Press International, Moscow, 19 April 2005, in *Washington Times*; "Secret Lives," Aviva Films, 2000, <www.secretlives.org>.

TURKEY, BRITISH INVASION OF

204

By the end of 1914, the war in France had settled into a deadlock. With both Allied and Central powers anchoring their flanks on the English Channel and the Swiss border, defenses in depth were the rule. Some in the British government believed that the war might have to be won elsewhere, or that at least the Allies should pose a sufficient threat to make Germany withdraw troops and weaken their position in France. The Russians were having little success against Germany, so that front seemed unlikely to bring any luck. First Lord of the Admiralty Winston Churchill suggested an attack against Germany's ally, Turkey. Turkey had its fingers in many pies: a new attack against the Caucasus to threaten Russia, an abortive move against the Suez Canal,

and a defensive stand against a British force moving up from the Persian Gulf. Certainly, Churchill argued, a direct thrust against the Turkish capital at Constantinople should be enough to disrupt the Turkish military and panic its government into surrender. Secretary of State for War Lord Kitchener blocked any attempt to siphon off soldiers from the fighting in France, so Churchill stated that the victory could be won by the Royal Navy alone. Churchill proposed to destroy the forts that guarded the Dardanelles, the passageway to Constantinople and the Black Sea, after which a naval force could cruise up to the Turkish capital and bombard the city at leisure. He was certain that naval gunfire could destroy the forts. When the Turks had joined the war the previous November, a British naval raid against the straits met virtually no resistance from the obsolescent Turkish defenses, so the Turkish government should surrender at gunpoint with little trouble. Once Turkey had been removed from the war, Churchill argued, a direct supply line to and from Russia would be open, and the Balkan States that had allied themselves with Germany should cave in quickly to Allied pressure and threaten Germany's other ally, Austria-Hungary. The British Cabinet reluctantly approved.

The force that gathered at the Greek island of Lemnos in February 1915 was made up of both British and French battleships. Though they were allies, the French had no intention of allowing Britain to control the straits alone. Under overall British command, the armada sailed to the mouth of the Dardanelles and began bombarding the forts. Little did the British know that the previous November's raid had alerted the Turks to the weakness of their defenses and, under the direction of German adviser Field Marshal Colmar von der Goltz, they had been working steadily ever since to improve their fortifications.

The Allies began bombarding the forts, and were surprised to find no return fire until they drew close to shore. The first few hours of shelling had had little effect, and the Allies withdrew to wait out some bad weather. When they returned on 25 February, the shelling continued with irregular results. Some forts were

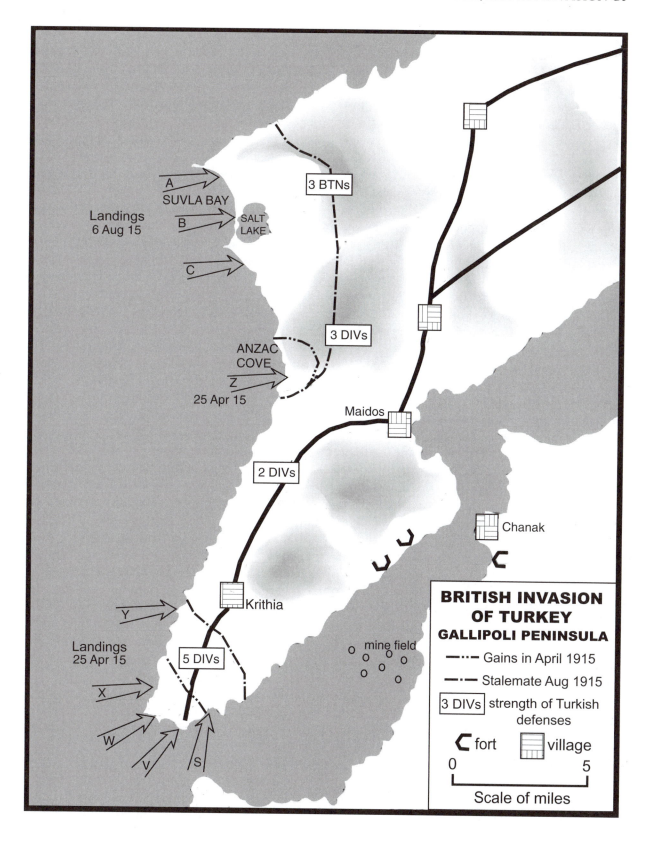

Landings
6 Aug 15

A

SUVLA BAY

B

SALT
LAKE

C

3 BTNs

3 DIVs

ANZAC
COVE

Z

25 Apr 15

Maidos

2 DIVs

Chanak

Krithia

Landings
25 Apr 15

Y

5 DIVs

X

W

V

S

mine field

BRITISH INVASION OF TURKEY
GALLIPOLI PENINSULA

—··— Gains in April 1915

—·— Stalemate Aug 1915

3 DIVs strength of Turkish defenses

C fort   village

0   5

Scale of miles

silenced by the naval guns, then blown apart by landing parties. Others survived erratic shelling with little problem. Turkish return fire was bothersome, but not dangerous. It was not artillery fire, however, that turned the tide, but mines. The Allies knew the Turks had sown the straits with mines, and had brought along minesweepers to take care of the problem. But the art of minesweeping was in its infancy, and a secret Turkish operation in a previously cleared area proved the Allies' undoing. On 18 March the ships sailed in to run the length of the straits and ran straight into the new minefield. Within a few hours, three ships were sunk and three were badly damaged. The naval forces withdrew. Had they pushed forward past this point, the mission may well have been successful, because the Turks were almost out of ammunition. The navy had failed, and called for the army.

Oddly enough, the government in London had been preparing forces for the campaign. Kitchener's early resistance turned to grudging acceptance, and 75,000 men, many from the Australia and New Zealand Army Corps (Anzacs), were assigned to land on the Gallipoli Peninsula. Sir Ian Hamilton was given command of the operation, though he was allowed little time to prepare; the government wanted results in a hurry. Because Hamilton found the base at Lemnos unfit for a major operation, he redirected the troops' convoys to Alexandria, Egypt. The ships had to be unloaded and reloaded in an attempt to repair the haphazard loading done in England. Finally, the expedition got under way in mid-April 1915. Hamilton decided to land forces at five spots along the peninsula, plus a French diversionary force on the Asiatic side of the mouth of the straits. This multiple landing would allow the troops to swarm over the peninsula and capture the forts, thereby giving the navy the opportunity to sail by unhindered. Rarely has the expression "So close and yet so far" had such meaning in military history as it did on 25 April 1915. The Turkish defenders, though outnumbering the attackers, were mostly held in reserve at the neck of the peninsula. At some beaches, stiff resistance forced slow progress, but at others there was little or no resistance. The Turks were unprepared for

multiple landings, and aggressive action would have given the Allies an easy victory. Hamilton, onboard ship, had reports from all the beaches, but he preferred to have the local commanders respond to individual circumstances. Local commanders were operating on a preset timetable, and did not take advantage of opportunities because inland advances were scheduled for later. While the British, Anzacs, and French stayed on the beaches, whether through Turkish resistance or lack of leadership, the Turks were able to reinforce. By the time assaults were made, the Turks shot down the attackers in huge numbers. The quick, easy operation soon turned into a miniature version of the trench warfare of France.

Through the summer of 1915, the men on the beaches made little or no headway against Turkish defenses, which grew constantly stronger. Reinforcements sent in August repeated the failings of April: easy landings against little resistance, followed by enough hesitation to allow the Turks time to react. The 35,000 men committed in August ended up stuck on the beaches under punishing fire just like their comrades earlier. From beginning to end, the operation to force the straits suffered from a lack of planning and preparation. For example, the navy was sent in to capture Constantinople, though it is impossible for ships to take or hold targets on land. The amphibious operations were experimental to a great extent because the troops taking part had no previous training. Actually, the landings were successful; it was the push off the beaches that failed. The troops, both British and Anzac, were recent inductees in combat for the first time, and their lack of experience led to much confusion during and immediately after the landings. Although both Allies and Turks made mistakes, the Turks made fewer and won the battle. The Allies successfully evacuated in December.

The invasion reinforced the Turks' morale and strengthened their resolve to support Germany. Now veterans with a success under their belts, the Turkish troops transferred to Mesopotamia to take part in the successful siege of Kut-al-Amara, in which the Sixth Indian Division was captured after the longest siege in

British history. For the losing side, there are only a series of might-have-beens. As the battle took place, representatives of Britain, France, and Russia were dividing up the Ottoman Empire among them; Constantinople and the straits were to have gone to Russia, and the Russians would have attained their centuries-old dream of warm-water access for their navy. If the Western Allies could have used this passage to reinforce or resupply the Russians, would the Eastern Front have held? Would the Russian Revolution have taken place? Would the Balkan States have abandoned the Central Powers in order to grab what they could from a struggling Austria-Hungary? The future of Eastern Europe may well have been much different had the British Royal Navy in March or the soldiers on the ground in April 1915 seized opportunities that would have given them a relatively easy victory.

See also Mesopotamia, British Invasion of; Russia, German Invasion of.

References: Bush, Eric, *Gallipoli* (London: George Allen & Unwin, 1975); Fewster, Kevin, *A Turkish View of Gallipoli* (Richmond, Victoria, Australia: Hodja, 1985); Moorehead, Alan, *Gallipoli* (New York: Harper & Brothers, 1956).

SECTION TWO: BIBLIOGRAPHY

BIBLIOGRAPHY

Abbot, John S. C., *Life of Napoleon*, 4 vols. (New York: Harper & Brothers, 1855–1856).

Adams, James Truslow, *Building the British Empire* (New York: Scribner's Sons, 1938).

Addington, Larry, *Patterns of War through the Eighteenth Century* (Bloomington: Indiana University Press, 1990).

Adkin, Mark, *Urgent Fury: The Battle for Grenada* (Lexington, MA: D. C. Heath, 1989).

Alden, Richard, *The American Revolution* (New York: Harper & Row, 1954).

Allan, John, *The Cambridge Shorter History of India* (Delhi: S. Chand, 1964).

Allsen, Thomas, *Mongol Imperialism* (Berkeley: University of California Press, 1987).

American Committee to Save Bosnia, "A Summary of the Crisis in Bosnia," Mostar Online, www.geocities.com/Heartland/1935/crisis.html, 19 December 2005.

Anderson, David, *Histories of the Hanged: The Dirty War in Kenya and the End of Empire* (New York: W. W. Norton, 2005).

Anderson, David, lecture at School of Oriental and African Studies, London, 13 January 2005, www.royalafricansociety. org/reports publications/recent_meetings/histories maumau, 14 November 2005.

Arbrnan, Holger, *The Vikings* (New York: Praeger, 1961).

Armstrong, Karen, *Holy War* (New York: Macmillan, 1988).

Arnbrose, Stephen, *D-Day, June 6, 1944* (New York: Simon &. Schuster, 1994).

————, *Eisenhower: Soldier and Statesman* (New York: Simon & Schuster, 1990).

Arnold, James, *Napoleon Conquers Austria: The 1809 Campaign for Vienna* (Westport, CT Praeger, 1995).

Arrian, *The Campaigns of Alexander*, trans. Aubrey de Selincourt (New York: Penguin, 1958).

Audric, John, *Angkor and the Khmer Empire* (London: R. Hale, 1972).

Badri, Hasan, *The Ramadan War, 1973* (Boulder, CO: Westview Press, 1978).

Badsey, Steven, "Ashanti War," in Richard Holmes, ed., *Oxford Companion to Military History* (Oxford: Oxford University Press, 2001).

Bagnall, Nigel, *The Punic Wars* (London: Hutchinson, 1990).

Baines, J., and J. Malek, *Atlas of Ancient Egypt* (New York: Facts on File, 1980).

Baker, G. R, *Hannibal* (New York: Barnes &. Noble, 1967).

Balsdon, J. R. V. D., *Rome: The Story of an Empire* (New York: McGraw-Hill, 1970).

Barker, A. J., *The Civilizing Mission* (New York: Dial Press, 1968).

————, *The Neglected War* (London: Cassel & Co., 1967).

Barker, Elizabeth, *British Policy in Southeast Europe in the Second World War* (New York: Barnes & Noble, 1976).

Barker, John, *Justinian and the Later Roman Empire* (Madison: University of Wisconsin Press, 1966).

Bar-Kochva, Bezalel, *The Seleucid Army* (London: Cambridge University Press, 1976).

Barnes, Timothy, *The New Empire of Diocletian and Constantine* (Cambridge, MA: Harvard University Press, 1982).

Barnett, Corelli, *The Desen Generais* (London: Viking, 1960).

Barraclough, Geoffrey, *The Crucible of Europe* (Berkeley: University of California Press, 1976).

Bartha, Antal, *Hungarian Society in the Ninth and Tenth Centuries*, trans. K. Baazs (Budapest: Akademiai Kiado, 1975).

Basham, A. L., *The Wonder That Was India* (New York: Taplinger, 1954).

Beaufre, Andre, *The Suez Expedition 1956*, trans. Richard Barry (New York: Praegei, 1969).

Beny, Roloff, *Island Ceylon* (London: Thames & Hudson, 1970).

Berdan, Frances, *The Aztecs of Central Mexico* (New York: Holt, Rinehart & Winston, 1982).

Berton, Pierre, *The Invasion of Canada* (Boston: Little, Brown, 1980).

Best, Geoffrey, *War and Society in Revolutionary Europe, 1770–1870* (New York: St. Martin's Press, 1982).

Beven, Edwyn, *A History of Egypt under the Ptolemaic Dynasty* (London: Methuen & Co., 1927).

Bidwell, Shelford, *The Chindit War* (New York: Macmillan, 1980).

Bilgrami, Ashgar, *Afghanistan and British India, 1793–1907* (New Delhi: Sterling Press, 1972).

Birtle, A. J., *Sicily* (Washington: U. S. Army Center for Military History, 1993).

Blackwell, James, *Thunder in the Desert* (New York: Bantam Books, 1991).

Boaz, John, ed., *The US Attack on Afghanistan* (Farmington Hills, MI: Greenhaven, 2005).

Bolger, Daniel, *Americans at War, 1975–1986: An Era of Violent Peace* (Novato, CA: Presidio Press, 1988).

Bona, Istvan, *The Dawn of the Dark Ages: The Gepids and the Lombards* (Budapest: Corvina Press, 1976).

Borza, Eugene, *In the Shadow of Olympus: The Emergence of Macedon* (Princeton, NJ: Princeton University Press, 1990).

Bosworth, A. B., *Conquest and Empire* (New York: Cambridge University Press, 1988).

Boulger, Demetrius, *The History of China*, 2 vols. (Freeport, NY: Books for Libraries, 1898).

Bowie, Robert, *Suez, 1956* (London: Oxford University Press, 1974).

Bradford, Ernie, *Julius Caesar: The Pursuit of Power* (New York: Morrow, 1984).

Breuer, William, *Retaking the Philippines* (New York: St. Martin's Press, 1986).

Brewer, William B., *Operation Torch* (New York: St. Martin's Press, 1985).

Briggs, Lawrence, *The Ancient Khmer Empire* (Philadelphia: The Philosophical Society, 1951).

Brion, Marcel, *Attila: The Scourge of God* (New York: Robert McBride & Co., 1929).

Britt, Albert Sidney, *The Wars of Napoleon* (Wayne, NJ: Avery Publishing Group, 1985).

Brown, R. Allen, *The Normans* (New York: St. Martin's Press, 1984).

Browning, Robert, *The Byzantine Empire* (New York: Scribner, 1980).

————, *Justinian and Theodora* (London: Weidenfeld & Nicolson, 1971).

Bullock, Alan, *Hitler: A Study in Tyranny* (New York: Harper, 1953).

Bullough, Donald, *The Age of Charlemagne* (New York: Putnam, 1965).

Burn, A. R., *Persia and the Greeks: The Defence of the West* (London: Arnold, 1962).

Bury, J. B., S. A. Cook, and F. E. Adcocks, eds., *The Cambridge Ancient History: The Assyrian Empire* (Cambridge: Cambridge University Press, 1923–1939).

Bury, J. B., *The Invasion of Europe by the Barbarians* (New York: Russell & Russell, 1963).

Bush, Eric, *Gallipoli* (London: George Allen & Unwin, 1975).

Buxton, David, *The Abyssinians* (New York: Praeger, 1970).

Byford-Jones, W, *The Lightning War* (Indianapolis: Bobbs-Merrill, 1968).

Byng, Edward, *The World of the Arabs* (Plainview, NY: Books for Libraries, 1974).

Byrnes, Rita M., ed., *Uganda: A Country Study* (Washington, DC: Government Printing Office, 1992).

Byron, Robert, *The Byzantine Achievement* (New York: Russell & Russell, 1964).

Caesar, Julius, *Commentaries*, trans. John Warrington, (New York: Heritage Press, 1955).

————, *The Gallic War*, trans. H. J. Edwards (Cambridge, MA: Harvard University Press, 1966).

Caffrey, Kate, *Out in the Midday Sun: Singapore, 1941–1945* (New York: Stein & Day, 1973).

Cain, P. J., *British Imperialism: Innovation and Expansion, 1688–1914* (London: Longmans, 1993).

Campbell, J. B., *The Roman Army, 31 B.C.– A.D. 337* (London: Routledge, 1994).

Cannon, Terry, *Vietnam: A Thousand Years of Struggle* (San Francisco: People's Press, 1969).

Capon, Edmund, *T'ang China* (London: Macdonald Orbis, 1989).

Carmichael, Joel, *A History of Russia* (New York: Hippocrene Books, 1990).

Carr, William, *The Origin of the Wars of German Unification* (London: Longman, 1991).

Carrasco, David, *Montezuma's Mexico* (Niwot: University of Colorado Press, 1992).

Carrell, Paul, *Hitler Moves East, 1941–1943* (Boston: Little, Brown & Co., 1965).

————, *Invasion: They're Coming*, trans. E. Osers (New York: E. E. Dutton, 1960).

Carrion, Arturo Morales, *Puerto Rico, a Political and Cultural History* (New York: Norton, 1983).

Carver, Sir Michael, *The War Lords: Military Commanders of the Twentieth Century* (Boston: Little, Brown & Co., 1976).

Cate, Curtis, *The War of Two Emperors* (New York: Random House, 1984).

Caven, Brian, *The Punic Wars* (London: Weidenfeld & Nicolson, 1980).

Cawkwell, George, *Philip of Macedon* (Boston: Faber & Faber, 1978).

Ceram, C. W., *The Secret of the Hittites*, trans. Richard Winston and Clara Winston (New York: Alfred A. Knopf, 1956).

Cervi, Mario, *The Hollow Legions: Mussolini's Blunder in Greece*, trans. Eric Mosbacher (Garden City, NY: Doubleday, 1971).

Chamberlain, Muriel, *Britain and India* (Hamden, CT: Archon Books, 1974).

Chambers, James, *The Devil's Horsemen* (New York: Atheneum, 1979).

Chandler, David, *The Campaigns of Napoleon* (New York: Macmillan, 1966).

Charles, E., *A History of Spain* (New York: Free Press, 1966).

Charles-Picard, Gilbert, and Collette Picard, *The Life and Death of Carthage*, trans. Dominique Collon (London: Sidgwick & Jackson, 1968).

Charol, Michael, *The Mongol Empire: Its Rise and Legacy* (London: George Allen & Unwin, 1961).

Chattopadhyay, Bhaskar, *Kushana State and Indian Society* (Calcutta: Punthi Pustak, 1975).

Chejne, Anwar, *Muslim Spain: Its History and Culture* (Minneapolis: University of Minnesota Press, 1974).

Chidsey, Donald B., *The War in the North: An Informal History of the American Revolution in and Near Canada* (New York: Crown Publishers, 1967).

Chirovsky, Nicolas, *A History of the Russian Empire* (New York: Philosophical Library, 1973).

Churchill, Winston, *The Gathering Storm* (Boston: Houghton Mifflin, 1948).

Clark, Alan, *Barbarossa* (New York: Morrow, 1965).

Clark, Mark, *Calculated Risk* (New York: Harper, 1950).

Claypole, William, *Caribbean Story, 2 vols.* (San Juan, PR: Longman Caribbean, 1989).

Codrington, Humphrey, *A Short History of Ceylon* (Freeport, NY: Books for Libraries, 1926).

Coedes, G., *The Making of Southeast Asia*, trans. H. M. Wright (Berkeley: University of California Press, 1966).

Cohen, Daniel, *Conquerors on Horseback* (Garden City, NY: Doubleday, 1970).

Cohen, Roger, Stephen Kinzer, and Elaine Sciolino, in *Macmillan Atlas of War and Peace: Special Reports by Correspondents of the New York Times* (New York: Macmillan, 1996).

Coles, Harry L., *The War of 1812* (Chicago: University of Chicago Press, 1965).

Collier, Basil, *Japan at War: An Illustrated History of the War in the Far East* (London: Sidgwick & Jackson, 1975).

Collier, Richard, *Duce!* (New York: Viking, 1971).

Collins, John, *America's Small Wars* (Washington: Brassey's, 1991).

Collins, Robert, *Europeans in Africa* (New York: Knopf, 1971).

Connelly, Owen, *Blundering to Glory* (Wilmington: Scholarly Resources, 1987).

Connor, Seymour, *North America Divided* (New York: Oxford University Press, 1971).

Conroy, Hilary, *The Japanese Seizure of Korea, 1869–1910* (Philadelphia: University of Pennsylvania Press, 1960).

Coonaughton, R. M., *The War of the Rising Sun and the Tumbling Bear* (London: Routledge, 1991).

Costello, John, *The Pacific War, 1941–1945* (New York: Quill, 1982).

Cotterell, Arthur, *The First Emperor of China* (London: Macmillan, 1981).

Crankshaw, Edward, *Maria Theresa* (New York: Viking, 1969).

Cunliffe, Barry, *Rome and Her Empire* (London: Constable, 1994 [1978]).

Curtin, Jeremiah, *The Mongols: A History* (Westport, CT: Greenwood Press, 1972).

Dabrowski, Roman, *Mussolini: Twilight and Fall* (New York: Roy Publishers, 1956).

Davis, Paul K., *Ends and Means: The British Mesopotamia Campaign and Commission* (Rutherford, NJ: Fairleigh Dickinson University Press, 1994).

Department of Defense, "Into Afghanistan: Rooting out Terrorists," United States Department of Defense, http://www.defenselink.mil/home/features/1092004a.html (21 November 2005).

Department of State, "Background Notes: Somalia," Bureau of African Affairs, U.S. Department of State, www.state.gov/r/pa/ei/bgn/2863.htm, 18 November 2005.

Diaz del Castillo, Bernal, *The Discovery and Conquest of Mexico* (London: Routledge, 1928).

Diffie, Bailey, *A History of Colonial Brazil* (Malabar, FL: R. E. Krieger, 1987).

Donald, A. H., *Republican Rome* (New York: Frederick Praeger, 1966).

Donnelly, Thomas, Margaret Roth, and Caleb Baker, *Operation Just Cause: The Storming of Panama* (New York: Lexington Books, 1991).

Dorey, T. A. and D. R. Dudley, *Rome against Carthage* (London: Seeker & Warburg, 1971).

Dorries, Hermann, *Constantine the Great* (New York: Harper & Row, 1972).

Dowart, Jeffrey, *The Pigtail War* (Amherst, MA: University of Massachusetts Press, 1975).

Drinkwater, J. F., *Roman Gaul* (London: Groom Helm, Ltd., 1983).

Dudley, David, *The Romans: 850 B.C.–A.D. 337* (New York: Knopf, 1970).

Duffy, Chris, *The Military Life of Frederick the Great* (New York: Atheneum, 1986).

Duffy, Christopher, *Red Storm on the Reich: The Soviet March on Germany, 1945* (New York: Atheneum, 1991).

Duffy, James, *Portuguese Africa* (Cambridge, MA: Harvard University Press, 1968).

Dunnigan, James, and Albert Nofi, *Victory at Sea* (New York: Morrow, 1995).

Dupuy, R. E., *An Outline History of the American Revolution* (New York: Harper & Row, 1975).

Dupuy, Trevor, *Elusive Victory: The Arab-Israeli Wars, 1947–74* (New York: Harper & Row, 1978).

Dyer, Gwen, *A History of the Vikings* (Oxford: Oxford University Press, 1968).

Earl, Donald C., *The Age of Augustus* (New York: Crown, 1968).

Eccles, W. J., *France in America* (East Lansing: Michigan State University Press, 1990).

Eddy, J. J., *Britain and the Australian Colonies* (Oxford: Clarendon, 1969).

Edwards, E. S., ed., *The Cambridge Ancient History* (Cambridge: Cambridge University Press, 1980).

Eisenhower, Dwight, *Crusade in Europe* (Garden City, NY: Doubleday, 1948).

Eisenhower, John, *So Far from God* (New York: Random House, 1989).

enteruganda.com, "Political History of Uganda," www.enteruganda.com, 27 December 2005.

Erfurth, Waldemar, *Warfare in the Far North* (Washington: Center for Military History, 1987).

Errington, R., *The Dawn of Empire: Rome's Rise to World Power* (New York: Cornell University Press, 1972).

Fage, J. D., *A History of Africa*, 3rd ed. (New York: Routledge, 1995 [1978]).

————, *A History of West Africa* (London: Cambridge University Press, 1969).

Falls, Cyril, *The First 3000 Years* (New York: Viking, 1960).

Farwell, Byron, *Queen Victoria's Little Wars* (New York: Harper and Row, 1972)

Fehrenbach, T. R., *This Kind of War* (New York: Macmillan, 1963).

Ferreira, Eduardo, *Portuguese Colonialism in Africa* (Paris: UNESCO, 1974).

Fewster, Kevin, *A Turkish View of Gallipoli* (Richmond, Victoria, Australia: Hodja, 1985).

Fieldhouse, D. K., *The Colonial Empires* (New York: Dell, 1966).

Finley, M. I., et al., *A History of Sicily* (New York: Viking Penguin, 1987).

Finnegan, Richard, *Ireland: The Challenge of Conflict* (Boulder: Westview Press, 1983).

Fischer, Fritz, *War of Illusions* (London: Chatto & Windus, 1975).

Flanagan, Edward, *The Battle for Panama: Inside Operation Just Cause* (McLean, VA: Brassey's, 1993).

Florinsky, Michael, *Russia: A History and an Interpretation* (New York: Macmillan, 1947).

Fontenot, Gregory, *On Point: The United States Army in Operation Iraqi Freedom* (Annapolis: Naval Institute Press, 2005).

Foster, Edward, *Alexandria: A History and a Guide* (Gloucester: Doubleday & Co., 1968).

Franzius, Enno, *History of the Byzantine Empire* (New York: Funk & Wagnalls, 1968).

Freeman, Edward, *The History of the Norman Conquest of England* (Chicago: University of Chicago Press, 1974).

Friedel, Frank, *The Splendid Little War* (New York: Dell, 1962).

Friedman, Norman, *Desert Victory* (Annapolis, MD: Naval Institute Press, 1991).

Friend, Theodore, *The Blue-Eyed Enemy: Japan against the West in Java and Luzon, 1942–1945* (Princeton: Princeton University Press, 1988).

Frost, Alan, *Convicts and Empire* (Oxford: Oxford University Press, 1980).

Fry, Plantagenet, *Roman Britain, History and Sites* (Totawa, NJ: Barnes and Noble, 1984).

Fuller, J. F. C., *Military History of the Western World*, vol. 1 (New York: Minerva, 1954).

Furneaux, Rupert, *The Battle of Saratoga* (New York: Stein & Day, 1971).

————, *The Invasion of 1066* (Englewood Cliffs, NJ: Prentice Hall, 1974).

Gabriel, Richard, *The Culture of War* (New York: Greenwood Press, 1990).

————, *From Sumer to Rome* (New York: Greenwood Press, 1991).

Gallo, Max, *Mussolini's Italy*, trans. Charles Markmann (New York: Macmillan, 1973).

Garland, Albert, *Sicily and the Surrender of Italy* (Washington: U.S. Army Center for Military History, 1965).

Gates, John M., *Schoolbooks and Krags: The United States Army in the Philippines* (New York: Greenwood Press, 1973).

Gaubert, Henri, *Moses and Joshua, Founders of the Nation* (New York: Hastings House, 1969).

Gelb, Norman, *Desperate Venture: The Story of Operation Torch* (London: Hodder & Staughton, 1992).

Gibbs, M. B., *Napoleon's Military Career* (Chicago: Werner Co., 1895).

Gimbutas, Marija, *The Slavs* (New York: Praeger, 1971).

Glantz, David, and Jonathan House, *When Titans Clashed* (Lawrence: University of Kansas Press, 1995).

Glick, Thomas, *Islamic and Christian Spain in the Early Middle Ages* (Princeton: Princeton University Press, 1979).

globalsecurity.com, "The 1978 Revolution and the Soviet Invasion," GlobalSecurity.org, http://www.globalsecurity.org/military/world/afghanistan/cs-invasion.htm, 20 November 2005.

Gokhale, Balkrishna, *Ancient India: History and Culture* (Bombay and New York: Asia Publishing House, 1959).

Gordon, David, *The Passing of French Algeria* (London: Oxford University Press, 1966).

Grant, Michael, *The History of Ancient Israel* (New York: Scribner, 1984).

————, *The Rise of the Greeks* (New York: Scribner's Sons, 1987).

Grau, Lester, *The Bear Went Over the Mountain: Soviet Combat Tactics in Afghanistan* (Washington: National Defense University Press, 1996).

Green, Peter, *Alexander of Macedon* (Los Angeles: University of California Press, 1991).

Gregory of Tours, *History of the Franks*, trans. Ernest Brehaut (New York: Norton, 1969).

Griffiths, E. J., *The British Impact on India* (Hamden, CT Archon Books, 1965).

Gruber, Ira, *The Howe Brothers and the American Revolution* (New York: Atheneum, 1972).

Gruber, Ruth, *Israel on the Seventh Day* (New York: Hill & Wang, 1968).

Gruen, E. S., ed., *Imperialism in the Roman Republic* (New York: Holt, Rinehart & Winston, 1970).

Guderian, Heinz, *Panzer Leader* (New York: E. P. Dutton, 1957).

Hahn, Emily, *Raffles of Singapore, a Biography* (Garden City, NY: Doubleday, 1946).

Haidar, Muhammad, *A History of the Moghuls of Central Asia* (New York: Praeger, 1970).

Haines, C. G. and R. J. S. Hoffman, *The Origins and Background of World War II* (New York: Oxford University Press, 1947).

Hallenbeck, Jan, *Pavia and Rome: The Lombard Monarchy and the Papacy in the Eighth Century* (Philadelphia: American Philosophical Society, 1982).

Hallett, Robin, *Africa to 1875* (Ann Arbor: University of Michigan Press, 1970).

Hamilton, Allen Lee, *Sentinel of the Southern Plains* (Fort Worth: TCU Press, 1990).

Hammer, Ellen, *The Struggle for Indochina* (Stanford: Stanford University Press, 1955).

Hammond, N. G. L., *Alexander the Great: King, Commander, and Statesman* (Park Ridge, NJ: Noyes Press, 1974).

Hamshere, Cyril, *The British in the Caribbean* (Cambridge, MA: Harvard University Press, 1972).

Harlow, Vincent, ed., *History of East Africa*, 2 vols. (Oxford: Clarendon Press, 1965).

Harrison, John, *Akhbar and the Mughal Empire* (St. Paul, MN: Greenhaven Press, 1980).

Hartendorp, A. V. H., *The Japanese Occupation of the Philippines* (Manila: Bookmark, 1967).

Hartog, Leo, *Genghis Khan, Conqueror of the World* (New York: St. Martin's Press, 1989).

Hassel, Arthur, *Louis XIV and the Zenith of French Monarchy* (Freeport, NY: Books for Libraries, 1972).

Hatada, Takahashi, *A History of Korea*, trans. Warren Smith and Benjamin Hazard (Santa Barbara: ABC-Clio, 1969).

Hatton, R. M., *Charles XII of Sweden* (London: Weidenfeld & Nicolson, 1968).

Hawkes, Jacquetta, *Pharaohs of Egypt* (New York: American Heritage, 1965).

Hayes. W., *The Scepter of Egypt* (Cambridge, MA: Harvard University Press, 1959).

Heather, Peter, *Goths and Romans* (Oxford: Clarendon, 1991).

Heckman, Wolf, *Rommel's War in Africa* (Garden City, NY: Doubleday, 1981).

Held, Joseph, *Hunyadi: Legend and Reality* (New York: Columbia University Press, 1985).

Henderson, Keith, *The Fall of the Aztec Empire* (Denver: Denver Museum of Natural History, 1993).

Henissary, Paul, *Wolves in the City: The Death of French Algeria* (New York: Simon & Schuster, 1970).

Henthorn, William, *Korea: The Mongol Invasions* (Leiden: E. J. Brill, 1963).

Hepple, Alexander, *South Africa: A Political and Economic History* (London: Pall Mall Press, 1966).

Herzog, Chaim, *War of Atonement, October 1973* (Boston: Little, Brown & Co., 1975).

Hi, Hsi-sheng, *Nationalist China at War* (Ann Arbor: University of Michigan Press, 1982).

Higham, Robin, *Diary of a Disaster: British Aid to Greece, 1940–41* (Lexington: University of Kentucky Press, 1986).

Hignett, Charles, *Xerxes' Invasion of Greece* (Oxford: Clarendon, 1963).

Hiskett, M., and Nehemia Levtzion, *Ancient Ghana and Mali* (London: Methuen, 1973).

Hochschild, Adam, *King Leopold's Ghost* (New York: Houghton Mifflin, 1998).

Holder, P A., *The Roman Army in Britain* (New York: St. Martin's Press, 1982).

Holland, Jack, *The Order of Rome* (London: Cassell, 1980).

Holt, P. M., *The Cambridge History of Islam*, 2 vols. (Cambridge: Cambridge University Press, 1970).

Home, Alastair, *Napoleon, Master of Europe, 1805–1807* (New York: Morrow, 1979).

————, *To Lose a Battle: France, 1940* (Boston: Little, Brown & Co., 1969).

Hookham, Hilda, *A Short History of China* (New York: St. Martin's Press, 1970).

Hosch, Edgar, *The Balkans*, trans. Tania Alexander (New York: Crane, Russak & Co., 1972).

Hough, Richard, and Denis Richards, *The Battle of Britain* (New York: Norton, 1989).

Howard, Michael, *The Franco-Prussian War* (New York: Collier, 1961).

Howarth, David, *1066: The Year of the Conquest* (New York: Viking Penguin, 1977).

Howe, George, E, *Northwest Africa: Seizing the Initiative in the West* (Washington: Office of the Chief of Military History, 1957).

Hoyt, Edwin, *Guerrilla* (New York: Macmillan, 1981).

Hsu, Immanuel, *The Rise of Modern China* (New York: Oxford University Press, 1975).

Huart, Clement, *Ancient Persian and Iranian Civilization* (New York: Barnes and Noble, 1972).

Hucker, Charles, *The Ming Dynasty: Its Origins and Evolving Institutions* (Ann Arbor: University of Michigan Press, 1978).

Hyma, Albert, *A History of the Dutch in the Far East* (Ann Arbor, MI: George Wair Publishing Co., 1953).

Ienaga, Saburo, *The Pacific War, 1931–1945* (New York: Random House, 1978).

Innes, Hammond, *The Conquistadors* (New York: Knopf, 1969).

Isadore of Seville, *The History of the Goths, Vandals and Suevi*, trans. Guido Donini and Gordon Ford (Leiden: E. J. Brill, 1970).

Israel, Jonathan, *Dutch Primacy in World Trade, 1585–1740* (Oxford: Clarendon, 1989).

———, *The Dutch Republic: Its Rise, Greatness, and Fall, 1477–1806* (Oxford: Oxford University Press, 1995).

Jackson, Robert, *Dunkirk: The British Evacuation, 1940* (New York: St. Martin's Press, 1976).

James, Edward, *The Franks* (New York: Blackwell, 1988).

Jewell, Derek, ed., *Alamein and the Desert War* (London: Times Newspapers, 1967).

Jones, A. H. M., and Elizabeth Monroe, *A History of Ethiopia* (Oxford: Clarendon, 1955).

Jones, A. H. M., *Augustus* (New York: Norton, 1970).

Kagan, Donald, *On the Origins of War* (New York: Doubleday, 1995).

Kakar, M. Hassan, *Afghanistan: The Soviet Invasion and the Afghan Response, 1979–1982.* (Berkeley: University of California Press, 1995).

Kamen, Henry, *The War of Succession in Spain, 1700–15* (Bloomington: Indiana University Press, 1969).

Karnow, Stanley, *In Our Image: America's Empire in the Philippines* (New York: Random House, 1989).

Karugire, Samwari, *A Political History of Uganda* (Exeter, NH: Heinemann, 1980).

Kee, Robert, *Ireland: A History* (New York: Little, Brown & Co., 1982).

Keegan, John, *The Iraq War* (New York: Knopf, 2004).

———, *The Mask of Command* (New York: Viking, 1987).

———, *Six Armies in Normandy* (New York: Viking, 1982).

Keen, Benjamin, and Mark Wasserman, *A Short History of Latin America* (Boston: Houghton Mifflin, 1984).

Kenyalogy.com, "History," www.kenyalogy.com, 20 December 2005.

King, Anthony, *Roman Gaul and Germany* (Berkeley: University of California Press, 1990).

Kinross, Patrick, *The Ottoman Centuries* (New York: Morrow, 1977).

Klug, Foster, "Leaders to Commemorate the End of Bosnian War," Associated Press News Service, 21 November 1995.

Knights, Michael, *Operation Iraqi Freedom and the New Iraq* (Washington, DC: Institute for Near East Policy, 2004).

Koch, H. W, ed., *The Origins of the First World War* (London: Macmillan, 1972).

———, *The Seljuks of Anatolia*, trans. Gary Leiser (Salt Lake City: University of Utah Press, 1992).

Kumar, Baldev, *The Early Kusanas* (New Delhi: Sterling Publishers, 1973).

Kwanten, Luc, *Imperial Nomads* (Philadelphia: University of Pennsylvania Press, 1979).

Laessoe, Jorgen, *People of Ancient Assyria, Their Inscriptions and Correspondence* (London: Routledge & Kegan Paul, 1963).

LaFeber, Walter, *The American Age* (New York: Norton, 1989).

Lamb, Harold, *The Crusades*, 2 vols. (Garden City, NY: Doubleday, 1931).

———, *Cyrus the Great*, (New York: Doubleday and Co., 1960).

———, *Hannibal* (New York: Doubleday, 1958).

———, *March of the Barbarians* (New York: Literary Guild, 1940).

———, *Tamurlane, the Earth Shaker* (New York: R. M. McBride, 1928).

Lane Fox, Robin, *The Search for Alexander* (Boston: Little, Brown & Co., 1980).

Lane-Pool, Stanley, *Medieval India under Muhammadan Rule* (Calcutta: Susil Gupta, 1951).

Langley, Michael, *Inchon Landing* (New York: New York Times Books, 1979).

Lasko, Peter, *The Kingdom of the Franks* (New York: McGraw-Hill, 1971).

Lawson, Philip, *The Imperial Challenge: Quebec and Britain in the Age of the American Revolution* (Montreal: McGill-Queens University Press, 1990).

Layn, H. R., *The Vikings in Britain* (Oxford: Blackwell, 1995).

Layton, Edward, *"And I Was There": Pearl Harbor and Midway—Breaking the Secrets* (New York: Morrow, 1985).

Leckie, Robert, *Strong Men Armed* (New York: Random House, 1962).

Leckie, William, *The Military Conquest of the Southern Plains* (Norman: University of Oklahoma Press, 1963).

Lee, Maurice, *Road to Resolution: Scotland under Charles I* (Urbana: University of Illinois Press, 1985).

Lehman, Johannes, *The Hittites: People of a Thousand Gods*, trans. J. M. Brownjohn (New York: Viking, 1977).

Levack, Brian, *The Formation of the British State* (Oxford: Clarendon, 1987).

Lewis, Michael, *The Spanish Armada* (New York: Thomas Y. Crowell, 1968).

Liddell Hart, Basil, *History of the Second World War* (New York: Putnam, 1970).

Lineberry, William, *East Africa* (New York: Wilson, 1968).

Liss, Peggy K., *Mexico under Spain, 1521–1556* (Chicago: University of Chicago Press, 1975).

Liu, E. E., *A Military History of Modern China* (Princeton: Princeton University Press, 1956).

Logorici, Anton, *The Albanians* (Boulder, CO: Westview Press, 1977).

Lone, Stewart, *Japan's First Modern War* (New York: St. Martin's Press, 1994).

Lord, Walter, *The Dawn's Early Light* (New York: Norton, 1972).

————, *Incredible Victory* (New York: Harper & Row, 1967).

Lossky, Andrew, *Louis XIV and the French Monarchy* (New Brunswick, NJ: Rutgers University Press, 1994).

Lowe, C. J. and E. Marzari, *Italian Foreign Policy, 1870–1940* (London: Routledge & Kegan Paul, 1975).

Lundin, Charles, *Finland in the Second World War* (Bloomington: Indiana University Press, 1957).

Macartney, C. A., *The Magyars in the Ninth Century* (Cambridge: Cambridge University Press, 1968).

Macaulay, Neill, *Dom Pedro* (Durham, NC: Duke University Press, 1986).

Macksey, Kenneth, *Invasion* (New York: Macmillan, 1980).

MacMullen, Ramsay, *Constantine* (New York: Dial Press, 1969).

MacQueen, J. G., *The Hittites and Their Contemporaries in Asia Minor* (London: Thames & Hudson, 1968).

MacQueen, James, *Babylon* (New York: Praeger, 1965).

Mahon, John K., *The War of 1812* (Gainesville: University Presses of Florida, 1972).

Majdalany, Fred, *The Battle of Cassino* (Boston: Houghton Mifflin, 1958).

Manchester, William, *American Caesar* (Boston: Little, Brown & Co., 1978).

Manz, Beatrice, *The Rise and Rule of Tamurlane* (Cambridge: Cambridge University Press, 1989).

Markham, Felix, *Napoleon* (New York: New American Library, 1963).

————, *Napoleon and the Awakening of Europe* (London: English Universities Press, 1954).

Marks, Richard, *Cortes: The Great Adventurer and the Fate of Aztec Mexico* (New York: Knopf, 1993).

Marlowe, John, *Cromer in Egypt* (London: Elek, 1970).

Marques, A. H. de Olivera, *History of Portugal* (New York: Columbia University Press, 1976).

Marsden, John, *The Fury of the Northmen* (London: Kyle Cathie, 1993).

Martin, Colin, *The Spanish Armada* (New York: Norton, 1988).

Mason, Philip, *A Matter of Honour* (London: Jonathan Cape, 1974).

Mason, R. H. P. and J. G. Caiger, *History of Japan* (New York: Free Press, 1972).

Massie, Robert, *Peter the Great, His Life and World* (New York: Knopf, 1980).

Matthew, Eva, *The Mediterranean World in Ancient Times* (New York: Ronald Press, 1951).

Mattingly, Garrett, *The Armada* (Boston: Houghton Mifflin, 1959).

Mayo, Linda, *Bloody Buna* (Garden City, NY: Doubleday, 1974).

McKenzie, W. M., *Outline of Scottish History* (London: Adam & Charles Black, 1907).

McLeod, A. L., *The Pattern of New Zealand Culture* (Ithaca, NY: Cornell University Press, 1968).

Means, Philip A., *Fall of the Inca Empire and the Spanish Rule in Peru, 1530–1780* (New York: Gordian Press, 1971).

Meditz, Sandra W., and Tim Merrill, eds., "Zaire, a Country Study, Federal Research Division, Library of Congress (Washington: GPO, 1994).

Metz, Helen Chapin, *Libya, A Country Study* (Washington, DC: Government Printing Office, 1989).

————, *Somalia: A Country Study* (Washington, DC: Government Printing Office, 1993).

Meyer, W. C. and W. L. Sherman, *The Course of Mexican History* (New York: Oxford University Press, 1979).

Micheletti, Eric, *Special Forces: War on Terrorism* (Paris: Histoire and Collections, 2003).

Miles, William, *Imperial Burdens* (Boulder, CO: L. Rienner Publishers, 1995).

Miller, James, *A History of Ancient Israel and Judah* (Philadelphia: Westminster Press, 1968).

Miller, Stuart, *"Benevolent Assimilation": The American Conquest of the Philippines* (New Haven, CT: Yale University Press, 1982).

Millis, Walter, *Martial Spirit* (New York: Literary Guild, 1931).

Minns, Ellis, *Scythians and Greeks* (Cambridge: Cambridge University Press, 1913).

Mintz, Max, *The Generals of Saratoga: John Burgoyne and Horatio Gates* (New Haven, CT: Yale University Press, 1990).

Mokhtar, G., *Ancient Civilizations of Africa* (Paris: UNESCO, 1990).

Mookerji, Radha, *Chandragupta Maurya and His Times* (Delhi: Motilal Banarsidass, 1966).

Moorehead, Alan, *Gallipoli* (New York: Harper & Bros., 1956).

Morgan, David, *The Mongols* (Oxford: Blackwell, 1986).

Morris, Donald, *The Washing of the Spears* (New York: Simon & Schuster, 1965).

Morris, Eric, *Circles of Hell* (London: Hutchinson, 1993).

Morris, William, *Hannibal: Soldier, Statesman, Patriot* (New York: Knickerbocker Press, 1978).

Morrison, Samuel E., *The Two-Ocean War* (New York: Little, Brown & Co., 1963).

Moshref, Rameen, "The Role of Afghanistan in the Fall of the USSR," Afghanistan online, http://www.afghan-web.com/history/articles/ussr.html, 22 November 2005; npr.org, "Iraq," www.npr.org, 28 December 2005.

Mukherjee, Bratindra, *The Rise and Fall of the Kushana Empire* (Calcutta: Firma KLM, 1988).

Muller, Herbert, *The Loom of History* (New York: Harper & Bros., 1958).

Newitt, Marilyn, *Portugal in Africa* (London: Longmans, 1981).

Nish, Ian, *Japan's Struggle with Internationalism* (New York: K. Paul International, 1993).

Nissen, Henrik, *Scandinavia during the Second World War*, trans. Thomas Munch-Petersen (Minneapolis: University of Minnesota Press, 1983).

North, Martin, *The Old Testament World* (Philadelphia: Fortress Press, 1962).

Nottingham, Anthony, *Scramble for Africa: The Great Trek to the Boer War* (London: Constable, 1970).

O'Ballance, Edgar, *The Algerian Insurrection* (Hamden, CT: Archon Books, 1967).

Obolensky, Dimitri, *Byzantium and the Slavs* (London: Variorum Reprints, 1971).

Oliver, Roland, *A Short History of Africa* (New York: New York University Press, 1962).

OnWar.com, "Armed Conflict Events Data: Asante," http://www.onwar.com/aced/ nation/all/asante/findex.htm, 28 October 2005.

OnWar.com, "First Jihad of the 'Mad Mullah' 1899–1905," www.onwar.com/ aced/ data/ mike/madmullah1899.htm, 10 December 2005.

Orel, Harold, ed., *Irish History and Culture* (Lawrence: University of Kansas Press, 1976).

Ovendale, Ritchie, *Origins of the Arab-Israeli Wars* (London: Longmans, 1984).

Owen, David E., *British Opium Policy in China and India* (Hamden, CT Archon Books, 1968).

Painter, Sydney, and Brian Tierney, *Western Europe in the Middle Ages* (New York: Knopf, 1983).

Pakenham, Thomas, *The Scramble for Africa* (New York: Random House, 1991).

Palmer, Alan, *Napoleon in Russia* (New York: Simon & Schuster, 1967).

Palmer, John J. N., *England, France, and Christendom, 1377–99* (Chapel Hill: University of North Carolina Press, 1972).

Parker, Geoffrey, ed., *The Thirty Years War* (London: Routledge & Kegan Paul, 1984).

Paul the Deacon, *History of the Langobards*, trans. W. D. Foulke (Philadelphia: University of Pennsylvania Press, 1974).

Payne, Pierre, *The Holy Sword* (New York: Harper, 1959).

Payne, Robert, *The Life and Death of Adolph Hitler* (New York: Praeger, 1973).

Payne, Stanley, *A History of Spain and Portugal* (Madison: University of Wisconsin Press, 1973).

Pearson, Michael, *Those Damned Rebels: The American Revolution as Seen through British Eyes* (New York: Putnam, 1972).

Perlman, Samuel, *Philip and Athens* (New York: Barnes & Noble, 1973).

Petrow, Richard, *Bitter Years: The Invasion and Occupation of Denmark and Norway* (New York: Morrow, 1974).

Porter, Bernard, *The Lion's Share* (London: Longmans, 1975).

Prado, Caio, *The Colonial Background of Modern Brazil* (Berkeley: University of California Press, 1967).

Prange, Gordon, *Miracle at Midway* (New York: McGraw-Hill, 1982).

Prawdin, Michael, *Builders of the Moghul Empire* (London: Allen & Unwin, 1963).

Procopius, *The Secret History of Justinian*, trans. Richard Atwater (Ann Arbor: University of Michigan Press, 1961).

Randle, Robert, *Geneva 1954* (Princeton: Princeton University Press, 1969).

Rice, Eugene, *The Foundation of Early Modern Europe, 1460–1559* (New York: Norton, 1970).

Rice, Tamara, *The Seljuks in Asia Minor* (New York: Praeger, 1961).

Richter, Michael, *Medieval Ireland* (New York: St. Martin's Press, 1988).

Riedlmayer, Andras, "A Brief History of Bosnia-Herzegovina," Mostar Online, www.geocities.com/Heartland/1935/history.html, 19 December 2005.

Ritter, E. A., *Shaka Zulu* (London: Longmans, 1955).

Ritter, Gerhard, *Frederick the Great, a Historical Profile* (Berkeley: University of California Press, 1970).

Robb, Theodore, ed., *The Thirty Years War* (Lexington, MA: Heath, 1972).

Robert, Michael, *Sweden's Age of Greatness, 1632–1718* (New York: St. Martin's Press, 1973).

Robinson, Neville, *Villagers at War* (Canberra: Australian National University, 1981).

Robinson, R. E. and J. A. Gallagher, *Africa and the Victorians* (New York: Macmillan, 1961).

Roeder, Ralph, *Juarez and His Mexico*, 2 vols. (New York: Viking, 1947).

Romanus, Charles, *Time Runs out in CBI* (Washington: Office of the Chief of Military History, 1958).

Rossabi, Morris, *Khubilai Khan: His Life and Times* (Berkeley: University of California Press, 1987).

Rostovtzeff, M., *Iranians and Greeks in Southern Russia* (New York: Russell & Russell, 1969).

Rutherford, Ward, *The Russian Army in World War I* (London: Gordon Cremones, 1975).

Ryan, N. J., *A History of Malaysia and Singapore* (London: Oxford University Press, 1976).

Saggs, H. W. E., *The Might That Was Assyria* (London: Sidgwick & Jackson, 1984).

Salmon, Edward, *A History of the Roman World from 30 B.C. to A.D. 138* (London: Methuen, 1972).

Salway, Peter, *Roman Britain* (New York: Oxford University Press, 1981).

Saunders, J. J., *The History of the Mongol Conquests* (New York: Barnes &. Noble, 1971).

Savory, Roger, *Iran under the Safavids* (New York: Cambridge University Press, 1980).

Schwab, Peter, *Haile Selassie: Ethiopia's Lion of Judah* (Chicago: Nelson-Hall, 1979).

Scullard, Howard H., *A History of the Roman World: From 753 to 146 B.C.* (London: Methuen & Co., 1969).

Searle, Eleanor, *Predatory Kinship and the Creation of Norman Power* (Berkeley: University of California Press, 1988).

Seignobos, Charles, *The World of Babylon* (New York: Leon Amiel, 1975).

Selby, John, *Shaka's Heirs* (London: George Allen & Unwin, 1971).

Sen, Siba Pada, *The French in India* (Calcutta: University of Calcutta Press, 1947).

Serjeant, R. B., *Studies in Arabian History and Civilisation* (London: Variorum Reprints, 1981).

Severin, Timothy, *The Golden Antilles* (New York: Knopf, 1970).

Sharma, G. N., *Mewar and the Mughal Emperors* (Agra: Shiva Lal Agarwala, 1962).

Shaw, A. G. L., *Convicts and the Colonies* (London: Faber & Faber, 1966).

Shaw, Stanford J., and Ezel Kural Shaw, *History of the Ottoman Empire and Modern Turkey*, vol. II (Cambridge: University Press, 1977).

Shaw, Stanford, *The History of the Ottoman Empire and Turkey* (Cambridge: Cambridge University Press, 1976).

Sherwin-White, Susan, *From Samarkand to Sardis* (London: Duckworth, 1993).

Shirer, William, *The Collapse of the Third Republic* (New York: Simon & Schuster, 1969).

————, *The Nightmare Years* (New York: Little, Brown & Co., 1984).

————, *The Rise and Fall of the Third Reich* (New York: Simon & Schuster, 1960).

Showalter, Dennis, *Tannenberg: Clash of Empires* (Hamden, CT: Archon Books, 1991).

Singletary, Otis, *The Mexican War* (Chicago: University of Chicago Press, 1960).

Slim, William, *Defeat into Victory* (New York: D. McKay, 1961).

Smith, Dennis Mack, *A History of Sicily* (New York: Viking, 1968).

Smith, Gaddis, *The Last Years of the Monroe Doctrine, 1945–1993* (New York: Hill & Wang, 1994).

Smith, Jonathan Riley, *The Crusades* (New Haven: Yale University Press, 1987).

Smith, Robert, *Triumph in the Philippines* (Washington: Office of the Chief of Military History, 1963).

Smith, Woodruff, *The German Colonial Empire* (Chapel Hill: University of North Carolina Press, 1978).

Sonino, Paul, *Louis XIV and the Origins of the Dutch War* (New York: Cambridge University Press, 1988).

Spence, Jonathan, ed., *From Ming to Ching* (New Haven: Yale University Press, 1979).

Spielman, John, *The City and the Crown: Vienna and the Imperial Court, 1600–1740* (West Lafayette, IN: Purdue University Press, 1993).

Stannard, David, *American Holocaust* (New York: Oxford University Press, 1992).

Steeds, David, *China, Japan, and Nineteenth Century Britain* (Dublin: Irish University Press, 1977).

Steele, Ian, *Warpaths: Invasions of North America* (New York: Oxford University Press, 1994).

Stephens, Morse, *The Story of Portugal* (New York: AMS Press, 1971).

Stokesbury, James, *A Short History of the Korean War* (New York: Morrow, 1988).

Sweets, John, *Choices in Vichy France* (New York: Oxford University Press, 1986).

Sydenham, M. J., *The First French Republic, 1792–1804* (Berkeley: University of California Press, 1973).

Sykes, Sir Percy, *Persia* (Oxford: Clarendon, 1922).

Tarle, Eugene, *Napoleon's Invasion of Russia in 1812* (New York: Farrar, Straus & Giroux, 1971).

Tarn, W. W., *Alexander the Great* (Cambridge: Cambridge University Press, 1948).

Taylor, F. L., *The Art of War in Italy, 1494–1529* (Cambridge: Cambridge University Press, 1921).

Taylor, Keith, *The Birth of Vietnam* (Berkeley: University of California Press, 1983).

Taylor, Telford, *Munich: The Price of Peace* (Garden City, NY: Doubleday, 1979).

Thompson, E. A., *The Goths in Spain* (Oxford: Clarendon, 1969).

————, *Romans and Barbarians* (Madison: University of Wisconsin Press, 1982).

Thompson, Virginia, *French Indo-China* (New York: Macmillan, 1937).

Thomson, Arthur, *The Story of New Zealand* (New York: Praeger, 1970).

Toland, John, *But Not in Shame* (New York: Random House, 1961).

Tompkins, Stuart, *Russia through the Ages* (New York: Prentice Hall, 1940).

Tong, James, *Disorder under Heaven* (Stanford: Stanford University Press, 1991).

Townsend, Mary Evelyn, *Origins of Modern German Colonialism* (New York: Howard Fertig, 1974).

Trask, David, F., *The War with Spain in 1898* (New York: Macmillan, 1981).

Treasure, G. R. R., *Seventeenth Century France* (London: Rivington's, 1966).

Tresidder, Argus, *Ceylon: An Introduction to the Resplendent Land* (Princeton, NJ: Van Nostrand, 1960).

Trimingham, J. S., *Islam in West Africa* (London: Oxford University Press, 1962).

Tuchman, Barbara, *The Guns of August* (New York: Macmillan, 1962).

———, *Stilwell and the American Experience in China* (New York: Macmillan, 1970).

Twitchett, Denis, and John Fairbank, eds., *The Cambridge History of China*, vols. 9 and 10 (New York: Cambridge University Press, 1993).

Twitchett, Denis, and Michael Loewe, eds., *The Cambridge History of China*, vol. 1, The Ch'in and Han Empires (New York: Cambridge University Press, 1978).

Utley, Robert, *Frontier Regulars* (New York: Macmillan, 1973).

Vader, John, *New Guinea: The Tide Is Stemmed* (New York: Ballantine, 1971).

Vale, Malcolm, *English Gascony, 1399–1453* (London: Oxford University Press, 1970).

Vambery, Arminius, *Hungary in Ancient, Medieval and Modern Times* (Hallandale, FL: New World Books, 1972).

Van Creveld, Martin, *Hitler's Strategy 1940–41: The Balkan Clue* (Cambridge: Cambridge University Press, 1973).

Van Seeters, J., *The Hyksos* (New Haven: Yale University Press, 1966).

Vlekke, Bernard, *The Story of the Dutch East Indies* (Cambridge, MA: Harvard University Press, 1945).

von Moltke, Graf Helmuth, *The Franco-German War of 1870–71* (New York: Harper Brothers, 1901).

Walder, David, *The Short Victorious War* (London: Hutchinson, 1973).

Waley, D., *The Italian City-Republics* (New York: Longmans, 1988).

Warmington, B. H., *Carthage: A History* (London: Robert Hale, 1960).

Warner, Denis, *The Tide at Sunrise* (New York: Charterhouse, 1974).

Warren, Harris, *Paraguay and the Triple Alliance* (Austin, TX: Institute of Latin American Studies, 1978).

Wedgwood C. V., *The Thirty Years War* (Gloucester, MA: P. Smith, 1969).

Wei, Cheng, *Mirror to the Son of Heaven*, ed. and trans. Howard Wechsler (New Haven: Yale University Press, 1974).

Wheatcroft, Andrew, *The Ottomans* (London: Viking, 1993).

Wheeler, Radha, *Early India and Pakistan* (New York: Praeger, 1959).

Wheeler, Robert, *Early India and Pakistan to Ashoka* (New York: Praeger, 1959).

White, John, *Cortez and the Fall of the Aztec Empire* (New York: St. Martin's Press, 1971).

Williams, John, *The Rise and Fall of the Paraguayan Republic* (Austin, TX: Institute of Latin American Studies, 1979).

Wiseman, Anne, and Peter Wiseman, *Julius Caesar: The Battle for Gaul* (Boston: David R. Godine, 1980).

Wolpert, Stanley, *India* (Englewood Cliffs, NJ: Prentice Hall, 1965).

Wolseley, Field Marshal Viscount, *Story of a Soldier's Life*, vol. 2 (Westminster: Archibald Constable & Co., 1903).

Wood, Derek, and Derek Dempster, *The Narrow Margin* (New York: Coronet, 1969).

Woodward, Bob, *The Commanders* (New York: Simon & Schuster, 1991).

Wourinen, John, ed., *Finland and World War II, 1939–1944* (Westport, CT: Greenwood Press, 1983).

Wright, John L., *Libya: A Modern History* (London: Croom Helm, 1982).

Wright, Ronald, *Stolen Continents* (Boston: Houghton Mifflin, 1992).

Wrong, George McKinnon, *Canada and the American Revolution* (New York: Macmillan, 1935).

———, *The Rise and Fall of New France* (New York: Octagon Books, 1970 [1928]).

Yoshihashi, Takehiko, *Conspiracy at Mukden* (New Haven, CT: Yale University Press, 1963).

Young, Donald, *The Battle of Bataan* (Jefferson, NC: McFarland, 1992).

Ziemke, Earl, *Stalingrad to Berlin: The German Defeat in the East* (Washington: Center For Military History, 1968).

SECTION THREE: READINGS

Introduction

For almost as long as there has been warfare, there have been those who practice it and those that attempt to limit it. Declarations of war, peace treaties, humanitarian limitations on weaponry and military practices, and diplomatic agencies such as the United Nations have all played roles in how war is initiated, conducted, and (possibly) limited. An oft-pursued goal is that of limiting international conflicts and affirming human rights. "Rules of war" have been proposed, codified, and broken throughout history, but slowly international standards have developed to such an extent that unwarranted invasions or terrorist attacks can find little legal standing or world support. Treaties, conventions, and international law have created, in modern times, a degree of accountability. Many governments limit the war powers of their leaders; the *United States Constitution*, for example, provides no specific power for war-making for the president other than simply "commander-in-chief," while declarations of war and military funding must be approved by congress. On a larger scale, groups of governments occasionally bind themselves to fight wars (e.g., the Axis powers of World War II) or to establish peace and guarantee safety (e.g., the 1928 *Pact of Paris*). Nations also have worked together to place peaceful coexistence on a firmer footing through meetings and conferences, as in the *International Peace Conferences of 1899 and 1907*.

The following collection of documents attempts to illustrate views of war and attempts at regulating war as expressed through individuals and groups. From ancient declarations of battlefield prowess such as the *Armant Stela* of Thutmose III to the extremely specific terms of the *Dayton Peace Accords*, it becomes clear that warfare and attempts to control it are both inherent in human society.

Paul Davis, 2006

Text of the Armant Stela

1456 B.C.

Source: Pritchard, James B. (ed.)
Ancient Near Eastern Texts Relating to the Old Testament
©1969 by Princeton University Press.
Reprinted by permission of Princeton University Press.

Details of the Asiatic Campaigns of Thutmose III, Egyptian Pharoah of the 18ᵗʰ Dynasty.

Horus of Edfu, great god, lord of heaven, may he give life!
Words to be spoken: `I have given you all life and dominion, all health, and all valour and strength.'

Month, lord of Thebes. The good god, lord of action, Menkheperre, given life forever, Tjenenut.

Praising the god four times, so that he may be given life. Words to be spoken: `I have given you all life and dominion, all health, all joy, while the kingship of the Two Lands is under your command. May you live like Re!' Words to be spoken: `I have given you millions of years, while all foreign lands are under your feet.'

Source: M.J. Nederhof

Son of Re, his beloved, Tuthmosis, ruler of truth, given life forever. Live Horus: Mighty Bull, Appearing in Thebes; the Two Goddesses: Enduring of Kingship, like Re in Heaven; the Horus of Gold: Majestic of Appearances, Mighty of Strength; the King of Upper and Lower Egypt, Lord of the Two Lands, Lord of Making Offerings: Men-kheper-Re; the Son of Re, of his Body: Thut-mose Heqa-Maat, beloved of Montu, Lord of Thebes, Residing in Hermonthis, living forever.

Year 22, 2nd month of the second season, day 10. Summary of the deeds of valor and victory which this good god performed, being every effective deed of heroism, beginning from the first generation; that which the Lord of the Gods, the Lord of Hermonthis, did for him: the magnification of his victories, to cause that his deeds of valor be related for millions of years to come, apart from the deeds of heroism which his majesty did at all times. If (they) were to be related all together by their names, they would be (too) numerous to put them into writing

Source: J.B. Pritchard

When he shoots at a copper target, all wood is splintered like a papyrus reed. His Majesty offered an example thereof in the temple of Amun, with a target of hammered copper of three digits in thickness; when he had shot his arrow there, he caused protrusion of three palms behind it, so as to cause the followers to pray for the proficiency of his arms in valour and strength. I'm telling you what he did, without deception and without lie, in front of his entire army, and there is no word of exaggeration therein.

When he spent a moment of recreation, hunting in any foreign land, the quantity that he captured was greater than what the entire army achieved. He slew seven lions by shooting in an instant. He captured a herd of twelve wild bulls in an hour at the time of breakfast, their tails behind him. He killed 120 elephants in the foreign country of Nija when he came from Naharina.

He crossed the river Euphrates, and trampled the towns on its banks, which were destroyed by fire forever. He erected a stela of victory on its [...] side. He captured a rhinoceros by shooting in the southern land of Taseti, after he had gone to Miu to seek out him who had rebelled against him in that land. He erected his stela there as he had done at the ends [...]

Source: M.J. Nederhof

His majesty made no delay in proceeding to the land of Djahi, to kill the treacherous ones who were in it and to give things to those who were loyal to him; witness, indeed, [their] names, each [country] according to its time. His majesty returned on each occasion, when his attack had been effected in valor and victory, so that he caused Egypt to be in its condition as (it was) when Re was in it as king.

[Year 22, 4th month of the second season, day...Proceeding] from Memphis, to slay the countries of the wretched Retenu, on the first occasion of victory. It was his majesty who opened its roads and foxed its every way for his army, after it had made [rebellion, gathered in Megid]do. His majesty entered upon that road which becomes very narrow,' as the first of his entire army, while every country had gathered, standing prepared at its mouth. ... The enemy quailed, fleeing headlong to their town, together with the prince who was in... (15)... to them, beseeching [breath], their goods upon their backs. His majesty returned in gladness of heart, with this entire land as vassal... [Asia]tics, coming at one time, bearing [their] tribute...

The Peace of Nicias

Jona Lendering
www.livius.org

In March 421, the Peace of Nicias was signed, which marked the end of the Archidamian War. It is called after the Athenian negotiator Nicias; no doubt, the Spartans had another name for the document. Its main point was that Athens and Sparta would keep what they had, although there were some adjustments: Sparta would return Amphipolis to Athens, and the Athenians would give up the occupation of Pylos. Thucydides, who was fascinated by the problems of chronology, notes that the treaty was signed "just ten years, with the difference of a few days, after the first invasion of Attica and the beginning of this war" (History of the Peloponnesian War, 5.20.1).

There are two types of successful peace treaty. The first is possible if one side has been completely defeated and can no longer recover. In that case, the victor can dictate terms that will never be challenged (e.g., the end of the Second World War). The second type is possible when all parties are involved, understand the political and military realities, see their vital interests respected, and are willing to negotiate on minor points (e.g., the Peace of Westphalia or the Congress of Vienna). The Peace of Nicias did not belong to these categories. Sparta had gone to war to put an end to Athenian supremacy but the Delian League was still alive; moreover, at Sphacteria it had become clear that Sparta was not invincible.

However, although Athens had won the war, it had not destroyed Sparta, which was still a powerful state. Moreover, not all parties that had been involved agreed to the treaty. For example, Sparta's ally Thebes refused to agree, and the inhabitants of Amphipolis, who were supposed to return to the Athenian alliance, were not willing to do so. Sparta made promises that it could not keep. Moreover, it betrayed its allies Corinth and Megara, because it accepted the Athenian occupation of territories that belonged to these cities.

Almost immediately after the treaty had been signed, it collapsed. Corinth embarked upon an ambitious diplomatic offensive that was directed against Sparta; Thebes simply refused to sign; Sparta was unable to give back Amphipolis, and Athens did not return Pylos. As a result of these tensions, the Athenians accepted Alcibiades' advice to join the coalition of the democratic states Argos, Mantinea, and Elis. Athens now had allies on the Peloponnese, and it may have looked as if the Spartan alliance, the Peloponnesian League, was about to collapse.

In 418, the Spartan king Agis II attacked Mantinea and Argos. Now, Athens was faced with a difficult choice: would it help its ally Sparta, or would it help its democratic allies? It choose the second option and was willing to take up arms against Sparta in the battle of Mantinea. That Agis won the fight was important -it restored Spartan influence on the Peloponnese and discredited democracy- but the deeper significance of the battle was that the Peace of Nicias had come to an end, three years after it had been signed.

Below, you can read the text of the treaty, which has been included in Thucydides' History of the Peloponnesian War (5.18.1-19.2, 23.1-24.1; Rex Warner's translation). There are two texts: the real treaty that ended the war, and a document in which Sparta and Athens concluded a defensive alliance.

The Peace of Nicias

The Athenians, the Spartans and their allies made treaty and swore to it, city by city, as follows:

- With regard to the Panhellenic temples, everyone who wishes, according to the customs of his country, to sacrifice in them, to travel to them, to consult the oracles, or to attend the games shall be guaranteed security in doing so, both by sea and by land. At Delphi the consecrated ground and the temple of Apollo and the Delphians themselves shall be governed by their own laws, taxed by their own state, and judged by their own judges, both the people and the territory, according to the custom of the place.
- The treaty is to be in force between the Athenians, with their allies, and the Spartans, with their allies, for fifty years without fraud or damage by land or sea.
- It shall not be lawful to take up arms with the intent to do injury either for the Spartans and their allies against the Athenians and their allies, or for the Athenians and their allies against the Spartans and their allies, in any way or by any means whatever.
- If any dispute should arise between them, they are to deal with it by law and by oath, as may be agreed between them.
- The Spartans and their allies are to give back Amphipolis to the Athenians. In the case of all cities given back by the Spartans to the Athenians, the inhabitants shall have the right to go where they please taking their property with them.
- These cities are to pay the tribute fixed by Aristides [1] and are to be independent. So long as they pay the tribute, it shall not be lawful for the Athenians and their allies to take up arms against these cities, once the treaty has been made. The cities referred to are Argilus, Stagirus, Acanthus, Scolus, Olynthus, and Spartalus.[2] These cities are to be allied neither to Sparta nor to Athens. If, however, the Athenians persuade the cities to do so, it shall be lawful for the Athenians to make them their allies, provided that the cities themselves are willing.
- The Mecyberneans, the Sanaeans, and Singaeans shall inhabit their own cities, as shall the Olynthians and Acanthians.
- The Spartans and their allies shall give back Panactum to the Athenians.
- The Athenians shall give back Coryphasium [=Sphacteria], Cythera, Methana, Ptelium, and Atalanta to the Spartans; also all Spartans who are in prison in Athens or in any other prison in the Athenian dominions.
- The Athenians shall let go the Peloponnesians besieged in Scione and all others in Scione who are allies of Sparta, and those whom Brasidas sent in there, and any other allies of Sparta who are in prison in Athens or in any other prison in the Athenian dominions.
- The Spartans shall and their allies shall in the same way give back all Athenians or allies of Athens whom they have in their hands. With regard to Scione, Torone, Sermyle, and any other cities in Athenian hands, the Athenians may act as they shall see fit.[3]
- The Athenians shall take an oath to the Spartans and their allies, city by city. The oath shall be the most binding one that exists in each city, and seventeen representatives on each side are to swear it. The words of the oath shall be these: "I shall abide by the terms of the treaty honestly and sincerely." In the same way, the Spartans and their allies

- shall take an oath to the Athenians. This oath is to be renewed annually by both sides.
- Pillars are to be set up at Olympia, Pythia, the Isthmus, in the Acropolis at Athens, and in the temple at Amyclae in Lacedaemon.
- If any point connected with any subject at all has been overlooked, alterations may be made, without any breach of oath, by mutual agreement and on due consideration by the two parties, the Athenians and the Spartans.
- The treaty comes into effect from the 27th day of the month of Artemisium at Sparta, Pleistolas holding the office of ephor; and at Athens from the 25th day of the month of Elaphebolium, in the archonship of Alcaeus.
- Those who took the oath and poured the libations were as follows:
- For the Spartans: Pleistoanax, Agis, Pleistolas, Damagetus, Chionis, Metagenes, Acanthus, Daithus, Ischagoras, Philocharidas, Zeuxidas, Antiphus, Tellis, Alcindas, Empedias, Menas, and Laphilus.
- For the Athenians: Lampon, Isthmonicus, Nicias, Laches, Euthydemus, Procles, Pythodorus, Hagnon, Myrtilus, Thrasycles, Theagenes, Aristocrates, Iolcius, Timocrates, Leon, Lamachus, and Demosthenes.

The Defensive Alliance

Sparta and Athens shall be allies for fifty years, under the conditions to be set out

- In case of any enemy invasion of Spartan territory or hostile action against the Spartans themselves, the Athenians are to come to the aid of Sparta in the most effective way possible, according to their resources.
- But if by this time the enemy enemy has laid waste the country and gone away, then that city shall be held to be in a state of war with both Sparta and Athens and shall be punished by them both. Peace shall be made by Sparta and Athens jointly and simultaneously. These provisions are to be carried out honestly, promptly, and sincerely.
- In case of any enemy invasion of Athenian territory or hostile action against the Athenians themselves, the Spartans are to come to the aid of Athens in the most effective way possible, according to their resources.
- But if by this time the enemy enemy has laid waste the country and gone away, then that city shall be held to be in a state of war with both Sparta and Athens and shall be punished by them both. Peace shall be made by Sparta and Athens jointly and simultaneously. These provisions are to be carried out honestly, promptly, and sincerely.
- In case of a rising of the slaves, the Athenians are to come to the aid of Sparta with all their strength, according to their resources.
- This treaty shall be sworn to by the same people on either side who took the oath on the previous treaty. The oath shall be renewed every year by the Spartans going to Athens for the Dionysia and by the Athenians going to Sparta for the Hyacinthia.[4]
- Each party shall set up a pillar, the one at Sparta to be near the statue of Apollo at Amyclae, the one at Athens near the statue of Athena on the Acropolis.
- If the Spartans and the Athenians should wish to add or take away anything from the terms of this alliance, they may do it jointly together without any breach of oath.

- Those who took the oath for the
  Spartans were Pleistoanax, Agis,
  Pleistolas, Damagetus, Chionis,
  Metagenes, Acanthus, Daithus,
  Ischagoras, Philocharidas, Zeuxidas,
  Antiphus, Tellis, Alcindas,
  Empedius, Menas, and Laphilus, and
  for the Athenians Lampon,
  Isthmonicus, Nicias, Laches,
  Euthydemus, Procles, Pythodorus,
  Hagnon, Myrtilus, Thrasycles,
  Theagenes, Aristocrates, Iolcius,
  Timocrates, Leon, Lamachus, and
  Demosthenes.

Note 1:
When the Delian League was founded.
Note 2:
Towns on the Chalcidice that had been
forced out of the Delian League by Brasidas.
Note 3:
The inhabitants of Scione were massacred.
Note 4:
Religious festivals.

Truce of God - Bishopric of Terouanne, 1063

from Oliver J. Thatcher, and Edgar Holmes McNeal, eds., *A Source Book for Medieval History*, (New York: Scribners, 1905), pp. 417-418

Drogo, bishop of Terouanne, and count Baldwin [of Hainault] have established this peace with the cooperation of the clergy and people of the land.

Dearest brothers in the Lord, these are the conditions which you must observe during the time of the peace which is commonly called the truce of God, and which begins with sunset on Wednesday and lasts until sunrise on Monday.

1. During those four days and five nights no man or woman shall assault, wound, or slay another, or attack, seize, or destroy a castle, burg, or villa, by craft or by violence.

2. If anyone violates this peace and disobeys these commands of ours, he shall be exiled for thirty years as a penance, and before he leaves the bishopric he shall make compensation for the injury which he committed. Otherwise he shall be excommunicated by the Lord God and excluded from all Christian fellowship.

3. All who associate with him in any way, who give him advice or aid, or hold converse with him, unless it be to advise him to do penance and to leave the bishopric, shall be under excommunication until they have made satisfaction.

4. If any violator of the peace shall fall sick and die before he completes his penance, no Christian shall visit him or move his body from the place where it lay, or receive any of his possessions.

5. In addition, brethren, you should observe the peace in regard to lands and animals and all things that can be possessed. If anyone takes from another an animal, a coin, or a garment, during the days of the truce, he shall be excommunicated unless he makes satisfaction. If he desires to make satisfaction for his crime he shall first restore the thing which he stole or its value in money, and shall do penance for seven years within the bishopric. If he should die before he makes satisfaction and completes his penance, his body shall not be buried or removed from the place where it lay, unless his family shall make satisfaction for him to the person whom he injured.

6. During the days of the peace, no one shall make a hostile expedition on horseback, except when summoned by the count; and all who go with the count shall take for their support only as much as is necessary for themselves and their horses.

7. All merchants and other men who pass through your territory from other lands shall have peace from you.

8. You shall also keep this peace every day of the week from the beginning of Advent to the octave of Epiphany and from the beginning of Lent to the octave of Easter, and from the feast of Rogations [the Monday before Ascension Day] to the octave of Pentecost.

9. We command all priests on feast days and Sundays to pray for all who keep the peace, and to curse all who violate it or support its violators.

10. If anyone has been accused of violating the peace and denies the charge, he shall take the communion and undergo the ordeal of hot iron. If he is found guilty, he shall do penance within the bishopric for seven years.

Decree of the Emperor Henry IV Concerning a Truce of God; 1085 A.D.

Source:
Henderson, Ernest F.
Select Historical Documents of the Middle Ages
London : George Bell and Sons, 1896

http://www.yale.edu/lawweb/avalon/medieval/dechenry.htm

1. [Doeberl, " Monumenta Germaniae Selecta," Bd. 3,p. 49].
Whereas in our times the holy church has been afflicted beyond measure by tribulations through having to join in suffering so many oppressions and dangers, we have so striven to aid it, with God's help, that the peace which we could not make lasting by reason of our sins, we should to some extent make binding by at least exempting certain days. In the year of the Lord's incarnation, 1085, in the 8th indiction, it was decreed by God's mediation, the clergy and people unanimously agreeing: that from the first day of the Advent of our Lord until the end of the day of the Epiphany, and from the beginning of Septuagesima until the 8th day after Pentecost, and throughout that whole day, and on every Thursday, Friday, Saturday, and Sunday, until sunrise on Monday, and on the day of the fast of the four seasons, and on the eve and the day itself of each of the apostles-moreover on every day canonically set apart, or in future to be set apart for fasting or for celebrating,-this decree of peace shall be observed. The purpose of it is that those who travel and those who remain at home may enjoy the greatest possible security, so that no one shall commit murder or arson, robbery or assault, no man shall injure another with a whip or a sword or any kind of weapon, and that no one, no matter on account of what wrong he shall be at feud, shall, from the Advent of our Lord to the 8th day after Epiphany, and from Septuagesima until the 8th day after Pentecost, presume to bear as weapons a shield, sword, or lance-or, in fact, the burden of any armour. Likewise on the other days-namely, on Sundays, Thursdays, Fridays, Saturdays, and on the eve and day of each of the apostles, and on every day canonically fixed, or to be fixed, for fasting or celebrating,-it is unlawful, except for those going a long distance, to carry arms; and even then under the condition that they injure no one in any way. It, during the space for which the peace has been declared, it shall be necessary for any one to go to another place where that peace isn't observed, he may bear arms; provided, nevertheless, that he harm no one unless he is at. tacked and has to defend himself. Moreover, when he returns, he shall lay aside his weapons again. If it shall happen that a castle is being besieged, the besiegers shall cease from the attack during the days included in the peace, unless they are attacked by the besieged, and are obliged to beat them back.

Fulcher of Chartres

Urban II (1088-1099)
Speech at Council of Clermont
1095

Source:
Bongars, Gesta Dei per Francos, 1, pp. 382
f., trans in Oliver J. Thatcher, and Edgar
Holmes McNeal, eds., *A Source Book for
Medieval History*, (New York: Scribners,
1905), 513-17

[adapted from Thatcher] Here is the one by
the chronicler Fulcher of Chartres. Note
how the traditions of the peace and truce of
God - aimed at bringing about peace in
Christendom - ties in directly with the call
for a Crusade.

Most beloved brethren: Urged by necessity,
I, Urban, by the permission of God chief
bishop and prelate over the whole world,
have come into these parts as an ambassador
with a divine admonition to you, the
servants of God. I hoped to find you as
faithful and as zealous in the service of God
as I had supposed you to be. But if there is in
you any deformity or crookedness contrary
to God's law, with divine help I will do my
best to remove it. For God has put you as
stewards over his family to minister to it.
Happy indeed will you be if he finds you
faithful in your stewardship. You are called
shepherds; see that you do not act as
hirelings. But be true shepherds, with your
crooks always in your hands. Do not go to
sleep, but guard on all sides the flock
committed to you. For if through your
carelessness or negligence a wolf carries
away one of your sheep, you will surely lose
the reward laid up for you with God. And
after you have been bitterly scourged with
remorse for your faults-, you will be fiercely
overwhelmed in hell, the abode of death. For
according to the gospel you are the salt of
the earth [Matt. 5:13]. But if you fall short
in your duty, how, it may be asked, can it be
salted? O how great the need of salting! It is
indeed necessary for you to correct with the
salt of wisdom this foolish people which is so
devoted to the pleasures of this -world, lest
the Lord, when He may wish to speak to
them, find them putrefied by their sins
unsalted and stinking. For if He, shall find
worms, that is, sins, In them, because you
have been negligent in your duty, He will
command them as worthless to be thrown
into the abyss of unclean things. And
because you cannot restore to Him His great
loss, He will surely condemn you and drive
you from His loving presence. But the man
who applies this salt should be prudent,
provident, modest, learned, peaceable,
watchful, pious, just, equitable, and pure.
For how can the ignorant teach others? How
can the licentious make others modest? And
how can the impure make others pure? If
anyone hates peace, how can he make
others peaceable ? Or if anyone has soiled
his hands with baseness, how can he cleanse
the impurities of another? We read also that
if the blind lead the blind, both will fall into
the ditch [Matt. 15:14]. But first correct
yourselves, in order that, free from blame ,
you may be able to correct those who are
subject to you. If you wish to be the friends
of God, gladly do the things which you know
will please Him. You must especially let all
matters that pertain to the church be
controlled by the law of the church. And be
careful that simony does not take root
among you, lest both those who buy and
those who sell [church offices] be beaten
with the scourges of the Lord through
narrow streets and driven into the place of
destruction and confusion. Keep the church
and the clergy in all its grades entirely free
from the secular power. See that the tithes
that belong to God are faithfully paid from
all the produce of the land; let them not be
sold or withheld. If anyone seizes a bishop let
him be treated as an outlaw. If anyone seizes
or robs monks, or clergymen, or nuns, or
their servants, or pilgrims, or merchants, let
him be anathema [that is, cursed]. Let
robbers and incendiaries and all their
accomplices be expelled from the church
and anthematized. If a man who does not

give a part of his goods as alms is punished with the damnation of hell, how should he be punished who robs another of his goods? For thus it happened to the rich man in the gospel [Luke 16:19]; he was not punished because he had stolen the goods of another, but because he had not used well the things which were his.

"You have seen for a long time the great disorder in the world caused by these crimes. It is so bad in some of your provinces, I am told, and you are so weak in the administration of justice, that one can hardly go along the road by day or night without being attacked by robbers; and whether at home or abroad one is in danger of being despoiled either by force or fraud. Therefore it is necessary to reenact the truce, as it is commonly called, which was proclaimed a long time ago by our holy fathers. I exhort and demand that you, each, try hard to have the truce kept in your diocese. And if anyone shall be led by his cupidity or arrogance to break this truce, by the authority of God and with the sanction of this council he shall be anathematized."

After these and various other matters had been attended to, all who were present, clergy and people, gave thanks to God and agreed to the pope's proposition. They all faithfully promised to keep the decrees. Then the pope said that in another part of the world Christianity was suffering from a state of affairs that was worse than the one just mentioned. He continued:

"Although, O sons of God, you have promised more firmly than ever to keep the peace among yourselves and to preserve the rights of the church, there remains still an important work for you to do. Freshly quickened by the divine correction, you must apply the strength of your righteousness to another matter which concerns you as well as God. For your brethren who live in the east are in urgent need of your help, and you must hasten to give them the aid which has often been promised them. For, as the most of you have heard, the Turks and Arabs have attacked them and have conquered the territory of Romania [the Greek empire] as far west as the shore of the Mediterranean and the Hellespont, which is called the Arm of St. George. They have occupied more and more of the lands of those Christians, and have overcome them in seven battles. They have killed and captured many, and have destroyed the churches and devastated the empire. If you permit them to continue thus for awhile with impurity, the faithful of God will be much more widely attacked by them. On this account I, or rather the Lord, beseech you as Christ's heralds to publish this everywhere and to persuade all people of whatever rank, foot-soldiers and knights, poor and rich, to carry aid promptly to those Christians and to destroy that vile race from the lands of our friends. I say this to those who are present, it meant also for those who are absent. Moreover, Christ commands it.

"All who die by the way, whether by land or by sea, or in battle against the pagans, shall have immediate remission of sins. This I grant them through the power of God with which I am invested. O what a disgrace if such a despised and base race, which worships demons, should conquer a people which has the faith of omnipotent God and is made glorious with the name of Christ! With what reproaches will the Lord overwhelm us if you do not aid those who, with us, profess the Christian religion! Let those who have been accustomed unjustly to wage private warfare against the faithful now go against the infidels and end with victory this war which should have been begun long ago. Let those who for a long time, have been robbers, now become knights. Let those who have been fighting against their brothers and relatives now fight in a proper way against the barbarians. Let those who have been serving as mercenaries for small pay now obtain the eternal reward. Let those who have been wearing themselves out in both body and soul now work for a double honor. Behold! on this side will be the sorrowful and poor, on that, the rich; on this side, the enemies of the Lord, on that, his friends. Let those who go not put off the journey, but rent their lands and collect money for their expenses; and as soon as winter is over and spring comes, let hem eagerly set out on the way with God as their guide."

Peace of the Land Established by Frederick Barbarossa

Between 1152 and 1157 A.D.

Source:
Henderson, Ernest F.
Select Historical Documents of the Middle Ages
London : George Bell and Sons, 1896

(Altmann u. Bernheim, "Ausgewahlte Urkunden," p. 150. Berlin, 1891.)

Frederick by the grace of God emperor of the Romans, always august, to the bishops, dukes, counts, margraves and all to whom these letters shall come: sends his favour, peace, and love.

Inasmuch as by the ordination of the divine mercy we ascend the throne of the royal majesty, it is right that in our works we altogether obey Him by whose gift we are exalted. Therefore we, desiring the divine as well as the human laws to remain in vigour, and endeavouring to exalt the churches and ecclesiastical persons, and to defend them from tile incursions and invasions of every one, do wish to preserve to all persons whatever their rights, and do by the royal authority indicate a peace, long desired and hitherto necessary to the whole earth, to be observed throughout all parts of our kingdom. In what manner, moreover, this same peace is to be kept and observed, will be clearly shown from what follows.

1. If any one, within the term fixed for the peace, shall slay a man, he shall be sentenced to death, unless by wager of battle he can prove this, that he slew him in defending his own life. But if this shall be manifest to all, that he slew him not of necessity but voluntarily, then neither through wager of battle nor in any other manner shall he keep himself from being condemned to death. But if a violator of the peace shall flee the face of the judge, his movable possessions shall be confiscated by the judge and dispensed among the people; but his heirs shall receive the heritage which he held; this condition being imposed, that a promise shall be given under oath to the effect that that of the peace shall never, henceforth, by their mill or consent receive any emolument from it. But if late; the heirs, neglecting the rigour of the law, shall allow him to have his heritage, the count shall hand over that same heritage to the rule of the king and shall receive it from the king under the name of a benefice.

2. If any one wound another after the proclamation of the peace, unless he prove by wager of battle that he did this while defending his life, his hand shall be amputated and he shall be sentenced as has been explained above: the judge shall most strictly prosecute him and his possessions according to the rigour of justice.

3. If any one take another and without shedding blood beat him with rods, or pull out his hair or beard, he shall pay by way of composition 10 pounds to him on whom the injury is seen to have been inflicted, and 80 pounds to the judge. But if without striking him he shall boldly attack him "asteros hant," as it is vulgarly called, viz., with hot hand, and shall maltreat him with contumelious words, he shall compound with 10 pounds for such excess and shall pay 10 to the judge. And whoever, for an excess, shall engage to pay 20 pounds to his judge, shall hand over his estate to him as a pledge, and within four weeks shad pay the money required; and if within four weeks he neglect to hand over his estate, his heirs, if they wish, may receive his heritage, and shall pay to the count the 20 pounds within six weeks; but if not, the count shall assign that heritage to the power of the king, shall restore the claims of those who proclaim them, and shall receive the estate from the king under the title of a benefice.

4. If a clerk be charged with violating the peace and be openly known and published as doing so, or if he keep companionship with a violator of the peace and be convicted of these things in the presence of his bishop and by sufficient testimony: to the count in

whose county this same clerk has perpetrated this he shall pay 20 pounds, and for so great an excess he shall make satisfaction to the bishop according to the statutes of the canons. If, moreover, that same clerk shall be disobedient, he shall not only be deprived of his office and ecclesiastical benefice, but also he shall be considered an outlaw.

5. If a judge through clamour of the people shall have followed any violator of the peace to the city of any lord that same lord whose city it is known to be shall produce him to render justice; but if he shall mistrust his own innocence and shall fear to come before the face of the judge,-if he have a dwelling in the city, his lord shall under oath, place all his movable goods at the disposition of the judge, and in future, as an outlaw, not receive him in his house; but if he have not a dwelling in his city, his lord shall cause him to be placed in security, and afterwards the judge, with the people, shall not desist from prosecuting him as a violator of the peace.

6. If two men contend for the possession of one benefice and one of them produces the man who invested him with that benefice, his testimony, if the investor acknowledge having given the investiture, shall be received first by the count; and if the man can prove by suitable witnesses that he obtained this same benefice without plunder, the occasion for controversy being removed, he shall hold it; but if in the presence of the judge he be convicted of plunder, he shall doubly pay the plunder, and shall be deprived of the benefice, unless, justice and judgment dictating, he may in the future seek to obtain it again.

7. If three or more contend for the same benefice, each one producing different investors, the judge in whose presence the case is carried on shall require of two men of good testimony dwelling in the province of these same litigants, that they swear by an oath which of them, without plunder, has been the possessor of that benefice; and, the truth of the matter being known from their testimony, the possessor shall quietly obtain his benefice unless, justice and judgment dictating, another shall snatch it from his hand.

8. If a rustic charge a knight with violating the peace he shall swear by his hand that he does this not willingly but of necessity; the knight shall clear himself by the hand of four.

9. If a knight charge a rustic with violating the peace, the rustic- shall swear by his hand that he has done this not willingly but of necessity; the rustic shall choose one of two things: whether he shall show his innocence by a divine or a human judgment, or whether he shall expurgate himself by six suitable witnesses whom the judge shall choose.

10. If for violation of the peace, or in any capital matter, a knight wishes to engage in wager of battle against a knight, permission to fight shall not be granted to him unless he can prove that front of old he himself, and his parents as well, have by birth been lawful knights.

11. After the nativity of St. Mary each count shall choose for himself seven men of good testimony, and shall wisely make arrangements for each province, and shall usefully provide for what price, according to the quality, the grain is to be sold at different times; but whoever contrary to his ruling, within the term of the year, shall presume to sell a measure for a higher price, shall be considered a violator of the peace, and shall pay as many times thirty pounds to the count as the number of measures he shall have been convicted of selling.

12. If any rustic shall carry as weapons either a lance or a sword, the judge within whose jurisdiction he shall be found to belong shall either take away the weapons, or shall receive 20 shillings for them from the rustic.

13. A merchant passing through the province on business may tie his sword to his saddle, or place it above his vehicle, not in order to injure the innocent, but to defend himself from the robber.

14. No one shall spread his nets or his nooses, or any other instruments for taking

game, except for taking bears, boars and wolves.

15. In going to the palace of the count no knight shall bear arms unless invited by the count. Public robbers and convicts shall be condemned to the old sentence.

16. Whoever shall treat his advowson or any other benefice unbecomingly, and shall have been warned by his lord and do not amend, continuing in his insolence,-he shall be deprived by a judicial order as well of his advowson as of his benefice; and if he afterwards, with bold daring, shall invade his advowson or benefice, he shall be considered a violator of the peace.

17. If any one shall have stolen 5 shillings, or its equivalent,-he shall be hung with a rope; if less he shall be flayed with whips, and his hair pulled out with a pincers.

18. If the ministeriales of any lord have a conflict among themselves, the count or judge in whose district they do this shall carry on the law and the judgments in the matter.

19. Whoever, in passing through the land, wishes to feed his horse, may with impunity take, for the defection and refreshment of his horse, as much as he can reach when he stands in a place directly adjoining the road. It is lawful for any one to take, for his convenience and necessary use, grass and green wood; but without any devastation.

Henderson's Note

Document issued by Frederick Barbarossa. It will be seen from § 10 that knights of good family might still engage in wager of battle against their equals, although, in other respects a breach of the peace was to be severely punished.

Constitution of the United States of America

Article I, Section 8.

The Congress shall have Power To lay and collect Taxes, Duties, Imposts and Excises, to pay the Debts and provide for the common Defence and general Welfare of the United States; but all Duties, Imposts and Excises shall be uniform throughout the United States;
To borrow Money on the credit of the United States;

To regulate Commerce with foreign Nations, and among the several States, and with the Indian Tribes;

To establish an uniform Rule of Naturalization, and uniform Laws on the subject of Bankruptcies throughout the United States;

To coin Money, regulate the Value thereof, and of foreign Coin, and fix the Standard of Weights and Measures;
To provide for the Punishment of counterfeiting the Securities and current Coin of the United States;

To establish Post Offices and post Roads;
To promote the Progress of Science and useful Arts, by securing for limited Times to Authors and Inventors the exclusive Right to their respective Writings and Discoveries;

To constitute Tribunals inferior to the supreme Court;

To define and punish Piracies and Felonies committed on the high Seas, and Offences against the Law of Nations;

To declare War, grant Letters of Marque and Reprisal, and make Rules concerning Captures on Land and Water;

To raise and support Armies, but no Appropriation of Money to that Use shall be for a longer Term than two Years;

To provide and maintain a Navy;

To make Rules for the Government and Regulation of the land and naval Forces;
To provide for calling forth the Militia to execute the Laws of the Union, suppress Insurrections and repel Invasions;

To provide for organizing, arming, and disciplining, the Militia, and for governing such Part of them as may be employed in the Service of the United States, reserving to the States respectively, the Appointment of the Officers, and the Authority of training the Militia according to the discipline prescribed by Congress;

To exercise exclusive Legislation in all Cases whatsoever, over such District (not exceeding ten Miles square) as may, by Cession of particular States, and the Acceptance of Congress, become the Seat of the Government of the United States, and to exercise like Authority over all Places purchased by the Consent of the Legislature of the State in which the Same shall be, for the Erection of Forts, Magazines, Arsenals, dock-Yards, and other needful Buildings;

--And
To make all Laws which shall be necessary and proper for carrying into Execution the foregoing Powers, and all

other Powers vested by this Constitution in the Government of the United States, or in any Department or Officer thereof.

***

Article II, Section 2
The President shall be Commander in Chief of the Army and Navy of the United States, and of the Militia of the several States....
He shall have Power, by and with the Advice and Consent of the Senate, to make Treaties, provided two thirds of the Senators present concur....

Final Act of the International Peace Conference

The Hague, 29 July 1899

The International Peace Conference, convoked in the best interests of humanity by His Majesty the Emperor of All the Russias, assembled, on the invitation of the Government of Her Majesty the Queen of the Netherlands, in the Royal House in the Wood at The Hague on 18 May 1899.
The Powers enumerated in the following list took part in the Conference, to which they appointed the delegates named below:

(Here follow the names of delegates)

In a series of meetings, between 18 May and 29 July 1899, in which the constant desire of the delegates above-mentioned has been to realize, in the fullest manner possible, the generous views of the august initiator of the Conference and the intentions of their Governments, the Conference has agreed, for submission for signature by the plenipotentiaries, on the text of the Convention and Declarations enumerated below and annexed to the present Act:
I. Convention for the peaceful adjustment of international differences.
II. Convention regarding the laws and customs of war on land.
III.Convention for the adaptation to maritime warfare of the principles of the Geneva Convention of 22 August 1864.
IV. Three Declarations:
1. To prohibit the launching of projectiles and explosives from balloons or by other similar new methods.
2. To prohibit the use of projectiles, the only object of which is the diffusion of asphyxiating or deleterious gases.
3. To prohibit the use of bullets which expand or flatten easily in the human body, such as bullets with a hard envelope, of which the envelope does not entirely cover the core or is pierced with incisions.

These Conventions and Declarations shall form so many separate Acts. These Acts shall be dated this day, and may be signed up to 31 December 1899, by the Plenipotentiaries of the Powers represented at the International Peace Conference at The Hague.

Guided by the same sentiments, the Conference has adopted unanimously the following Resolution:
"The Conference is of opinion that the restriction of military charges, which are at present a heavy burden on the world, is extremely desirable for the increase of the material and moral welfare of mankind."
It has besides formulated the following ' Voeux ':
1. The Conference, taking into consideration the preliminary step taken by the Swiss Federal Government for the revision of the Geneva Convention, expresses the wish that steps may be shortly taken for the assembly of a special Conference having for its object the revision of that Convention.
This wish was voted unanimously.
2. The Conference expresses the wish that the questions of the rights and duties of neutrals may be inserted in the program of a Conference in the near future.
3. The Conference expresses the wish that the questions with regard to rifles and naval guns, as considered by it, may be studied by the Governments with the object of coming to an agreement respecting the employment of new types and calibers.
4. The Conference expresses the wish that the Governments, taking into consideration the proposals made at the Conference, may examine the possibility of an agreement as to the limitation of armed forces by land and sea, and of war budgets.
5. The Conference expresses the wish that the proposal, which contemplates the

declaration of the inviolability of private property in naval warfare, may be referred to a subsequent Conference for consideration. 6. The Conference expresses the wish that the proposal to settle the question of the bombardment of ports, towns, and villages by a naval force may be referred to a subsequent Conference for consideration. The last five wishes were voted unanimously, saving some abstentions.

In faith of which, the Plenipotentiaries have signed the present Act, and have affixed their seals thereto.

Done at The Hague, 29 July 1899, in one copy only, which shall be deposited in the Ministry for Foreign Affairs, and of which copies, duly certified, shall be delivered to all the Powers represented at the Conference.

(Here follow signatures)

Final Act of the Second International Peace Conference

The Hague, 18 October 1907

The Second International Peace Conference, proposed in the first instance by the President of the United States of America, having been convoked, on the invitation of His Majesty the Emperor of All the Russias, by Her Majesty the Queen of the Netherlands, assembled on 15 June 1907, at The Hague, in the Hall of the Knights, for the purpose of giving a fresh development to the humanitarian principles which served as a basis for the work of the First Conference of 1899.

The following Powers took part in the Conference, and appointed the delegates named below:

(Here follow the names of delegates)

At a series of meetings, held from 15 June to 18 October 1907, in which the above delegates were throughout animated by the desire to realize, in the fullest possible measure, the generous views of the august initiator of the Conference and the intentions of their Governments, the Conference drew up, for submission for signature by the plenipotentiaries, the text of the Conventions and of the Declaration enumerated below and annexed to the present Act.

I. Convention for the pacific settlement of international disputes.

II. Convention respecting the limitation of the employment of force for the recovery of contract debts.

III. Convention relative to the opening of hostilities.

IV. Convention respecting the laws and customs of war on land.

V. Convention respecting the rights and duties of neutral powers and persons in case of war on land.

VI. Convention relative to the status of enemy merchant ships at the outbreak of hostilities.

VII. Convention relative to the conversion of merchant ships into warships.

VIII. Convention relative to the laying of automatic submarine contact mines.

IX. Convention respecting bombardment by naval forces in time of war.

X. Convention for the adaptation to naval war of the principles of the Geneva Convention.

XI. Convention relative to certain restrictions with regard to the exercise of the right of capture in naval war.

XII. Convention relative to the creation of an International Prize Court.

XIII. Convention concerning the rights and duties of neutral Powers in naval war.

XIV. Declaration prohibiting the discharge of projectiles and explosives from balloons.

These Conventions and Declarations shall form so many separate Acts. These Acts shall be dated this day, and may be signed up to 30 June 1908, at The Hague, by the Plenipotentiaries of the Powers represented at the Second Peace Conference.

The Conference, actuated by the spirit of mutual agreement and concession characterizing its deliberations, has agreed upon the following Declaration, which, while reserving to each of the Powers represented full liberty of action as regards voting, enables them to affirm the principles which they regard as unanimously admitted:

It is unanimous:

1. In admitting the principle of compulsory arbitration.

2. In declaring that certain disputes, in particular those relating to the interpretation and application of the provisions of international agreements, may be submitted to compulsory arbitration without any restriction.

Finally, it is unanimous in proclaiming that, although it has not yet been found feasible to conclude a Convention in this sense, nevertheless the divergences of opinion which have come to light have not exceeded the bounds of judicial controversy, and that, by working together here during the past four months, the collected Powers not only have learnt to understand one another and to draw closer together, but have succeeded in the course of this long collaboration in evolving a very lofty conception of the common welfare of humanity.

The Conference has further unanimously adopted the following Resolution:
"The Second Peace Conference confirms the Resolution adopted by the Conference of 1899 in regard to the limitation of military expenditure; and inasmuch as military expenditure has considerably increased in almost every country since that time, the Conference declares that it is eminently desirable that the Governments should resume the serious examination of this question."
It has besides expressed the following ' Voeux ':
1. The Conference recommends to the Signatory Powers the adoption of the annexed draft Convention for the creation of a Judicial Arbitration Court, and the bringing it into force as soon as an agreement has been reached respecting the selection of the judges and the constitution of the Court.
2. The Conference expresses the opinion that, in case of war, the responsible authorities, civil as well as military, should make it their special duty to ensure and safeguard the maintenance of pacific relations, more especially of the commercial and industrial relations between the inhabitants of the belligerent States and neutral countries.
3. The Conference expresses the opinion that the Powers should regulate, by special treaties, the position, as regards military charges, of foreigners residing within their territories.
4. The Conference expresses the opinion that the preparation of regulations relative to the laws and customs of naval war should figure in the programme of the next Conference, and that in any case the Powers may apply, as far as possible, to war by sea the principles of the Convention relative to the laws and customs of war on land.
Finally, the Conference recommends to the Powers the assembly of a Third Peace Conference, which might be held within a period corresponding to that which has elapsed since the preceding Conference, at a date to be fixed by common agreement between the Powers, and it calls their attention to the necessity of preparing the programme of this Third Conference a sufficient time in advance to ensure its deliberations being conducted with the necessary authority and expedition.
In order to attain this object the Conference considers that it would be very desirable that, some two years before the probable date of the meeting, a preparatory committee should be charged by the Governments with the task of collecting the various proposals to be submitted to the Conference, of ascertaining what subjects are ripe for embodiment in an international regulation, and of preparing a programme which the Governments should decide upon in sufficient time to enable it to be carefully examined by the countries interested. This committee should further be entrusted with the task of proposing a system of organization and procedure for the Conference itself.

In faith whereof the Plenipotentiaries have signed the present Act and have affixed their seals thereto.

Done at The Hague, 18 October 1907, in a single copy, which shall remain deposited in the archives of the Netherlands Government, and duly certified copies of which shall be sent to all the Powers represented at the Conference.

(Here follow signatures)

General Pact for the Renunciation of War- Signed at Paris

27 August 1928

1. The President of the German Reich, the President of the United States of America, His Majesty the King of the Belgians, the President of the French Republic, His Majesty the King of Great Britain, Ireland and the British Dominions beyond the Seas, Emperor of India, His Majesty the King of Italy, His Majesty the Emperor of Japan, the President of the Republic of Poland, the President of the Czechoslovak Republic Deeply sensible of their solemn duty to promote the welfare of mankind;
Persuaded that the time has come when a frank renunciation of war as an instrument of national policy should be made to the end that the peaceful and friendly relations now existing between their peoples may be perpetuated
Convinced that all changes in their relations with one another should be sought only by pacific means and be the result of a peaceful and orderly process and that any signatory power which shall hereafter seek to promote its national interests by resort to war should be denied the benefits furnished by this treaty
Hopeful that, encouraged by their example, all the other nations of the world will join in this humane endeavor and by adhering to the present treaty as soon as it comes into force bring their peoples within the scope of its beneficent provisions, thus uniting the civilized nations of the world in a common renunciation of war as an instrument of their national policy;
Have decided to conclude a treaty and for that purpose have appointed as their respective plenipotentiaries:
The President of the German Reich:
Dr. Gustav Stresemann, Minister of Foreign Affairs; The President of the United States of America:

The Hon. Frank B. Kellogg, Secretary of State; His Majesty the King of the Belgians: Mr. Paul Hymans, Minister of Foreign Affairs, Minister of State: The President of the French Republic:
Mr. Aristide Briand, Minister for Foreign Affairs;
His Majesty the King of Great Britain, Ireland and the British Dominions beyond the Seas, Emperor of India:
For Great Britain and Northern Ireland and all parts of the British Empire which are not separate members of the League of Nations: The Right Hon. Lord Cushendun, Chancellor of the Duchy of Lancaster, Acting Secretary of State for Foreign Affairs;

For the Dominion of Canada:
The Right Hon. William Lyon Mackenzie King, Prime Minister and Minister for External Affairs;
For the Commonwealth of Australia:
The Hon. Alexander John McLachlan, Member of the Executive Federal Council For the Dominion of New Zealand:
The Hon. Sir Christopher James Parr, High Commissioner for New Zealand in Great Britain;
For the Union of South Africa:
The Hon. Jacobus Stephanus Smit, High Commissioner for the Union of South Africa in Great Britain;
For the Irish Free State:
Mr. William Thomas Cosgrave, President of the Executive Council;
For India:
The Right Hon. Lord Gushendun, Chancellor of the Duchy of Lancaster, Acting Secretary of State for Foreign Affairs;

His Majesty the King of Italy:
Count Gaetano Manzoni, his Ambassador Extraordinary and Plenipotentiary at Paris. His Majesty the Emporer of Japan:
Count Uchida, Privy Councillor; The President of the Republic of Poland:
Mr. A. Zaleski, Minister for Foreign Affairs; The President of the Czechoslovak Republic:

Dr. Eduard Benes, Minister for Foreign Affairs; who, having communicated to one another their full powers found in good and due form have agreed upon the following articles:

ARTICLE 1

The high contracting parties solemnly declare in the names of their respective peoples that they condemn recourse to war for the solution of international controversies, and renounce it as an instrument of national policy in their relations with one another.

ARTICLE 2

The high Contracting parties agree that the settlement or solution of all disputes or conflicts of whatever nature or of whatever origin they may be, which may arise among them, shall never be sought except by pacific means.

ARTICLE 3

The present treaty shall be ratified by the high contracting parties named in the preamble in accordance with their respective constitutional requirements, and shall take effect as between them as soon as all their several instruments of ratification shall have been deposited at Washington.

This treaty shall, when it has come into effect as prescribed in the preceding paragraph, remain open as long as may be necessary for adherence by all the other powers of the world. Every instrument evidencing the adherence of a power shall be deposited at Washington and the treaty shall immediately upon such deposit become effective as between the power thus adhering and the other powers parties hereto.

It shall be the duty of the Government of the United States to furnish each government named in the preamble and every government subsequently adhering to this treaty with a certified copy of the treaty and of every instrument of ratification or adherence. It shall also be the duty of the Government of the United States telegraphically to notify such governments immediately upon the deposit with it of each instrument of ratification or adherence.

In faith whereof the respective plenipotentiaries have signed this treaty in the French and English languages, both texts having equal force, and hereunto affix their seals.

Done at Paris, the twenty-seventh day of August in the year one thousand nine hundred and twenty-eight.

[SEAL] GUSTAV STRESEMANN[SEAL] FRANK B KELLOGG[SEAL] PAUL HYMANS[SEAL] ARI BRIAND[SEAL] CUSHENDUN[SEAL] W. L. MACKENZIE KING[SEAL] A J MCLACHLAN[SEAL] C. J. PARR[SEAL] J S. SMIT[SEAL] LIAM T.MACCOSGAIR[SEAL] CUSHENDUN[SEAL] G. MANZONI[SEAL] UCHIDA[SEAL] AUGUST ZALESKI[SEAL] DR EDWARD BENES

Directive No. 1 for the Conduct of the War

Berlin, 31 August 1939

SUPREME COMMANDER OF THE ARMED FORCES MOST SECRET

1. Now that all the political possibilities of disposing by peaceful means of a situation on the Eastern Frontier which is intolerable for Germany are exhausted, I have determined a solution by force.

2. The attack on Poland is to be carried out in accordance with the preparations made for Case White, with the alterations which result, where the Army is concerned, from the fact that it has in the meantime almost completed it. dispositions; Allotment of tasks and the operational target remain unchanged.

Date of attack: September 1, 1939.

Time of attack: 4:45 A.M.

This timing also applies to the operation at Gdynia, Bay of Danzig and the Dirschau Bridge.

3. In the West it is important that the responsibility for the opening of hostilities should rest squarely on England and France. For the time being insignificant frontier violations should be met by purely local action.

The neutrality of Holland, Belgium, Luxembourg and Switzerland, to which we have given assurances, must be scrupulously observed.

On land, the German Western Frontier is not to be crossed without my express permission.

At sea, the same applies for all warlike actions or actions which could be regarded as such.

4. If Britain and France open hostilities against Germany, it is the task of the Wehrmacht formations operating in the West to conserve their forces as much as possible and thus maintain the conditions for a victorious conclusion of the Operations against Poland. Within these limits enemy forces and their military-economic resources are to be damaged as much as possible. Orders to go over to the attack I reserve, in any case, to myself.

The Army will hold the West Wall and make preparations to prevent its being outflanked in the north through violation of Belgian or Dutch territory by the Western powers . . .

The Navy will carry on warfare against merchant shipping, directed mainly at England . . . The Air Force is, in the first place, to prevent the French and British Air Forces from attacking the German Army and the German Lebensraum.

In conducting the war against England, preparations are to be made for the use of the Luftwaffe in disrupting British supplies by sea, the armaments industry, and the transport of troops to France. A favorable opportunity is to be taken for an effective attack on massed British naval units, especially against battleships and aircraft carriers. Attacks against London are reserved for my decision.

Preparations are to be made for attacks against the British mainland, bearing in mind that partial success with insufficient forces is in all circumstances to be avoided.

ADOLF HITLER

Proclamation by Adolf Hitler, Chancellor of the Reich, to the German Army

September 1, 1939

The Polish State has refused the peaceful settlement of relations which I desired, and has appealed to arms. Germans in Poland are persecuted with bloody terror and driven from their houses. A series of violations of the frontier, intolerable to a great Power, prove that Poland is no longer willing to respect the frontier of the Reich.

In order to put an end to this lunacy, I have no other choice than to meet force with force from now on. The German Army will fight the battle for the honour and the vital rights of reborn Germany with hard determination. I expect that every soldier, mindful of the great traditions of eternal German soldiery, will ever remain conscious that he is a representative of the National-Socialist Greater Germany. Long live our people and our Reich!

Three-Power Pact among Germany, Italy, and Japan, Signed at Berlin

September 27, 1940

The governments of Germany, Italy and Japan, considering it as a condition precedent of any lasting peace that all nations of the world be given each its own proper place, have decided to stand by and co-operate with one another in regard to their efforts in greater East Asia and regions of Europe respectively wherein it is their prime purpose to establish and maintain a new order of things calculated to promote the mutual prosperity and welfare of the peoples concerned.

Furthermore, it is the desire of the three governments to extend co-operation to such nations in other spheres of the world as may be inclined to put forth endeavours along lines similar to their own, in order that their ultimate aspirations for world peace may thus be realized.

Accordingly, the governments of Germany, Italy and Japan have agreed as follows:

ARTICLE ONE

Japan recognizes and respects the leadership of Germany and Italy in establishment of a new order in Europe.

ARTICLE TWO

Germany and Italy recognize and respect the leadership of Japan in the establishment of a new order in greater East Asia.

ARTICLE THREE

Germany, Italy and Japan agree to co-operate in their efforts on aforesaid lines. They further undertake to assist one another with all political, economic and military means when one of the three contracting powers is attacked by a power at present not involved in the European war or in the Chinese-Japanese conflict.

ARTICLE FOUR

With the view to implementing the present pact, joint technical commissions, members which are to be appointed by the respective governments of Germany, Italy and Japan will meet without delay.

ARTICLE FIVE

Germany, Italy and Japan affirm that the aforesaid terms do not in any way affect the political status which exists at present as between each of the three contracting powers and Soviet Russia.

ARTICLE SIX

The present pact shall come into effect immediately upon signature and shall remain in force 10 years from the date of its coming into force. At the proper time before expiration of said term, the high contracting parties shall at the request of any of them enter into negotiations for its renewal.

In faith whereof, the undersigned duly authorized by their respective governments have signed this pact and have affixed hereto their signatures.

Done in triplicate at Berlin, the 27th day of September, 1940, in the 19th year of the fascist era, corresponding to the 27th day of the ninth month of the 15th year of Showa (the reign of Emperor Hirohito).

Text of Franklin D. Roosevelt's Speech to Congress and the Nation Following the Japanese Attack on Pearl Harbor

8 December 1941

Mr. Vice President, Mr. Speaker, Members of the Senate, and of the House of Representatives:

Yesterday, December 7th, 1941 -- a date which will live in infamy -- the United States of America was suddenly and deliberately attacked by naval and air forces of the Empire of Japan.

The United States was at peace with that nation and, at the solicitation of Japan, was still in conversation with its government and its emperor looking toward the maintenance of peace in the Pacific.

Indeed, one hour after Japanese air squadrons had commenced bombing in the American island of Oahu, the Japanese ambassador to the United States and his colleague delivered to our Secretary of State a formal reply to a recent American message. And while this reply stated that it seemed useless to continue the existing diplomatic negotiations, it contained no threat or hint of war or of armed attack.

It will be recorded that the distance of Hawaii from Japan makes it obvious that the attack was deliberately planned many days or even weeks ago. During the intervening time, the Japanese government has deliberately sought to deceive the United States by false statements and expressions of hope for continued peace.

The attack yesterday on the Hawaiian islands has caused severe damage to American naval and military forces. I regret to tell you that very many American lives have been lost. In addition, American ships have been reported torpedoed on the high seas between San Francisco and Honolulu.

Yesterday, the Japanese government also launched an attack against Malaya.

Last night, Japanese forces attacked Hong Kong.

Last night, Japanese forces attacked Guam.

Last night, Japanese forces attacked the Philippine Islands.

Last night, the Japanese attacked Wake Island.

And this morning, the Japanese attacked Midway Island.

Japan has, therefore, undertaken a surprise offensive extending throughout the Pacific area. The facts of yesterday and today speak for themselves. The people of the United States have already formed their opinions and well understand the implications to the very life and safety of our nation.

As commander in chief of the Army and Navy, I have directed that all measures be taken for our defense. But always will our whole nation remember the character of the onslaught against us.

No matter how long it may take us to overcome this premeditated invasion, the American people in their righteous might will win through to absolute victory.

I believe that I interpret the will of the Congress and of the people when I assert that we will not only defend ourselves to the uttermost, but will make it very certain that this form of treachery shall never again endanger us.

Hostilities exist. There is no blinking at the fact that our people, our territory, and our interests are in grave danger.

With confidence in our armed forces, with the unbounding determination of our people, we will gain the inevitable triumph -- so help us God.

I ask that the Congress declare that since the unprovoked and dastardly attack by Japan on Sunday, December 7th, 1941, a state of war has existed between the United States and the Japanese empire.

Selections from the Charter of the United Nations

WE THE PEOPLES OF THE UNITED NATIONS DETERMINED to save succeeding generations from the scourge of war, which twice in our lifetime has brought untold sorrow to mankind, and to reaffirm faith in fundamental human rights, in the dignity and worth of the human person, in the equal rights of men and women and of nations large and small, and to establish conditions under which justice and respect for the obligations arising from treaties and other sources of international law can be maintained, and to promote social progress and better standards of life in larger freedom, AND FOR THESE ENDS to practice tolerance and live together in peace with one another as good neighbours, and to unite our strength to maintain international peace and security, and to ensure, by the acceptance of principles and the institution of methods, that armed force shall not be used, save in the common interest, and to employ international machinery for the promotion of the economic and social advancement of all peoples, HAVE RESOLVED TO COMBINE OUR EFFORTS TO ACCOMPLISH THESE AIMS Accordingly, our respective Governments, through representatives assembled in the city of San Francisco, who have exhibited their full powers found to be in good and due form, have agreed to the present Charter of the United Nations and do hereby establish an international organization to be known as the United Nations.

CHAPTER I

PURPOSES AND PRINCIPLES

Article 1

The Purposes of the United Nations are:

1. To maintain international peace and security, and to that end: to take effective collective measures for the prevention and removal of threats to the peace, and for the suppression of acts of aggression or other breaches of the peace, and to bring about by peaceful means, and in conformity with the principles of justice and international law, adjustment or settlement of international disputes or situations which might lead to a breach of the peace;

2. To develop friendly relations among nations based on respect for the principle of equal rights and self-determination of peoples, and to take other appropriate measures to strengthen universal peace;

3. To achieve international co-operation in solving international problems of an economic, social, cultural, or humanitarian character, and in promoting and encouraging respect for human rights and for fundamental freedoms for all without distinction as to race, sex, language, or religion; and

4. To be a centre for harmonizing the actions of nations in the attainment of these common ends.

Article 2

The Organization and its Members, in pursuit of the Purposes stated in **Article 1**, shall act in accordance with the following Principles.

1. The Organization is based on the principle of the sovereign equality of all its Members.

2. All Members, in order to ensure to all of them the rights and benefits resulting from membership, shall fulfill in good faith the obligations assumed by them in accordance with the present Charter.

3. All Members shall settle their international disputes by peaceful means in such a manner that international peace and security, and. justice, are not endangered.

4. All Members shall refrain in their international relations from the threat or use of force against the territorial integrity or political independence of any state, or in any other manner inconsistent with the Purposes of the United Nations.

5. All Members shall give the United Nations every assistance in any action it takes in accordance with the present Charter, and shall refrain from giving assistance to any state against which the United Nations is taking preventive or enforcement action.

6. The Organization shall ensure that states which are not Members of the United Nations act in accordance with these Principles so far as may be necessary for the maintenance of international peace and security.

7. Nothing contained in the present Charter shall authorize the United Nations to intervene in matters which are essentially within the domestic jurisdiction of any state or shall require the Members to submit such matters to settlement under the present Charter; but this principle shall not prejudice the application of enforcement measures under **Chapter VII**.

***

CHAPTER V

THE SECURITY COUNCIL

Composition

Article 23

1. The Security Council shall consist of fifteen Members of the United Nations. The Republic of China, France, the Union of Soviet Socialist , the United Kingdom of Great Britain and Northern Ireland, and the United States of America shall be permanent members of the Security Council. The General Assembly shall elect ten other Members of the United Nations to be non-permanent members of the Security Council, due regard being specially paid, in the first in- stance to the contribution of Members of the United Nations to the maintenance of inter- national peace and security and to the other purposes of the Organization, and also to equitable geographical distribution.

2. The non-permanent members of the Security Council shall be elected for a term of two years. In the first election of the non-permanent members after the increase of the membership of the Security Council from eleven to fifteen, two of the four additional members shall be chosen for a term of one year. A retiring member shall not be eligible for immediate re-election.

3. Each member of the Security Council shall have one representative.

Functions and Powers

Article 24

1. In order to ensure prompt and effective action by the United Nations, its Members confer on the Security Council primary responsibility for the maintenance of international peace and security, and agree that in carrying out its duties under this responsibility the Security Council acts on their behalf.

2. In discharging these duties the Security Council shall act in accordance with the Purposes and Principles of the United Nations. The specific powers granted to the Security Council for the discharge of these duties are laid down in Chapters **VI, VII, VIII**, and **XII**.

3. The Security Council shall submit annual and, when necessary, special reports to the General Assembly for its consideration.

Article 25

The Members of the United Nations agree to accept and carry out the decisions of the Security Council in accordance with the present Charter.

Article 26

In order to promote the establishment and maintenance of international peace and security with the least diversion for armaments of the world's human and economic resources, the Security Council shall be responsible for formulating, with the assistance of the Military Staff Committee referred to in **Article 47**, plans to be submitted to the Members of the United-Nations for the establishment of a system for the regulation of armaments.

Voting

Article 27

1. Each member of the Security Council shall have one vote.
2. Decisions of the Security Council on procedural matters shall be made by an affirmative vote of nine members.
3. Decisions of the Security Council on all other matters shall be made by an affirmative vote of nine members including the concurring votes of the permanent members; provided that, in decisions under **Chapter VI**, and under paragraph 3 of **Article 52**, a party to a dispute shall abstain from voting.

Procedure

Article 28

1. The Security Council shall be so organized as to be able to function continuously. Each member of the Security Council shall for this purpose be represented at times at the seat of the Organization.
2. The Security Council shall hold meetings at which each of its members may, if it so desires, be represented by a member of the government or by some other specially designated representative.
3. The Security Council may hold meetings at such places other than the seat of the Organization as in its judgment will best facilitate its work.

Article 29

The Security Council may establish such subsidiary organs as it deems necessary for the performance of its functions.

Article 30

The Security Council shall adopt its own rules of procedure, including the method of selecting its President.

Article 31

Any Member of the United Nations which is not a member of the Security Council may participate, without vote, in the discussion of any question brought before the Security Council whenever the latter considers that the interests of that Member are specially affected.

Article 32

Any Member of the United Nations which is not a member of the Security Council or any state which is not a Member of the United Nations, if it is a party to a dispute under consideration by the Security Council, shall be invited to participate, without vote, in the discussion relating to the dispute. The Security Council shall any down such conditions as it deems just for the participation of a state which is not a Member of the United Nations.

CHAPTER VI

PACIFIC SETTLEMENT OF DISPUTES

Article 33

1. The parties to any dispute, the continuance of which is likely to endanger the maintenance of international peace and security, shall, first of a, seek a solution by negotiation, enquiry, mediation, conciliation, arbitration, judicial settlement, resort to regional agencies or arrangements, or other peaceful means of their own choice.

2. The Security Council shall, when it deems necessary, call upon the parties to settle their dispute by such means.

Article 34

The Security Council may investigate any dispute, or any situation which might lead to international friction or give rise to a dispute, in order to determine whether the continuance of the dispute or situation is likely to endanger the maintenance of international peace and security.

Article 35

l. Any Member of the United Nations may bring any dispute, or any situation of the nature referred to in **Article 34**, to the attention of the Security Council or of the General Assembly.

2. A state which is not a Member of the United Nations may bring to the attention of the Security Council or of the General Assembly any dispute to which it is a party if it accepts in advance, for the purposes of the dispute, the obligations of pacific settlement provided in the present Charter.

3. The proceedings of the General Assembly in respect of matters brought to its attention under this Article will be subject to the provisions of Articles 11 and 12.

Article 36

1. The Security Council may, at any stage of a dispute of the nature referred to in Article 33 or of a situation of like nature, recommend appropriate procedures or methods of adjustment.

2. The Security Council should take into consideration any procedures for the settlement of the dispute which have already been adopted by the parties.

3. In making recommendations under this Article the Security Council should also take into consideration that legal disputes should as a general rule be referred by the parties to the International Court of Justice in accordance with the provisions of the Statute of the Court.

Article 37

1. Should the parties to a dispute of the nature referred to in Article 33 fail to settle it by the means indicated in that Article, they shall refer it to the Security Council.

2. If the Security Council deems that the continuance of the dispute is in fact likely to endanger the maintenance of international peace and security, it shall decide whether to take action under Article 36 or to recommend such terms of settlement as it may consider appropriate.

Article 38

Without prejudice to the provisions of Articles 33 to 37, the Security Council may, if all the parties to any dispute so request, make recommendations to the parties with a view to a pacific settlement of the dispute.

CHAPTER VII

ACTION WITH RESPECT TO THREATS TO THE PEACE, BREACHES OF THE PEACE, AND ACTS OF AGGRESSION

Article 39

The Security Council shall determine the existence of any threat to the peace, breach of the peace, or act of aggression and shall make recommendations, or decide what measures shall be taken in accordance with Articles 4 and 42, to maintain or restore international peace and security.

Article 40

In order to prevent an aggravation of the situation, the Security Council may, before making the recommendations or deciding upon the measures provided for in Article 39, call upon the parties concerned to comply with such provisional measures as it deems necessary or desirable. Such provisional measures shall be without prejudice to the rights, claims, or position of the parties concerned. The Security Council shall duly take account of failure to comply with such provisional measures.

Article 41

The Security Council may decide what measures not involving the use of armed force are to be employed to give effect to its decisions, and it may call upon the Members of the United Nations to apply such measures. These may include complete or partial interruption of economic relations and of rail, sea, air, postal, telegraphic, radio, and other means of communication, and the severance of diplomatic relations.

Article 42

Should the Security Council consider that measures provided for in Article 41 would be inadequate or have proved to be inadequate, it may take such action by air, sea, or land forces as may be necessary to maintain or restore international peace and security. Such action may include demonstrations, blockade, and other operations by air, sea, or land forces of Members of the United Nations.

Article 43

1. All Members of the United Nations, in order to contribute to the maintenance of international peace and security, undertake to make available to the Security Council, on its and in accordance with a special agreement or agreements, armed forces, assistance, and facilities, including rights of passage, necessary for the purpose of maintaining international peace and security.
2. Such agreement or agreements shall govern the numbers and types of forces, their degree of readiness and general location, and the nature of the facilities and assistance to be provided.
3. The agreement or agreements shall be negotiated as soon as possible on the initiative of the Security Council. They shall be concluded between the Security Council and Members or between the Security Council and groups of Members and shall be subject to ratification by the signatory states in accordance with their respective constitutional processes.

Article 44

When Security Council has decided to use force it shall, before calling upon a Member not represented on it to provide armed forces in fulfilment of the obligations assumed under Article 43, invite that Member, if the Member so desires, to participate in the decisions of the Security Council concerning the employment of contingents of that Member's armed forces.

Article 45

In order to enable the Nations to take urgent military measures, Members shall hold immediately available national air-force contingents for combined international enforcement action. The strength and degree of readiness of these contingents and plans for their combined action shall be determined, within the limits laid down in the special agreement or agreements referred to in Article 43, by the Security Council with the assistance of the Military Committee.

Article 46

Plans for the application of armed force shall be made by the Security Council with the assistance of the Military Staff Committee.

Article 47

1. There shall be established a Military Staff Committee to advise and assist the Security Council on questions relating to the Security Council's military requirements for the maintenance of international peace and security, the employment and command of forces placed at its disposal, the regulation of armaments, and possible disarmament.
2. The Military Staff Committee consist of the Chiefs of Staff of the permanent members of the Security Council or their representatives. Any Member of the United Nations not permanently represented on the Committee shall be invited by the Committee to be associated with it when the efficient discharge of the Committee's responsibilities re- quires the participation of that Member its work.
3. The Military Staff Committee be responsible under the Security Council for the strategic direction of any armed forces paced at the disposal of the Security Council. Questions relating to the command of such forces shall be worked out subsequently.
4. The Military Staff Committee, with the authorization of the security Council and after consultation with appropriate regional agencies, may establish sub-commit- tees.

Article 48

1. The action required to carry out the decisions of the Security Council for the maintenance of international peace and security shall be taken by all the Members of the United Nations or by some of them, as the Security Council may determine.
2. Such decisions shall be carried out by the Members of the United Nations directly and through their action in the appropriate

international agencies of which they are members.

Article 49

The Members of the United Nations shall join in affording mutual assistance in carrying out the measures decided upon by the Security Council.

Article 50

If preventive or enforcement measures against any state are taken by the Security Council, any other state, whether a Member of the United Nations or not, which finds itself confronted with special economic problems arising from the carrying out of those measures shall have the right to consult the Security Council with regard to a solution of those problems.

Article 51

Nothing in the present Charter shall impair the inherent right of individual or collective self-defence if an armed attack occurs against a Member of the United Nations, until the Security Council has taken measures necessary to maintain international peace and security. Measures taken by Members in the exercise of this right of self-defence shall be immediately reported to the Security Council and shall not in any way affect the authority and responsibility of the Security Council under the present Charter to take at any time such action as it deems necessary in order to maintain or restore international peace and security.

Chapter VIII

REGIONAL ARRANGEMENTS

Article 52

1. Nothing in the present Charter the existence of regional arrangements or agencies for dealing with such matters relating to the maintenance of international peace and security as are appropriate fur regional action, provided that such arrangements or agencies and their activities are consistent with the Purposes and Principles of the United Nations.

2. The Members of the United Nations entering into such arrangements or constituting such agencies shall make every effort to achieve pacific settlement of local disputes through such regional arrangements or by such regional agencies before referring them to the Security Council.

3. The Security Council shall encourage the development of pacific settlement of local disputes through such regional arrangements or by such regional agencies either on the initiative of the states concerned or by reference from the Security Council.

4. This Article in no way the application of Articles 34 and 35.

Article 53

1. The Security Council shall, where appropriate, utilize such regional arrangements or agencies for enforcement action under its authority. But no enforcement action shall be taken under regional arrangements or by regional agencies without the authorization of the Security Council, with the exception of measures against any enemy state, as defined in paragraph 2 of this Article, provided for pursuant to **Article 107** or in regional arrangements directed against renewal of aggressive policy on the part of any such state, until such time as the Organization may, on request of the Governments concerned, be charged with the responsibility for preventing further aggression by such a state.

2. The term enemy state as used in paragraph 1 of this Article applies to any state which during the Second World War has been an enemy of any signatory of the present Charter.

Article 54

The Security Council shall at all times be kept fully informed of activities undertaken or in contemplation under regional arrangements or by regional agencies for the maintenance of international peace and security.

***

CHAPTER XI

DECLARATION REGARDING NON-SELF-GOVERNING TERRITORIES

Article 73

Members of the United Nations which have or assume responsibilities for the administration of territories whose peoples have not yet attained a full measure of self-government recognize the principle that the interests of the inhabitants of these territories are paramount, and accept as a sacred trust the obligation to promote to the utmost, within the system of international peace and security established by the present Charter, the well- being of the inhabitants of these territories, and, to this end:
a. to ensure, with due respect for the culture of the peoples concerned, their political, economic, social, and educational advancement, their just treatment, and their protection against abuses;
b. to develop self-government, to take due account of the political aspirations of the peoples, and to assist them in the progressive development of their free political institutions, according to the particular circumstances of each territory and its peoples and their varying stages of advancement;
c. to further international peace and security;
d. to promote constructive measures of development, to encourage research, and to co-operate with one another and, when and where appropriate, with specialized international bodies with a view to the practical achievement of the social, economic, and scientific purposes set forth in this Article; and
e. to transmit regularly to the Secretary-General for information purposes, subject to such limitation as security and constitutional considerations may require, statistical and other information of a technical nature relating to economic, social, and educational

conditions in the territories for which they are respectively responsible other than those territories to which Chapters XII and XIII apply.

Article 74

Members of the United Nations also agree that their policy in respect of the territories to which this Chapter applies, no less than in respect of their metropolitan areas, must be based on the general principle of good-neigh-bourliness, due account being taken of the interests and well-being of the rest of the world, in social, economic, and commercial matters.

***

CHAPTER XIV

THE INTERNATIONAL COURT OF JUSTICE

Article 92

The International Court of Justice shall be the principal judicial organ of the United Nations. It shall function in accordance with the annexed Statute, which is based upon the Statute of the Permanent Court of International Justice and forms an integral part of the present Charter.

Article 93

1. All Members of the United Nations are facto parties to the Statute of the International Court of Justice.
2. A state which is not of the United Nations may become a party to the Statute of the International Court of Justice on to be determined in each case by the General Assembly upon the recommendation of the Security Council.

Article 94

1. Each Member of the United Nations undertakes to comply with the decision of the International Court of Justice in any case to which it is a party.
2. If any party to a case fails to perform the obligations incumbent upon it under a judgment rendered by the Court, the other

party may have recourse to the Security Council, which may, if it deems necessary, make recommendations or decide upon measures to be taken to give to the judgment.

Article 95

Nothing in the present Charter shall prevent Members of the United Nations from entrusting the solution of their differences to other tribunals by virtue of agreements already in existence or which may be concluded in the future.

Article 96

1. The General Assembly or the Security Council may request the International Court of Justice to give an advisory opinion on any legal question.
2. Other organs of the United Nations and specialized agencies, which may at any time be so authorized by the General Assembly, may also request advisory opinions of the Court on legal questions arising within the scope of their activities.

***

DONE at the city of San Francisco the twenty-sixth day of June, one thousand nine hundred and forty-five.

Universal Declaration of Human Rights

Adopted and proclaimed by General Assembly Resolution 217 A (III) of 10 December 1948

On December 10, 1948 the General Assembly of the United Nations adopted and proclaimed the Universal Declaration of Human Rights the full text of which appears in the following pages. Following this historic act the Assembly called upon all Member countries to publicize the text of the Declaration and "to cause it to be disseminated, displayed, read and expounded principally in schools and other educational institutions, without distinction based on the political status of countries or territories."

PREAMBLE

Whereas recognition of the inherent dignity and of the equal and inalienable rights of all members of the human family is the foundation of freedom, justice and peace in the world,

Whereas disregard and contempt for human rights have resulted in barbarous acts which have outraged the conscience of mankind, and the advent of a world in which human beings shall enjoy freedom of speech and belief and freedom from fear and want has been proclaimed as the highest aspiration of the common people,

Whereas it is essential, if man is not to be compelled to have recourse, as a last resort, to rebellion against tyranny and oppression, that human rights should be protected by the rule of law,

Whereas it is essential to promote the development of friendly relations between nations,

Whereas the peoples of the United Nations have in the Charter reaffirmed their faith in fundamental human rights, in the dignity and worth of the human person and in the equal rights of men and women and have determined to promote social progress and better standards of life in larger freedom,

Whereas Member States have pledged themselves to achieve, in co-operation with the United Nations, the promotion of universal respect for and observance of human rights and fundamental freedoms,

Whereas a common understanding of these rights and freedoms is of the greatest importance for the full realization of this pledge,

Now, Therefore THE GENERAL ASSEMBLY proclaims THIS UNIVERSAL DECLARATION OF HUMAN RIGHTS as a common standard of achievement for all peoples and all nations, to the end that every individual and every organ of society, keeping this Declaration constantly in mind, shall strive by teaching and education to promote respect for these rights and freedoms and by progressive measures, national and international, to secure their universal and effective recognition and observance, both among the peoples of Member States themselves and among the peoples of territories under their jurisdiction.

Article 1.

All human beings are born free and equal in dignity and rights. They are endowed with reason and conscience and should act towards one another in a spirit of brotherhood.

Article 2.

Everyone is entitled to all the rights and freedoms set forth in this Declaration, without distinction of any kind, such as race, colour, sex, language, religion, political or other opinion, national or social origin, property, birth or other status. Furthermore, no distinction shall be made on the basis of the political, jurisdictional or international status of the country or territory to which a person belongs, whether it be independent, trust, non-self-governing or under any other limitation of sovereignty.

Article 3.
Everyone has the right to life, liberty and security of person.

Article 4.
No one shall be held in slavery or servitude; slavery and the slave trade shall be prohibited in all their forms.

Article 5.
No one shall be subjected to torture or to cruel, inhuman or degrading treatment or punishment.

Article 6.
Everyone has the right to recognition everywhere as a person before the law.

Article 7.
All are equal before the law and are entitled without any discrimination to equal protection of the law. All are entitled to equal protection against any discrimination in violation of this Declaration and against any incitement to such discrimination.

Article 8.
Everyone has the right to an effective remedy by the competent national tribunals for acts violating the fundamental rights granted him by the constitution or by law.

Article 9.
No one shall be subjected to arbitrary arrest, detention or exile.

Article 10.
Everyone is entitled in full equality to a fair and public hearing by an independent and impartial tribunal, in the determination of his rights and obligations and of any criminal charge against him.

Article 11.
(1) Everyone charged with a penal offence has the right to be presumed innocent until proved guilty according to law in a public trial at which he has had all the guarantees necessary for his defence.

(2) No one shall be held guilty of any penal offence on account of any act or omission which did not constitute a penal offence, under national or international law, at the time when it was committed. Nor shall a heavier penalty be imposed than the one that was applicable at the time the penal offence was committed.

Article 12.
No one shall be subjected to arbitrary interference with his privacy, family, home or correspondence, nor to attacks upon his honour and reputation. Everyone has the right to the protection of the law against such interference or attacks.

Article 13.
(1) Everyone has the right to freedom of movement and residence within the borders of each state.

(2) Everyone has the right to leave any country, including his own, and to return to his country.

Article 14.
(1) Everyone has the right to seek and to enjoy in other countries asylum from persecution.

(2) This right may not be invoked in the case of prosecutions genuinely arising from non-political crimes or from acts contrary to the purposes and principles of the United Nations.

Article 15.
(1) Everyone has the right to a nationality.

(2) No one shall be arbitrarily deprived of his nationality nor denied the right to change his nationality.

Article 16.
(1) Men and women of full age, without any limitation due to race, nationality or religion, have the right to marry and to found a family. They are entitled to equal rights as to marriage, during marriage and at its dissolution.

(2) Marriage shall be entered into only with the free and full consent of the intending spouses.

(3) The family is the natural and fundamental group unit of society and is entitled to protection by society and the State.

Article 17.
(1) Everyone has the right to own property alone as well as in association with others.

(2) No one shall be arbitrarily deprived of his property.

Article 18.
Everyone has the right to freedom of thought, conscience and religion; this right includes freedom to change his religion or belief, and freedom, either alone or in community with others and in public or private, to manifest his religion or belief in teaching, practice, worship and observance.

Article 19.
Everyone has the right to freedom of opinion and expression; this right includes freedom to hold opinions without interference and to seek, receive and impart information and ideas through any media and regardless of frontiers.

Article 20.
(1) Everyone has the right to freedom of peaceful assembly and association.

(2) No one may be compelled to belong to an association.

Article 21.
(1) Everyone has the right to take part in the government of his country, directly or through freely chosen representatives.

(2) Everyone has the right of equal access to public service in his country.

(3) The will of the people shall be the basis of the authority of government; this will shall be expressed in periodic and genuine elections which shall be by universal and equal suffrage and shall be held by secret vote or by equivalent free voting procedures.

Article 22.
Everyone, as a member of society, has the right to social security and is entitled to realization, through national effort and international co-operation and in accordance with the organization and resources of each State, of the economic, social and cultural rights indispensable for his dignity and the free development of his personality.

Article 23.
(1) Everyone has the right to work, to free choice of employment, to just and favourable conditions of work and to protection against unemployment.

(2) Everyone, without any discrimination, has the right to equal pay for equal work.

(3) Everyone who works has the right to just and favourable remuneration ensuring for himself and his family an existence worthy of human dignity, and supplemented, if necessary, by other means of social protection.

(4) Everyone has the right to form and to join trade unions for the protection of his interests.

Article 24.
Everyone has the right to rest and leisure, including reasonable limitation of working hours and periodic holidays with pay.

Article 25.
(1) Everyone has the right to a standard of living adequate for the health and well-being of himself and of his family, including food, clothing, housing and medical care and necessary social services, and the right to security in the event of unemployment, sickness, disability, widowhood, old age or other lack of livelihood in circumstances beyond his control.

(2) Motherhood and childhood are entitled to special care and assistance. All children, whether born in or out of wedlock, shall enjoy the same social protection.

Article 26.
(1) Everyone has the right to education. Education shall be free, at least in the elementary and fundamental stages. Elementary education shall be compulsory. Technical and professional education shall be made generally available and higher education shall be equally accessible to all on the basis of merit.

(2) Education shall be directed to the full development of the human personality and to the strengthening of respect for human rights and fundamental freedoms. It shall promote understanding, tolerance and friendship among all nations, racial or religious groups, and shall further the activities of the United Nations for the maintenance of peace.

(3) Parents have a prior right to choose the kind of education that shall be given to their children.

Article 27.
(1) Everyone has the right freely to participate in the cultural life of the community, to enjoy the arts and to share in scientific advancement and its benefits.

(2) Everyone has the right to the protection of the moral and material interests resulting from any scientific, literary or artistic production of which he is the author.

Article 28.
Everyone is entitled to a social and international order in which the rights and freedoms set forth in this Declaration can be fully realized.

Article 29.
(1) Everyone has duties to the community in which alone the free and full development of his personality is possible.

(2) In the exercise of his rights and freedoms, everyone shall be subject only to such limitations as are determined by law solely for the purpose of securing due recognition and respect for the rights and freedoms of others and of meeting the just requirements of morality, public order and the general welfare in a democratic society.

(3) These rights and freedoms may in no case be exercised contrary to the purposes and principles of the United Nations.

Article 30.
Nothing in this Declaration may be interpreted as implying for any State, group or person any right to engage in any activity or to perform any act aimed at the destruction of any of the rights and freedoms set forth herein.

The North Atlantic Treaty
Washington D.C. - 4 April 1949

The Parties to this Treaty reaffirm their faith in the purposes and principles of the <u>Charter of the United Nations</u> and their desire to live in peace with all peoples and all governments.

They are determined to safeguard the freedom, common heritage and civilisation of their peoples, founded on the principles of democracy, individual liberty and the rule of law. They seek to promote stability and well-being in the North Atlantic area.

They are resolved to unite their efforts for collective defence and for the preservation of peace and security. They therefore agree to this North Atlantic Treaty :

Article 1
The Parties undertake, as set forth in the <u>Charter of the United Nations</u>, to settle any international dispute in which they may be involved by peaceful means in such a manner that international peace and security and justice are not endangered, and to refrain in their international relations from the threat or use of force in any manner inconsistent with the purposes of the United Nations.

Article 2
The Parties will contribute toward the further development of peaceful and friendly international relations by strengthening their free institutions, by bringing about a better understanding of the principles upon which these institutions are founded, and by promoting conditions of stability and well-being. They will seek to eliminate conflict in their international economic policies and will encourage economic collaboration between any or all of them.

Article 3
In order more effectively to achieve the objectives of this Treaty, the Parties, separately and jointly, by means of continuous and effective self-help and mutual aid, will maintain and develop their individual and collective capacity to resist armed attack.

Article 4
The Parties will consult together whenever, in the opinion of any of them, the territorial integrity, political independence or security of any of the Parties is threatened.

Article 5
The Parties agree that an armed attack against one or more of them in Europe or North America shall be considered an attack against them all and consequently they agree that, if such an armed attack occurs, each of them, in exercise of the right of individual or collective self-defence recognised by <u>Article 51 of the Charter of the United Nations</u>, will assist the Party or Parties so attacked by taking forthwith, individually and in concert with the other Parties, such action as it deems necessary, including the use of armed force, to restore and maintain the security of the North Atlantic area.

Any such armed attack and all measures taken as a result thereof shall immediately be reported to the Security Council. Such measures shall be terminated when the Security Council has taken the measures necessary to restore and maintain international peace and security .

Article 6 (<u>1</u>)
For the purpose of Article 5, an armed attack on one or more of the Parties is deemed to include an armed attack:

- on the territory of any of the Parties in Europe or North America, on the Algerian Departments of France (<u>2</u>), on the territory of or on the Islands under the jurisdiction of any of the Parties in the North Atlantic area north of the Tropic of Cancer;
- on the forces, vessels, or aircraft of any of the Parties, when in or over these territories or any other area in Europe in which occupation forces of any of the Parties were stationed on the date when the Treaty entered into force or the Mediterranean Sea or the North Atlantic area north of the Tropic of Cancer.

Article 7

This Treaty does not affect, and shall not be interpreted as affecting in any way the rights and obligations under the Charter of the Parties which are members of the United Nations, or the primary responsibility of the Security Council for the maintenance of international peace and security.

Article 8

Each Party declares that none of the international engagements now in force between it and any other of the Parties or any third State is in conflict with the provisions of this Treaty, and undertakes not to enter into any international engagement in conflict with this Treaty.

Article 9

The Parties hereby establish a Council, on which each of them shall be represented, to consider matters concerning the implementation of this Treaty. The Council shall be so organised as to be able to meet promptly at any time. The Council shall set up such subsidiary bodies as may be necessary; in particular it shall establish immediately a defence committee which shall recommend measures for the implementation of Articles 3 and 5.

Article 10

The Parties may, by unanimous agreement, invite any other European State in a position to further the principles of this Treaty and to contribute to the security of the North Atlantic area to accede to this Treaty. Any State so invited may become a Party to the Treaty by depositing its instrument of accession with the Government of the United States of America. The Government of the United States of America will inform each of the Parties of the deposit of each such instrument of accession.

Article 11

This Treaty shall be ratified and its provisions carried out by the Parties in accordance with their respective constitutional processes. The instruments of ratification shall be deposited as soon as possible with the Government of the United States of America, which will notify all the other signatories of each deposit. The Treaty shall enter into force between the States which have ratified it as soon as the ratifications of the majority of the signatories, including the ratifications of Belgium, Canada, France, Luxembourg, the Netherlands, the United Kingdom and the United States, have been deposited and shall come into effect with respect to other States on the date of the deposit of their ratifications. (²)

Article 12

After the Treaty has been in force for ten years, or at any time thereafter, the Parties shall, if any of them so requests, consult together for the purpose of reviewing the Treaty, having regard for the factors then affecting peace and security in the North Atlantic area, including the development of universal as well as regional arrangements under the Charter of the United Nations for the maintenance of international peace and security.

Article 13

After the Treaty has been in force for twenty years, any Party may cease to be a Party one year after its notice of denunciation has been given to the Government of the United States of America, which will inform the Governments of the other Parties of the deposit of each notice of denunciation.

Article 14

This Treaty, of which the English and French texts are equally authentic, shall be deposited in the archives of the Government of the United States of America. Duly certified copies will be transmitted by that Government to the Governments of other signatories.

Footnotes :

1. The definition of the territories to which Article 5 applies was revised by Article 2 of the Protocol to the North Atlantic Treaty on the accession of Greece and Turkey signed on 22 October 1951.
2. On January 16, 1963, the North Atlantic Council noted that insofar as the former Algerian Departments

of France were concerned, the relevant clauses of this Treaty had become inapplicable as from July 3, 1962.

3. The Treaty came into force on 24 August 1949, after the deposition of the ratifications of all signatory states.

Excerpts from The Dayton Peace Accords: General Framework Agreement for Peace in Bosnia and Herzegovina

Table of Content

Articles

The Republic of Bosnia and Herzegovina, the Republic of Croatia and the Federal Republic of Yugoslavia (the "Parties"),

Recognizing the need for a comprehensive settlement to bring an end to the tragic conflict in the region,

Desiring to contribute toward that end and to promote an enduring peace and stability,

Affirming their commitment to the Agreed Basic Principles issued on September 8, 1995, the Further Agreed Basic Principles issued on September 26, 1995, and the cease-fire agreements of September 14 and October 5, 1995,

Noting the agreement of August 29, 1995, which authorized the delegation of the Federal Republic of Yugoslavia to sign, on behalf of the Republika Srpska, the parts of the peace plan concerning it, with the obligation to implement the agreement that is reached strictly and consequently,

Have agreed as follows:

Article I

The Parties shall conduct their relations in accordance with the principles set forth in the United Nations Charter, as well as the Helsinki Final Act and other documents of the Organization for Security and Cooperation in Europe. In particular, the Parties shall fully respect the sovereign equality of one another, shall settle disputes by peaceful means, and shall refrain from any action, by threat or use of force or otherwise, against the territorial integrity or political independence of Bosnia and Herzegovina or any other State.

Article II

The Parties welcome and endorse the arrangements that have been made concerning the military aspects of the peace settlement and aspects of regional stabilization, as set forth in the Agreements at Annex 1-A and Annex 1-B. The Parties shall fully respect and promote fulfillment of the commitments made in Annex 1-A, and shall comply fully with their commitments as set forth in Annex 1-B.

Article III

The Parties welcome and endorse the arrangements that have been made concerning the boundary demarcation between the two Entities, the Federation of Bosnia and Herzegovina and Republika Srpska, as set forth in the Agreement at Annex 2. The Parties shall fully respect and promote fulfillment of the commitments made therein.

Article IV

The Parties welcome and endorse the elections program for Bosnia and Herzegovina as set forth in Annex 3. The Parties shall fully respect and promote fulfillment of that program.

Article V

The Parties welcome and endorse the arrangements that have been made concerning the Constitution of Bosnia and Herzegovina, as set forth in Annex 4. The Parties shall fully respect and promote fulfillment of the commitments made therein.

Article VI

The Parties welcome and endorse the arrangements that have been made concerning the establishment of an arbitration tribunal, a Commission on Human Rights, a Commission on Refugees and Displaced Persons, a Commission to Preserve National Monuments, and Bosnia and Herzegovina Public Corporations, as set forth in the Agreements at Annexes 5-9. The Parties shall fully respect and promote fulfillment of the commitments made therein.

Article VII

Recognizing that the observance of human rights and the protection of refugees and displaced persons are of vital importance in achieving a lasting peace, the Parties agree to and shall comply fully with the provisions concerning human rights set forth in Chapter One of the Agreement at Annex 6, as well as the provisions concerning refugees and displaced persons set forth in Chapter One of the Agreement at Annex 7.

Article VIII

The Parties welcome and endorse the arrangements that have been made concerning the implementation of this peace settlement, including in particular those pertaining to the civilian (non-military) implementation, as set forth in the Agreement at Annex 10, and the international police task force, as set forth in the Agreement at Annex 11. The Parties shall fully respect and promote fulfillment of the commitments made therein.

Article IX

The Parties shall cooperate fully with all entities involved in implementation of this peace settlement, as described in the Annexes to this Agreement, or which are otherwise authorized by the United Nations Security Council, pursuant to the obligation of all Parties to cooperate in the investigation and prosecution of war crimes and other violations of international humanitarian law.

Article X

The Federal Republic of Yugoslavia and the Republic of Bosnia and Herzegovina recognize each other as sovereign independent States within their international borders. Further aspects of their mutual recognition will be subject to subsequent discussions.

Article XI

This Agreement shall enter into force upon signature.

DONE at Paris, this 14 day of December, 1995, in the Bosnian, Croatian, English and Serbian languages, each text being equally authentic.

For the Republic of Bosnia and Herzegovina
For the Republic of Croatia

For the Federal Republic of Yugoslavia
Witnessed by:

European Union Special Negotiator
For the French Republic
For the Federal Republic of Germany
For the Russian Federation
For the United Kingdom of Great Britain
and Northern Ireland
For the United States of America
Annexes:

Table of Contents

The Republic of Bosnia and Herzegovina, the Federation of Bosnia and Herzegovina, and the Republika Srpska (hereinafter the "Parties") have agreed as follows:

Article I: General Obligations

The Parties undertake to recreate as quickly as possible normal conditions of life in Bosnia and Herzegovina. They understand that this requires a major contribution on their part in which they will make strenuous efforts to cooperate with each other and with the international organizations and agencies which are assisting them on the ground. They welcome the willingness of the international community to send to the region, for a period of approximately one year, a force to assist in implementation of the territorial and other militarily related provisions of the agreement as described herein.

The United Nations Security Council is invited to adopt a resolution by which it will authorize Member States or regional organizations and arrangements to establish a multinational military Implementation Force (hereinafter "IFOR"). The Parties understand and agree that this Implementation Force may be composed of ground, air and maritime units from NATO and non- NATO nations, deployed to Bosnia and Herzegovina to help ensure compliance with the provisions of this Agreement (hereinafter "Annex"). The Parties understand and agree that the IFOR will begin the implementation of the military aspects of this Annex upon the transfer of authority from the UNPROFOR Commander to the IFOR Commander (hereinafter "Transfer of Authority"), and that until the Transfer of Authority, UNPROFOR will continue to exercise its mandate.

It is understood and agreed that NATO may establish such a force, which will operate under the authority and subject to the direction and political control of the North Atlantic Council ("NAC") through the NATO chain of command. They undertake to facilitate its operations. The Parties, therefore, hereby agree and freely undertake to fully comply with all obligations set forth in this Annex.

It is understood and agreed that other States may assist in implementing the military aspects of this Annex. The Parties understand and agree that the modalities of those States' participation will be the subject of agreement between such participating States and NATO.

The purposes of these obligations are as follows:
to establish a durable cessation of hostilities. Neither Entity shall threaten or use force against the other Entity, and under no circumstances shall any armed forces of either Entity enter into or stay within the territory of the other Entity without the consent of the government of the latter and of the Presidency of Bosnia and Herzegovina. All armed forces in Bosnia and Herzegovina shall operate consistently with the sovereignty and territorial integrity of Bosnia and Herzegovina;

to provide for the support and authorization of the IFOR and in particular to authorize the IFOR to take such actions as required, including the use of necessary force, to ensure compliance with this Annex, and to ensure its own protection; and

to establish lasting security and arms control measures as outlined in Annex 1-B to the General Framework Agreement, which aim to promote a permanent reconciliation between all Parties and to facilitate the achievement of all political arrangements agreed to in the General Framework Agreement.

The Parties understand and agree that within Bosnia and Herzegovina the obligations undertaken in this Annex shall be applied equally within both Entities. Both Entities shall be held equally responsible for compliance herewith, and both shall be equally subject to such enforcement action by the IFOR as may be necessary to ensure implementation of this Annex and the protection of the IFOR.

Article II: Cessation of Hostilities

The Parties shall comply with the cessation of hostilities begun with the agreement of October 5, 1995 and shall continue to refrain from all offensive operations of any type against each other. An offensive operation in this case is an action that includes projecting forces or fire forward of a Party's own lines. Each Party shall ensure that all personnel and organizations with military capability under its control or within territory under its control, including armed civilian groups, national guards, army reserves, military police, and the Ministry of Internal Affairs Special Police (MUP) (hereinafter "Forces") comply with this Annex. The term "Forces" does not include UNPROFOR, the International Police Task Force referred to in the General Framework Agreement, the IFOR or other elements referred to in Article I, paragraph 1 (c).

In carrying out the obligations set forth in paragraph 1, the Parties undertake, in particular, to cease the firing of all weapons and explosive devices except as authorized by this Annex. The Parties shall not place any additional minefields, barriers, or protective obstacles. They shall not engage in patrolling, ground or air reconnaissance forward of their own force positions, or into the Zones of Separation as provided for in Article IV below, without IFOR approval.

The Parties shall provide a safe and secure environment for all persons in their respective jurisdictions, by maintaining civilian law enforcement agencies operating in accordance with internationally recognized standards and with respect for internationally recognized human rights and fundamental freedoms, and by taking such other measures as appropriate. The Parties also commit themselves to disarm and disband all armed civilian groups, except for authorized police forces, within 30 days after the Transfer of Authority.

The Parties shall cooperate fully with any international personnel including investigators, advisors, monitors, observers, or other personnel in Bosnia and Herzegovina pursuant to the General Framework Agreement, including facilitating free and unimpeded access and movement and by providing such status as is necessary for the effective conduct of their tasks.

The Parties shall strictly avoid committing any reprisals, counter-attacks, or any unilateral actions in response to violations of this Annex by another Party. The Parties shall respond to alleged violations of the provisions of this Annex through the procedures provided in Article VIII.

Article III: Withdrawal of Foreign Forces

All Forces in Bosnia and Herzegovina as of the date this Annex enters into force which are not of local origin, whether or not they are legally and militarily subordinated to the Republic of Bosnia and Herzegovina, the Federation of Bosnia and Herzegovina, or Republika Srpska, shall be withdrawn together with their equipment from the territory of Bosnia and Herzegovina within thirty (30) days. Furthermore, all Forces that remain on the territory of Bosnia and Herzegovina must act consistently with the territorial integrity, sovereignty, and political independence of Bosnia and Herzegovina. In accordance with Article II, paragraph 1, this paragraph does not apply to UNPROFOR, the International Police Task Force referred to in the General Framework Agreement, the IFOR or other elements referred to in Article I, paragraph 1 (c).

In particular, all foreign Forces, including individual advisors, freedom fighters, trainers, volunteers, and personnel from neighboring and other States, shall be withdrawn from the territory of Bosnia and Herzegovina in accordance with Article III, paragraph 1.

Article IV: Redeployment of Forces

The Republic of Bosnia and Herzegovina and the Entities shall redeploy their Forces in three phases:

Phase I

The Parties immediately after this Annex enters into force shall begin promptly and proceed steadily to withdraw all Forces behind a Zone of Separation which shall be established on either side of the Agreed Cease-Fire Line that represents a clear and distinct demarcation between any and all opposing Forces. This withdrawal shall be completed within thirty (30) days after the Transfer of Authority. The precise Agreed Cease-Fire Line and Agreed Cease- Fire Zone of Separation are indicated on the maps at Appendix A of this Annex.

The Agreed Cease-Fire Zone of Separation shall extend for a distance of approximately two (2) kilometers on either side of the Agreed Cease-Fire Line. No weapons other than those of the IFOR are permitted in this Agreed Cease-Fire Zone of Separation except as provided herein. No individual may retain or possess any military weapons or explosives within this four kilometer Zone without specific approval of the IFOR.

Violators of this provision shall be subject to military action by the IFOR, including the use of necessary force to ensure compliance. In addition to the other provisions of this Annex, the following specific provisions shall also apply to Sarajevo and Gorazde:

Sarajevo

Within seven (7) days after the Transfer of Authority, the Parties shall transfer and vacate selected positions along the Agreed Cease- Fire Line according to instructions to be issued by the IFOR Commander.

The Parties shall complete withdrawal from the Agreed Cease-Fire Zone of Separation in Sarajevo within thirty (30) days after the Transfer of Authority, in accordance with Article IV, paragraph 2. The width of this Zone of Separation will be approximately one (l) kilometer on either side of the Agreed Cease-Fire Line. However, this Zone of Separation may be adjusted by the IFOR Commander either to narrow the Zone of Separation?to take account of the urban

area of Sarajevo or to widen the Zone of Separation up to two (2) kilometers on either side of the Agreed Cease-Fire Line to take account of more open terrain.

Within the Agreed Cease-Fire Zone of Separation, no individual may retain or possess any weapons or explosives, other than a member of the IFOR or the local police exercising official duties as authorized by the IFOR in accordance with Article IV, paragraph 2(b).

The Parties understand and agree that violators of subparagraphs (1), (2) and (3) above shall be subject to military action by the IFOR, including the use of necessary force to ensure compliance.

Gorazde

The Parties understand and agree that a two lane all-weather road will be constructed in the Gorazde Corridor. Until such road construction is complete, the two interim routes will be used by both Entities.

The Grid coordinates for these alternate routes are (Map References: Defense Mapping Agency 1:50,000 Topographic Line Maps, Series M709, Sheets 2782-1, 2782-2, 2782-3, 2782-4, 2881-4, 2882-1, 2882-2, 2882-3, and 2882-4; Military Grid Reference System grid coordinates referenced to World Geodetic System 84 (Horizontal Datum):

Interim Route 1: From Gorazde (34TCP361365), proceed northeast following Highway 5 along the Drina River to the Ustipraca area (34TCP456395). At that point, proceed north on Highway 19-3 through Rogatica (34TCP393515) continuing northwest past Stienice (34TCP294565) to the road intersection at Podromanija (34TCP208652). From this point, proceed west following Highway 19 to where it enters the outskirts of Sarajevo (34TBP950601).

Interim Route 2: From Gorazde (34TCP361365), proceed south following Highway 20. Follow Highway 20 through Ustinkolina (34TCP218281). Continue south following Highway 20 passing Foca along the west bank of the Drina River (34TCP203195) to a point (34TCP175178) where the route turns west following Highway 18. From this point, follow Highway 18 south of Miljevina (34TCP097204) continuing through Trnovo (34TBP942380) north to the outskirts of Sarajevo where it enters the town at Vaskovici (34TBP868533).

There shall be complete freedom of movement along these routes for civilian traffic. The Parties shall only utilize these interim routes for military forces and equipment as authorized by and under the control and direction of the IFOR. In this regard, and in order to reduce the risk to civilian traffic, the IFOR shall have the right to manage movement of military and civilian traffic from both Entities along these routes.

The Parties understand and agree that violators of subparagraph (1) shall be subject to military action by the IFOR, including the use of necessary force to ensure compliance.

The Parties pledge as a confidence building measure that they shall not locate any Forces or heavy weapons as defined in paragraph 5 of this Article within two (2) kilometers of the designated interim routes. Where those routes run in or through the designated Zones of Separation, the provisions relating to Zones of Separation in this Annex shall also apply.

The Parties immediately after this Annex enters into force shall begin promptly and proceed steadily to complete the following activities within thirty (30) days after the Transfer of Authority or as determined by the IFOR Commander: (1) remove, dismantle or destroy all mines, unexploded ordnance, explosive devices, demolitions,

and barbed or razor wire from the Agreed Cease-Fire Zone of Separation or other areas from which their Forces are withdrawn; (2) mark all known mine emplacements, unexploded ordnance, explosive devices and demolitions within Bosnia and Herzegovina; and (3) remove, dismantle or destroy all mines, unexploded ordnance, explosive devices and demolitions as required by the IFOR Commander.

The IFOR is authorized to direct that any military personnel, active or reserve, who reside within the Agreed Cease-Fire Zone of Separation register with the appropriate IFOR Command Post referred to in Article VI which is closest to their residence.

PHASE II (AS REQUIRED IN SPECIFIC LOCATIONS)
This phase applies to those locations where the Inter-Entity Boundary Line does not follow the Agreed Cease-Fire Line.

In those locations in which, pursuant to the General Framework Agreement, areas occupied by one Entity are to be transferred to another Entity, all Forces of the withdrawing Entity shall have forty-five (45) days after the Transfer of Authority to completely vacate and clear this area. This shall include the removal of all Forces as well as the removal, dismantling or destruction of equipment, mines, obstacles, unexploded ordnance, explosive devices, demolitions, and weapons. In those areas being transferred to a different Entity, in order to provide an orderly period of transition, the Entity to which an area is transferred shall not put Forces in this area for ninety (90) days after the Transfer of Authority or as determined by the IFOR Commander. The Parties understand and agree that the IFOR shall have the right to provide the military security for these transferred areas from thirty (30) days after the Transfer of Authority until ninety-one (91) days after the Transfer of Authority, or as soon as possible as determined by the

IFOR Commander, when these areas may be occupied by the Forces of the Entity to which they are transferred. Upon occupation by the Entity to which the area is transferred, a new Zone of Separation along the Inter-Entity Boundary Line as indicated on the map at Appendix A shall be established by the IFOR, and the Parties shall observe the same limitations on the presence of Forces and weapons in this Zone as apply to the Agreed Cease-Fire Zone of Separation.

The IFOR is authorized to direct that any military personnel, active or reserve, who reside within the Inter-Entity Zone of Separation register with the appropriate IFOR Command Post referred to in Article VI which is closest to their residence.

GENERAL. The following provisions apply to Phases I and II:

In order to provide visible indication, the IFOR shall supervise the selective marking of the Agreed Cease-Fire Line and its Zone of Separation, and the Inter-Entity Boundary Line and its Zone of Separation. Final authority for placement of such markers shall rest with the IFOR. All Parties understand and agree that the Agreed Cease-Fire Line and its Zone of Separation and the Inter-Entity Boundary Line and its Zone of Separation are defined by the maps and documents agreed to as part of the General Framework Agreement and not the physical location of markers.

All Parties understand and agree that they shall be subject to military action by the IFOR, including the use of necessary force to ensure compliance, for:

failure to remove all their Forces and unauthorized weapons from the four (4) kilometer Agreed Cease-Fire Zone of Separation within thirty (30) days after the Transfer of Authority, as provided in Article IV, paragraph 2(a) and (b) above;

failure to vacate and clear areas being transferred to another Entity within forty-five (45) days after the Transfer of Authority, as provided in Article IV, paragraph 3(a) above;

deploying Forces within areas transferred from another Entity earlier than ninety (90) days after the Transfer of Authority or as determined by the IFOR Commander, as provided in Article IV, paragraph 3(a) above;

failure to keep all Forces and unauthorized weapons outside the Inter-Entity Zone of Separation after this Zone is declared in effect by the IFOR, as provided in Article IV, paragraph 3(a) above; or

violation of the cessation of hostilities as agreed to by the Parties in Article II.

PHASE III

The Parties pledge as confidence building measures that they shall:

within 120 days after the Transfer of Authority withdraw all heavy weapons and Forces to cantonment/barracks areas or other locations as designated by the IFOR Commander. "Heavy weapons" refers to all tanks and armored vehicles, all artillery 75 mm and above, all mortars 81 mm and above, and all anti-aircraft weapons 20 mm and above. This movement of these Forces to cantonment/barracks areas is intended to enhance mutual confidence by the Parties in the success of this Annex and help the overall cause of peace in Bosnia and Herzegovina.

within 120 days after the Transfer of Authority demobilize Forces which cannot be accommodated in cantonment/barracks areas as provided in subparagraph (a) above. Demobilization shall consist of removing from the possession of these personnel all weapons, including individual weapons, explosive devices, communications equipment, vehicles, and all other military equipment. All personnel belonging to these Forces shall be released from service and shall not engage in any further training or other military activities.

Notwithstanding any other provision of this Annex, the Parties understand and agree that the IFOR has the right and is authorized to compel the removal, withdrawal, or relocation of specific Forces and weapons from, and to order the cessation of any activities in, any location in Bosnia and Herzegovina whenever the IFOR determines such Forces, weapons or activities to constitute a threat or potential threat to either the IFOR or its mission, or to another Party. Forces failing to redeploy, withdraw, relocate, or to cease threatening or potentially threatening activities following such a demand by the IFOR shall be subject to military action by the IFOR, including the use of necessary force to ensure compliance, consistent with the terms set forth in Article I, paragraph 3.

Article V: Notifications

Immediately upon establishment of the Joint Military Commission provided for in Article VIII, each Party shall furnish to the Joint Military Commission information regarding the positions and descriptions of all known unexploded ordnance, explosive devices, demolitions, minefields, booby traps, wire entanglements, and all other physical or military hazards to the safe movement of any personnel within Bosnia and Herzegovina, as well as the location of lanes through the Agreed Cease-Fire Zone of Separation which are free of all such hazards. The Parties shall keep the Joint Military Commission updated on changes in this information.

Within thirty (30) days after the Transfer of Authority, each Party shall furnish to the Joint Military Commission the following specific information regarding the status of

its Forces within Bosnia and Herzegovina and shall keep the Joint Military Commission updated on changes in this information:

location, type, strengths of personnel and weaponry of all Forces within ten (10) kilometers of the Agreed Cease-Fire Line and Inter-Entity Boundary Line. maps depicting the forward line of troops and front lines;

positions and descriptions of fortifications, minefields, unexploded ordnance, explosive devices, demolitions, barriers, and other man-made obstacles, ammunition dumps, command headquarters, and communications networks within ten (10) kilometers of the Agreed Cease-Fire Line or Inter-Entity Boundary Line;

positions and descriptions of all surface to air missiles/launchers, including mobile systems, anti-aircraft artillery, supporting radars and associated command and control systems;

positions and descriptions of all mines, unexploded ordnance, explosive devices, demolitions, obstacles, weapons systems, vehicles, or any other military equipment which cannot be removed, dismantled or destroyed under the provisions of Article IV, paragraphs 2(d) and 3(a); and

any further information of a military nature as requested by the IFOR.

Within 120 days after the Transfer of Authority, the Parties shall furnish to the Joint Military Commission the following specific information regarding the status of their Forces in Bosnia and Herzegovina and shall keep the Joint Military Commission updated on changes in this information:

location, type, strengths of personnel and weaponry of all Forces;

maps depicting the information in sub-paragraph (a) above;

positions and descriptions of fortifications, minefields, unexploded ordnance, explosive devices, demolitions, barriers, and other man-made obstacles, ammunition dumps, command headquarters, and communications networks; and

any further information of a military nature as requested by the IFOR.

Article VI: Deployment of the Implementation Force

Recognizing the need to provide for the effective implementation of the provisions of this Annex, and to ensure compliance, the United Nations Security Council is invited to authorize Member States or regional organizations and arrangements to establish the IFOR acting under Chapter VII of the United Nations Charter. The Parties understand and agree that this Implementation Force may be composed of ground, air and maritime units from NATO and non-NATO nations, deployed to Bosnia and Herzegovina to help ensure compliance with the provisions of this Annex. The Parties understand and agree that the IFOR shall have the right to deploy on either side of the Inter-Entity Boundary Line and throughout Bosnia and Herzegovina.

The Parties understand and agree that the IFOR shall have the right:

to monitor and help ensure compliance by all Parties with this Annex (including, in particular, withdrawal and redeployment of Forces within agreed periods, and the establishment of Zones of Separation);

to authorize and supervise the selective marking of the Agreed Cease-Fire Line and its Zone of Separation and the Inter-Entity Boundary Line and its Zone of Separation as

established by the General Framework Agreement;

to establish liaison arrangements with local civilian and military authorities and other international organizations as necessary for the accomplishment of its mission;

and to assist in the withdrawal of UN Peace Forces not transferred to the IFOR, including, if necessary, the emergency withdrawal of UNCRO Forces.

The Parties understand and agree that the IFOR shall have the right to fulfill its supporting tasks, within the limits of its assigned principal tasks and available resources, and on request, which include the following:

to help create secure conditions for the conduct by others of other tasks associated with the peace settlement, including free and fair elections;

to assist the movement of organizations in the accomplishment of humanitarian missions;

to assist the UNHCR and other international organizations in their humanitarian missions;

to observe and prevent interference with the movement of civilian populations, refugees, and displaced persons, and to respond appropriately to deliberate violence to life and person; and,

to monitor the clearing of minefields and obstacles.

The Parties understand and agree that further directives from the NAC may establish additional duties and responsibilities for the IFOR in implementing this Annex.

The Parties understand and agree that the IFOR Commander shall have the authority, without interference or permission of any Party, to do all that the Commander judges necessary and proper, including the use of military force, to protect the IFOR and to carry out the responsibilities listed above in paragraphs 2, 3 and 4, and they shall comply in all respects with the IFOR requirements.

The Parties understand and agree that in carrying out its responsibilities, the IFOR shall have the unimpeded right to observe, monitor, and inspect any Forces, facility or activity in Bosnia and Herzegovina that the IFOR believes may have military capability. The refusal, interference, or denial by any Party of this right to observe, monitor, and inspect by the IFOR shall constitute a breach of this Annex and the violating Party shall be subject to military action by the IFOR, including the use of necessary force to ensure compliance with this Annex.

The Army of the Republic of Bosnia and Herzegovina, the Croat Defense Council Forces, and the Army of Republika Srpska shall establish Command Posts at IFOR brigade, battalion, or other levels which shall be co-located with specific IFOR command Vocations, as determined by the IFOR Commander. These Command Posts shall exercise command and control over all Forces of their respective sides which are located within ten (10) kilometers of the Agreed Cease-Fire Line or Inter-Entity Boundary Line, as specified by the IFOR. The Command Posts shall provide, at the request of the IFOR, timely status reports on organizations and troop levels in their areas.

In addition to co-located Command Posts, the Army of the Republic of Bosnia and Herzegovina, the Croat Defense Council Forces, and the Army of Republika Srpska shall maintain liaison teams to be co-located with the IFOR Command, as determined by the IFOR Commander, for the purpose of

fostering communication, and preserving the overall cessation of hostilities.

Air and surface movements in Bosnia and Herzegovina shall be governed by the following provisions:

The IFOR shall have complete and unimpeded freedom of movement by ground, air, and water throughout Bosnia and Herzegovina. It shall have the right to bivouac, maneuver, billet, and utilize any areas or facilities to carry out its responsibilities as required for its support, training, and operations, with such advance notice as may be practicable. The IFOR and its personnel shall not be liable for any damages to civilian or government property caused by combat or combat related activities. Roadblocks, checkpoints or other impediments to IFOR freedom of movement shall constitute a breach of this Annex and the violating Party shall be subject to military action by the IFOR, including the use of necessary force to ensure compliance with this Annex.

The IFOR Commander shall have sole authority to establish rules and procedures governing command and control of airspace over Bosnia and Herzegovina to enable civilian air traffic and non- combat air activities by the military or civilian authorities in Bosnia and Herzegovina, or if necessary to terminate civilian air traffic and non- combat air activities.

The Parties understand and agree there shall be no military air traffic, or non-military aircraft performing military missions, including reconnaissance or logistics, without the express permission of the IFOR Commander. The only military aircraft that may be authorized to fly in Bosnia and Herzegovina are those being flown in support of the IFOR, except with the express permission of the IFOR. Any flight activities by military fixed- wing or helicopter aircraft within Bosnia and Herzegovina without the express permission of the IFOR Commander are subject to military action by the IFOR, including the use of necessary force to ensure compliance.

All air early warning, air defense, or fire control radars shall be shut down within 72 hours after this Annex enters into force, and shall remain inactive unless authorized by the IFOR Commander. Any use of air traffic, air early warning, air defense or fire control radars not authorized by the IFOR Commander shall constitute a breach of this Annex and the violating Party shall be subject to military action by the IFOR, including the use of necessary force to ensure compliance.

The Parties understand and agree that the IFOR Commander will implement the transfer to civilian control of air space over Bosnia and Herzegovina to the appropriate institutions of Bosnia and Herzegovina in a gradual fashion consistent with the objective of the IFOR to ensure smooth and safe operation of an air traffic system upon IFOR departure.

The IFOR Commander is authorized to promulgate appropriate rules for the control and regulation of surface military traffic throughout Bosnia and Herzegovina, including the movement of the Forces of the Parties. The Joint Military Commission referred to in Article VIII may assist in the development and promulgation of rules related to military movement.

The IFOR shall have the right to utilize such means and services as required to ensure its full ability to communicate and shall have the right to the unrestricted use of all of the electromagnetic spectrum for this purpose. In implementing this right, the IFOR shall make every reasonable effort to coordinate with and take into account the needs and requirements of the appropriate authorities.

All Parties shall accord the IFOR and its personnel the assistance, privileges, and immunities set forth at Appendix B of this Annex, including the unimpeded transit through, to, over and on the territory of all Parties.

All Parties shall accord any military elements as referred to in Article I, paragraph l(c) and their personnel the assistance, privileges and immunities referred to in Article VI, paragraph 11.

Article VII: Withdrawal of UNPROFOR

It is noted that as a consequence of the forthcoming introduction of the IFOR into the Republic of Bosnia and Herzegovina, the conditions for the withdrawal of the UNPROFOR established by United Nations Security Council Resolution 743 have been met. It is requested that the United Nations, in consultation with NATO, take all necessary steps to withdraw the UNPROFOR from Bosnia and Herzegovina, except those parts incorporated into the IFOR.

Article VIII: Establishment of a Joint Military Commission

A Joint Military Commission (the "Commission") shall be established with the deployment of the IFOR to Bosnia and Herzegovina.

The Commission shall:

Serve as the central body for all Parties to this Annex to bring any military complaints, questions, or problems that require resolution by the IFOR Commander, such as allegations of cease-fire violations or other noncompliance with this Annex.
Receive reports and agree on specific actions to ensure compliance with the provisions of this Annex by the Parties.

Assist the IFOR Commander in determining and implementing a series of local transparency measures between the Parties.

The Commission shall be chaired by the IFOR Commander or his or her representative and consist of the following members:

the senior military commander of the forces of each Party within Bosnia and Herzegovina;

other persons as the Chairman may determine;

each Party to this Annex may also select two civilians who shall advise the Commission in carrying out its duties;

the High Representative referred to in the General Framework Agreement or his or her nominated representative shall attend Commission meetings, and offer advice particularly on matters of a political- military nature.

The Commission shall not include any persons who are now or who come under indictment by the International Tribunal for the Former Yugoslavia.

The Commission shall function as a consultative body for the IFOR Commander. To the extent possible, problems shall be solved promptly by mutual agreement. However, all final decisions concerning its military matters shall be made by the IFOR Commander.

The Commission shall meet at the call of the IFOR Commander. The High Representative may when necessary request a meeting of the Commission. The Parties may also request a meeting of the Commission.

The IFOR Commander shall have the right to decide on military matters, in a timely

fashion, when there are overriding considerations relating to the safety of the IFOR or the Parties' compliance with the provisions of this Annex.

The Commission shall establish subordinate military commissions for the purpose of providing assistance in carrying out the functions described above. Such commissions shall be at the brigade and battalion level or at other echelons as the local IFOR Commander shall direct and be composed of commanders from each of the Parties and the IFOR. The representative of the High Representative shall attend and offer advice particularly on matters of a political-military nature. The local IFOR Commander shall invite local civilian authorities when appropriate.

Appropriate liaison arrangements will be established between the IFOR Commander and the High Representative to facilitate the discharge of their respective responsibilities.

Article IX: Prisoner Exchanges
The Parties shall release and transfer without delay all combatants and civilians held in relation to the conflict (hereinafter "prisoners"), in conformity with international humanitarian law and the provisions of this Article.

The Parties shall be bound by and implement such plan for release and transfer of all prisoners as may be developed by the ICRC, after consultation with the Parties. The Parties shall cooperate fully with the ICRC and facilitate its work in implementing and monitoring the plan for release and transfer of prisoners.
No later than thirty (30) days after the Transfer of Authority, the Parties shall release and transfer all prisoners held by them.

In order to expedite this process, no later than twenty-one (21) days after this Annex enters into force, the Parties shall draw up comprehensive lists of prisoners and shall provide such lists to the ICRC, to the other Parties, and to the Joint Military Commission and the High Representative. These lists shall identify prisoners by nationality, name, rank (if any) and any internment or military serial number, to the extent applicable.

The Parties shall ensure that the ICRC enjoys full and unimpeded access to all places where prisoners are kept and to all prisoners. The Parties shall permit the ICRC to privately interview each prisoner at least forty-eight (48) hours prior to his or her release for the purpose of implementing and monitoring the plan, including determination of the onward destination of each prisoner.

The Parties shall take no reprisals against any prisoner or his/her family in the event that a prisoner refuses to be transferred. Notwithstanding the above provisions, each Party shall comply with any order or request of the International Tribunal for the Former Yugoslavia for the arrest, detention, surrender of or access to persons who would otherwise be released and transferred under this Article, but who are accused of violations within the jurisdiction of the Tribunal. Each Party must detain persons reasonably suspected of such violations for a period of time sufficient to permit appropriate consultation with Tribunal authorities.

In those cases where places of burial, whether individual or mass, are known as a matter of record, and graves are actually found to exist, each Party shall permit graves registration personnel of the other Parties to enter, within a mutually agreed period of time, for the limited purpose of proceeding to such graves, to recover and evacuate the bodies of deceased military and civilian personnel of that side, including deceased prisoners.

Article X: Cooperation

The Parties shall cooperate fully with all entities involved in implementation of this peace settlement, as described in the General Framework Agreement, or which are otherwise authorized by the United Nations Security Council, including the International Tribunal for the Former Yugoslavia.

Article XI: Notification to Military Commands

Each Party shall ensure that the terms of this Annex, and written orders requiring compliance, are immediately communicated to all of its Forces.

Article XII: Final Authority to Interpret

In accordance with Article I, the IFOR Commander is the final authority in theatre regarding interpretation of this agreement on the military aspects of the peace settlement, of which the Appendices constitute an integral part.

Article XIII: Entry into Force

This Annex shall enter into force upon signature.

For the Republic of Bosnia and Herzegovina
For the Federation of Bosnia and Herzegovina
For the Republika Srpska

Endorsed:

For the Republic of Croatia

Endorsed:

For the Federal Republic of Yugoslavia

Annex 1B - Agreement on Regional Stabilization

The Republic of Bosnia and Herzegovina, the Republic of Croatia, the Federal Republic of Yugoslavia, the Federation of Bosnia and Herzegovina, and the Republika Srpska (hereinafter the "Parties") have agreed as follows:

Article I: General Obligations

Article II: Confidence- and Security-Building Measures in Bosnia and Herzegovina

Article III: Regional Confidence- and Security-Building Measures

Article IV: Measures for Sub-Regional Arms Control

Article V: Regional Arms Control Agreement

Article VI: Entry into Force

Article I: General Obligations

The Parties agree that establishment of progressive measures for regional stability and arms control is essential to creating a stable peace in the region. To this end, they agree on the importance of devising new forms of cooperation in the field of security aimed at building transparency and confidence and achieving balanced and stable defense force levels at the lowest numbers consistent with the Parties' respective security and the need to avoid an arms race in the region. They have approved the following elements for a regional structure for stability.

Article II: Confidence- and Security-Building Measures in Bosnia and Herzegovina

Within seven days after this Agreement (hereinafter "Annex") enters into force, the Republic of Bosnia and Herzegovina, the Federation of Bosnia and Herzegovina, and

the Republika Srpska shall at an appropriately high political level commence negotiations under the auspices of the Organization for Security and Cooperation in Europe (hereinafter "OSCE") to agree upon a series of measures to enhance mutual confidence and reduce the risk of conflict, drawing fully upon the 1994 Vienna Document of the Negotiations on Confidence- and Security-Building Measures of the OSCE. The objective of these negotiations is to agree upon an initial set of measures within forty-five (45) days after this Annex enters into force including, but not necessarily limited to, the following:

restrictions on military deployments and exercises in certain geographical areas; restraints on the reintroduction of foreign Forces in light of Article III of Annex 1-A to the General Framework Agreement;

restrictions on locations of heavy weapons;

withdrawal of Forces and heavy weapons to cantonment/barracks areas or other designated locations as provided in Article IV of Annex 1-A;

notification of disbandment of special operations and armed civilian groups;

notification of certain planned military activities, including international military assistance and training programs;

identification of and monitoring of weapons manufacturing capabilities;

immediate exchange of data on the holdings of the five Treaty on Conventional Armed Forces in Europe (hereinafter "CFE") weapons categories as defined in the CFE Treaty, with the additional understanding that artillery pieces will be defined as those of 75mm calibre and above; and

immediate establishment of military liaison missions between the Chiefs of the Armed

Forces of the Federation of Bosnia and Herzegovina and the Republika Srpska;

Article III: Regional Confidence- and Security-Building Measures

To supplement the measures in Article II above on a wider basis, the Parties agree to initiate steps toward a regional agreement on confidence- and security-building measures. The Parties agree:

not to import any arms for ninety (90) days after this Annex enters into force;

not to import for 180 days after this Annex enters into force or until the arms control agreement referred to in Article IV below takes effect, whichever is the earlier, heavy weapons or heavy weapons ammunition, mines, military aircraft, and helicopters.

Heavy weapons refers to all tanks and armored vehicles, all artillery 75 mm and above, all mortars 81 mm and above, and all anti-aircraft weapons 20 mm and above.

Article IV: Measures for Sub-Regional Arms Control

Recognizing the importance of achieving balanced and stable defense force levels at the lowest numbers consistent with their respective security, and understanding that the establishment of a stable military balance based on the lowest level of armaments will be an essential element in preventing the recurrence of conflict, the Parties within thirty (30) days after this Annex enters into force shall commence negotiations under the auspices of the OSCE to reach early agreement on levels of armaments consistent with this goal. Within thirty (30) days after this Annex enters into force, the Parties shall also commence negotiations on an agreement establishing voluntary limits on military manpower.

The Parties agree that the armaments agreement should be based at a minimum on the following criteria: population size, current military armament holdings, defense needs, and relative force levels in the region.

The agreement shall establish numerical limits on holdings of tanks, artillery, armored combat vehicles, combat aircraft, and attack helicopters, as defined in the relevant sections of the CFE Treaty, with the additional understanding that artillery pieces will be defined as those of 75 mm calibre and above.

In order to establish a baseline, the Parties agree to report within thirty (30) days after this Annex enters into force their holdings as defined in sub-paragraph (a) above, according to the format prescribed in the 1992 Vienna Document of the OSCE.

This notification format shall be supplemented to take into account the special considerations of the region.

The Parties agree to complete within 180 days after this Annex enters into force the negotiations above on agreed numerical limits on the categories referred to in paragraph 2(a) of this Article. If the Parties fail to agree to such limits within 180 days after this Annex enters into force, the following limits shall apply, according to a ratio of 5:2:2 based on the approximate ratio of populations of the Parties:

the baseline shall be the determined holdings of the Federal Republic of Yugoslavia (hereinafter the "baseline");

the limits for the Federal Republic of Yugoslavia shall be seventy-five (75) percent of the baseline;

the limits for the Republic of Croatia shall be thirty (30) percent of the baseline;

the limits for Bosnia and Herzegovina shall be thirty (30) percent of the baseline; and

the allocations for Bosnia and Herzegovina will be divided between the Entities on the basis of a ratio of two (2) for the Federation of Bosnia and Herzegovina and one (1) for the Republika Srpska.

The OSCE will assist the Parties in their negotiations underArticles II and IV of this Annex and in the implementation and verification (including verification of holdings declarations) of resulting agreements.

Article V: Regional Arms Control Agreement

The OSCE will assist the Parties by designating a special representative to help organize and conduct negotiations under the auspices of the OSCE Forum on Security Cooperation ("FSC") with the goal of establishing a regional balance in and around the former Yugoslavia. The Parties undertake to cooperate fully with the OSCE to that end and to facilitate regular inspections by other parties. Further, the Parties agree to establish a commission together with representatives of the OSCE for the purpose of facilitating the resolution of any disputes that might arise.

Article VI: Entry into Force

This Annex shall enter into force upon signature.

For the Republic of Bosnia and Herzegovina

For the Republic of Croatia

For the Federal Republic of Yugoslavia

For the Federation of Bosnia and Herzegovina

For the Republika Srpska

Annex 2 - Agreement on Inter-Entity Boundary Line and Related Issues (With Appendix)

The Republic of Bosnia and Herzegovina, the Federation of Bosnia and Herzegovina and the Republika Srpska (the "Parties") have agreed as follows:

Article I: Inter-Entity Boundary Line

Article II: Adjustment by the Parties

Article III: Rivers

Article IV: Delineation and Marking

Article V: Arbitration for the Brcko Area

Article VI: Transition

Article VII: Status of Appendix

Article VIII: Entry into Force

Article I: Inter-Entity Boundary Line

The boundary between the Federation of Bosnia and Herzegovina and the Republika Srpska (the "Inter-Entity Boundary Line") shall be as delineated on the map at the Appendix.

Article II: Adjustment by the Parties

The Parties may adjust the Inter-Entity Boundary Line only by mutual consent. During the period in which the multinational military Implementation Force ("IFOR") is deployed pursuant to Annex 1-A to the General Framework Agreement, the Parties shall consult with the IFOR Commander prior to making any agreed adjustment and shall provide notification of such adjustment to the IFOR Commander.

Article III: Rivers

Where the Inter-Entity Boundary Line follows a river, the line shall follow natural changes (accretion or erosion) in the course of the river unless otherwise agreed. Artificial changes in the course of the river shall not affect the location of the Inter-Entity Boundary Line unless otherwise agreed. No artificial changes may be made except by agreement among the Parties.

In the event of sudden natural changes in the course of the river (avulsion or cutting of new bed), the line shall be determined by mutual agreement of the Parties. If such event occurs during the period in which the IFOR is deployed, any such determination shall be subject to the approval of the IFOR Commander.

Article IV: Delineation and Marking

The line on the 1:50,000 scale map to be provided for the Appendix delineating the Inter-Entity Boundary Line, and the lines on the 1:50,000 scale map to be provided for Appendix A to Annex 1-A delineating the Inter-Entity Zone of Separation and the Agreed Cease-Fire Line and its Zone of Separation, which are accepted by the Parties as controlling and definitive, are accurate to within approximately 50 meters. During the period in which the IFOR is deployed, the IFOR Commander shall have the right to determine, after consultation with the Parties, the exact delineation of such Lines and Zones, provided that with respect to Sarajevo the IFOR Commander shall have the right to adjust the Zone of Separation as necessary.

The Lines and Zones described above may be marked by representatives of the Parties in coordination with and under the supervision of the IFOR. Final authority for placement of such markers shall rest with the IFOR. These Lines and Zones are defined by the maps and documents agreed to by the Parties and not by the physical location of markers.

Following entry into force of this Agreement, the Parties shall form a joint commission, comprised of an equal number of representatives from each Party, to prepare an agreed technical document containing a precise description of the Inter-Entity Boundary Line. Any such document prepared during the period in which the IFOR is deployed shall be subject to the approval of the IFOR Commander.

Article V: Arbitration for the Brcko Area

The Parties agree to binding arbitration of the disputed portion of the Inter-Entity Boundary Line in the Brcko area indicated on the map attached at the Appendix. No later than six months after the entry into force of this Agreement, the Federation shall appoint one arbitrator, and the Republika Srpska shall appoint one arbitrator. A third arbitrator shall be selected by agreement of the Parties' appointees within thirty days thereafter. If they do not agree, the third arbitrator shall be appointed by the President of the International Court of Justice. The third arbitrator shall serve as presiding officer of the arbitral tribunal.

Unless otherwise agreed by the Parties, the proceedings shall be conducted in accordance with the UNCITRAL rules. The arbitrators shall apply relevant legal and equitable principles.

Unless otherwise agreed, the area indicated in paragraph 1 above shall continue to be administered as currently.

The arbitrators shall issue their decision no later than one year from the entry into force of this Agreement. The decision shall be final and binding, and the Parties shall implement it without delay.

Article VI: Transition

In those areas transferring from one Entity to the other in accordance with the demarcation described herein, there shall be a transitional period to provide for the orderly transfer of authority. The transition shall be completed forty-five (45) days after the Transfer of Authority from the UNPROFOR Commander to the IFOR Commander, as described in Annex 1-A.

Article VII: Status of Appendix

The Appendix shall constitute an integral part of this Agreement.

Article VIII: Entry into Force

This Agreement shall enter into force upon signature.

For the Republic of Bosnia and Herzegovina

For the Federation of Bosnia and Herzegovina

For the Republika Srpska

Endorsed:

For the Republic of Croatia

Endorsed:

For the Federal Republic of Yugoslavia

Appendix to Annex 2

The Appendix to Annex 2 consists of this document together with

a 1:600,000 scale UNPROFOR road map consisting of one map sheet, attached hereto; and

a 1:50,000 scale Topographic Line Map, to be provided as described below.

On the basis of the attached 1:600,000 scale map, the Parties request that the United States Department of Defense provide a 1:50,000 scale Topographic Line Map,

consisting of as many map sheets as necessary, in order to provide a more precise delineation of the Inter-Entity Boundary Line. Such map shall be incorporated as an integral part of this Appendix, and the Parties agree to accept such map as controlling and definitive for all purposes.

For the Republic of Bosnia and Herzegovina

For the Federation of Bosnia and Herzegovina

For the Republika Srpska

Endorsed:

For the Republic of Croatia

Endorsed:

For the Federal Republic of Yugoslavia

[MAP NOT AVAILABLE]

Annex 5 - Agreement on Arbitration

The Federation of Bosnia and Herzegovina and the Republika Srpska agree to honor the following obligations as set forth in the Agreed Basic Principles adopted at Geneva on September 8, 1995, by the Republic of Bosnia and Herzegovina, the Republic of Croatia, and the Federal Republic of Yugoslavia, the latter representing also the Republika Srpska:

Paragraph 2.4. "The two entities will enter into reciprocal commitments. . .(c) to engage in binding arbitration to resolve disputes between them."

Paragraph 3. "The entities have agreed in principle to the following:... 3.5 The design and implementation of a system of arbitration for the solution of disputes between the two entities."

For the Federation of Bosnia and Herzegovina

For the Republika Srpska

Annex 6 - Agreement on Human Rights

The Republic of Bosnia and Herzegovina, the Federation of Bosnia and Herzegovina and the Republika Srpska (the "Parties") have agreed as follows:

Chapter One: Respect for Human Rights

Article I: Fundamental Rights and Freedoms

Article II: Establishment of the Commission

Article III: Facilities, Staff and Expenses

Article IV: Human Rights Ombudsman

Article V: Jurisdiction of the Ombudsman

Article VI: Powers

Article VII: Human Rights Chamber

Article VIII: Jurisdiction of the Chamber

Article IX: Friendly Settlement

Article X: Proceedings before the Chamber

Article XI: Decisions

Article XII: Rules and Regulations

Article XIII: Organizations Concerned with Human Rights

Article XIV: Transfer

Article XV: Notice

Article XVI: Entry into Force

Article I: Fundamental Rights and Freedoms

The Parties shall secure to all persons within their jurisdiction the highest level of internationally recognized human rights and fundamental freedoms, including the rights and freedoms provided in the European Convention for the Protection of Human Rights and Fundamental Freedoms and its Protocols and the other international agreements listed in the Appendix to this Annex. These include:

The right to life.

The right not to be subjected to torture or to inhuman or degrading treatment or punishment.

The right not to be held in slavery or servitude or to perform forced or compulsory labor.

The rights to liberty and security of person.

The right to a fair hearing in civil and criminal matters, and other rights relating to criminal proceedings.

The right to private and family life, home, and correspondence.

Freedom of thought, conscience and religion.

Freedom of expression.

Freedom of peaceful assembly and freedom of association with others.

The right to marry and to found a family. The right to property.

The right to education.

The right to liberty of movement and residence.

The enjoyment of the rights and freedoms provided for in this Article or in the international agreements listed in the Annex to this Constitution secured without discrimination on any ground such as sex, race, color, language, religion, political or other opinion, national or social origin, association with a national minority, property, birth or other status.

Chapter Two: The Commission on Human Rights

Part A: General

Article II: Establishment of the Commission

To assist in honoring their obligations under this Agreement, the Parties hereby establish a Commission on Human Rights (the "Commission"). The Commission shall consist of two parts: the Office of the Ombudsman and the Human Rights Chamber.

The Office of the Ombudsman and the Human Rights Chamber shall consider, as subsequently described:

alleged or apparent violations of human rights as provided in the European Convention for the Protection of Human Rights and Fundamental Freedoms and the Protocols thereto, or

alleged or apparent discrimination on any ground such as sex, race, color, language, religion, political or other opinion, national or social origin, association with a national minority, property, birth or other status arising in the enjoyment of any of the rights and freedoms provided for in the international agreements listed in the Appendix to this Annex, where such violation is alleged or appears to have been committed by the Parties, including by any official or organ of the Parties, Cantons, Municipalities, or any individual acting under the authority of such official or organ.

The Parties recognize the right of all persons to submit to the Commission and to other human rights bodies applications concerning alleged violations of human rights, in accordance with the procedures of this Annex and such bodies. The Parties shall not undertake any punitive action directed against persons who intend to submit, or have submitted, such allegations.

Article III: Facilities, Staff and Expenses

The Commission shall have appropriate facilities and a professionally competent staff. There shall be an Executive Officer, appointed jointly by the Ombudsman and the President of the Chamber, who shall be responsible for all necessary administrative arrangements with respect to facilities and staff. The Executive Officer shall be subject to the direction of the Ombudsman and the President of the Chamber insofar as concerns their respective administrative and professional office staff.

The salaries and expenses of the Commission and its staff shall be determined jointly by the Parties and shall be borne by Bosnia and Herzegovina. The salaries and expenses shall be fully adequate to implement the Commission's mandate. The Commission shall have its headquarters in Sarajevo, including both the headquarters Office of the Ombudsman and the facilities for the Chamber. The Ombudsman shall have at least one additional office in the territory of the Federation and the Republika Srpska and at other locations as it deems appropriate. The Chamber may meet in other locations where it determines that the needs of a particular case so require, and may meet at any place it deems appropriate for the inspection of property, documents or other items.

The Ombudsman and all members of the Chamber shall not be held criminally or civilly liable for any acts carried out within the scope of their duties. When the Ombudsman and members of the Chamber are not citizens of Bosnia and Herzegovina, they and their families shall be accorded the same privileges and immunities as are enjoyed by diplomatic agents and their families under the Vienna Convention on Diplomatic Relations.

With full regard for the need to maintain impartiality, the Commission may receive assistance as it deems appropriate from any governmental, international, or non-governmental organization.

Part B: Human Rights Ombudsman

Article IV: Human Rights Ombudsman

The Parties hereby establish the Office of the Human Rights Ombudsman (the "Ombudsman").

The Ombudsman shall be appointed for a non-renewable term of five years by the Chairman- in-Office of the Organization for Security and Cooperation in Europe (OSCE), after consultation with the Parties. He or she shall be independently responsible for choosing his or her own staff. Until the transfer described in Article XIV below, the Ombudsman may not be a citizen of Bosnia and Herzegovina or of any neighboring state. The Ombudsman appointed after that transfer shall be appointed by the Presidency of Bosnia and Herzegovina.

Members of the Office of the Ombudsman must be of recognized high moral standing and have competence in the field of international human rights.

The Office of the Ombudsman shall be an independent agency. In carrying out its mandate, no person or organ of the Parties may interfere with its functions.

Article V: Jurisdiction of the Ombudsman

Allegations of violations of human rights received by the Commission shall generally be directed to the Office of the Ombudsman, except where an applicant specifies the Chamber.

The Ombudsman may investigate, either on his or her own initiative or in response to an allegation by any Party or person, non-governmental organization, or group of individuals claiming to be the victim of a violation by any Party or acting on behalf of alleged victims who are deceased or missing, alleged or apparent violations of human rights within the scope of paragraph 2 of Article II. The Parties undertake not to hinder in any way the effective exercise of this right.

The Ombudsman shall determine which allegations warrant investigation and in what priority, giving particular priority to allegations of especially severe or systematic violations and those founded on alleged discrimination on prohibited grounds. The Ombudsman shall issue findings and conclusions promptly after concluding an investigation. A Party identified as violating human rights shall, within a specified period, explain in writing how it will comply with the conclusions.

Where an allegation is received which is within the jurisdiction of the Human Rights Chamber, the Ombudsman may refer the allegation to the Chamber at any stage. The Ombudsman may also present special reports at any time to any competent government organ or official. Those receiving such reports shall reply within a time limit specified by the Ombudsman, including specific responses to any conclusions offered by the Ombudsman.

The Ombudsman shall publish a report, which, in the event that a person or entity does not comply with his or her conclusions and recommendations, will be forwarded to the High Representative described in Annex 10 to the General Framework Agreement while such office exists, as well as referred for further action to the Presidency of the appropriate Party. The Ombudsman may also initiate proceedings before the Human Rights Chamber based on such Report. The Ombudsman may also intervene in any proceedings before the Chamber.

Article VI: Powers

The Ombudsman shall have access to and may examine all official documents, including classified ones, as well as judicial and administrative files, and can require any person, including a government official, to cooperate by providing relevant information, documents and files. The Ombudsman may attend administrative hearings and meetings of other organs and may enter and inspect any place where persons deprived of their liberty are confined or work.

The Ombudsman and staff are required to maintain the confidentiality of all confidential information obtained, except where required by order of the Chamber, and shall treat all documents and files in accordance with applicable rules.

Part C: Human Rights Chamber

Article VII: Human Rights Chamber

The Human Rights Chamber shall be composed of fourteen members.

Within 90 days after this Agreement enters into force, the Federation of Bosnia and Herzegovina shall appoint four members and the Republika Srpska shall appoint two members. The Committee of Ministers of the Council of Europe, pursuant to its resolution (93)6, after consultation with the Parties, shall appoint the remaining members, who shall not be citizens of Bosnia and Herzegovina or any neighboring state, and shall designate one such member as the President of the Chamber.

All members of the Chamber shall possess the qualifications required for appointment to high judicial office or be jurists of recognized competence. The members of the Chamber shall be appointed for a term of five years and may be reappointed. Members appointed after the transfer described in Article XIV below shall be appointed by the Presidency of Bosnia and Herzegovina.

Article VIII: Jurisdiction of the Chamber

The Chamber shall receive by referral from the Ombudsman on behalf of an applicant, or directly from any Party or person, non-governmental organization, or group of individuals claiming to be the victim of a violation by any Party or acting on behalf of alleged victims who are deceased or missing, for resolution or decision applications concerning alleged or apparent violations of human rights within the scope of paragraph 2 of Article II.

The Chamber shall decide which applications to accept and in what priority to address them. In so doing, the Chamber shall take into account the following criteria:

Whether effective remedies exist, and the applicant has demonstrated that they have been exhausted and that the application has been filed with the Commission within six months from such date on which the final decision was taken.

The Chamber shall not address any application which is substantially the same as a matter which has already been examined by the Chamber or has already been submitted to another procedure or international investigation or settlement.

The Chamber shall also dismiss any application which it considers incompatible with this Agreement, manifestly ill-founded, or an abuse of the right of petition.

The Chamber may reject or defer further consideration if the application concerns a matter currently pending before any other international human rights body responsible for the adjudication of applications or the decision of cases, or any other Commission established by the Annexes to the General Framework Agreement.

In principle, the Chamber shall endeavor to accept and to give particular priority to allegations of especially severe or systematic violations and those founded on alleged discrimination on prohibited grounds.

Applications which entail requests for provisional measures shall be reviewed as a matter of priority in order to determine (1) whether they should be accepted and, if so (2) whether high priority for the scheduling of proceedings on the provisional measures request is warranted.

The Chamber may decide at any point in its proceedings to suspend consideration of, reject or strike out, an application on the ground that (a) the applicant does not intend to pursue his application; (b) the matter has been resolved; or (c) for any other reason established by the Chamber, it is no longer justified to continue the examination of the application; provided that such result is consistent with the objective of respect for human rights.

Article IX: Friendly Settlement

At the outset of a case or at any stage during the proceedings, the Chamber may attempt to facilitate an amicable resolution of the matter on the basis of respect for the rights and freedoms referred to in this Agreement.

If the Chamber succeeds in effecting such a resolution it shall publish a Report and forward it to the High Representative described in Annex 10 to the General Framework Agreement while such office exists, the OSCE and the Secretary General of the Council of Europe. Such a Report shall include a brief statement of the facts and the resolution reached. The report of a resolution in a given case may, however, be confidential in whole or in part where necessary for the protection of human rights or with the agreement of the Chamber and the parties concerned.

Article X: Proceedings before the Chamber

The Chamber shall develop fair and effective procedures for the adjudication of applications. Such procedures shall provide for appropriate written pleadings and, on the decision of the Chamber, a hearing for oral argument or the presentation of evidence. The Chamber shall have the power to order provisional measures, to appoint experts, and to compel the production of witnesses and evidence.

The Chamber shall normally sit in panels of seven, composed of two members from the Federation, one from the Republika Srpska, and four who are not citizens of Bosnia and Herzegovina or any neighboring state. When an application is decided by a panel, the full Chamber may decide, upon motion of a party to the case or the Ombudsman, to review the decision; such review may include the taking of additional evidence where the Chamber so decides. References in this Annex to the Chamber shall include, as appropriate, the Panel, except that the power to develop general rules, regulations and procedures is vested in the Chamber as a whole.

Except in exceptional circumstances in accordance with rules, hearings of the Chamber shall be held in public.

Applicants may be represented in proceedings by attorneys or other representatives of their choice, but shall also be personally present unless excused by the Chamber on account of hardship, impossibility, or other good cause.

The Parties undertake to provide all relevant information to, and to cooperate fully with, the Chamber.

Article XI: Decisions

Following the conclusion of the proceedings, the chamber shall promptly issue a decision, which shall address:
whether the facts found indicate a breach by the Party concerned of its obligations under this Agreement; and if so
what steps shall be taken by the Party to remedy such breach, including orders to cease and desist, monetary relief (including pecuniary and non-pecuniary injuries), and provisional measures.

The Chamber shall make its decision by a majority of members. In the event a decision by the full Chamber results in a tie, the President of the Chamber shall cast the deciding vote.

Subject to review as provided in paragraph 2 of Article X, the decisions of the Chamber shall be final and binding.

Any member shall be entitled to issue a separate opinion on any case.

The Chamber shall issue reasons for its decisions. Its decisions shall be published and forwarded to the parties concerned, the High Representative described in Annex 10 to the General Framework Agreement while such office exists, the Secretary General of the Council of Europe and the OSCE.

The Parties shall implement fully decisions of the Chamber.

Article XII: Rules and Regulations

The Chamber shall promulgate such rules and regulations, consistent with this Agreement, as may be necessary to carry out its functions, including provisions for preliminary hearings, expedited decisions on provisional measures, decisions by panels of the Chamber, and review of decisions made by any such panels.

Chapter Three: General Provisions

Article XIII: Organizations Concerned with Human Rights

The Parties shall promote and encourage the activities of non- governmental and international organizations for the protection and promotion of human rights.

The Parties join in inviting the United Nations Commission on Human Rights, the OSCE, the United Nations High Commissioner for Human Rights, and other intergovernmental or regional human rights missions or organizations to monitor closely the human rights situation in Bosnia and Herzegovina, including through the establishment of local offices and the assignment of observers, rapporteurs, or other relevant persons on a permanent or mission-by- mission basis and to provide them with full and effective facilitation, assistance and access.

The Parties shall allow full and effective access to non- governmental organizations for purposes of investigating and monitoring human rights conditions in Bosnia and Herzegovina and shall refrain from hindering or impeding them in the exercise of these functions.

All competent authorities in Bosnia and Herzegovina shall cooperate with and provide unrestricted access to the organizations established in this Agreement; any international human rights monitoring mechanisms established for Bosnia and Herzegovina; the supervisory bodies established by any of the international agreements listed in the Appendix to this Annex; the International Tribunal for the Former Yugoslavia; and any other organization authorized by the U.N. Security

Council with a mandate concerning human rights or humanitarian law.

Article XIV: Transfer

Five years after this Agreement enters into force, the responsibility for the continued operation of the Commission shall transfer from the Parties to the institutions of Bosnia and Herzegovina, unless the Parties otherwise agree. In the latter case, the Commission shall continue to operate as provided above.

Article XV: Notice

The Parties shall give effective notice of the terms of this Agreement throughout Bosnia and Herzegovina.

Article XVI: Entry into Force

This Agreement shall enter into force upon signature.

For the Republic of Bosnia and Herzegovina

For the Federation of Bosnia and Herzegovina

For the Republika Srpska

Appendix: Human Rights Agreements

1948 Convention on the Prevention and Punishment of the Crime of Genocide

1949 Geneva Conventions I-IV on the Protection of the Victims of War, and the

1977 Geneva Protocols I-II thereto

1950 European Convention for the Protection of Human Rights and Fundamental Freedoms, and the Protocols thereto

1951 Convention relating to the Status of Refugees and the 1966 Protocol thereto

1957 Convention on the Nationality of Married Women

1961 Convention on the Reduction of Statelessness

1965 International Convention on the Elimination of All Forms of Racial Discrimination

1966 International Covenant on Civil and Political Rights and the 1966 and 1989 Optional Protocols thereto

1966 Covenant on Economic, Social and Cultural Rights

1979 Convention on the Elimination of All Forms of Discrimination against Women

1984 Convention against Torture and Other Cruel, Inhuman or Degrading Treatment or Punishment

1987 European Convention on the Prevention of Torture and Inhuman or Degrading Treatment or Punishment

1989 Convention on the Rights of the Child

1990 Convention on the Protection of the Rights of All Migrant Workers and Members of Their Families

1992 European Charter for Regional or Minority Languages

1994 Framework Convention for the Protection of National Minorities.

Annex 11 - Agreement on International Police Force

The Republic of Bosnia and Herzegovina, the Federation of Bosnia and Herzegovina, and the Republika Srpska (the "Parties") have agreed as follows:

Article I: Civilian Law Enforcement

As provided in Article III(2)(c) of the Constitution agreed as Annex 4 to the General Framework Agreement, the Parties shall provide a safe and secure environment for all persons in their respective jurisdictions, by maintaining civilian law enforcement agencies operating in accordance with internationally recognized standards and with respect for internationally recognized human rights and fundamental freedoms, and by taking such other measures as appropriate.

To assist them in meeting their obligations, the Parties request that the United Nations establish by a decision of the Security Council, as a UNCIVPOL operation, a U.N. International Police Task Force (IPTF) to carry out, throughout Bosnia and Herzegovina, the program of assistance the elements of which are described in Article III below.

Article II: Establishment of the IPTF

The IPTF shall be autonomous with regard to the execution of its functions under this Agreement. Its activities will be coordinated through the High Representative described in Annex 10 to the General Framework Agreement.

The IPTF will be headed by a Commissioner, who will be appointed by the Secretary General of the United Nations in consultation with the Security Council. It shall consist of persons of high moral standing who have experience in law enforcement. The IPTF Commissioner may request and accept personnel, resources, and assistance from states and international and nongovernmental organizations.

The IPTF Commissioner shall receive guidance from the High Representative.

The IPTF Commissioner shall periodically report on matters within his or her responsibility to the High Representative, the Secretary General of the United Nations, and shall provide information to the IFOR Commander and, as he or she deems appropriate, other institutions and agencies.

The IPTF shall at all times act in accordance with internationally recognized standards and with respect for internationally recognized human rights and fundamental freedoms, and shall respect, consistent with the IPTF's responsibilities, the laws and customs of the host country.

The Parties shall accord the IPTF Commissioner, IPTF personnel, and their families the privileges and immunities described in Sections 18 and 19 of the 1946 Convention on the Privileges and Immunities of the United Nations. In particular, they shall enjoy inviolability, shall not be subject to any form of arrest or detention, and shall have absolute immunity from criminal jurisdiction. IPTF personnel shall remain subject to penalties and sanctions under applicable laws and regulations of the United Nations and other states.

The IPTF and its premises, archives, and other property shall be accorded the same privileges and immunities, including inviolability, as are described in Articles II and III of the 1946 Convention on the Privileges and Immunities of the United Nations.

In order to promote the coordination by the High Representative of IPTF activities with those of other civilian organizations and agencies and of the (IFOR), the IPTF Commissioner or his or her representatives may attend meetings of the Joint Civilian Commission established in Annex 10 to the General Framework Agreement and of the Joint Military Commission established in Annex 1, as well as meetings of their subordinate commissions. The IPTF Commissioner may request that meetings of appropriate commissions be convened to discuss issues within his or her area of responsibility.

Article III: IPTF Assistance Program

IPTF assistance includes the following elements, to be provided in a program designed and implemented by the IPTF Commissioner in accordance with the Security Council decision described in Article I(2):

monitoring, observing, and inspecting law enforcement activities and facilities, including associated judicial organizations, structures, and proceedings;
advising law enforcement personnel and forces;

training law enforcement personnel;
facilitating, within the IPTF' s mission of assistance, the Parties' law enforcement activities;

assessing threats to public order and advising on the capability of law enforcement agencies to deal with such threats.

advising governmental authorities in Bosnia and Herzegovina on the organization of effective civilian law enforcement agencies; and

assisting by accompanying the Parties' law enforcement personnel as they carry out their responsibilities, as the IPTF deems appropriate.

In addition to the elements of the assistance program set forth in paragraph 1, the IPTF will consider, consistent with its responsibilities and resources, requests from the Parties or law enforcement agencies in Bosnia and Herzegovina for assistance described in paragraph 1.

The Parties confirm their particular responsibility to ensure the existence of social conditions for free and fair elections, including the protection of international personnel in Bosnia and Herzegovina in connection with the elections provided for in Annex 3 to the General Framework Agreement. They request the IPTF to give priority to assisting the Parties in carrying out this responsibility.

Article IV: Specific Responsibilities of the Parties

The Parties shall cooperate fully with the IPTF and shall so instruct all their law enforcement agencies.

Within 30 days after this Agreement enters into force, the Parties shall provide the IPTF Commissioner or his or her designee with information on their law enforcement agencies, including their size, location, and force structure. Upon request of the IPTF Commissioner, they shall provide additional information, including any training, operational, or employment and service records of law enforcement agencies and personnel.

The Parties shall not impede the movement of IPTF personnel or in any way hinder, obstruct, or delay them in the performance of their responsibilities. They shall allow IPTF personnel immediate and complete access to any site, person, activity, proceeding, record, or other item or event in Bosnia and Herzegovina as requested by the IPTF in carrying out its responsibilities under this Agreement. This shall include the right to monitor, observe, and inspect any site or facility at which it believes that police, law enforcement, detention, or judicial activities are taking place.

Upon request by the IPTF, the Parties shall make available for training qualified personnel, who are expected to take up law enforcement duties immediately following such training.

The Parties shall facilitate the operations of the IPTF in Bosnia and Herzegovina, including by the provision of appropriate assistance as requested with regard to transportation, subsistence, accommodations, communications, and other facilities at rates equivalent to those provided for the IFOR under applicable agreements.

Article V: Failure to Cooperate

Any obstruction of or interference with IPTF activities, failure or refusal to comply with an IPTF request, or other failure to meet the Parties' responsibilities or other obligations in this Agreement, shall constitute a failure to cooperate with the IPTF.

The IPTF Commissioner will notify the High Representative and inform the IFOR Commander of failures to cooperate with the IPTF. The IPTF Commissioner may request that the High Representative take appropriate steps upon receiving such notifications, including calling such failures to the attention of the Parties, convening the Joint Civilian Commission, and consulting with the United Nations, relevant states, and international organizations on further responses.

Article VI: Human Rights

When IPTF personnel learn of credible information concerning violations of internationally recognized human rights or fundamental freedoms or of the role of law enforcement officials or forces in such violations, they shall provide such information to the Human Rights Commission established in Annex 6 to the General Framework Agreement, the International Tribunal for the Former Yugoslavia, or to other appropriate organizations.

The Parties shall cooperate with investigations of law enforcement forces and officials by the organizations described in paragraph 1.

Article VII: Application

This Agreement applies throughout Bosnia and Herzegovina to law enforcement agencies and personnel of Bosnia and Herzegovina, the Entities, and any agency, subdivision, or instrumentality thereof. Law enforcement agencies are those with a mandate including law enforcement, criminal investigations, public and state security, or detention or judicial activities.

Article VIII: Entry into Force

This Agreement shall enter into force upon signature.

For the Republic of Bosnia and Herzegovina

For the Federation of Bosnia and Herzegovina

For the Republika Srpska

Not-so-Sacred Borders

By James Kitfield
Reprinted with permission from National
Journal, November 11, 1999. Copyright
2006 National Journal. All rights reserved.

As the United States and its NATO allies
stood on the brink of war against Yugoslavia
in the waning days of March, lawyers rose to
sudden prominence in the high councils of
the alliance. Everyone understood that an
attack would violate a fundamental precept
of international law, and set a new
precedent for the use of military force.
For the first time, Western nations would be
intervening militarily against an
independent nation not because it posed a
direct threat to neighbors, but because it
persecuted an ethnic minority within its own
borders. In striking Belgrade, NATO would
bypass the United Nations and ignore the
fundamental principles of sovereignty and
the "Great Powers" consensus that are at the
core of the United Nations charter.
In a March 23 letter to Senate Majority
Leader Trent Lott, R-Miss., White House
National Security Adviser Samuel R.
"Sandy" Berger justified going to war on the
grounds that Serbian strongman Slobodan
Milosevic was a repeat offender under
international law and a direct threat to the
stability of the region. "It is important to
note that Serbian President Milosevic
initiated an aggressive war against the
independent nation of Croatia in 1991;
against the independent nation of Bosnia-
Herzegovina in 1992; and is currently
engaged in widespread repression of Kosovo,
whose constitutional guarantees of
autonomy he unilaterally abrogated in
1989," wrote Berger. "Arguments based on
Serbian 'sovereignty' are undercut by this
history."

Whatever the merit of its moral
underpinnings, NATO's war with Yugoslavia
crossed an important threshold in
international law. The sanctity of national
sovereignty has largely governed nation-state
relations for the past half-century. The
Allies specifically cited sovereignty as they
fought the wars of aggression that haunted
the first half of the 20th century, in their
hope of breaking the historic pattern in
which strong nations exploited the weak.
And interventions on behalf of ethnic
minorities don't have an entirely noble
history. Adolf Hitler justified his seizure of
the Sudetenland in Czechoslovakia by
claiming persecution of ethnic Germans
there.

The visceral opposition to the
Kosovo conflict on the part of Russia, China,
and India revealed just how uncomfortable
some nations still are with the apparent
abandonment of the principle of sovereignty,
especially during a period of unrivaled U.S.
military power. They point to the U.N.
charter, which enshrines and protects
sovereignty unless the five Great Powers on
the Security Council agree to breach it.
Donald Kagan, a professor of history at Yale
University, sees the Kosovo conflict as an
important marker. "That the United States
and its allies were willing to intervene
militarily in what were the agreed borders of
a sovereign state was unusual and very rare,
and it raises the question of, where do we go
from here," said Kagan. "I see it as part of the
effort, since the end of the Cold War, to
establish new rules for the international
order that reduce the chance for war. I think
NATO was saying sovereignty has limits,
and the world will not sit by idly again and
watch while a Hitler or Mao murders
millions. At the same time, we shouldn't
erode the principle of sovereignty lightly.
Nation-states have been, are now, and will
remain fundamental building blocks of
international order."
The establishment of the nation-state as a
building block of the international system--
including each country's independence and
its primacy over its citizenry that are at the
heart of sovereignty--dates back to the
Treaty of Westphalia in 1648, which ended
Europe's bloody Thirty Years' War. The
Westphalian system respected the territorial

integrity of each nation-state, even one that had lost a war, and held that states may not interfere in the internal affairs of other states. While imperialist powers showed little compunction about intervening in "less-civilized" nations, such actions were seen among the major powers as an abrogation of accepted international norms.

After the trauma of World War II, the principle of sovereignty was codified in the U.N. charter. States would be sanctioned for acts of force against other states unless in self-defense, but within their borders, they were free to act. In the U.N. conventions on genocide and torture, however, nations also assumed a legal obligation to uphold basic human rights. And Chapter VII of the U.N. charter endorses collective action to counter "threats to international peace and security," such as internal actions that might cause massive refugee flows that could destabilize neighboring countries. In truth, as with most founding documents, the U.N. charter is subject to interpretation.

"What's happened is that the Chapter VII provisions of the U.N. charter have been interpreted more and more broadly in recent years to justify interventions in places like Somalia and Kosovo," said Stephen Garrett, a professor at the Monterey Institute of International Studies in California. "There are also contradictions between the early parts of the U.N. charter that talk about nation-state rights, and those sections which refer to the duty of the international community to uphold human rights. There's definite tension and ambiguity there." Giving veto power to each of the five permanent Security Council members--the United States, Great Britain, France, Russia, and China--was the U.N. founders' way of precluding international action in the absence of Great Power consensus. And it worked; but it largely kept the United Nations from intervening in conflicts during the Cold War. All of that changed when the East-West standoff ended, and U.S. leaders saw an opportunity to use the collective will of the international community to turn back nation-state aggression by Iraq over Kuwait. New World Order "The United Nations had been set up to deal with one of the great scourges of mankind, which was nation-state aggression, but the Cold War had derailed its ability to deal with the problem," said Brent Scowcroft, former national security adviser to President George Bush. "In 1991, we suddenly saw a new vista where consensus was possible within the U.N. to counter nation-state aggression. That was the new world order we were talking about. What we didn't perceive was the extent to which conflicts of the 1990s would be about civil wars, internal disputes, and the breakup of countries."

In attempting to cope with humanitarian disaster and instability provoked by internal conflict in places like Somalia, Rwanda, Haiti, and Bosnia, the United States and its allies found themselves subtly reinterpreting the concepts of nation-state sovereignty and intervention. And in each case, the United Nations gave its blessing to international intervention. The process culminated in the Kosovo conflict, when NATO found itself confronting massive "ethnic cleansing" and regional destabilization in Europe growing out of a conflict on which a consensus among the Great Powers was impossible. NATO decided that national and humanitarian interests outweighed sovereignty and even U.N. collectivism.

"NATO was faced with a pragmatic question of whether the principle of sovereignty required it to sit on the sidelines of a humanitarian tragedy that was destabilizing the region, and which could possibly bring NATO partners Greece and Turkey into conflict," said Zbigniew Brzezinski, a White House national security adviser in the Carter Administration and senior analyst at the Center for Strategic and International Studies. "I would argue that was too costly a price to pay for the principle of sovereignty."

In the wake of the Kosovo conflict, a number of prominent leaders have called for an international review of the definition of a "just war," and a rewriting of the U.N. charter to facilitate humanitarian interventions.

"There is an emerging international law that countries cannot hide behind sovereignty and abuse people without expecting the rest of the world to do something about it," Kofi Annan, U.N. secretary-general, said in a May 22 speech in Stockholm, Sweden. Former NATO Secretary General Javier Solana echoes Annan's views: "We're moving into a system of international relations in which human rights, rights of minorities every day, are much more important. More important even than sovereignty."

But there is danger in consigning sovereignty to the history books. Weakening the sanctity of borders could undermine the international norms that have kept naked state-on-state aggression largely at bay in recent decades. Nations should also be wary of announcing new international principles that they lack the will to defend. On the other hand, if even a few architects of future genocide and "ethnic cleansing" feel, as a result of Kosovo, less certain of international indifference, then the war may have established a precedent worth fighting for.

"By bypassing the United Nations and disregarding the principle of sovereignty because of Serbia's internal treatment of its own people, I think NATO's actions in the Kosovo conflict do represent a significant paradigm shift," said Garrett of the Monterey Institute. "That doesn't mean we're going to see lots of similar humanitarian interventions, or interventions in Great Powers such as China and Russia. However, the days of absolute sovereignty--when governments could abuse their own people with total impunity--are gone forever."

Frontline: Give War a Chance
The Uses of Military Force

By Jim Mokhiber and Rick Young
Courtesy WGBH Educational Foundation,
Copyright © 1999 WGBH/FRONTLINE

As von Clausewitz famously put it, war is politics pursued by other means. Behind this dictum, however, lies a messy mix of questions regarding military force and its use to achieve foreign policy goals.

In the United States, this debate--which frequently pits the military versus the "civilian" arms of the government, including the State Department and the White House--has resurfaced with each major conflict and intervention since the second World War.

As **Alexander George** has written, in the wake of the ambiguous results of the Korean War of the early 1950s, one school of thought began to argue that the United States should "never again" fight such an inconclusive war of half-measures. Either the United States should commit to using "all or nothing" to win or it should avoid armed intervention abroad altogether. By contrast, other foreign policy strategists contended that incertain cases in which important US interests were at stake, it would be necessary to call on military force to wage "limited wars" to defend them.

The Vietnam War crystallized this strategic debate, and imprinted indelible lessons upon a generation of future military leaders. For many, the failure in Vietnam began early on with the the gradual escalation of involvement, the constrained application of force, and the meddling of politicians in war's operational details. "The war in Vietnam was not lost in the field, nor was it lost on the front pages of the New York Times or on the college campuses," Vietnam author, Major H.R. McMaster has written. "It was lost in Washington, D.C., even before Americans assumed sole responsibility for the fighting in 1965 and before they realized the country was at war."

Through its so-called "hollow force years" of the 1970s and beyond, the military faced new missions and further humiliations. During the Carter administration, the failed hostage rescue attempt in Iran in 1980 undermined the military's prestige. Moreover, despite the vast military build-up of the Reagan years, the 1983 bombing of the US Marine barracks in Lebanon, at a loss of 241 lives, encouraged another stock taking. The "lessons" of the Vietnam War and Beirut loomed large in November of 1984, when Reagans Secretary of Defense Caspar Weinberger gave an **influential speech** embracing many of the military's concerns. The "Weinberger doctrine" contained six points sharply limiting the use of combat forces:

- Either the United States' or its close allies' vital national interests had to be at risk;
- The war had to be fought "wholeheartedly, with the clear intention of winning";
- We should employ decisive force in the pursuit of clearly defined political and military objectives;
- We must constantly reassess whether the use of force is necessary and appropriate;
- There must be a "reasonable assurance" of Congressional and public support;
- Force should be used only as a last resort.

Immensely influential within military circles, Weinberger's formulation was challenged by diplomats including Secretary of State George Shultz. Shultz worried that American diplomacy, not backed up by credible threats of force, would be hamstrung by the military's supposed reluctance to become involved in "limited" wars.

Admittedly, the Reagan administration's application of the Weinberger doctrine was never as orthodox as the defense secretary's six criteria might suggest. The repeated confrontations with Libya throughout the

1980s are but one example of the administration's willingness to calibrate military force to fit limited strategic goals. It was the Persian Gulf War in 1990-1991 that seemed to validate many of Weinberger's central points: the United States had a clear and vital interest in the region's oil, military action was largely supported by the public, Congress and key allies, and evicting the Iraqi's from Kuwait was the kind of well-defined, achievable objective the military could embrace. Most importantly, the American victory suggested that the use of decisive amounts of firepower and troops would avoid the incremental escalation that contributed to the debacle in Vietnam.

Nevertheless, late in his administration George Bush began grappling with the challenges inherent in the United States position as the sole superpower in a post-cold war world. Speaking at West Point in January 1993, Bush offered a more flexible set of guidelines while reiterating the need to maintain a clear and achievable mission. The most notable articulation of policy on use of force came not from Bush, however, but from the Chairman of the Joint Chiefs of Staff, Colin Powell. A Vietnam War veteran, former military assistant to Secretary Weinberger and Gulf War hero, Powell stressed the "lessons learned" in Vietnam and reiterated the insistence on using force only when objectives are clearly defined and results reasonably achievable. And while Powell accepted the post-cold war need for the military to undertake peacekeeping and humanitarian missions, he posed a series of questions, or tests, that should be asked in situations which required the use of "violent" force:

> Is the political objective we seek to achieve important, clearly defined and understood? Have all other nonviolent policy means failed? Will military force achieve the objective? At what cost? Have the gains and risks been analyzed? How might the situation that we seek to alter, once

it is altered by force, develop further and what might be the consequences?

Drawing on his Gulf War experience, Powell trumpeted the application of "overwhelming force" - a catch-phrase that has come to describe what is now refered to as the Powell doctrine. He criticized the "so-called experts" who called for "a little surgical bombing or a limited attack." History, he wrote, has not been kind to this approach to war-making.

In 1993, with the arrival of President Clinton, doctrine governing the use of military force faced several key tests. None would prove more lasting than Somalia, where in October 1993, the United States' involvement took a turn toward disaster. From its origins as a limited humanitarian effort during the Bush administration, the Somalia intervention had evolved into a broader peace-keeping mission - a mission that was shattered when 18 lightly-armed troops were killed in a firefight with guerillas loyal to Mogadishu warlords. The strong military and public reactions to the televised images of a helicopter pilots body being dragged through the streets led to a rapid American pull-out.

The Somalia experience engulfed deliberations within the Clinton Administration over how to deal with the deteriorating civil war in Bosnia. As a presidential candidate, Clinton had sharply criticized President Bush's failure to stop the bloodshed in the Balkans. However, once in office, Clinton's campaign rhetoric ran head-long into the cautionary questioning of General Powell, who had publicly voiced concerns about intervention in Bosnia. While Clinton did mobilize some 20,000 troops in 1994, in an effort to help build democracy in Haiti, administration policy on Bosnia muddled along for more than two years. Finally in mid-1995, the bombing of a Sarajevo marketplace touched off what was, at the time, NATO's largest military action-- "Operation Deliberate Force." Diplomats claimed victory when the two-week calibrated bombing campaign, assisted by an aggressive Croat-Muslim offensive on the ground, pushed the Bosnian Serbs to the negotiating table and, ultimately, to the Dayton Peace Accords.

Based in part on the Bosnian experience, Clinton's national security adviser Anthony Lake gave a speech in early 1996, outlining the beginnings of a new force doctrine. Once again, the ultimate goal was to avoid "Vietnam-like quagmires" and muddled interventions such as Lebanon and Somalia. Nevertheless, Lake's speech suggested that the post-cold war world required a broader and more flexible policy regarding the use of force than was outlined in either the Weinberger or Powell doctrines.

To better define what constituted an area of US national interest, Lake listed seven broad sets of circumstances for using force ranging from a direct attack on the United States or its allies to curtailing drug trafficking and ending gross abuses of human rights. When it came to actually using force, Lake came up with three key principles:

- Credible threats of force can be as effective as force itself;
- The "selective but substantial use of force is sometimes more appropriate than its massive use";
- Carefully defined exit strategies should accompany every foreign intervention.

Lake placed particular emphasis on the last point, and argued that "tightly tailored military missions and sharp withdrawal deadlines must be the norm." Calling his policy "tough love" and warning against "dangerous hubris," Lake argued that the US could not "build other nations. But where our own interests are engaged, we can help nations build themselves and give them the time to make a start of it." In the case of Bosnia, Lake saw the US troops staying to enforce a one-year "window of opportunity" that would expire at the end of 1996.

On the ground in Bosnia, the administration's policy would be sorely tested as the senior military and diplomatic officials -- Admiral Leighton "Snuffy" Smith and Ambassador Richard Holbrooke -- battled over the implementation of the hard-won Dayton Accords. For "maximalists" like Holbrooke, Dayton's lesson was that force had been essential to stopping the war, and would be needed to support efforts to build a new peace. By contrast, Smith argued that the military had been given a more limited mandate and resources, and he warned against the kind of "mission-creep" that he believed had characterized previous intervention disasters, like Somalia, Beirut and Vietnam.

Both opinions reflected the reality that while shooting in Bosnia had subsided, a stable peace that would allow for the exit of American troops had not been achieved. Indeed, in late 1997 President Clinton finally announced that, after missing several deadlines, no further dates for troop withdrawal would be set.

As violence escalated in Kosovo in early 1999, following the collapse of the Rambouillet peace talks, the Clinton Administration and its NATO allies turned again to the peace-building formula that had won agreement at Dayton: a calibrated and escalating air campaign designed to force a peace agreement. However, Serb recalcitrance in Kosovo, including the continued mass expulsion of ethnic Albanians, has proven a tough test of the administration's new "bombs for peace" strategy-- bringing to the fore the central and recurring questions about when, where and how military force should be used.

September 11, 2001: Attack on America Joint Resolution 63 - Introduced in the House

September 13, 2001

Resolved by the Senate and House of Representatives of the United States of America in Congress assembled, (Introduced in the House)
HJ 63 IH
107th CONGRESS
1st Session
H. J. RES. 63
Declaring that a state of war exists between the United States and any entity determined by the President to have planned, carried out, or otherwise supported the attacks against the United States on September 11 , 2001, and authorizing the President to use United States Armed Forces and all other necessary resources of the United States Government against any such entity in order to bring the conflict to a successful termination.
IN THE HOUSE OF REPRESENTATIVES
September 13, 2001
Mr. WELDON of Pennsylvania (for himself, Mr. SCHAFFER, Mr. PETERSON of Pennsylvania, Mr. GILMAN, and Mr. BARTLETT of Maryland) introduced the following joint resolution; which was referred to the Committee on International Relations
----

JOINT RESOLUTION
Declaring that a state of war exists between the United States and any entity determined by the President to have planned, carried out, or otherwise supported the attacks against the United States on September 11 , 2001, and authorizing the President to use United States Armed Forces and all other necessary resources of the United States Government against any such entity in order

to bring the conflict to a successful termination.
Resolved by the Senate and House of Representatives of the United States of America in Congress assembled,
SECTION 1. FINDINGS.
Congress finds the following:
(1) On September 11 , 2001, terrorists hijacked and destroyed 4 civilian aircraft, crashing 2 of them into the towers of the World Trade Center in New York City, and a third into the Pentagon outside Washington, D.C.
(2) Thousands of innocent Americans were killed and injured as a result of these attacks, including the passengers and crew of the 4 aircraft, workers in the World Trade Center and in the Pentagon, rescue workers, and bystanders.
(3) These attacks destroyed both towers of the World Trade Center, as well as adjacent buildings, and seriously damaged the Pentagon.
(4) These attacks were by far the deadliest terrorist attacks ever launched against the United States, and, by targeting symbols of American strength and success, clearly were intended to intimidate our Nation and weaken its resolve.
(5) Article I, section 8, of the United States Constitution vests in Congress the power to declare war.
SEC. 2. DECLARATION OF WAR.
Congress hereby declares that a state of war exists between the United States of America and any entity determined by the President to have planned, carried out, or otherwise supported the attacks against the United States on September 11 , 2001.
SEC. 3. AUTHORIZATION OF USE OF ARMED FORCES.
The President is authorized to use United States Armed Forces and all other necessary resources of the United States Government against any entity determined by the President to have planned, carried out, or otherwise supported the attacks against the United States on September 11 , 2001, in

order to bring the conflict to a successful
termination.

Source:
U.S. Government Website

Supreme Court Cases Reviewing the War and Treaty Powers of the U.S. Constitution

Reprinted with permission of
Douglas O. Linder.
Article posted at
www.law.umkc.edu/faculty/projects/ftrials/
conlaw/warandtreaty.htm

Introduction -War Powers

The Constitution divides war powers between the Congress and the President. This division was intended by the framers to ensure that wars would not be entered into easily: it takes two keys, not one, to start the engine of war.

The Constitution's division of powers leaves the President with some exclusive powers as Commander-in-Chief (such as decisions on the field of battle), Congress with certain other exclusive powers (such as the ability to declare war and appropriate dollars to support the war effort), and a sort of "twilight zone" of concurrent powers. In the zone of concurrent powers, the Congress might effectively limit presidential power, but in the absence of express congressional limitations the President is free to act. Although on paper it might appear that the powers of Congress with respect to war are more dominant, the reality is that Presidential power has been more important--in part due to the modern need for quick responses to foreign threats and in part due to the many-headed nature of Congress.

The Supreme Court has had relatively little to say about the Constitution's war powers. Many interesting legal questions--such as the constitutionality of the "police action" in Korea or the "undeclared war" in Viet Nam-- were never decided by the Court. (Although the Supreme Court had three opportunities to decide the constitutionality of the war in Viet Nam, it passed on each one.)

During the Civil War, the Court issued two significant opinions interpreting the war powers. In the Prize Cases (1863), the Court on a 5 to 4 vote upheld President Lincoln's order blockading southern ports-- even though the order was issues prior to a formal declaration of war on the Rebel states by Congress. The Court found Lincoln's action authorized by a 1795 Act allowing the President to call out troops to suppress an insurrection. The dissenters argued the President's action were unconstitutional, as a blockade is quite different that an action merely directed at those participating in an insurrection. Three years later, in Ex Parte Milligan, the Court found unconstitutional Lincoln's order authorizing trial by a military tribunal of Lambdin P. Milligan, an Indiana lawyer accused of stirring up support for the Confederacy. The Court ruled that civilians must be tried in civilian courts, even during time of war, so long at least as the civilian courts are open and operating. The Court also found the President lacked authority to declare martial law in Indiana. Four concurring justices argued that even though the President did not have the power to order a military trial of Milligan in the absence of congressional action, the power to authorize use of military tribunals did reside in Congress under its war power.

In 1942, in Ex Parte Quirin, the Court considered the constitutionality of an order of President Roosevelt authorizing trial by military commission of eight German Nazi saboteurs arrested after entering the United States. The eight had planned to blow up munitions factories and military installations in the United States. The Court, voting 8 to 0, upheld the legality of trying the Germans (who the Court found to be unlawful combatants) in a military tribunal without the usual safeguards of the 5th and 6th Amendments. The Court found the authorization of trial by tribunal supported by legislation enacted by Congress, and noted that it need not decide whether a presidential order of trial by commission would be constitutional in the absence of congressional action.

In Hamilton v Kentucky Distilleries (1919), the Court considered the constitutionality of a federal law, enacted under the war power of Congress, prohibiting the sale and distribution of distilled spirits. Congress said the Act was necessary "for the purpose of conserving the man power of the Nation, and to increase efficiency in the production of arms, munitions, ships, food, and clothing for the army and navy." Justice Brandeis, writing for the Court, found the restriction to be within the war powers of Congress and that the Act was not a taking requiring just compensation. The Court said that although at some time after the cessation of hostilities the restriction must come to an end, it would be reluctant to conclude that the war power was no longer effective so long as some troops remained abroad and some other wartime measures remained in effect.

On June 28, 2004, the Court ruled in two important cases challenging actions of the Bush Administration taken subsequent to the 9-11 acts of terrorism. In Hamdi v Rumsfeld, the Court ruled that Congress, in its 2001 Authorization for the Use of Military Force, had given the President had the power to declare an American citizen an "enemy combatant" and deny him a trial in federal court. Justice O'Connor, writing for the majority did, however, indicate that such persons cannot be held indefinitely and were entitled to contest the determination of their status with the assistance of counsel. Justice Scalia, somewhat surprisingly dissented, arguing that the Constitution entitled Hamdi to a criminal trial. He concluded:

"The Founders well understood the difficult tradeoff between safety and freedom. "Safety from external danger," Hamilton declared, "is the most powerful director of national conduct. Even the ardent love of liberty will, after a time, give way to its dictates. The violent destruction of life and property incident to war; the continual effort and alarm attendant on a state of continual danger, will compel nations the most attached to liberty, to resort for repose and security to institutions which have a tendency to destroy their civil and political rights. To be more safe, they, at length, become willing to run the risk of being less free." The Federalist No. 8, p. 33.

The Founders warned us about the risk, and equipped us with a Constitution designed to deal with it.

Many think it not only inevitable but entirely proper that liberty give way to security in times of national crisis-that, at the extremes of military exigency, inter arma silent leges. Whatever the general merits of the view that war silences law or modulates its voice, that view has no place in the interpretation and application of a Constitution designed precisely to confront war and, in a manner that accords with democratic principles, to accommodate it. Because the Court has proceeded to meet the current emergency in a manner the Constitution does not envision, I respectfully dissent.

The Court in Hamdi did conclude, however, that under due process principles that citizens designated as enemy combatants were entitled to a written statement of the basis for that declaration, as well as a right to challenge it before a neutral decision-maker in a timely manner. In the other 9-11 case, Rasul v Bush, the Court ruled 6 to 3 that aliens detained in Guatanamo, Cuba had the right to challenge their detention in American courts, in part because the United States had exclusive jurisdiction and control over the base in Cuba.

Treaty Power

The case of Missouri v Holland (1920) presented the Court with an opportunity to define the reach of the treaty power. Missouri challenged the federal government's regulation of the hunting of migratory birds, including its setting of seasons, hunting methods, and limits. The regulations were adopted under the Migratory Bird Treaty Act, implementing a treating signed by the United States and Great Britain (for Canada). The Court upheld the regulations, even though they were not supported by specific Article I powers of Congress, as a reasonable implication of the President's Article II power to "make treaties." The Court cautioned, however, that the treaty-implementing power could not be used as an excuse for regulating activities that were not "a proper subject of regulation."

Just-war Theory

Reprinted with permission from Alexander Moseley. Article originally appeared at the Internet Encyclopedia of Philosophy (http://www.utm.edu/research/iep/)

Just-war theory deals with the justification of how and why wars are fought. The justification can be either theoretical or historical. The theoretical aspect is concerned with ethically justifying war and forms of warfare. The historical aspect, or the "just war tradition" deals with the historical body of rules or agreements applied (or at least existing) in various wars across the ages. For instance international agreements such as the Geneva and Hague conventions are historical rules aimed at limiting certain kinds of warfare. It is the role of ethics to examine these institutional agreements for their philosophical coherence as well as to inquire into whether aspects of the conventions ought to be changed.

1. Introduction

Historically, the just-war tradition—a set of mutually agreed rules of combat—commonly evolves between two similar enemies. When enemies differ greatly because of different religious beliefs, race, or language, war conventions have rarely been applied. It is only when the enemy is seen to be a people with whom one will do business in the following peace that tacit or explicit rules are formed for how wars should be fought and who they should involve. In part the motivation is seen to be mutually beneficial—it is preferable to remove any underhand tactics or weapons that may provoke an indefinite series of vengeance acts. Nonetheless, it has been the concern of the majority of just war theorists that such asymmetrical morality should be denounced, and that the rules of war should apply to all equally; that is, just war theory should be universal.

The just-war tradition is as old as warfare itself. Early records of collective fighting indicate that some moral considerations were used by warriors. They may have involved consideration of women and children or the treatment of prisoners. Commonly they invoked considerations of honour: some acts in war have always been deemed dishonourable, whilst others have been deemed honourable. Whilst the specifics of what is honourable differ with time and place, the very fact of one moral virtue has been sufficient to infuse warfare with moral concerns.

The just war theory also has a long history. Whilst parts of the Bible hint at ethical behaviour in war and concepts of just cause, the most systematic exposition is given by Saint Thomas Aquinas. In the Summa Theologicae Aquinas presents the general outline of what becomes the just war theory. He discusses not only the justification of war, but also the kinds of activity that are permissible in war. Aquinas's thoughts become the model for later Scholastics and Jurists to expand. The most important of these are: Francisco de Vitoria (1486-1546), Francisco Suarez (1548-1617), Hugo Grotius (1583-1645), Samuel Pufendorf (1632-1704), Christian Wolff (1679-1754), and Emerich de Vattel (1714-1767). In the twentieth century it has undergone a revival mainly in response to the invention of nuclear weaponry and American involvement in the Vietnam war. The most important contemporary texts include Michael Walzer's Just and Unjust Wars (1977), Barrie Paskins and Michael Dockrill The Ethics of War (1979), Richard Norman Ethics, Killing, and War (1995), Brian Orend War and International Justice (2001) and Michael Walzer on War and Justice (2001), as well as seminal articles by Thomas Nagel "War and Massacre", Elizabeth Anscombe "War and Murder", and a host of others, commonly found in the journals Ethics or The Journal of Philosophy and Public Affairs.

Since the terrorist attacks on the USA on 9/11 academics have turned their attention to just war once again with international and national conventions developing and consolidating the theoretical aspects of the conventions - just war theory has become a popular topic in International Relations, Political Science, Philosophy, Ethics, and Military History courses. Conference proceedings are regularly published, offering readers a breadth of issues that the topic stirs: e.g., Alexander Moseley and Richard Norman, eds. Human Rights and Military Intervention, Paul Robinson, ed., Just War in a Comparative Perspective, Alexsander Jokic, ed., War Crimes and Collective Wrongdoing. What has been of great interest is that in the headline wars of the past decade, the dynamic interplay of the rules and conventions of warfare not only remain intact on the battlefield but their role and hence their explication have been awarded a higher level of scrutiny and debate. Generals have extolled their troops to adhere to the rules, soldiers are taught the just war conventions in the military academies, yet war crimes continue - genocidal campaigns have been waged by mutually hating peoples, leaders have waged total war on ethnic groups within or without their borders, and individual soldiers or guerilla bands have committed atrocious, murderous, or humiliating acts. Yet increasingly, the rule of law - the need to hold violators and transgressors responsible for their actions in war - is making headway onto the battlefield. In chivalrous times, the Christian crusader could seek absolution for atrocities committed in war; today, the law courts are less forgiving. Nonetheless, the idealism of those who seek the imposition of law and responsibility on the battlefield (cf. Geoffrey Robinson's Crimes Against Humanity (1999)), often runs ahead of the traditions and customs that demean or weaken the justum bellum that may exist between warring factions. And in some cases, no just war conventions exist at all. In such cases, the ethic of war is considered, or is implicitly held to be, beyond the norms of peaceful ethics and therefore deserving a separate moral realm where "fair is foul and foul is fair" (Shakespeare, Macbeth I.i). In such examples (e.g, Rwanda 1994), a people's justification of destructiveness and killing to whatever relative degree they hold to be justifiable in this amoral world, triumphs over attempts to establish the laws of peaceful interaction into this separate bloody realm, and in some wars, people fighting for their land or nation prefer to pick up the cudgel rather than the rapier, as Leo Tolstoy notes in War and Peace (Book 4.Ch.2), to sidestep the etiquette or war in favour securing their land from occupational or invading forces.

Against the just war (justum bellum) are those of a skeptical persuasion who do not believe that morality can or should exist in war. There are various positions against the need or the possibility of morality in war. Generally, consequentialists and act utilitarians may claim that if victory is sought then all methods should be employed to ensure it is gained at a minimum of expense and time. Arguments from 'military necessity' are of this type; for example, to defeat Germany in World War II, it was deemed necessary to bomb civilian centers, or in the US Civil War, for General Sherman to burn Atlanta. However, intrinsicists may also decree that no morality can exist in the state of war, for they may claim it can only exist in a peaceful situation in which recourse exists to conflict resolving institutions. Or intrinsicists may claim that possessing a just cause (the argument from righteousness) is a sufficient condition for pursuing whatever means are necessary to gain a victory or to punish an enemy. A different skeptical argument, one advanced by Michael Walzer, is that the invention of nuclear weapons alters war so much that our notions of morality—and hence just-war theories—become redundant. However, against Walzer, it can be reasonably argued that although such weapons change the nature of warfare they do not dissolve the need to consider their use within a moral framework.

Whilst sceptical positions may be derived from consequentialist and intrinsicist positions, they need not be. Consequentialists can argue that there are long-term benefits to having a war convention. For example, by fighting cleanly, both sides can be sure that the war does not escalate, thus reducing the probability of creating an incessant war of counter-revenges. Intrinsicists can argue that certain spheres of life ought never to be targeted in war; for example, hospitals and densely populated suburbs. The inherent problem with both ethical models is that they become either vague or restrictive when it comes to war. Consequentialism is an open-ended model, highly vulnerable to pressing military needs to adhere to any code of conduct in war: if more will be gained from breaking the rules than will be lost, the consequentialist cannot but demur to military necessity. On the other hand, intrinsicism can be so restrictive that it permits no flexibility in war: whether it entails a Kantian thesis of respecting others or a classical rights position, intrinsicism produces an inflexible model that would restrain warrior's actions to the targeting of permissible targets only. In principle such a prescription is commendable, yet the nature of war is not so clean cut when military targets can be hidden amongst civilian centers.

Against these two ethical positions, just war theory offers a series of principles that aim to retain a plausible moral framework for war. From the just war (justum bellum) tradition, theorists distinguish between the rules that govern the justice of war (jus ad bellum) from those that govern just and fair conduct in war (Jus In Bello). The two are by no means mutually exclusive, but they offer a set of moral guidelines for waging war that

are neither unrestricted nor too restrictive. The problem for ethics involves expounding the guidelines in particular wars or situations.

2. The Jus Ad Bellem Convention

The principles of the justice of war are commonly held to be: having just cause, being declared by a proper authority, possessing right intention, having a reasonable chance of success, and the end being proportional to the means used. One can immediately detect that the principles are not wholly intrinsicist nor consequentialist—they invoke the concerns of both models. Whilst this provides just war theory with the advantage of flexibility, the lack of a strict ethical framework means that the principles themselves are open to broad interpretations. Examining each in turn draws attention to the relevant problems.

Possessing just cause is the first and arguably the most important condition of jus ad bellum. Most theorists hold that initiating acts of aggression is unjust and gives a group a just cause to defend itself. But unless 'aggression' is defined, this proscription is rather open-ended. For example, just cause resulting from an act of aggression can ostensibly be responses to a physical injury (e.g., a violation of territory), an insult (an aggression against national honor), a trade embargo (an aggression against economic activity), or even to a neighbor's prosperity (a violation of social justice). The onus is then on the just war theorist to provide a consistent and sound account of what is meant by just cause. Whilst not going into the reasons of why the other explanations do not offer a useful condition of just cause, the consensus is that an initiation of physical force is wrong and may justly be resisted. Self-defense against physical aggression, therefore, is putatively the only sufficient reason for just cause. Nonetheless, the principle of self-defense can be extrapolated to anticipate probable acts of aggression, as well as in assisting others against an oppressive government or from another external threat (interventionism). Therefore, it is commonly held that aggressive war is only permissible if its purpose is to retaliate against a wrong already committed (e.g., to pursue and punish an aggressor), or to pre-empt an anticipated attack.

The notion of proper authority seems to be resolved for most of the theorists, who claim it obviously resides in the sovereign power of the state. But the concept of sovereignty raises a plethora of issues to consider here. If a government is just, i.e., it is accountable and does not rule arbitrarily, then giving the officers of the state the right to declare war is reasonable. However, the more removed from a proper and just form a government is, the more reasonable it is that its sovereignty disintegrates. A historical example can elucidate the problem: when Nazi Germany invaded France in 1940 it set up the Vichy puppet regime. What allegiance did the people of France under its rule owe to its precepts and rules? A Hobbesian rendition of almost absolute allegiance to the state entails that resistance is wrong; whereas a Lockean or instrumentalist conception of the state entails that a poorly accountable, inept, or corrupt regime possesses no sovereignty, and the right of declaring war (to defend themselves against the government or from a foreign power) is wholly justifiable. The notion of proper authority therefore requires thinking about what is meant by sovereignty, what is meant by the state, and what is the proper relationship between a people and its government.

The possession of right intention is ostensibly less problematic. The general thrust of the concept being that a nation waging a just war should be doing so for the cause of justice and not for reasons of self-interest or aggrandizement. Putatively, a just war cannot be considered to be just if

reasons of national interest are paramount or overwhelm the pretext of fighting aggression. However, possessing right intention masks many philosophical problems. According to Kant, possessing good intent constitutes the only condition of moral activity, regardless of the consequences envisioned or caused, and regardless, or even in spite, of any self interest in the action the agent may have. The extreme intrinsicism of Kant can be criticized on various grounds, the most pertinent here being the value of self-interest itself. At what point does right intention separate itself from self-interest? On the one hand, if the only method to secure peace is to annex a belligerent neighbor's territory, political aggrandizement is intimately connected with the proper intention of maintaining the peace. On the other hand, a nation may possess just cause to defend an oppressed group, and may rightly argue that the proper intention is to secure their freedom, yet such a war may justly be deemed too expensive or too difficult to wage; i.e., it is not ultimately in their self-interest to fight the just war. On that account, some may demand that national interest is paramount: only if waging war on behalf of freedom is also complemented by the securing of economic or other military interests should a nation commit its troops. The issue of intention raises the concern of practicalities as well as consequences, both of which should be considered before declaring war.

The next principle is that of reasonable success. This is another necessary condition for waging just war, but again is insufficient by itself. Given just cause and right intention, the just war theory asserts that there must be a reasonable probability of success. The principle of reasonable success is consequentialist in that the costs and benefits of a campaign must be calculated. However, the concept of weighing benefits poses moral as well as practical problems as evinced in the following questions. Should one not go to the aid of a people or declare war if there is no conceivable chance of success? Is it right to comply with aggression because the costs of not complying are too prohibitive? Is it not sometimes morally necessary to stand up to a bullying larger force, as the Finns did when Russia invaded in 1940, for the sake of national self-esteem? Besides, posturing for defense may sometimes make aggression itself too costly, even for a much stronger side. However, the thrust of the principle of reasonable success emphasizes that human life and economic resources should not be wasted in what would obviously be an uneven match. For a nation threatened by invasion, other forms of retaliation or defense may be available, such as civil disobedience, or even forming alliances with other small nations to equalize the odds. Historically, many nations have overcome the probability of defeat: the fight may seem hopeless, but a charismatic leader or rousing speech can sometimes be enough to stir a people into fighting with all their will. Winston Churchill offered the British nation some of the finest of war's rhetoric when it was threatened with defeat and invasion by Nazi Germany in 1940. For example: "Let us therefore brace ourselves to do our duty, and so bear ourselves that, if the British Commonwealth and its Empire lasts for a thousand years, men will still say, 'This was their finest hour.'" ....And "What is our aim?....Victory, victory at all costs, victory in spite of all terror; victory, however long and hard the road may be; for without victory, there is no survival." (Speeches to Parliament, 1940).

The final guide of jus ad bellum, is that the desired end should be proportional to the means used. This principle overlaps into the moral guidelines of how a war should be fought, namely the principles of Jus In Bello. With regards to just cause, a policy of war requires a goal, and that goal must be proportional to the other principles of just cause. Whilst this commonly entails the minimizing of war's destruction, it can also invoke general balance of power considerations. For example, if nation A invades a land belonging to the people of nation B, then B has just cause to take the land back. According to the principle of proportionality, B's counter-attack must not invoke a disproportionate response: it should aim to retrieve its land. That goal may be tempered with attaining assurances that no further invasion will take place. But for B to invade and annex regions of A is nominally a disproportionate response, unless (controversially) that is the only method for securing guarantees of no future reprisals. For B to invade and annex A and then to continue to invade neutral neighboring nations on the grounds that their territory would provide a useful defense against other threats is even more unsustainable.

On the whole the principles offered by jus ad bellum are useful guidelines. Philosophically however they invoke a plethora of problems by either their independent vagueness or by mutually inconsistent results. They are nonetheless a useful starting point for ethics and remain a pressing concern for statesmen and women.

3. The Principles Of Jus In Bello

The rules of just conduct fall under the two broad principles of discrimination and proportionality. The principle of discrimination concerns who are legitimate targets in war, whilst the principle of proportionality concerns how much force is morally appropriate. One strong implication of being a separate topic of analysis for just war theorists, is that a nation fighting an unjust cause may still fight justly, or vice versa. A third principle can be added to the traditional two, namely the principle of responsibility, which demands an examination of where responsibility lies in war.

In waging war it is considered unfair and unjust to attack indiscriminately since non-combatants or innocents are deemed to stand outside the field of war proper. Immunity from war can be reasoned from the fact that their existence and activity is not part of the essence of war, which is killing combatants. Since killing itself is highly problematic, the just-war theorist has to proffer a reason why combatants become legitimate targets in the first place, and whether their status alters if they are fighting a just or unjust war. Firstly, a theorist may hold that being trained and/or armed constitutes a sufficient threat to combatants on the other side. Voluntarists may invoke the boxing ring analogy: punching another individual is not morally supportable in a civilized community, but those who voluntarily enter the boxing ring renounce their right not to be hit. Similarly, those who join an army renounce their rights not to be targeted in war; the rights of non-combatants (civilians, or 'innocents') remain intact and therefore they cannot be justly attacked. Others, avoiding a rights analysis, may argue that those who join the army (or who have even been pressed into conscription) come to terms with being a target, and hence their own deaths. This is argued for example by Barrie Paskins and Michael Dockrill in The Ethics of War (1979). However, since civilians can just as readily come to terms with their own deaths, their argument is not sufficient to defend the principle of discrimination. Rights-based analyses are more productive, especially those that focus on the renouncing of rights by combatants by virtue of their war status, leaving a sphere of immunity for civilians.

Warfare sometimes unavoidably involves civilians. Whilst the principle of discrimination argues for their immunity from war, the practicalities of war provoke the need for a different model. The doctrine of double effect offers a justification for killing civilians in war, so long as their deaths are not intended but are accidental. Targeting a military establishment in the middle of a city is permissible according to the doctrine of double effect, for the target is legitimate. Civilian casualties are a foreseeable but accidental effect. Whilst the doctrine provides a useful justification of 'collateral damage' to civilians, it raises a number of issues concerning the justification of foreseeable breaches of immunity, as well as the balance to strike between military objectives and civilian casualties.

Another problem arises in defining who is a combatant and who is not. Usually combatants carry arms openly, but guerrillas disguise themselves as civilians. Michael Walzer, in his Just and Unjust Wars (1977) claims that the lack of identification does not give a government the right to kill indiscriminately—the onus is on the government to identify the combatants. Others have argued that the nature of modern warfare dissolves the possibility of discrimination. Civilians are just as necessary causal conditions for the war machine as are combatants, therefore, they claim, there is no moral distinction in targeting an armed combatant and a civilian involved in arming or feeding the combatant. The distinction is, however, not closed by the nature of modern economies, since a combatant still remains a very different entity from a non-combatant, if not for the simple reason that the former is presently armed (and hence has renounced rights or is prepared to die, or is a threat), whilst the civilian is not. On the other hand, it can be argued that being a civilian does not necessarily mean that one is not a threat and hence not a legitimate target. If Mr Smith is the only individual in the nation to possess the correct combination that will detonate a device, then he becomes not only causally efficacious in the firing of a weapon of war, but also morally responsible; reasonably he also becomes a legitimate military target. His job effectively militarizes his status. The underlying issues that ethical analysis must deal with involve the logical nature of an individual's complicity, or aiding and abetting the war machine, with greater weight being imposed on those logically closer than those logically further from the war machine in their work. At a deeper level, one can consider the role that civilians play in supporting an unjust war; to what extent are they morally culpable, and if they are culpable to some extent, does that mean they may become legitimate targets? This invokes the issue of collective versus individuality responsibility that is in itself a complex topic.

The second principle of just conduct is that any offence should remain strictly proportional to the objective desired. This principle overlaps with the proportionality principle of just cause, but it is distinct enough to consider it in its own light. Proportionality for Jus In Bello requires tempering the extent and violence of warfare to minimise destruction and casualties. It is broadly utilitarian in that it seeks to minimize overall suffering, but it can also be understood from other moral perspectives, for instance, from harboring good will to all (Kantian ethics), or acting virtuously (Aristotelian ethics). Whilst the consideration of discrimination focuses on who is a legitimate target of war, the principle of proportionality deals with what kind of force is morally permissible. In fighting a just war in which only military targets are attacked, it is still possible to breach morality by employing disproportionate force against an enemy. Whilst the earlier theoreticians, such as Thomas Aquinas, invoked the Christian concepts of charity and mercy, modern theorists may invoke either consequentialist or intrinsicist prescriptions, both are which remain problematic as the foregoing discussions have noted. However, it does not seem morally reasonable to completely gun down a barely armed belligerent tribe. At the battle of Omdurman in the Sudan, six machine gunners killed thousands of dervishes—the gunners may have been in the right to defend themselves, but the principle of proportionality demands that a battle ends before it becomes a massacre. Similarly, following the battle of Culloden,

Cumberland ordered "No Quarter", which was not only a breach of the principle of discrimination, for his troops were permitted to kill the wounded as well as supporting civilians, but also a breach of the principle of proportionality, since the battle had been won, and the Jacobite cause effectively defeated on the battle field.

The principles of proportionality and discrimination aim to temper war's violence and range. They are complemented by other considerations that are not taken up in the traditional exposition of Jus In Bello, especially the issue of responsibility.

Jus In Bello requires that the agents of war be held responsible for their actions. This ties in their actions to morality generally. Some, such as Saint Augustine argues against this assertion: "who is but the sword in the hand of him who uses it, is not himself responsible for the death he deals." Those who act according to a divine command, or even God's laws as enacted by the state and who put wicked men to death "have by no means violated the commandment, 'Thou shalt not kill.'" Whilst this issue is connected to the concepts of just cause, it does not follow that individuals waging a just, or unjust war, should be absolved of breaching the principles of just conduct. Readily it can be accepted that soldiers killing other soldiers is part of the nature of warfare, but when soldiers turn their weapons against non-combatants, or pursue their enemy beyond what is reasonable, then they are no longer committing legitimate acts of war but acts of murder. The principle of responsibility re-asserts the burden of abiding by rules in times of peace on those acting in war. The issues that arise from this principle include the morality of obeying orders (for example, when one knows those orders to be immoral), as well as the status of ignorance (not knowing of the effects of one's actions).

The foregoing has described the main tenets of the just war theory, as well as some of the problems that it entails. The theory bridges theoretical and applied ethics, since it demands an adherence, or at least a consideration of meta-ethical conditions and models, as well as prompting concern for the practicalities of war. A few of those practicalities have been mentioned here. Other areas of interest are: hostages, innocent threats, international blockades, sieges, the use of weapons of mass destruction or of anti-personnel weapons (e.g., land mines), and interventionism.

SECTION FOUR: HISTORICAL TIMELINE OF ENTRIES

Entry Title	Beginning	Ending
Sargon the Great	r. 2334 BCE	2279 BCE
Hittites	1900 BCE	1200 BCE
Egypt, Hyksos Invasion of	1750 BCE	1567 BCE
India, Aryan Invasion of	1500s BCE?	500s BCE?
Palestine, Egyptian Invasions of	1500s BCE	1269 BCE
Canaan, Israelite Invasion of	13th Century BCE	1050? BCE
Assyrian Empire	1300 BCE	612 BCE
Kush, Expansion of	725 BCE	350 CE
Scythians	700 BCE	300 BCE
Philip of Macedon	640 BCE	602 BCE
Augustus, Caesar	63 BCE	14 CE
Chaldean (Neo-Babylonian) Empire, Expansion of	612 BCE	539 BCE
Cyrus the Great	590? BCE	529 BCE
Carthage, Expansion of	553 BCE	146 BCE
Axum, Expansion of	500 BCE	6th Century CE
Greece, Persian Invasion of	492 BCE	479 BCE
Alexander the Great	356 BCE	323 BCE
Egypt, Alexander's Conquest of	334 BCE	342 BCE
Persia, Alexander's Conquest of	334 BCE	327 BCE
India, Alexander's Invasion of	326 BCE	325 BCE
Seleucid Empire	323 BCE	250 BCE
Mauryan Empire	321 BCE	184 BCE
Ptolemaic Dynasty	305 BCE	30 BCE
Sicily, Roman Conquest of (First Punic War)	264 BCE	241 BCE
Hannibal	247 BCE	183 BCE
Ch'in Dynasty	221 BCE	206 BCE
Italy, Carthaginian Invasion of (Second Punic War)	218 BCE	202 BCE
Vietnam, Chinese Conquest of	218 BCE	907 CE
Spain, Roman Conquest of	209 BCE	409 CE
Han Dynasty	206 BCE	220 CE
Carthage, Roman Invasion of (Third Punic War)	149 BCE	146 BCE
Caesar, Julius	100 BCE	44 BCE
Gaul, Roman Conquest of	58 BCE	49 BCE
Britain, Roman Conquest of	55 BCE	410 CE
Germany, Roman Invasion of	12 BCE	14 CE
India, Kushan Invasion of	50	250
Visigoths	3rd Century	711

Entry Title	Beginning	Ending
Constantine, Emperor	274	337
Huns	4th Century	454
Gupta Empire	320	480
Byzantine Empire	330	1453
Vandals	350	435
Ostrogoths	370	540
Franks	5th Century	800
Avars	400	805
Justinian	483	565
Lombards	539	773
Khmer Kingdom	600	1863
T'ang Dynasty	618	907
Middle East, Muslim Conquest of the	634	750
Bulgars	635	969
Carolingian Dynasty	640	899
Songhay, Expansion of	670	1591
Spain, Muslim Conquest of	710	1492
England, Viking Conquest of	789	954
Ireland, Viking Invasions of	840	1000
France, Viking Invasion of	849	911
Russia, Establishment and Expansion of	862	1097
Magyars	896	955
Crusades	10th through	13th Centuries
India, Muslim Invasion of	10th Century	1526
China, Khitan Invasion of	950	11th Century
Turks	977	1260s
Ghaznavids	977	1040
Seljuks	1040	1260s
Italy and Sicily, Norman Conquest of	1042	1194
Ghana, Almoravid Invasion of	1054	1163
Britain, Norman Invasion of	1066	1066
Genghis Khan	1167?	1227
Ireland, English Invasion of	1168	1169
China, Mongol Conquest of	1206	1294
Kubilai Khan	1215	1294
Middle East, Mongol Invasion of the	1219	1337
Russia, Mongol Conquest of	1223	1480
Uzbeks	1227	1868
Mali, Expansion of	1230	1400s
Korea, Mongol Invasion of	1234	1361

Entry Title	Beginning	Ending
Europe, Mongol Invasion of	1240	1241
Japan, Mongol Invasions of	1274	1284
Scotland, English Conquest of	1296	1707
Ottoman Empire	1299	1922
Hundred Years' War	1336	1452
Tamurlane	1336	1405
Mexico, Aztec Conquest of	1350	1521
Ming Dynasty	1368	1644
Indians of North America, U.S. Conquest of	15th Century	1890
Africa, Portuguese Occupation of	1440	1975
Cortes, Hernan	1485	1547
Western Hemisphere, Spanish Occupation of	1492	1898
Caribbean, European Occupation of	**1492**	19th Century
Bahamas	1650	1973
Bermuda	1612	1973
Cuba	1492	1898
French West Indies	17th Century	---
Hispaniola (Spanish/French)	1492/1697	1821/1804
Jamaica	1509	---
Puerto Rico	1509	1898
U.S. Virgin Islands (Spanish/Danish)	1555/1733	1917
British Virgin Islands (Dutch/British)	1648/1672	---
Italy, French Invasions of	1494	1552
Brazil, Portuguese Colonization of	1500	1825
Ceylon, Portuguese Occupation of	1505	1656
Austria, Turkish Invasion of	1521	1699
North America, French Occupation of	1524	1763
Moghul Empire	1526	1707
Cyprus, Ottoman invasion of	1570	1878
Portugal, Spanish Occupation of	1580	1668
England, Spanish Invasion of (Spanish Armada)	1588	1588
Africa, Dutch Occupation in	1595	1815
East Indies, Dutch Occupation of the	1596	1815
North America, British Occupation of	1607	1783
Ching (Manchu) Dynasty	1616	1912
Thirty Years War	1618	1648

Entry Title	Beginning	Ending
Singapore, British Occupation of	1819	1958
Algeria, French Occupation of	1830	1962
China, British Invasion of (Opium War)	1839	1842
Mexico, U.S. Invasion of	1846	1848
Africa, German Occupations in	1848	1918
New Zealand, British Occupation of	1860	1907
Indochina, French Occupation of	1862	1956
Mexico, French Occupation of	1862	1867
Paraguayan War	1864	1870
France, Prussian Invasion of (Franco-Prussian War)	1870	1871
Ashanti, British Conquest of	1873	1874
Congo, Belgian Occupation of	1879	1960
War of the Pacific	1879	1883
Zululand, British Invasion of	1879	1906
MacArthur, Douglas	1880	1964
Mussolini, Benito	1883	1945
Kenya, British Occupation of	1887	1963
Hitler, Adolf	1889	1945
Somalia, Italian Occupation of	1889	1941
Eisenhower, Dwight David	1890	1969
Uganda, British Occupation of	1890	1961
Korea, Japanese Invasion of (Sino-Japanese War)	1894	1895
Cuba, U.S. Invasion of	1898	1902
<u>Latin America, US Interventions In</u>	1898	2000
Cuba	1898	1934
Dominican Republic	1907	1934
El Salvador	1981	1992
Guatemala	1954	1954
Hispaniola	1915/1994	1934/1994
Nicaragua	1913	1933
Panama	1903	2000
Philippines, U.S. Occupation of the	1898	1946
Puerto Rico, U.S. Invasion of	1898	---
Manchuria, Japanese Invasion of (1904) (Russo-Japanese War)	1904	1905
Libya, Italian Occupation of	1912	1943

Entry Title	Beginning	Ending
East Africa, British Invasion of	1914	1918
France, German Invasion of	1914	1918
Mesopotamia, British Invasion of	1914	1918
Russia, German Invasion of	1915	1918
Turkey, British Invasion of	1915	1916
Albania, Italian Conquest of	1926	1943
Manchuria, Japanese Invasion of (1931)	1931	1945
Ethiopia, Italian Invasion of	1934	1941
Rhineland, Nazi Occupation of the	1936	1945
China, Japanese Invasion of	1937	1945
Austria, Nazi Occupation of	1938	1945
Czechoslovakia, Nazi Occupation of	1938	1945
Finland, Soviet Invasion of	1939	1945
Poland, Nazi Conquest of	1939	1944
Britain, Nazi Invasion of (Battle of Britain)	1940	1940
Egypt, Italian Invasion of	1940	1943
France, Nazi Invasion of	1940	1944
Norway and Denmark, Nazi Invasion of	1940	1945
Greece, Nazi Invasion of	1941	1945
Philippines, Japanese Invasion of the	1941	1945
Singapore and Malaya, Japanese	1941	1945
Soviet Union, Nazi Invasion of the	1941	1943
Burma, Japanese Invasion of	1942	1945
Dutch East Indies, Japanese Invasion of	1942	1945
Midway, Japanese Invasion of	1942	1942
New Guinea, Japanese Invasion of	1942	1945
North Africa, U.S. Invasion of	1942	1945
Pacific Islands, U.S. Conquest of	**1942**	**1945**
Solomon Islands	1942	1943
Gilbert and Marshall Islands	1943	1944
Mariana Islands	1944	1944
Iwo Jima and Okinawa	1945	1945
Italy, Allied Invasion of	1943	1945
Sicily, Allied Invasion of	1943	1945
France, Allied Invasion of	1944	1945
Germany, Soviet Invasion of	1944	1945

Entry Title	Beginning	Ending
Philippines, U. S. Invasion of the	1944	1945
South Korea, North Korean Invasion of (Korean War)	1950	1953
Sinai, Israeli Invasion of (1956) (Suez Crisis)	October, 1956	March, 1957
Sinai, Israeli Invasion of (1967) (Six-Day War)	6/5/67	6/10/67
Israel, Arab Invasion of (Yom Kippur War)	1972	1972
Cyprus, Turkish Invasion of	1974	1983
Afghanistan, Soviet Invasion of	1979	1989
Grenada, U.S. Invasion of	1983	1983
Panama, U.S. Invasion of	1989	1989
Kuwait, Iraqi Invasion of	1990	1991
Bosnia-Herzegovinia, Serbian Invasion of	1992	1995
Afghanistan, UN Invasion of	2001	2002
Iraq, coalition Invasion of	2003	---

SECTION FIVE: INDEX